Principles of Money, Banking, and Financial Markets

Principles of Money, Banking, and Financial Markets

Fourth, Revised Edition

Lawrence S. Ritter
William L. Silber

BASIC BOOKS, INC., PUBLISHERS NEW YORK

". . . be careful in teaching,
for error in teaching amounts to deliberate sin."

The *Mishnah*
Pirkei Avot, 4

Library of Congress Cataloging in Publication Data
Ritter, Lawrence S.
   Principles of money, banking, and financial
markets.
   Includes bibliographical references and index.
   1. Money. 2. Banks and banking. 3. Finance.
   I. Silber, William L. II. Title.
HG221.R536 1983   332   82–72962
ISBN 0–465–06342–X

For
Jonathan, *who likes to win*
Danny, *who likes his way*
Tammy, *who likes people*
and for
Steve *and* **Peter**
With Love

Acknowledgments

The first three editions of this book generated a number of communications from students and teachers. Some were favorable, others critical, but all helped us prepare this fourth edition. We would like to thank the following for taking the time and effort to help improve this revision:

Eddie Ary, *Ouachita Baptist University*
William T. Baldwin *Eastern Kentucky U.*
John Bay, *University of Southern Maine*
Ralph T. Byrns, *Metropolitan State College*
John A. Carlson, *Purdue University*
Arthur D. Chesler, *Kentucky Wesleyan*
Thomas C. Chiang, *Drexel University*
Dale Cloninger, *U. of Houston at Clear Lake*
Bob Curl, *Northwest Nazarene College*
Robert M. Domine, *University of Michigan*
James S. Earley, *U. of California, Riverside*
William P. Field, Jr., *Nicholls State University*
Stanley Fischer, *M. I. T.*
Ian Giddy, *Columbia University*
John B. Guerard, Jr., *University of Texas*
Jerry W. Gustafson, *Beloit College*
Philip J. Hahn, *Youngstown State U.*
Gabriel Hawawini, *Baruch College of CUNY*
Naphtali Hoffman, *Elmira College*
Robert S. Holbrook, *University of Michigan*
Edward J. Kane, *Ohio State University*
Jimmie King, Jr., *Tuskegee Institute*
Gregor Lazarcik, *State U. of New York at Genesco*
Darryl W. Lowry, *Roanoke College*
Morgan J. Lynge, *U. of Illinois at Urbana*
H. Brian Moehring, *U. of the Redlands*
Robert L. Moore, *Harvard University*
Douglas W. Morrill, *Centenary College of Louisiana*

Alan Norton, *St. John Fisher College*
Braxton I. Patterson, *U. of Wisconsin at Oshkosh*
Thomas J. Pierce, *California State College at San Bernardino*
Dean Popp, *San Diego State College*
Alan Rabin, *University of Tennessee*
Deborah E. Robbins, *Wellesley College*
John M. Sapinsley, *Rhode Island College*
Donald J. Schilling, *University of Missouri*
Carole Scott, *West Georgia College*
Edward Shapiro, *University of Toledo*
Milton M. Shapiro, *California State Polytechnic*
Thomas J. Shea, *Springfield College*
Cathy Sherman, *University of Texas*
William O. Shropshire, *Oglethorpe University*
Theodore R. Snyder, Jr., *University of New England*
Milton H. Spencer, *Wayne State University*
Charles E. Staley, *State U. of New York at Stony Brook*
H. Joe Story, *Pacific University*
Harry C. Symons, *Ursinus College*
Ronald L. Teigen, *University of Michigan*
John Thorkelson, *University of Connecticut*
Kenneth N. Townsend, *Hampden-Sydney College*
Pearl S. Vogel, *Sacred Heart University*
Joan Walters, *Fairfield University*
Douglas A. Wion, *Lock Haven State College*
Stuart Wood, *Tulane University*

How to Use This Book:
Notes to the Instructor

In preparing this fourth edition we were greatly influenced by a questionnaire we sent to instructors throughout the United States and Canada. Over two hundred responses were received, and the comments and suggestions are reflected throughout the text. The only dimension that was left untouched was the casual conversational style that we were strongly encouraged to maintain.

The improvements that were made are both substantive and pedagogical. Substantively, new chapters have been added on many timely subjects, including International Banking, the Payments Mechanism, Nonbank Financial Institutions, Budget Deficits and the Money Supply, and Hitting the Money Supply Targets. New sections have also been added to existing chapters on such topics as Treasury Bill Yields and Auctions, the Glass-Steagall Act, Real vs. Nominal Interest Rates, Aggregate Demand and Supply, Expectations and Monetary Policy, and Financial Futures.

Pedagogically, a considerable amount of material has been added, including illustrative news clippings, but at the same time the text has been streamlined, and many sections have been consolidated. For example, the Monetarist-Keynesian dialogue is now developed within the Aggregate Demand and Supply framework. As a result of these changes, the total length of the book has been reduced by about 15 percent. A summary has been added at the end of each chapter, highlighting the chapter's main points. The separate *Instructor's Manual* has been expanded considerably and now also includes a substantial *Test Bank*. The *Study Guide* by Gabriel Hawawini has been completely revised and updated. We think that this entire package will permit you to tailor your course to meet the needs of your students.

The specific organization of the book reflects the way we would teach a course in Money and Banking or Financial Institutions and Markets. However, we realize that there are alternative ways to organize such a course, ways that would involve a different ordering of chapters. We have, therefore, written the book with the ideal of flexibility in mind. Although every instructor can best structure his or her own course, here are some illustrative examples of the ways this book can be adapted to different approaches.

Part I forms the foundation for all future topics. Thus the chapters in Part I might all be assigned in the beginning of the course. Alternatively, each of the chapters in Part I can be used to initiate subsequent parts of the book. For example, Chapter 2 belongs with Part IV, Chapter 3 with Part II, Chapter 4 with Part III, and Chapter 5 with Part V.

The two major types of course organization are (1) a financial institutions and markets and central banking emphasis, and (2) a monetary theory and policy emphasis. The ordering of the chapters as they appear in the Table of Contents reflects the first type of approach: financial institutions and markets and central banking. Even within each of these categories, it is possible to emphasize different subjects. Here are some suggestions:

1. *Financial institutions and markets and central banking:* After the Basics in Part I, Parts II and III present a comprehensive analysis of the business of financial intermediaries and the art of central banking. A limited amount of theory on the role of money in the economy is given in Chapters 1 and 2 to provide the proper framework for the discussion of central banking.

When the formal presentation of monetary theory begins in Part IV, it is possible to reduce the emphasis on theory by eliminating Chapters 19 and 21; these chapters construct and then apply IS-LM analysis, but the rest of the book is written so that the omission of this material will not interrupt its continuity or intelligibility.

It is also possible to move more quickly into financial markets by going directly to Part V ("Financial Markets and Interest Rates") after Part I or after any subsequent part.

Many professors seem to prefer teaching Parts I, II, and III in sequence, then moving to Part V and possibly even VI before backtracking to Part IV ("Monetary Theory").

2. *Monetary theory and policy:* After Part I is completed, monetary theory can be introduced immediately by going directly to Part IV. One can then backtrack to Parts II and III, which discuss financial institutions and central banking, and then continue with Part V ("Financial Markets and Interest Rates"). In fact, Chapters 25 and 26 in Part V ("Forecasting Interest Rates" and "The Structure of Interest Rates") could be brought into a theory-oriented course much earlier, right after Part IV.

3. *International aspects:* It is possible to put all of Part VI ("International Finance") virtually anywhere one wishes, provided the basics in Part I have been covered. The international chapters, for example, could easily follow Part III ("The Art of Central Banking") or Part IV ("Monetary Theory").

We hope that you find both the new and continuing features of the book useful teaching devices. If you have any comments or suggestions for the next edition, we would appreciate hearing from you.

LSR
WLS

About the Authors

LAWRENCE S. RITTER is Professor of Finance and Economics at the undergraduate and graduate Schools of Business of New York University. A former Chief of the Domestic Research Division of the Federal Reserve Bank of New York, he has served as a consultant to the U.S. Treasury, the Federal Deposit Insurance Corporation, the Board of Governors of the Federal Reserve System, the American Bankers Association, and the Association of Reserve City Bankers. He has been the Editor of the *Journal of Finance* and is a past President of the American Finance Association. Professor Ritter is also the author of numerous articles in professional journals.

WILLIAM L. SILBER is Professor of Economics and Finance at the Graduate School of Business Administration at New York University and a Research Associate with the National Bureau of Economic Research. A former Senior Staff Economist with the President's Council of Economic Advisers, he has served as a consultant to the Board of Governors of the Federal Reserve System, the President's Commission on Financial Structure and Regulation, the U.S. Senate Committee on the Budget, the House Committee on Banking, Currency and Housing, the Justice Department, the Federal Reserve Bank of New York, the Federal Home Loan Bank Board, the National Commission on Electronic Funds Transfers, and the Department of Housing and Urban Development. He is an Associate Editor of the *Review of Economics and Statistics* and is the author of five books and numerous articles in professional journals.

Contents

Part I   The Basics

Part III   The Art of Central Banking

Part IV   Monetary Theory

Part V   Financial Markets and Interest Rates

Part I
The Basics

1
Money and the Economy

THE LACK OF MONEY is the root of all evil," said George Bernard Shaw. Although that may be something of an exaggeration, there have been numerous periods in history when it appeared to be more true than false. There have also been rather lengthy episodes when the opposite seemed true: when economic disruption apparently stemmed not from too little money, but from too *much* of it.

From this line of thought, the question naturally arises: What is the "right" amount of money? Not too little, not too much, but just right. And how can we go about getting it?

Questions of this sort used to be considered heresy, back in the days when the economy was viewed as a marvel of perpetual motion, sparked by divine inspiration in the form of gold (which gave money intrinsic value) and human intelligence (which told us to stay out of the way and let things work out by themselves). Flanked by the twin eternal verities—the gold standard and the balanced budget—laissez faire reigned supreme. Let nature take its course, and everything will turn out for the best in this best of all possible worlds.

Today we are no longer so sure. Aggregate spending on the nation's output of new goods and services—the economy's gross national product (GNP)—is no longer seen as inevitably producing full

2

employment without inflation, a high rate of economic growth, balance in international payments, and all the other things we expect our economy to yield. We have experienced too many instances of GNP falling short of the mark, or overshooting it, to retain blind faith in any built-in self-correcting thermostat. So today we often try to influence the course of economic events. We tinker, meddle, turn switches, push buttons, pull levers, and try to make things better.

But are they really any better? The answer is far from clear. Nevertheless, for many people the issue now is not *whether* the government should intervene, but how, when, and to what extent. The ends are not particularly new—high employment, price stability, economic growth, and balance of payments equilibrium—but the means are. The means most frequently used today to influence the economy's direction are *monetary policy,* with which this book is directly concerned, and *fiscal policy,* about which we will also have a fair amount to say. How well do they work? Are they appropriate to achieve their purposes? Can they be improved?

As a first approximation, monetary policy involves regulating the money supply and conditions in financial markets to achieve the goals of national economic policy. Fiscal policy involves changing government spending and tax rates for similar purposes. Let's set the stage for exploring these issues by providing a first look at the supply of money and its relationship to economic activity.

The Supply of Money

What *is* money, anyway? And how much of it do we actually have?

Money is just what you think it is—what you spend when you want to buy something. The Indians used beads, Eskimos used fishhooks, and we use *currency* (coins and dollar bills) and, most of all, checking accounts.

Money is used (1) as a means of payment—a medium of exchange —but it has other functions as well. It is also used (2) as a store of value, when people hold on to it, and (3) as a standard of value (a unit of account) when people compare prices and thereby assess relative values. But most prominently money is what you can spend, a generally acceptable medium of exchange that you can use to buy things or settle debts.

How large a money supply do we have? It amounted to $440 billion at the end of 1981, roughly $125 billion in the form of currency and about $315 billion in checkable deposits at banks and other financial institutions. This definition of money—currency outside banks plus checking accounts—is frequently called M1 (to distinguish it from three other definitions of money, M2, M3, and L, which we will get to in a moment). If you want to know what the money supply is *today,* add about 5 percent per annum to that figure since the end of 1981 and you probably won't be far off. Or else do what we did: Look it up in the latest issue of the *Federal Reserve Bulletin.*

Since currency and checking accounts are spendable at face value virtually anywhere, at any time, they are the most "liquid" assets a person can have. A liquid asset is something you can turn into the generally acceptable medium of exchange quickly without taking a loss—as compared with illiquid assets which can be sold or liquidated on short notice only at a substantially lower price. Currency and checking accounts are the most liquid assets you can have (because they *are* the medium of exchange), but they are not the only liquid assets around. Savings deposits and government bonds are rather liquid, although you can't spend them directly. To spend them, you first have to exchange them for money. At the other extreme, real estate and vintage automobiles typically rank fairly low on the liquidity scale: If you have to sell quickly, you're likely to take a beating on the deal.

Thus liquidity is a continuum, ranging from currency and checkable deposits at the top of the scale to a variety of frozen assets at the bottom. As a result, what we call "money" is not a fixed and immutable thing, like what we call water (H_2O), but to a great extent is a matter of judgment; there are several different definitions of money, each of which drops one notch lower on the liquidity scale in drawing the line between "money" and "all other assets." Table 1 summarizes four different definitions of the money supply.

M1 refers to the most liquid of all assets—currency plus all types of checking accounts at financial institutions. Until the mid–1970s, commercial banks were the only financial institutions permitted to issue checking accounts (sometimes called demand deposits). Now, the so-called thrift or deposit-type institutions—mutual savings

Table 1 Four Definitions of the Money Supply (end of 1981)

M1	Currency outside banks ($125 billion) plus demand deposits at commercial banks and at all thrift institutions ($235 billion) plus other checkable deposits at banks and thrifts ($75 billion) plus traveler's checks ($5 billion)	$440 billion
M2	Add small-denomination time deposits ($850 billion) plus passbook savings deposits ($340 billion) at all depository institutions, plus money market mutual funds shares ($150 billion), plus bank overnight repurchase agreements and Eurodollars ($40 billion)	1,820 billion
M3	Add large-denomination ($100,000 and over) time deposits at all depository institutions ($300 billion), plus bank long-term repurchase agreements	2,190 billion
L	Add long-term Eurodollars, bankers' acceptances, commercial paper, Treasury bills, U.S. savings bonds, and other liquid Treasury securities	2,640 billion

SOURCE: *Federal Reserve Bulletin.*

NOTE: Money market mutual funds, repurchase agreements, and Eurodollars are all explained and discussed in subsequent chapters.

banks, savings and loan associations, and credit unions—have entered the picture as well. However, more than 95 percent of all demand deposits are still in commercial banks.

In addition, as Table 1 indicates, other checkable deposits, such as Negotiable Order of Withdrawal (NOW) and Automated Transfer Service (ATS) accounts, are also considered part of M1. These interest-bearing checking accounts were made available to individuals and households during the 1970s as banks and thrifts circumvented the prohibition of paying interest on demand deposits. Since M1 is confined to these highly liquid assets, ones that can be used in an unrestricted way as a means of payment, it is the narrowest definition of money (as well as the most traditional one, by the way).

M2 drops just a shade lower on the liquidity scale by adding assets that are most easily and most frequently transferred into checking accounts when a payment is about to be made. This category includes household savings accounts and small (under $100,000) time deposits; it also includes overnight repurchase agreements and Eurodollars that businesses hold on a temporary basis.[1] The most spectacular growth item in the 1970s in this category was money market mutual funds. Businesses and households use these funds directly to write large checks (above $500); these funds can also be transferred easily to regular checking accounts for smaller disbursements. It will not be surprising, in fact, if money market mutual funds eventually work their way into the M1 definition of money. But that will depend on the evolving financial practices of businesses and individuals.

M3 adds primarily large-denomination time deposits (and long-term repurchase agreements) to M2. Unlike passbook savings deposits, these time deposits, more commonly known as certificates of deposit (CDs), have a scheduled maturity date—such as six months or two years—and if you want to withdraw your funds earlier you suffer a substantial penalty by having to forfeit part of the accumulated interest. For most businesses that hold large CDs, therefore, they are a less liquid source of funds than regular passbook savings accounts.

Finally, we come to L, which simply adds a number of short-term securities, such as Treasury bills and savings bonds, to M3. The L stands for liquidity, which is what this category is supposed to represent.

So what is the money supply in the United States? Is it $440 billion (M1) or $2,640 billion (L), or something in between? Each definition of money has its adherents, but by and large most economists prefer the narrow definition of the money supply—M1—because that and only that is generally acceptable as a means of payment. Once you go beyond currency and checking accounts, it is hard to find a logical place to stop, since many things (bonds, stocks, waterbeds) contain liquidity in varying degree. Throughout this book, therefore, we will

[1]These financial assets as well as the others mentioned here will be defined carefully and discussed at length in Part II.

for the most part stick to the narrow definition of money—currency plus checkable deposits.[2]

Who Determines Our Money Supply?

Why do we have $440 billion of money in the United States? Who, or what, determines how much there will be?

Regardless of what you may have heard, the amount of gold does *not* determine the money supply. Indeed, it has very little influence on it. In 1968 the last remaining link between the money supply and gold was severed when a law requiring 25 percent gold backing behind most of our currency was repealed. If that is all news to you, it is a good indication of just how unimportant the connection between gold and money has always been, at least in our lifetime.

Both currency and checking accounts can be increased (or decreased) without any relation to gold. Does that disturb you? Does it lead you to distrust the value of your money? Then send it to us. We'll be delighted to pay you ninety cents on the dollar, which should be a bargain if you believe all you read about a dollar being worth only sixty cents, or fifty cents, or whatever the latest figure may be.[3]

If gold is not the watchdog, then who (or what) does determine how much money we will have?

The monetary authority in most countries is called the central

[2]Which is not to say that M1 is a perfect measure of how much of the means of payment is in existence. As just one example of its shortcomings, notice that M1 does not include any estimate of existing bank "overdraft" facilities (which are arrangements that allow people to write checks—legally—even when they don't have enough in their checking accounts to cover them). These as well as other funds available for immediate payment are not included in M1 mainly because of the absence of reliable data on them.

[3]Actually, when you read that the dollar is worth only fifty cents it provides a clue to why gold has little to do with the *value* of money, in addition to having little to do with determining the amount outstanding. Money is valuable only because you can buy things with it—like clothes and books and stereos. The value of a dollar is therefore determined by the prices of the things we buy. When people say a dollar is worth only fifty cents they mean that a dollar can now buy what fifty cents could have bought a few years ago (because prices have doubled).

bank. A central bank does not deal directly with the public; it is rather a bank for banks, and it is responsible for the execution of national monetary policy. In the United States the central banking function is carried out by the Federal Reserve System, created by Congress in 1913. It consists of 12 district Federal Reserve Banks, scattered throughout the country, and a Board of Governors in Washington. This hydra-headed monster, which some view as benign but others consider an ever lurking peril, possesses ultimate authority over the money supply.

As noted above, the money supply (M1) consists of currency and checking accounts. *Currency* is manufactured by money factories—the Bureau of Engraving and Printing and the Mint—and then shipped under heavy guard to the U.S. Treasury and the Federal Reserve for further distribution. For the most part it enters circulation when people and business firms cash checks at their local banks. Thus it is the public that ultimately decides what proportion of the money supply will be in the form of currency, with the Federal Reserve Banks wholesaling the necessary coins and paper to local banks. The Federal Reserve is not particularly concerned with the fraction of the money supply that is in one form or another, but rather with the *total* of checkable deposits plus currency.[4]

As Table 1 shows, most of the money supply (almost three-quarters of it) is in the form of *demand deposits* or other checking accounts. These deposits come into being, as we shall see in Chapter 3, when banks extend credit—that is, when they make loans or buy

---

[4]Just in case you're curious, here are some miscellaneous facts about coins and currency: Coins are manufactured by the U.S. Mint, which has production facilities in Philadelphia, Denver and San Francisco. All currency is manufacturd by the U.S. Bureau of Engraving and Printing in Washington, D.C. The largest denomination of currency now issued is the $100 bill; there used to be $500, $1,000, $5,000, and $10,000 bills in circulation, but they were all discontinued in 1945. The average life of a $1 bill is about a year and a half, before getting torn or worn out, which is why the government started issuing the Susan B. Anthony dollar coins in 1979. Coins last much longer than currency. Banks send worn-out bills back to the Federal Reserve, which destroys them, and then distributes newly printed bills in their place. With a population of 230 million, the $125 billion of coin and currency in circulation at the end of 1981 amounted to an average of more than $500 for each man, woman, and child in the country. Which means, if you stop to think about it, that there must be an awful lot of dollar bills stashed away *somewhere.*

securities. Checking deposits vanish, as silently as they came, when banks contract credit—when loans are repaid or banks sell securities. It is precisely here, through its <u>ability to control bank behavior</u>, that the <u>Federal Reserve</u> wields its primary authority over the money supply and thereby implements monetary policy.

This process of money creation by banks, under the influence of the Federal Reserve, will be discussed at greater length in the following chapters. But before we get into the details, we should back off for a moment and ask why all the fuss? Why is money so important to begin with?

The Importance of Money I: Man Beats Barter

What good is money in the first place? To appreciate the importance of money in an economic system, it is instructive to speculate on what the economy might look like without it. In other words, why was money invented (by Sir John Money in 3016 B.C.)?

For one thing, without money individuals in the economy would have to devote more time to buying what they want and selling what they don't. In other words, people would have less time to work and play. A barter economy is one without a medium of exchange or a unit of account (the measuring rod function of money). Let's see what it might be like in a barter economy.

Say you are a carpenter and agree to build a bookcase for your neighbor. Your friend happens to raise chickens and pays you with four dozen eggs. You decide to keep a dozen for yourself, so you now have three dozen to exchange for the rest of the week's groceries. All you must do is find a grocer who is short on eggs.

What's more, you have to remember that a loaf of bread exchanges for six eggs (it also exchanges for eleven books of matches or three boxes of crayons or one Yankee Yearbook, but never mind because you don't have any of these things to spare). And of course all the other items on the grocer's shelf have similar price tags—the tags are bigger than the items.

Along comes money and simplifies matters. Workers are paid in something called money, which they can then use to pay their bills and make their purchases (medium of exchange). We no longer need price tags giving rates of exchange between an item and everything else that might conceivably be exchanged for it. Instead, prices of goods and services are expressed in terms of money, a common denominator (unit of account).

The most important thing about the medium of exchange is that every person must be confident that it can be passed on—that it is generally acceptable in trade. Paradoxically, a person will accept the medium of exchange only when certain that it can be passed on to someone else. One key characteristic is that the *uncertainty* over its value in trade must be very *low*. People will be more willing to accept the medium of exchange if they are certain what it is worth in terms of things they really want. The uncertainty of barter transactions makes people wary of exchange: If I want to sell my house and buy a car and you want to do just the reverse, we might be able to strike a deal except for the fact that you've got shifty eyes and are likely to rip me off by passing me a lemon; hence no deal; I'm uncertain about the value of the thing I accept in exchange. The medium of exchange, which is handled often in many transactions, becomes familiar to us all and can be checked carefully for fraud, thereby reducing uncertainty in trading.

Closely related to the low-uncertainty-high-exchangeability requirement is the ability to hold on to the medium of exchange without its deteriorating in value. It must be a good store of value, or as soon as I accept the medium of exchange I'll try to get rid of it, lest it be worth fewer and fewer goods and services tomorrow or the day after. Thus if price inflation gets out of hand and I have little confidence that the medium of exchange will hold its value, I'll be reluctant to accept it in exchange; in other words, it won't be the medium of exchange for very long. If that happens, we'll begin to slip back into barter.

The medium of exchange also usually serves as a unit of account. In other words, the prices of all other goods are expressed in terms of, say, dollars. Without such a unit of account, you'd have to remember the exchange ratios of soap for bread, knives for shirts, and bookcases for haircuts (and haircuts for soap). The unit of account reduces the information you have to carry around in your brain—freeing that limited space for creative speculation.

So money is a good thing. It frees people from spending too much time running around bartering goods and services, and allows them to undertake other endeavors—production, relaxation, contemplation, and temptation.

It is important to emphasize, once again, that people use the medium of exchange—money—not because it has any intrinsic value but because it can be exchanged for things to eat, drink, wear, and play with. The *value* of a unit of money is determined, therefore, by the prices of each and every thing—more accurately, the average level of all prices. If prices go up, a unit of money (a dollar) is worth less because it will buy less; if prices go down—use your imagination —a dollar is worth more because it will buy more.

The Importance of Money II: Financial Institutions and Markets

Money also contributes to economic development and growth, by stimulating both saving and investment and facilitating transfers of funds out of the hoards of savers and into the hands of borrowers who want to undertake investment projects but do not have enough of their own money to do so. Financial markets give savers a variety of ways to lend to borrowers, thereby increasing the volume of both saving and investment and encouraging economic growth.

People who save are often not the same people who can see and exploit profitable investment opportunities. In an economy without money, the only way a person can invest (buy productive equipment) is by consuming less than his income (saving). Similarly, in an economy without money the only way a person can save—that is consume less than his income—is by acquiring real goods directly.

The introduction of money, however, permits separation of the act of investment from the act of saving: money makes it possible for a person to invest without first refraining from consumption (saving), and likewise makes it possible for a person to save without also investing. People can now invest who are not fortunate enough to have their own savings.

In a monetary economy, a person simply accumulates savings in cash (money is a store of value). Through financial markets, this surplus cash can be lent to a business firm borrowing the funds to invest in new equipment, equipment it might not have been able to buy if it did not have access to borrowed funds. Both are better off —the saver receives interest payments, and the business firm presumably would not borrow and invest the money unless it expected to earn a return over and above the interest cost. And the economy is also better off: the only way an economy can grow is by allocating part of its resources to the creation of new and better productive facilities.

In an advanced economy such as ours, this channeling of funds from savers to investors, through financial markets, reaches highly complex dimensions. A wide variety of financial instruments, such as stocks, bonds, and mortgages, are utilized as devices through which borrowers can gain access to the surplus funds of savers. Various markets specialize in trading one or another of these financial instruments.

And financial institutions have sprung up—such as commercial banks, savings banks, savings and loan associations, credit unions, insurance companies, mutual funds, and pension funds—that act as middlemen in transferring funds from ultimate lenders to ultimate borrowers. Such financial institutions, or financial intermediaries, as they are often called, themselves borrow from saver-lenders and then turn around and lend the funds to borrower-investors. They mobilize the savings of many small savers and package them for sale to the highest bidders. In the process, again both ultimate saver-lenders and ultimate borrower-investors gain: savers have the added option of acquiring savings deposits or pension rights, which are less risky than individual stocks or bonds, and business firm borrowers can tap large sums of money from a single source.

None of this would be possible were it not for the existence of money, the one financial asset that lies at the foundation of the whole superstructure.[5] But once we have this unique thing called money, we also have the problem of controlling it.

[5]Strictly speaking it is theoretically possible for transfers between savers and investors to occur within a barter framework. Thus credit arrangements could exist without money. But only the existence of money permits the complex and efficient channeling of funds between savers and investors.

Uncontrolled, it may cause hyperinflation or disastrous depression, and thereby cancel its blessings. If price inflation gets out of hand, for example, money ceases to be a reliable store of value and therefore becomes a less efficient medium of exchange. People become reluctant to accept cash in payment for goods and services, and when they do accept it, they try to get rid of it as soon as possible. As we noted above, the value of money is determined by the price level of the goods money is used to purchase. The higher the prices, the more dollars one has to give up to get real goods or buy services. Inflation (rising prices) reduces the value of money. Hyperinflation (prices rising at a fast and furious pace) reduces the value of money by a lot within a short time span. Hence people don't want to hold very much cash—they want to exchange it for goods as quickly as possible. Thus if money breaks down as a store of value, it starts to deteriorate as a medium of exchange as well, and we start to slip back into barter. People spend more time exchanging goods and less time producing, consuming, and enjoying them. Severe depression causes different but no less serious consequences.

So once we have money, the question constantly challenges us: *How much* of it should there be?

How Large Should the Money Supply Be?

In theory, the answer is simple enough. Presumably the supply of money affects the rate of spending, and therefore we should have enough money so that we buy, at current prices, all the goods and services the economy is able to produce. If we spend less, we will have idle capacity and idle people; if we spend more, we will wind up with higher prices but no more real goods or services. In other words, we need a money supply large enough to generate just the right amount of spending to give us a GNP that represents full employment at stable prices. More money than that would mean more spending and inflation, and less money would mean less spending and recession or depression.

In practice, unfortunately, the answer is not nearly that simple. In the first place, decisions about the appropriate level of the money supply are often linked with the notion of countercyclical monetary policy: that is, a monetary policy that varies the amount of money in the economy, presumably increasing it (or, more realistically, increasing the rate at which it is growing) during a recession, to stimulate spending; and decreasing it (or increasing it at a less than normal rate) during a boom, to inhibit spending. As we will see in subsequent chapters, there is considerable debate over the desirability of such attempts at economic stabilization.

The more fundamental issue for us is to understand how changes in the money supply can influence people's *spending* in a consistent way. What a change in the money supply can do is alter people's *liquidity.* Money, after all, is the most liquid of all assets. A liquid asset, as mentioned above, is something that can be turned into cash —that is, sold or "liquidated"—quickly, with no loss in dollar value. Money already *is* cash. You can't get more liquid than that!

Since monetary policy alters the liquidity of the public's portfolio of total assets—including, in that balance sheet, holdings of real as well as financial assets—it should thereby lead to portfolio readjustments that involve spending decisions. An increase in the money supply implies that the public is more liquid than formerly; a decrease in the money supply implies that the public is less liquid than before. If the public had formerly been satisfied with its holdings of money relative to the rest of its assets, a change in that money supply will presumably lead to readjustments throughout the rest of its portfolio.[6]

In other words, these changes in liquidity should lead to more (or less) spending on either real assets (cars and television sets) or financial assets (stocks and bonds). If spending on real assets expands, demand for goods and services increases, and GNP is directly affected. If spending on financial assets goes up, the increased demand for stocks and bonds drives up securities prices. Higher securities prices mean lower interest rates. The fall in interest rates may induce more spending on housing and on plant and equipment

---

[6]Of course, if monetary policy could increase the money supply while all other assets of the public remained unchanged, people would not only be more liquid but also wealthier. As we will see in Chapter 4, however, monetary policy can only alter the composition of the public's assets but cannot change its total wealth *directly.*

"Frank, how did you ever find this *guru?"*

Drawing by D. Fradon;
© 1968 The New Yorker Magazine, Inc.

(investment spending), thereby influencing GNP through that route.[7]

Underlying the effectiveness of monetary policy, therefore, is its impact on the liquidity of the public. But whether a change in the supply of liquidity actually does influence spending depends on what is happening to the demand for liquidity. If the supply of money is increased but the demand expands even more, the addi-

---

[7]Since it will come up again and again, it is worth devoting a moment to the *inverse* relationship between the *price* of an income-earning asset and its effective *rate of interest* (or yield). For example, a long-term bond that carries a fixed interest payment of $10 a year, and costs $100, yields an annual interest rate of 10 percent. However, if the price of the bond were to rise to $200, the current yield would drop to 10/200, or 5 percent. And if the price of the security were to fall to $50, the current yield would rise to 10/50, or 20 percent. Conclusion: A rise (or fall) in the price of a bond is reflected, in terms of sheer arithmetic, in an automatic change in the opposite direction in the effective rate of interest. To say the price of bonds rose or the rate of interest fell is saying the same thing in two different ways. We will return to this concept in Chapter 5.

tional money will be held and not spent. "Easy" or "tight" money is not really a matter of increases or decreases in the money supply in an absolute sense, but rather increases or decreases relative to the demand for money. In the past decade we have had few periods in which the money supply actually decreased for any sustained length of time, yet we have had many periods of tight money because the *rate* of growth was so small that the demand for money rose faster than the supply.

If people always respond in a consistent manner to an increase in their liquidity (the proportion of money in their portfolio), the Federal Reserve will be able to gauge the impact on GNP of a change in the money supply. But if people's spending reactions vary unpredictably when there is a change in the money supply, the central bank will never know whether it should alter the money supply a little or a lot (or even at all!) to bring about a specified change in spending.

The relationship between changes in the money supply and induced changes in spending brings us to the speed with which money is spent, its rate of turnover or velocity. When the Federal Reserve increases the money supply by $1 billion, how much of an effect will this have on people's spending, and thereby on GNP? Say we are in a recession, with GNP $20 billion below prosperity levels. Can the Fed induce a $20 billion expansion in spending by increasing the money supply by $2 billion? Or will it take a $10 billion . . . or a $15 billion . . . increase in the money supply to do the job?

Velocity: The Missing Link

Clearly, this is the key puzzle that monetary policy must solve if it is to operate effectively. After all, the central bank is not in business to change the money supply just for the sake of changing the money supply. Money is only a means to an end, and the end is the total volume of spending—which should be sufficient to give us high employment but not so great as to produce excessively rising prices.

When the Federal Reserve increases the money supply, the recipients of this additional liquidity *probably* spend some of it on goods and services, increasing GNP. The funds thereby move from the original recipients to the sellers of the goods and services. Now *they* have more money than before, and if they behave the same way as the others, they too are *likely* to spend some of it. GNP thus rises further, and at the same time the money moves on to yet another set of owners, who in turn *may* also spend part of it, thereby increasing GNP again. Over a period of time, say a year, a multiple increase in spending and GNP could thus flow from an initial increase in the stock of money.

This relationship between the increase in GNP over a period of time and the initial change in the money supply is important enough to have a name: the velocity of money. Technically speaking, velocity is found, after the process has ended, by dividing the cumulative increase in GNP by the initial increase in the money supply.

Similarly, we can compute the velocity of the *total* amount of money in the country by dividing total GNP (not just the increase in it) by the *total* money supply. This gives us the average number of times each dollar turns over to buy goods and services during the year. In 1981, for example, with a GNP of $2,920 billion and an average money supply of $430 billion, the velocity of money was 2,920 divided by 430, or 6.8 per annum. Each dollar, on the average, was spent 6.8 times in purchasing goods and services during 1981.

With this missing link—velocity—now in place, we can reformulate the problem of monetary policy more succinctly. The Federal Reserve controls the supply of money. Its main job is to regulate the flow of spending. The flow of spending, however, depends not only on the supply of money but also on that supply's rate of turnover, or velocity, and this the Federal Reserve does *not* have under its thumb. Since any given supply of money might be spent faster or slower—that is, velocity might rise or fall—a rather wide range of potential spending could conceivably flow from any given stock of money.

If it weren't for the complications introduced by velocity, decisions about the appropriate money supply would be fairly simple, and there would be little disagreement among rational people. However, complications there are, and a central problem of monetary theory is the exploration of exactly what determines the velocity of money—or, looked at another way, what determines the volume of spending that flows from a change in the supply of money. As we shall see, disagreements over the determinants and behavior of velocity underlie part of the debate over economic stabilization policy.

A Preview

We now have an overall view of the role of money in economic activity. To help you keep track of where we'll be going, here is how the remainder of the book is arranged. Each of the remaining chapters of this introductory section (Part I, "The Basics") corresponds to more detailed discussions that appear later on in the book.

Chapter 2 focuses on perhaps the most fundamental, and historically most popular, problem for monetary economics: the relationship between money and inflation. This discussion is broadened in Part IV with the development of monetary theory and the alternative views of Monetarists and Keynesians on money, inflation, interest rates, and economic activity.

Chapter 3 introduces the fundamentals of commercial banks and money creation. Correspondingly, all of Part II is devoted to a more comprehensive analysis of what all types of financial institutions do and how they work, with special emphasis on commercial banks. Similarly, Chapter 4 introduces the Federal Reserve, and Part III provides an in-depth view of Federal Reserve policy-making.

The basis for understanding the financial system in general is set forth in Chapter 5. On that groundwork a more detailed analysis of financial markets is presented in Part V; here the structure of interest rates and the interrelationships among markets is given extensive treatment.

In Part VI we look at the role of money in international finance. The balance of payments enters the picture here, as well as exchange rates and the function of gold in the world's monetary system.

Summary

1. Money serves a number of functions in the economy. Perhaps the most important is its use as a medium of exchange. It also serves as a store of value and as a unit of account. In general, money is considered the most liquid asset because it can be spent at face value virtually anywhere at any time.

2. The precise definition of the asset called money varies with the economic system. In the United States we have four definitions: M1, M2, M3, and L. Each represents a slightly different definition of liquidity and spendability. M1 is the narrowest and most popular definition: the sum of currency and all checkable deposits at banks and thrift institutions. This is the definition we use throughout the book unless we say otherwise.

3. Without money the economy would have to rely on the more cumbersome barter system to exchange goods and services. It would also mean that only a primitive mechanism would exist for channeling savings into productive investments. The level of economic welfare would be lower on both counts.

4. Control over the money supply rests with the central bank. In the United States the central banking function is carried out by the Federal Reserve System, which is charged with regulating the supply of money so that we have enough spending to generate full employment without inflation. Control over inflation is crucial for maintaining the value of money, since an increase in the price level erodes the purchasing power of money.

5. The relationship between money and spending depends upon how frequently people turn over their cash balances. This "rate of turnover" of money is called velocity. *If* people hold a predictable fraction of income and wealth in the form of money balances, then it will be possible to influence spending in a consistent way by altering the money supply.

Suggestions for Further Reading

An excellent summary of money in exchange systems is Chapter 2 of Mark J. Flannery and Dwight M. Jaffee, *The Economic Implications of an Electronic Monetary Transfer System* (Lexington, Mass.: Lexington Books, 1973). *Money, Information, and Uncertainty,* by Charles A. E. Goodhart (New York: Barnes & Noble, 1975), discusses the role of money with special emphasis on risk and uncertainty. Robert Clower's collection of essays, *Monetary Theory: Selected Readings* (New York: Penguin, 1970), focuses specifically on the foundations of money. His introduction is especially good.

If you want to step back a bit and view things from a broader perspective, we recommend Norman Angell, *The Story of Money* (New York: Frederick A. Stokes Co., 1929); and Paul Einzig, *Primitive Money,* 2d edition (New York: Oxford University Press, 1966). For a fascinating illustration of the need for money, and the functions it performs, read R. A. Radford, "The Economic Organization of a P.O.W. Camp," *Economica* (November 1945).

2

Money and Inflation

CONSUMER PRICES ARE now more than *seven* times higher than in the late 1930s, when many of your parents were born. They are more than triple what they were in 1963, when many of you were born. Since 1963 prices have risen at an annual average rate of 6½ percent a year; at that rate, which looks modest by the standards of recent years, prices *double* every 11 years.[1]

As for the future, a recent popular book forecasts that "by 1992 the average secretary will be earning over $25,000 a year, and by the year 2030 over $600,000 a year. But prices will rise just as rapidly; by the year 2030, $10 bills will be considered small change, barely enough to buy a cup of coffee."[2] That sounds absurd until you think about it. In fact, an average annual inflation rate of only 8.6 percent would make those numbers a reality.

---

[1] As a special bonus, we give you "the rule of 72" for growth rates. If something (anything) is growing at a compound annual rate of x percent, to find out how many years it will take to *double,* divide 72 (the magic number) by x. For example, if prices are rising at 6.5 percent a year, they will double in $72 \div 6.5 = 11$ years. It isn't precise to the dot, but it's a useful rule of thumb.

While we're on such things, here's another rule of thumb: if you listen carefully to a cricket, the number of times it chirps in 15 seconds plus 37 equals the temperature in degrees Fahrenheit. Where else can you get such neat information?

[2] David Wallechinsky, Amy Wallace, and Irving Wallace, *The Book of Predictions* (New York: William Morrow & Company, 1980), page 261.

Who is responsible for inflation? Is money the culprit? Can we bring an inflationary spiral to a halt if we clamp down on the money supply? This overview of money and inflation will provide some insight into one of the oldest issues in monetary economics. The previous chapter focused on money and the overall economy; here we want to focus on a more specific issue: how money influences prices.

Too Much Money Chasing Too Few Goods

The classic explanation of inflation is that "too much money is chasing too few goods." The diagnosis implies the remedy; stop creating so much money and inflation will disappear.

Such a diagnosis has been painfully accurate during those hard-to-believe episodes in history when runaway hyperinflation skyrocketed prices out of sight and plunged the value of money to practically zero. Example: Prices quadrupled in revolutionary America between 1775 and 1780, when the Continental Congress opened the printing presses and flooded the country with currency. The phrase "not worth a continental" remains to this day. Germany after World War I was even more extreme; prices in 1923 were 34 billion times what they had been in 1921. In Hungary after World War II, it took 1.4 nonillion pengö in 1946 to buy what one pengö could purchase a few years earlier (one nonillion equals 1,000,000,000,000,000,000,-000,000,000,000).

Pathological breakdowns of this sort are impossible unless they are fueled by continuous injections of new money in ever increasing volume. In such cases money is undoubtedly the inflation culprit, and the only way to stop the avalanche from gathering momentum is to slam a quick brake on the money creation machine.

However, hyperinflation is not what we have been experiencing in this country in recent years. During World War II consumer prices rose by about 30 percent. In the immediate postwar years (1945–1949), after wage and price controls were removed, they climbed another 30 percent. None of this was unexpected or particularly unusual. Prices typically rise in wartime and immediately thereafter.

The unusual thing about prices and World War II is not that they rose so much during and immediately after it, but that they have never declined since. Quite the contrary—prices have continued onward and upward to this day, virtually without interruption, producing the longest period of continuous inflation in American history. In all prior times of war, prices had gone up during and immediately after hostilities, but then had fallen back somewhat. Not this time. In all prior peacetimes, price increases had been interrupted from time to time by occasional corrective periods of stable or declining prices. No longer.

From 1950 through 1980, the cost of living increased in every year but one (1955). The annual rate of inflation over the entire thirty-year period averages out at more than 4 percent per year. This is not hyperinflation. It is not like America in 1775, Germany in 1923, or Hungary in 1946. This is a different sort of animal—nibbling away doggedly, insistently, without pause, at the purchasing power of the dollar. Prices do not skyrocket, they only creep—some years 6 percent, some years 10 percent—but always in the same direction, always up, up, up.

This type of inflation is something new. Is money the culprit here, too? Can creeping inflation, like hyperinflation, be stopped simply by slamming the brakes on the money supply? To work our way around these questions, it will be helpful to examine the recent inflation process a bit more closely.

Demand Pull

We understand fairly clearly—as well as anything is understood in economics, anyway—why the price level rises when aggregate demand exceeds the limits of the economy's full capacity output. This is the orthodox inflation setting, exemplified in starkest form in wartime when we simply cannot produce enough goods and services to satisfy all would-be purchasers at existing prices. The excessive spending (in relation to the available supply of goods and services) bids up prices, thereby eliminating some potential buyers and, in effect, rationing the available short supply among those able and willing to pay more.

War thus generates the classic form of demand-pull inflation, with competition among buyers for the available goods and services driving prices higher. People are put to work producing war goods —which are bought by the government—but the incomes they receive, unless siphoned off by higher taxes, are as available as ever for the purchase of private consumer goods and services. At the same time, the output of civilian goods is curtailed as war production takes precedence.

Part of the reason for our inability to eliminate the inching up of prices is simply that we have never really brought World War II to a complete end. An entire generation has grown up that has never fully known peace. Intermittently, in the past thirty years, the financial, manpower, and matériel resources of the nation have been mobilized in an effort to produce both guns *and* butter. Budget deficits, shortages, and accelerated consumer and business buying plans have periodically converged, with the swollen aggregate demand outpacing the economy's productive capacity.

Cost Push

But that cannot be the whole story. There have been periods of relative tranquillity, primarily in the late 1950s and early 1960s, and just after the Vietnam war ended, when international tensions eased and slack developed in the economy. But even then prices continued upward. For example, aggregate demand from government, business, and consumers was in no sense excessive during the years 1974 and 1975. If anything, demand was sluggish. Unemployment averaged about 7 percent of the civilian labor force during that two-year period; nevertheless, consumer prices rose by 12 percent in 1974 and by 7 percent in 1975.

Why should prices rise when spending is slow and we are far below full employment of our labor force and full capacity utilization of our industrial plant? In past years, before World War II, these

were the very times when prices *fell* and the impact of prior inflation was to some extent ameliorated. Some new ingredients have
evidently entered the picture since the 1930s, and drastically altered
the economy's response mechanism.

One such ingredient is the economic strength of labor unions. The
American Federation of Labor was founded in 1886, but the real
power of trade unions to influence money-wages came with the
passage of the Wagner Act and related legislation half a century
later. On the basis of government encouragement of unionism as a
declared principle of public policy, the expansion of the economy
from the depression of the 1930s into the war boom of the 1940s
carried with it an enormous growth in union membership. The
ranks of organized labor jumped from 3 million members in 1933 to
9 million in 1940 and 15 million in 1946. Today, union rolls list about
25 million members. The Taft-Hartley Act of 1947 corrected some
union abuses, but it put hardly a dent in their newfound power to
extract wage increases in excess of productivity growth, thereby
generating higher production costs.

A second new ingredient—closely related to the economic power
of organized labor, although not so recent an arrival—is the substantial market power of big business. Because of the nature of modern
technology, which often results in lower unit production costs as the
scale of operations expands, a few large firms dominate many major
manufacturing industries. Their size enables these industrial giants
to exert a degree of control over their prices that would be impossible in a thoroughgoing competitive environment, thereby permitting them, to some extent, to pass on cost increases to their customers.

A third new ingredient is the Employment Act of 1946, under
which the government assumed responsibility for maintaining high
employment through the use of its monetary, fiscal, and related
powers. According to the Employment Act, "it is the continuing
policy and responsibility of the federal government to use all practi-
cable means . . . to promote maximum employment, production, and
purchasing power." Without the support of the Employment Act,
neither Big Labor nor Big Business, individually or in concert, could
sustain a wage-price spiral for very long. In the absence of the Employment Act, labor would have to take more seriously the possibility that it might be jacking up money-wages too far—that excessive

wage demands might force businessmen to cut back on their hiring. Businessmen would similarly have to guard against pricing their products out of the market. But such restraints are relaxed by the presence of Big Government standing ready to "insure prosperity" with injections of purchasing power should employment or sales decline too far.

Finally, in the past few years these three ingredients driving up prices have been joined by a fourth element: *imported* inflation. When the international oil cartel raised oil prices 400 percent late in 1973, we suddenly realized that our domestic price level has become extremely sensitive to actions quite beyond our control. Political extortion in the form of the 1973 Arab oil embargo had devastating economic impact. The prices that we have to pay for certain key imports from abroad—like oil and some other raw materials—have a pervasive influence on our own cost of living. When an international cartel, like the Organization of Petroleum Exporting Countries (OPEC), sets artificially high prices for its products and successfully limits its output to keep those prices up, the consequences include higher consumer prices in the United States (and elsewhere), regardless of the state of our domestic economy.

All this has created an environment of inflationary expectations. Such expectations feed on themselves by forcing labor and business to enter contractual arrangements that pass on higher wages and prices in a never ending spiral. The old-fashioned pattern of demand-pull inflation—excess aggregate spending, greater than the economy's productive capacity, pulling prices up—has not disappeared. But demand-pull (or buyers') inflation has been joined in the postwar period by a new form of inflation—cost-push (or sellers') inflation. Even when aggregate spending subsides, prices still rise. The distinguishing feature of cost-push or sellers' inflation is a rising price level while the economy is still below a full employment (full capacity) rate of production.

Money and Creeping Inflation

Unlike hyperinflation, money is not so obviously the culprit when it comes to the real problem of our times, creeping inflation. Take, for example, the five decades from 1930 to 1980:

"I've called the family together to announce that, because of inflation, I'm going to have to let two of you go."

Drawing by Joseph Farris;
© 1974 The New Yorker Magazine, Inc.

1. During the 1930s, the money supply (M1) increased by 35 percent, but consumer prices *fell* 20 percent.

2. In the 1940s, the money supply increased by 200 percent, but prices rose by "only" 70 percent.

3. The 1950s provide the best fit: the money supply and prices both rose by about 25 percent.

4. However, in the 1960s the relationship deteriorated again: the money supply increased by 45 percent, but consumer prices by less than 30 percent.

5. During the 1970s, the money supply rose by 90 percent, while prices rose by 105 percent.

On balance, the data imply that money has a lot to do with creeping inflation. People will not be able to continue buying the same amount of goods and services at higher and higher prices unless the money supply increases. If the money supply today were no larger than it was in 1950 ($115 billion), prices would have stopped rising long ago—and so would real economic activity.

More specifically, an increase in the money supply is a *necessary* condition for the continuation of inflation, creeping or otherwise. But it is not a *sufficient* condition. Increases in the money supply will not raise prices if velocity falls (as in the 1930s). Even if velocity remains constant, an increase in the money supply will not raise prices if production expands. When we are in a depression, for example, the spending stimulated by an increase in the money supply is likely to raise output and employment rather than prices. Furthermore, in the short run at least—and sometimes the short run is a matter of several years—increased spending and inflation can be brought about by increases in velocity without any increase in the money supply.

Let us end this section with a summary statement of the role of money in the inflation process. Does more money *always* lead to inflation? No, but it can under certain circumstances, and if the increase is large enough it probably will. Case 1: If the central bank expands the money supply while we are in a recession, the increased spending it induces is likely to lead to more employment and a larger output of goods and services rather than to higher prices. Case 2: As we approach full employment and capacity output, increases in the money supply become more and more likely to generate rising prices. However, if this increase is only large enough to provide funds for the enlarged volume of transactions accompanying real economic growth, inflation still need not result. Case 3: Only when the money supply increases under conditions of high employment *and* exceeds the requirements of economic growth can it be held primarily responsible for kindling an inflationary spiral.

The time horizon and the extent of inflation are also relevant. In the short run, an increase in monetary velocity alone (generated by increasing government or private spending), with a constant or even declining money supply, can finance a modest rate of inflation. The longer the time span, however, and the higher prices rise, the less likely that velocity can do the job by itself. Over the longer run, the money supply must expand for inflation to persist.

Conclusions: More money does not always lead to inflation (Cases 1 and 2), but sometimes it does (Case 3). In the short run, inflation can make some headway without any change in the money supply, but rising prices cannot proceed too far too long unless inflation is fueled by an expanding money supply.

The Trade-off Between Price Stability and Employment

Since inflation is not something we want any more of, and since the monetary tools to curb it are at hand, why don't we just put a firm brake on the money supply and stop these never ending increases in the cost of living?

We hesitate because of an apparent conflict of national objectives. The cost of price stability—in terms of the unemployment necessary to get it—is too high. If we pursued monetary policies with the determination necessary to put a total and complete brake on inflation, we would probably find ourselves with catastrophic rates of unemployment, at least in the short run. We do not want any more inflation, but we do not want any more depressions either, and so far we seem unable to find a solution to the problem of stopping rising prices without simultaneously bringing on at least a recession.

To put the problem succinctly, it appears that we cannot have both price stability and high employment at the same time. If we want stable prices, we have to sacrifice high employment. And if we want a high level of employment, we have to give up stable prices. Exactly what are the terms of this trade-off?

Chart 1 shows the rate of inflation and its associated rate of unemployment for every year from 1964 through 1981. In 1975, for example, we had 8½ percent unemployment and 7 percent inflation. In 1978, we had 6 percent unemployment but 9 percent inflation. Less unemployment but more inflation.

The freehand trend lines showing the relationship between unemployment and inflation are known as Phillips Curves, after

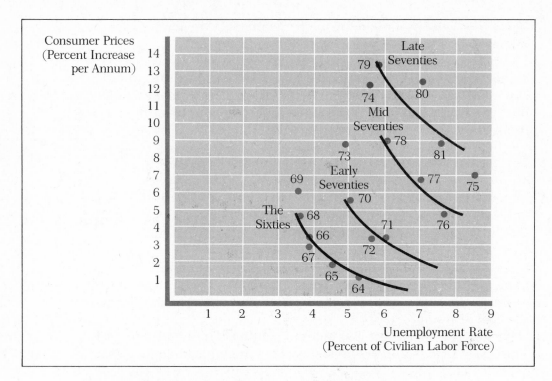

Chart 1 / Prices and Employment: The Trade-Off

their popularizer, Professor A. W. Phillips. The Phillips Curve for the 1960s indicates that to obtain absolute price stability then would have required unemployment approaching 7 percent. In the early 1970s, absolute price stability would have meant unemployment closer to 9 percent. In the late 1970s and early 1980s, matters grew even worse.

The optimum choice among this array of less-than-happy alternatives is not amenable to a purely economic solution. If we move to the left on one of the curves and choose low unemployment, some people will be hurt by the resulting inflation. On the other hand, if we move toward the right and choose something close to stable prices, other people will be hurt by the resulting unemployment. An economist, as an economist, has no basis for judging which is better. Resolution of this conflict of interests fundamentally involves personal value judgments and assessments of the social implications of the alternatives more than it involves economics.[3]

Why has the Phillips Curve been shifting to the right since the 1960s, compounding our problems? One answer is that the trade-off between stable prices and high employment has gotten worse because of structural changes that have taken place in the economy. These include a changed composition of the labor force, an expansion in the demand for skilled labor but not for unskilled, more aggressive union behavior, increased market power in the hands of the large corporations, and the international oil cartel.

But there is another possibility—no Phillips Curve at all. The trade-off between stable prices and high employment is illusory. That towering iconoclast, Milton Friedman, has pounced on yet another victim!

Is There Really a Phillips Curve?

With respect to the underlying data, Chart 2 is exactly the same as Chart 1. However, instead of visualizing a series of rightward-shifting Phillips Curves, Chart 2 has a freehand trend line that shows price stability and low unemployment as *compatible* rather than incompatible. According to the trend line in Chart 2, the best way to reduce unemployment is by *lowering* the rate of inflation, not raising it. In other words, different people looking at the same facts come to diametrically opposite conclusions (not for the first time!).

The reasoning of Friedman and others goes something like this: Government policies to reduce unemployment do indeed initially generate rising prices. For a while, some reduction in unemployment can be bought with higher prices. But wage earners soon realize that rising prices are eroding the value of their pay raises. If they were satisfied with 3 percent pay raises when prices were stable, now they will want more to keep pace with inflation. If we assume that 4 percent inflation has been generated, for example, workers

[3]The chart does not show, for example, that for many years the black unemployment rate has been approximately twice the national average. Black teenage unemployment is typically six or seven times the overall jobless rate.

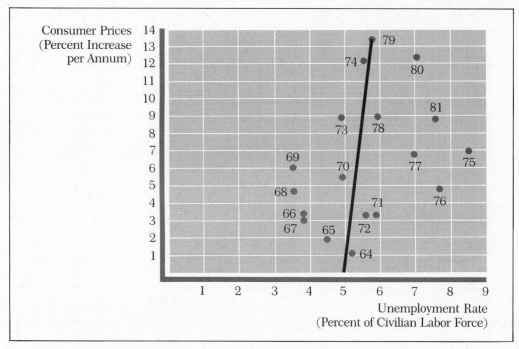

Chart 2 / Stable Prices and Low Unemployment: They Go Together, After All.

will want 7 percent pay raises to get a 3 percent *real* wage increase. If employers believe they can pass on such a wage increase in the form of higher prices, they will grant it—thereby making the inflation worse. Then, as the day follows the night, unions will want even larger money-wage increases next year to wind up with another real wage hike. Thus expectations of further inflation snowball through round after round of ever growing wage settlements promptly followed by corresponding price increases.

This has become known as the "accelerationist" hypothesis. It implies that ever increasing rates of inflation will be required to maintain unemployment at its lower level. It also suggests that if and when unemployment rises, the inflationary expectations that caused the spiral will remain for a while, thereby leaving us with *both* high unemployment and high inflation.

On such grounds, Friedman argues that there is no true trade-off between employment and prices, because in the long run you can't fool all of the people very much of the time. You may be able to buy some additional employment with higher prices for a while, but as soon as workers catch on that their pay raises are more imaginary than real, either the inflation will accelerate or businessmen will begin to lay off workers. In either case, the Phillips curve doesn't give the correct answer to the question of how high prices would rise if employment were increased by a given amount.

What should be done?

Nothing, says Friedman. Keep the money supply under tight control to reduce inflation and then let the economy find its own "natu-

"What, no Phillips curve!"

ral" rate of unemployment. Don't try to lower unemployment by countercyclical policies, because they'll only produce inflation. It will only help for a short while, and the more you do it the worse things will get.[4]

Is all this true? To some extent, yes. But most of the evidence points to a rather long run—such as five years—before all the employment effects of increased inflation are wiped out. We can still use inflation to buy some employment—but less than we thought and for a shorter time.

Summary

1. Inflation has been our major economic problem ever since the end of World War II.

2. In cases of hyperinflation, the money supply is clearly the main culprit.

3. Responsibility is not so clear with respect to creeping inflation. Demand-pull and cost-push elements have both been involved in the creeping inflation we have had since World War II. Among the cost-push elements are the strength of labor unions, the market power of big business, and the tactics of OPEC.

4. Increases in the money supply are a necessary but not a sufficient condition for creeping inflation. More money does not always lead to inflation, because velocity can fall and output can expand. In the long run, however, inflation cannot continue unless it is fueled by an expanding money supply.

5. Policy-makers do not clamp down on the money supply and put a stop to inflation because of an apparent conflict between the national objectives of stable prices and high employment. The Phillips Curve analysis shows that stopping inflation would mean substantial unemployment.

[4]An early presentation of this argument is in Milton Friedman, "The Role of Monetary Policy," *American Economic Review* (March 1968).

6. But is there really a Phillips Curve? Friedman and others argue that there may be in the short run but not in the long run. They conclude that in the long run the best way to get high employment is to pursue policies that yield stable prices.

Suggestions for Further Reading

The original article by A. W. Phillips describing the trade-off between inflation and unemployment is "The Relation Between Unemployment and the Rate of Change in Money Wage Rates in the United Kingdom, 1861–1957," *Economica* (1958). A classic survey of demand-pull versus cost-push inflation is by Paul Samuelson and Robert Solow, "Analytical Aspects of Anti-Inflation Policy," *American Economic Review* (May 1960). More recently, see David Laidler and Michael Parkin, "Inflation: A Survey," *Economic Journal* (December 1975). Many excellent articles dealing with inflation and the controversy between "structuralists" and "accelerationists" can be found in various issues of the *Brookings Papers on Economic Activity* since 1970.

Three good books devoted entirely to inflation are R. J. Ball, *Inflation and the Theory of Money* (Chicago: Aldine, 1965); James A. Trevithick and Charles Mulvey, *The Economics of Inflation* (New York: Wiley, 1975); and Thomas M. Humphrey, *Essays on Inflation* (Federal Reserve Bank of Richmond, 1979). Humphrey's Chapter 6, "Changing Views of the Phillips Curve," is particularly worth reading.

Finally, a very useful and readable small volume is G. L. Bach, *The New Inflation* (Providence, R.I.: Brown University Press, 1973).

3
Commercial Banking and Deposit Creation

THE BIBLE BEGINS with the creation of heaven and earth. Money and banking textbooks also begin with creation—the creation of money by commercial banks. Creation *ex nihilo* is the explanation in both cases. We are not qualified to demonstrate the biblical creation "out of nothing," so we'll confine ourselves to showing how banks create money out of nothing. To see how it works, let's go into the banking business ourselves.

The Business of Banking

Commercial banks, as we saw in Chapter 1, are the habitat of almost all of the country's demand deposits (checking accounts). Since demand deposits are money, that looks like an intriguing business to get involved in. First we'll have to get together enough of our friends to back us, since you need a lot of money to begin with before you can start a bank. Poor people don't open banks (at least not legally).

While we're dreaming, we may as well go all out and assume we can raise $5 million, that the various legal formalities are satisfied, and that our bank is chartered as a member of the Federal Reserve System. For $1 million we buy a building and refurbish it like a spooky castle in Transylvania, hire six tellers and talk them into wearing monster masks (like Dracula, Frankenstein, and Ritter and Silber), and employ a sour-faced accountant who graduated from embalming school and knows more about formaldehyde than accounts receivable. One overcast and gloomy day we open our doors for business. The accountant reluctantly stops reading *Horror Comics* long enough to show us the bank's balance sheet on opening morning:

ASSETS		LIABILITIES AND NET WORTH	
Cash	$4,000,000	Net Worth	$5,000,000
Building, etc.	1,000,000		

This looks nice, but it could be better. Too much cash. Doesn't earn any interest. So we immediately take three-quarters of the cash and buy government bonds with it. The T-account, showing the *changes* that occur in our balance sheet, looks like this:

A		L & NW
Cash	− $3,000,000	
Government bonds	+ 3,000,000	

Next, for purposes that will become clear shortly, we take another $900,000 and ship it to our regional Federal Reserve Bank, to open up a deposit in our bank's name:

A		L & NW
Cash	−$900,000	
Deposit in Fed	+ 900,000	

During the course of the first few days, we gleefully welcome long lines of new depositors who open up accounts with us by depositing $2 million worth of checks drawn on *other* banks—where they are closing out their accounts, because they like our ambience better. Our T-account for these deposits is as follows:

A		L & NW	
Cash items in process of collection	+$2,000,000	Demand deposits	+$2,000,000

A demand deposit in a bank is an asset for the depositor. It is part of his wealth. For the bank, however, it is a *liability,* a debt, because we are obligated to pay it—indeed, to pay it *on demand.* A demand deposit must be paid any time the depositor wishes, either by handing out currency across the counter or by transferring the funds to someone else upon the depositor's order. That is precisely what a check is: a depositor's order to a bank to transfer his funds to whomever is named on the check, or to whomever has endorsed it on the back.

We now have $2 million of checks drawn on other banks that our new customers have deposited with us. We have to "collect" these checks—so far they are just "cash items in process of collection." If we had the time, we could take each check to the bank on which it is drawn, ask for currency over the counter, and then haul it back to our own bank. Since this would get tedious if we had to do it every day, what we do instead is what other banks do—rely on the Federal Reserve to help us in the check collection process. Federal Reserve Banks play a pivotal role in collecting checks, so vital that we must digress a moment to see how they do it.

There are twelve Federal Reserve Banks around the country—in New York, Atlanta, Dallas, Minneapolis, San Francisco, and so on. Every commercial member bank is affiliated with one of them. The Federal Reserve Banks themselves have little direct contact with the public; mostly they deal with the government and with commercial banks. Through facilities they provide, however, checks are efficiently collected and funds transferred around the country. The primary collection vehicle is the deposit that each member bank maintains with its regional Federal Reserve Bank, which is one reason we deposited $900,000 in our Federal Reserve Bank two T-accounts back.

Let's see how the collection process works. We take the $2 million worth of checks our new customers have deposited, checks drawn on other banks, and ship the whole batch of them to the Federal Reserve Bank. The Fed credits us with these checks by increasing our "deposit in the Fed" by that amount. At the same time, it *deducts* $2 million from the "deposits in the Fed" of the banks on which the checks were drawn. It then sends these checks to the appropriate banks, with a slip notifying them of the deduction, and the banks in turn deduct the proper amounts from their depositors' accounts. The

"Come right in. What makes you think we're not a member of the Federal Reserve System?"

T-accounts of the whole check collection process look like this, with the arrows showing the direction in which the checks move:

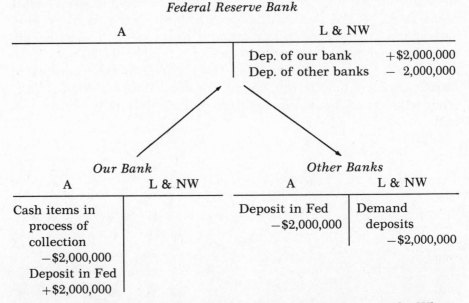

Federal Reserve Bank

A	L & NW	
	Dep. of our bank	+$2,000,000
	Dep. of other banks	− 2,000,000

Our Bank

A	L & NW
Cash items in process of collection −$2,000,000 Deposit in Fed +$2,000,000	

Other Banks

A	L & NW
Deposit in Fed −$2,000,000	Demand deposits −$2,000,000

We can summarize this collection process in a few words. When a bank receives a check drawn on another bank, it gains deposits in the Fed equal to the amount of the check. Conversely, the bank on which the check was drawn loses deposits in the Fed of the same amount.[1] We will see soon that deposits in the Fed are part of a bank's *reserves.* We can rephrase the above into an important banking principle: *When a bank receives a check drawn on another bank, it gains reserves equal to the amount of the check. Conversely, the bank on which the check was drawn loses reserves of the same amount.*

Two minor complications. One: What if some of the banks involved are not members of the Federal Reserve System? No problem. All financial institutions that accept checkable deposits, whether they are member banks or not, must hold reserves in the form of either vault cash or deposits with the Fed (or with another

[1]Notice that the deposits of member banks in the Federal Reserve Bank are *liabilities* of the Federal Reserve Bank (although assets of the commercial banks), just as deposits of the public in a commercial bank are liabilities of the bank (although assets of the depositors).

bank that in turn holds them with the Fed). So they will either clear checks directly through the Fed or through arrangements with a so-called correspondent bank that holds such reserves. Two: What if the two commercial banks involved are in different Federal Reserve Districts, so they have deposits in two *different* Federal Reserve Banks? Again no problem. The Federal Reserve has its own Inter-District Settlement Fund, where the twelve Federal Reserve Banks all hold accounts, and they settle up in such cases by transferring balances among themselves on the books of the Inter-District Settlement Fund.

So where do we stand now? Let's take a look at our bank's balance sheet, after all the above transactions have been incorporated into it:

A		L & NW	
Cash	$ 100,000	Demand deposits	$2,000,000
Deposit in Fed	2,900,000	Net worth	5,000,000
Government bonds	3,000,000		
Building, etc.	1,000,000		

Looking at this balance sheet reminds us that commercial banks have to hold part of their assets in the form of *reserves*. As mentioned above, all banks are required to hold reserves—*in the form of either cash or deposits in the Fed*—as specified by the Board of Governors of the Federal Reserve.

In particular, the Fed's regulations require that banks must hold cash and/or deposits in the Fed at least equal to a designated percentage of their demand deposit liabilities—3 percent of demand deposits on the first $25 million of deposits and 12 percent of any additional demand deposits.

How does our bank stand with respect to reserves? To simplify matters, let's assume from here on that all banks, ours included, have to hold reserves equal to a flat 10 percent of demand deposits, regardless of how much demand deposits they have. According to actual regulations, we should hold reserves of only 3 percent, since we haven't exceeded the $25 million deposit level yet; but let's assume, for illustrative purposes, that instead of a sliding scale for reserve requirements it is simply 10 percent.

We *have* reserves—cash and/or deposits in the Fed—of $3 million. With demand deposits of $2 million, we *need* reserves equal to 10 percent of that figure, or $200,000, to satisfy our legal obligation. Thus we have *excess* reserves of $2.8 million. That simple calculation, computing the amount of a bank's excess reserves, is crucially important in the banking business.

What should we do now? Unfortunately, with this balance sheet we are not too profitable. We have a lot of excess reserves that are earning no interest, and not enough earning assets. All we have in the way of interest-bearing assets is the $3 million of government bonds we bought practically before we opened our doors. Banks make profits mostly by making loans. Surely we can hustle up some good loans—preferably to people who don't need the money, because they are obviously the ones who deserve it most (and are most likely to pay us back).

Let's assume we can find enough creditworthy borrowers who want to take out loans. Then a big question faces us: *How much can we safely lend?*

Deposit Expansion: The Single Bank

To answer the question of how much we can safely lend, we need to know two things: (1) how much excess reserves we have, and (2) what happens when we make a loan. We already know how much excess reserves we have—$2.8 million. So let's take a moment to examine what happens when we make a loan.

When a bank lends, the borrower does not ordinarily take the proceeds in hundred-dollar bills; he or she takes a brand-new checking account instead. On the bank's balance sheet, loans (an asset) and demand deposits (a liability) both rise. A bank *creates* a demand deposit when it lends. In effect, since demand deposits are money, banks create money.

How much, then, can we lend? Since the only limit on our creation of demand deposits appears to be the requirement that we hold a 10 percent reserve, a superficial answer would be that we can lend—and create demand deposits—up to a limit of ten times our excess reserves. We have excess reserves of $2.8 million, so why not lend ten times that, or $28 million? If we did, here is what would happen:[2]

	A		L & NW	
Loans	+$28,000,000		Demand deposits	+$28,000,000

And our new balance sheet would look like this:

	A		L & NW	
Reserves {	Cash	$ 100,000	Demand deposits	$30,000,000
	Deposit in Fed	2,900,000	Net worth	5,000,000
	Government bonds	3,000,000		
	Loans	28,000,000		
	Building, etc.	1,000,000		

We now have some good news and some bad news. First the good news: We have a fairly large amount of demand deposit liabilities —$30 million—and our reserves, at $3 million, are legally sufficient to support them. It appears we have found a veritable gold mine. In business hardly a month, only a $5 million investment, and here we are collecting the interest on $3 million of government bonds *and* $28 million of loans.

But wait a minute, because here comes the bad news: We haven't really looked into what happens *after* a borrower takes out a loan. Most borrowers don't take out loans, and pay interest on them, just to leave the funds sitting there. They want to *spend* the money. (Gulp!) And when they do, they'll write checks on those brand-new demand deposits, the checks will probably be deposited in *other* banks by their recipients, and when they clear through the Federal Reserve we'll *lose reserves.* (Remember that a bank on which a

[2]Actually, a bank would typically "discount" the loan—that is, deduct the interest in advance, giving the borrowers somewhat less than $28 million. For the sake of convenience, let's ignore this detail.

check is drawn loses reserves equal to the amount of the check.) Thus, for our bank:

A		L&NW	
Deposit in Fed	−$28,000,000	Demand deposits	−$28,000,000

If our deposits in the Fed are only $2.9 million to begin with, we can hardly stand by calmly while they fall by $28 *million*. We'll wind up in jail instead of on the Riviera. Something has clearly gone very wrong. What has gone wrong, obviously, is that we miscalculated our lending limit, the amount we could safely lend— "safely" meaning without endangering our legal reserve position.

What, then, is our safe lending limit? It is the amount of reserves we can afford to lose, and we already know what that is: our *excess* reserves. *A commercial bank can lend up to the amount of its excess reserves, and no more.* If it tries to lend more, it will find itself with inadequate reserves as soon as the borrowers spend the proceeds of the loans and the checks are collected through the Federal Reserve's check-collection facilities.

So let's start over again. Our excess reserves are $2.8 million. If we lend that amount, our balance sheet entry is:

A		L & NW	
Loans	+$2,800,000	Demand deposits	+$2,800,000

When the borrowers spend the funds, assuming the checks are deposited in other banks, we have:

A		L & NW	
Deposit in Fed	−$2,800,000	Demand deposits	−$2,800,000

Which leaves our balance sheet as follows:

A			L & NW	
Reserves { Cash	$ 100,000		Demand deposits	$2,000,000
Deposit in Fed	100,000		Net worth	5,000,000
Government bonds	3,000,000			
Loans	2,800,000			
Building, etc.	1,000,000			

Now, after all checks have cleared, we end up with deposits of $2 million and reserves of $200,000, which is right on the dot—our reserves equal one-tenth of our deposits. But notice that we got there by shrinking our reserves, *not* by blowing up our deposits (as in the previous disastrous example). We shrank our reserves by lending an amount equal to the excess, which resulted in an equivalent reduction in our reserves in the ordinary course of events.[3]

Notice also that the purchase of securities would have the same effect on reserves as lending, except that it would probably occur more rapidly. If we bought securities for the bank, we would generally not open a deposit account for the seller, but simply pay him with a check drawn on the bank (payable via our account at the Fed). As soon as the check cleared, our reserves would fall by that amount.

The conclusion of this section is worth emphasizing: A single commercial bank cannot safely lend (or buy securities) in an amount greater than its excess reserves, as calculated *before* it makes the loan. But it *can* lend or buy securities up to the amount

[3]Calculation of excess reserves to estimate our lending ability should always be made *prior* to extending new loans, without including the reserves needed to support the new loan-created deposits. For example, after we made the $2.8 million of loans noted above, demand deposits went up by the same amount, so that required reserves rose by $280,000. But that $280,000 increase in required reserves does not affect our lending ability, because so long as those $2.8 million of deposits are there, our reserves are more than ample. It is not until those loan-created deposits disappear—when the borrowers write checks on their new deposits—that our reserves will drop, as the checks are collected in favor of other banks through the Federal Reserve. By that time, however, we won't need reserves against those deposits, since they will no longer be on our books.

of its excess reserves without endangering its legal reserve position.

The individual bank can therefore create money (demand deposits), but only if it has excess reserves to begin with. As soon as it has created this money—in our case, $2.8 million—it *loses* it to another bank when the money is spent. This is the key to the difference between the ability of a single bank to create money as compared with the banking system as a whole.

Deposit Expansion: The Banking System

When we lent our $2.8 million and created demand deposits of that amount for the borrowers, they soon spent the funds, and we lost both the newly created deposits and reserves of a like amount. That ended *our* ability to lend. But in the check-clearing process, some other banks *gained* $2.8 million of deposits and reserves, and those other banks can expand *their* lending, for now *they* have excess reserves.

Let's simplify our calculations at this point and assume that instead of having excess reserves of $2.8 million, and lending that amount, we had excess reserves of only $1,000, and had lent that. This will make the numbers easier to work with. When the checks cleared, some other banks would have gained $1,000 of deposits and reserves, and those other banks could now continue the process, for they now have excess reserves. If the entire $1,000 were deposited in one bank (Bank B), that bank's T-account would look like this:

Bank B

A		L & NW	
Deposit in Fed	+$1,000	Demand deposits	+$1,000

Bank B can now extend credit and create additional demand deposits. Assuming it was all loaned up (zero excess reserves) before it received this deposit, how much could Bank B lend? Less than we did, because its excess reserves are not $1,000 but only $900—it has new reserves of $1,000, but it needs $100 additional as reserves against the $1,000 deposit.

If Bank B does indeed make a $900 loan, we should start to sense what is going to happen. Its loans and deposits will both rise by $900, and when the borrowers spend the funds its *reserves* and deposits will both fall by the same amount. Net result: Its demand deposits will drop back to $1,000, its reserves to $100, and its lending (and money-creating) ability will be exhausted.

However, when Bank B's borrowers spend their $900, giving checks to people who deposit them in other banks (such as Bank C), the very clearing process that takes reserves and deposits away from Bank B transfers them *to* Bank C:

Bank C

A		L & NW	
Deposit in Fed	+$900	Demand deposits	+$900

Now Bank C can carry the torch. It can lend, and create new demand deposits, up to the amount of *its* excess reserves, which are $810. As the process is repeated, Bank D can lend $729 (creating that much additional demand deposits), Bank E can lend $656.10, Bank F $590.49, and so on. Because the reserve requirement is 10 percent, each bank in the sequence gets excess reserves, lends, and creates new demand deposits equal to 90 percent of the preceding one. If we add $1,000 + $900 + $810 + $729 + $656.10 + . . . the summation of the series approaches $10,000.

When expansion has approached its $10,000 limit, the banking *system* will have demand deposits that are a multiple of its reserves —demand deposits will be $10,000 on the liabilities side and reserves $1,000 on the asset side for all banks taken together. (At the same time, of course, banks will also have $9,000 in other assets—loans in our example.) For the banking system, this final stage is reached not by shrinking reserves, as in the case of a single bank, but by blowing up deposits. The key: While each individual commercial bank loses reserves after it lends—in the check-clearing process—some bank always gains the reserves another bank loses, so reserves for the entire banking system do not change. They just get transferred from bank to bank. However, as banks lend more and more, demand deposit liabilities grow, thereby reducing *excess* reserves even though the total reserves of the system do not change. This continuous decline in excess reserves eventually sets a limit on further expansion. (Although we promised creation *ex nihilo,* we didn't say it could go on forever.)

In more general terms, how much can the banking system expand demand deposits? While a single commercial bank can lend (and create demand deposits) only up to the amount of its excess reserves, the banking *system* can create demand deposits up to a *multiple* of an original injection of excess reserves.

The particular expansion multiple for the banking system depends on the prevailing required reserve ratio. In our example, with a reserve requirement of 1/10, the multiple is ten (an original increase of $1,000 in excess reserves can lead to an eventual $10,000 increase in demand deposits). If the reserve requirement were 1/5, the multiple would be five (an original increase of $1,000 in excess reserves could lead to a potential $5,000 increase in demand deposits). In general, *the multiple is always the reciprocal of the reserve requirement ratio.* In brief, for the entire banking system:

$$\text{original excess reserves} \times \frac{1}{\text{reserve ratio}} = \frac{\text{potential change in}}{\text{demand deposits}}$$

We can derive this formula more formally. We have been assuming that each bank lends out all of its excess reserves. The process of deposit expansion can continue until all excess reserves become required reserves because of deposit growth; then no more deposit expansion can take place. At that point, total reserves (R) will equal the required reserve ratio on demand deposits (r_{dd}) times total demand deposits (DD). That is:

$$R = r_{dd} \times DD$$

Dividing both sides of the equation by r_{dd} (which is a legal operation even in the banking business) produces:

$$\frac{R}{r_{dd}} = \frac{r_{dd} \times DD}{r_{dd}}$$

or

$$R \times \frac{1}{r_{dd}} = DD$$

Using the familiar delta sign to denote change-in, we have:

$$\Delta R \times \frac{1}{r_{dd}} = \Delta DD$$

where the change in reserves initially produces excess reserves in that amount until demand deposits are created in sufficient magnitude by the banks to put all the reserves in the required category.[4]

Deposit Contraction

A change in demand deposits can, of course, be down as well as up, negative as well as positive. If we start with a *deficiency* in reserves in the formula, a negative excess, the potential change in demand deposits is negative rather than positive. Instead of money being *created* by banks when they lend or buy securities, money is *destroyed* as bank loans are repaid or securities sold.

When someone repays a bank loan, the bank has fewer loans outstanding and at the same time deducts the amount repaid from the borrower's demand deposit balance. There are fewer demand deposits in existence; money has disappeared. Similarly, if a bank

[4]An even more formal derivation of the relationship between changes in reserves and changes in deposits uses the formula for the sum of the (geometric) series discussed above in the text. In particular, the change in demand deposits due to an increase in reserves can be expressed as follows:

$$\Delta DD = \Delta R \left[1 + (1 - r_{dd}) + (1 - r_{dd})^2 + \ldots + (1 - r_{dd})^n \right]$$

There is a formula (white and bubbly) which gives the sum of the geometric progression within the brackets. As n gets infinitely large, the formula becomes:

$$\frac{1}{1 - (1 - r_{dd})} = \frac{1}{r_{dd}}$$

or, believe it or not:

$$\Delta DD = \Delta R \times \frac{1}{r_{dd}}$$

sells a bond to one of its own depositors, it takes payment by reducing the depositor's checking account balance. If it sells a bond to a depositor in another bank, the other bank winds up with fewer demand deposit liabilities.

The potential multiple contraction in demand deposits follows the same principles discussed above for the potential expansion of demand deposits, with one exception: the entire downward multiple change in demand deposits could conceivably take place in one single bank.

Say that a bank has a $1,000 reserve deficiency. It is then faced with two stark alternatives: It must either (a) increase its reserves by $1,000 or (b) decrease its demand deposits by ten times $1,000, or $10,000 (assuming a reserve requirement of 10 percent).

Let's take the second alternative first. The bank could decrease its demand deposits by the entire $10,000 by demanding repayment of that many loans, or by selling that many securities to its own depositors. Loans (or bonds) would drop by $10,000 on the asset side, demand deposits would drop by the same amount on the liabilities side, and the reserve deficiency would be eliminated. In this case, the single bank alone bears the entire multiple decrease in the money supply.

It is more likely that the bank will choose the first option, increasing its reserves by $1,000. One way it could go about this is by borrowing $1,000 in reserves from the Federal Reserve, an alternative we will discuss more fully in Chapters 4 and 13. Another way is by selling $1,000 of bonds on the open market, making the reasonable assumption that they will be bought by depositors in other banks (our bank being just a little fish in a veritable sea of banks). After the checks are cleared, its deposits in the Fed will be $1,000 higher and its reserves will be adequate once again.

But the reserves gained by Bank A will be another bank's loss. Some other bank—the bank where the purchaser of the bond kept his account—has lost $1,000 of deposits and $1,000 of reserves. Assuming that this second bank, Bank B, had precisely adequate reserves before this transaction, it now has a $900 reserve deficiency. It has lost $1,000 of reserves, but its requirements are $100 lower because it has also lost $1,000 of demand deposits, so its deficiency is only $900.

Bank B will now have no choice but to (a) get $900 in additional reserves, or (b) reduce its demand deposits by ten times $900, or $9,000. If it sells $900 of bonds to depositors in other banks, it gets its reserves, but in doing so it puts the other banks $810 in the hole. Thus the multiple contraction process continues very much like the multiple expansion process ($1,000 + $900 + $810 + $729 + $656.10 + . . .), and the summation of the series again approaches $10,000. At each stage, the bank that sells securities gains reserves, but at the expense of other banks, since the buyers of the bonds pay by checks that are cleared via the transfer of reserves on the books of the Federal Reserve Banks. Reserve deficiencies are shuffled from bank to bank, just as in the expansion process reserve excesses are shuffled from one bank to another.

There is a difference, however. When banks get *excess* reserves, they *may* lend more and increase the money supply; when they have *deficient* reserves, they *must* reduce their demand deposits. We usually assume that banks will want to lend out all of their excess reserves, and expand demand deposits to the maximum, because they earn interest on the loans generated in the process. But there can be exceptions, as we will see in subsequent chapters.

Control over bank reserves thus gives the Federal Reserve considerable power over the money supply. If the Fed can inject excess reserves into the banking system, it can *permit* commercial banks to expand the money supply by a multiple of the injection. If it can impose a deficit reserve position on the banking system, it can *force* a multiple reduction in the money supply.

We now turn to the Fed's tricks of the trade. Later, in Chapter 15, we will return to bank deposit creation and add a few complicating elements we have so far ignored in the interest of simplicity.

Summary

1. All banks are legally required to hold reserves, either in the form of vault cash or as deposits in their local Federal Reserve Bank.

2. When a bank receives a check drawn on another bank, it gains reserves (through the clearing process) equal to the amount of the check. Conversely, the bank on which the check is drawn loses reserves of the same amount.

3. A single bank can safely lend, and create demand deposits, up to the amount of its excess reserves.

4. However, the banking system can lend, and create demand deposits, up to a multiple of an original injection of excess reserves. The multiple is the reciprocal of the reserve requirement ratio.

5. A bank with deficient reserves must either (a) increase its reserves by the amount of the deficiency or (b) reduce its demand deposits by a multiple of the deficiency. Again, the multiple is the reciprocal of the reserve requirement.

6. Banks with excess reserves *may* lend more and increase the money supply. Banks with deficient reserves *must* either increase their reserves or reduce their demand deposits.

Suggestions for Further Reading

In case you feel you don't have a firm grasp of the basic principles underlying deposit expansion and contraction, try pp. 2–13 in Dorothy M. Nichols's excellent pamphlet, *Modern Money Mechanics: A Workbook on Deposits, Currency, and Bank Reserves,* which is available free from the Federal Reserve Bank of Chicago (P.O. Box 834, Chicago, Illinois 60690).

4

A Bird's-Eye View of the Federal Reserve

THE FEDERAL RESERVE—twelve regional Federal Reserve Banks and a Board of Governors in Washington—possesses ultimate control over bank lending and the money supply. It exercises this authority through its power to alter the reserves of banks and other deposit-type financial institutions, regardless of whether they like it or not. The Fed manipulates reserves in several different ways, none of which—contrary to what you may have heard—are particularly dramatic.

It is *not* true, for instance, that the Federal Reserve has experienced safecrackers scattered throughout the United States, whose job it is to break into vaults in the dead of night and remove stacks of hundred-dollar bills when the Fed wants to reduce reserves, or add stacks of hundreds when it wants to increase them. That is simply not the way the Federal Reserve operates. Besides, it would foul up everybody's bookkeeping, and since the whole monetary system is based on bookkeeping, as you're starting to see, it would be self-defeating.

Neither is it true that the Fed places self-destruct tape recordings in secret hiding places, instructing undercover agents to undertake perilous missions designed to confuse bank presidents so that they think they have more (or less) excess reserves than they actually have. The Federal Reserve has denied these rumors as total fabrications.

The central bank's methods are more prosaic (at least so far as we know). It alters bank excess reserves either by changing reserve *requirements* relative to deposits, or by changing the actual *amount* of reserves the banks hold. In this chapter we will take a first look at these methods, and then go into them in greater depth in Chapter 13.

Reserve Requirements

Within boundaries established by Congress, the Federal Reserve's Board of Governors can specify the reserve requirements that banks and other deposit-type institutions must hold against deposits. Congressional limits are that reserves must be between 8 and 14 percent of demand deposits, and between 0 and 9 percent of business-owned time and savings deposits. Such reserves, as we have seen, must be held in the form of vault cash and/or deposits in a regional Federal Reserve Bank.

Lowering the demand deposit required reserve ratio—for example, from 14 to 10 percent—does two things. First, it instantly and automatically increases banks' excess reserves, since less reserves are now required against any given volume of demand deposits. A bank with demand deposits of $1,000 and reserves of $140 would be all loaned up were the reserve requirement 14 percent; lowering it to 10 percent suddenly provides $40 of excess reserves. More excess reserves, of course, enable banks to make more loans, buy more securities, and expand demand deposits.

In addition, lowering the required reserve ratio also increases the demand deposit expansion *multiplier* for the entire banking system, since, as we saw in Chapter 3, the multiplier is in fact the reciprocal of the required reserve ratio. The smaller the ratio, the larger its reciprocal. Thus a decrease in the required reserve ratio from 14 percent to 10 percent would raise the deposit expansion multiplier from about seven to ten.

Raising reserve requirements—for example, from 10 to 14 percent

—would have the opposite effects. It would create reserve deficiencies, or at least reduce excesses, *and* lower the potential for multiple expansion. Putting banks into a deficit reserve position would *force* them to call in loans and sell securities, bringing about a reduction in demand deposits, while smaller excesses would at least restrain lending and deposit creation.

Discounting and the Discount Rate

The Federal Reserve may also alter the excess reserves of banks and other depository institutions by changing the actual amount of reserves they hold. One way this is accomplished is through the discount mechanism—which amounts to the Fed lending reserves, temporarily, to the banks. The Fed charges an interest rate, called the discount rate, on such loans. In other words, banks faced with reserve deficits can temporarily borrow reserves from their regional Federal Reserve Bank at a price (the discount rate).

Say that a bank in Cucamonga, California, has a reserve deficiency of $1,000 (it needs $1,000 more reserves than it has). Rather than take the drastic step of calling in loans, and preferring not to sell securities, it can borrow the reserves it needs from the Federal Reserve Bank of San Francisco at the prevailing discount rate. If it did so, the T-accounts would look like this:

Federal Reserve Bank

A		L & NW	
Loan to Cucamonga Bank	+$1,000	Deposit of Cucamonga Bank	+$1,000

Cucamonga Commercial Bank

A		L & NW	
Deposit in Fed	+$1,000	Due to Fed	+$1,000

When a businessman borrows from a bank, he receives a brand-new deposit at the bank. A bank is in the same position relative to the Federal Reserve: when it borrows from its friendly neighborhood Federal Reserve Bank, it receives a brand-new deposit at the Fed which increases its legal reserves.[1] The ability to borrow these reserves—to discount from the Fed—means that the Cucamonga bank does not have to call in loans or sell securities, and the money supply can remain unchanged.

A bank might also be more aggressive and borrow enough reserves to move into an *excess* reserve position, to make additional loans and thereby increase the money supply. The Fed generally frowns on such behavior, and tries to discourage it by establishing ground rules as to when it is proper for banks to utilize the discount facility. In general, it is OK if a bank does so only once in a while in order to adjust a deficit reserve position. It is not OK if a bank borrows frequently and in order to *expand* its earning assets.

More important, the Federal Reserve tries to influence the willingness of banks to borrow reserves by changing the interest rate it charges on such loans (the discount rate). A lower discount rate will make the borrowing of reserves more attractive to banks, and a higher discount rate will make it less attractive.

A shortcoming of the discount mechanism for injecting or withdrawing reserves is that the initiative as to whether or not to borrow from the Fed rests not with the Fed but with the banks.

Banks will want to borrow reserves only when they need them. If they already have ample reserves, there is no reason for them to borrow more, no matter how low the discount rate. During the 1930s and 1940s, for example, when banks generally had substantial excess reserves, the discount mechanism rusted from disuse and changes in the discount rate became irrelevant. In recent decades, however, excess reserves have declined and discounting has once again become common, so that changes in the discount rate are more important as a tool of Federal Reserve policy. Nevertheless, since the initiative still rests with the banks rather than the Fed, the

---

[1]Notice again that the Cucamonga bank's deposit in the Fed is an asset of the Cucamonga bank, but a liability of the Fed (just as your deposit in a local bank is your asset but the bank's liability).

discount process is not a very efficient instrument for the Federal Reserve to use in injecting or withdrawing reserves when *it* wishes to do so.

Open Market Operations

The most important way the Federal Reserve alters the actual amount of reserves the banks hold is not by discounting, but by frequent buying and selling of government securities—better known as open market operations. Undertaken at its own initiative, open market operations are the mainstay of Federal Reserve policy.

About $700 billion worth of marketable government securities are outstanding. They are held as investments by the public—by individuals, corporations, financial institutions, and so on. Over $100 billion are held by the Federal Reserve System. These government securities came into being when the United States Treasury had to borrow to finance past budget deficits. Some are long-term bonds, running fifteen or twenty years until maturity, and others are shorter term, all the way down to government securities called Treasury bills that are issued for only a few months. The existence of this pool of widely held marketable securities, with many potential buyers and sellers, offers an ideal vehicle through which the Federal Reserve can affect bank reserves. Federal Reserve purchases of government securities increase bank reserves, and Federal Reserve sales decrease them. Here's how it works:

When the Federal Reserve *buys* $1,000 of government securities, much as you might buy a stock or a bond on one of the stock exchanges, it pays with a check drawn on itself. *If the Fed buys the securities directly from a commercial bank*—say from a bank in Succasunna, N.J.—the Succasunna bank sends the Fed's check to its regional Federal Reserve Bank (the Federal Reserve Bank of Philadelphia), and has its deposit at the Fed—its reserves—increased by $1,000. Its excess reserves rise by the full amount of the transaction, and with more excess reserves it can make more loans and increase its demand deposits.

The T-accounts for a Federal Reserve purchase of government securities directly from a commercial bank are:

Federal Reserve

A		L & NW	
Govt. securities	+$1,000	Deposit of Succasunna Bank	+$1,000

Succasunna Commercial Bank

A		L & NW
Deposit in Fed	+$1,000	
Govt. securities	−1,000	

But what the central bank giveth, the central bank can taketh away. When the Federal Reserve *sells* government securities out of its portfolio, it *gets paid* for them, and everything is reversed. Say the Fed sells $1,000 of government securities directly to our friendly Succasunna bank—the Succasunna bank now has gained $1,000 worth of securities, which is good, but it has to pay for them, which is bad. The Fed takes payment by deducting that sum from the Succasunna bank's deposit at the Federal Reserve, thus diminishing its reserves. If you were to draw up the T-accounts for the transaction, everything would be exactly the same as the T-accounts above, except that every plus sign would become a minus and every minus sign a plus. The Succasunna bank's excess reserves fall by the full amount of the transaction; if it had no excess reserves, now it has a $1,000 reserve deficiency.

Note that the Federal Reserve could achieve the same ends—that is, change bank reserves—by buying or selling any asset, such as record albums or any type of bond or stock. The reason for limiting its open market operations to the purchase and sale of government securities is quite obvious: Who would determine whether the Federal Reserve should buy Bob Dylan or Barry Manilow? General Motors stock or IBM? The Federal Reserve is smart enough, at least in this respect, not to get in the public's hair.

Of course, when the Federal Reserve buys (or sells) government securities, it has no assurance that a bank will be the other party to the transaction. But it doesn't matter whether the securities the Fed buys are being sold by a bank or by someone else, nor is it important whether the securities the Fed sells are ultimately bought by a bank or by someone else. In either case, when the Fed buys, bank reserves go up, and when the Fed sells, bank reserves go down.

For example, *suppose that when the Fed bought $1,000 of government securities, the seller of the securities wasn't the Succasunna bank but an insurance company in Mishawaka, Indiana.* It wouldn't matter if the insurance company were in Chillicothe, Ohio, Waxahachie, Texas, Tallahatchie, Mississippi, or even Punxsutawney, Pennsylvania. However, *this* insurance company happens to be in Mishawaka, Indiana.[2]

In any case, when the Fed buys it still pays for the securities with a check drawn on itself. When the insurance company deposits the check in its local commercial bank, the Mishawaka bank now has the Federal Reserve's check (an asset), and it gives the insurance company a demand deposit. In turn, the Mishawaka bank sends the check to its regional Federal Reserve Bank (the Federal Reserve Bank of Chicago), and receives in exchange a $1,000 addition to its reserves.

The T-account for the insurance company shows that it now has $1,000 less in government securities, and $1,000 more in its demand deposit account at its local commercial bank. For the Federal Reserve and the Mishawaka bank, the T-accounts for such a Federal Reserve purchase look like this:

Federal Reserve

A		L & NW	
Govt. securities	+$1,000	Deposit of Mishawaka Bank	+$1,000

[2]Speaking of place names reminds us of Zzyzx Road (believe it or not), which you will encounter on Interstate 15 about fifty miles out of Barstow on the way to Las Vegas.

Mishawaka Commercial Bank

A		L & NW	
Deposit in Fed	+$1,000	Demand deposit of Ins. Co.	+$1,000

Notice that in this case the commercial bank's excess reserves go up, but not by the full amount of the transaction. The bank has $1,000 more of reserves, but it needs $100 more (assuming a 10 percent reserve requirement) because its deposits have gone up by $1,000; thus its *excess* reserves have risen by $900. However, the money supply has *already* risen by $1,000, so the ultimate potential effect on the money supply is the same regardless of where the Fed buys its securities:

1. If the Fed buys $1,000 of government securities directly from commercial banks, bank excess reserves rise by the full $1,000 and the banking system can then create $10,000 of new money (assuming a 10 percent reserve requirement);

2. If the Fed buys from nonbanks, bank excess reserves rise by only $900 and the banking system can create $9,000 of new money—but the money supply has already gone up by $1,000, and $9,000 + $1,000 also equal $10,000. So, in the end, the ultimate effect on the money supply of either type of open market purchase turns out to be the same.[3]

Commercial banks are unable to do anything to offset these measures. If the Fed wants to reduce bank reserves by open market sales, there is nothing the banks can do about it. By lowering its selling price, the Fed can always unearth a buyer. Since it is not in business to make a profit, the Fed is free to alter its selling price as it wishes. And while any single commercial bank can replenish its own re-

---

[3]Similarly, were the Fed to *sell* securities to an insurance company, everything would be exactly the same as the T-accounts immediately above, except the signs would be reversed. Our Mishawaka bank would find its excess reserves diminished by $900 (not by $1,000, because although its reserves would be $1,000 lower, its deposit liabilities would also be that much lower). When the Fed sells securities directly to commercial banks, on the other hand, bank excess reserves fall by the full amount of the sale. However, in both cases the potential effect on the money supply is the same.

serves by selling securities to other banks—or to individuals who keep their accounts in other banks—the reserves of the other banks will then decline. Reserves replenished by one bank are lost by others. Total bank reserves must fall by the value of the securities sold by the Federal Reserve.

As suggested in Chapter 1 (see footnote 6 in that chapter), it should now be clear why a contraction or expansion in the money supply via pure monetary policy does not change the total size of the public's portfolio (its wealth) directly. The public gives up an asset, or incurs a liability, as part of the very process through which currency or demand deposits rise; the reverse occurs when demand deposits decline. For example, if the money supply is increased by Federal Reserve open market purchases of securities, the increased demand deposit acquired by the public is offset by the reduction in its holdings of government securities (they were purchased by the Federal Reserve). In any subsequent expansion of demand deposits by bank lending or security purchases, the public acquires an asset (demand deposits) but either creates a liability against itself in the form of a bank loan or sells to the bank an asset of equal value, such as a government bond.

A Step Back

It's time to step back a moment and look at where we are. We've seen that the central bank can affect the ability of banks to lend and buy securities, and thereby to create (or destroy) money. It can do this by changing bank required reserve ratios, or by changing the actual amount of bank reserves—by altering the discount rate and, most important, by open market operations. When banks are put in a deficit reserve position, they *must* take steps to reduce their demand deposit liabilities; when banks are given excess reserves, on the other hand, they *may* lend more, buy more securities, and increase the money supply—but the Fed cannot compel them to do so.

Why does the Fed engage in all these shenanigans? Because the money supply is important. Changes in the money supply alter people's liquidity and probably affect their spending, and spending

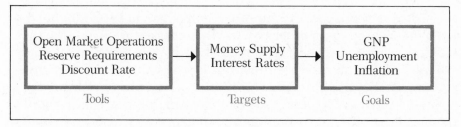

Open Market Operations Reserve Requirements Discount Rate	Money Supply Interest Rates	GNP Unemployment Inflation
Tools	Targets	Goals

Chart 1 / The Fed's Game Plan

helps determine whether we're going to have recession or inflation (or both!). In addition, by changing the ability and eagerness of banks to lend and buy securities, the Fed affects the terms on which banks lend—the interest rate. And this also influences spending by consumers and business firms: higher interest rates discourage borrowing and spending, while lower rates do the opposite.

Schematically, the Federal Reserve's game plan, at least as a first approximation, looks something like Chart 1.

The job of the Federal Reserve looks rather simple. In fact, it is far more complex than it appears, as we shall see in Part III.

Summary

1. The Federal Reserve regulates bank lending and the money supply through its control over bank reserves.

2. By changing the required reserve ratio, the Fed alters bank excess reserves and simultaneously changes the deposit expansion multiplier for the entire banking system. Lower required reserve ratios mean easier money, while higher ratios imply tighter money.

3. By changing the discount rate, the Fed affects the willingness of banks to borrow reserves from the Federal Reserve.

4. Most important, by buying or selling government securities (called open market operations), the Fed supplies banks with additional reserves or takes away some of their reserves. Fed

buying increases bank reserves (easier money), while Fed selling decreases them (tighter money).

5. By changing bank reserves and thereby the money supply, the
   Fed alters people's liquidity and, it is hoped, their spending on
   goods and services, which in turn helps determine GNP, the
   level of unemployment, and the rate of inflation.

Suggestions for Further Reading

See the suggestions at the end of Chapter 13 (page 206).

5
Financial Markets and Interest Rates

FINANCIAL MARKETS are basically the same as other kinds of markets. People buy and sell, bargain and hassle, win and lose, just as in the flea markets of Casablanca and Amsterdam or the gold markets of London and Zurich. In financial markets they buy and sell securities —like stocks and bonds—which are less tangible than hot bracelets or cold gold bars but are no less valuable. Stocks and bonds can be very valuable indeed, even though they are nothing but pieces of paper.

The Function of Financial Markets

Financial markets are the transmission mechanism between saver-lenders and borrower-spenders. Through a wide variety of techniques, instruments, and institutions, financial markets mobilize the savings of millions and channel them into the hands of borrower-spenders who need more funds than they have on hand. Financial markets are conduits through which those who do not spend all their income can make their excess funds available to those who want to spend more than their income.

Saver-lenders stand to benefit because they earn interest or dividends on their funds. Borrower-investors stand to gain because they get access to money to carry out investment plans they otherwise could not finance (and that presumably yield more than the interest they pay). Without financial markets, savers would have no choice but to hoard their excess money, and borrowers would be unable to realize any investment plans except those they could finance by themselves.

Financial markets give savers additional options besides that of simply holding their savings in the form of cash. They can, if they wish, *buy securities* with the money. Similarly, through financial markets borrowers can finance their investment plans even though they may not have previously accumulated funds to draw upon. They can *sell securities* to obtain the funds they need.

Schematically, Figure 1 illustrates in simplified form the flow of funds from ultimate saver-lenders, through financial markets, to ultimate borrower-spenders. Ultimate lenders are on the left, ultimate borrowers on the right. Funds flow from left to right, either directly (from ultimate lenders to ultimate borrowers via financial markets) or indirectly (through financial institutions, such as banks and insurance companies). The liabilities issued by ultimate borrowers, known as *primary securities,* flow in the opposite direction, from right to left, as they are purchased by either ultimate lenders (direct finance) or financial institutions (indirect finance).

Ultimate lenders are typically households, although from time to time business firms and governmental bodies—federal, state, and local—also lend substantial amounts. *Ultimate borrowers* are mostly business firms and governments, although households are also important as consumer credit and mortgage borrowers. The financial market in which the transaction takes place generally takes its name from the borrowers' side of the market, more specifically from the particular kind of primary security involved—the government bond market, the municipal bond market, the mortgage market, the corporate bond market, the stock market, and so on. Sometimes, however, it is the lender who gives the market its name, as, for example, the market for bank loans.

The existence of highly developed, widely accessible, and smoothly functioning financial markets is of crucial importance in

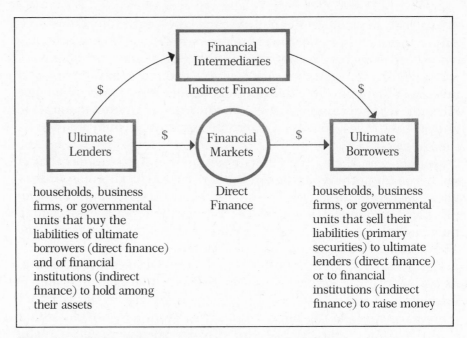

Figure 1 / Flows of Funds From Lenders to Borrowers

transmitting savings into the hands of those desiring to make investment expenditures. Those who can visualize and exploit potentially profitable investment opportunities are frequently not the same people who generate current saving. If the financial transmission mechanism is underdeveloped, inaccessible, or imperfect, the flow of funds from household saving to business investment will be impeded, and GNP will fall below its potential.

Assume, for example, that a significant portion of otherwise feasible investment plans is not undertaken because of lack of financing, due to the failure of financial markets to channel funds effectively from savers able to lend to business firms anxious to borrow. The end result of reduced investment spending is likely to be a level of GNP far below what could have been reached had financial markets operated more effectively.

A concrete example of the failure of financial markets to channel funds effectively arises when there is a lack of adequate information about borrowers seeking funds and/or lenders wanting to lend them. This highlights the main function of any market—to bring buyers and sellers together. In financial markets, it is buyers and sellers of credit. If some potential borrowers, for example, are unaware of financial markets—or if knowledge about sources of funds is not widely disseminated—then some investments which could have been undertaken won't be (there are savers who would have willingly lent the funds at rates of interest equal to, or less than, what investors would have been willing to pay).

A similar situation could arise as far as savers are concerned. Some may not be aware of lending opportunities. Instead of being put to work, funds are put under the mattress and less investment takes place (which in turn lowers saving as income declines). But well-developed financial markets do not permit such waste and inefficiency.

Securities brokers, dealers, and stock exchanges are some of the institutional arrangements that develop to help bring together buyers and sellers of financial assets. In addition to these trading facilities, financial intermediaries also step in to help set matters right.

The Role of Financial Intermediaries

Financial intermediaries are nothing more than financial institutions—commercial banks, savings banks, savings and loan associations, credit unions, pension funds, insurance companies, and so on—that act as middlemen, transferring funds from ultimate lenders to ultimate borrowers. They borrow from Peter in order to lend to Paul. (Actually, that cliché has been around for so long that Paul is way over his head in debt by now; his credit rating is lower than Chrysler's.) What all financial intermediaries have in common is that they acquire funds by issuing their own liabilities to the public (saving deposits, savings and loan shares), and then turn around and use this money to buy primary securities (stocks, bonds, mortgages) for themselves.

Because these institutions exist, savers who do not want to hoard their cash under a mattress, but who feel hesitant about purchasing corporate bonds or stocks or mortgages (primary securities) because they feel that these assets are perhaps too risky or too illiquid—or because they don't know about the availability of such items—have a third choice. They can "purchase" savings deposits or savings and loan shares. In that way they can hold a relatively safe and quite liquid financial asset, yet still earn *some* interest income. At the same time, corporations and potential homeowners can sell their bonds, stocks, and mortgages—to the financial intermediaries rather than to the original savers themselves. Financial intermediaries, in brief, "intermediate" between ultimate saver-lenders and ultimate borrowers.

Financial intermediation, or indirect finance, is precisely this process: Savers deposit funds with financial institutions rather than directly buying bonds or mortgages, and the financial institutions, in turn, lend to the ultimate borrowers.

Disintermediation is the reverse: Savers take funds out of deposit accounts, or reduce the amounts they normally put in, and invest directly in primary securities such as stocks and bonds.

Financial institutions are in a better position than individuals to bear and spread the risks of primary security ownership. Because of their large size, intermediaries can diversify their portfolios and minimize the risk involved in holding any one security. They are experts in evaluating borrower credit characteristics. They employ skilled portfolio managers and can take advantage of administrative economies in large-scale buying and selling.

Competition among financial intermediaries forces interest rates to the lowest level compatible with the intermediaries' evaluation of the risks of security ownership. These yields are lower than if the primary securities were held by individual investors, who are unable to minimize their risks as efficiently.

The growth in financial intermediaries has been spectacular in the post–World War II period. Time and savings deposits in commercial banks have grown from $30 billion at the end of World War II to $900 billion at the end of 1981, and savings and loan shares have increased from less than $10 billion to over $500 billion.

It is worth noting that since financial intermediation tends to lower interest rates, or at least to moderate any increase, it has been highly beneficial to our rate of economic growth.[1] A high rate of

---

[1]In recent years financial intermediation has grown but interest rates have frequently risen, because "all other things" have not remained constant. (In Parts IV and V we discuss these "other things.") Without financial intermediation, interest rates would have risen even higher.

economic growth requires a large volume of real investment. The lower the rate of interest that ultimate borrowers must pay, the greater their expenditure on real investment.

The beneficial effect of intermediation on economic growth can also be seen from the viewpoint of risk bearing. Intermediaries are better able than individuals to bear the risks of lending out capital. As was previously stressed, ability to diversify, economies of scale, and expertise in lending account for this comparative advantage of institutions over individuals. As financial intermediaries own a larger and larger portion of the marketable securities outstanding, the subjective risk borne by the economy is lowered, interest rates are reduced, and more real investment takes place. Funds are channeled from ultimate lenders, through intermediaries, to ultimate borrowers more efficiently than if the intermediaries did not exist. In Part II we will examine the operations of financial institutions in greater detail.

Having surveyed the function of financial markets and the role that financial intermediaries play in those markets, it is time to turn to a brief examination of the markets themselves. Generally, a distinction is drawn between the market for long-term securities (more than a year in original maturity), called the "capital market," and the market for shorter-term issues, the "money market."

The Capital Market

Stocks, bonds, and mortgages are the major kinds of primary securities in the capital market. Corporate *stocks* are evidences of ownership in a business firm. Since they are not debt instruments, they have no maturity date at all and pay an income (called dividends) that depends on the corporation's profitability. *Bonds,* unlike stocks, represent indebtedness; they promise to pay a certain number of dollars (called interest) each year for a stated number of years, and then repay the principal amount at maturity. *Mortgages* are debts incurred by someone borrowing to purchase land or buildings, with the land or building serving as security, or collateral. Like bonds,

Table 1 The Capital Market: Securities Outstanding (end of 1981)

Type of Instrument	Amount Outstanding*
Corporate stocks (at market value)	$1,500
Residential mortgages	1,160
Corporate bonds	530
U.S. Government securities (marketable, long-term)	480
Consumer loans	410
Commercial and farm mortgages	380
Bank business loans	360
State and local government bonds	320
U.S. Government Agency securities	230

*In billions of dollars.
SOURCE: Federal Reserve Flow of Funds Accounts and *Federal Reserve Bulletin*.

mortgages are debt instruments and promise to pay interest for a stated number of years and repay the principal at maturity. Mortgages are frequently amortized, which means that the principal is gradually repaid, along with the interest, during the life of the mortgage.

By far the largest sector of the capital market, in terms of dollar volume of securities outstanding, is the stock market, as Table 1 indicates. About 70 percent of all the outstanding stocks are owned by individuals, without the benefit of financial intermediation; the rest are held by such institutional investors as pension funds, mutual funds, and insurance companies (in that order).

Mortgages are usually divided into residential (one-to-four-family and multifamily homes) and commercial and farm mortgages. Most one-to-four-family home mortgages—some of which are insured by the Federal Housing Authority or guaranteed by the Veterans' Administration—are financed by savings and loan associations and savings banks, but commercial banks are also important lenders in this area. Multifamily mortgages are purchased mostly by thrift institutions (savings and loan associations and savings banks) and life insurance companies, commercial mortgages mainly by life insurance companies and commercial banks.

In the corporate bond market, life insurance companies are the main lenders (they own more than a third of the corporate bonds), followed by pension and retirement funds and households (direct finance). State and local government bonds, on the other hand, are bought primarily for their tax-exempt feature, since their interest is exempt from federal income taxes: Commercial banks own half of the total outstanding, followed by wealthy individuals (again direct finance) and property and casualty insurance companies.

U.S. Government securities are generally bought by a wide variety of purchasers, including the Federal Reserve, commercial banks, individuals, and foreigners. The same is true of the securities of various government agencies (such as the Federal Home Loan Banks, the Federal National Mortgage Association, and the Federal Land Banks); most of these are guaranteed, formally or informally, by the full faith and credit of the federal government.

In many of these sectors of the capital market, active trading takes place daily for outstanding issues—especially for stocks and for U.S. Government securities, to a lesser extent for corporate and for municipal (state and local) bonds. Trading is facilitated by a variety of institutions, including securities dealers and brokers, with expensive communications facilities, under the watchful eye of government regulators (such as the Securities and Exchange Commission). We will explore the functioning of all these markets in greater depth in Chapter 28.

In other sectors, such as consumer credit and bank business loans, there is virtually no secondary market at all—that is, no trading in outstanding securities—so that these securities have little marketability and liquidity. In the residential mortgage market, government-sponsored programs such as the Government National Mortgage Association pass-through program have facilitated a secondary market in mortgages (see Chapter 28), thereby giving home mortgages a degree of liquidity they formerly lacked.

Trading is most active, as noted, in the stock and bond markets, but even there it does not compare with the dollar volume of turnover that daily characterizes the money market, especially with respect to Treasury bills.

The Money Market

In contrast to the capital market, with its long-term securities, the money market specializes in short-term instruments that almost by definition are highly liquid—that is, readily marketable, with little possibility of loss. If you need to raise cash quickly and are forced to dispose of long-term securities, you can take a beating; but if you have short-term securities, chances are you can sell them without taking much of a loss. The short-term securities will mature pretty soon anyway, so if you can hold off a little while you can redeem them at face value when they mature. In addition, it is simply a fact of life, embedded in the mathematics of bond yields and prices, that for long-term securities a small change in interest rates involves a large change in price, whereas for short-term securities even a large change in yield involves only a small change in price.

Example: A rise in yield from 10 to 12 percent on a $10,000 face value thirty-year bond bearing a 10 percent coupon involves a fall in price from $10,000 to $8,348. A similar rise in yield on a three-month security of similar coupon involves a fall in price from $10,000 to only $9,770.[2]

For this reason, business firms and others with temporary surplus funds buy money market instruments rather than long-term securities. They purchase short-term money market securities and thus earn interest without much risk exposure. Commercial banks are particularly important participants in the money market, both as lenders and borrowers, as they adjust their legal reserve positions, invest temporarily idle balances, or sell some of their securities to raise funds in anticipation of forthcoming business demands for loans.

U.S. Treasury bills are the most liquid money market instrument, with about $250 billion outstanding. Treasury bills are short-term debts of the U.S. Government. Typically, they are issued for three months or six months or a year. They are highly marketable and actively traded by both financial and nonfinancial institutions. Treasury bills have been around since 1929.

In 1961 they were joined by bank CDs, when the First National

[2]For a more general proof, see the last section of this chapter.

City Bank of New York (now Citibank) introduced the large-denomination ($100,000 and over) negotiable certificate of deposit. As Table 2 indicates, there are now more CDs outstanding than Treasury bills. Negotiable CDs are deposits and thus liabilities of the issuing banks. But they are interest-earning assets to the corporations that hold them; they are attractive to corporate treasurers since they are readily marketable through dealers who specialize in buying and selling them. Thus a corporate treasurer who needs cash quickly can sell off CDs before they mature. The negotiable CD offers corporate treasurers an alternative to Treasury bills or other money market instruments. By raising the rate they pay on CDs, banks can entice corporate surplus funds that might otherwise go into Treasury bills.

Commercial paper is also largely held by corporate treasurers. It represents short-term liabilities of *prime* business firms and finance companies. Bankers' acceptances, the least important of the main money market instruments, arise mostly in the course of international trade transactions.

In addition to the above, the daily purchase and sale of "Federal funds" (member bank reserves at the Federal Reserve Banks) is also of major importance in the money market, particularly with respect to the role of commercial banks. In a typical Federal funds transaction, a bank with excess reserves will sell some of its excess to a bank with deficient reserves, on an overnight basis and at an agreed-upon interest rate. We will encounter Federal funds in a number of chapters; just remember, Federal funds as the term is used here has no necessary connection with the U.S. Treasury.

Table 2 The Money Market: Securities Outstanding (end of 1981)

Type of Instrument	Amount Outstanding*
Negotiable bank CDs (large denomination)	300
U.S. Treasury bills	250
Commercial paper	160
Bankers' acceptances	70

*In billions of dollars.
SOURCE: Federal Reserve Flow of Funds Accounts and *Federal Reserve Bulletin*.

Asset Prices and Yields

Before leaving this chapter, it is useful to have at least a nodding acquaintance with the calculation of bond prices and yields. For example, suppose you pay $900 for a $1,000-face-value 5 percent-coupon bond that will mature in ten years and that you expect to hold until maturity. *What annual interest rate will you be getting on that security?*

To begin with, you have to be careful to keep clear which interest rate you are talking about. At a minimum, it is important to distinguish between (1) the coupon rate, (2) the current yield, and (3) the yield to maturity.

1. *The coupon rate* is 5 percent, which merely means that printed on the face of the bond is the statement that each year the holder will get a payment equal to 5 percent of the $1,000 face value, or $50. If you had paid the $1,000 face value for the bond, you would indeed be getting 5 percent interest. But bond prices rise and fall. In this case, you are paying only $900; so although the coupon rate specifies 5 percent, you will actually be getting more than 5 percent because you paid less than $1,000. But how much more?

2. *The current yield* is calculated as the annual dollar interest payment divided by the price you paid for the bond, or $50/$900 = 5.56 percent. It looks appealing but actually it is rarely quoted because it is inexact except under rather restrictive assumptions. Specifically, it fails to take into account receipts accruing beyond a one-year time horizon, including the fact that when the bond matures, in ten years, you will have a $100 capital gain. (You paid only $900, but when the bond matures it will be redeemed at its $1,000 face value.)

3. *The yield to maturity*—the most widely used interest rate in the bond markets—takes into account the elements that the current yield neglects. To fully understand it, however, we will have to back up a moment and realize the implications of that venerable cliché: *time is money.* Like most clichés, it succinctly expresses a fundamental truth.

If you deposit $100 in a bank at 5 percent annual interest, what is your deposit worth after a year? The answer, of course, is $105. More formally: $100 (1 + .05) = $105. What is it worth after two years?

Due to compounding (receiving interest on interest), it becomes $105 (1 + .05) = $110.25. What the second year really amounts to is $100 (1 + .05) (1 + .05), or $100 (1 + .05)^2 = $110.25. On the same basis, after three years the deposit would be worth $100 (1 + .05)^3, after four years $100 (1 + .05)^4, and so on.

If $100 today at 5 percent interest is worth $105 a year from now, and $110.25 two years from now, we can *work backward* and say that $105 a year from now must be worth only $100 today, and that $110.25 two years from now must also be worth only $100 today. In the previous paragraph, we applied an interest rate to increase a present sum into the future; now, when we work backward, we are *discounting* to reduce a future sum back to its present value (time is money). Putting it a bit more formally, we have simply transposed the previous paragraph's

$$\$100 \ (1 + .05) = \$105 \qquad \text{into} \qquad \$100 = \frac{\$105}{(1 + .05)}$$

$$\text{and} \quad \$100 \ (1 + .05)^2 = \$110.25 \quad \text{into} \qquad \$100 = \frac{\$110.25}{(1 + .05)^2}.$$

With that as background, we can now understand—at least intuitively—the general formula for the price or present value (P) of a fixed-income security which pays a dollar coupon (C) in each of n years and has a face value (F) which will be paid off at maturity n years from now. The general formula for the present value or price of such a security is:

$$P = \frac{C_1}{(1 + r)} + \frac{C_2}{(1 + r)^2} + \frac{C_3}{(1 + r)^3} + \cdots + \frac{C_n}{(1 + r)^n}$$

$$+ \frac{F_n}{(1 + r)^n}$$

In our example, we already know the price or present value ($900), the coupon payments ($50), the face value ($1,000), and the number of years to maturity (10). Thus:

$$\$900 = \frac{\$50}{(1 + r)} + \frac{\$50}{(1 + r)^2} + \frac{\$50}{(1 + r)^3} + \cdots + \frac{\$50}{(1 + r)^{10}}$$

$$+ \frac{\$1000}{(1 + r)^{10}}$$

What we do *not* know is *r*—the particular rate of discount that will make the sum of all the expected future payments equal to the present value (or price) of $900. That particular *r* is called the *yield to maturity.* In corporation finance textbooks it is also called the internal rate of return.

What is *r* in this case?

We could figure it out by trial and error, trying one discount rate (say 5 percent) and then another (6 percent) until we find the one that makes all the terms on the right-hand side of the formula add up to $900. But that would be a time-consuming process. It would be a lot quicker (and easier) to look it up in a book of bond tables, where it is all figured out for us. There the yield to maturity in this particular case turns out to be 6.37 percent. That is the answer we have been searching for: 6.37 percent is the effective annual interest rate you will be getting on this security.[3]Put in terms of our previous forward-looking example: Investing $900 at 6.37 percent would generate coupon payments of $50 per year for ten years and a $1,000 payment at the end of ten years.

To summarize: A payment that is due to you in one year is discounted by $(1 + r)$, one due in two years by $(1 + r)^2$, one due in three years by $(1 + r)^3$, and so on; with a given *r,* the longer away the payment the smaller its present value (time is money!). The yield to maturity (or internal rate of return) of 6.37 percent is the rate of discount that will make the sum of the present values of all future payments equal to the price (of $900). The $900 price therefore consists of the sum of the discounted present values of all the expected future payments.

4.   We can use this example to illustrate the important *inverse relationship between bond prices and yields.* As early as Chapter 1 (see footnote 7), we mentioned that "a rise (or fall) in the price of a bond is reflected, in terms of sheer arithmetic, in an automatic change in the opposite direction in the effective rate of interest. To say the price of bonds rose or the rate of interest fell is saying the same thing in two different ways."

This is clearly seen by looking at our general formula for the present value or price of a bond. If the coupon (*C*) and the face value

---

[3]Bond tables are generally constructed on the assumption of semiannual interest payments. If you work this problem on a hand calculator, assuming only one interest payment a year, you will get 6.38 percent.

(F) are fixed, a higher price (P) must imply a lower yield to maturity (r). Similarly, a lower P must imply a higher r.

For instance, what if you paid not $900 but $950 for the bond we have been discussing? What yield to maturity would you be getting then? Substitute $950 for $900 in our illustration above. The yield to maturity, according to bond tables, would fall to 5.66 percent. What if you paid only $850? Then the yield to maturity would rise to 7.13 percent.

In our example, we have assumed that we know P and want to find the resulting interest rate. We could do it the other way around: we could assume we want to get a certain target rate of interest and then search for whatever price would provide it. For instance, enter 7 percent as a target rate of interest in the formula above, and then find the price that would provide that yield to maturity (assuming, of course, that C and F are fixed). The answer must be a price *below* $900, since $900 only gives us a 6.37 percent yield. (The answer, according to bond tables, is that in this case a price of $858 would produce a 7 percent yield to maturity.)

In this connection, the special case of a consol—or perpetuity— deserves a paragraph or two of its own because it illustrates this principle so clearly. A consol is a bond with no maturity date at all. It promises that the holder will receive a fixed annual dollar payment forever, with no redemption date. In that case, with n approaching infinity, our general present value formula collapses (you'll have to take our word for it) into simply:

$$P = \frac{C}{r}$$

Here it becomes obvious that, with C given (at say $50), the price ($P$) and the rate of interest (r) have to move inversely. If P falls, r must rise; and if P rises, r must fall.

5. We can also use our general formula above, for the present value or price of a bond, to explain why *a given change in interest rates affects long-term bond prices so much more than it affects the prices of short-term securities.* In the money market section of this chapter, we noted that "it is simply a fact of life, embedded in the mathematics of bond yields and prices, that for long-term securities a small change in interest rates involves a large change in price, whereas for short-term securities even a large change in yield involves only a small change in price."

This fact—the longer a bond's maturity, the more its price will be affected by a change in the general level of interest rates—has enormous implications for capital gains and losses. When all interest rates fall, short and long term, long-term securities rise dramatically in price, not short-term ones. Similarly, when all interest rates rise across the board, long-term bonds—not the shorter ones—drop drastically in price. In other words, you could get rich quick with long bonds, but you could also go down the drain.

Our general formula explains why this is so, when the change in interest rates is the same throughout the maturity range. The formula shows that the price or present value of a bond consists of the sum of the discounted present values of all of its future payments. With a short-term security, you will receive only a few future payments; thus a change in the discount factor (r) will have relatively little impact on the price. The longer the maturity of a security, however, the greater will be the impact of a change in r on the price because a larger number of future payments will be discounted, and for a longer period of time. The longer period of time is important: remember that discounting a payment due ten years hence isn't just discounting (dividing) by $(1 + r)$ but by $(1 + r)^{10}$.

6.   Finally, a word of warning. Thus far we have talked only about nominal interest rates, but *it is important to distinguish between nominal and "real" rates.* The 6.37 percent yield to maturity on our bond is a nominal rate of interest; it measures the return on the *dollars* invested in terms of the *dollars* received. The "real" rate of interest is defined as the nominal rate minus the rate of inflation—because inflation means that you will get back dollars that are worth less (in terms of purchasing power) than the dollars you originally paid out. In our example, if inflation proceeds at a constant rate of 5 percent a year, then the *real* rate of interest is 6.37 percent minus 5 percent or only 1.37 percent. If inflation is *greater* than 6.37 percent per annum, the real rate of interest would actually be *negative* —which was indeed the case in the late 1970s.

Summary

1. Financial markets are the transmission mechanism between saver-lenders and borrower-spenders. Ultimate lenders supply

funds to ultimate borrowers either directly, by buying primary securities, or indirectly, by buying the liabilities of financial intermediaries which in turn buy the primary securities.

2. Well-functioning financial markets facilitate the growth of GNP by giving both lenders and borrowers options they would not otherwise have, thereby increasing both saving and investment.

3. Financial intermediation involves financial institutions acquiring funds from the public by issuing their own liabilities and then using the funds to buy primary securities. Disintermediation is the reverse: savers take their funds out of financial institutions and buy the primary securities themselves.

4. Financial intermediation leads to lower interest rates because financial institutions can bear the risks of primary security ownership better than individuals. They also have economies of scale and more skilled portfolio management than is available to most individuals acting on their own.

5. The capital market refers to the market for long-term securities, such as corporate stocks and bonds. The money market refers to the market for short-term securities (one year or less in original maturity), such as Treasury bills and negotiable bank CDs. Money market instruments are more liquid than capital market securities.

6. The yield to maturity of a security is that rate of discount that will make the sum of the present values of all future payments equal to its price. Conversely, the present value or price of a security consists of the sum of the discounted present values of all its expected future payments.

7. The present value formula shows why there is an inverse relationship between bond prices and yields. It also shows why a given change in interest rates affects the prices of long-term bonds more than the prices of short-term securities.

8. It is important to distinguish between nominal and "real" interest rates. The real rate of interest is the nominal rate minus the rate of inflation. When the inflation rate is greater than the nominal interest rate, the real interest rate becomes negative.

Suggestions for Further Reading

The overall perspective of this chapter is derived primarily from John G. Gurley, "Financial Institutions in the Saving-Investment Process," *Proceedings of the 1959 Conference on Saving and Residential Financing* (United States Savings and Loan League, 1959). A very popular introduction to this general area is Dorothy M. Nichols, *Two Faces of Debt* (Federal Reserve Bank of Chicago).

For more on financial institutions, in terms of their activities and the composition of their assets and liabilities, see Robert P. Black and Doris E. Harless, *Nonbank Financial Institutions* (Federal Reserve Bank of Richmond); Raymond W. Goldsmith, *Financial Intermediaries in the American Economy Since 1900* (Princeton, N.J.: Princeton University Press, 1958); and Murray E. Polakoff, Thomas Durkin, et al., *Financial Institutions and Markets,* 2nd ed. (Boston: Houghton Mifflin, 1981). For a formal econometric investigation into financial institutions, see William L. Silber, *Portfolio Behavior of Financial Institutions* (New York: Holt, Rinehart and Winston, 1970).

The operations of the money and capital markets are explored in greater depth in *Money Market Instruments* (Federal Reserve Bank of Cleveland); *Instruments of the Money Market* (Federal Reserve Bank of Richmond); Wesley Lindow, *Inside the Money Market* (New York: Random House, 1972); and William C. Freund, *Investment Fundamentals* (Washington, D.C.: American Bankers Association, 1970).

There is also a lot of useful information in Yale L. Meltzer, *Putting Money to Work: An Investment Primer* (Englewood Cliffs, N.J.: Prentice-Hall, 1976); and in Marcia Stigum, *The Money Market: Myth, Reality, and Practice* (Homewood, Ill.: Dow Jones–Irwin, 1978).

On interest, discount, and related matters see Gary E. Clayton and Christopher B. Spivey, *The Time Value of Money* (Philadelphia: W. B. Saunders, 1978).

Appendix

Treasury Bills: Auctions and Yields

Treasury bills are such important money market instruments that it is worth taking a moment to see how they are issued and how their yields are calculated. Treasury bills do not carry a coupon entitling the holder to periodic interest payments, so the only way to get interest on them is to buy them at less than face (redemption) value. The interest earned is the difference between the purchase price and the price received when the bill is sold or redeemed at maturity. This difference is really a capital gain, but it is treated as interest income by the only people who count—the Internal Revenue Service.

Treasury bills typically have original maturities of three months, six months, or one year. The U.S. Treasury borrows money by selling bills at regularly scheduled auctions. Auctions for new three-month and six-month bills are held once a week and for new one-year bills once a month. Potential buyers who bid a high enough price get them and unsuccessful bidders don't. Of course, an unsuccessful bidder can always buy some afterward from one of the successful bidders.

The best way to see how the process works is to examine a typical Treasury bill auction. Table 1 in this appendix shows the results of the regular weekly auction of three-month and six-month bills that was held on Monday, May 10, 1982.

Before the auction, the Treasury announced that it would sell $4.7 billion of three-month bills and an equal amount of six-month bills (see the second line of the table). Some potential buyers, fearful of not getting their bills by competitive bidding, submitted noncompetitive tenders (line 3), which guaranteed they would receive them at the *average* price resulting from the auction. Since $1.2 billion of noncompetitive tenders were submitted for the three-month bill, the Treasury had to use competitive bidding only for the remaining $3.5 billion; and since $1.0 billion of such orders were submitted for the six-month bill, the Treasury had to sell only the remaining $3.7 billion competitively (line 4).

Competitive bids can be submitted at any Federal Reserve Bank or Branch until 1:30 P.M. on the day of the auction. At that time the Treasury closes the books and begins ranking the bids from the highest price on down. Table 1 shows that $13.9 billion of bids (both competitive and noncompetitive) were received for the three-month bills and $14.8 billion for the six-month issue—in both cases about triple what the Treasury wanted to sell.

The highest bid for the three-month bill was $96.917 for a $100 face value bill. (Actually, $10,000 is the minimum denomination for Treasury bills, so $96.917 really means $9,691.70. However, it is easier to do the calculations on the basis of $100 rather than $10,-000.) Everyone bidding at that price was a successful bidder. The Treasury continued to accept bids at lower and lower prices until they aggregated $3.5 billion for three-month bills and $3.7 billion for six-month bills. At that point—the stop-out price—the auction is over and those who submitted lower bids get nothing.

Since the successful bidders bought their bills at different prices, they will be receiving different yields. Two kinds of yield computations are used in the Treasury bill market: (1) yield on a discount basis and (2) the coupon equivalent yield (also called the bond equivalent yield).

Yield on a discount basis is calculated as the difference between the face value and the purchase price (let's call this D) divided by the face value. For example, Table 1 shows that high bidders for the new three-month bill received a $100 face value Treasury bill for $96.917. They paid $96.917 but in three months they'll get back $100. The difference (D) is $3.083:

$$\frac{3.083}{100} = 3.083\%$$

Table 1 Results of Treasury Bill Auction Held on May 10, 1982

	Three-month bills	Six-month bills
Amount applied for at auction	$13.9 billion	$14.8 billion
Amount scheduled to be sold	$ 4.7 billion	$ 4.7 billion
Noncompetitive tenders	$ 1.2 billion	$ 1.0 billion
Sales by competitive bidding	$ 3.5 billion	$ 3.7 billion
High price paid at auction	$96.917	$93.798
Yield on a discount basis	12.196%	12.201%
Coupon equivalent yield	12.759%	13.188%
Average price paid at auction	$96.904	$93.780
Yield on a discount basis	12.248%	12.236%
Coupon equivalent yield	12.814%	13.229%
Low price paid (stop-out price)	$96.896	$93.775
Yield on a discount basis	12.280%	12.246%
Coupon equivalent yield	12.849%	13.240%

SOURCE: United States Treasury.

However, all yields are commonly understood to be on an *annual* basis. Three-month bills are really 13-week bills; they mature 91 days from issue date. Assuming as a rough approximation that a year has 360 days, a yield of 3.083 percent for 91 days can be annualized by multiplying it by 360/91 or 3.956. Thus the annual yield on a discount basis for the three-month Treasury bill high bidders is 3.083% × 3.956 = 12.196% (see Table 1).

The general formula for calculating yield on a discount basis is:

$$\frac{D}{\text{face value}} \times \frac{360}{\text{number days to maturity}}$$

As another illustration, take the low bidders for the six-month bill. Six-month Treasury bills are really 26-week bills; they mature 182 days from issue date. Three- and six-month bills are always auctioned on a Monday, issued on Thursday of the same week, and mature on Thursday either 13 or 26 weeks later. This particular six-month bill would ordinarily mature on November 11, 1982. Since that is a national holiday (Veterans Day), it will mature one day later, on November 12.

Thus its annual yield on a discount basis would be:

$$\frac{6.225}{100} \times \frac{360}{183} = 12.246\% \text{ (see Table 1)}$$

Yields have been quoted on a discount basis in the money market for generations. They keep being used because custom and tradition are hard to overcome. Nevertheless, the yield on a discount basis is a poor indicator of the *true* yield for two reasons. First of all, an investor doesn't pay the full face value of a bill when buying it, so it shouldn't be the denominator in the first term of the expression. Second, there aren't 360 days in a year, so it shouldn't be the numerator in the second term of the equation.

Coupon equivalent yield corrects for these two flaws in yield on a discount basis. The formula for calculating the coupon equivalent yield is:

$$\frac{D}{\text{purchase price}} \times \frac{365}{\text{number days to maturity}}$$

For example, the low bidders for the six-month bill who paid $93.775 for a $100 face value security received a coupon equivalent yield of:

$$\frac{6.225}{93.775} \times \frac{365}{183} = 13.240 \text{ percent (see Table 1)}$$

As Table 1 shows, coupon equivalent yield is always *larger* than yield on a discount basis because the denominator of the first term is necessarily smaller (it is the purchase price instead of the face value) and the numerator of the second term is larger (365 rather than 360).

More generally, the formula for calculating the true yield of any Treasury bill is

$$\frac{F - P}{P} \div t$$

Where F is the face value, P is the purchase price, and t is the maturity in fractions of a year (¼, ½, etc.). In fact, this formula can be used to calculate the annual rate of growth for anything. In the case of a Treasury bill it calculates the annual rate of growth of an initial sum of money (P) into a final amount (F).

Part II
Intermediaries and Banks

6

What Financial Intermediaries Do

IN CHAPTER 5 we saw what financial intermediation is all about. Since savers are often wary of buying stocks, bonds, or mortgages, because they consider these assets too risky or illiquid, they acquire instead the relatively safe and liquid deposits of financial institutions. In turn, the financial institutions buy the stocks, bonds, and mortgages (primary securities). Financial institutions can minimize the risks involved better than individuals because their size enables them to diversify their portfolios more easily and because they have experts who can better evaluate the riskiness of various financial assets.

In this and the following four chapters we will examine how the major financial institutions function—how they acquire funds, what they do with the money once they get it, and how the profit motive and the regulatory environment influence their behavior. In this chapter we will take a broad look at each type of institution.

We are most interested in exactly how these institutions *intermediate* between saver-lenders and borrower-spenders. So we will pay special attention to the *composition* of their liabilities and assets, because they acquire funds from saver-lenders by "selling" their own liabilities, and then turn around and obtain earning assets when they disperse the funds to borrower-lenders. By paying a lower

86

interest rate when they acquire funds than they charge when dispersing them, financial institutions hope to make a profit on the differential.

Financial Institutions in Profile

Although all financial institutions have a lot in common, there are also substantial differences among them. Ranked in terms of asset size, for example, as in Table 1, commercial banks are easily the largest. In addition to sheer size, the composition of liabilities and assets also differs significantly from one type of financial institution to another.

1. *Commercial banks* are the most prominent of all financial institutions. There are about 15,000 of them, ranging from the Bank of America, with close to $100 billion in deposits, to thousands of small banks scattered throughout the country, many of which have less than $5 million in deposits.

They are not only the largest but also the most widely diversified in terms of both liabilities and assets. Their major source of funds

Table 1 Financial Institutions, Ranked by Asset Size (end of 1981)

Institution	Asset Size*
Commercial banks	$1,520
Savings and loan associations	660
Life insurance companies	510
Private noninsured pension funds	310
State and local government retirement funds	230
Sales and consumer finance companies	220
Property and casualty insurance companies	200
Mutual savings banks	180
Money market mutual funds	150
Credit unions	70
Mutual funds	70

*Total financial assets, in billions of dollars.
SOURCE: Federal Reserve Flow of Funds Accounts.

used to be demand deposits, but in the past two decades savings and time deposits—including certificates of deposit—have become even more important than demand deposits.

With these funds they buy a wide variety of assets, ranging from short-term government securities to long-term business loans and home mortgages. Because of their importance we will devote all of Chapters 8 and 10 to commercial banks.

2. *Savings and loan associations* (S&Ls) have traditionally acquired almost all their funds through savings deposits—usually called shares instead of deposits—and used them to make home mortgage loans. This was their original purpose—to encourage family thrift and home ownership. For the most part, S&Ls are still oriented in these directions, but changes are taking place rapidly. The Banking Act of 1980—formally known as the Depository Institutions Deregulation and Monetary Control Act of 1980—granted them the power to issue checking accounts (usually called NOW—for negotiable order of withdrawal—accounts) and also to make consumer loans.

There are about 5,000 savings and loan associations in the United States, extending from coast to coast. They have encountered serious problems in recent years because such a large proportion of their liabilities is in the form of savings deposits—which in effect are payable on demand—while so many of their assets consist of long-term mortgages, a lot of them acquired years ago when interest rates were much lower.

Typically they pay an interest rate of say 6 percent for their savings deposits and then turn around and make home mortgage loans at a higher rate, say 10 percent. The 4 percent differential is supposed to cover their operating costs and yield a profit. However, imagine the problems they face when short-term interest rates rise to say 14 percent: they are caught in a profit squeeze because they have to pay 14 percent to get new money, and also to prevent an outflow of their existing deposits, while their assets are still earning 10 percent (or even less) because most of them were acquired long ago.

We will examine the savings and loan industry and its difficulties in more detail in Chapter 7.

3. *Mutual savings banks* are practically identical with savings and loans except that there are only about 500 of them and they are

concentrated mostly on the East Coast. Both are often called "thrift institutions." As their name implies, mutual savings banks are legally structured as "mutuals" or "cooperatives," with the depositors or shareholders "owning" the institution.

Like S&Ls, they have traditionally obtained most of their funds in the form of savings deposits and used the money mainly to make home mortgages. However, the Banking Act of 1980 also gave them the power to issue demand deposits (NOW accounts) and to make consumer and some business loans.

Since mutual savings banks are so similar to S&Ls, they face identical problems when interest rates rise. They have to pay more to get new money, and to retain a lot of what they have, but the return they get on most of their assets fails to rise correspondingly since these are long-term mortgages acquired years ago.

4. *Life insurance companies* rank third in asset size, right after commercial banks and S&Ls. They insure people against the financial consequences of death, receiving their funds in the form of periodic payments (called premiums) that are based on mortality statistics. They can predict with a high degree of actuarial accuracy how much money they will have to pay out in benefits this year, next year, even ten or twenty years from now. They invest accordingly, aiming for the highest yield consistent with safety over the long run. Thus a high percentage of their assets is in the form of long-term corporate bonds and long-term mortgages, although the mortgages are typically on commercial rather than residential properties.

5. *Pension and retirement funds* are similar to life insurance companies in that they are mainly concerned with the long run rather than the short run. Their inflow of money comes from working people building a nest egg for their retirement years. Like life insurance companies, pension and retirement funds are able to predict with a high degree of accuracy how much they will have to pay out in pensions (called annuities) for many years into the future. Since they face few short-term uncertainties, they invest mainly in long-term corporate bonds and high-grade stocks.

6. *Property and casualty insurance companies,* on the other hand, are more likely to encounter short-run liquidity needs. They insure homeowners against burglary and fire, car owners against theft and collision, and business firms against negligence lawsuits,

"I'll bet a $5,000 savings and loan deposit that you've got the Old Maid."

among other things. With the premiums they receive—big ones from car owners under twenty-five years old—they buy high-grade municipal and corporate bonds, high-grade stocks, and short-term money market instruments (for liquidity).

7. *Sales and consumer finance companies* specialize in lending money for people to buy cars and take vacations and for business firms to help them finance their inventories. Many of them, like the General Motors Acceptance Corporation, are owned by a manufacturing firm and lend money mainly to help retailers and customers

buy that firm's products. Others, like Household Finance and Beneficial Finance, mainly make small consumer loans. They get their funds by selling their own short-term IOUs (called commercial paper) to business firms with funds to invest for a short while, as well as by selling their own long-term bonds.

8. *Credit unions* are generally included, along with S&Ls and mutual savings banks, in the category of "thrift institutions." There are over 20,000 of them, some in every state in the Union, most quite small but a few with assets exceeding $1 million. They are organized as cooperatives for people with some sort of common interest, such as employees of a particular company or members of a particular labor union or fraternal order or church. Credit union members buy shares, which are the same as deposits, and this makes them eligible to borrow from the credit union.

Until recently credit unions offered only savings deposits and made only consumer loans. Like S&Ls and mutual savings banks, however, they have had their powers broadened considerably by the Banking Act of 1980. They can now offer checking accounts (called credit union share drafts) and also make long-term mortgage loans.

9. *Mutual funds* are almost exclusively stock market–related institutions. Pooling the funds of many people of moderate means, the fund's management invests the money in a wide variety of stocks, thereby obtaining diversification that individuals acting alone probably could not achieve. Shareholders can always redeem or sell back their shares if they wish, but the price they'll receive from the fund depends on what has happened to the stocks it holds. Buying shares in a mutual fund is thus much more risky than buying a savings deposit or a money market instrument, like a Treasury bill, but it is less risky than buying stocks on your own.

10. *Money market mutual funds* are something else again. They are the growth phenomena of the 1970s and early 1980s. From only $2 billion in 1974 they exploded to $45 billion by 1978 and then to a startling $150 billion by 1981. They are like the old-fashioned kind of mutual fund, described above, in that people buy shares in a fund. However, the fund's management does not invest the money in the stock market. Instead, it is put into highly liquid short-term money market instruments, such as large-size bank negotiable CDs, Treasury bills, and high-grade commercial paper.

Why have money market mutual funds grown so fantastically in recent years? Obviously the extrordinarily high short-term money market interest rates available in the late 1970s and early 1980s must have had something to do with it. But that alone is only a partial explanation. For the full answer, we have to bring into the picture something called Regulation Q—the interest rate ceilings imposed on savings and time deposits by federal law. Let's examine Regulation Q for a moment and see how, among other consequences, it gave birth to a new kind of financial institution.

The Pervasive Effects of Regulation Q

Through Regulation Q the Federal Reserve sets the legal maximum interest rates that commercial banks are allowed to pay on their time and savings deposit liabilities. The maximum interest rates that savings banks and savings and loan associations may offer depositors are also regulated. (In addition, until recently banks were prohibited from paying any interest at all on checking deposits—in effect, the checking deposit interest rate ceiling was set at zero.)

Regulation Q was enacted in the Banking Act of 1933, on the ground that excessive interest rate competition for deposits during the 1920s had undermined the soundness of the banking system. It was believed that competition among commercial banks for funds had driven deposit rates up too high. To cover their costs, banks acquired high-yielding but excessively risky low-quality assets. This deterioration in the quality of bank portfolios, it was said, contributed to the collapse of the banking system in the early 1930s. Abolition of interest rate competition for deposits, by setting legal rate ceilings, was seen as rooting out the basic element weakening the banking system.

Similar arguments were responsible for the imposition of comparable ceilings over S&Ls and savings banks starting in 1966, although, in an effort to reward S&Ls and savings banks for their home mortgage concentration, the ceiling on their deposit rates is set ¼ percent higher than at commercial banks. Thus S&Ls and savings banks have been given a competitive edge in attracting depositors' funds. For example, in March of 1982 commercial banks were allowed to pay passbook savings depositors no more than 5¼ percent interest; thrift institutions could pay no more than 5½ percent.

In retrospect, it is not at all clear that the historical experience which led to Regulation Q was correctly interpreted at the time. Interest rates on bank time and savings deposits actually declined during the 1920s, and thorough investigation since has failed to substantiate any appreciable deterioration in the quality of bank assets during that period.

Regulation Q has effectively prevented aggressive, well-managed banks from offering depositors more attractive interest rates than the bank next door. Aggressive banks that would like to compete for funds by bidding more for deposits have been legally prohibited from doing so, which also means, of course, that depositors have simultaneously been deprived of the enlarged options that more vigorous price competition among banks would offer them. It is true that banks have been known to give away toasters, radios, and a two-year subscription to *Mad* magazine in order to attract deposits. But how do banks reach those who don't eat bread, can't stand the radio, and have foresworn serious reading?[1]

Regulation Q has also caused intermittent financial *dis*intermediation—as during the tight-money episodes of the 1960s and 1970s, and again in 1981. During those periods, money market interest rates rose but deposit interest rates were held down by Regulation Q. With deposit interest rates substantially below open market rates, savers stopped moving funds *into* financial institutions—instead, they moved them *out.* People took money out of savings accounts and put funds directly into money market instruments and other primary securities, thereby bypassing the intermediaries. This behavior is known as financial disintermediation. Financial intermediation describes savers depositing funds with financial institutions, which then turn around and buy primary securities (such as bonds, stocks, and mortgages). Financial disintermediation is the reverse: savers take funds *out* of their deposit accounts, or reduce the amounts they normally put in, and directly buy the primary securities themselves.

[1]In addition, Regulation Q discriminates against the small saver. Higher interest rates are permitted on large deposits (over $100,000) than on small ones. See Edward J. Kane, "Short-Changing the Small Saver," *Journal of Money, Credit and Banking* (November 1970).

Disintermediation put the intermediaries under severe pressure. With substantial withdrawals and minimal inflows of new funds, their profit position was threatened, their solvency was endangered, and their ability to lend evaporated.

The disintermediation effects of Regulation Q have been softened in the past few years by several regulatory changes. In 1970 the Federal Reserve eliminated the rate ceilings on large-size ($100,000 and over) negotiable CDs that mature in less than three months, in order to ease money market pressures stemming from the collapse of the Penn Central Railroad. And in 1973 the Fed eliminated the ceilings on longer-maturity large-size CDs as well.

Equally important, especially in forestalling disintermediation during the tight-money episode of 1978–1979, was a newly permitted six-month money market time certificate that commercial banks and thrift institutions were allowed to issue starting in mid-1978. The interest rate on these is tied to the Treasury bill rate, so that depositors can receive high money market yields without withdrawing their funds from the depository institutions. They can merely shift their funds for six months in the same bank or S&L from a passbook savings account to a money market time certificate. So far, however, these are not permitted in denominations below $10,000, leaving smaller depositors out in the cold.

Money market mutual funds are the private sector's answer to this under-$10,000 gap. They are a new kind of financial institution that has arisen in response to the restrictions of Regulation Q. With large depositors able to get the benefits of high money market rates—since large CDs of $100,000 and over were freed from deposit rate ceilings in 1970 and 1973, and with both Treasury bills and money market time certificates available in denominations no lower than $10,000 —there was room for ingenuity and innovation on behalf of small depositors.

This ingenuity was provided, beginning in the early 1970s, by money market mutual funds: they gather together the funds of many small savers, in batches as small as $1,000 and $2,000, and then proceed to buy high-yielding large-size CDs and other money market instruments, such as commercial paper, in denominations of $25,000, $50,000, and $100,000. Since they are not subject to Regulation Q, the money market funds can pass these high yields on to their shareholders. By pooling their funds, small savers are thus able to gain access to money market yields that Regulation Q otherwise prevents them from realizing. Most money market mutual funds even provide limited checking account facilities for their shareholders. Remember, however, that these money market funds are not insured by any federal agency. Nevertheless, by the end of 1981 they had grown to $150 billion in total assets. And to the government's consternation, no one regulates them very much (at least not so far).

The Banking Act of 1980 promises to put an end to Regulation Q. The Act established a Depository Institutions Deregulation Committee which is to gradually phase out interest rate ceilings on time and savings deposits and eliminate them entirely by April 1, 1986. But don't cheer too soon: Congress could always change its mind at the last minute. (However, the Act did put an end to the ban against paying interest on checking deposits by permitting all depository institutions to offer NOW accounts, which are in effect interest-bearing checking accounts.)

Financial Institutions Are Becoming More Alike

So far in this chapter we have emphasized the differences among financial institutions, traditional distinctions that have deep historical and institutional roots. But in recent years these differences have been eroding, making depository institutions increasingly alike. By the year 1990 it will be difficult to tell them apart.

For instance:

1. Traditionally, demand deposits have been the exclusive province of commercial banks, with other deposit-type institutions legally barred from offering checking account facilities. In the 1970s, however, thrift institutions began offering NOW accounts, which are just checking accounts under another name. The Banking Act of 1980 confirmed their right to do so, with the result that now S&Ls, mutual savings banks, and credit unions all offer some type of checking account. Even money market mutual funds have gotten into the act, though they are not mentioned in the Banking Act of 1980.

2. Traditionally, only commercial banks made business loans and savings banks specialized in mortgage lending, credit unions in consumer loans. However, the Banking Act of 1980 enlarged the lending powers of all the thrifts, so that now S&Ls and savings banks can make consumer and business loans and credit unions can make mortgage loans.

The net result of all these changes is that the traditional specialization of financial institutions is breaking down. Financial institutions are becoming more general and more alike. In a sense, they are all in the process of becoming commercial banks—dealing in checking accounts as well as savings deposits and becoming more diversified in their assets as well as their liabilities.

The Level of Intermediary Output

Early in this chapter we mentioned that financial intermediaries earn profits on the differential between interest rates on assets and liabilities. Indeed, the optimal level of savings and loan shares, or savings bank deposits, from the viewpoint of management, is determined by the interest rate earned on assets compared with the rate paid on liabilities. At some point, for example, it would no longer pay savings institutions to attract deposits—namely, when the interest return on their assets no longer exceeds the rate paid on their liabilities. Only if the rate earned on assets goes up will they raise deposit rates in order to attract liabilities—and this is as it should be. A financial intermediary is like any other firm. The level of operations (deposits or loans) should be determined by the familiar marginal-revenue-equals-marginal-cost condition of traditional price theory.

Back in Chapter 3, however, when discussing the level of demand deposits for commercial banks, we hardly mentioned the rate of interest. Instead, the level of demand deposits supplied by commercial banks was given by the volume of reserves times the deposit multiplier (the reciprocal of the required reserve ratio). The deposit multiplier approach assumes that an increase in reserves will always be loaned out, until all reserves wind up in the required category. A lower required reserve ratio means more demand deposits, and more reserves mean more demand deposits.

It is obvious that we cannot apply the deposit multiplier analysis to all other types of deposits. If we did, it would suggest that the level of liabilities should be infinite—a required reserve ratio of zero and one divided by zero is infinity—a ridiculously unrealistic proposition that not even an economist could promote with a good conscience. Clearly, therefore, the marginal-revenue-marginal-cost approach is correct for determining the level of liabilities at nonbank financial institutions: that is what sets the upper limit to savings bank size, for example, just as it sets the upper limit to the size of any firm in the economy. So why not for the demand deposits of banks, at least as they are traditionally described?

The only justification for using the multiplier approach for demand deposits at banks is that marginal-revenue-marginal-cost calculations are not relevant. We can count on commercial bankers lending out all of their reserves, until none are in the excess category, only if they are in a position where marginal revenue *exceeds* marginal cost. That has been true traditionally because of two legal regulations: (1) no interest is permitted on bank demand deposits, which holds down marginal cost; and (2) bank required reserves limit bank lending. Banks would love to increase their loans and deposits until marginal revenue falls to the point where it equals marginal cost. For every additional dollar loaned out in such circumstances, profits go up. Why don't the banks do it? Because they are constrained by the required reserve ratio and the fixed volume of reserves.

The truth about the determination of the volume of demand deposits lies somewhere between the basic deposit-multiplier approach and the marginal-revenue-equals-marginal-cost approach. As we will see in Chapter 15 and its Appendix, the level of demand deposits can also be a function of interest rates. For example, commercial banks will borrow reserves from the Fed when the interest rate on bank loans (marginal revenue) goes up. Similarly, if rates fall to low enough levels, banks may just sit with excess reserves rather than incurring any risks by making loans or buying securities. And this situation occurred quite dramatically in the 1930s.

A *compleat* treatment of the determination of the supply of demand deposits is basically similar to the treatment of savings deposits and savings and loan shares. The multiplier approach is, indeed, oversimplified. Moreover, the changing financial environment discussed in this chapter suggests that further amendments may soon be required.

Summary

1. Commercial banks are the largest of all financial institutions in terms of asset size, followed by savings and loan associations, life insurance companies, and pension and retirement funds. The fastest growing of all have been the money market mutual funds.

2. Commercial banks are not only the largest but also the most widely diversified in both their liabilities and their assets. However, the Banking Act of 1980 (the Depository Institutions Deregulation and Monetary Control Act) broadened the asset and liability powers of the thrift institutions, so they are rapidly becoming more and more like commercial banks.

3. Regulation Q, which sets legal maximum interest rates on time and savings deposits, has been responsible for reducing competition among depository institutions and for stimulating the recent rapid growth of money market mutual funds. When market interest rates rise above Regulation Q's ceilings, depositors withdraw their funds from depository institutions, or put in less than usual, and move their money into primary securities either on their own or via money market mutual funds (financial disintermediation).

4. Regulation Q is scheduled to expire in 1986, but don't believe it until it happens. However, the ban against paying interest on demand deposits has been virtually eliminated by allowing all depository institutions to offer NOW accounts.

5. The level of intermediary liabilities is determined by the interest rate earned on assets compared with the interest rate paid

on liabilities. The traditional demand deposit multiplier approach to bank liabilities stems primarily from regulatory restrictions that are in the process of change.

Suggestions for Further Reading

For more on financial institutions and what they do, see Robert P. Black and Doris E. Harless, *Nonbank Financial Institutions* (Federal Reserve Bank of Richmond, 1975). Two classics on financial intermediaries are the book by John G. Gurley and Edwin S. Shaw, *Money in a Theory of Finance* (Washington, D.C.: Brookings Institution, 1960), and the article by James Tobin, "Commercial Banks as Creators of Money," in *Banking and Monetary Studies,* ed. Deane Carson (Homewood, Ill.: Irwin, 1963).

If you want to know more about the administration of Regulation Q over the years, a convenient source is the article by Adrian W. Throop which takes up just about the whole November 1974 issue of the Federal Reserve Bank of Dallas *Business Review.* You can find the current Regulation Q rate ceilings in the statistical section in the back of any recent *Federal Reserve Bulletin* (usually they are on page A9 in a table labeled "Maximum Interest Rates Payable on Time and Savings Deposits at Federally Insured Institutions"). With respect to demand deposits, see Bryon Higgins, "Interest Payments on Demand Deposits: Historical Evolution and Current Controversy," Federal Reserve Bank of Kansas City *Monthly Review* (July-August 1977).

For a careful historical survey of legislative developments regarding financial institutions, see Jean M. Lovati, "The Growing Similarity Among Financial Institutions," Federal Reserve Bank of St. Louis *Review* (October 1977).

7

The Regulation and Structure of Deposit Institutions

AS WE HAVE already seen, one of the major influences on financial institutions is the regulatory environment within which they operate. In this chapter we look at the structure and regulation of depository institutions—commercial banks, thrift institutions (S&Ls, mutual savings banks, and credit unions), and money market mutual funds. Actually money market funds are not really deposit institutions, at least not in the full sense the others are, but they do offer checking account facilities and are included on that basis.

Since commercial banks are so much bigger than the others, and occupy such a pervasive role in the functioning of the economy, most of the chapter is devoted to them. A number of questions spring to mind. Is the banking industry structured so as to best serve the financial needs of a changing and growing economy? Is there enough competition and flexibility in banking to make it a dynamic and innovative industry, responsive to private needs and public goals? Are banks safe places for your money? Who supervises them, in what ways and for what purposes?

After we have looked at the banking system, we will turn to the structure and regulation of thrift institutions and money market funds.

The Dual Banking System

The American banking system is known as a "dual" banking system, not because its origins have anything to do with the historic encounter between Alexander Hamilton and Aaron Burr in 1804, but because its main feature is side-by-side federal and state chartering (and supervision) of commercial banks. It has no counterpart in any other country. Indeed, it arose quite by accident in the United States, the unexpected result of legislation in the 1860s that was intended to shift the authority to charter banks from the various state governments to the federal government.

The National Currency Act of 1863, the National Bank Act of 1864, and related post–Civil War legislation established a new federally chartered banking system, under the supervision of the Comptroller of the Currency (within the U.S. Treasury). The idea was to drive the existing state-chartered banks out of business by imposing a prohibitive tax on their issuance of state banknotes (currency issued by state-chartered banks), which in those days was the principal form of circulating money. However, the plot was foiled in the nick of time and state-chartered banks survived and eventually flourished—because public acceptance of demand deposits in lieu of currency enabled the state banks to make loans and create money, despite their inability to issue banknotes.

Thus today we have a dual banking system: federally chartered banks, under the aegis of the Comptroller of the Currency, and state-chartered banks, under the supervision of each of the various states. Federally chartered banks are for the most part larger institutions, but state-chartered banks are more numerous. In mid-1981, as Table 1 indicates, roughly two-thirds of the commercial banks had state charters, but the one-third with national charters held over half the assets in the banking system.

In 1913, with the passage of the Federal Reserve Act, another supervisory layer was added as national banks were required to

Table 1 Status of Insured Commercial Banks, 1981
(dollars in billions)

All Commercial Banks	Number of Banks 14,443		Total Assets $1,584	
	No.	Percent	Amount	Percent
National banks	4,453	31	$897	57
State banks	9,990	69	687	43
F.R. member banks	5,471	38	1,178	74
Nonmember banks	8,972	62	406	26

SOURCE: *Federal Reserve Bulletin.* Data for June 30, 1981.

become member banks of the Federal Reserve System, while state banks were permitted the option of joining or not. At present, as can be inferred from Table 1, most state banks are not members of the Federal Reserve System. Nevertheless, member banks, both state and national, hold 74 percent of the total assets in the banking system.

An additional supervisory structure was laid atop the edifice with the establishment of federal deposit insurance in the 1930s. All Federal Reserve member banks, which includes all national banks, are required to be insured by the Federal Deposit Insurance Corporation (FDIC), while state nonmembers retain the option of having federal deposit insurance or not. Virtually all banks, however, have chosen to have federal deposit insurance coverage because it would be impossible to attract deposits without it. (We will return to the FDIC later in this chapter.)

As matters now stand, a national bank is subject to the supervisory authority of the Comptroller of the Currency, the Federal Reserve, and the FDIC. A state member bank is subject to the regulatory authority of the state in which it is located (usually exercised through a state banking commission), the Federal Reserve, and the FDIC. A state bank that is not a member of the Federal Reserve is subject to its state's regulations plus the FDIC. A unique feature of the system is that the regulated can choose their regulator: state banks can shift to national charters and vice versa, state member banks can shift to nonmember status and vice versa. An economic historian might be able to detect the application of Gresham's law to bank supervision: bad regulators drive out good regulators.[1]

The justification for the dual banking system—side-by-side federal and state bank regulation—is that it is supposed to foster change and innovation by providing alternative routes through which banks can seek charters and do business. It is claimed that a dual banking system is more responsive to the evolving banking needs of the economy than a single system would be. The validity of these arguments is difficult to assess, but whatever their merits no one has been marching in the streets demanding change in the status quo. The dual banking system seems to be working tolerably well, regardless of its logic.

Multiple Federal Authorities

The dual banking system has aroused considerably less controversy than the existence of multiple and sometimes conflicting supervisory authorities at the federal level. Dispute among the federal banking agencies was especially marked during the regime of James J. Saxon as Comptroller of the Currency, from late 1961 to late 1966. The Comptroller repeatedly sought to depart from established

[1]Since every money and banking textbook should tell you what Gresham's law is— and since this is as good a chance as any—here it is. Sir Thomas Gresham (1519–1579), financial adviser to Queen Elizabeth I, is said to have coined the phrase "bad money drives good money out of circulation"—meaning that if two types of money of the same denomination serve as media of exchange, one containing less valuable (or debased) metal and the other containing more valuable metal, the coins containing the less valuable metal will remain in circulation while the more valuable coins will be hoarded. The bad money (less valuable intrinsic content) will drive the good money (more valuable intrinsic content) out of circulation, because everyone will try to hold on to the more valuable and pass on the less valuable.

Concrete examples of Gresham's law occur daily. Dimes and quarters minted in 1965 and since have been 75 percent copper and 25 percent nickel bonded to a pure copper core; previously they had been 90 percent silver and 10 percent copper. In light of the relatively high price of silver, the intrinsic value of a coin minted in 1965 or later is much less than one minted before 1965. The result, à la Gresham, is that post-1964 dimes and quarters remain in circulation while an estimated $2½ billion of the more valuable earlier coins have disappeared into private hoards.

The Comptroller repeatedly sought to depart from established precedent. . .

precedent, only to be met by resistance from the more conservative Federal Reserve and FDIC.

The Federal Reserve and the Comptroller clashed frequently over the interpretation of certain laws. Relations between the FDIC and the Comptroller were also strained, even though the Comptroller is one of the three members of the FDIC's Board of Directors. Amity was not furthered by the Comptroller's refusal, after a while, to attend FDIC Board meetings.

Different interpretations of the same statutes and intermittent dissension that has punctuated relations among the federal supervisory agencies have led many to recommend that all federal chartering, examination, and supervisory responsibilities be combined in a single agency. The proposal has always foundered, however, on lack of consensus as to which agency—the Federal Reserve, the FDIC, or the Comptroller of the Currency—is most appropriate. Notice that consolidation at the federal level would not affect the dual banking system, since state chartering and supervision would continue to exist.

Despite the fact that one study group after another has seen fit to recommend unification at the federal level—disagreeing only in how that unification might best be achieved—the existing tripartite arrangement remains. In 1978 Congress attempted to achieve some coordination by establishing a five-member Federal Financial Institutions Examination Council. The Council consists of a member of the Federal Reserve Board, the Comptroller of the Currency, and the chairmen of the FDIC, the Federal Home Loan Bank Board, and the National Credit Union Administration. Its purpose is to try to develop uniform reporting, examination, and regulatory standards for all financial institutions supervised by federal agencies.

The present system is defended by some on the grounds that divided federal authority, like the dual banking system, provides an element of flexibility, fostering innovation and change, that would be lacking were all federal banking powers concentrated in one agency. On the other hand, if there is to be federal supervision of banking at all, it would appear axiomatic that it should be consistent in application and operated at minimum cost—which implies that one supervisory body is preferable to three, especially when they tend to disagree among themselves.

It has to be admitted, however, as an argument in favor of the status quo, that federal regulatory agencies, in general, have not compiled a particularly outstanding record for imaginative leadership, for stimulating innovation, or even for protecting (not to mention furthering) the public interest. While a forward-looking, able, and conscientious single federal banking authority would undoubtedly be an improvement over present arrangements, lack of these qualities in a consolidated agency might only make matters worse.

Deposit Insurance and the FDIC

It is time for more detail on the Federal Deposit Insurance Corporation (FDIC) and its crucial role in banking today. Although it may be hard to believe nowadays, bank failures were a common event before the FDIC was established on January 1, 1934. During the 1920s bank failures averaged about 600 a year, and during the years 1930–1933 over 2,000 a year! Read that sentence over again, so you really appreciate how huge those numbers are, and get some idea of how many people lost their life savings as bank after bank disappeared. At the end of 1933 there were fewer than 15,000 commercial banks remaining out of 30,000 that had been in existence in 1920. Since the end of World War II, on the other hand, bank failures have averaged around twelve a year. On the basis of that record, the FDIC is probably the most successful and worthwhile government agency ever established.[2]

The Banking Acts of 1933 and 1935 were responsible for many things, including the creation of the FDIC to insure deposits (demand, passbook savings, and time) at commercial and mutual savings banks. Companion legislation created the Federal Savings and Loan Insurance Corporation to do the same for savings and loan associations, and in 1970 the National Credit Union Administration initiated deposit insurance for federally chartered credit unions. FDIC deposit insurance became effective in 1934, with coverage limited to $2,500 per depositor per bank. This was raised to $5,000 in mid-1934, $10,000 in 1950, $15,000 in 1966, $20,000 in 1969, $40,000 in 1974, and $100,000 in 1980.

According to FDIC survey data, the present coverage provides full insurance for about 99 percent of the *depositors* in insured banks. With respect to the dollar volume of deposits, however, the 1 percent of depositors not fully covered hold *uninsured* balances that consti-

[2]The typical point of view of the banking community in 1933, with respect to the feasibility of federal deposit insurance, was summarized in the gloomy conclusion that "the plan is inherently fallacious ... one of those plausible, but deceptive, human plans that in actual application only serve to render worse the very evils they seek to cure." (*The Guaranty of Bank Deposits,* Economic Policy Commission, American Bankers Association, 1933, p. 43.) On this basis, organized banking groups generally opposed legislation establishing the FDIC.

tute a third of the dollar value of total deposits. In other words, although almost all depositors are fully insured (i.e., they have less than $100,000 in their accounts in any single bank), a third of the deposits in terms of dollar volume are not insured. A $150,000 negotiable certificate of deposit (CD), for example, would be insured for $100,000 and uninsured for the $50,000 balance.

Although nominal insurance coverage is $100,000 per depositor per bank, in fact actual coverage may be greater (never less), depending on the procedure used by the FDIC in taking over a failed bank. The FDIC may allow the bank to go into receivership, the so-called "payoff" method. In such cases the FDIC sends its agents to the bank, verifies the deposit records, and then pays out funds directly to each depositor up to a limit of $100,000. Thereafter the FDIC shares, on a pro rata basis with the claims of depositors in excess of their insurance and with the other creditors, in the residual proceeds realized from liquidation of the failed bank's assets. The FDIC reports that, after liquidation, those with deposits in excess of the insurance limit have usually received back over ninety cents on the dollar, but often only after a wait of several years.

Alternatively, the FDIC may succeed in merging the failed bank with a healthy one, the so-called "assumption" method. The deposits of the failed bank are assumed by another bank into which the distressed one is merged, and are made available in full to the depositors. The FDIC may assist in this procedure by making loans to the bank taking over, or relieving it of some of the weaker assets of the failed bank. In such cases the FDIC has in effect completely insured all depositors to the *full* amount of their deposits, regardless of the technical insurance coverage limit.

The original capital of the FDIC was provided by a levy on the Treasury and the Federal Reserve Banks, amounting to $289 million, which was fully repaid in 1948. In addition, insured banks are assessed annually one-twelfth of 1 percent of their *total* deposits (not just their insured deposits). With continued growth of the insurance fund to about $12 billion, the effective rate of these assessments has been reduced by rebates which the FDIC annually returns to the banks. Thus the effective assessment rate in recent years has generally been no more than about one-thirtieth of 1 percent of a bank's total deposits.

Were the banking system to collapse, an insurance fund of $12 billion is obviously insufficient to pay off several hundred billion dollars of currently insured deposits. The FDIC has additional legislative authority to borrow up to $3 billion from the U.S. Treasury in case of emergency, but such numbers are really meaningless. The reasoning underlying the FDIC does not involve calculations of actuarial probability, but rather the basic premise that the very existence of federal deposit insurance eliminates the possibility of large-scale bank failure. By insuring deposits under the auspices of the Federal Government, with the implied support of the United States Treasury to whatever extent necessary, the FDIC has successfully eliminated the old-fashioned "run on the bank" by frightened depositors that formerly heralded another bank failure. If people hear their bank is "in trouble" now, they hardly pay attention. They're insured, so who cares? Thanks to this simple but effective device, savings have been made safe and the banking system has prospered in the last 50 years as never before.

However, a word of caution. Although apprehensive depositors no longer form long lines waiting to withdraw their funds from a bank that is rumored to be "in trouble," a less obvious but very large deposit drain can still occur through the failure of corporate treasurers to renew outstanding large-size negotiable certificates of deposit. Corporate treasurers are exceedingly careful about which banks they put their funds in, since large-size CDs ($100,000 and over) are only insured up to the $100,000 insurance limit. Similarly, large corporate checking accounts will be transferred quickly from a bank in trouble to one that is safe.

For example, New York's Franklin National Bank lost half a billion dollars of CDs between May and October of 1974, the five-month interval between the time it became known that the bank was in trouble and when it was finally officially declared insolvent by the Comptroller of the Currency and the FDIC. When Franklin National's CDs came due, corporate treasurers simply failed to renew them (they let them "run off"), so that $500 million of the bank's $2 billion of deposits left silently and invisibly, without any line at all forming in front of the tellers' windows. So a "run on the bank" is not entirely a thing of the past, after all! It should be noted, however, that in this case the infection did not spread, and there was no financial panic; no other bank was affected by Franklin National's difficulties.[3]

Bank Size Distribution and the McFadden Act

The objectives of bank supervision, regulation, and insurance are to protect the safety of depositors' funds and promote a viable and smoothly functioning banking system—one that will encourage saving, channel funds from savers to borrowers, enable borrowers to get funds on reasonable terms, and foster economic stability and growth. All of this means that the objectives of bank supervision, regulation, and insurance are to make sure that banks are both safe and competitive. The FDIC and bank examinations are designed to insure safety, while other aspects of supervision are intended to promote competition.

In down-to-earth terms, competitive conditions mean that customers can shop around—that they have alternatives. For example, are the opportunities open to depositors sufficiently varied to give them an array of choices with respect to deposit terms and yields, so they can pick those that best fit their particular needs? Similarly, do borrowers who are refused a loan at one bank have alternatives open to them—other banks to which they can turn? Do banks actively seek customers, either depositors or borrowers, by offering more service or better terms than rival banks are offering?

As we have mentioned before (in Chapter 6), probably the most competition-inhibiting element in banking at the present time is Regulation Q, which prohibits banks from paying depositors more than specified maximum interest rates on deposits. But Regulation Q is run a close second by the prevailing network of laws and regulations regarding branch banking, laws that have resulted in a size

[3]Nor did any Franklin National depositor lose a penny when the bank folded (although the bank's stockholders lost plenty). The institution was taken over by the European-American Bank, which is owned by a consortium of six large European banks. As far as depositors were concerned, the only difference was that their new checks were baby blue instead of passionate pink. This is an example of the assumption method of handling a failed bank, as described above.

distribution of commercial banks that is unique to this country.

With more than 14,000 commercial banks in the United States, there would appear to be, on the face of it, a high degree of robust competition in banking. However, as Table 2 indicates, a large percentage of banks are very small institutions, with less than $25 million of assets per bank. Indeed, about 7,200 of the banks in the country—50 percent of them—are that small (see lines 1 and 2 in the table). These 7,200 banks have only 6 percent of the aggregate assets in the banking system. Most of them are in small, one-bank towns.

At the other end of the scale, about 350 large banks (the last two lines of Table 2), only 2 percent of the total, have 60 percent of all bank assets.

If this large number of very small banks were the product of natural evolution, it would indicate that the optimum (low-cost) size bank is probably a very small institution. Their large numbers would attest to their competitive viability.

In fact, the reason for so many very small banks in this country does not have much to do with their successful adaptation to changing economic needs or their innovative capabilities. It is that most of them are *sheltered* from competition by state antibranching statutes, to which the federal banking authorities defer. Many very small banks would be unable to remain in business if a large bank opened up a branch next door. The fact that in many states the large

Table 2 Size Distribution of Insured Commercial Banks (end of 1980)

Asset Size	No. of Banks	% of Total Banks	% of Total Assets
Less than $10 million	2,569	18	1
$10–25 million	4,651	32	5
$25–50 million	3,546	25	8
$50–100 million	1,969	14	9
$100–500 million	1,354	9	17
$500 million–1 billion	159	1	7
Over $1 billion	187	1	53
TOTALS	14,435	100	100

SOURCE: FDIC.

bank is legally prohibited from doing so is what permits many small banks to survive.

The McFadden Act of 1927 prohibits banks from branching across state lines and permits national banks to branch within a state only to the same extent as state-chartered banks. At present, about a dozen states, mostly in the Midwest, permit only unit banking—that is, no branches at all are allowed. Another dozen states allow only some limited form of branching. The remaining states permit unlimited statewide branching. In summary, *the McFadden Act prohibits interstate branching everywhere and requires that a federally chartered bank abide by the branching laws of the state in which it is headquartered.*[4]

The result is that the McFadden Act and state antibranching statutes, not economic circumstances, are the principal determinants of the number of banks in the United States. The fact that there are over 14,000 independent commercial banks bears witness to the *absence,* not the presence, of vigorous competition. If there were fewer banks, and more of them were close to optimum size, the general public would be better served. The proof is that almost half the banks in the country are in the dozen no-branching states, where the average bank size is much smaller than in unlimited branching states.

Closely related to the branching issue is that of new entry into the banking industry. By law, both federal and state banking authorities typically evaluate a number of conditions before chartering a new bank. These include the adequacy of its capital structure, the general character of its management, its future earnings prospects, and the convenience and needs of the community it proposes to serve. (Further, the well-known liquidity index is given due consideration: namely, the number of state legislators on the bank's board of directors multiplied by the number of Little League baseball teams it proposes to sponsor.)

Few would dispute the necessity of maintaining standards of capital adequacy, or the need for determining that the management of

---

[4]Actually, federal branching laws are contained not only in the McFadden Act of 1927 but also in the National Bank Act of 1864, the Banking Act of 1933, and the Douglas Amendment to the Bank Holding Company Act of 1956. However, in financial circles the McFadden Act is commonly understood as meaning the whole network of restrictive federal branching laws.

a proposed new bank, and their backers, are honest people, without underworld connections. (Not to mention the desirability of a rating higher than 3π on the liquidity index.) But the other two elements in the screening process—the future earnings prospects of a proposed new bank and the convenience and needs of the community in which it would be located—in effect shield existing banking institutions from the rigors (and vitality) of competition more than they serve the interests of the public at large.

The purpose of both an earnings prospects criterion and a convenience and needs criterion is supposedly the prevention of bank failures. But measures that insulate all banks from the slightest chance of failure are also measures that discourage financial innovation, circumscribe management decision-making, and stifle the benefits to the general public that can flow from competitive rivalry. These are a high price to pay, particularly when federal deposit insurance protection has eliminated the widespread distress that bank failures formerly caused.[5]

Do the Giant Banks Pose a Monopoly Threat?

So far we have emphasized that there are probably too many very small banks in the United States, too small for efficient operation. What about the other end of the scale—where each of a few Giant Banks has over $18 *billion* in assets? This handful of banks, one-tenth of 1 percent of all the banks in the country, holds one-third of all the banking system's assets. Do these fifteen Giants, listed in Table 3, pose a clear and present monopoly danger?

Opinions differ on this, of course, but at this stage in history the Giant Banks appear to be more benign than malignant. Not because they are particularly generous, home loving, or patriotic—at least no more so than any of us—but simply because, large as they are, they

[5]Sam Peltzman has concluded, for example, that in recent decades regulatory restriction has reduced the rate of entry "by a third to a half below what it otherwise would have been." See his "Bank Entry Regulation: Its Impact and Purpose," in *Studies in Banking Competition and Banking Structure* (Comptroller of the Currency, 1966).

Table 3 The Fifteen Giants

Bank	Assets*
Bank of America (San Francisco)	$119
Citibank (New York)	105
Chase Manhattan (New York)	77
Manufacturers Hanover (New York)	54
Morgan Guaranty (New York)	53
Continental Illinois (Chicago)	45
Chemical (New York)	44
First National (Chicago)	33
Bankers Trust (New York)	32
Security Pacific (Los Angeles)	30
Crocker (San Francisco)	22
Wells Fargo (San Francisco)	21
First Interstate (Los Angeles)	20
Marine Midland (Buffalo)	19
Mellon (Pittsburgh)	18

*In billions of dollars, end of 1981.
SOURCE: *The American Banker.*

still face sufficient competition to keep them in line. Close on their heels are another two dozen banks with assets between $5 and $18 billion, and close behind *them* come another hundred with assets between $2 and $5 billion.

The monopoly threat is further ameliorated in this country by legislation that forbids banking and industrial operations by the same firm. In some other countries—Japan is the outstanding example—giant banks are affiliated with giant manufacturing firms under common ownership, representing a vast concentration of economic power. If Chase Manhattan Bank, Xerox, and IBM could merge into a huge combine, as is permissible in Japan—where they are called *zaibatsus*—then we would really have something to worry about.

One development of the past twenty years that contributed to the fear of bigness in banking is the growth of one-bank holding companies. In the late 1960s and early 1970s all the nation's large banks converted their corporate structure to holding company form, with the holding company owning the bank as well as other subsidiaries.

The primary motivation for the growth of one-bank holding companies was not an attempt to form vast financial-industrial combines, like Japan's *zaibatsus.* The underlying reasons were much more mundane: an effort on the part of American banks to evolve into new functional areas—such as data processing activities, insurance services, mutual fund sales, investment advisory services, and so on—in which, *as banks,* they could not fully participate. Faced with legal and regulatory constraints on their ability, as banks, to move into diversified financial activities, they turned to the holding company format as a way out. The holding company becomes an umbrella, sheltering under a single corporate structure the bank and various affiliated subsidiaries that can legally offer an array of financial services.

The apparition of potential *zaibatsus* was put to rest once and for all by congressional legislation in 1970 regulating one-bank holding companies. That legislation specified that the holding companies must confine their activities to fields "so closely related to banking as to be a proper incident thereto." The supervisory body is the Board of Governors of the Federal Reserve System. Thus one-bank holding companies cannot engage in manufacturing, communications, or any other industry not "closely related" to banking.

The future activities of one-bank holding companies are still unclear. The Federal Reserve, pursuant to the 1970 legislation, has ruled that they may engage in certain specified activities, such as some forms of insurance underwriting, acting as an investment or financial adviser, and providing bookkeeping or data processing services. But litigation continues in the courts; for example, in 1971 the Supreme Court decided that one-bank holding companies could not operate their own mutual funds, and in 1976 the Federal Reserve decided that they should not be permitted to operate travel agencies, because that activity is not "closely related" to banking. The outcome of other suits, still pending, will be a crucial factor in deciding the shape of banking in the future.

One thing that has already happened, however, is that the venerable geographic restrictions that have inhibited banking for so long appear to have been irrevocably breached. National banks still cannot branch across state lines and cannot branch in a state except as that state's laws permit its state-chartered banks to branch. However, the geographic limitations that the McFadden Act places on branches do not apply to nonbank subsidiaries. Under the one-bank holding company umbrella, both national and state banks can establish bank-related subsidiaries and affiliates anywhere in the country. New York banks now have mortgage company subsidiaries in Florida, California banks have finance company affiliates in Texas, and Chicago banks have loan production offices in New York. Whether this breakdown of traditional geographic restrictions will eventually extend to banks themselves, resulting in nationwide commercial bank branching, remains to be seen. But the first step in that direction has definitely been taken.

Savings and Loan Associations and Mutual Savings Banks

Savings and loan associations may be federally or state chartered. Of the roughly 5,000 S&Ls in existence, slightly more than half are chartered by the states in which they operate and the rest by the federal government. Virtually all of them, however, are members of the Federal Home Loan Bank System (FHLBS), which is comparable for S&Ls to what the Federal Reserve System is for commercial banks. The Federal Home Loan Bank System, like the Federal Reserve System, consists of twelve regional Banks plus a supervisory Board in Washington.

The Federal Home Loan Bank Board regulates S&Ls by chartering them, conducting examinations, and reviewing applications for branches and mergers. Branching fundamentally depends on state laws, but it tends to be much more liberal for S&Ls than for commercial banks, and branching across state lines is not uncommon.

The Federal Home Loan Bank System also supports S&Ls by making loans to them when they are otherwise short of funds; the FHLBS raises the money in the open market by selling its own securities and then uses the funds to make loans to savings and loan associations. While Federal Reserve discount window lending to commercial banks is usually expected to be repaid fairly rapidly, Federal Home Loan Bank loans to S&Ls are often for extended periods of time.

Deposit insurance for S&Ls, up to $100,000 per depositor, is provided by the Federal Savings and Loan Insurance Corporation (FSLIC). While the bank-related FDIC is an independent agency, the FSLIC is a subsidiary of the Federal Home Loan Bank System and its policies are determined by the Federal Home Loan Bank Board. At the end of 1980, the FSLIC insurance fund amounted to $6.5 billion.

Mutual savings banks were the first thrift institutions in the country: the first ones were founded in 1816 (the Provident Institution for Savings in Boston and the Saving Fund Society in Philadelphia), whereas the first S&L was not organized until fifteen years later (the Oxford Provident Building Association in Philadelphia). Nowadays, though, for most practical purposes savings banks and savings and loans are hard to tell apart except by their names.

The 500 mutual savings banks, concentrated on the Eastern Seaboard, are almost all state chartered, since federal chartering of savings banks was not begun until 1978. Because most are state chartered, they are state regulated and state supervised. However, they are insured by the FDIC, rather than by the FSLIC, up to the standard $100,000 per depositor.

Under the Depository Institutions Deregulation and Monetary Control Act of 1980, otherwise known as the Banking Act of 1980, both S&Ls and mutual savings banks must hold reserves against their checking account and business time deposit liabilities, as specified by the Federal Reserve; as a *quid pro quo,* they have full access to temporary borrowing from the Federal Reserve when needed.

As mentioned in the previous chapter, both S&Ls and mutual savings banks have had serious difficulties in recent years, owing to the rise in the general level of interest rates. Their liabilities are mostly short term while their assets are chiefly sunk in relatively low-yielding fixed-interest long-term mortgages. In the early 1980s a number of them were merged, with FSLIC or FDIC assistance, to create financially stronger institutions. In some cases, in what may be the wave of the future, an ailing thrift institution was merged into, or acquired by, a financially healthy commercial bank. Some of the mergers also took place across state lines.

As an aside, it is useful to note that there are a number of government-sponsored efforts to support the activities of mortgage-related financial institutions. Perhaps the most popular is the Federal National Mortgage Association, also known as Fannie Mae, established by Congress in 1938. It later became part of the Department of Housing and Urban Development (HUD) and in 1968 became a privately owned corporation with certain ties to the government. Fannie Mae buys mortgages from S&Ls and other institutions that no longer wish to hold them as investments, and finances these so-called secondary market operations primarily by issuing bonds to the public.

Fannie Mae's performance in the mortgage market is complemented by the work of Ginnie Mae, more properly called the Government National Mortgage Association. A relative newcomer to the mortgage market scene, Ginnie Mae was established by Congress in 1968 as part of HUD. Since 1970, Ginnie Mae has made a name in connection with the "pass-through program." Instead of buying mortgages and financing these acquisitions by issuing her own securities, Ginnie Mae guarantees the timely payment of interest and principal on packages or pools of mortgages that are insured by the Federal Housing Administration (FHA) or the Veterans Administration (VA). These pools of mortgages are put together by private mortgage originators such as savings and loan associations. GNMA pass-through securities are attractive to such investors as pension funds and insurance companies because of their government guarantee and liquidity. The pass-through program has made mortgages look very much like bonds to some investors, thereby broadening the source of mortgage funds.

In 1970, Congress established the Federal Home Loan Mortgage Corporation (FHLMC) as a subsidiary of the Federal Home Loan Bank System. Dubbed Freddie Mac by the investment community, this latest creation does just about what Ginnie Mae does, except that instead of FHA-VA mortgage-backed securities, Freddie Mac creates participation certificates in conventional mortgages and sells them to ultimate investors. As with Ginnie Mae, the objective is to attract heretofore nontraditional funds into the mortgage market by packaging individual mortgage loans into a bondlike instrument.

All these government and government-sponsored agencies are very active, especially during periods of tight money, in helping to finance mortgage activity. This has, in fact, led to concern in the capital markets over the "federalization of the mortgage market."

Credit Unions

The first credit union in this country was established in Manchester, New Hampshire, in 1909. Credit unions now number 20,000, making them the most numerous of the thrift institutions. They have not been subject to the same problems as S&Ls and mutual savings banks because the bulk of their lending has always taken the form of relatively short-term consumer loans.

Credit unions may be federally or state chartered, but the majority have federal charters. State-chartered institutions are regulated and supervised by the states in which they operate and the federally chartered ones by the National Credit Union Administration in Washington. The National Credit Union Share Insurance Fund, run by the National Credit Union Administration, provides deposit insurance (up to $100,000 per depositor) for both state and federally chartered credit unions.

As with savings and loans and mutual savings banks, the Banking Act of 1980 provides that credit unions must hold reserves against their checking accounts as specified by the Federal Reserve. In return, they have access to the temporary borrowing (discounting) facilities of the Fed.

Money Market Mutual Funds

There are now more than thirty money market mutual funds that have assets of over $1 billion each, as compared with none only ten years ago. As the previous chapter explained, the explosion of money market funds is directly attributable to Regulation Q: when money market interest rates rise above Regulation Q's deposit interest rate ceilings, depositors withdraw their funds from depository institutions and move their money into high-yielding short-term money market securities, either on their own or via money market mutual funds. They began to do this in the early 1970s and they are still doing it.

You will not find a money market mutual fund with a drive-in window at your local shopping center because all transactions are by mail, phone, or some related form of telecommunication. They are not regulated or supervised by any banking-type agency, either state or federal, and since they have no brick-and-mortar branches there are no regulations about where they can locate. However, as mutual funds they do come under the overall regulation of the Securities and Exchange Commission in Washington, which provides protection to shareholders against fraudulent practices and other potential abuses. Shares in money market mutual funds are not insured by any governmental agency.[6]

Since money market funds generally offer checking account privileges—in most cases only for checks of $500 or more—their "deposits" or shares are included as part of the money supply (M2). However, they are not subject to the reserve requirements that the Federal Reserve enforces on all other institutions offering demand deposits. So far the Fed has not strongly protested this anomaly.

Summary

1. The United States has a dual banking system, involving side-by-side federal and state chartering and supervision of commercial banks. State-chartered banks are more numerous, while federally chartered banks are larger. It is claimed that a dual banking system is more responsive to the evolving banking needs of the economy than a single system would be.

2. Multiple federal supervisory authorities—the Federal Reserve, the Comptroller of the Currency, and the FDIC—frequently cause confusion and conflict. There is general agreement that one federal supervisory authority would be preferable to three,

[6]The main difference between money market mutual funds and other depository institutions is that the money funds (like all mutual funds) do not have any capital (or surplus) on their balance sheets. In other words, money funds distribute all of their earnings on assets to their shareholders (less a management fee). Other financial intermediaries retain some portion of their earnings to build up capital. One consequence of this difference is that the return earned on money funds can never be fixed; it must always fluctuate with earnings on assets.

but there is no consensus as to which one of the three would be best.

3. FDIC insurance of bank depositors has eliminated the old-fashioned "run" on a bank in trouble, but deposits can still evaporate as holders of a bank's CDs let them run off.

4. The McFadden Act of 1927 prohibits interstate branching and requires that a federally chartered bank abide by state branching laws. One result is that the United States has more than 14,000 commercial banks, most of them very small institutions.

5. The Giant Banks appear to pose no near-term monopoly threat, especially since one-bank holding companies must confine their activities to fields "closely related" to banking.

6. Savings and loan associations are supervised by the Federal Home Loan Bank Board and insured by the FSLIC. Mutual savings banks are mostly state supervised and insured by the FDIC. Credit unions are supervised by the National Credit Union Administration and insured by the National Credit Union Share Insurance Fund.

7. Money market mutual funds come under the overall supervision of the Securities and Exchange Commission. So far they have escaped the reserve requirements of the Federal Reserve even though their shares are included as part of the money supply (M2).

Suggestions for Further Reading

The literature on bank structure is extensive. The classic in the field is David Alhadeff's *Monopoly and Competition in Banking* (Berkeley: University of California Press, 1954). Also see his "Barriers to Bank Entry," *Southern Economic Journal* (April 1974). Recent changes in bank structure are discussed in Donald T. Savage, "Developments in Banking Structure," *Federal Reserve Bulletin* (February 1982).

The McFadden Act is analyzed in *Geographic Restrictions on Commercial Banking in the United States: The Report of the President* (Washington: Government Printing Office, 1981). The entire Summer 1980 issue of the *Journal of Bank Research* is also devoted to it.

On problems of bank regulation, Marriner Eccles' analysis of many years ago is still sound and up to date: it is in his autobiography, *Beckoning Frontiers* (New York: Knopf, 1951), pp. 266–286. A very useful book on regulation and its historical development is Carter H. Golembe and David S. Holland, *Federal Regulation of Banking* (Washington: Golembe Associates, 1981). Also highly recommended: Elbert V. Bowden, *Revolution in Banking* (Richmond, Va: Robert F. Dame, 1980).

Closely related to structure and regulation is the role of bank examination. On this see George J. Benston's monograph, *Bank Examination* (New York University, Institute of Finance, 1973). And if you get a chance, be sure to see W. C. Fields (as Egbert Sousé) in the movie *The Bank Dick.* Franklin Pangborn plays the part of the bank examiner, J. Pinkerton Snoopington.

8

Commercial Bank Asset and Liability Management

BANKS are business firms. Banks may not look like Frisbee factories, but then King Kong doesn't look much like Rudolph the Red-nosed Reindeer either. They are both animals, nevertheless.

Like Frisbee manufacturers, bankers buy inputs, massage them a bit, burn a little incense, say the magic words, and out pops some output from the oven. If their luck holds, they can sell the finished product for more than it cost to buy the raw materials in the first place.

For a banker, the raw material is money. He buys it at a long counter he sets up in the store, then rushes around to the back, sits down behind a huge desk (a little out of breath), and sells it as soon as he can to someone else. If he's really good at his business, sometimes he can even sell it back to the same person he bought it from (a trick bankers picked up from Los Angeles used-car salesmen).

About the only way you can tell whether a banker is buying money or selling it is to observe him in his native habitat and see whether he's standing up or sitting down. For some unknown reason, probably an inherited trait, bankers always stand up when they buy money (take your deposit), but invariably sit down when they sell it (make loans or buy securities). In this chapter we'll look first at what happens when they're sitting down, and then at what they do when they stand up.

Uses of Bank Funds

Tables 1 and 2 show the major trends in the past twenty years in uses of bank funds. Table 1 contains the dollar amounts and Table 2 the relative percentages. What trends do they show?

Banks have obviously cut way back on the proportion of their funds in cash assets (which includes their deposits in the Federal Reserve) and their holdings of government securities—from 44 percent of total assets in 1960 to only 24 percent in 1980. These have been replaced chiefly by loans of all sorts, which are up from 46 percent of total assets in 1960 to 59 percent in 1980.

Bank holdings of government securities are often called their "secondary reserves," because they are highly marketable and can be liquidated on short notice. Aside from the long-run decline in holdings of government securities, there are also cyclical fluctuations that are not captured by Tables 1 or 2. Traditionally, banks buy government securities during recessions, when private loan demand is slack, and then sell them off during business recoveries, when private loan demand is vigorous. Thus bank holdings of government securities show a countercyclical pattern, rising when business conditions decline and falling when the business cycle is

Table 1 Assets of Insured Commercial Banks, 1960–1980
(In billions of dollars)

	1960	1970	1980
Cash assets	52	93	202
U.S. govt. and agency securities	61	75	163
State and local govt. securities	17	69	146
Other securities	3	3	15
Business loans	43	112	283
Mortgage loans	29	73	263
Consumer loans	26	66	182
Other loans	19	63	184
Miscellaneous assets	6	22	101
TOTAL	256	576	1,539

SOURCE: FDIC *Annual Reports.* All figures are as of year end.

Table 2 Assets of Insured Commercial Banks, 1960–1980 (Percentage distribution)

	1960	1970	1980
Cash assets	20	16	13
U.S. govt. and agency securities	24	13	11
State and local govt. securities	7	12	9
Other securities	1	1	1
Business loans	17	19	18
Mortgage loans	11	13	17
Consumer loans	10	11	12
Other loans	8	11	12
Miscellaneous assets	2	4	7
TOTAL	100	100	100

SOURCE: Table 1.

on the upswing. Loans in general, and business loans in particular, move in the opposite direction—that is, in harmony with the business cycle.

Why is it that no *stocks* are included among bank assets? Why no GE, IBM, GM, or TWA? (Not to mention NYU, UCLA, and SMU, none of which has had a decent football team for years.) The reason is that commercial banks have traditionally been barred by law from owning stocks, on the ground that stocks are too risky. This prohibition dates from the National Currency Act of 1863 and the National Bank Act of 1864, and has been reaffirmed repeatedly in subsequent legislation. Banks *do* buy billions of dollars worth of stocks, but not for themselves—they buy them for the trusts, estates, and pension funds that they manage for others. Such trust department holdings are not included among a bank's own assets.

Sources of Bank Funds

Tables 3 and 4 show the major trends over the past twenty years in sources of bank funds. Table 3 contains the dollar amounts and Table 4 the relative percentages.

Table 3 Liabilities and Capital of Insured Commercial Banks, 1960–1980
(In billions of dollars)

	1960	1970	1980
Demand deposits	156	247	432
Passbook savings deposits	55	99	201
Time deposits*	18	110	321
Large-size negotiable CDs	0	26	238
Miscellaneous liabilities	6	54	239
Equity capital	21	40	108
TOTAL	256	576	1,539

*Excluding large-size ($100,000 and over) negotiable certificates of deposit.
SOURCE: FDIC *Annual Reports* and *Federal Reserve Bulletin.* All figures are as of year end.

Table 4 Liabilities and Capital of Insured Commercial Banks, 1960–1980
(Percentage distribution)

	1960	1970	1980
Demand deposits	61	43	28
Passbook savings deposits	22	17	13
Time deposits	7	19	21
Large-size negotiable CDs	0	5	15
Miscellaneous liabilities	2	9	16
Equity capital	8	7	7
TOTAL	100	100	100

SOURCE: Table 3.

Notice first how demand deposits, which used to be *the* major source of bank funds—61 percent in 1960—have slipped in importance, declining to 28 percent by 1980. This decline is traceable to the legal prohibition against banks paying interest on demand deposits, combined with the general increase in interest rates on other types of assets over the postwar period. Individuals and business firms are reluctant to hold any more demand deposits than they really need for their day-to-day payments. They have learned that it pays to economize on their checking accounts, since to hold more than is absolutely necessary means sacrificing interest income.

Savings and time deposits, on the other hand, have expanded from only 29 percent of bank funds in 1960 to 49 percent in 1980. Savings and time deposits are frequently lumped together, but in the tables we have disaggregated them into three components: passbook savings deposits, time deposits (not counting large-size negotiable certificates of deposit), and large-size ($100,000 and over) negotiable CDs. One reason for the separation is that their relative growth rates have differed considerably over the period.

Passbook savings deposits are the traditional form of savings account, held mostly by individuals and nonprofit organizations. A little blue (sometimes green) passbook has been the standard symbol of a savings account for generations, and until the late 1960s such passbook accounts represented the bulk of total commercial bank savings and time deposits. Time deposits consist of certificates of deposit with a scheduled maturity date, and are held by business firms as well as by individuals. They have swept well ahead of passbook savings deposits in recent years.

With passbook savings accounts, funds can be withdrawn from the savings account at any time. Technically, thirty days' notice is required prior to a withdrawal, although this requirement is universally waived. On the other hand, if depositors want to withdraw funds from a time deposit before the scheduled maturity date they are subject to substantial penalties, such as the forfeiture of interest. Why, then, have time certificates of deposit become so popular in recent years?

The reason is our old friend Regulation Q. Banks are permitted to offer higher yields on time certificates than on passbook savings. In early 1982, for example, a commercial bank could legally offer a potential depositor only 5¼ percent interest on a regular passbook savings account. But it could offer 14 percent on a six-month money market time deposit. Because of such interest differentials, time deposits have grown much more popular than the traditional passbook savings account, as Tables 1 and 2 indicate.

The growth of time deposits was given particular impetus by the "invention" of the *negotiable* certificate of deposit in 1961. Usually issued in denominations of $100,000 and over, the negotiable CD can

"And here's an extra 'substantial penalty' for the early withdrawal of your time deposit!"

Drawing by D. Fradon; © 1975 The New Yorker Magazine, Inc.

be sold if one has to raise cash before it matures. Thus it serves as an alternative to Treasury bills for the corporate treasurer with excess funds to invest for a short time. Regulation Q has not applied to large-size negotiable CDs since 1973. At the end of 1981, $300 billion of corporate funds were invested in large-size negotiable CDs, a money market instrument that was not even in existence in 1960.

Tables 3 and 4 also show a huge increase in "miscellaneous" liabilities over the past twenty years. These include a wide variety of *nondeposit* sources of funds, such as:

1. Borrowings from the Federal Reserve (at the discount rate).
2. Borrowings in the Federal funds market, with banks in need of reserves borrowing some from banks that have an excess (at the Federal funds rate).
3. Borrowings by banks from their foreign branches, from their parent holding companies, and from their subsidiaries and affiliates.

4. Repurchase agreements: the sale of securities that banks have agreed to buy back at a later date (often the next day). When banks sell securities to corporations under agreements to repurchase—called RPs or "repos"—the banks commit themselves to buy the securities back on a specified future date at a predetermined price. In effect, since the bank has the use of the funds until the securities are repurchased, the bank is borrowing funds with the securities as collateral; the interest rate is determined by the difference between today's selling price and tomorrow's higher repurchase price. With overnight RPs, the bank gains access to short-term funds, which it hopes to use profitably, and the corporation earns interest while sacrificing virtually no liquidity. When such a transaction is made between a bank and one of its own corporate depositors, the bank's balance sheet shows a rise in borrowings and a corresponding drop in demand deposit liabilities.[1]

Bank Capital

The final source of funds on Tables 3 and 4 is equity capital, which means the difference between total assets and total liabilities on a bank's balance sheet.[2] The function of equity capital is to serve as a buffer, so that if a bank experiences hard times depositors will not be immediately affected. As in any business, equity capital serves as a cushion against adversity. (In return, of course, stockholders also get the fruits of prosperity.)

[1]The widespread growth of overnight RPs in recent years has increased skepticism regarding the value of the M1 money supply figures as a reliable measure of liquidity in the economy. See William L. Silber, *Commercial Bank Liability Management* (Chicago: Association of Reserve City Bankers, 1978), pages 42–45, and Gillian Garcia and Simon Pak, "Some Clues in the Case of the Missing Money," *American Economic Review* (May 1979).

[2]This measure of equity capital has no necessary connection with the value of a bank as measured by the price of its stock in the stock market. Accountants and finance majors worry about such discrepancies but we don't have to.

As Table 4 shows, equity capital has held at a stable 7 or 8 percent of total sources of funds for many years. But meanwhile the overall riskiness of bank assets has increased. Bank examiners measure the riskiness of bank portfolios by subtracting cash assets and U.S. government securities from total assets. Thus, as Table 2 shows, 56 percent of bank assets were risk assets in 1960, 71 percent in 1970, and 76 percent in 1980. The ratio of the dollar amount of equity capital to risk assets (from Tables 3 and 1) is shown in Table 5.

Table 5 Equity Capital to Risk Assets, 1960–1980*

	1960	1970	1980
(1) Equity capital	$ 21	$ 40	$108
(2) Risk assets	$143	$408	$1,174
(1) ÷ (2)	15%	10%	9%

*Equity capital and risk assets in billions of dollars.
SOURCE: Tables 3 and 1.

It is clear from Table 5 that the ratio of equity capital to risk assets has been declining. This has led many bank regulators to question the adequacy of bank capital today, and to suggest that banks go about rebuilding their capital positions (by retained earnings and new stock flotations) so as to regain the levels of capital relative to risk assets that were typical fifteen or twenty years ago.

Bankers, on the other hand, typically prefer to operate with less rather than more equity. Because equity is usually more expensive than deposits or other short-term borrowed funds, a bank's profitability is enhanced the less it relies on equity and the more on deposits and other debt. As a result, there is constant conflict between bankers and the supervisory authorities as to how much bank capital is appropriate.

Liquidity and Profitability

Bank management is a never ending tug of war—between liquidity and safety, on the one hand, and earnings and profitability on the other. The reason: the more liquid an asset, the less it is likely to yield. But banks are business firms, with stockholders; presumably they want to earn profits. Why not forget about liquidity, then, and buy only high-yielding (less liquid) assets? Because, due to the unique structure of their liabilities, banks *need* liquidity—that is, they need assets that are quickly convertible into cash, with little or no loss in value. So bank management faces an endless conflict (a conflict of interest?).

The nature of bank liabilities confirms their need for liquidity on the asset side. Demand deposits, for example, are all payable, as their name implies, on *demand.* And so are passbook savings deposits, for all practical purposes. Thus, a far larger proportion of commercial bank liabilities is payable on demand than is the case with any other type of business. But, of course, if a bank holds only highly liquid assets to meet any conceivable volume of withdrawals, it will probably not cover its costs and will have to go out of business.

Tables 6 and 7 show the income and expenses of all insured commercial banks since 1960. Notice how interest *expenses* have grown —to 70 percent of total costs in 1980, five times larger than salaries and wages.

Having to *pay out* so much in interest puts added pressure on bank portfolio decision-makers to acquire assets that *return* enough in interest to make the bank a profitable enterprise. This illustrates concretely the dilemma constantly facing bankers: They must maintain liquidity (because of the nature of their liabilities), and yet they are always tempted to reduce liquidity (to generate profits).

By almost any measure, bank liquidity has declined substantially over the years 1960–1980. One traditional rule-of-thumb measure that is widely used to gauge bank liquidity is the ratio of total loans to total deposits. A lower loan/deposit ratio indicates a rise in bank liquidity, a higher loan/deposit ratio a decline in bank liquidity. If you compare the data in Tables 1 and 3, you will find that the loan/ deposit ratio rose from 51 percent in 1960 to 65 percent in 1970 and to 77 percent in 1980.[3]

For the banking *system*—all the banks taken together—ultimate

---

[3]For 1960, 117/229 = 51%; for 1970, 314/482 = 65%; and for 1980, 912/1192 = 77%. These figures are for all insured commercial banks. Larger banks typically have higher loan/deposit ratios than smaller ones.

Table 6 Operating Income, Expenses, and Net Income of Insured Commercial Banks, 1960–1980
(In billions of dollars)

	1960	1970	1980
Operating Income			
Interest on loans	6.8	24.0	152.0
Interest on securities	2.3	6.5	23.1
Service charges and fees	.8	2.0	7.5
Trust department income	.5	1.1	2.7
Other operating income	.3	1.1	5.5
TOTAL	10.7	34.7	190.8
Operating Expenses			
Salaries and wages	2.9	7.7	24.7
Interest on deposits	1.8	10.5	98.4
Interest on other borrowed funds	—	2.0	21.7
Other operating expenses	2.2	7.4	26.5
TOTAL	6.9	27.6	171.3
Net Operating Income	3.8	7.1	19.5
Securities gains (losses)	(.4)	(.1)	(.5)
Taxes	1.4	1.9	5.0
Net After-Tax Income	2.0	5.1	14.0

SOURCE: FDIC *Annual Reports.*

liquidity is provided by the Federal Reserve. But what about an *individual* commercial bank? How can a single commercial bank best provide for its liquidity needs without excessively impairing its profitability?

Liability Management

The 1960s witnessed a dramatic change in bank liquidity practices. Until then, provision for liquidity had been sought almost entirely on the asset side of the balance sheet. Banks stocked up with liquid assets, especially short-term government securities, and then sold

Table 7 Operating Income and Expenses of Insured Commercial Banks, 1960–1980
(Percentage distribution)

	1960	1970	1980
Operating Income			
Interest on loans	63	69	80
Interest on securities	21	19	12
Service charges and fees	8	6	4
Trust department income	5	3	1
Other operating income	3	3	3
TOTAL	100	100	100
Operating Expenses			
Salaries and wages	42	28	14
Interest on deposits	26	38	57
Interest on other borrowed funds	—	7	13
Other operating expenses	32	27	16
TOTAL	100	100	100

SOURCE: Table 6.

them off when they needed funds. The single exception to this principle was occasional resort to Federal Reserve discounting.

Starting in the early 1960s, however, banks began increasingly to draw their liquidity from the *liabilities* side of the balance sheet. *Instead of taking their liability structure as given and tailoring their assets to fit, they began to take a target asset growth as given and adjust their liabilities to suit their needs.* Liability management became the most important banking development of the 1960s. It was facilitated by the growth of the negotiable CD market, which started in early 1961.

More and more during the 1960s, banks—especially the larger ones—came to rely on their ability to buy (borrow) money when necessary as a means of meeting whatever liquidity needs might arise. Why store up liquidity in short-term, low-yielding assets, when it could always be bought in the market when needed? Why turn away creditworthy potential borrowers with talk of being "loaned up"—only to see them get loans from competitors—when the necessary funds could always be bought by selling new CDs?

The expansion of the Federal funds market during the 1960s also played a significant role in the development of bank liability management. In a traditional Federal funds transaction, a bank with excess reserves will sell some of its excess to a bank with deficient reserves, on an overnight basis and at an agreed-upon interest rate. In addition, Federal funds are transferred on the same day a transaction is concluded.

For a bank seeking to make up a reserve deficiency, the Federal funds market is an alternative to borrowing from the Federal Reserve through the discount window or to selling off short-term assets. Since borrowing at the discount window is an alternative to buying Federal funds, the interest rate on Federal funds never rose above the discount rate (until the mid-1960s). If the Federal funds rate went above the discount rate, a bank needing reserves would merely use the discount window instead of buying Federal funds from another commercial bank.

Since the mid-1960s, however, the daily Federal funds rate has rarely been *below* the discount rate. This is because in recent years the market has changed its nature. It used to involve only banks making temporary last-minute adjustments in their reserves. Now a number of large banks use the Federal funds market to make virtually continuous net purchases, even when they are not faced with a reserve shortage; they are using the Federal funds market to acquire funds on a more or less permanent basis. Thus Federal funds are just another bank liability (included under Miscellaneous liabilities in Tables 3 and 4) used to expand lending ability.

The paradoxical result is that the shortest of all money market transactions—the overnight purchase of Federal funds—has become in many respects more like a capital market than a money market instrument. This serves as a good lesson in why you cannot draw a hard and fast line between the two. Virtually all financial markets are interconnected and interrelated, in one way or another. We will return to these interactions in Chapter 26, when we examine the determinants of the structure of interest rates—why some interest rates are higher than others, and what causes changes in their relationships.

"Our main bank is right near your home, and we have fifteen other
handy branches with all the latest push-button systems. We'll give you
top interest rates and lollipops on your 'rainy-day' savings account. You
can also have a safe-deposit box that no one but you is allowed to open.
You'll get free 'stop-and-bank' souvenirs, such as little silver Empire
State Buildings and Abraham Lincolns. There is a brand-new
playground next to your bank, and you'll get a chance to win one of the
grand sweepstakes prizes—hi-fi stereo, color television, or two weeks for
two in Mexico City."

Drawing by Booth; © 1974 The New Yorker Magazine, Inc.

Discretionary Funds Management

The central focus of bank management today is a modified form of liability management, best described as discretionary funds management. It revolves around the strategic employment of interest-sensitive funds—whether liabilities *or* assets—that can be increased or decreased at the bank's initiative.

Bank management in relatively large institutions meets at least monthly, often weekly, to project expected movements in *non*discretionary funds—anticipated inflows and outflows that are beyond the bank's immediate control. These would include expected extensions or repayments of business loans, projected inflows and outflows of time and savings deposits, and so on. The result of all these nondiscretionary flows is either a projected *net outflow* of funds or a projected *net inflow,* which the bank must accommodate in the short run. An expected net outflow means funds must be raised to fill the gap; an expected net inflow means there are surplus funds to dispose of.

It is the *discretionary* liabilities and assets that will be used to raise funds or dispose of them, as the case might be. If a bank needs to raise funds, it might buy Federal funds, sell Treasury bills, sell securities under repurchase agreements, or borrow through CDs or from the Federal Reserve. If it has funds to dispose of, funds it does not want to keep idle, it might sell Federal funds, buy Treasury bills, lower its CD rate and let CDs run off, and so on. Whether a discretionary item is an asset or a liability is relatively unimportant in the bank's financing decision. The most basic consideration is to raise funds at minimum cost or to allocate a surplus to maximize profits.

These alternative sources of funds all stand on a common footing in that each of them can—at a price—supply a dollar of liquidity which is just as good as a dollar of liquidity acquired from any other source. In brief, at any one time a choice exists among an array of alternatives as to how liquidity might be acquired. It is more profitable to make this choice in terms of relative costs and risks than to worry about whether it is assets or liabilities that are involved.

Finally, it should be emphasized that fundamental to the state of bank liquidity are three basic factors that are often overlooked: (1) federal monetary-fiscal policies, to maintain a prosperous economy in which the anticipated income of borrowers will actually be realized so that they are able to repay their loans on time; (2) federal deposit insurance protection, which has successfully eliminated the old-fashioned "run on the bank" that used to spark liquidity crises; and (3) the Federal Reserve itself, in times of unforeseen widespread financial emergency, standing by as a "lender of last resort" through its open market operations and discount facilities.

Summary

1. Over the past twenty years, commercial banks have sharply reduced their holdings of government securities in favor of loans of all sorts. However, their government securities still show countercyclical fluctuations.

2. On the liabilities side, demand deposits and passbook savings deposits, which were 83 percent of bank liabilities in 1960, dropped to 41 percent in 1980. Their place was taken by time deposits, large-size negotiable CDs, and miscellaneous liabilities, such as Federal funds purchases and the sale of securities under repurchase agreements.

3. The ratio of equity capital to risk assets has been falling, and so has bank liquidity as measured by the loan/deposit ratio.

4. Bank management is a continuous tug of war between liquidity and profitability. Banks need liquidity because such a large proportion of their liabilities is payable on demand, but typically the more liquid an asset the less it yields in interest.

5. Liability management replaced asset management in the 1960s as the main method of providing for bank liquidity. In turn, exclusive reliance on liability management has been superseded by discretionary funds management, incorporating both assets and liabilities and choosing among alternatives on the basis of relative costs and risks.

Suggestions for Further Reading

The problems of bank liquidity are discussed in surprisingly modern terms in Walter Bagehot's classic *Lombard Street* (New York: Scribner's, 1873; reprinted, Homewood, Ill.: Irwin, 1962), and in Lloyd W. Mints, *A History of Banking Theory* (University of Chicago Press, 1945).

For more up-to-date treatments of bank asset and liability management, see William L. Silber, *Commercial Bank Liability Management* (Chicago: Association of Reserve City Bankers, 1978), and Paul S. Nadler, *Commercial Banking in the Economy,* 3rd ed. (New York: Random House, 1979).

A good bibliography on the subject of bank capital is in Ronald D. Watson's informative "Insuring Some Progress in the Bank Capital Hassle," Federal Reserve Bank of Philadelphia *Business Review* (July/August 1974).

Appendix

Managing a Bank's Money Position

The legal obligation to hold reserves leads to the problem of managing a bank's reserve position—usually called managing its "money position." This appendix explains how a bank's "money desk" manager goes about the job of meeting those requirements.

First, the simple rules of the game:

1. All banks have to hold required reserves against both their demand and business or non-personal time deposit liabilities.

2. Only two assets can be used to fulfill these requirements, namely cash in vault and deposits in the regional Federal Reserve Bank. Neither of these earn any interest, so while a bank must hold enough reserves to meet its requirements it has an incentive not to hold any more than that.

A complicating factor is that reserve requirements are not imposed against a bank's total demand deposits but against its *net* demand deposits. Net demand deposits are a bank's total demand deposit liabilities minus both (a) cash items in process of collection and (b) demand balances due *from* domestic banks. Both of these deductions are *asset* items on a bank's balance sheet. Deducting them from a bank's total demand deposit liabilities avoids requiring reserves twice against what is really the same deposit. In other words, by allowing these two deductions the Fed avoids double counting of demand deposit liabilities of the banking system to the public.

For example, take the asset item "cash items in process of collection." Say you have an account in the King Kong National Bank and you write a check and give it to a storekeeper who deposits it in the Godzilla State Bank on the other side of town. This is a new demand deposit liability for Godzilla, but until the check clears King Kong still has your demand deposit on its books too. In fact, for the moment King Kong doesn't even know you have written that check, so it is still figuring you have the same demand deposit and is still holding the required reserve against it. If both banks had to hold reserves against these deposits, they would both be holding reserves against what really amounts to one and the same deposit. What Godzilla, the storekeeper's bank, does until the check clears is list an offsetting item on the asset side of its balance sheet, namely "cash item in process of collection." This is subtracted from its total demand deposits when it computes its net demand deposits, so for now only King Kong has to hold reserves against this deposit. Then when the check clears in a day or so, several things happen: the King Kong National Bank receives your check back, cancels it, and removes your demand deposit from its books; and the Godzilla State Bank removes the entry "cash items in process of collection" from its assets (because the check is no longer "in process" of collection—it has actually been collected). Now King Kong no longer has the deposit and no longer has to keep reserves against it. The deposit is now officially at Godzilla and that is the bank that has to hold reserves against it.

Similar logic—avoiding double counting of the banking system's demand deposit liabilities to the public—is also behind the other deduction, "demand balances due *from* domestic banks." These are simply interbank deposits as carried on the books (as assets) of the *depositing* bank. Say you deposit a $100 check in your account at King Kong National. Also let's say that King Kong is a correspondent of a large city bank, the Bank of America (also known as the Mighty Joe Young Bank and Trust Company). A correspondent bank holds deposits with another bank usually to facilitate check clearing and for other services. King Kong therefore may very well make a $100 deposit of its own in the Bank of America. When King Kong does this, it enters an asset on its books "demand balance due from the Bank of America." King Kong deducts this from its total demand deposits when calculating its net demand deposits, because in effect it has shifted the deposit to the Bank of America. It is the Bank of America that must now hold reserves against this $100 deposit.

Once a bank's net demand and business time deposits are determined, the level of required reserves can be calculated based on the applicable required reserves ratio. The money desk manager's job is to hit that target level of reserves right on the nose. A *lower* than target volume of reserves will penalize the bank, because banks that are deficient in their reserves have to pay a penalty on the deficiency to the Federal Reserve. A *higher* than target volume of reserves will also penalize the bank in the form of foregone income, since excess reserves earn no interest.

A money desk manager who wants to *increase* a bank's reserves will start selling assets, like Treasury bills, or borrowing money—in the Federal funds market, via CDs, or maybe at the Fed's discount window. Naturally, the least-cost alternative will be the most attractive: it would be cheaper to sell Treasury bills that are yielding 10 percent than to borrow in the Federal funds market at 12 percent. To *reduce* reserves a money desk manager would do the opposite: buy Treasury bills, sell Federal funds, or perhaps pay off any outstanding indebtedness at the Federal Reserve discount window.

Why is the money desk manager's job so difficult? Because so many things that affect a bank's reserve balance are not within the bank's control. After all, every check that is written by a depositor of the bank—or received by a depositor—and that clears through the Federal Reserve alters the bank's reserves. If a large corporate depositor writes a big check, the bank's reserves fall; if many large corporate depositors do so, the bank's reserves fall a lot. The opposite happens if depositors receive checks and send them in to the bank to be credited to their accounts—then the bank's reserves at the Fed rise. A large bank will have thousands of such transactions each day, often with unpredictable net effects on its reserves. You can always tell who the money position managers are in large banks: they have glazed eyes and they twitch a lot. But there are compensations: they get paid well and have long vacations.

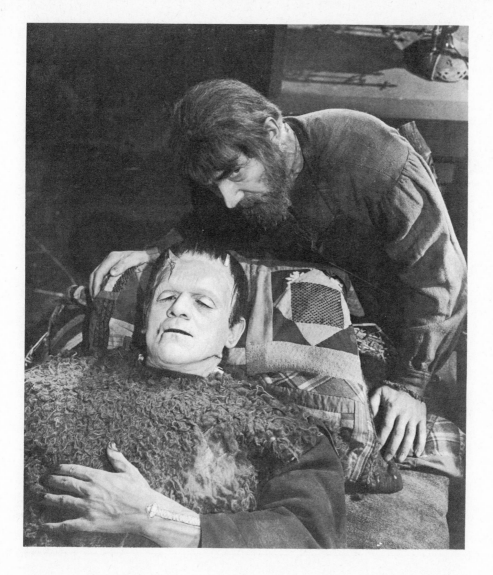

"Psst, we need reserves bad . . . get in there and buy some Fed funds."

9

Nondeposit Financial Institutions

ONCE UPON A TIME, so the story goes, there used to be deposit financial institutions and nondeposit financial institutions and never the twain did meet. Those days are fast disappearing. The sharp differences between deposit and nondeposit institutions are fading as various financial institutions aggressively invade each other's territory. In this chapter we will look at each of the major nondeposit financial institutions as well as at the overlaps and conflicts that are now erupting.

Life Insurance Companies

The first life insurance company in the United States was established shortly before the Revolutionary War and is still in existence (the Presbyterian Ministers' Fund). There are now about 1,800 life insurance companies in the country, with assets in excess of $500 billion at the end of 1981. Some are among the largest and best-known corporations in the world, like Prudential Insurance Company and Metropolitan Life, with assets at the end of 1980 of $60 billion and $50 billion respectively.

Life insurance companies are structured as either stock companies or mutual associations. In stock companies the business is owned and controlled by regular stockholders; in mutuals ownership and control technically rests with the policyholders. Over 90 percent of the life insurance companies now in existence are stock companies, but the mutuals are much larger and control more than half of the assets. Both Prudential and Metropolitan Life, for example, are organized as mutuals.

Life insurance companies are supervised and regulated almost entirely by the states in which they operate. Regulation covers virtually every aspect of the business, including sales practices, premium rates, the calculation of reserves (not the same as bank reserves), and allowable investments. A company must be licensed and file reports in all states in which it sells life insurance. Regulation is usually by a state insurance commissioner who is sometimes also the state banking commissioner.

Firms marketing life insurance used to specialize almost exclusively in selling "whole life" policies to individuals. Such policies have a constant premium through the entire life of the policy, which is higher than actuarial probabilities warrant in the early years of the policy but gradually becomes lower than required by actuarial probabilities later on. (Actuaries are statisticians who specialize in mortality probabilities.) Since the earlier premiums are higher than necessary in terms of actuarial statistics, whole life policies build up reserves. These reserves provide savings that yield a cash value the policyholder can borrow against or take outright at any time by canceling the policy.

Whole life policies contrast with "term" life insurance, in which premiums are relatively low at first but then rise as people grow older to keep in step with the higher statistical probability of dying. Term life insurance policies are pure insurance and involve no reserves or savings element.

For a number of years, the savings feature of whole life insurance has produced a rate of return to policyholders that has been well below yields obtainable on alternative investments, such as Treasury bills or money market mutual funds. As a result there has been a pronounced shift by the public away from whole life policies in favor of strictly term insurance. Term insurance gives the same amount of protection at a generally lower premium; with the money they save in premiums, people can buy an asset that yields a higher rate of return than provided by the savings component of a whole life policy.

In response, the life insurance industry has begun to change its ways drastically, to recapture the funds it used to receive but which are now flowing elsewhere. It has redesigned its product, selling more group insurance (through employers, for example) than policies to individuals, and inventing new kinds of insurance policies that offer higher yields than were formerly available. For example, some new types of policies combine term life insurance with investment in a money market fund or something similar, like a stock market mutual fund. To facilitate these adaptations to a changing environment, a number of life insurance companies have acquired firms with expertise in money market funds, the stock market, and related areas. In 1981 Prudential merged with Bache Halsey Stuart Shields, a member firm of the New York Stock Exchange; American Express, which owns the Fireman's Fund Life Insurance Company, similarly acquired a large stock exchange firm, Shearson Loeb Rhoades.

In line with these developments, life insurance companies have also altered their investment policies. Traditionally, they used premiums they received on policies (over what they paid in benefits) mainly to buy long-term corporate bonds and commercial mortgages. Lately, however, they have branched out into riskier ventures, such as common stocks and real estate. Metropolitan Life, for instance, paid $400 million in 1981 to buy the Pan Am Building in New York City.

Pension Funds

A lot of people are financially better off dead than alive, because when they die their life insurance policies pay out a hefty amount. The problems arise when they stay alive too long after they've finished their working careers and find out that social security doesn't come anywhere close to meeting their day-to-day retirement needs, not to mention buying an occasional luxury item. Pension plans are intended to fill this gap, enabling retirees to maintain a decent standard of living.

Private pension plans are run by a trustee—possibly a bank, an insurance company, or a pension fund manager—whose job is to administer the pension arrangements agreed to by a single employer or group of employers and their employees. All pension plans involve the twin problems of *vesting* and *funding* of future benefits.

An employee's pension benefits are said to be vested when the employee can leave the job and still retain pension benefits already earned. Many firms require that a person be on the payroll for ten years before future benefits are vested; if he or she quits or is fired after nine years, all pension rights are forfeited. Other plans provide for something like 25 percent vesting after so many years, with a gradual increase to 100 percent after so many additional years. The specific provisions about vesting are obviously among the most important clauses in any pension plan contract. Employers generally prefer to delay vesting as long as possible so that an employee will think twice (or three times) before quitting to go elsewhere.

Equally important are the stipulations about funding. A pension liability is fully funded when enough money has been set aside so that, after earning an assumed rate of return, it will be sufficient to pay the promised pension when it comes due. Because of the power of compound interest over time, the entire final amount does not have to be set aside today. If the money is expected to earn 10 percent interest, then only $1,000 has to be set aside today to fully fund a pension of $1,100 due a year from now ... or a pension of $17,450 due thirty years from now (because $1,000 \, (1 + .10)^{30} = \$17,450$).[1]

Given those figures—$1,100 a year from now or $17,450 thirty years from now, and an assumed 10 percent yield—if *less* than $1,000 is set aside today, then the pension is said to be only partly funded. Many companies have a low level of funding, planning to meet their pension commitments mainly out of current earnings when the pensions come due. This works, of course, only if earnings remain sufficient to meet such liabilities. Clearly, the higher the

[1]See the final section of Chapter 5.

level of funding the safer the pension. The social security system, for instance, is largely unfunded. It pays current pensions mainly out of current social security tax receipts, which is one reason it is in trouble.

Because of abuses and mismanagement in many private pension plans, in 1974 Congress enacted the Employee Retirement Income Security Act (ERISA), which established minimum reporting, disclosure, vesting, funding, and investment standards to safeguard employee pension rights. The same legislation also created the Pension Benefit Guaranty Corporation—known, believe it or not, as Penny Benny—which is a sort of pension FDIC. It guarantees some pension benefits in case a company goes bankrupt or is otherwise unable to meet its accrued pension liabilities.

In addition to employer-sponsored pension plans, individuals are also given tax incentives to set up their own pension plans—Keogh Plans for self-employed people and Individual Retirement Accounts (IRAs) for anyone who works.[2] These are usually established in the form of a deposit account in a bank or thrift institution or in the form of shares in a mutual fund of some sort, with the interest or dividends tax-deferred until retirement.

Property and Casualty Insurance Companies

Property and casualty insurance companies cannot plan ahead as easily as life insurance companies because they have no equivalent to actuarial mortality tables to tell them how much they will probably have to pay out every year into the indefinite future. About 3,000 companies nationwide offer insurance against casualties such as automobile accidents, fire, theft, personal negligence, malpractice, hailstorms, floods, and almost anything else you can dream up. Lloyd's of London, it is said, will insure against *any* contingency—at a price.

[2]Keogh Plans are named after Representative Eugene F. Keogh of New York, who sponsored the legislation that created pension plans for self-employed individuals.

Automobile liability insurance is the most important of all forms of property and casualty insurance in dollar terms. The most unusual of all is probably the retroactive fire insurance the MGM Grand Hotel in Las Vegas purchased *after* its disastrous 1980 fire; since there was uncertainty about how much the fire might cost the hotel as the result of negligence lawsuits, the hotel insured itself against payments above a certain amount. The second most unusual is probably the strike insurance the major league baseball owners wisely bought before the start of the 1981 season—it put them in a comfortable bargaining position when the players went on strike for seven weeks that year.

Property and casualty insurance companies, like life insurance companies, are regulated and supervised almost exclusively by the states in which they operate. There is little federal involvement. State insurance commissions set ranges for rates, enforce operating standards, and exercise overall supervision over company policies.

Their investment policies reflect the fact that they are fully taxed and that casualty losses can be highly variable. Thus they are heavy buyers of tax-free municipal bonds and liquid short-term securities.

Securities Brokers and Dealers and Investment Bankers

Neither securities brokers and dealers nor investment bankers are listed as major financial institutions in Table 1 of Chapter 6, because they have relatively small amounts of assets of their own. However, they are crucially important as middlemen in the distribution and trading of huge amounts of securities, including corporate stocks, bonds, state and local government securities, and U.S. Government securities.

The difference between investment bankers on the one hand and brokers and dealers on the other involves the distinction between *primary* and *secondary* securities markets. Primary markets refer to the sale and distribution of securities when they are *originally issued* by the money-raising corporation or governmental unit. Secondary markets involve the *subsequent trading* of those securities once they are already outstanding. The New York Stock Exchange is an example of a secondary market.

Investment bankers operate in primary markets, selling and distributing new stocks and bonds directly from the issuing corporations to their original purchasers. Brokers and dealers are involved in secondary markets, trading "used" or already outstanding securities.

The difference between brokers and dealers is that brokers do not buy or sell for their own account. They are pure middlemen, matching buyers and sellers of a particular security and earning a commission fee for bringing the two together. Dealers, on the other hand, "take positions" in securities: they buy them for their own account hoping to resell at a higher price. If they are wrong, and the price falls before they can unload, their hoped-for profit becomes a loss instead.

Many of the nationwide stock exchange firms, like Merrill Lynch, act in all of these capacities. They are called stockbrokers, or brokerage houses, because they act as agents in executing orders to buy or sell securities on the various stock exchanges. At times they also act as dealers and at other times as investment bankers. We will return to all these matters in Chapter 28, when we explore the functioning of securities markets in detail.

Our main interest at the moment, however, is in the ways in which a number of large stock exchange firms have branched out in the last few years to provide new kinds of financial services that used to be considered beyond their province. Merrill Lynch was the innovator, starting the ball rolling in 1977 with its Cash Management Account (CMA). The CMA consists of a financial package that includes a credit card, instant loans, check-writing privileges, investment in a money market mutual fund, and complete record keeping—including monthly statements (see the accompanying newspaper article). This brings brokerage houses close to being in the banking business. Can banks respond to the challenge by turning around and going into the securities or money market fund business themselves? So far the answer is no, and the reason they can't is called Glass-Steagall.

The Glass-Steagall Act

The Banking Act of 1933, known as the Glass-Steagall Act, separated commercial banking and investment banking, where the latter refers specifically to issuing, underwriting, selling, or distributing new stock and bond offerings of corporations. Commercial banks had become deeply involved in the sale and distribution of new stock and bond offerings in the 1920s, not always with happy results. There were suspicions that banks on occasion dumped new offerings into trust funds that they managed because they couldn't sell them to anyone else. To avoid such conflicts of interest, the Banking Act of 1933 divorced commercial from investment banking. Banks involved in both areas were forced to choose one or the other.[3]

Commercial banks are still permitted to distribute new offerings of federal government securities and "full faith and credit" general obligations of state and local governments. But Glass-Steagall forbids them to get involved in new offerings of corporate stocks or bonds or municipal revenue bonds. Revenue bonds differ from general municipal obligations in that they are not backed by the full taxing power of the state or local government; bondholders have a claim only on the revenues of the specific project being financed, such as a toll road or a state university dormitory (maybe even yours). The Act has also been interpreted as meaning that commercial banks cannot offer mutual funds, including money market mutual funds.

Commercial banks believe they are being discriminated against by the provisions of the Glass-Steagall Act. After all, securities firms and investment bankers—not to mention life insurance companies—have penetrated their deposit and checking account business via money market mutual funds and CMAs, but commercial banks can't penetrate the securities business with stock or money market mutual funds or by distributing new municipal revenue bonds or new corporate securities of any sort.

[3]The Banking Act of 1933 is called the Glass-Steagall Act after its two principal sponsors, Senator Carter Glass of Virginia and Representative Henry B. Steagall of Alabama. While we're at it, Representative Louis T. McFadden was from Pennsylvania. Quick now: what was the McFadden Act? (Check Chapter 7.)

Merrill Lynch's C.M.A. Boom

Service Mix Is Imitated; Banks Irked

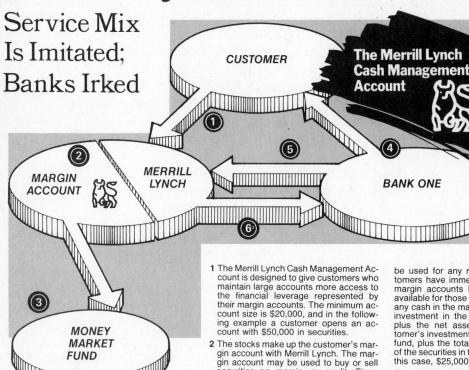

CUSTOMER

The Merrill Lynch Cash Management Account

① ⑤ ④

② MARGIN ACCOUNT

MERRILL LYNCH

BANK ONE

⑥

③ MONEY MARKET FUND

By KENNETH B. NOBLE

Four years ago, Merrill Lynch, Pierce, Fenner & Smith introduced an innovative new product that combined its traditional brokerage margin account with checkwriting and Visa card privileges tied to a money market mutual fund.

Most of its customers though were more mystified than dazzled by the ingenuity of the product, and it was greeted with widespread indifference.

The novelty of money funds—which pool the money of investors and place it in various liquid assets—has long since worn off and the huge success of Merrill Lynch's marketing gamble, called a Cash Management Account, has propelled the firm into the leading edge of the revolution in financial services that is transforming Wall Street.

1 The Merrill Lynch Cash Management Account is designed to give customers who maintain large accounts more access to the financial leverage represented by their margin accounts. The minimum account size is $20,000, and in the following example a customer opens an account with $50,000 in securities.

2 The stocks make up the customer's margin account with Merrill Lynch. The margin account may be used to buy or sell securities on margin, or credit. Since Merrill Lynch is normally allowed to lend customers half of the value of the securities in the account, in this case the margin account represents $25,000 in available credit.

3 Credit balances—from stock sales or dividends, bond interest, cash deposits —are automatically invested in a money market fund at the beginning of each week.

4 The customer also opens checking and Visa credit card accounts with Bank One of Columbus, Ohio, a commercial bank that provides the retail banking services for Merrill Lynch's C.M.A. customers. Since the checks and the Visa card can

The Cash Management Account program is multiplying at a remarkable pace—almost 110,000 of its 300,000 accounts have been added so far this year alone. Investment in the C.M.A. money trust—the cornerstone of the program from which funds are invested into the

be used for any retail purchases, customers have immediate access to their margin accounts because the amount available for those purchases is equal to: any cash in the margin account awaiting investment in the money market fund, plus the net asset value of the customer's investment in the money market fund, plus the total available loan value of the securities in the margin account (in this case, $25,000).

5 Bank One processes the customer's checking and credit card transactions, receiving from Merrill Lynch daily updates on available cash.

6 Merrill Lynch receives daily reports on the customer's purchases from Bank One, and pays the bank on behalf of the C.M.A. customer. Payment to the bank comes first from any free cash in the margin account and then from the redemption of shares in the money market fund. If those amounts do not cover the purchase, Merrill Lynch pays for the purchase by lending the customer sufficient funds through the available loan value of the securities in the margin account.

money market—is more than $6 billion —double the amount in reserve a year ago.

"C.M.A.'s could be the most important innovation in financial packaging since the creation of the mutual fund," said Adrian L. Banky, senior vice president

---

News Item / Stock exchange firms have branched out in the last few years to provide new kinds of financial services

and general manager of the Securities Industry Association, a trade group. "It's quite possible that the concept may still be refined. It's the threshold that may open doors to many other kinds of financial services."

At the same time, this blend of banking and broker services has created considerable consternation among bankers, some of whom have complained that the Merrill Lynch bull is nosing into their china shops.

Nothwithstanding such grumblings, Merrill Lynch's C.M.A. program is the envy of most of the financial services community and has spawned a host of eager imitators.

In recent weeks such major commercial brokerage firms as Dean Witter Reynolds and Shearson Loeb Rhoades and regional firms, including the Advest Group, based in Hartford, and A.G. Edwards of St. Louis, have announced plans for C.M.A.-type accounts.

Another adaptation of the C.M.A. concept is a product being developed jointly by Bache Halsey Stuart Shields and its recent merger partner, the Prudential Insurance Company of America. For the last two years, Prudential has been working on a "family account"—a total package of five or six insurance policies including automobile or homeowners coverage, for instance—that would enable the customer to make a single monthly payment for all policies using the same computer system that Bache is utilizing to develop its answer to the Merrill Lynch C.M.A.'s.

Although it is "premature to say exactly how Prudential's product will mesh with Bache's money market funds," said Frank Hoenemeyer, chief investment officer and vice chairman of Prudential, "I think it is inevitable for a large number of consumers to want some of the convenience of the one-stop shopping kind of thing. We don't think that those kinds of services are for everybody, but as life becomes more complicated, people are looking for ways to simplify their financial life, and the Cash Management-type account is certainly one step in the direction of simplification."

Even some banks have leapt into the competitive fray. Last week, the Provident National Bank, Philadelphia's fifth largest, announced its own C.M.A.-type account, which offers a free, no-minimum-balance interest-paying NOW —or negotiable order of withdrawal—account and automatically transfers cash balances in its trust, agency and custody accounts to money market funds.

Merrill Lynch hurdled the complex legal barriers preventing brokerage firms from offering banking-type investments by carefully separating the essential broker-dealer services from the services normally performed by a commercial bank.

To be eligible for a Cash Management Account, the customer must place at least $20,000 in cash or securities, or a combination of both, in a margin account through which securities may be bought and sold. The C.M.A. customer is required to execute three agreements. The first is a C.M.A. agreement with Merrill Lynch. Second, the customer opens up a margin account. This agreement also opens an account with its C.M.A. money trust—the money market fund, of which the State Street Bank and Trust Company of Boston is the custodian and the First Jersey National Bank of Jersey City is the transfer and dividend-dispersing agent. Finally, a Visa account and checkwriting account are opened at Bank One of Columbus, Ohio.

What makes the C.M.A. account different from the traditional account is that it permits the customer to write a check or use Visa credit on the margin account. Since the brokerage firm is not a bank and cannot directly issue checking accounts, the checks are actually drawn on Bank One.

The margin account allows the customer to purchase stock on credit. If there are insufficient funds in the margin account, Merrill Lynch automatically provides credit up to the amount the Federal Reserve Board permits securities firms to lend on margin.

Can Borrow Up to 50 Percent

Currently, the Fed's margin requirements are up to 50 percent. Thus, an individual with $20,000 worth of marginable securities in a C.M.A. account can automatically borrow up to $10,000.

In most of the 35 states in which C.M.A. accounts are now available—all 50 states are expected to be covered by the end of the year—there is no minimum checkwriting requirement, though the prospectus states that the account is not intended to be used as an alternative to a checking account.

In 1977 the Colorado State Banking Board brought suit to force Merrill Lynch to apply for a charter, arguing that the brokerage firm was engaged in the business of banking. After much wrangling, a compromise was agreed upon—checks written in Colorado are limited to amounts of $200 or more.

Each Monday, all liquid assets received from investments in the account during the previous week are transferred to the C.M.A. money trust. Funds placed in the trust are then invested by Merrill Lynch in money market instruments such as Treasury bills and bank certificates of deposit. The customer receives the interest earned on the money in the trust minus a management fee of three-eighths of a percentage point of the trust's net assets that is paid to Merrill Lynch at an annualized rate.

Once a check or credit card slip is returned to Merrill Lynch by a merchant, it debits its customer's principal money market account.

Free From Ceilings on Rates

Conscious of the increasing competition, the banking industry is trying to develop strategies to limit the spread of money market funds—the heart of the C.M.A. program. Unlike banks, the money funds are free from federally imposed interest rate ceilings and from the ban on interstate banking.

Most distressing from the perspective of the banks is the C.M.A. program's potential for attracting the deposits of affluent customers—the most lucrative aspect of consumer banking.

There have been assertions that the C.M.A. program violates the Glass-Steagall Act, the Federal law designed to prevent an overlapping of investment and commercial banking.

The American Bankers Association, the main banking trade group, has already drafted proposed legislation in this area, and the current push for reform of the act is apparently gaining momentum because of changes in the financial markets. But most analysts believe that the current political drift toward deregulation in the financial services industry would probably weaken rather then fortify the barriers between the banking and investment community.

In light of the breakdowns in barriers separating financial institutions that have occurred over the past decade, it is likely that new legislation in the 1980s will carry that trend even further and permit commercial banks to gain a foothold in the securities business. Many observers expect that before long banks will be able to compete by being empowered to offer their own mutual funds and to sell and distribute new municipal revenue bonds.

Summary

1. Life insurance companies used to specialize in selling whole life policies to individuals. Whole life policies involve a savings element while term life insurance does not. Since that savings feature has produced a relatively low rate of return, there has been a pronounced shift on the part of the public in favor of term insurance.

2. In response, the life insurance industry has begun to emphasize group rather than individual insurance and to invent new kinds of policies that offer higher yields. Some combine term insurance with investment in a money market or stock market mutual fund. This helps explain why Prudential bought Bache and American Express acquired Shearson Loeb Rhoades. It also explains why life insurance companies have been moving into somewhat riskier investments.

3. Two crucial aspects of private pension plans are the provisions regarding vesting and funding. Because of abuses in these areas, in 1974 Congress enacted the Employee Retirement Income Security Act (ERISA) in an attempt to safeguard employee pension rights. The same Act also created the Pension Benefit Guaranty Corporation to provide a limited form of insurance coverage for pension funds.

4. Securities brokers and dealers and investment bankers have recently branched out into new kinds of financial services, such as Merrill Lynch's Cash Management Account (CMA), which includes checking account privileges as well as a variety of other financial services.

5. The Banking Act of 1933, usually called the Glass-Steagall Act, divorced investment and commercial banking. As a result, commercial banks are unable to offer their own money market or stock market mutual funds or sell and distribute newly issued corporate securities or municipal revenue bonds.

Suggestions for Further Reading

A useful source for information about all nondeposit financial institutions is Robert P. Black and Doris E. Harless, *Nonbank Financial Institutions* (Federal Reserve Bank of Richmond, 1975).

On insurance in particular, two good references are the annual *Life Insurance Fact Book* (Washington, D.C.: American Council on Life Insurance) and *Insurance Facts* (New York: Insurance Information Institute). On a practical level, see *The Consumers Union Report on Life Insurance,* 4th ed. (New York: Holt, Rinehart & Winston, 1980). A highly readable and to some extent controversial book is Andrew Tobias, *The Invisible Bankers,* subtitled "Everything the Insurance Industry Never Wanted You to Know" (New York: Simon & Schuster, 1982).

With respect to pension funds, see Peter F. Drucker, *The Unseen Revolution: How Pension Fund Socialism Came to America* (New York: Harper and Row, 1976); William C. Greenough and Francis P. King, *Pension Plans and Public Policy* (New York: Columbia University Press, 1976); and Dan M. McGill, *Fundamentals of Private Pensions,* 4th ed. (Homewood, Ill.: Irwin, 1979).

On the Banking Act of 1933 (Glass-Steagall), see Larry R. Mote, "Banks and the Securities Markets," Federal Reserve Bank of Chicago *Economic Perspectives* (March/April 1979); and Henry C. Wallich, "Reflections on Glass-Steagall," in his *Monetary Policy and Practice* (Lexington, Mass.: Lexington Books, 1982).

10

International Banking

ONLY TWENTY YEARS ago, United States banks, with few exceptions, stayed within their own national borders. The field of international banking was dominated by British banks. But things have changed dramatically. Now many large U.S. banks do a significant part of their business overseas; indeed, a number of them earn *more* of their income from their international than from their domestic operations.

American Banks Abroad

In 1960, only eight United States banks had branches abroad, with the assets of those branches totaling less than $4 billion. By 1980, only twenty years later, almost 200 American banks had established foreign branches, with the assets of those branches exceeding $400 billion. What accounts for this remarkable expansion of U.S. banks into foreign countries?

One reason is the rapid growth of foreign trade and of U.S. multinational corporations that took place during the sixties and seventies. American firms engaged in importing or exporting, and Ameri-

155

can multinationals with subsidiaries and affiliates abroad, often need banking services overseas. Foreign banks can do the job if necessary, but a branch of an American bank abroad can be even more convenient: there are no language problems; the firm and the branch share common business customs and practices; and in the case of multinationals the parent firm and parent bank may already have ties with each other of long standing.

In addition to branches abroad, U.S. banks also participate in international financing through Edge Act corporations, which are domestic subsidiaries engaged strictly in international banking operations. Congress passed the Edge Act in 1919 (named after Senator Walter Edge of New Jersey) to allow U.S. banks to establish special subsidiaries to facilitate their involvement in international finance. Edge Act corporations are located in the United States, but they are exempt from the McFadden Act's prohibition against interstate branching, so that a bank can have Edge Act subsidiaries in several different states—one in Florida, for example, specializing in financing trade with Latin America, one in New York, one on the West Coast, and so on.

Eurodollars

The spread of international trade and the growth of American multinationals between 1960 and 1980 encouraged branching by American banks overseas, but these were not the only factors stimulating the establishment of foreign branches. As usual, our old friend Regulation Q played a part as well.

In the 1960s, when Regulation Q still imposed interest-rate ceilings on large-size CDs, European banks were able to offer more attractive yields to potential depositors than U.S. banks were allowed to pay. Not only are there no interest-rate ceilings in most countries abroad, but in addition reserve requirements and other regulations are typically less onerous than in the United States. As a result, foreign banks could outbid American banks for time deposits.

These deposits in foreign banks—mainly in London during the 1960s—not only paid higher yields than American banks could offer but, as an added inducement for convenience and safety, were recorded as payable *in dollars* rather than in pounds or francs or whatever the money of the host country happened to be. Naturally enough, such deposits came to be known as *Eurodollars.* The term has since been broadened to mean deposits in banks abroad—still mostly in London but now in other places in Europe and in Asia and the Caribbean as well—that are on the banks' books as payable in U.S. dollars rather than in the money of the country where the bank is located.

Eurodollars are created when an American transfers a dollar deposit from an American bank to a foreign bank and keeps it there *in dollars* (rather than switching to pounds, say, if the bank to which the money is transferred is in London). Eurodollars are also created when a foreign holder of a deposit in a U.S. bank does the same thing, as when a French exporter gets paid with a check drawn on an American bank and deposits the check in a Paris bank with instructions to retain it as a dollar deposit instead of exchanging it into an equivalent amount of francs. Why would anyone want to do this? Because dollars are still considered safer than most other kinds of money and are still more generally acceptable in international transactions than any other kind of money.

In self-defense, many American banks decided to open their own branches abroad in order to escape domestic regulations and to bid for funds on a more equal basis with their foreign competition. During periods of tight money, when their ordinary domestic sources of funds dried up because of Federal Reserve restraint, Regulation Q, and financial disintermediation, American banks turned around and borrowed these Eurodollars back from their foreign branches as one aspect of their growing reliance on liability management. Eurodollars are now an integral and accepted part of overall global bank asset and liability management.

At the end of 1981, the foreign branches of U.S. banks held total assets of $460 billion. Of this total, $160 billion was in London branches and $150 billion in branches in the Bahamas and the Cayman Islands in the Caribbean. Branches in London are easy to understand: London has been an international financial center for centuries and remains the heart of the Eurodollar market. But how did the Bahamas and the Caymans ever get into the act?

The Bahamas and the Caymans are tax havens, with almost zero taxation and practically no regulation. Virtually all the assets in branches there are held not by full-service branches but by "shell" branches—primarily bookkeeping operations, with fund-raising and lending decisions emanating from the banks' head offices in the United States. A rise in British taxes in the early 1970s led to a substantial shift in bookings from London to the Bahamas. The Cayman Islands subsequently came into the picture when the Bahamas achieved their independence, giving rise to anxiety (since proven unfounded) that this might lead to increased Bahamian regulation and taxation.

Domestically Based International Banking Facilities

In late 1981, in an effort to bring some of this offshore Eurodollar business back home, the Federal Reserve approved International Banking Facilities (IBFs) on American soil. Caribbean branches have flourished because they operate in an environment almost entirely free from regulation and taxation. The purpose of IBFs is to offer banks comparable conditions here and thus lure offshore banking back to the United States. Thus both American and foreign banks can now have IBFs that are within the geographic confines of the United States but are regulated as though they were located abroad. In effect, an IBF is a domestic branch that is treated by the Federal Reserve as if it were a foreign branch. Their transactions are considered offshore transactions, free from such domestic regulations as reserve requirements, interest rate ceilings, and deposit insurance assessments.

It is not necessary for a parent bank to open up a separate office to establish an IBF. Essentially, IBFs are bookkeeping operations, just like shell branches. A bank wanting to start an IBF simply notifies the Federal Reserve and then segregates its IBF assets, liabilities, and related transactions from all others. This creates a new set of books that are exempt from the usual rules and regulations that apply to domestic transactions. Moreover, many states have enacted legislation exempting the income of IBFs from state and local taxes, thereby providing an environment that closely resembles tax havens abroad.

So much for the good news; the bad news is that the services of IBFs are not available to domestic residents. IBFs can only transact business that is international in nature with respect to both sources and uses of funds. They are permitted to accept deposits from and lend funds to foreign-based customers only. Foreign subsidiaries of American multinationals are included among the eligible depositors and borrowers provided the funds do not come from domestic sources and are not used for domestic purposes.

Thus far IBFs have been a resounding success. Although they have been allowed only since December 1981, by the middle of 1982 they already had assets exceeding $100 billion, mostly at the expense of Caribbean branches.

Foreign Banks in the United States

Just as U.S. banks have a major presence abroad, so foreign banks play a significant role in this country. For example, in 1981 fully 20 percent of the dollar volume of all commercial bank business loans in the United States was made by branches or subsidiaries of foreign-owned banks.

Of the fifteen Giant Banks listed in Table 3 of Chapter 7, two are foreign-owned: Crocker National Bank of San Francisco is British-owned and Marine Midland of Buffalo is owned by the Hong Kong and Shanghai Banking Corporation. In addition, such large and well-known banks as Union Bank of Los Angeles and the National Bank of North America (New York) are British-owned; California First Bank of San Francisco is Japanese-owned; and the European-American Bank (New York), successor to the failed Franklin National Bank, is owned by a consortium of six foreign banks whose home bases are Austria, Belgium, England, France, Germany, and the Netherlands. All in all, more than 400 affiliates of foreign banks are currently operating in the United States.

Foreign banks do business here through four main organizational forms: they may open a *branch* of the parent bank, open or buy a *subsidiary* bank, establish an *agency*, or open a *representative office*. A branch is an integral part of the foreign bank and usually carries that bank's name. A subsidiary is legally separate from the foreign bank that owns its stock; the subsidiary usually has its own charter and may or may not carry the name of its foreign owner. Both branches and subsidiaries are full-service banking institutions. Agencies have more limited powers than either branches or subsidiaries; they can make loans but cannot accept deposits. Representative offices cannot accept deposits *or* make loans; they mostly make contacts with potential customers of the parent organization (by holding dinner parties) and perform public relations functions (by sponsoring rock or philharmonic concerts). Foreign banks can also complicate matters further by having Edge Act corporations in the United States and they may also establish their own IBF here.

Until 1978, foreign banks operating in the United States were largely unregulated. They did not have to hold reserves with the Fed, were able to branch across state lines, and had numerous other rights and privileges denied to domestic banks. This was changed by the International Banking Act of 1978, which brought foreign banks under essentially the same federal regulations that apply to domestic banks.

Some Observations

It is obvious that the world of international banking no longer consists of many separate and distinct national banking systems. The banks of most major countries operate in the territory of most other major countries. American banks have branches and subsidiaries worldwide, while in turn the large banks of other nations operate freely in the United States. The Eurodollar market reinforces these relationships and binds them together, communicating, virtually instantaneously, financial pressures from New York to London to Singapore to the Bahamas.

These ties provide numerous benefits in terms of capital mobility, but they also raise questions with respect to the ability of nations to control their own financial destinies. Complex issues are just below the surface, issues that involve regulation versus competition, control versus freedom, sovereignty versus the world economy. There may be fairly simple philosophic resolutions to many of these potential conflicts, but in practice the answers are less clear cut.

For example, it has become increasingly difficult to manage a domestic economy with orthodox monetary policies in isolation from the world economy. It is widely realized that individual states, such as Michigan and Oklahoma, cannot by themselves impose price controls or minimum wage laws for fear of business moving elsewhere, where opportunities are more attractive. Similarly, interrelated banking and financial systems mean that individual nations can no longer act with financial impunity, disregarding the international ramifications of their actions.

We will return to many of these problems when we get to Part VI and look at the subject of international finance in more detail.

Summary

1. Many large American banks now earn more of their income from their international operations than from their domestic side. Close to 200 American banks have branches or subsidiaries abroad, with assets of $460 billion in foreign branches at the end of 1981.

2. In addition to branches abroad, American banks also participate in international financing through Edge Act corporations, which are subsidiaries located in the United States that specialize in the financing of foreign trade.

3. American regulation helped create the Eurodollar market. Eurodollars are deposits in banks abroad (no longer just in Europe) that are carried on the banks' books in dollars, rather than in the money of the countries where the banks are located. As one aspect of their liability management, American banks use their foreign branches to bid for Eurodollars, then the parent bank borrows these funds back when other sources of funds dry up or become relatively more expensive.

4. Since late 1981 American banks have been allowed to establish International Banking Facilities (IBFs) in the United States. IBFs are shell branches located here but treated for regulatory and tax purposes as though they were abroad. They have been permitted in order to recapture some of the offshore Eurodollar business that has flourished in tax havens such as the Bahamas and the Cayman Islands.

5. Just as American banks have a major presence abroad, so foreign-owned banks play a significant role in this country. In 1981, for example, 20 percent of the dollar volume of all commercial bank business loans was made by foreign-owned institutions. The International Banking Act of 1978 brought foreign banks in the United States under essentially the same federal regulations that apply to domestic banks.

6. The integration of banking and financial markets worldwide provides many benefits but simultaneously raises troubling questions regarding future national financial self-determination.

Suggestions for Further Reading

Recent developments in international banking are discussed in Warren E. Moskowitz, "Global Asset and Liability Management at Commercial Banks," *Quarterly Review* of the Federal Reserve Bank of New York (Spring 1979); and Gerald H. Anderson, "Current Developments in the Regulation of International Banking," Federal Reserve Bank of Cleveland *Economic Review* (January 1980). In a more popular vein, Anthony Sampson's *The Money Lenders* (New York: Viking Press, 1982) is informative, controversial, and fun to read.

If you want to learn more about Eurodollars, see Milton Friedman, "The Eurodollar Market: Some First Principles," Morgan Guaranty *Survey* (October 1969); *Eurodollars: The Money Market Gypsies* by Jane Sneddon Little (New York: Harper and Row, 1975); and Anatol B. Balbach and David H. Resler, "Eurodollars and the U.S. Money Supply," in the Federal Reserve Bank of St. Louis *Review* (June/July 1980).

11

The Payments System

THE PAYMENTS SYSTEM has become a rather glamorous topic, with focus on the technological revolution that promises to replace checks with electronic messages and turn bankers into robots. It was only about a hundred years ago that checks displaced currency as the dominant means of payment in the economy, sparking a revolution of its own. To provide a perspective on current and future developments, therefore, it is useful to review briefly the evolution of the payments system during the past century. We can then turn to a science fiction view of the payments system of the future—ever mindful that today's science fiction is tomorrow's reality.

A Paper Payments System

Back in Chapter 1 we showed how monetary exchange is superior to a barter-based system. In particular, using a medium of exchange to consummate transactions cuts down the time needed for exchange. It also facilitates trade among strangers because the medium of exchange is readily identifiable and acceptable in the settle-

163

ment of obligations. But the contribution of monetary exchange depends, in part, on exactly what serves as money in such a system. For example, in the good old days gold and other metals served as money because only they were readily acceptable in trade. Paper currency came into the picture because coins and bullion were cumbersome media of exchange. As long as the banks that issued the currency could redeem it in "real money"—the underlying metal—paper currency was acceptable in trade and served as a more convenient means of payment.

But even currency has its drawbacks as a medium of exchange. It is still fairly bulky—$10,000,000 even in $100 bills fills quite a few suitcases—and it can be easily stolen. Settling obligations by shipping currency can be inconvenient as well as expensive. Coin and currency are a substantial improvement over barter, but consummating a transaction in cash is still costly, especially when payments must be made over some distance.

Checks came into use precisely to overcome such costs. A check is simply an order to a bank to shift funds from one person's account to someone else's. Instead of paying out $10,000 in $100 bills to buy a new de luxe compact car, a check orders a bank to shift $10,000 from the buyer's checking account to the car dealer's account. The transaction can be completed without currency ever moving out of the bank's safekeeping. And that's the way most transactions are done nowadays. Payments are made via debits and credits on a bank's books rather than through an exchange of cash.

The actual check-based payments system is complicated by the fact that buyers and sellers do not usually have checking accounts at the same bank. Thus when a check is drawn on one bank ordering payment to an account at another bank, the individual banks must settle accounts with each other. Many of the institutional wrinkles in the current payment system arose in connection with interbank settlement of claims.

The local clearinghouse is the oldest institution used to settle interbank claims. Representatives from banks in each city gather once (or twice) a day to settle via a single exchange of cash the net inflow or outflow required against all other local banks. The advantage is that only *net* cash balances are exchanged. Thus if Banc One (Columbus, Ohio) is presented with $10 million in checks drawn by its depositors and holds $9 million in checks drawn on other local banks, it will have to ante up only $1 million, the net debit to other members of the clearinghouse.

Processing checks drawn against out-of-town (nonclearinghouse) banks is more complicated. To accomplish this efficiently, banks maintain checking accounts with each other—called correspondent balances. For example, when a Chicago bank receives a check drawn against a bank in Toledo, Ohio, it will forward the check for collection to a Chicago institution that is the Toledo bank's correspondent—or to the correspondent of a correspondent. In this way a check is eventually debited to the proper bank, although it may take a rather circuitous trip in the process. Nevertheless, about 30 percent of our checks are currently collected through the network of correspondent balances.

By far the most dominant force in the check collection system is the Federal Reserve System. When the Fed was established in 1914, one of its main functions was to facilitate the check collection process, especially for out-of-town checks. In fact, the Federal Reserve operates a nationwide clearinghouse for settling interbank transfers of funds. As we saw in Chapter 3, checks are collected by debiting and crediting member bank reserves on the books of the regional Federal Reserve Banks. The Fed operates regional check processing centers (RCPCs) to sift and tabulate the mass of paper generated by the checking system.

To facilitate transfers of reserves between banks in different regions, the Federal Reserve uses a sophisticated telecommunications system for sending messages between regional Federal Reserve Banks. Back in 1918 this wire transfer system consisted only of leased telegraph lines; today it is a network of interconnected computer systems that route orders to transfer funds between banks within nanoseconds.[1] In fact, the Fed's wire transfer system, together with an interbank communications system known as the Bank Wire, permits corporations and individuals to make "payments by wire" rather than by check. Most Eurodollar transactions are settled through the New York Clearing House Association's CHIPS, a computerized worldwide telecommunications transfer system (CHIPS stands for Clearinghouse Interbank Payments System).

---

[1] A nanosecond is one-billionth of a second.

The use of electronic communications to transfer funds, rather than written orders on pieces of paper, is thus already with us. In addition to direct wire transfers of funds, there are automated clearinghouses (ACHs) which process computer tape orders to pay rather than checks. Thus far the ACHs are most often used for preauthorized standard payments, such as monthly mortgage or utility bills, or to receive direct credits of salary checks and social security payments.

The payments system of today is a mixture of paper, electronics, and, of course, plastic. While credit cards look like an improvement over checks, because only one payment at the end of the month substitutes for lots of small checks, the fact of the matter is that credit card transactions generate at least as much paper as checks. The merchant receives a slip, the buyer receives a copy, and so does the bank. Bank credit cards are used with automated teller machines (ATMs) to withdraw currency when needed, but the evolution to a *complete* electronic funds transfer system (EFTS) has not yet occurred. The final step requires all purchases and sales of goods and services to be processed by point of sale (POS) terminals connected on line with a bank's computer. Payments for goods and services would be made at the checkout counter by debiting the buyer's bank account and crediting the seller's. Some POS terminals have been experimented with in recent years, although they have not picked up many adherents.

There is little doubt that electronics will make further inroads on paper as the primary mechanism for settling transactions. The cost of processing the sheer volume of paper will continue to spur innovative practices. To provide a flavor of what it might be like in the Ultimate Payments System (UPS?), let's take a somewhat fanciful view of how it might work out. Be careful, it may be closer than you think.

The Payments System of the Future

A few decades from now, coins will probably still be with us for inserting into vending machines that we can then shake and bang to release our aggressions. But checks may well have vanished.

Check payment, as we have just seen, is really nothing more than a bookkeeping operation to begin with. As a method of dispersing information about how the books should be kept, checks are—in light of present and foreseeable technology—notoriously cumbersome, slow, unreliable, and inefficient.

More in keeping with the twenty-first century will be a vast nationwide balance sheet and clearing system in which debits and credits can be rung up virtually instantaneously by electronic impulse. Every individual and every transacting organization of whatever sort will be tagged at birth with a number and a slot on the "books" of a computerized nationwide accounting and payments system, a National Ledger, as it were.

Credits and debits to each individual account will be made by the insertion of a twenty-first-century version of a credit card into a twenty-first-century version of a telephone or teletype. Instead of a written piece of paper instructing a bank to credit this account and debit that one—that is, a check, with its necessary physical routing from place to place—the insertion of a plastic card into the appropriate receptacle will automatically credit and debit both accounts instantaneously. With high-speed computers, magnetic tape storage, remote feed-ins, and satellite transmission, it should not be too difficult to devise a system whereby the proper code will serve as a means of verifying the validity of the electronic instructions to the Great Master Bookkeeper in the Sky.

Eliminating checks would be only one of the many advantages that would emerge from such a system. All financial assets are nothing more than a representation of someone else's liability or evidence of equity. Current practice, which consists of inscribing same on embossed parchment, has been absurd for at least two generations. There is no need for stocks and bonds to look like Pronouncements of State by King Henry VIII. As everyone is fully aware, a simple computer print-out would do just as well. However, by the year 2000 even that will not be necessary, since it will all be recorded automatically on the magnetic tape of the National Ledger as soon as a stock or bond is sold or a transaction made.

A National Ledger payments system will be possible in a surprisingly few years. Already its introduction depends more on costs and financial evaluations regarding its profitability than on purely technological considerations. It remains to be seen whether the necessary services will be provided by one firm, an association of private financial and nonfinancial firms, or the government, alone or in partnership with private enterprise.

With methods of communication and the dissemination of information perfected to the ultimate degree by the year 2000, in all likelihood, financial markets will finally take on the characteristics of the purely competitive markets that economists have been talking about in classrooms since the days of Adam Smith. Instead of simple buy and sell orders, or bid and offered quotations, potential buyers and sellers of financial assets will be able electronically to transmit complete demand and supply schedules to a central clearing computer, specifying the amounts of various securities they wish to buy or sell at a range of alternative prices.

Of course, this in itself would not be quite sufficient to meet classroom standards for a purely competitive market, since one of the prerequisites for such a market is that the participants possess perfect foresight regarding the future as well as perfect knowledge of the present. But even that might be incorporated by feeding probability forecasts into the Giant Maw of the computer. Is it too far-fetched to suggest that such forecasts might even involve some of the parapsychological techniques—like clairvoyance and precognition—currently under study at some of our most prestigious universities and on several all-night radio programs?

Economic policy-making will also mean something quite different in the twenty-first century from what it means today. Monetary and fiscal policy are far too uncertain in their impact for use in the Century of Efficiency that will follow the present Century of Progress.

By that time, all assets and liabilities as recorded on the National Ledger will be subject to increase or decrease by any given percentage by Executive Order, thereby instantaneously altering the wealth of every individual and every business firm in the country. If aggregate spending does not respond promptly in the direction and amount desired, further asset-valuation adjustments can be fine-tuned until the reaction of the private sector conforms to what is deemed necessary to assure the Good Life for all.

Given human nature, this may possibly give rise to the problem of "valuation evasion"—that is, an illegal market in which assets are valued and transactions effected at prices other than those re-

Judge Refuses Man's Request To Let Him Become a Number

MINNEAPOLIS, Feb. 13—A district court judge today denied the request of a Minneapolis man who wanted his name changed to a number, saying that it would be "an offense to basic human dignity."

Michael Herbert Dengler filed a petition in October seeking to assume legally the name 1069, which he said he had used for more than four years. Mr. Dengler cited philosophical reasons for his request, saying that each of the numerals had symbolic significance to him. Taken together, he said, the numerals "describe what is inherent in me."

He was out of town and could not be reached for comments on the ruling.

Mr. Dengler, a 32-year-old former resident of North Dakota, had twice been denied such permission by courts in that state. The North Dakota Supreme Court conceded that "One Zero Six Nine" might qualify as a name, but balked at his use of numerals instead of words.

Opened Checking Account

However, after Mr. Dengler moved to Minnesota he opened a checking account as 1069, and he displays a Social Security card also identifying him by number. He said he had little trouble passing checks bearing the unusual name.

"I just write the check and say, 'Would I write a bad check with a name like this?'" he said.

But Mr. Dengler said that he had been discriminated against by potential employees and utility companies that refused to accept his number as a name. In an interview for a job at a large corporation, a personnel officer reportedly told him: "You come in here with a name. We'll give you a number."

Mr. Dengler's attorney, Timothy Geck, said at a court hearing in Minneapolis that several utilities had refused to give his client services as 1069 without a court order making it official. The Northwestern Bell Telephone Company, for example, would give Mr. Dengler only an unlisted telephone number as 1069, Mr. Geck said.

Judge Donald Barbeau of Hennepin County District Court said he believed Mr. Dengler was sincere in his philosophical motives for requesting the change, but said that he could not "in good conscience add to today's inhumanity by giving it the stamp of judicial approval."

"Dehumanization is widespread and affects our culture like a disease in epidemic proportions," Judge Barbeau wrote in his opinion. "To allow the use of a number instead of a name would only provide additional nourishment upon which the illness of the dehumanization is able to feed and grow to the point where it is totally incurable."

Mr. Geck said, after learning of the decision, that "there is a very good likelihood" that Mr. Dengler would appeal the ruling to the Minnesota Supreme Court.

News Item / The Twenty-First Century?

Update: Mr. Dengler did indeed appeal to the Minnesota Supreme Court, which ruled in 1980 that he could not use the name 1069 but that one zero six nine was permissible. The court noted that this would be much like Juan Nyen.

New York Times, February 14, 1978

corded on the National Ledger. The result would be the accumulation of unrecorded wealth for those involved in such dealings. If this gains currency, so to speak, an entire underground financial system —complete with (unreported) deposits, handwritten checks, and a subterranean check-routing network—is likely to spring up in opposition to the more efficient computerized and satellite-supervised official payments system.

The most effective remedy to prevent such undermining of the common welfare would be to bar all participants in Financial Subversion from access to the National Ledger. Practitioners of too-private enterprise would thus be consigned to deserved financial ostracism as Subverters of the National Happiness.

Such a solution would have the self-evident virtue of safeguarding the Sinews of our Efficiency, while at the same time being consistent with the preservation of our Cherished Freedoms.

Summary

1. An efficient payments system reduces the cost of completing transactions by devising low cost media of exchange to replace higher cost means of payment. Checks are a less costly payments mechanism than either currency or metal, hence checks have dominated both during much of the twentieth century.

2. Check clearing among banks is facilitated by a number of institutional arrangements, including clearinghouses, correspondent balances, and the Federal Reserve System.

3. A number of electronic transfer mechanisms currently supplement the system of check collection. The Federal Reserve's wire transfer system is the oldest. More recently, computer transfers through automated clearinghouses have become routine for standardized payments.

4. What some refer to as an "electronic funds transfer system" (EFTS) is nothing more than an extension of these electronic payment orders to still other areas of the economy. Point of sale terminals that are hooked up directly to bank computers would do the job, but they have met with little success thus far.

5. The payments system of the future is limited only by the confines of current imagination. One thing will surely be with us, however: a subterranean economy to circumvent excessive control and documentation. "The more things change, the more they remain the same" is true of the payments system as well as everything else.

Suggestions for Further Reading

A number of articles in various issues of the *Federal Reserve Bulletin* have described the payments mechanism, including: Earl Hamilton, "An Update on the Automated Clearinghouse" (July 1979); James Brundy, David Humphrey, and Myron Kwast, "Check Processing at the Federal Reserve Offices" (February 1979); and George Mitchell and Raymond Hodgdon, "Federal Reserve and the Payments System" (February 1981). For an interesting historical study see Kenneth Garbade and William Silber, "The Payment System and Domestic Exchange Rates: Technological Versus Institutional Change," *Journal of Monetary Economics* (January 1979).

For a discussion of the payments system of tomorrow see: Lawrence Ritter and Thomas Atkinson, "Monetary Theory and Policy in the Payments System of the Future," *Journal of Money, Credit, and Banking* (November 1970); and Mark J. Flannery and Dwight M. Jaffee, *The Economic Implications of an Electronic Monetary Transfer System* (Lexington, Mass.: Lexington Books, 1973).

But for the real truth first read Aldous Huxley's *Brave New World* (New York: Harper & Row, 1932) and George Orwell's *1984* (New York: Harcourt, Brace, 1949). Then go see Stanley Kubrick's *2001: A Space Odyssey* and Charlton Heston in *Planet of the Apes*.

Part III
The Art of Central Banking

12
Who's in Charge Here?

MONETARY POLICY is the responsibility of the Federal Reserve, but to whom is the Federal Reserve responsible? We saw in Chapter 1 that the money supply should be set to give us full employment without inflation. The Federal Reserve checks the money supply, but who checks the Fed?

The answer to that question is so complex that if we unravel it successfully (which is not too likely a prospect), we will either have unveiled one of the great socioeconomic creations in the annals of civilization, comparable to the invention of inside plumbing, or unmasked one of the most devious schemes ever contrived by the mind of man to camouflage the true locus of clandestine power.

According to some, the Federal Reserve is responsible to the Congress. But it is the President, not Congress, who appoints the seven members of the Board of Governors of the Federal Reserve System, who occupy the stately building at Twentieth Street and Constitution Avenue, Washington, D.C. The President also selects from among those seven the Chairman of the Board of Governors, the principal policy-maker of the central bank.

On that basis, one might surmise that the Federal Reserve is responsible to the executive branch of government, in the person of the President. However, since each member serves a fourteen-year term, the current President can appoint only two of the seven-member Board of Governors, unless there are deaths or resignations. Even the Chairman may be the appointee of the previous administration. Furthermore, it is Congress that created the Federal Reserve (not in its own image) in 1913, and it is Congress, not the President, that has the authority to alter its working mandate at any time. In 1935, for example, Congress chose to throw two administration representatives off the Board of Governors—the Secretary of the Treasury and the Comptroller of the Currency, both of whom had been ex officio members—simply because they were representatives of the executive branch.

Others, more cynical, have suggested that the Federal Reserve is mostly responsible to the private banking community, primarily the 5,400 commercial banks that are member banks of the Federal Reserve System. The member banks do in fact choose the presidents of each of the twelve regional Federal Reserve banks, including the President of the most aristocratic of all, the Federal Reserve Bank of New York. It may or may not be significant that the annual salary of the President of the Federal Reserve Bank of New York is $130,000 while that of the Chairman of the Board of Governors in Washington is $60,000.

Who's in charge here? Who indeed? In Chapter 1 we noted how bank lending and the money supply affect economic activity. In Chapter 4 we showed how the central bank could control bank lending and the money supply (if it wanted to). And we will devote all of Part IV to a more detailed discussion of the role of money in economic activity. Before going any further, however, let's see who should get the accolades for the successes and the blame for the mistakes.

Formal Structure

The statutory organization of the Federal Reserve System is a case study in those currently popular concepts, decentralization and the blending of public and private authority. A deliberate attempt was made in the enabling congressional legislation, the 1913 Federal

Reserve Act, to diffuse power over a broad base—geographically, between the private and public sectors, and even within the government—so that no one person, group, or sector, either inside or outside the government, could exert enough leverage to dominate the direction of monetary policy.

As noted in Figure 1, the Board of Governors of the Federal Reserve System consists of seven members, appointed by the President with the advice and consent of the Senate. To prevent presidential board-packing, each member is appointed for a term of fourteen years, with one term expiring at the end of January in each even-numbered year. Furthermore, no two board members may come from the same Federal Reserve District. The Chairman of the Board of Governors, chosen from among the seven by the President, serves a four-year term. However, his term is not concurrent with the presidential term, so an incoming President could find himself saddled with an already appointed Chairman for part of his first term in office. The Board is independent of the congressional appropriations process and partly exempt from audit by the government's watchdog, the General Accounting Office, since its operating funds come from the earnings of the twelve regional Federal Reserve banks.

The regional Federal Reserve banks, one in each Federal Reserve District, are geographically dispersed throughout the nation—the Federal Reserve Bank of New York, the Federal Reserve Bank of Kansas City, the Federal Reserve Bank of San Francisco, and so on (see Figure 2). Each Federal Reserve Bank is privately owned by the member banks in its district, the very commercial banks it is charged with supervising and regulating. Each member commercial bank is required to buy stock in its district Federal Reserve Bank equal to 6 percent of its own capital and surplus. Of this 6 percent, 3 percent must be paid in and 3 percent is subject to call by the Board of Governors. However, the profits accruing to ownership are limited by law to a 6 percent annual dividend on paid-in capital stock. The member bank stockholders elect six of the nine directors of their district Federal Reserve Bank, and the remaining three are appointed from Washington by the Board of Governors. These nine directors, in turn, choose the president of their Federal Reserve Bank, subject to the approval of the Board of Governors.

The directors of each Federal Reserve Bank also select a person, always a commercial banker, to serve on the Federal Advisory Coun-

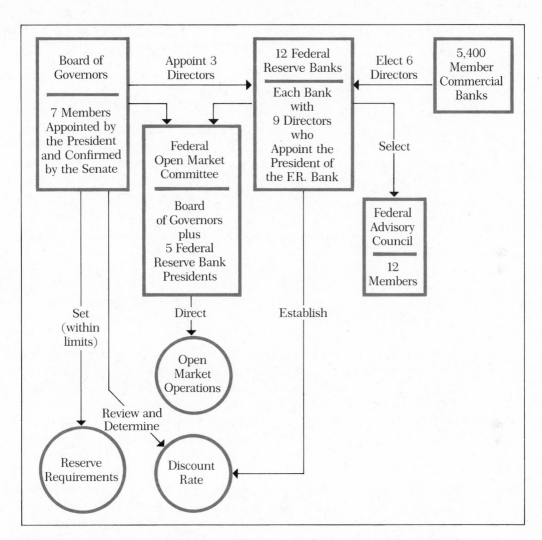

Figure 1 / The Formal Structure and Policy Organization of the Federal Reserve System

cil, a statutory body consisting of a member from each of the twelve Federal Reserve districts. The Federal Advisory Council consults quarterly with the Board of Governors in Washington and makes recommendations regarding the conduct of monetary policy.

Legal authority is similarly diffused with respect to the *execution*

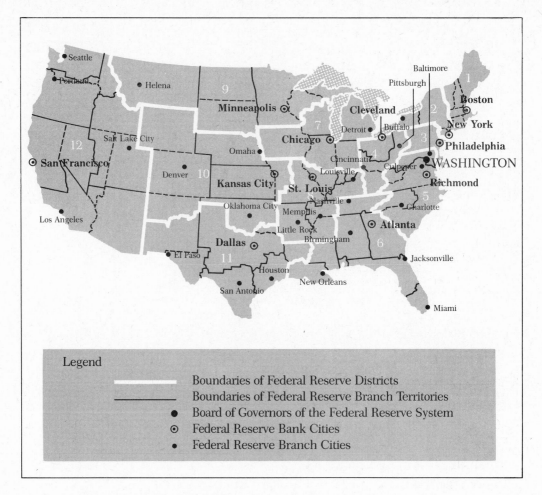

Figure 2 / The Federal Reserve System

SOURCE: *Federal Reserve Bulletin.* Drawn by R. W. Galvin, Cart.
NOTE: Hawaii and Alaska are in the Twelfth Federal Reserve District.

of monetary policy, as Figure 1 indicates. The Board of Governors has the power to set reserve requirements on commercial bank time and demand deposits, for example, but it cannot set them outside the bounds of the specific limits imposed by Congress.

Open market operations are directed by a body known as the Federal Open Market Committee (FOMC), composed of the seven-member Board of Governors plus five of the Reserve Bank presidents. Since the members of the Board of Governors are appointed by the White House, and the Reserve Bank presidents are appointed by the directors of each Federal Reserve Bank, who are (six of nine) elected by the member commercial banks, the diffusion of authority over open market operations spans the distance from the White House to the member bank on Main Street. In addition, although the FOMC directs open market operations, they are executed at the trading desk of the Federal Reserve Bank of New York by a person who appears to be simultaneously an employee of the FOMC and the Federal Reserve Bank of New York.

Legal authority over discount rates is even more confusing. Discount rates are "established" every two weeks by the directors of each regional Federal Reserve Bank, but they are subject to "review and determination" by the Board of Governors. The distinction between "establishing" discount rates and "determining" them is a fine line indeed, and it is not surprising that confusion occasionally arises as to precisely where the final authority and responsibility lie.

The Realities of Power

So much for the Land of Oz. Actually, the facts of life are rather different, as the more realistic Figure 3 illustrates.

By all odds, the dominant figure in the formation and execution of monetary policy is the Chairman of the Board of Governors of the Federal Reserve System, currently Paul A. Volcker. He is the most prominent member of the Board itself and the most influential member of the FOMC, and he is generally recognized by both Congress and the public at large as *the* spokesman for the Federal Reserve System. Although the Federal Reserve Act appears to put all seven members of the Board of Governors on more or less equal footing, over the past fifty years the strong personalities, outstanding abilities, and determined devotion to purpose of the chairmen —first Marriner S. Eccles, then William McChesney Martin, Jr., later Arthur F. Burns, and now Paul Volcker—have made them

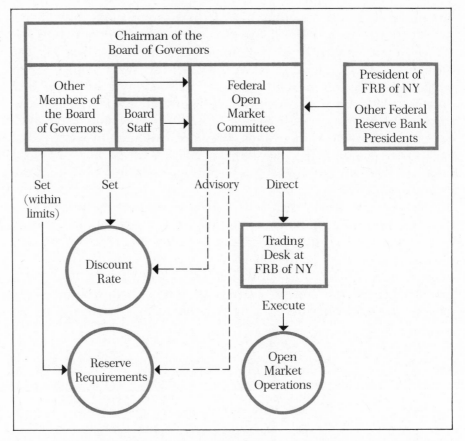

Figure 3 / The Realities of Power Within the Federal Reserve System

rather more equal than the others. As adviser to the President, negotiator with Congress, and final authority on appointments throughout the system, with influence over all aspects of monetary policy in his capacity as Chairman of both the Board of Governors and the FOMC, the Chairman for all practical purposes is the embodiment of the central bank in this country.

The other six members of the Board of Governors also exercise a substantial amount of authority, more so than is indicated in the formal paper structure of the system, because with the passage of time primary responsibility for monetary policy has become more centralized and concentrated in Washington. When the Federal Reserve Act was passed in 1913, it was thought that the Federal Reserve System would be mainly a passive service agency, supplying currency when needed, clearing checks, and providing a discount facility for the convenience of the private commercial member banks. At that time there was no conception of monetary policy as an active countercyclical force. Open market operations were unknown and reserve requirements were fixed by law, with no flexibility permitted. Since then, of course, the central bank has shifted from passive accommodation to active regulation, from the performance of regional service functions to the implementation of national economic policy. This shift has been accompanied, naturally enough, by a rise in the power of the centralized Board of Governors in Washington and a corresponding decline in the role of the regional Federal Reserve Banks and their "owners," the commercial banks.

It would not be unrealistic to describe the central bank today as headquartered in Washington, with twelve field offices throughout the nation. These field offices may be known by the rather imposing name of Federal Reserve Banks, and they do indeed retain a certain degree of autonomy in expressing their views on the wisdom of various policies. But even so they essentially amount to little more than branches of the Washington headquarters.

Closely related to the Board of Governors in the informal power structure, and deriving influence through that association, is the Board's professional staff of economic experts and advisers. The long tenure in the Federal Reserve System of many senior staff economists, their familiarity with Federal Reserve history, and their expertise in monetary analysis give them a power base that is to a large extent founded on the respect with which they, as individuals, are held throughout the System. Through daily consultation with the individual Governors and written and oral presentations before each meeting of the FOMC, staff personnel exert an indefinable but significant influence on the ultimate decision-making process. In fact, in recent years three members of the Board's staff have been elevated to the Board itself, via presidential nomination (Robert Holland in 1973, Charles Partee in 1976, and Lyle Gramley in 1980).[1]

Aside from the Board of Governors, its Chairman, and its staff, the only other body playing a major role in Federal Reserve policy-making is the FOMC, which meets every four weeks in Washington. Of the twelve members on the FOMC, a majority of seven are the Board of Governors themselves. The other five are Reserve Bank presidents. The President of the Federal Reserve Bank of New York is a permanent member of the FOMC, and the other eleven Federal Reserve Bank presidents alternate the remaining four seats among themselves.

The statutory authority of the FOMC is confined to the direction of open market operations, but in recent years it has become the practice to bring all policy matters under review at FOMC meetings. Although only five of the Reserve Bank presidents are entitled to vote at any one time, typically all twelve attend every meeting and participate in the discussion. Thus potential reserve-requirement and discount-rate changes are, in effect, decided upon within the FOMC, with the twelve Reserve Bank presidents participating in an advisory capacity. The Board of Governors, however, always has the final say on reserve requirements and discount rates if matters should come to a showdown, particularly since legal opinion appears to be that, in case of disagreement, the Board's power to "review and determine" discount rates overrides the authority of the individual Reserve Banks to "establish" them.

Once the FOMC decides on the appropriate open market policy, actual execution of the policy directive until the next meeting is the responsibility of the Account Manager at the Federal Reserve Bank of New York's trading desk. He is called the Account Manager because he manages the System Open Market Account, which includes all the securities holdings of the Federal Reserve System. Since the FOMC's instructions are often couched in rather broad language, the Account Manager has to translate these instructions into actual daily purchases and sales of Treasury securities. In the process, at least a modest amount of leeway and personal interpreta-

---

[1]In 1978, Nancy Teeters became the first woman member of the Board of Governors. The first black member of the Board was Andrew Brimmer, who was appointed in 1966.

tion is inevitable, as subsequent chapters will show.

Like that of the Account Manager, the unique position of the President of the Federal Reserve Bank of New York in the hierarchy stems from his role and status in the nation's financial center. If he is inclined to use this leverage, as Allan Sproul did a generation ago and Benjamin Strong before him, the President of the New York Reserve Bank can mount a substantial challenge even to the Chairman of the Board of Governors. Since such a challenge would have little legal foundation, it would have to be based on the prestige of the presidency of the Federal Reserve Bank of New York and the forcefulness of the person who holds the position.

But where, in the corridors of power, does this leave the member banks, the directors of each Federal Reserve Bank, and the Federal Advisory Council? Pretty much shut out, if the truth be known.

The member banks do indeed "own" their district Federal Reserve Bank, but such stockholding is mostly symbolic and carries none of the usual attributes of ownership. The member banks also have a major voice in electing the directors of their Reserve Bank, but the directors in turn have responsibilities that are largely ceremonial. True, they appoint the members of the Federal Advisory Council, but the Federal Advisory Council serves mostly a public relations purpose and has little to do with actual policy-making. The directors of each Federal Reserve Bank also choose the president of their Reserve Bank, subject to the approval of the Board of Governors. But the "subject to approval" clause has meant, in practice, that the most the directors can really do is submit a list of nominees for the position of president. On several occasions the choice of the directors of a Federal Reserve Bank has not met with approval from Washington; such cases have made very clear exactly where ultimate authority is lodged.

The Problem of Federal Reserve Independence

The fact that ultimate authority over monetary policy resides in Washington brings to the fore the relationship between the central bank and the other branches of government also responsible for overall national economic policy—the Congress and the administration, the latter personified by the President.

The Federal Reserve is a creature of the Congress. The Constitution gives Congress the power "to coin money and regulate the value thereof." On this basis, in 1913 Congress created the Federal Reserve as the institution delegated to administer that responsibility on its behalf. Congress requires periodic accountability by the Federal Reserve and has the authority to amend the enabling legislation, the Federal Reserve Act, any time it sees fit.

Essentially, Congress has given the Federal Reserve a broad mandate to regulate the monetary system in the public interest, and then has more or less stood aside and let the monetary authorities pursue this objective on their own and to the best of their abilities. Congress has also attempted to minimize interference from the administration by giving each member of the Board of Governors a fourteen-year term, thereby sharply limiting any single President's influence over the board.

This semiindependent status of the central bank is a source of continuous friction. Some members of Congress believe that the Federal Reserve has carried its "independence" much too far. There has been some concern over its freedom from congressional appropriations and its partial exemption from standard government audit. Also, the Federal Reserve's responsibility on occasion for tight money and high interest rates has stimulated some intensive questioning at congressional hearings, including frequent scoldings of Federal Reserve officials by populist-minded congressmen who get uptight about tight money.

Others, in Congress and out, have complained that the Federal Reserve simply has not done a very good job, that we would all be better off if Congress laid down some guidelines or rules to limit the discretion available to the monetary authorities in conducting their business. We will discuss such proposals in Chapter 20.

The relationship between the central bank and the President has also aroused considerable controversy. Many feel that the Federal Reserve should be a part of the executive branch of government, responsible to the President, on the ground that monetary policy is an integral part of national economic policy, and monetary policy should therefore be coordinated at the highest level (that is, by the President), along with fiscal policy, as a component part of the administration's total program for economic growth and stability.

To do otherwise, it is charged, is both undemocratic and divisive —undemocratic because monetary policy is too important to be run by an elite group of experts insulated from the political process, and divisive because monetary and fiscal policy should not work at cross-purposes. Since fiscal policy proposals are clearly within the President's domain, monetary policy should be as well. A Federal Reserve independent of presidential authority conflicts with the administration's responsibility to promulgate and coordinate an overall economic program.

On the other hand, the case for central bank independence from the President rests on the pragmatic basis that subordination of the central bank to the executive branch of government invites excessive money creation and consequent inflation. The charge that an independent Federal Reserve is undemocratic is countered by the reminder that the central bank is still very much responsible to Congress, which can amend the Federal Reserve Act any time it wishes. In addition, the President holds frequent meetings with the Chairman of the Board of Governors, the Secretary of the Treasury, and the Chairman of the Council of Economic Advisors.

It is feared by many, and not without historical justification, that if the monetary authority is made the junior partner to the President or the Treasury (the fiscal authority), monetary stability will be sacrificed to the government's revenue needs—the government will be tempted to seek the easy way out in raising funds, by printing money or borrowing excessively at artificially low interest rates, in preference to the politically more difficult route of raising taxes or cutting back on government spending. The sole purpose of an independent monetary authority, in brief, is to forestall the natural propensity of governments to resort to inflation.

Still to Come

The rest of Part III takes an intensive look at Federal Reserve methods of control. Back in Chapter 4 ("A Bird's-Eye View of the Federal Reserve"), we glanced at the three main instruments of Federal

The President holds frequent meetings with the Chairman of the Board of Governors, the Secretary of the Treasury, and the Chairman of the Council of Economic Advisors.

Reserve policy—reserve requirements, the discount rate, and open market operations. It's time to revisit each and see more fully how the Fed goes about its business.

These policy instruments do not exhaust the Fed's arsenal of weapons. In addition to the general or quantitative controls, the Fed also exercises some selective or qualitative controls. For example, it sets maximum interest rates banks may pay to depositors, which we

WHITE HOUSE WARNS FED AGAINST LIFTING OF INTEREST RATES

Without Addressing Central Bank, Statement Says Further Rise Could Endanger Recovery

By JOHN H. ALLAN

In an unusual move, the White House yesterday warned the Federal Reserve Board—without directly addressing it directly—against raising interest rates and thus hurting the economy.

The warning, coming just a short while before the Federal Reserve released banking statistics that strongly indicated further rate increases were imminent, appeared to revive the dormant conflict between the Administration and the nation's monetary authorities.

It also cast doubt on the chances of Arthur F. Burns's reappointment as chairman of the Federal Reserve when his term expires early next year. Even before the White House statement, many businessmen and economists had expressed the opinion that Dr. Burns's reappointment was in danger.

White House Issues Notice

The White House made its position known in a "notice to the press" that mentioned the Federal Reserve only in a reference to the central bank's role in setting growth targets for the nation's money supply. The statement, however, cautioned the central bank in unmistakable language.

"Rapid growth of the money supply is a matter of concern when it occurs in the context of very rapid economic expansion, high employment and a worsening outlook for inflation," the statement said. "Those are not the circumstances we face presently," it emphasized.

The statement was written in response to a reporter's request at a news briefing Wednesday for the Administration's views on short-term interest rates and the money supply. Normally, a White House reply would await the next scheduled news briefing, but in this case, the White House chose to distribute its comments in a special, general release.

Dr. Burns, meanwhile, was in Kansas City, Mo., yesterday for a meeting of the directors of the Federal Reserve bank there. A spokesman said that the Fed chairman was aware of the White House statement but would make no comment on it.

The White House warning was one of the most direct of the continuing maneuvers of several branches of the Federal Government to chip away at the independence of the Federal Reserve, an agency that works on its own to promote economic growth while maintaining stability in the purchasing power of the dollar. The Fed's conduct in pursuing these aims affects jobs and inflation, touching everyone in some degree.

In recent years, Congress has moved to circumscribe the Federal Reserve's power by making it report twice a year on monetary policy and its targets for money supply growth.

The Carter Administration has urged that the Federal Reserve chairman's term in office run concurrently with the President's. Mr. Burns, last appointed to the chairmanship in 1974 by former President Nixon, comes up for reappointment in January.

Higher short-term rates, the White House said, could divert money from savings accounts and impair mortgage lending for housing, which has been a particularly strong element in the economic recovery. It noted that higher interest rates had already "unsettled" the stock market, although it conceded that so far they had not "seriously damaged" the overall recovery.

Short-term interest rates have been climbing steadily since late July, largely as the result of the Federal Reserve's effort to slow down expansion of the nation's money supply—the amount of currency in circulation plus the funds on deposit in checking accounts at banks.

News Item / Who's in Charge Here?

New York Times, October 21, 1977

examined in Chapter 6. And it regulates margin (or down payment) requirements on stock market credit; we discuss this in Chapter 27.

Summary

1. The dominant figure in the formation and execution of monetary policy is the Chairman of the Board of Governors of the Federal Reserve System. The Federal Open Market Committee is the major policy-making body within the System. It is composed of the seven members of the Board of Governors and five Reserve Bank presidents.

2. The Federal Reserve is accountable to the Congress but is legally independent of the executive branch of government. This semiindependent status of the Federal Reserve has been a source of frequent conflict. It is defended on the ground that the central bank must have considerable independence to counteract the natural propensity of governments to resort to inflationary methods of financing themselves.

Suggestions for Further Reading

For a formal description of the Federal Reserve's structure, read Chapter 2 of the sixth edition of *The Federal Reserve System: Purposes and Functions* (Washington, D.C.: Board of Governors of the Federal Reserve System, 1974). On the internal workings of the Fed, see C. R. Whittlesey, "Power and Influence in the Federal Reserve System," *Economica* (February 1963); David P. Eastburn, "The Federal Reserve as a Living Institution," in *Men, Money, and Policy: Essays in Honor of Karl R. Bopp* (Federal Reserve Bank of Philadelphia, 1970); and Jane W. D'Arista, *Federal Reserve Structure and the Development of Monetary Policy* (Staff Report, House Committee on Banking and Currency, U.S. Congress, 1971). A particularly interesting study on the internal operations of the Federal Reserve is by Thomas Havrilesky, William P. Yohe, and David Schirm, "The Economic Affiliations of Directors of Federal Reserve District Banks," in *Social Science Quarterly* (December 1973).

For the real flavor and excitement of central banking, two books are *must* reading: Marriner Eccles's autobiography, *Beckoning Frontiers* (New York: Knopf, 1951); and the *Selected Papers of Allan Sproul,* published by the Federal Reserve Bank of New York in 1980 (you can get a copy of the Sproul book for free if you write to the Federal Reserve Bank of New York and ask for it). Marriner Eccles was a member of the Board of Governors from 1934 to 1951 and its Chairman from 1934 to 1948. Allan Sproul was President of the Federal Reserve Bank of New York from 1941 to 1956.

13

The Instruments of Central Banking

IN CHAPTER 4 you were introduced to the Fed's three main policy instruments: reserve requirements, the discount rate, and open market operations. In the last chapter you learned how the Fed works. Now it's time to get better acquainted with the tools of the trade.

First, though, a word of warning: As you get to know them better, try not to get emotionally involved. The discount rate, especially, can be quite appealing. Deep down, however, it has almost no capacity for a meaningful relationship. Take our word for it. Long ago, a member of the Board of Governors fell for the discount rate hook, line, and sinker. When he encountered nothing but cold indifference he became despondent and after repeated rejections committed suicide (by hanging himself from an old T-account that was stored in the attic of the Federal Reserve Building). Naturally, the whole affair was hushed up.

Reserve Requirements

It was thought many years ago that the purpose of reserve requirements was to provide for bank liquidity, solvency, and safety. It was believed that if banks held reserves against their deposits, this would make the banks more liquid and depositors' funds more safe. But reserve requirements, at 12 percent, are much too low to accomplish those ends, which are better achieved in other ways anyway (as by federal deposit insurance).

As seen today, the primary function of reserve requirements is to serve as an instrument of monetary control. First, the reserve ratio, as we saw in Chapter 3, provides a linkage between the volume of reserves and the level of demand deposits. The linkage is the deposit multiplier—which, remember, is the reciprocal of the required reserve ratio. Second, by varying the required reserve ratio, the Federal Reserve can instantly change bank excess reserves. Such changes are thought to be so powerful that they are used sparingly, for fear they may produce too great an effect. The increase of ½ of 1 percentage point in required reserves against demand deposits in July of 1973, for example, shifted $850 million of reserves from the excess category, where they could have been used for loan and deposit expansion, to the required category, where they were immobilized. When reserve requirements are changed, the Fed usually undertakes some offsetting open market operations to soften the powerful impact.

The Banking Act of 1980 specifies that *all* depository institutions —savings banks, savings and loans, and credit unions, as well as *all* commercial banks, whether members of the Federal Reserve System or not—are subject to the Fed's reserve requirements.

The Act specifies that each depository institution must hold reserves as follows:

1. Against *demand deposits* and similar checking-type accounts (such as NOW accounts and automatic transfers from savings to demand deposits), reserves equal to:

    a. 3 percent of its *first $25 million* of demand deposits.[1]

---

[1]The $25 million figure will be adjusted upward annually by 80 percent of the percentage increase in *total* transactions accounts in the country. Example: if total transactions accounts in the country rise by 5 percent, the $25 million figure will be increased by 80 percent of 5 percent, which equals 4 percent. Four percent of $25 million equals $1 million. Accordingly, at the beginning of 1982 the amount was increased from $25 million to $26 million. It can be expected to increase by about that much every year.

b. 12 percent of its demand deposits *in excess of that amount.*
The Fed can vary this within a range of 8 to 14 percent, and
under emergency circumstances can go as high as 18 percent.

2. Against *time and savings deposits,* reserves equal to:
   a. 3 percent of its *business-owned* time and savings deposits.
   The Fed can vary this within a range of zero to 9 percent.
   Thus far, the Fed has ruled that the 3 percent requirement
   should be applied only to such deposits with an original maturity of less than four years; longer maturities have no reserve requirement.
   b. Reserve requirements against *personal* time and savings
   deposits, which used to exist, have been eliminated.

3. Against its *borrowing from foreign banks or branches abroad:*
   reserves equal to 3 percent of the amount borrowed.

Since the same reserve requirements apply to nonmember as well
as member commercial banks, membership in the Federal Reserve
System has become essentially irrelevant. The problem of dropouts
from the Federal Reserve System that occurred during the 1960s and
1970s has been resolved. Banks can no longer escape the requirement to hold zero interest-bearing reserves by leaving the System.
Also, since the same requirements apply to thrift institutions as to
commercial banks, the distinction between them—as pointed out in
earlier chapters—has become less important.[2]
How crucial are reserve requirements for monetary policy? What
would happen if the Federal Reserve eliminated reserve requirements entirely in order to increase bank profits?

---

[2]Recall that reserve requirements are satisfied by holding vault cash or deposits in
a bank's regional Federal Reserve Bank, neither of which earns any interest. Higher
reserve requirements thus lower bank profitability by increasing the proportion of
assets that yield no income.
  The differential impact of reserve requirements on bank profitability was one of
the main reasons behind passage of the Banking Act of 1980. Until it was enacted in
March of 1980, the Fed's reserve requirements applied only to commercial banks and,
further, only to those commercial banks that were members of the Federal Reserve
System.

Actually, even without formal reserve requirements the Fed would still be in business. Financial institutions would still need both cash to meet customer withdrawals and balances in the Fed to clear checks. As long as they have a demand for claims against the central bank, and as long as the central bank controls the supply of such claims (via open market operations), monetary policy could still work. While changing reserve requirements would be out the window as a tool of monetary policy if there were no formal requirements, the Fed would still influence the System.

There is one qualification: The size of the multiplier relationship between reserves and money supply might fluctuate considerably. This would make the job of controlling the money supply more difficult. Not impossible, but more difficult. And as we will see in Chapter 15, things are already tough enough.

Discounting

The Banking Act of 1980 also contains provisions regarding discounting: specifically, it enlarges access to borrowing from the Federal Reserve to *all* depository institutions that now have to hold reserves—which means nonmember as well as member commercial banks and thrift institutions also. Previously, only member

---

The adverse effect of the Fed's reserve requirements on their earnings led many member banks to reconsider their membership in the Federal Reserve System. Of the roughly 14,000 commercial banks in the United States, about one-third are chartered by the federal government (national banks) and two-thirds are chartered by the state in which they operate (state banks). National banks are *required* to be members of the Federal Reserve System, but state banks are free to join the System or not, as they wish.

During the 1960s and 1970s many state banks withdrew from the Federal Reserve System, giving up their membership to escape the Fed's onerous reserve requirements, and some national banks even turned in their national charters and took out state charters for the same reason. State-administered reserve requirements were typically much lower than the Fed's requirements.

banks had access to discounting, although in emergencies others could sometimes use it too. Now, however, the Act provides that nonmember banks and thrift institutions have the same access to borrowing from the Federal Reserve that member banks have, and on exactly the same terms.

Stepping back a moment, it is worth noting that discounting and the discount rate have a long and distinguished history in the evolution of central banking. Indeed, discounting was considered the *main* instrument of central banking throughout the nineteenth century and the first three decades of the twentieth. It reached its apogee in terms of prestige in 1931 (the same year that "The Star-Spangled Banner" was declared the national anthem by act of Congress). At that time, England's Macmillan Committee, somewhat carried away by the splendor of it all, reported that the discount rate "is an absolute necessity for the sound management of a monetary system, and is a most delicate and beautiful instrument for the purpose."[3] This was just at the time—1931—when the monetary system of virtually every country was collapsing into ruins, whether it had a delicate and beautiful discount rate or not.

It should be mentioned at the start that discount policy has two dimensions: the first is *price,* the discount rate, the rate of interest the Federal Reserve charges financial institutions when they borrow from the Fed. The second dimension has to do with the *quantity* of Federal Reserve lending, including Federal Reserve surveillance over the amount that each institution borrows and the reasons why it borrows. Let us examine quantity first and price second—each, in its turn, has been credited with the mystique of power that surrounds discounting.

Historically, the primary function of a central bank has been to stand ready to supply liquidity—promptly and in abundance—whenever the economy is in danger of coming apart at the seams because of a shortage of cash. While that is no longer its sole function, it is still one of its most important. The central bank is the ultimate source of liquidity in the economy, since its power over bank reserves can increase (or decrease) the ability of the banking

[3]*Report of the Committee on Finance and Industry* (London: His Majesty's Stationery Office, 1931), p. 97.

system to create money. No one else can do this job, so it is the central bank that must be responsible for supplying funds promptly on those rare but crucial occasions when liquidity shortages threaten economic stability. "Financial panics," the history books call them. Because of this responsibility, the central bank has traditionally been called the "lender of last resort."[4]

When the Federal Reserve Act was passed in 1913, its principal feature was setting up a discounting mechanism—facilities through which member banks could temporarily borrow funds from the Fed. Until that time there had been no such mechanism available (indeed, until then there was no central bank in this country). It is also worth noting that open market operations were unknown then (they were not understood or used until the 1920s), and bank reserve requirements could not be varied by the Federal Reserve (they were fixed by Congress; legislation permitting the Fed to alter reserve requirements, within limits, was not enacted until the 1930s). Thus the *only* monetary policy instrument contained in the original Federal Reserve Act was discount policy.

The new discount facilities were intended to prevent a recurrence of the financial panics that had periodically plagued the United States during the 1800s and early 1900s. Such financial crises were typically ignited when some banks failed, and frightened depositors in other banks rushed to exchange their checking accounts for currency. Until 1934 there was no such thing as federal deposit insur-

---

[4]The principle of the central bank as "lender of last resort" was eloquently articulated as long ago as 1873 by Walter Bagehot in *Lombard Street,* the first full-blown exposition of what central banking is all about. Many of his ideas stemmed from Henry Thornton's *An Enquiry into the Nature and Effects of the Paper Credit of Great Britain,* which was published in 1802.

Two relatively recent examples of this "crisis function" of discounting occurred in 1970 and 1974. In 1970, when the Penn Central Railroad went bankrupt, the Fed stepped in and made loans freely available to avert a collapse of lending in the short-term money market—a lot of lenders had been afraid that other large firms might go bankrupt also, and were reluctant to make loans without lots of collateral just in case the loans turned sour. And in 1974 the Fed made $1.7 billion of emergency credit available to New York's Franklin National Bank when that institution got into big trouble, and by so doing reassured the public that the entire banking system was not on the verge of collapse. Eventually Franklin National went down the drain anyway, but there was no financial panic and no depositor lost a penny.

ance; if your bank went down the drain, you went with it. Faced with a "run on the bank," banks would have to call in loans and sell securities to raise cash to meet depositor withdrawals, which would endanger still other banks. Such infectious liquidity crises often jeopardized the entire financial system, since—as we saw in Chapter 3—calling in loans and selling securities to depositors in other banks merely shifts reserve shortages like a hot potato from one bank to another.

The new discount facilities instituted by the passage of the Federal Reserve Act in 1913 were supposed to provide a vehicle through which the Federal Reserve could quickly inject funds precisely where needed in order to stop a panic from spreading. Banks threatened with cash drains could borrow what they needed from the Fed —the lender of last resort. Thus they could get more reserves without any other bank losing them, and thereby prevent the infection from becoming a plague. (For the T-accounts of discounting, see Chapter 4.)

However, when the showdown came, after the stock market crash of 1929, the discount mechanism could not stem the tide. In the four years 1930–1933, more than 9,000 commercial banks failed, almost 40 percent of all the banks in the country. Ah, the good old days!

What went wrong? Lots of things, including the Federal Reserve's lack of experience in dealing with such a gargantuan economic collapse, its failure to use open market operations in sufficient volume, and the absence of appropriate federal fiscal policies.

In the ordinary course of events, however, bank use of the discount facility is rather routine, not at all panic-oriented, with banks borrowing here and there to make short-run adjustments in their reserves with no fuss or bother. As when a bank finds itself with an unexpected reserve deficit and needs to borrow ten million or so to tide itself over for a few days.

The Fed has always stressed that ordinary run-of-the-mill borrowing of this sort (as contrasted with crisis situations) should not be used *too* often to get banks out of reserve difficulties. Banks should run their affairs so they do not have to rely on the Fed to bail them out every few weeks. Or, as the Federal Reserve usually puts it, discounting is considered a privilege, not a right, and privileges should not be abused. Federal Reserve surveillance enforces the "privilege, not a right" concept by checking up on banks that borrow

"There's a run on the bank!"

Drawn by Robt. Day; © 1969 The New Yorker Magazine, Inc.

too much or too frequently.[5] A bank is supposed to borrow only because of *need,* and not go out and make a *profit* on the deal.

In particular, the Fed is sensitive to the possibility that banks may borrow from it and then turn around and use the money to purchase higher-yielding securities, such as a bank borrowing from the Fed at a 10 percent discount rate and then using the funds to buy a short-term security yielding 12 percent. That's a no-no! Nor does the

---

[5]In 1973, however, the Fed introduced a special "seasonal borrowing privilege" that encourages small banks to borrow at the discount window to cover most of their recurring reserve needs arising from seasonal swings in loans or deposits (as happens to banks in agricultural and resort areas).

Fed like it when a bank borrows from it too often, in effect using the discount facility as a more or less permanent source of funds.

In practice, it is not always so easy to determine whether a bank is borrowing because of "need" or to make a "profit." A bank faced with a reserve deficiency can cover it by borrowing funds from the Fed *or* by selling some securities in the money market. Relative rates of interest will be a key determining element in deciding between these alternatives. Say the discount rate is 10 percent and the short-term securities the bank is holding are yielding 12 percent. The bank will be tempted, naturally enough, to utilize the least-cost alternative in adjusting its reserve position—to borrow at 10 percent from the Fed rather than to sell off securities yielding 12 percent. Is this bank borrowing because of "need" or for "profit"? It isn't going out and buying *additional* securities yielding 12 percent; it's just not disposing of the ones it already has. The need is there, but least-cost methods of satisfying it are also relevant.

One Fed method of preventing "abuse" of the discount facility is tighter surveillance procedures. Another way is simply to raise the price of borrowing—which brings us to the discount rate itself.

The Discount Rate and Market Interest Rates

The objective of changing the discount rate is just what the Federal Reserve says it is: A higher discount rate discourages borrowing from the Fed, and a lower discount rate encourages it. These results flow from the least-cost alternatives facing banks with reserve deficiencies. A higher discount rate makes it relatively more advantageous to sell securities to get additional reserves, and a lower discount rate makes it relatively more advantageous to borrow from the Fed. Actually, "higher" and "lower" in absolute terms are not as important as the relationship between the discount rate and market interest rates. Discounting is discouraged (by cost considerations) when the discount rate is *above* other short-term interest rates, and encouraged when it is *below* market interest rates.[6]

[6]See R. Alton Gilbert, "Benefits of Borrowing from the Federal Reserve when the Discount Rate is Below Market Interest Rates," Federal Reserve Bank of St. Louis *Review* (March 1979).

Fed Reprimands Some New York Banks For Abusing Their Borrowing Privileges

By EDWARD P. FOLDESSY
Staff Reporter of THE WALL STREET JOURNAL

The Federal Reserve Bank of New York has reprimanded some large banks in New York for abusing their borrowing privilege at its discount window.

It was learned that the New York Fed has told a number of money-center banks to stay out of the discount window unless there wasn't any reasonable alternative available.

According to sources, the problem arose because of the currently low discount rate, the interest rate charged by the Fed on loans to member commercial banks. That rate has been at 5¾% since August. By contrast, the rate on federal funds, uncommitted reserves banks lend one another, has been hovering around 6½%.

For many banks, the rate differential was too much of a lure. At least some banks, it was understood, borrowed from the Fed at the lower rate and reloaned the money in the federal funds market, a "no-no" by Fed standards.

The Federal Reserve considers discount borrowings as a privilege, not a right. And it expects money market banks to use the federal funds market for their needs when such funds are reasonably available. But many banks had continued to use the discount window when funds were relatively abundant.

The identity of the banks that were reprimanded couldn't be obtained. Figures previously released by the Fed showed that the 10 largest New York banks had borrowed more than $1.1 billion from the discount window last Wednesday, almost a third of the total such borrowings of $3.4 billion from all Federal Reserve district banks. The $3.4 billion borrowing was the largest for any single day since Sept. 25, 1974, when borrowings totaled $5.04 billion.

At least some analysts said the heavy borrowings could force the Fed to boost the discount rate to 6% or 6¼% to bring it closer in line with the federal funds rate.

News Item / Discounting: A Right or a Privilege?

Wall Street Journal, October 25, 1977

In some countries the discount rate is kept above short-term market interest rates at all times (a "penalty rate"), as a means of restraining excessive commercial bank use of the central bank's borrowing facilities. In the United States, on the other hand, the discount rate is usually, although not always, held below the Treasury bill rate, so that the Fed has to rely more on surveillance to prevent "abuse of the discount privilege."

How does a change in the discount rate affect market interest rates? The two are not *directly* connected. A higher or lower discount rate alters bank borrowing, thereby changing bank reserves, bank lending, the money supply, and finally market interest rates. However, this is a rather weak linkage, since the effects on reserves and the money supply of a change in the discount rate are small compared with the effects of the two other tools available to the Federal Reserve.

And yet there does appear to be a connection between the discount rate and market interest rates. As can be seen in Chart 1, there is a relationship between the discount rate and short-term interest rates, such as the Federal funds rate and the yield on Treasury bills.

Careful examination, however, reveals that *changes* in the Federal funds rate and in Treasury bill yields typically *precede* changes in the discount rate. The Federal funds rate and Treasury bill yields rise, probably because of Federal Reserve open market operations, and then—after they have risen quite a while and often quite a bit —the discount rate moves up. Or bill rates fall and then the discount rate is lowered. In other words, a change in the discount rate is likely to come *after* a basic change in market interest rates has already occurred. This is not *always* true, of course, but it is *generally* the case.

One possible way that changes in the discount rate might directly affect market interest rates is through the "announcement effect" produced when a discount rate change comes unexpectedly. An unanticipated rise in the discount rate is likely to lead bondholders to expect tight money and higher interest rates (lower bond prices). They sell bonds to avoid capital losses, thus hastening the drop in bond prices and the rise in interest rates.

The key is that the rise in the discount rate under such circumstances generates expectations regarding future interest rates. But if the public had already observed tightening in the credit markets prior to the change in the discount rate, due to open market operations, the actual announcement itself would produce very little reaction. In fact, the bond markets might be relieved of uncertainty, and interest rates might fall back a bit. The change in the discount rate thus usually confirms what is going on, but does not initiate it.

The 1980 period covered in Chart 1 shows that the discount rate

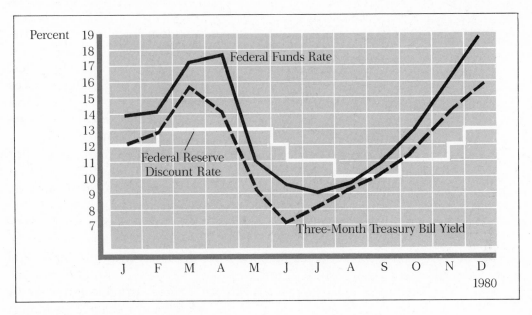

Chart 1 / Togetherness, 1980

was a penalty rate, well above other short-term rates, only in the middle of the year. Both early and late in the year it was significantly below both the Treasury bill yield and the Federal funds rate. In fact, when the discount rate was lower than the Treasury bill yield and the Federal funds rate, predictable consequences followed. The differentials produced an irresistible urge for banks to adjust their reserve positions by borrowing from the Fed rather than by borrowing from each other in the Federal funds market or by selling Treasury bills. Borrowing from the Fed averaged over $2 billion daily in March and November, as compared with only $400 million in mid-year when the discount rate was a true penalty rate.

Realizing what was happening and why, the Federal Reserve added a special 3 percent surcharge to the discount rate during early and late 1980. The surcharge was levied on large banks that used the discount facility too frequently. "Too frequently" was defined as borrowing in successive weeks or in more than four weeks in a calendar quarter.

Conducting Open Market Operations

In Chapter 4 we saw how open market operations affect bank reserves, but we didn't spend any time then on how the Fed actually does its buying and selling of government securities. It's time for a look behind the scenes to see just how the process works.

Although monetary policy is made in Washington, open market operations are actually conducted in New York—in a well-guarded trading room on the eighth floor of the Federal Reserve Bank of New York, which is only a few blocks from Wall Street. The Federal Open Market Committee (FOMC) in Washington decides on the general aims and objectives of monetary policy, but then it is up to the New York Federal Reserve Bank's Peter Sternlight, Manager of the System Open Market Account, to do the actual buying and selling to carry out the FOMC's intentions.

Sternlight's location in the heart of the New York financial district puts him in close contact with the government securities dealers with whom the Fed does business when it buys or sells government securities. Every morning of the work week the Account Manager meets with some of the securities dealers to get the "feel of the market"—and even the opening handshakes (firm or limp? dry or sweaty palms?) probably give him a hint of whether the market is likely to be strong or weak, bullish or bearish. It is said that on occasion Sternlight has been known to shock the dealers by the judicious use of one of those little hand buzzers that they sell in novelty shops.

Feedback from the securities dealers is only one component of the vast array of data and information marshaled by the Account Manager in mapping his plans for open market operations on any given day. His starting point, of course, is the stance of monetary policy as expressed by the FOMC with respect to bank reserves, the money supply, and interest rates. Given these targets, it is Sternlight's job to figure out how to achieve them by open market operations— should he buy or sell, how much, from or to whom, and when?

Each morning, a little after 9:30, the Account Manager receives a report on the reserve position of the banking system as of the night before. An additional indicator of what is happening in the market for bank reserves is provided by the Federal funds rate, the rate charged on reserves loaned from one bank to another. If many banks have excess reserves and only a few have deficiencies, the Federal funds rate is likely to fall because there will be many eager lenders and few borrowers. On the other hand, if many banks have reserve deficiencies and only a few are in surplus, the rate will rise because there will be many eager borrowers and few lenders. The Federal funds rate thus provides the Fed with a sensitive barometer of bank reserve conditions.

A little later in the morning, the Account Manager is provided with a detailed projection by his research staff. It covers movements in various items that can affect the reserve position of the banking system—including currency holdings of the public (which show considerable seasonal variation), deposits in foreign accounts at the Federal Reserve Banks, and other technical factors. A change in any of these can cause reserves to go up or down and thereby affect bank lending capabilities, interest rates, and growth in the money supply. For example, as the public cashes checks in order to hold more currency, commercial banks must pay out vault cash and thereby suffer a loss in reserves.

A call is also made to the U.S. Treasury to determine what is likely to happen to Treasury balances in tax and loan accounts at commercial banks—deposits of the U.S. government generated by tax payments of the public and receipts from bond sales—and to find out what is likely to happen to Treasury balances at the Federal Reserve Banks, from which most government expenditures are made. As funds are shifted from Treasury tax and loan accounts in commercial banks to Treasury balances at the Federal Reserve, the commercial banking system loses reserves.[7]

By 11:00 A.M., Peter Sternlight has a good idea of money market conditions, including what is happening to interest rates, and of anticipated changes in the reserve position of the banking system. He also knows what the FOMC wants. If the FOMC had asked for moderate growth in reserves to sustain moderate growth in the money supply, and all the other technical factors just discussed are expected to pour a large volume of reserves into the banking system, he may decide that open market *sales* are necessary to prevent an

---

[7]The discussion of the last two paragraphs on the impact of various items on bank reserves will be explained in detail in the next chapter.

excessive (more than moderate) expansion in reserves. If, on the other hand, he expects to find reserves going up too little or even declining as a result of these other forces, he may engage in large-scale open market purchases. It is clear, therefore, why knowledge of the amount of government securities that the Federal Reserve bought or sold on a given day, or during a given week, in itself tells us almost nothing about the overall posture or intent of monetary policy. Many purchases and sales are used to offset technical influences on reserves.

At 11:15 it is time for a daily long-distance conference call with a member of the Board of Governors in Washington and one of the Federal Reserve Bank presidents. Sternlight outlines his plan of action for the day and explains the reasons for his particular strategy. Once his decision is approved, the purchase or sale of securities (usually Treasury bills) takes place. The Account Manager instructs the traders in the trading room of the Federal Reserve Bank of New York to call the thirty-five or so government securities dealers and ask them for firm bids for stated amounts of specific maturities of government securities (in the case of an open market sale) or for their selling price quotations for stated amounts of specific maturities (in the case of an open market purchase). While the Federal Reserve does not engage in open market operations to make a profit, it still insists on getting the most for its money, and it is assured of that by vigorous competition among the various dealers in government securities.

The Account Manager may instruct his traders to buy or sell securities outright—that is, involving no additional commitments. Or he may decide that he prefers to inject or withdraw reserves only *temporarily,* say for two or four days. One type of open market operation is particularly well suited to the temporary injection of reserves—namely, buying government securities *under repurchase agreements.* With a "repo" the Fed buys the security with an agreement that the seller repurchase it on a specific date in the future, usually within a week or so.[8] When the Fed buys, reserves go up; but when the security is sold back to the dealer a week or so later, reserves drop back down again.

[8]The term repo takes its name from the dealer's point of view. That is, the dealer sells to the Fed under an agreement to repurchase the securities.

A "reverse repo" is designed to do the opposite. It *withdraws* reserves from the banking system temporarily. With a reverse repo, also called a matched sale-purchase agreement, the Fed sells securities but simultaneously agrees to buy them back at a specific date in the future. When the Fed sells, reserves fall; but when the Fed buys the securities back, reserves are restored.

In recent years, the Fed has relied to an increasing extent on repos and reverse repos. In terms of the dollar volume of open market operations, they now exceed outright purchases and sales by twenty or thirty to one.

It takes only about half an hour for the traders to complete their "go-around" of the market and execute the open market operation. By 12:30 the Account Manager and his staff are back to monitoring bank reserve positions via the Federal funds rate and to keeping track of trends in financial markets in general. If necessary to implement the original objective, the manager is prepared to engage in further open market operations during the afternoon.

Summary

1. The 1980 legislation put all depository institutions on an equal footing. Commercial bank or thrift, member or nonmember, all are subject to the Fed's reserve requirements on an equal basis. Until the 1980 legislation, the Fed's reserve requirements applied only to commercial banks that were members of the Federal Reserve System.

2. The same legislation also affected discounting by opening access to borrowing from the central bank to all depository institutions that now have to hold reserves.

3. Discounting and the discount rate have a long and distinguished history, dating back to the nineteenth-century concept of the central bank as the ultimate "lender of last resort."

4. When the discount rate is below market interest rates, profit motivations encourage commercial banks to adjust their reserve positions by borrowing from the central bank.

5. Open market operations are not conducted in Washington but at the Federal Reserve Bank of New York. Repos and reverse repos have become much more important than outright purchases and sales in recent years.

Suggestions for Further Reading

Two informative articles on reserve requirements are William Poole and Charles Lieberman, "Improving Monetary Control," *Brookings Papers on Economic Activity* (No. 2, 1972); and George Garvy, "Reserve Requirements Abroad," Federal Reserve Bank of New York *Monthly Review* (October 1973).

A good survey of the evolution of thinking behind discounting and the discount rate can be found in Murray E. Polakoff, "Federal Reserve Discount Policy and Its Critics," in *Banking and Monetary Studies,* ed. Deane Carson (Homewood, Ill.: Irwin, 1963). The standard works in this field are W. W. Riefler, *Money Rates and Money Markets in the United States* (New York: Harper, 1930); R. C. Turner, *Member Bank Borrowing* (Columbus: Ohio State University Press, 1938); and Warren L. Smith, "The Discount Rate as a Credit Control Weapon," *Journal of Political Economy* (April 1958). A formal statistical analysis of member bank borrowing is Stephen M. Goldfeld and Edward J. Kane, "The Determinants of Member Bank Borrowing," *Journal of Finance* (September 1966). A recent article that explores in some detail the seminal ideas of Henry Thornton and Walter Bagehot is well worth reading; see Thomas M. Humphrey, "The Classical Concept of the Lender of Last Resort," Federal Reserve Bank of Richmond *Economic Review* (January/February 1975).

The Federal Reserve has also conducted a full-scale study of discounting. It published the results in 1971 and 1972 in three volumes under the overall title *Reappraisal of the Federal Reserve Discount Mechanism.*

An explanation from A to Z of the formulation and execution of open market operations is found in Paul Meek, *Open Market Operations* (Federal Reserve Bank of New York, 1978). Although Meek is close to the center of the action, the trials and tribulations of trying to control the money supply can be gotten straight from the horse's mouth; see former Account Manager Alan Holmes, "Operational Constraints on the Stabilization of Money Supply Growth," in *Controlling Monetary Aggregates* (Federal Reserve Bank of Boston, 1969).

14

Understanding Movements in Bank Reserves

ADDING AND SUBTRACTING bank reserves are simple matters when all that's needed are pluses and minuses on textbook T-accounts. But in the real world simple T-accounts are replaced by complicated balance sheets that frequently seem to hide the truth. To understand the specific factors influencing bank reserves, we must look at the balance sheet of the Federal Reserve. To keep from being at the mercy of the accountants, we must translate the balance sheet into the bank reserve equation. Actually, it is the depository institutions' reserve equation, since thrift institutions as well as commercial banks must now hold reserves with the Fed. These items are sufficiently important to the interpretation of monetary policy that they appear in part every Monday in the *Wall Street Journal* and in full every month in the *Federal Reserve Bulletin.*

In the previous chapter we noted that both open market operations and lending at the discount window can change the volume of bank reserves and, therefore, the potential level of the money supply. Not surprisingly, we will see that both open market operations and discounting show up in specific items on the Fed's balance sheet. But there are other entries on the Fed's balance sheet that can offset or exacerbate these movements in reserves. Some are not even under the discretionary control of the Federal Reserve. Thus it becomes obvious that only the Fed's balance sheet can help explain why the central bank sometimes has difficulty controlling total bank reserves.

As if this weren't sufficiently complicated, it is also true that activities of the U.S. Treasury can add or absorb bank reserves. It is, therefore, necessary to expand the determinants of bank reserves beyond the Fed's balance sheet to get the entire picture. This expanded view goes by the rather imposing name of the bank (or depository institutions) reserve equation. In fact, it is nothing more than a tally sheet of the sources and uses of reserves. Nevertheless, it is so crucial for monitoring trends in reserves that it is often billed as the fundamental framework of monetary control.

In the first two sections of this chapter we present the Fed's balance sheet and the monetary accounts of the U.S. Treasury. We use T-accounts to show how the specific items influence reserves. In the last two sections we combine these balance sheets into the reserve equation and show how it can be used to monitor Federal Reserve policies.

The Fed's Balance Sheet

Table 1 is the somewhat simplified balance sheet of the Federal Reserve System at the end of 1981.[1] Each of the items on both the assets and liabilities sides deserves some explanation, since each of them reflects something that has an effect on reserves.

The general proof of that last statement—that every item on the Fed's balance sheet has an effect on reserves—is so obvious it's easy to overlook. So here it is:

1. By definition, on *any* balance sheet, total assets = total liabilities (including net worth or "capital accounts").

2. With respect to the Fed, its total liabilities include reserves—they are "bank deposits" in the Fed—plus that part of "Federal Reserve notes outstanding" which is in bank vaults.

[1] If you look in the back of the *Federal Reserve Bulletin*, you will find the Fed's balance sheet in a table labeled "Federal Reserve Banks: Condition and Federal Reserve Note Statements."

3. Therefore, bank reserves must equal total Federal Reserve assets minus all other Federal Reserve liabilities (and capital accounts) besides bank reserves.

All of which can be put more formally:

Definition 1: Fed assets = Fed liabilities + Fed capital accounts

Definition 2: Fed liabilities = bank reserves + other Fed liabilities

Thus (by substitution): Fed assets = bank reserves + other Fed liabilities + capital accounts

Therefore (rearranging terms):

Bank Reserves = Fed assets −(other Fed liabilities + capital accounts)

At this point, it is clear that anything affecting a Fed asset or a Fed liability has to alter reserves *unless it is offset somewhere else in the balance sheet.* If total Fed assets rise, for example, and there are no changes in "other liabilities," then reserves have to rise. Or if Fed liabilities other than reserves rise, and no asset changes, then re-

Table 1 The Federal Reserve's Balance Sheet
(end of 1981; in billions of dollars)

Assets		Liabilities & Capital Accounts	
Gold certificates (including special drawing rights)	14.5	Federal Reserve notes outstanding	131.9
Cash	.4	Bank deposits (reserves)	25.2
Loans	1.6	U.S. Treasury deposits	4.3
U.S. govt. and agency securities		Foreign and other	
Owned outright	136.9	deposits	1.3
Held under repurchase agreements	3.4		
Cash items in process of collection	8.6	Deferred availability cash items	6.8
Miscellaneous assets	9.4	Miscellaneous liabilities and capital accounts	5.3
	174.8		174.8

SOURCE: *Federal Reserve Bulletin.*

serves have to fall. It all follows from the fundamental accounting identity: total assets = total liabilities plus capital accounts.

To understand the mechanics underlying the process, it will be useful to examine more closely each of the major items on the Fed's balance sheet. We will see exactly how increases in each of the Fed's assets expand bank reserves and how increases in "other liabilities" decrease bank reserves. We can then isolate the uncontrollable items that complicate the Fed's influence over reserves.

1. *Gold certificates (including special drawing rights),* equal to $14.5 billion in Table 1, are Federal Reserve assets that arise in connection with U.S. Treasury gold purchases, regardless of whether the gold is purchased from abroad or from domestic mines. Say the U.S. Treasury buys $100 million of newly mined gold from the Get Rich Quick Mining Company in Dodge City, Kansas. The Treasury pays for the gold with a check drawn on its deposit in the Federal Reserve; the Get Rich Quick Mining Company deposits the check in its local commercial bank, which sends it to the Fed for collection, and as a result bank reserves rise by $100 million, as we see in the following T-accounts:

U.S. Treasury		*Federal Reserve*		*Commercial Bank*	
A	L	A	L	A	L
Gold +$100 Dep. in FRB −$100			Dep. of commercial bank +$100	Dep. in FRB +$100	Dep. of mining co. + $100
			Dep. of Treas. −$100		

So far, this illustrates that if a Fed liability other than bank reserves falls, and there are no offsetting entries, then bank reserves must rise. But when gold is involved, that is not the end of the story. The Treasury has used up part of its checking account balance at the Fed. To replenish it, the Treasury issues to the Fed a "gold certificate" (a claim on the gold) equal in value to the dollar amount of gold purchased, and the Fed in exchange credits the Treasury's deposit account by a similar amount, as follows:

U.S. Treasury		Federal Reserve	
A	L	A	L
Dep. in FRB + $100	Gold certif. outstanding + $100	Gold certif. + $100	Dep. of Treas. + $100

In this latter transaction, Federal Reserve assets (namely, gold certificates) have risen but reserves are not affected, because a liability other than reserves (namely, Treasury deposits) has risen simultaneously.[2] However, the net result of both of these transactions is still an increase in bank reserves. (A gold *sale* by the Treasury would *reduce* bank reserves, with all the above entries being the same except opposite in sign.)[3]

2. *Cash* on the asset side of the Federal Reserve balance sheet consists of coin and currency issued by the U. S. Treasury (a liability of the Treasury) that the Fed happens to have in its vaults (equal to $.4 billion in Table 1). Mostly it consists of coins. If a bank sends a truckload of pennies to the Fed, cash goes up on the asset side of the Federal Reserve's balance sheet and reserves go up on the liability side.

3. *Loans* (or bank borrowings), totaling $1.6 billion in Table 1, have been examined in detail via T-accounts in Chapter 4. When banks borrow from the Fed the banks' reserves rise, and when they repay such debts their reserves decline.

4. *U.S. government and agency*[4] *securities* are acquired by the Fed when it engages in open market operations, as we saw in Chapter 4. When the Fed buys securities, bank reserves expand, and when the Fed sells securities, bank reserves contract.

[2]As you can see, this step is nothing more than a sterile bookkeeping operation since this "monetization of gold" comes *after* the gold stock has already affected bank reserves. In fact, some gold purchases are not "monetized" by the Treasury (no gold certificates are issued for them), and yet they affect bank reserves just the same.

[3]We will discuss "special drawing rights" (SDRs) in Chapter 32. They comprise only $3.3 billion of the $14.5 billion in Table 1. SDRs result from international monetary arrangements made in recent years. They are a supplement to gold in international finance, and an increase in U.S. holdings of SDRs affects bank reserves exactly the same as an inflow of gold.

[4]Agency issues are securities of government-sponsored institutions, such as the Federal Home Loan Banks and the Federal National Mortgage Association (see Chapter 7). Agency obligations account for only about $9.4 billion of the $140.3 billion in Table 1.

5. *Cash items in process of collection* on the asset side of the
Fed's balance sheet is an entry that arises in the course of clearing
checks. The entry "deferred availability cash items" on the liabilities side is generated by the same process. Although each of these
entries is rather obscure, the difference between them—"float"—is
more popular and has often caused serious short-term disruptions
in bank reserves. A somewhat detailed treatment, therefore, seems
worthwhile.

Let's take a specific example. Say you have an account in the Safe
& Sound National Bank and you see in the local newspaper that for
only $100 you can get an antique spittoon and bedpan (matching set,
last one left, accept no substitutes!). So you rush downtown and are
lucky enough to get them, paying the $100 by check. The antique
dealer has his checking account at the Last Laugh National Bank,
in a neighboring town. He deposits your check in Last Laugh, which
sends it in to the Fed for collection.

So far so good, and indeed we saw all this before in Chapter 3. But
in reality things are just a bit more complicated. Back in Chapter 3
we said that the Fed would simply add $100 to the Last Laugh Bank's
deposit in the Fed, deduct that amount from your Safe & Sound
Bank's reserve account, and that would be that. Although the end
results are accurate enough, the mechanics are not quite that simple, as the T-accounts below indicate:

Federal Reserve Bank

A	L
(a) Cash items in process of collection: Safe & Sound Bank +$100	Deferred availability cash items: Last Laugh Bank +$100
(b)	Deferred availability cash items: Last Laugh Bank −$100 Bank deposits: Last Laugh Bank +$100
(c) Cash items in process of collection: Safe & Sound Bank −$100	Bank deposits: Safe & Sound Bank −$100

When the Fed receives your check from Last Laugh, it doesn't *immediately* credit Last Laugh's reserve account and reduce Safe & Sound's reserve account. What it does is give Last Laugh "deferred availability" credit, meaning that Last Laugh's reserve account will be credited in due time, according to a prearranged time schedule. At the same time it considers the check "in process of collection" from Safe & Sound. Thus the first pair of entries, labeled (a), in the Fed's T-account above.

Next step: After a day or two, depending on the time schedule, Last Laugh will formally receive an addition to its reserve account—the

Cash items in process of collection.

pair of entries labeled (b) above. Notice that, for the moment, *after* step (b) but *before* step (c), "cash items in process of collection" on the Federal Reserve's balance sheet exceeds "deferred availability cash items" by $100. This $100 difference is known as Federal Reserve *float,* and it adds to total bank reserves because it means that one bank's reserves have been increased, but so far no other bank's reserves have been reduced.

Finally, when the check is actually collected from Safe & Sound, then Safe & Sound's reserve account will be reduced, which is step (c). At that time, "cash items in process of collection" will also decline, and both float and total reserves will fall by $100, returning to their original amounts.

Float—the difference on the Fed's balance sheet between the asset item "cash items in process of collection" and the liability item "deferred availability cash items"—arises because many checks are not collected within the time period established for crediting the reserves of banks depositing checks with the Fed. According to the time schedule now in use, all checks must be credited to a depositing bank's reserve account no later than two days after they are received by the Fed.

With respect to its effect on bank reserves, adding $1.8 billion at the end of 1981 according to Table 1, the importance of float is not so much that it exists but that it fluctuates considerably. Float usually rises, as shown in the news item at the end of the chapter, when bad weather grounds planes and causes delays in the mails, since this interferes with the delivery of checks en route for collection. A rise in Federal Reserve float increases total bank reserves, but such gains are temporary since subsequent declines in float reduce reserves.[5]

Note: On the Fed's balance sheet, the sum of bank borrowing, U.S. government and agency security holdings, and Federal Reserve float is frequently referred to as "Federal Reserve credit."

6. *Federal Reserve notes outstanding* are most of our $1, $2, $5, $10, and $20 bills (and so on up the ladder), an asset to those of us who are fortunate enough to have any. But to the Fed they are just

---

[5]As electronic debiting and crediting replaces checks as the means of transferring funds, the volatility of float will be a diminishing problem (see Chapter 11). For more details on float, see Arline Hoel, "A Primer on Federal Reserve Float," *Monthly Review* of the Federal Reserve Bank of New York (October 1975).

Federal Reserve Bank		Commercial Bank	
A	L	A	L
	F.R. notes outstanding +$100	Cash in vault +$100	
	Dep. of bank −$100	Dep. in FRB −$100	

another liability, totaling $131.9 billion in Table 1. When your local bank finds itself running short of currency, it cashes a check at its regional Federal Reserve Bank and the Fed sends an armored car to deliver some more tens and twenties. This is recorded as is shown above.[6]

When commercial banks or thrift institutions ship currency back to the Fed, of course, the entries are the same but opposite in sign. Which means that when the Fed receives an inflow of Federal Reserve notes, its assets do not rise; instead, its Federal Reserve note liabilities decline, because there are fewer Federal Reserve notes *outstanding*. (Federal Reserve notes in the possession of the Federal Reserve are just so much paper—if they are frayed or worn, they are burned; if they are still serviceable, they are stored awaiting the day when banks will want them again.)

So when the item "Federal Reserve notes outstanding" rises, bank deposits at the Fed fall, and vice versa. But these transactions—

---

[6]What if the Fed includes in its shipment some Treasury-issued coin or some Treasury-issued $5 or $10 bills? To the extent that this occurs, then instead of the Fed liability "Federal Reserve notes outstanding" rising, what happens is that the Fed asset "cash" falls. In *either* case, member bank deposits at the Fed fall.

shipments of currency back and forth between depository institutions and the Federal Reserve Banks—do not in themselves alter bank reserves. They just exchange one kind of reserve (a deposit at the Fed) for another (cash in vault). However, if the *public* decides to hold more currency—perhaps because Christmas is approaching and people need more coins and bills to spend—then bank reserves fall dollar for dollar with the currency drain:

Commercial Bank			*Public*	
A	L		A	L
Cash in vault − $100	Demand deposits − $100		Demand deposits −$100	
			Currency +$100	

When currency is returned to the banking system, as in the weeks after the Christmas season ends, then bank reserves rise dollar for dollar with the currency reflow. The T-accounts are the same as above, except opposite in sign. If the currency is then shipped back to the Fed, banks are merely exchanging reserves in the form of currency for reserves in the form of deposits at the Fed.

7. *U.S. Treasury deposits,* amounting to $4.3 billion in Table 1, are just what the name implies: deposits of the Treasury held in the Federal Reserve Banks. The Treasury keeps most of its working balances in "tax and loan accounts" at many commercial banks throughout the country. This is where tax payments and the receipts from bond sales are initially deposited. But when the Treasury wants to spend the money, it first shifts its funds to a Federal Reserve Bank and then writes a check on its balance at the Fed. The Treasury can shift its balances from commercial banks to the Fed prior to making payments by writing a check on its balance at commercial banks and giving the check to the Fed.[7]As a result, Treasury deposits at the Fed rise and bank reserves fall:

[7]The Treasury's balances are actually shifted by electronic instructions wired to banks, not by writing paper checks.

U.S. Treasury		Federal Reserve Bank		Commercial Banks	
A	L	A	L	A	L
Dep. in comm. bank −$100			Comm. bank dep. −$100	Dep. in FRB −$100	Dep. of Treasury −$100
Dep. in FRB +$100			Treasury dep. +$100		

However, when the Treasury actually spends the funds, then its deposits at the Fed fall and reserves rise again. Say the Treasury spends $100 on paper clips. It pays a supplier of paper clips with a check drawn on its balance at the Fed, the supplier deposits the check in his local commercial bank, the bank sends it in to the Fed, and—*voilà!*—as Treasury deposits at the Fed decline bank reserves are increased:

U.S. Treasury		Federal Reserve Bank		Commercial Banks	
A	L	A	L	A	L
Dep. in FRB −$100			Comm. bank dep. +$100	Dep. in FRB +$100	Demand dep. +$100
Paper clips +$100			Treasury dep. −$100		

This completes our analysis of bank reserves and the balance sheet of the Federal Reserve. In addition, however, many transactions of the U.S. Treasury also affect bank reserves. Some of these transactions we have already discussed, but they bear repeating from the independent viewpoint of the Treasury; others—like the issuance of Treasury currency—have not yet been taken into account. Let's turn to the Treasury's influence on bank reserves.

The U.S. Treasury's Monetary Accounts

First of all, strictly speaking, it is the Treasury, not the Fed, that officially buys and sells gold on behalf of the government. As we have seen, after it buys some gold, the Treasury usually issues an equal amount of gold certificates (a Treasury liability) and hands them to the Fed (for whom they are an asset), so that the Treasury can replenish its deposit account at the Fed. However, as the T-accounts at the beginning of this chapter show, it is really the gold purchase that increases bank reserves, not the subsequent issue of gold certificates. Since gold, per se, does not appear on the balance sheet of the Fed, we had to talk about the gold certificates while we were confining ourselves to the Fed's balance sheet. But now that we are bringing the Treasury explicitly into the picture, we can go right to the heart of the matter: When the Treasury buys gold, bank reserves rise, and when the Treasury sells gold, bank reserves fall.[8]

A second aspect of Treasury operations that affects bank reserves is changes in the Treasury's deposits at the Federal Reserve Banks. Since we have just seen the T-accounts illustrating this process, there is no need to repeat them.

Finally, we have to take account of the fact that the Treasury also issues a small amount of our currency and all of our coins. Actually, the Bureau of Engraving and Printing operates the printing presses for currency (this is not the same thing as the Government Printing Office, although for all practical purposes maybe there isn't much difference), and the Bureau of the Mint manufactures the coins in three coin factories that are located in Denver, Philadelphia, and San Francisco. Both of these bureaus are departments of the U.S. Treasury.

The impacts on bank reserves of changes in Treasury currency outstanding are the same as the effects of Federal Reserve notes.

---

[8]You can confirm the ultimate significance of gold rather than gold certificates by noting that if you were to consolidate the balance sheets of the Treasury and the Fed, gold certificates would cancel each other—since they are a liability of the Treasury and an asset of the Fed—leaving only the gold itself.

Thus the T-accounts presented above apply here as well. The reason is straightforward: there is no difference between currency that is in the form of Federal Reserve notes and currency (such as United States notes or silver certificates) and coin that is issued by the U.S. Treasury. Regardless of who issued it, all coin and currency in bank vaults count as reserves. Thus when the public decides it wants to hold more currency—because when going to the supermarket a $50 bill is needed rather than a $20—then bank reserves fall dollar for dollar with the drain of currency out of bank vaults into the purses of the public. It doesn't matter whether the currency leaving the banks is in the form of Federal Reserve notes or Treasury-issued money. And conversely, when the public redeposits its change—nickels, quarters, and a few dollar bills—back in the banking system, bank reserves rise dollar for dollar with the currency reflow regardless of the type of currency being redeposited.

The Bank Reserve Equation

We have now become acquainted with all the factors that affect bank reserves and we can put them together in a full and complete "bank reserve equation." The reserve equation is nothing more than a record of the sources and uses of bank reserves. It is actually rather simple to visualize conceptually, as long as you remember the accounting at the beginning of this chapter plus the fact that Treasury currency in bank vaults also counts as reserves.

Namely, bank reserves = total Fed assets *minus* all Fed liabilities and capital accounts *other than* those Fed liabilities that comprise bank reserves *plus* Treasury currency in bank vaults. This is usually put more formally, as in Table 2, but it amounts to the same thing.[9]

Table 2, the bank reserve equation, looks a bit different from Table 1, the Fed's balance sheet, but the differences are really minor. "Factors supplying reserves" in Table 2 correspond roughly to Federal

---

[9]You can find the reserve equation in the *Federal Reserve Bulletin* in a table labeled "Reserves of Depository Institutions: Reserve Bank Credit."

**Table 2 The Bank Reserve Equation
(end of 1981; in billions of dollars)**

Factors supplying reserves:

Federal Reserve credit:	
U.S. govt. and agency securities	140.3
Loans to member banks	1.6
Float	1.8
Miscel. Federal Reserve assets	9.4
Gold stock (including SDRs)	14.5
Treasury currency outstanding	14.5
	182.1

Less factors absorbing reserves:

Currency in circulation (i.e., outside the Federal Reserve, the Treasury, *and bank vaults*)	126.1
Treasury cash holdings	.4
Treasury, foreign, and other deposits with Federal Reserve Banks	5.6
Miscel. Federal Reserve liabilities and capital	5.3
	137.4

Equals bank reserves:

Bank deposits with Federal Reserve Banks	25.2
Currency in bank vaults	19.5
	44.7

SOURCE: *Federal Reserve Bulletin.*

Reserve assets, and "factors absorbing reserves" correspond roughly to Federal Reserve liabilities; in addition Treasury-issued coin and currency is also incorporated into Table 2.

In brief, Table 2, the bank reserve equation, is simply the consolidation of the Fed's balance sheet with the Treasury's monetary accounts. Some of the altered items are as follows. Federal Reserve float in Table 2 is the excess of the Fed asset from Table 1 called "cash items in process of collection" over the Fed liability "deferred availability cash items." Gold stock in Table 2 replaces gold certificates in Table 1 because, as we have seen, it is the purchase or sale of the gold itself that affects bank reserves, not the issuance of gold certificates. "Treasury currency outstanding" in Table 2, the only really new item as compared with Table 1, includes all Treasury-issued coin and currency regardless of who holds it; that is, it is counted here whether it is held by the public, commercial banks, the Federal Reserve, or even the Treasury itself. Thus under the "factors absorbing reserves" in Table 2 we include both Federal Reserve Notes and Treasury-issued currency as part of "Currency in circulation." This item absorbs reserves because it refers to currency held by the nonbank public—that is, currency that is *outside* the Federal Reserve, the Treasury, and the banks. Currency of any sort that may be held by the Treasury is included in the figure for "Treasury cash holdings."[10]

Thus, the bank reserve equation presented in Table 2 is really just a formal summary of the sources and uses of bank reserves. As we mentioned in the beginning of the chapter, it is obvious that other factors besides Federal Reserve decisions can influence bank reserves. This could cause problems for the Fed in controlling reserves and hence the money supply. The Federal Reserve, in fact, uses the reserve equation to keep track of these forces. Let's see how it is done.

[10]For more detail on the consolidation of the Fed's balance sheet with the Treasury's monetary accounts, see Arthur W. Samansky, *Statfacts: Understanding Federal Reserve Statistical Reports* (Federal Reserve Bank of New York, 1981). However, to *really* understand the accounting nitty-gritty you'll have to dig into the *Supplement to Banking and Monetary Statistics,* Section 10 (Board of Governors of the Federal Reserve System, 1962), pp. 1–13.

We should mention that in the bank reserve equation as actually published by the Federal Reserve, the term "currency in circulation" is defined as Federal Reserve Notes and Treasury-issued coin and currency held outside the Fed and the Treasury. In other words, "currency in circulation" as published by the Fed includes currency held by the banks as well as that held by the nonbank public. From the point of view of bank reserves this is illogical, as the Fed itself admits. It is illogical because "currency in circulation" is treated as an entry that reduces reserves in the reserve equation, but in fact currency held by banks is part of their reserves. The Fed's published version winds up with reserves held in the form of deposits at the Fed, to which vault cash is added back in to get total reserves. Our version corrects the structure of the reserve equation, redefining "currency in circulation" as only that currency held by the nonbank public. The Fed's reasons for its form of presentation are mainly historical, as explained on page 7 of the *Supplement to Banking and Monetary Statistics* mentioned above.

Putting It All to Use

In earlier chapters, when we related demand deposits to reserves via the simple deposit expansion multiplier (demand deposits = total reserves times the reciprocal of the demand deposit reserve ratio), we assumed that the Fed could control the volume of reserves by judicious use of open market operations. But from the reserve equation, we see that this is no simple matter. Movements in float, gold, Treasury deposits, currency in circulation, and the other variables listed in Table 2 have to be forecast and monitored. Only then can Fed open market operations hope to come close to the mark in terms of bank reserves. Open market operations, therefore, cannot be fully understood, or properly executed, without the bank reserve equation.

For example, if reserves are rising because of a temporary decline in the Treasury's balance at the Fed, open market sales may be used to *offset* such influences. Open market operations of this type are called *defensive* because they are aimed at defending a target level of reserves from "outside" influences. Another example would be increased purchases of government securities during December to offset seasonal increases in currency holdings by the public. December may mean mirth and cheer to most of us, but to practitioners of the dismal science in the Fed's trading room it means "pump up reserves to offset currency drains." The accompanying news item offers a specific example of defensive open market operations.

As we saw in the previous chapter there is a special type of open market operation that particularly lends itself to defensive uses, namely government securities bought under repurchase agreements. Under a repo the Fed buys the security with an agreement that the seller repurchase it on a specific date in the future (usually within seven days). As Table 1 indicates, $3.4 billion of government securities were held under repurchase agreements at the end of 1981. A reverse repo is designed to sop up reserves over a short interval; that is, the Fed sells government securities and agrees to repurchase them at some date in the near future (this is also called a matched sale-purchase agreement).

By their very nature, repos and reverse repos are *temporary* injections or deletions of reserves and might be interpreted as always being in the defensive category. But that would be falling into the well-known pitfall of identifying a specific Federal Reserve action with a particular objective. Never, never, never, do that. Once you do, the Fed denies it and then makes sure you're wrong by going out and doing just the opposite—using repos and reverse repos continuously to change reserves over a long period of time. In fact, in terms of volume of transactions, repos and reverses far outweigh outright purchases and sales.[11]

Which brings us to the *dynamic* variety of open market operations. Dynamic open market operations are aimed at either increasing or decreasing the overall level of bank lending capacity by changing the level of bank reserves. Even here, the volume of purchases or sales must be undertaken in light of movements in all the other factors in Table 2 that affect bank reserves. For example, if an increase in reserves is desired and the reserve equation shows that all other sources of reserves will be expanding, open market purchases may be completely unnecessary. For these reasons, it is not really possible for an outsider to distinguish defensive from dynamic open market operations, because the Fed is usually buying and/or selling on a continuous basis—sometimes offsetting "outside" influences on reserves, sometimes changing the total level of reserves, and sometimes even offsetting the offsetting changes. It is generally agreed, however, that the bulk of the Fed's open market operations are in the defensive category, making up as much as 80 or 90 percent of total purchases and sales.

Focusing on the Monetary Base

There has been considerable controversy over what specific variable the Fed should try to control in order to regulate the money supply. The control variable is often called an operating target, because it is the *immediate* objective of open market operations. We

[11]Table 1 shows that the volume of securities *held* under repurchase agreements at any given time is relatively small, but the number and volume of repo transactions are enormous. The reason they don't appear on the Fed's balance sheet is that repos expire and the securities are returned to their original owner.

FED MOVES ON RATES NOW TIED TO FACTORS OF TECHNICAL NATURE

CHECK CLEARING PROBLEM SEEN

Week's Increase in Money Supply Held Not Enough to Warrant Tightening of Policy

By JOHN H. ALLAN

The turmoil in the securities markets earlier this week that resulted from the perception that the Federal Reserve might have tightened monetary policy another notch may have been for nought.

That was the conclusion indicated by statistics released yesterday afternoon by the central bank at its weekly news conference. The nation's basic money supply rose $1.4 billion in the week ended Oct. 26, a fairly sizable increase but probably not enough to make the Fed change its policy.

Instead, the central bank's action last Monday appeared to be based more on offsetting some difficulty in clearing checks within the banking system.

'Float' Soars to Record

Because O'Hare Airport in Chicago was fogged in late last week, Federal Reserve "float"—extra reserves in the banking system resulting from checks in the process of collection—soared to a record $6.2 billion on Friday.

Consequently, the Fed drained reserves from the banking system on Monday by arranging so-called matched sale-purchase agreements and by selling Treasury bills for its own account.

The credit markets regard outright bill sales as something of a signal of monetary policy, and they jumped to the conclusion that the Federal Reserve was increasing short-term interest rates another notch in order to slow down what was presumed to be another big jump in the nation's money supply.

A spokesman for the New York Federal Reserve Bank described the credit markets' response to the Fed's action Monday as "fairly extreme" and acknowledged that the sale of Treasury bills "made more of an effect than it usually does."

The Federal Reserve System, he emphasized, "never tries to create such a situation; it tries to calm things."

Securities Markets Rally

Late yesterday afternoon, the Government securities markets rallied on this turn in the ongoing interpretation of the Federal Reserve's current strategy.

Still, the Fed yesterday reported that the basic money supply, which is known as M-1 and is made up of currency in circulation and mos checking-account balances, expanded to a record $334.6 billion in the latest week, while the broader money supply, known as M-2, increased $2.1 billion to average a record $801 billion.

As a result, M-1 showed an annual rate of growth over the latest 52 weeks of 7.6 percent and M-2 a 10.3 percent annual rate. Both presumably are higher than the maximums set by the Federal Reserve on Oct. 18 for the 12 months from the third quarter of 1977 to the third quarter of 1978, targets to be disclosed next Wednesday.

Since late July, the Federal Reserve has been nudging short-term interest rates higher in an effort to slow down the rate of growth of the money supply. Such growth, the monetary authorities contend, will make inflation worse.

This policy has drawn criticism from the Carter Administration and others. Yesterday, for example, Senator Hubert H. Humphrey asserted that monetary policy was not providing enough stimulus to the economy.

News Item / Even the Weather Can Cause "Defensive" Operations

New York Times, November 4, 1977

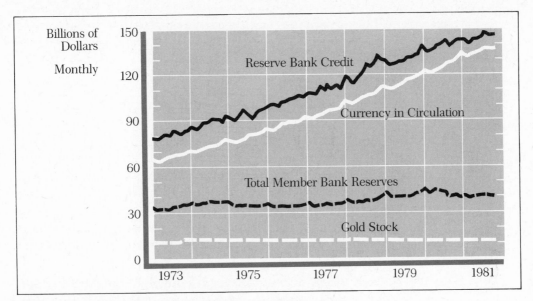

Chart 1 / Reserves and Related Items of Member Banks
SOURCE: Federal Reserve Chart Book

can show how to change Table 2 to focus on one popular alternative to bank reserves—the monetary base.

The definition of the monetary base is total reserves plus currency held by the nonbank public. The reserve equation can be altered quite easily to focus on the monetary base; just shift "currency in circulation" down to the bottom of Table 2, to join bank reserves. Then, in terms of Table 2, what we would have is (Federal Reserve credit + gold stock + Treasury currency outstanding) *less* (Treasury cash holdings + Treasury, foreign, and other deposits with the Federal Reserve Banks + miscellaneous Federal Reserve liabilities and capital) = the monetary base (i.e., member bank reserves + currency in circulation).

It is important to recognize that an open market operation, which changes the Fed's holdings of government securities in Table 2, produces a dollar for dollar change in bank reserves or the monetary base only if all the other items listed in Table 2 remain the same. Thus simply controlling the Fed's portfolio of government securities does not necessarily guarantee hitting a bank reserve or monetary base target. The advantages of alternative targets in helping the Fed achieve some goal of monetary growth will be explored in detail in the next chapter.

Summary

---

1. The main message of this chapter is that hitting a particular target for bank reserves takes a fair amount of work, planning, and coordination. The Fed cannot simply assume that changes in its holdings of government bonds will translate into reserve movements. The Fed must look at all the sources and uses of bank reserves.

2. We showed via T-accounts that all the items on the Federal Reserve's balance sheet as well as some U.S. Treasury operations have a potential effect on bank reserves. A convenient summary of the influences on bank reserves is provided by the bank reserve equation.

3. The most important item supplying reserves is U.S. government and agency securities held by the Federal Reserve. The largest alternative use of reserves is currency in circulation. Thus open market operations and the public's use of currency are key factors in the reserve equation. This does not imply, however, that the other entries can be ignored. Whenever these other factors fluctuate without warning, as float often does, there can be significant complications for the Federal Reserve.

4. The Fed maintains a particular target level of reserves by conducting *defensive* open market operations to offset movement in other items in the bank reserve equation. *Dynamic* open market operations are used to alter the overall level of reserves.

Suggestions for Further Reading

The best sources for details on the Federal Reserve's balance sheet and the factors affecting member bank reserves are Dorothy M. Nichols, *Modern Money Mechanics* (Federal Reserve Bank of Chicago, 1975), and Arthur Samansky, *Statfacts* (Federal Reserve Bank of New York, 1981). Both are available for the asking. See also Chapter 3 of *The Federal Reserve System: Purposes and Functions* (Board of Governors of the Federal Reserve System, 1974). Current and historical data can be found in the monthly *Federal Reserve Bulletin.* The distinction between defensive and dynamic open market operations was first made by Robert V. Roosa in *Federal Reserve Operations in the Money and Government Securities Markets* (Federal Reserve Bank of New York, 1956). This is still a useful booklet, but unless your library has it you are out of luck, because it is out of print.

15

Hitting
the Monetary
Targets

IN CHAPTER 13 we spoke of the important daily conference call between the manager of the System Open Market Account, located in the Federal Reserve Bank of New York, a member of the Board of Governors in Washington, D.C., and a president of one of the other Federal Reserve banks currently serving on the Federal Open Market Committee (FOMC). We have never listened in to what is said during one of these calls, but we can make a pretty good guess at the conversation, much as sports commentators are able to surmise what is said at those all-important conferences between the quarterback and his coach in the closing minutes of a game, or the even more important huddle between a pitcher and catcher with men on second and third and none out. It probably goes something like this:

OPERATOR: Kansas City and Washington are standing by, New York. Will you deposit $3.35, please?

NEW YORK: You mean it's our turn to pay? Hold on a minute, operator, we don't seem to have enough change here.

WASHINGTON: This is Chairman Volcker on the line.

NEW YORK: Sorry, there's no one here by that name.

WASHINGTON: No, you don't seem to understand, I'm Chairman Paul Volcker and I want . . .

NEW YORK: Hello, Paul. Sorry for the mix-up, but we've just hired a few Ph.D.s to man the phones, and they haven't gotten the hang of it quite yet.

WASHINGTON: I know just what you mean. Say, we've got a problem here. Our staff says the 6½ to 9 percent range for M1 should replace as the main target the 4 to 6½ percent range on M2. Or is it the other way around?

NEW YORK: Frankly, our people have urged me to look at the M3 numbers, trying to hit the fourth-quarter-to-fourth-quarter growth figures, rather than the two-month targets. They say the M1 ball game is over.

KANSAS CITY: Hello? Hello? When do we start?

As we said, we've never listened in, but the implication that the Federal Reserve is preoccupied with money supply targets is certainly authentic, and so is the uncertainty over precisely which monetary objective to shoot for. Ultimately, of course, the Fed is concerned with the performance of the economy—inflation, economic growth, and so on. But it uses money supply targets as a guideline in measuring the initial impact of its actions.

In the preceding three chapters we described who runs the Federal Reserve, the tools at the Fed's disposal, and the way Federal Reserve actions influence bank reserves. It is now time to put it all together to see how well the Federal Reserve meets its obligations. First, we take a more detailed look at the formulation of policy through what is known as the Federal Open Market Committee's directive. Second, we review the reasons for the particular "monetary aggregate" game plan that is followed. We then analyze the linkages between Fed operating targets and the money supply objectives. At the end we should have a pretty good idea of why the Fed sometimes has trouble hitting its targets.

The FOMC Directive

The FOMC meets in Washington about once every four weeks. At the beginning of each meeting the staff of the FOMC, comprising economists from the Board of Governors and the district Federal Reserve Banks, presents a review of recent economic and financial developments—what is happening to prices, unemployment, the balance of payments, interest rates, money supply, bank credit, and so on. Projections are also made for the months ahead. The meeting then proceeds to a discussion among the committee members; each expresses his or her views on the current economic and financial scene and proposes appropriate monetary policies.

The FOMC directive, embodying the committee's decision on the direction of monetary policy until the next meeting, is voted on toward the end of each meeting, with dissents recorded for posterity. If economic conditions are proceeding as expected the month before, and the current stance of monetary policy is still appropriate, the previous directive may remain unaltered. If conditions change, the directive is modified accordingly.

In recent years, the FOMC directive has usually contained five or six paragraphs. The first few review economic and financial developments, including the behavior of real output, inflation, monetary aggregates, and interest rates. The fourth or fifth paragraph then turns to a general qualitative statement of current policy goals. For example, at the last meeting of 1981, on December 21 and 22, the goals of the FOMC were set forth as follows:

> The Federal Open Market Committee seeks to foster monetary and financial conditions that will help to reduce inflation, promote a resumption of growth in output on a sustainable basis, and contribute to a sustainable pattern of international transactions.

While the statement of goals does not contain everything—we know that the FOMC is not trying to eliminate highway fatalities (at least not yet)—it does include virtually every objective of stabilization policy. This general statement of goals is rarely changed significantly. Toward the end of 1975, for example, when the country was in a deep recession, the phrase "encouraging economic expansion" replaced "to reduce inflation" as the first goal mentioned.

Immediately following this general statement, the directive presents long-run target ranges for the monetary aggregates that are thought to be consistent with the broadly stated goals. At the meeting of December 21, 1981, the annual targets were stated as follows:

The FOMC discusses its next step.

The Committee also tentatively agreed that for the period from the fourth quarter of 1981 to the fourth quarter of 1982 growth of M1, M2, and M3 within ranges of 2½ to 5½ percent, 6 to 9 percent, and 6½ to 9½ percent respectively, would be appropriate.

There are two important points to recognize in this statement. First, the goals for the monetary aggregates are stated for M1, M2, and M3, rather than focusing on a single measure of money supply. Second, the target growth ranges for each monetary aggregate are rather broad. These sources of flexibility reflect the Fed's uncertainty over the precise linkages between the monetary aggregates and the ultimate goals of policy.

The last order of business in the FOMC directive is to specify the immediate prescription for implementing these longer-run objectives. In that December 1981 meeting, the immediate targets were described:

> In the short run the Committee seeks behavior of reserve aggregates consistent with growth of M1 and M2 from November 1981 to March 1982 at annual rates of around 4 to 5 percent and 9 to 10 percent, respectively ... The Chairman may call for Committee consultation if it appears that pursuit of the monetary objectives and reserve paths ... is likely to be associated with a federal funds rate persistently outside the range of 10 to 14 percent.

Two points are worth emphasizing here. First, we now have money supply targets that are specified over a shorter time horizon. These targets usually set two-month growth rates for M1 and M2 that are designed to take into account "special events" that might call for deviations from the annual objectives. For example, previous shortfalls or overshooting in the annual growth paths are counteracted over these shorter intervals.

The second point to note is that while the Fed's short-run objectives are still couched in terms of money supply growth, the directive also mentions reserve targets to implement the desired growth in the aggregates. Thus in outlining its so-called operating targets, the Committee states (somewhat mysteriously) that behavior of reserve aggregates should be consistent with targeted money supply growth. The numerical reserve targets are not disclosed publicly with any greater precision; yet they are the focal point of the Fed's operating targets.

As we will see below, a number of other reserve targets are available, including total reserves, nonborrowed reserves, and even the broader monetary base. But the Fed never lets on exactly how much growth it would like to see in any particular measure. It keeps its options open because it is not quite certain about precisely how much reserve growth will produce the desired path in money supply.

The emphasis in this 1981 FOMC directive is clearly on the monetary and reserve aggregates. It wasn't always that way. Until the 1970s the Fed paid most of its attention to interest rates and money market conditions. The only surviving reference from that era is the specification of an expected range for the prevailing federal funds rate in the last line of the directive. Obviously the federal funds rate has been eclipsed by reserve targets; but it is plain to see that it has not disappeared totally. And this is not too surprising since the Fed's impact on reserves is simultaneously transmitted to the federal funds market, as we shall see in a moment.

The Fed's Strategy

Chart 1 summarizes the FOMC game plan as described in the directive. Notice that the ultimate goals are separated from the Fed's tools by two sets of intervening targets. These reserve and monetary targets are more immediately responsive to Federal Reserve actions than the ultimate goals of inflation and unemployment. Fed officials believe that by formulating these intermediate steps they can more easily and quickly judge whether they are on the right track, compared with waiting for a signal from overall economic activity. As

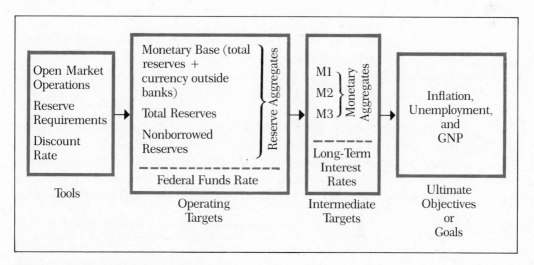

Chart 1 / The Fed's Game Plan

long as the linkages work reasonably well, it makes sense to use the intervening objectives.[1]

The Fed's plan is established in the following way (more or less): First, the rate of growth in GNP that is most consistent with the inflation/unemployment objective for the year is decided upon. Then the Fed sets the range for monetary growth that is expected to generate the target rate of GNP growth. Given that desired range for monetary growth—say 4 to 6 percent for M1—the Fed then sets a target range for the growth in reserves—say 3 to 5 percent—which will produce the desired rate of growth in money.

The key to the usefulness of both operating and intermediate targets rests with the connecting linkages on each side: from the tools to operating targets, from the operating targets to the intermediate targets, and finally to the ultimate goals. Each of these steps has been fraught with controversy in the past. In fact, in each of the target boxes in Chart 1 there is a list of alternative objectives that can be pursued. The operating targets include several possible reserve measures, while the intermediate targets list the conventional measures of money supply. In addition, below the dashed line in each of the boxes, the interest rate alternatives to the reserve and monetary aggregates are included as well. The advantages and disadvantages of these alternatives will be discussed in the next two sections.

Operating Targets: Reserves and the Federal Funds Market

Since October 1979, the Fed has focused its attention on reserves as the operating target. In particular, the first linkage in Chart 1 is between the Fed's tools and the level of reserves. Thus open market operations, the bread and butter of Fed policy, are executed so that a given level of reserves are made available to the banking system.

[1]For a contrary view on the value of such signals, see Benjamin M. Friedman, "The Inefficiency of Short-Run Monetary Targets for Monetary Policy," *Brookings Papers on Economic Activity,* No. 2, 1977.

In fact, using the reserve equation discussed in Chapter 14, the Fed buys or sells government securities (or does nothing) so that the net change in reserves on any day meets its objective. Presumably these reserves will be used by banks to support checking account balances, as described in Chapter 3.

Although this sounds like a fairly sensible procedure, it wasn't always the way the Fed played the game. Until October 1979, the impact on the interest rate in the federal funds market was the most important consideration in planning open market operations, at least in the short run. Since the federal funds market still reflects the initial impact of Fed policy, it is worth spending a few moments explaining in more detail how it works. Moreover, as we saw in the directive, even now the federal funds rate is viewed as something of a guideline for Fed policy.

Federal funds are immediately available funds that are loaned overnight between banks. Thus, in the simplest case, if Banc One (Columbus, Ohio) needs reserves, and First Third (Cincinnati) has an excess, then First Third can "sell" reserves to Banc One for immediate delivery. The reserves will be transferred on the books of the Federal Reserve System today, and will be returned tomorrow, unless another transaction is made. The interest rate charged on such overnight transactions is called the federal funds rate.[2] While federal funds are now used by banks for many purposes besides simple reserve adjustments (see the section on liability management in Chapter 8), our focus here is the way the federal funds rate reflects Fed pressure on bank reserves.

A simple example is as follows. Suppose the Fed sells securities because it wants to reduce bank reserves. If a customer of Banc One bought the securities, the bank will lose reserves. Its first response usually will be to replenish the reserves by an overnight purchase in the federal funds market. Since the Fed has made reserves less available, Banc One's efforts will force up the federal funds rate; the

[2]Alternatively, an overnight transfer of reserves can occur with a sale of government securities and an agreement to repurchase them (at a higher price, to reflect the interest rate) on the following day. The so-called "repo" market is closely linked with the federal funds market since they are both sources of overnight funds. In the rest of this discussion, we use the federal funds rate to represent all sources of overnight funds.

demand for reserves in the federal funds market will exceed the supply and the price (the interest rate) is pushed up.

Obviously, in this case the Fed's objective of reducing reserves is synonymous with an increased federal funds rate. The problem with using the federal funds rate as a target stems from the fact that it can sometimes induce inappropriate Federal Reserve actions. For example, suppose First Third is confronted with an increased demand for loans associated with an inflationary surge in economic activity. When the loan is made and demand deposits are created, First Third needs reserves. It turns to the federal funds market, where its efforts to borrow push up the rate. In this case, if the Federal Reserve had established a federal funds rate guideline, it would be induced to expand reserves to meet the demand. While this action would keep the federal funds rate on target, it would accommodate an inflationary surge in bank reserves.

Using a federal funds rate target didn't have to produce such mistakes. But the fact of the matter is that the procedure is prone to error, especially in an economy that is full of surprise shifts in demand for money and credit. Thus, beginning in October 1979, the Federal Reserve changed its focus to reserve targets, letting the federal funds rate find its own level—more or less. The cost has been greater fluctuations in the federal funds rate. And since the federal funds rate forms the base cost of funds to the financial system, other interest rates have become more volatile as well, as can be seen in Chart 2. The benefit, presumably, has been greater accuracy in monitoring the desired level of bank reserves. And that is important for controlling the money supply.

This brings us to the second linkage in the Fed's game plan—between reserves as the operating target and the various measures of money supply as intermediate targets. For those of you who still remember Chapter 3, there seems little cause for concern in this area. After all, we showed that demand deposits were a fixed multiple of total bank reserves. Therefore, as long as the Fed hits its reserves operating target there is little that can interfere with its M1 objective.

In point of fact, there are two major problem areas. First, the Federal Reserve is not able to control total reserves precisely. As we saw in Chapter 12, for example, banks can borrow reserves from their regional Federal Reserve Banks. Discounting adds to reserves just as open market operations do; but discounting is at the individual bank's initiative rather than the Fed's. Thus either First Third, Banc One, or even Chase, Citibank, or Continental Illinois can generate an increase in total reserves to support deposits. The Fed discourages such borrowing either by raising the discount rate or, after some demonstrated abuse, by refusing to lend to the offending bank. In the meantime, however, the level of reserves goes off track.

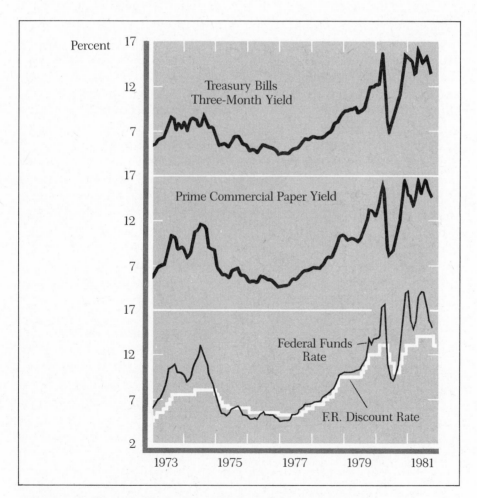

Chart 2 / Increased Volatility in Interest Rates Since 1979

The FOMC recognizes this problem, but still sets its reserve targets in terms of nonborrowed reserves—that is, total reserves less borrowed reserves. When borrowings balloon the total, the Fed uses its considerable influence to force banks to cut back. Of course, until the reduction is complete, the borrowed reserves can support a larger money supply than is consistent with Fed objectives.

The second problem in the linkage between the reserve operating target and the intermediate money supply objective has to do with instability in the multiplier relationship between reserves and deposits. The discussion back in Chapter 3 showed that demand deposits were equal to total reserves multiplied by the inverse of the required reserves ratio. But even there we hinted that the reserve multiplier might not be that stable. For example, if banks don't make loans based on all of their reserves, but hold some reserves in excess of what is required, the multiple expansion in deposits is cut short. More important, different sizes of banks have different required reserve ratios, as we noted in Chapter 13. Thus the volume of deposits that a given level of reserves can support depends, in part, on the mix of deposits between different classes of banks. Moreover, to the extent that the public withdraws currency from the banking system, the process of deposit creation with a given level of initial reserves is short-circuited; banks lose reserves dollar for dollar when currency leaks out of the system (see the T-accounts in Chapter 14). Finally, if M1 is the intermediate target, the reserve multiplier may be relatively simple, while if M2 or M3 is the preferred monetary aggregate (for reasons given in the next section), the reserve multiplier linkage may be much more complicated and even less predictable.

The details of various multiplier relationships are developed in the Appendix to this chapter. At this point it is sufficient to emphasize that the fixed multiplier approach is not quite the way the world works. A given level of total reserves can support more or less deposits depending upon (1) the mix of deposits with different reserve requirements; (2) the propensity of banks to hold excess reserves; and (3) the leakage of reserves into currency. In fact, the currency drain has led some critics to propose that the Fed focus its attention on the sum of reserves plus currency—the monetary base.

The truth is that the difference between total reserves and the monetary base as the operating target is less important than either of these versus nonborrowed reserves. The reason is that bank borrowings expand precisely when the Fed tries to contract reserves; similarly, borrowings contract precisely when the Fed tries to expand reserves. As we saw in Chapter 13, bank borrowings respond to the spread between the federal funds rate relative to the discount rate. Federal Reserve open market sales to reduce reserves push up the federal funds rate, sending banks scurrying to the discount window to pick up cheap funds. Thus closer control over total reserves requires some tinkering with the discount mechanism.[3] Until that happens, we'll just have to live with some slippage between Fed actions to control reserves and the induced impact on the monetary aggregates.[4]

Intermediate Targets: Which Money Supply?

It seems, from our discussion thus far, that the Fed has more than its share of trouble trying to control its reserve target. Unfortunately, this is only part of the story. The Fed must use its reserve target to hit a money supply objective. In Table 1 of Chapter 1 we described four series the Fed uses to monitor the money supply: M1, M2, M3, and L. Three of these measures, M1, M2, and M3, appear as potential intermediate targets in the chart we just looked at describing the Fed's game plan. The reason L is ruled out of our picture is that many of the items in L (Treasury bills, commercial paper, savings bonds) are totally unrelated to the level of reserves provided by the Federal Reserve, so the Fed cannot even try to control the L aggregate. And controllability is the first requirement of a good intermediate target.

The second requirement of an intermediate target is that it be closely linked with the ultimate goals of inflation and unemploy-

---

[3]There have been proposals to make the discount rate a true penalty rate; for example, it could be set at one percent above the federal funds rate. Thus far the Federal Reserve has resisted this logical solution, primarily out of historical sentiment (although the Fed always seems to give a fancier reason).
[4]A system of lagged rather than contemporaneous reserve accounting was in effect between 1968 and 1982, and that further complicated the relationship between reserves and money supply.

ment—or, more practically, the rate of growth in GNP. On this score, the potential for controversy lies in the linkages between the financial sector and real spending decisions. Both the theory and the empirical evidence for these linkages are discussed at length in Part IV. At this point we need only to recall the discussion in Chapter 1 about the velocity of money—the rate at which money balances are spent on real goods and services. The greater the stability and predictability of the velocity of a particular measure of the money supply, the better that monetary aggregate is as an intermediate target.

In the good old days, this used to be a relatively straightforward proposition. M1, consisting of currency and checking accounts, was widely acknowledged as the best measure of immediately spendable funds. Hence the linkage between M1 and GNP was accepted as the most reliable relationship between a financial aggregate and spending; hence, M1 was the best monetary target. But the growth of savings deposits and time deposits as close substitutes for checking accounts forced many economists to reconsider their devotion to the M1 definition. As far back as the mid-1950s, John Gurley and Edward Shaw, Keynesian economists at Stanford, popularized the notion that the deposit liabilities of savings and loan associations, mutual savings banks, and other financial intermediaries (see Chapter 7) must be monitored in order to get an accurate fix on whether monetary policy was expansionary or contractionary.[4] In recent years, with still newer financial instruments on the scene, the Gurley-Shaw argument would favor either the M2 or M3 definition of money. For somewhat different reasons, Milton Friedman has long advocated that both commercial bank demand deposits and savings deposits paint a better monetary picture than M1 alone. On the other hand, Monetarists Karl Brunner and Allan Meltzer have favored the narrower definition of money.[5]

---

[4]A theoretical treatment of their arguments is found in *Money in a Theory of Finance* (Washington, D.C.: Brookings Institution, 1960).

[5]For Friedman's views see M. Friedman and A. Schwartz, *A Monetary History of the United States* (Princeton University Press, 1963). Brunner's arguments appear in "The Role of Money and Monetary Policy," Federal Reserve Bank of St. Louis *Monthly Review* (July 1968) and Meltzer's view is in "The Demand for Money: The Evidence from the Time Series," *Journal of Political Economy* (June 1963).

The Fed has tried to measure the relative "moneyness" of M1, M2, and M3, as well as statistically isolating which has the closest linkage with GNP.[6] In an admirable demonstration of ecumenicism, however, the Fed lists all three definitions—M1, M2, and M3—as its intermediate targets.

There may be differences over the favored monetary aggregate, but there is agreement within the Federal Reserve System that focusing on the so-called aggregates as the intermediate target is superior to an interest rate objective. Thus the Fed does not consider the level of long-term interest rates on government, corporate, and other private debt a viable intermediate target for monetary policy. This is an apparent victory for Monetarist thinking over Keynesian analysis, as we will see in Part IV. We have, nevertheless, included long-term interest rates below the dashed line in the intermediate target box of Chart 1 to emphasize that they have been, and still are, a potential contact point between Fed activities and the ultimate goals of policy. In fact, it is useful to review the reason for the victory of the monetary aggregates over the level of interest rates, because you can never tell when interest rates will make a comeback; and then we'll know what we have to worry about.

The main virtue of using a monetary aggregate target is that it helps to insulate automatically the overall level of economic activity from unanticipated shifts in business or consumer spending. Thus if the Fed's ultimate goal is some level of nominal GNP that reflects its desired inflation/unemployment combination, pursuit of a monetary aggregate target will help to sustain that level of economic activity from uncontrolled shifts in spending. Let's look at an example of how the monetary aggregate target automatically provides stability compared with the interest rate target.

Suppose there is a burst of unanticipated investment spending because businessmen expect higher prices next year. As long as reserves and the money supply are kept on target, the jump in business demand for credit to carry out the spending plans will cause interest rates to rise. This will force others to rethink their spending plans, thereby mitigating the inflationary burst in the economy. But if the Fed had targeted on interest rates, then the unanticipated

[6]For trial investigations, see "A Proposal for Redefining the Monetary Aggregates," *Federal Reserve Bulletin* (January 1979).

jump in interest rates would require the Fed to push them back down again. Thus the Fed would be led to supply more bank reserves to support a higher level of money supply, thereby sanctioning an inflationary jump in economic activity. Thus interest rate targets are poor protection against unanticipated changes in real spending decisions.[7]

Congress is sufficiently impressed by the need to focus on the monetary aggregates to require the Federal Reserve to testify regarding its target growth rates for various measures of the money supply. Twice a year Fed representatives appear before the House and Senate Banking Committees to explain planned monetary objectives and to review recent results. Let's see how the Fed performed in 1981.

The Fed's Track Record

Judging whether the Federal Reserve has hit its monetary target would seem, at first glance, to be a fairly straightforward proposition. First you see what the Fed said it would do; you then compare that with what happened; and *voilà*—pass or fail, depending upon whether the Fed hit the bull's-eye. To see why things are not that simple requires some attention to the nitty-gritty details.

As we saw in the FOMC directive, the Fed sets target *ranges* for monetary growth. And in the past, these ranges have been rather wide, reflecting, no doubt, the well-known proverb: Big Target Means Sharp Shooter. Should the Fed be judged on whether it gets inside the rather broad ranges established for monetary growth, or should deviations from the mid-point be the relevant criterion? Second, the Fed sets both annual and two-month growth targets for M1,

[7]An interest rate target would, however, insulate the economy from unanticipated shifts in the demand for money. For example, if people reduced their cash balances and started to spend more, the declining demand for money would push down interest rates. The Fed would cut back on reserves and money supply if it were following an interest rate target, which is precisely what it should do to keep spending from accelerating. In this case, the interest rate target insulates the economy from unanticipated shifts in money demand. The victory of the money supply strategy stems from the belief that money demand is more predictable than business investment plans.

M2, and so on. Should their performance be based on the shorter- or longer-run objectives? Third, growth rates are notoriously sensitive to the starting point, the so-called base period. Should the growth in money during the year be measured from the average level of the previous year to the average level of the current year, or should it be measured from the fourth quarter of the previous year to the fourth quarter of the current year (which reflects the growth that took place *during* the current year)?

The proper answer to these questions should reflect the sensitivity of the ultimate goals of Fed policy to the errors implied by each measure. Since there is no consensus on this matter, we present the results according to the Fed's own preferred procedures.

Chart 3 shows the record for M1 and M2 during 1981.[8] The target annual rates of growth are fourth-quarter-to-fourth-quarter comparisons. Thus the target ranges appear in the picture as two rays emanating from the average level of the money supply during the fourth quarter of 1980. The lower line represents the lower limit on money growth and the upper line represents the higher limit. Thus for M1 there are target ranges of 3½ to 6 percent, while for M2 the growth targets are between 6 and 9 percent. The jagged line in each graph shows the actual path for M1 and M2 during 1981. Obviously the Fed missed both targets: M1 growth (at 2.3 percent) fell below the lower limit, and M2 growth (at 9.4 percent) was above the upper limit.

The variability in actual M1 and M2 growth during the course of the year seems just about as disturbing as missing the annual targets. This is especially true for M1, which actually declined for a while in the beginning of 1981, surged upward before mid-year, then took a nose dive, and finally ended the year on a space-flight trajectory.

The Fed explains these shortcomings in a number of ways. First, the stop-go growth pattern in money is not necessarily damaging to the economy as long as the shortfalls are temporary and the excesses are reversed. Second, while M1 growth during 1981 was deficient, that shortfall was balanced by the excess in M2 growth. Thus a broad consideration of the monetary aggregates leaves a better

---

[8]The chart is based on testimony by Paul Volcker before the Committee on Banking, Housing, and Urban Affairs, U.S. Senate, February 11, 1982.

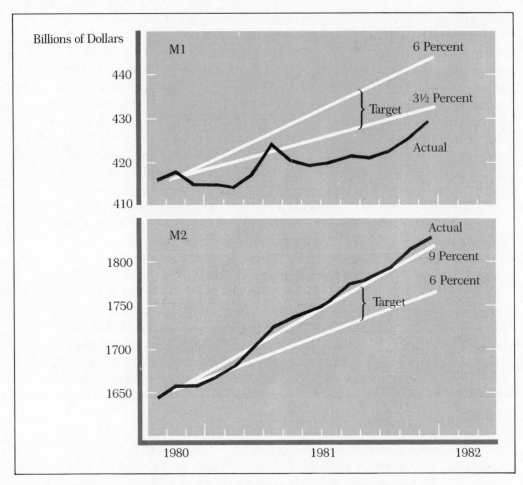

Chart 3 / Projected and Actual Growth Ranges for 1981

impression than a literal reading of each bit of evidence in isolation.

Congress, which is the ultimate judge of Fed performance, has so far not been terribly upset by the Fed's apparent imprecision. Were the committees convinced by the Fed's defense? Possibly. But a more likely explanation is that if monetary events turn out to precipitate a disaster, Congress will need a convenient scapegoat. And the Federal Reserve might fill that role quite well.

Summary

1. The Federal Reserve's strategy for implementing monetary policy is summarized in a directive issued about once a month by the Federal Open Market Committee. Operating targets for reserves are set so that the Fed can best hit its intermediate money supply targets. The money supply objectives are supposed to implement the Fed's ultimate goals in terms of inflation and unemployment.

2. The ideal operating target should be immediately responsive to such Fed tools as open market operations, and should link rather closely with the money supply. The Fed currently uses nonborrowed reserves as its operating objective; a stronger case can be made for focusing on total reserves (or the monetary base).

3. The federal funds rate reflects the initial thrust of changes in bank reserves. While the interest rate on federal funds used to be the main operating target, it often gave off unreliable signals. It was replaced in October 1979 by a reserve-based operating target.

4. The connection between reserves and the money supply is not quite as simple as Chapter 3's reserve multiplier would suggest. Currency drains and shifts among deposit classes complicate matters (see the Appendix to this chapter), as does the ability of banks to borrow at the discount window.

5. Focus on the monetary aggregates as intermediate targets stems from the stability and predictability of their linkage with overall economic activity. While the choice between M1, M2, and M3 as the best intermediate target is still open to debate, the Fed has clearly decided against an interest rate objective at this stage.

6. The Fed has not been terribly precise in hitting its money supply objectives, even after switching to reserve targeting since October 1979. Perhaps their execution will improve with practice.

Suggestions for Further Reading

A detailed study of everything you ever wanted to know about the monetary control procedures of the Fed is contained in a two-volume analysis entitled *New Monetary Control Procedures* (Board of Governors of the Federal Reserve System, February 1981). For those of you who don't want to read all of that, a nice review of the magnum opus (plural: opera) is the *Review Essay* by Stephen M. Goldfeld in the *Journal of Money, Credit and Banking* (February 1982). In addition, that particular issue of the *Journal of Money, Credit and Banking* contains an interesting debate on Fed policy: "Is the Federal Reserve's Monetary Control Policy Misdirected? A Debate," by Allan Meltzer, Robert Rasche, Stephen Axilrod, and Peter Sternlight. Finally, a summary of the Fed's strategy appears in Stephen Axilrod, "Monetary Policy, Money Supply and the Federal Reserve's Operating Procedures," *Federal Reserve Bulletin* (January 1982).

The literature on controlling the monetary aggregates is now in its third generation: see *Controlling Monetary Aggregates III* (Federal Reserve Bank of Boston, October 1980). A great deal of useful background material on targets and indicators is contained in *Improving the Monetary Aggregates: Report of the Advisory Committee on Monetary Statistics* (Board of Governors of the Federal Reserve System, June 1976); and "A Proposal for Redefining the Monetary Aggregates," *Federal Reserve Bulletin* (January 1979). The final definition of the aggregates (so far) is "The Redefined Monetary Aggregates," *Federal Reserve Bulletin* (February 1980).

The seminal article comparing the advantages and disadvantages of money supply targets versus interest rates is William Poole, "Optimal Choice of Monetary Policy Instruments in a Simple Stochastic Macro Model," *Quarterly Journal of Economics* (May 1970). For an English translation of the mathematics, see Poole's "Rules of Thumb for Guiding Monetary Policy" in *Open Market Policies and Operating Procedures,* Board of Governors of the Federal Reserve System (July 1971).

Appendix

Linking Money Supply and Reserves

The discussion of reserve multipliers in Chapter 3 suggested that it would be fairly easy for the Fed to generate just about any money supply it wanted. In this chapter we indicated that our earlier treatment was too naïve. We now show precisely where the complications arise.

By way of review, in terms of our formula from Chapter 3, a change in bank reserves (ΔR) times the reciprocal of the demand deposit reserve ratio (r_{dd}) gives us the maximum potential change in demand deposits (ΔDD). Say the reserve requirement against demand deposits is 15 percent and the Fed increases bank reserves by $1,000:

$$\Delta R \times \frac{1}{r_{dd}} = \Delta DD$$

$$\Delta R \times \frac{1}{.15} = \Delta DD$$

$$\Delta R \times 6\frac{2}{3} = \Delta DD$$

$$\$1,000 \times 6\frac{2}{3} = \$6,667$$

The actual change in demand deposits will reach the maximum of $6,667 as long as banks lend out all of their excess reserves. If we were to draw up a consolidated T-account for the entire banking system following this $1,000 injection of reserves, showing the changes that take place in the balance sheets of all banks taken together, our formula tells us it would look like this:

Final Position, All Banks Taken Together
($1,000 change in reserves; r_{dd} = 15 percent)

A		L & NW	
Reserves (cash + deposit in Fed)	+$1,000	Demand deposits	+$6,667
Loans and securities	+ 5,667		

But this is just the first approximation. Looking a bit deeper, we find that fundamental difficulties face the Fed in its efforts to control the money supply, even with such precision-like formulae. These problems can be categorized into three main complications.

1. *The simple case abstracts from the fact that, as demand deposits expand, the public is likely to want to hold part of its increased money supply in the form of currency.* When people need more currency, they simply go to their bank and cash a check. On the bank's balance sheet, both cash (an asset) and demand deposits (a liability) fall. The bank's excess reserves also fall by 85 percent of the withdrawal, assuming a 15 percent reserve ratio.

Notice that a $100 currency withdrawal does not directly change the public's money holdings; it simply switches $100 from demand deposits to dollar bills, leaving the total money supply unaltered. But it *does* deplete bank excess reserves by $85, because a $100 demand deposit uses up only $15 in reserves, whereas a $100 cash withdrawal subtracts a full $100 of reserves (remember that cash in bank vaults counts as reserves). Draining of currency into the hands of the public thus depletes bank reserves dollar for dollar and thereby cuts back the expansion potential of the banking system.

Let's assume that for every $1 in demand deposits, the public wants currency holdings of about 30 cents. That is, the ratio of currency to demand deposits (c/dd) is about 30 percent. This, of course, alters our demand deposit expansion formula. It is fairly easy to see the changes that are necessary: What we have to do is incorporate the currency/demand deposit ratio into the formula.

We continue to assume that banks lend out all their excess reserves. We saw in Chapter 3 that demand deposits could expand until all excess reserves become required reserves (because of deposit growth)—that is, until the demand deposit reserve requirement (r_{dd}) times the growth in demand deposits (ΔDD) equals the change in reserves (ΔR). But now, when reserves rise initially by ΔR, not only will they be absorbed by demand deposit growth, but in addition some of these reserves will *leave* the banking system as the public holds more currency (equal to c/dd times the growth in demand deposits). Although banks will still expand their demand deposits until all reserves are in the required category, *they will be unable to retain all of the initial change in reserves.* Since the initial injection of reserves eventually winds up as either required reserves or as currency held by the public, we have:

$$\Delta R = (r_{dd} \times \Delta DD) + (c/dd \times \Delta DD)$$

Factoring out the ΔDDs gives us:

$$\Delta R = (r_{dd} + c/dd) \times \Delta DD$$

and finally:

$$\Delta R \times \frac{1}{r_{dd} + c/dd} = \Delta DD$$

where the *initial change* in reserves (ΔR) is no longer fully retained within the banking system, because part leaks out into currency holdings outside the system. This total—reserves plus currency outside the banks—is the *monetary base* (B). When the Federal Reserve injects reserves, it is really adding to the monetary base, since some of these reserves will shift over into the form of currency holdings outside the banking system.

Let us now return, with our new formula, to our illustrative example. Assume a currency/demand deposit ratio of 30 percent, along with our 15 percent demand deposit reserve requirement, and our familiar injection of $1,000 of reserves by the Fed. However, due to the currency drain, the $1,000 of additional reserves are not all kept by the banks, so that in our new formula we should properly refer to a $1,000 increase in the monetary base (B) rather than reserves. What we get, after all is said and done, is a multiple expansion potential for demand deposits that is considerably smaller than before—now it is not 6.67, but only 2.22:[1]

$$\Delta B \times \frac{1}{r_{dd} + c/dd} = \Delta DD$$

$$\Delta B \times \frac{1}{.15 + .30} = \Delta DD$$

$$\Delta B \times \frac{1}{.45} = \Delta DD$$

$$\Delta B \times 2.22 = \Delta DD$$

$$\$1,000 \times 2.22 = \$2,222$$

Now an initial $1,000 injection of reserves produces an eventual maximum increase in demand deposits of only $2,222. If we again drew up a consolidated T-account for all banks, following a $1,000 initial boost to reserves, the final results would look like this:

Final Position, All Banks Taken Together
($1,000 initial change in reserves; r_{dd} = 15 percent;
and now adding cash drain: c/dd = 30 percent)

A		L & NW
Reserves (cash + deposit in Fed)	+ $333	Demand deposits + $2,222
Loans and securities	+ 1,889	

Memorandum: currency drain (i.e., currency outside the banks, held by the public): + $667

Notice that, because of the currency drain, the banking system *retains* as reserves only $333 of the original $1,000. With a 15 per-

[1]This multiplier is strictly correct only if ΔB is initially all reserves.

cent reserve requirement, this can support demand deposits of only $2,222. The other $667 has moved *out* of the banking system into the hands of the general public, on the premise that the public wants to hold 30 cents more currency when it gets $1 more demand deposits (667 = 30% of 2,222).

The total change in the M1 measure of the *money supply* due to the *initial* change in reserves (= change in the monetary base) is the sum of the change in demand deposits and the change in currency. We have just seen that currency goes up by 30 percent of 2,222, or more generally:

$$\Delta \text{ currency} = c/dd \times \Delta DD = c/dd \times \frac{1}{r_{dd} + c/dd} \times \Delta B$$

Hence, the total change in the money supply (ΔM) due to the initial change in reserves is:

$$\Delta M = \Delta DD + \Delta \text{currency}$$

$$= \frac{1}{r_{dd} + c/dd} \times \Delta B + \frac{c/dd}{r_{dd} + c/dd} \times \Delta B$$

which simplifies to:

$$\Delta M = \frac{1 + c/dd}{r_{dd} + c/dd} \times \Delta B$$

Using our numbers, the money supply multiplier is 2.889:

$$\Delta M = 2.889 \times \$1,000 = \$2,889$$

which is $2,222 in demand deposits and $667 in currency. This formula relating the change in money supply to an initial change in reserves is a lot more complicated than the simple inverse of the required reserve ratio derived in Chapter 3.

2. *In the second place, we have to recognize that banks have time deposits as well as demand deposits among their liabilities, and that these also require reserves.* To see how this affects the deposit multiplier, let's assume a reserve requirement on such deposits of 3 percent. While this is not as large as the reserve requirement against demand deposits, it does serve to absorb bank reserves and thereby further reduces the demand deposit expansion potential of

the system. Assume further that the public wants to hold a ratio of commercial bank time deposits to demand deposits (sd/dd) of about two to one. Since the reserve requirement against such deposits (r_{sd}) averages 3 percent, this has to affect our demand deposit expansion formula. Using the same logic as before, the new demand deposit multiplier turns out to be 1.961:[2]

$$\Delta B \times \frac{1}{r_{dd} + c/dd + sd/dd\ (r_{sd})} = \Delta DD$$

$$\Delta B \times \frac{1}{.15 + .30 + 2(.03)} = \Delta DD$$

$$\Delta B \times \frac{1}{.15 + .30 + .06} = \Delta DD$$

$$\Delta B \times \frac{1}{.51} = \Delta DD$$

$$\Delta B \times 1.961 = \Delta DD$$

$$\$1,000 \times 1.961 = \$1,961$$

[2]The derivation is as follows: The initial injection of reserves (ΔB) now gets absorbed by required reserves against demand deposits $(r_{dd} \times \Delta DD)$; by currency $(c/dd \times \Delta DD)$; and by required reserves against time deposits. The increase in time deposits (ΔSD) equals $sd/dd \times \Delta DD$, and reserves against time deposits equal $r_{sd} \times sd/dd \times \Delta DD$. Therefore, we have:

$$\Delta B = (r_{dd} \times \Delta DD) + (c/dd \times \Delta DD) + (sd/dd \times r_{sd} \times \Delta DD)$$

Factoring out the ΔDDs gives us:

$$\Delta B = [r_{dd} + c/dd + (sd/dd \times r_{sd})] \times \Delta DD$$

and finally:

$$\Delta B \times \frac{1}{r_{dd} + c/dd + (sd/dd)(r_{sd})} = \Delta DD$$

We can extend this expression to the M1 measure of the money supply as a whole (not just demand deposits) by adding the increase in currency in circulation to the increase in demand deposits:

$$\Delta M = \Delta DD + \Delta \text{currency} = \frac{1}{r_{dd} + c/dd + (sd/dd)\,(r_{sd})} \times \Delta B +$$

$$\frac{c/dd}{r_{dd} + c/dd + (sd/dd)\,(r_{sd})} \times \Delta B$$

which simplifies to:

$$\Delta M = \frac{1 + c/dd}{r_{dd} + c/dd + (sd/dd)\,(r_{sd})} \times \Delta B$$

If you work it out, you'll find that this yields an M1 money supply multiplier of 2.549.

The consolidated bank T-account for an initial $1,000 reserve increase under these circumstances is interesting:

Final Position, All Banks Taken Together
($1,000 initial change in reserves; $r_{dd} = 15$ percent;
currency drain $c/dd = 30$ percent; and now adding
time deposit growth: $sd/dd = 2$ and
$r_{sd} = 3$ percent)

A		L & NW	
Reserves (cash + deposit in Fed)	+ $412	Demand deposits	+ $1,961
For dem. deposits: + $ 294			
For sav. deposits: + 118			
Loans and securities	+ 5,471	Savings deposits	+ 3,922

Memorandum: currency drain (i.e., currency outside the banks, held by the public): + $588 (= 30% of $1,961)

These results—less demand deposits but more total deposits and more bank lending compared with the previous T-account—reflect two things. The currency drain is now less, so the banking system is retaining more reserves. (The currency drain is less even though the *c/dd* ratio is the same, because currency outflows depend on the growth of demand deposits only.) And time deposits, while they use up reserves and thereby inhibit potential demand deposit expansion, do not remove reserves from the banking system the way currency drains do; with time deposits, banks can continue lending, and indeed can lend even *more* than with an equivalent amount of demand deposits, because the reserve requirement against time deposits is lower. This suggests that the reserve multiplier consequences for broader money supply definitions are still more complicated than for M1.

3. *Finally, a last complication: We have been assuming that all banks are willing to expand their loans (or securities purchases) up to the full amount of their excess reserves.* This may not always be so. If some banks don't lend all their excess reserves (perhaps because they cannot find enough creditworthy borrowers), and don't buy additional securities (perhaps because they expect bond prices to fall), the whole sequence of lending and demand deposit creation cannot reach its theoretical maximum.

Banks that do not fully expand their loans won't lose all their excess reserves to other banks, so the other banks will be unable to lend as much. In addition, banks that do lend are likely to lose some reserves to the nonlenders, thereby rendering such reserves immobile. Thus the potential multiple can be realized only if *all* banks are willing to lend and/or buy securities up to the *full* amount of their excess reserves.

In the 1930s idle excess reserves were plentiful. In the past two decades most banks have stayed rather fully loaned up, so this has not been so much of a problem. Unused excess reserves have been small in amount and concentrated in small rural banks. But under some circumstances this might change. For example, it is quite possible that bank holdings of excess reserves could be a function of interest rates, high rates inducing banks to make more loans and hold less excess reserves, and low rates making it less costly for banks to hold excess reserves (they are not giving up much interest income by not lending). This raises the possibility that demand deposits and money supply are a function of interest rate levels.

What do all these complications mean for the Federal Reserve, these successive modifications of our original simple demand deposit expansion multiplier? (Remember when it was just the reciprocal of the demand deposit reserve requirement?) They mean, most important, that the Fed's ability to control the money supply, even in its narrow definition, is not nearly as precise as we had originally thought. As it attempts to control the money supply, the central bank has to deal with currency drains, time deposit growth, and bank holdings of idle excess reserves. We can get away with using sample numbers for the multipliers, but for the Fed that is simply not good enough. It has to predict with accuracy the various ratios for the coming weeks and months if it is to succeed in making the money supply what it wants it to be.

Suggestions for Further Reading

For a painstaking derivation of the demand deposit multipliers discussed in this Appendix, and a few others as well, see John T. Boorman and Thomas M. Havrilesky, *Money Supply, Money Demand, and Macroeconomic Models* (Boston: AHM, 1982), pp. 10–41. Also see Dorothy M. Nichols' pamphlet *Modern Money Mechanics: A Workbook on Deposits, Currency, and Bank Reserves* (Federal Reserve Bank of Chicago), pp. 29–31. For an advanced treatment with some historical perspective, see Phillip Cagan, *Determinants and Effects of Changes in the Stock of Money, 1875–1960* (New York: Columbia University Press, 1965).

16

Budget Deficits and the Money Supply

WHEN THE GOVERNMENT spends more than it receives in tax receipts it runs a deficit. The easiest way to finance the deficit is to print up the money and pay the bills. But that option is not open to the U.S. Treasury. Congress in its infinite wisdom conferred on the Federal Reserve System, not the U.S. Treasury, the responsibility of printing money and regulating its supply. What the Treasury *can* do is sell bonds and use the proceeds to meet its obligations, and in this process of carrying out its debt finance and spending functions, the Treasury can complicate the Fed's job.

In the first section of this chapter we examine the mechanics of how alternative procedures for financing government spending in general, and a deficit in particular, influence bank reserves and money supply. In the next section we confront the controversial issue of whether deficits are responsible for excessive growth in the money supply, and hence are inherently inflationary. Although the connection between deficits, the money supply, and inflation is part of the conventional wisdom, we will see that the linkages are far more subtle than most people would have us believe.

256

Financing Government Spending

It is useful to identify four ways available to the U.S. Treasury to finance government spending: (1) collecting taxes; (2) borrowing from the nonbank public; (3) borrowing from the banking system; and (4) borrowing from the Federal Reserve. Each method has somewhat different implications for bank reserves and the money supply.

1. *Taxation.* Assume the government decides to spend an additional $100 million on water pollution control equipment, and chooses to raise the money by levying taxes on everyone who takes more than one shower a week. As the taxes are collected, they are initially deposited in the Treasury's accounts at commercial banks throughout the country, called the Treasury's "tax and loan accounts." Thus demand deposits (DD) at commercial banks are transferred from private ownership to Treasury ownership. The relevant T-accounts look as follows:

T-Accounts for Taxation

U.S. Treasury		Fed. Res. Banks		Commercial Banks		Nonbank Public	
A	L	A	L	A	L	A	L
DD in comm. bank +$100					DD of Public − $100	DD in comm. bank − $100	Taxes due − $100
Taxes due − $100					DD of Treasury + $100		

As a result of this step alone, the money supply falls by $100 million since government deposits are not counted in the money supply.[1] Bank reserves, however, are not yet affected. But before the Treasury spends the money, it usually shifts the funds from the commercial banks to a Federal Reserve Bank so that it can make its disbursements from a central account. *This* step depletes total bank reserves by $100 million, as the following T-accounts show:

[1]The money supply is defined as currency and demand deposits owned by the nonbank public, because it is designed to measure the *private* sector's liquidity.

T-Accounts for Shifting Funds to the Federal Reserve

U.S. Treasury		Fed. Res. Banks		Commercial Banks		Nonbank Public	
A	L	A	L	A	L	A	L
DD in comm. bank − $100			Comm. bank dep. − $100	Dep. in FRB − $100	DD of Treasury − $100		
DD in FRB + $100			Treasury deposit + $100				

Having raised $100 million and shifted it from commercial banks to its account at the Federal Reserve, the government now spends it. When expenditures are made, the Treasury writes checks on its demand deposit account at the Fed to pay its suppliers. The suppliers deposit the checks in commercial banks, and the banks send the checks to the Fed for collection. The result is that the money supply *and* bank reserves go back up by $100 million:

T-Accounts for Government Spending

U.S. Treasury		Fed. Res. Banks		Commercial Banks		Nonbank Public	
A	L	A	L	A	L	A	L
DD in FRB − $100			Comm. bank deposit + $100	Dep. in FRB + $100	DD of public + $100	DD in comm. bank + $100	
Goods & services + $100			Treasury deposit − $100			Goods & services − $100	

By combining all the effects of acquiring funds via taxation and spending the money, we see that neither the money supply nor bank reserves are altered. The money supply falls when taxes are collected, but it rises by the same amount when the government spends the proceeds. Similarly, bank reserves at first decline when the

Treasury shifts the funds to its account at the Fed, but then reserves are replenished when the Treasury spends the money.[2]

2. *Borrowing from the nonbank public.* Alternatively, suppose people who take more than one shower a week amount to a substantial voting bloc (not very likely), and Congress decides it would be the better part of valor not to tax them. Instead, the Treasury finances its spending—now *deficit* spending—by borrowing, specifically by selling bonds to the nonbank public. The T-accounts are the same as for taxation, except this time people get a government security for their money instead of a receipt saying they paid their taxes:

T-Accounts for Borrowing from Nonbank Public

U.S. Treasury		Fed. Res. Banks		Commercial Banks		Nonbank Public	
A	L	A	L	A	L	A	L
DD in comm. bank + $100	Debt outst. + $100				DD of Public − $100	DD in comm. bank − $100	
					DD of Treasury + $100	Govt. bond + $100	

Again, as with taxation, this reduces the money supply, transferring it from the pockets of the public to the accounts of the Treasury. When the Treasury shifts the funds to the Fed, bank reserves are also reduced, but as soon as the government spends the funds the money supply and bank reserves bounce back to where they had been originally (we have already seen the T-accounts for both of these transactions). The net result: Just as in the case of taxation, after all is said and done neither the money supply nor bank reserves are altered (although this time the public does wind up with more government bonds than before).

[2]While the end result of the government's taxation and spending is to leave the money supply and bank reserves unchanged, the *timing* of the shifting of funds from tax and loan accounts at commercial banks to the Fed, and of subsequent expenditures, create reserve management problems for the Federal Reserve, as we saw in Chapter 14.

3. *Borrowing from the commercial banking system.* The Treasury need not sell its securities to the nonbank public. Instead of the public buying the securities, the commercial banks might buy them. The ultimate net effects of this depend on whether the commercial banks are (a) fully loaned up to begin with (zero excess reserves) or (b) have excess reserves. To see why this is so, let's examine each possibility.

(a)   If the banking system is fully loaned up to begin with, it will not be able to buy the government securities unless it first disposes of other assets. This is because the purchase of the government securities would result in an increase in Treasury demand deposits at commercial banks, against which required reserves must be held. To release sufficient reserves, private deposits have to be reduced by a corresponding amount. By selling $100 million of other investments to the public, the banks can now buy $100 million of government bonds from the Treasury. The relevant T-accounts are as follows, with the banks' liquidation of other investments above the dashed line and their subsequent acquisition of government securities below it:

T-Accounts for Borrowing from the Commercial Banking System
(Zero excess reserves)

U.S. Treasury		Fed. Res. Banks		Commercial Banks		Nonbank Public	
A	L	A	L	A	L	A	L
				"Other" securities − $100	DD of Public − $100	DD in comm. bank − $100 "Other" securities + $100	
DD in comm. banks + $100	Debt outst. + $100			Govt. bonds + $100	DD of Treasury + $100		

These transactions, by themselves, decrease the money supply, because the public has fewer deposits. (Although the Treasury has gained deposits, we have pointed out above that Treasury deposits are not counted as part of the money supply.) But, as in our previous cases, the Treasury shifts its funds to its account at the Fed and then spends them. When the funds are spent, the public's money holdings are restored to their former level. Once again, after all is said and done, there is no change in either total bank reserves or the money supply.

(b) On the other hand, if banks have excess reserves to begin with, then they will not have to dispose of other securities or call in loans in order to make room for their new purchases of Treasury securities. Thus that part of the T-accounts above the dashed line would not be necessary. The banks buy the Treasury bonds, open up a new deposit for the Treasury, the Treasury shifts its balance to the Fed, and then spends the money. When the Treasury spends, individuals receive brand-new demand deposits (for which they give up goods and services). Under these circumstances, financing a deficit by borrowing from the banks *increases the money supply* by as much as the deficit (but it does not alter total bank reserves).[3]

4. *Borrowing from the Federal Reserve.* The Treasury still has one option remaining; it could borrow the money directly from the Federal Reserve:

T-Accounts for Borrowing from the Federal Reserve

U.S. Treasury		Fed. Res. Banks		Commercial Banks		Nonbank Public	
A	L	A	L	A	L	A	L
DD in FRB + $100	Debt outst. + $100	Govt. bonds + $100	Treasury deposit + $100				

In this case the Treasury does not have to shift the funds to the Federal Reserve before spending them; they are already there. Also, this method of borrowing reduces neither the money supply nor bank reserves. The government merely sells some bonds to the Fed,

[3]Note that since banks had excess reserves to begin with, the money supply could have increased without any Treasury financing. The only role played by the deficit in this case is to induce banks to lend out all excess reserves.

gets a checking account for them, and is in business.[4] Painlessly. Thus, when the Treasury *spends* the funds, the public winds up with more demand deposits and the banks with more reserves, as our T-accounts for government spending (which we saw earlier) show. Indeed, this way of financing a deficit has the same effects as printing greenbacks.

Instead of borrowing from the Federal Reserve, the Treasury could conceivably do the same thing by printing currency, depositing it with the Fed, and then spending from its account at the Fed. The T-accounts for printing money are almost the same as those for borrowing from the Fed; the only difference is that the Treasury gives the Fed non-interest-bearing currency instead of interest-bearing bonds. But that is a meaningless difference, since at the end of the year the Federal Reserve turns over most of its interest earnings to the Treasury anyway.

T-Accounts for Printing Money

U.S. Treasury		Fed. Res. Banks		Commercial Banks		Nonbank Public	
A	L	A	L	A	L	A	L
DD in FRB + $100	Currency outst. + $100	Treasury currency + $100	Treasury deposit + $100				

In point of fact, there *is* a substantive difference between printing money and selling bonds to the Federal Reserve. And that has to do with the fact that except for minting new coins, the Treasury does not have the constitutional authority to issue currency. The Treasury *can* issue bonds, but it cannot force the Federal Reserve to buy them; that is the Federal Reserve's decision. And if the Federal

[4]In ordinary circumstances, the Treasury does not sell securities *directly* to the Federal Reserve. Rather, newly issued bonds are brought to market through auctions held by the Federal Reserve Banks. The Fed acts as the Treasury's fiscal agent—distributing issues to ultimate buyers (see the Appendix to Chapter 25 for a more complete discussion). Securities dealers buy newly issued Treasury obligations for their inventory, to distribute to their customers. Our example in the text would be implemented if the Federal Reserve bought back some of these newly issued securities from dealers.

Reserve refuses to buy the bonds and the Treasury must sell them to the nonbank public or to commercial banks with zero excess reserves, this will leave the money supply and bank reserves unchanged, as we saw above.

In the end, therefore, the Federal Reserve decides whether the Treasury's bond sale is tantamount to printing money or not. If the Fed buys the securities, new money is created; if the Fed refuses and the public buys the securities, no additional cash is created. Thus while the T-accounts of bond sales to the Fed and printing money by the Treasury are almost the same, the politics are not.

Can a Deficit Subvert Monetary Policy?

Obviously the deficit has to be financed in some way. We have just seen, however, that it is the Federal Reserve's prerogative to decide how much will come in the form of new money and how much must come through the ultimate sale of bonds to the public. The Fed makes the Treasury's financing job easier by "monetizing the debt," that is, by buying the newly issued securities. But turning new debt into new money may not be in the public interest. After all, in the long run, just about everyone agrees that excess money creation is inflationary (see Chapter 2). In fact, the reason Congress created the Federal Reserve was to keep the printing press away from the Treasury: to make deficit spending costly by forcing the Treasury to pay interest on its debt. In that way the inflationary consequences of a deficit would be mitigated.

When the Federal Reserve monetizes the debt by buying Treasury securities,[5] it lets the Treasury get to the printing presses through the back door. And that's precisely what Congress doesn't want (or at least says it doesn't).

There are some who contend that the Federal Reserve is often *forced* to accommodate excessive Treasury borrowing through new money creation. Despite the institutional separation between bond

[5]Note that it makes no difference whether the Fed buys some old securities when the Treasury sells new ones or whether the new securities are purchased. In either case, the Fed is monetizing some of the debt.

sales by the Treasury and money creation by the Federal Reserve, there is pressure on the Fed to monetize the deficit. That pressure stems from the fact that Treasury bond sales by themselves will raise interest rates. After all, the Treasury is a borrower just like everyone else. And when the Treasury comes to market it must induce individuals to part with their hard-earned dollars. The only way to do that is to raise the interest rate that is offered.

If the Federal Reserve is committed to a policy of holding down interest rates, then it has no choice but to buy Treasury securities whenever interest rates start to rise. But the only time the Federal Reserve made an open commitment to keep rates from rising was during and immediately after World War II. At that time the Federal Reserve agreed to peg the price of government securities to reduce the interest cost of financing the war. In effect, the Fed bought whatever bonds the public didn't want to hold; it monetized the deficit to whatever extent was necessary to keep interest rates from rising.[6]

The Federal Reserve extricated itself from the burden of blindly supporting the price of government securities through a compromise between the Treasury and the Federal Reserve which became known as the Treasury–Federal Reserve Accord. On March 4, 1951, the Federal Reserve and the Treasury issued a joint statement:

> The Treasury and the Federal Reserve System have reached full accord with respect to debt management and monetary policies to be pursued in furthering their common purpose to assure the successful financing of the Government's requirements and, at the same time, to minimize monetization of the public debt.

The key phrase for the Federal Reserve was the last one: "to minimize monetization of the public debt."

Chart 1 shows for the 1970s the behavior of two measures of the magnitude of federal deficits as well as the annual growth rate in the money supply. The dashed line is the ratio of federal debt to GNP, the dotted line is the annual rate of growth in federal debt, and the solid line is the annual rate of growth in M1. It is obvious from

---

[6]Note that pegging the price of bonds meant that the Fed lost control over its own holdings of bonds, hence it lost control over the supply of reserves. Whenever anyone wants to control the price of anything, control over the quantity bought or sold is lost in the process.

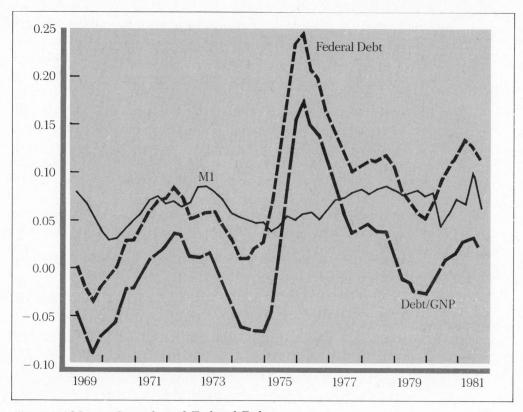

Chart 1 / Money Growth and Federal Debt

the chart that there is little or no relationship between the growth rate in the money supply and either indication of the importance of federal debt. Although there is little doubt that other measures of federal deficits could be developed, the implications of this simple overview is that large increases in federal deficits have had no persistent impact on money supply growth.

Chart 1 suggests no overall relationship between government debt and money growth, but that does not negate the fact that at times the deficit does cause trouble.[7] The picture is simply too broad to identify such effects. The fact that past deficits do not seem to have been excessively monetized by the Federal Reserve stems, in part, from

[7]For empirical evidence see Michael J. Hamburger and Burton Zwick, "Deficits, Money, and Inflation," *Journal of Monetary Economics,* January 1981.

the nature of the historical increase in government debt. Much of the deficit emerged during cyclical downturns in the economy, when reduced incomes generated smaller tax receipts. These deficits will not usually drive up interest rates because private credit demands are relatively low during recessionary periods. Thus there is little pressure on the Fed to monetize the automatic deficits that emerge in a recessionary economy. The real problem for the Federal Reserve occurs when the deficit expands during periods of economic expansion. Such deficits can be generated by an excessive increase in government spending; and that could very well lead to pressure on the Fed to monetize the debt.

To sum up: Deficits can at times be responsible for inducing faster growth in the money supply, but there is little evidence of such a systematic bias in recent years.

Summary

1. When the U.S. Treasury sells bonds to finance a deficit, the impacts on bank reserves and the money supply are different depending upon who buys the bonds. If either the nonbank public or banks with zero excess reserves buy the bonds, then the money supply and reserves remain unchanged. If banks with excess reserves buy the bonds, an increase in the money supply results. If the Federal Reserve buys the bonds, both bank reserves and money supply go up.

2. The purchase of newly issued bonds by the Federal Reserve is the modern-day equivalent of printing money to finance a deficit. The only new wrinkle is that it is the Federal Reserve, rather than the Treasury, that makes the ultimate decision to create more money.

3. A large deficit will induce the Federal Reserve to buy new Treasury securities if the deficit drives up interest rates when the Fed is trying to keep them down. This extreme case of "monetizing the debt" occurred during, and immediately after, World War II.

4. There is little formal evidence that deficits during the 1970s were persistently responsible for inducing an increased rate of growth in M1. It is possible, however, that over short intervals of time, deficits could elicit faster growth in money.

Suggestions for Further Reading

Most of the literature on the monetary effects of a deficit discusses the relationship between deficits and inflation. For the argument that deficits are benign in this respect, see Scott E. Hein, "Deficits and Inflation," Federal Reserve Bank of St. Louis *Review* (March 1981). Evidence to the contrary is in Michael J. Hamburger and Burton Zwick, "Deficits, Money and Inflation," *Journal of Monetary Economics* (January 1981). Finally, for an interesting psychological perspective with some history and economic statistics, see Thomas J. Sargent, "The Ends of Four Big Inflations," Conference Paper No. 90, National Bureau of Economic Research (January 1981).

Part IV

Monetary Theory

17

The Foundations
of Monetarism

THE FIRST QUESTION we asked in this book was: What is the "right" amount of money? The answer depends on how money influences the economy . . . which in turn depends upon what determines the overall level of spending. Monetarist and Keynesian economists have somewhat different views of the world in general and money in particular. This chapter and the others in Part IV explore the analytical foundations and empirical evidence that underlie their outlooks.

The origins of Monetarism lie in the Classical economics of Adam Smith (1723–1790) and his friends. The two cornerstones of the Classical system are Say's Law, which deals with interest rates, employment and production, and the Quantity Theory, which explains the role of money. Both concepts are essential to the proper functioning of the Classical world; both were attacked by John Maynard Keynes when the Classical wisdom was supposedly laid to rest in 1936; and both were resurrected by modern monetarism and refined during the 1970s and 1980s.

To understand the role of money according to Classical thinking, we must first see what determines GNP (the total value of goods and services produced). We start, therefore, with Say's law of markets and work our way toward the somewhat more famous quantity theory of money. Along the way we'll stop to consider some specifics: Classical interest theory as well as the demand for money.

Say's Law

Jean Baptiste Say (1767–1832) summarized the Classical school's income and employment theory with the now familiar maxim, "Supply creates its own demand." Dubbed Say's law (by Mrs. Say), it meant quite simply that the economy could never suffer from underemployment or succumb to Thomas Malthus' fear of under-consumption. Total spending (demand) would always be sufficient to justify production at a full employment GNP (supply). Here's why:

Given current technology, potential output of the economy is determined by the size of the labor force available to work with the existing stock of capital goods (plant and equipment). This production function, in technical terms, defines the total supply of goods and services that can be produced. Say argued that real output would be at the full employment level, since spending would always be great enough to buy all the goods and services that could be produced. Why? Because of the interplay of market forces, guided by what Adam Smith referred to as an "invisible hand."

If people who wanted to work couldn't find a job, they would offer their services for less money and would be snapped up by eager entrepreneurs. Entrepreneurs, finding it difficult to sell slow-moving items, would promptly lower their prices and watch their inventories disappear. Flexible wages and prices assured that all markets would be cleared, all goods sold, all people employed—except economists, who had nothing to do, since everything worked just fine without them. The interplay of market forces under the guiding principle of laissez faire (noninterference). The best of all possible worlds.

To represent Classical economics as having an entirely uniform outlook, however, would be unjust to some prominent precursors of modern Keynesian ideas. The Reverend Thomas Malthus (1766–1834) could hardly believe that *he,* a man of the cloth, was unable to see the invisible hand, so he proceeded to launch a sustained and vigorous attack on it. Spurning the microeconomic details, Malthus argued as follows: While the production of goods and services generates *income* in the same amount as total output, there does not seem to be anything to force *spending* to equal total production. Supply might create its own purchasing power (income), but not its own demand (spending). In particular, if people try to save too large a fraction of their income—more than firms want to invest—part of the goods produced will be left unsold, entrepreneurs will cut back their production, and unemployed labor and capital will result. This argument was later refined and formalized by Keynes, as we shall see in the next two chapters.[1]

However, the Classical economists cannot be disposed of so simply. People save part of their income, but such funds do not disappear. They are borrowed by entrepreneurs to use for capital investment projects. Savers receive interest on their funds and borrowers are willing to pay, as long as they expect to earn a return on their investment in excess of the rate of interest.

But what made the Classical economists so sure that all saving would actually be invested by entrepreneurs? If saving went up, would investment go up by the same amount? In Classical economics, *the rate of interest* is the key; according to Classical theory, the interest rate would fluctuate to make entrepreneurs *want to invest* what households *wanted to save.* As is emphasized in the Appendix to this chapter, this equality between desired saving and desired investment is sufficient to maintain production at the assumed level, in this case, full employment. The next section explains in greater detail this Classical theory of interest rate determination. It is really an elaboration of one of the market mechanisms underlying Say's law.

Classical Interest Theory

Saving, according to Classical economics, is a function of the rate of interest. The higher the rate of interest, the more will be saved (see Figure 1), since at higher interest rates people will be more willing to forgo present consumption. The rate of interest is an inducement

[1]There is a distinction between the accounting identity that income equals actual expenditure and the possibility that income may not equal *desired* expenditure. The Appendix to this chapter discusses these relationships, which are relevant both for Classical and Keynesian economics.

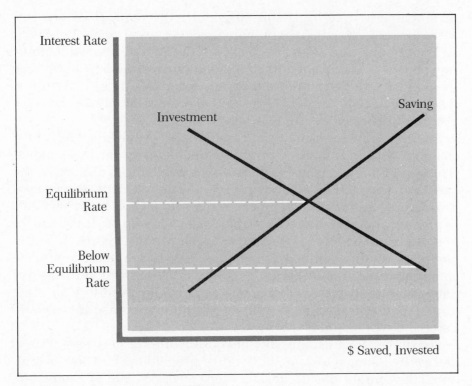

Figure 1 / Classical Interest Theory

to save, a reward for not giving in to one's baser instincts for instant gratification by consuming all one's income. It does not pay, by the way, to make too much of this Classical assumption, because Classical interest theory worked just as well if saving did not depend on the interest rate—that is, if saving were a vertical line in Figure 1.

As long as investment is a function of the rate of interest, increasing as the rate of interest declines (as illustrated by the negatively sloped investment line in Figure 1), Classical interest theory and Say's law remained alive and well. Let's take a closer look at why the amount of investment should increase with a fall in the rate of interest.

Investment in physical capital is undertaken because capital goods—buildings, machines, or anything which is not used up (consumed) immediately—produce services in the future. A new plant or machine is used by an entrepreneur to produce goods and services for sale. A businessman increases his capital stock (invests) if he expects his rate of return to exceed the rate of interest he must pay on the funds he borrows to make the investment. A lower rate of interest induces entrepreneurs to undertake more investment. They will accept projects of lower expected profitability, because the cost of borrowing funds is less.[2]

Figure 1 includes a supply of funds curve (people's saving) and a demand for funds curve (entrepreneurs' demand for investment). The rate of interest is in equilibrium (no tendency to change) at the point of intersection between saving and investment, where total saving is equal to investment: Everyone who wants to borrow funds is able to, and everyone who wants to lend can do so. If the rate of interest were below equilibrium, as shown in Figure 1, entrepreneurs would want more funds than savers are ready to provide and competition would force the interest rate upward. If the rate of interest were above equilibrium, savers would want to lend more funds than entrepreneurs want to invest, and competition would force the cost of funds downward.

But things don't usually stay in equilibrium for very long. If people really listened to some of the dire predictions of Thomas Malthus, they might decide to save more at every rate of interest, to provide for the day when population grows to the point where people cannot afford to smoke tobacco because they must eat it. The entire saving function would then shift to the right (Figure 2). At the old equilibrium interest rate, desired saving now exceeds the amount of investment that entrepreneurs are ready to make. That is precisely what Thomas Malthus said was wrong with the Classical system—people would spend too little in the form of consumption, they would save too much (more than entrepreneurs cared to invest), and unemployment would follow.

---

[2]The entrepreneur need not borrow for the interest rate to be important in his calculation. If he already has funds, his alternative to increasing his capital equipment is to lend the funds at the going rate of interest. At a lower rate of interest, lending becomes a less attractive use of the entrepreneur's funds and real investment becomes more attractive. The rate of interest *must* fall to elicit more investment spending because of our old friend from microeconomics, the law of diminishing returns. More investment means a larger capital stock, and, given the labor force and current technology, there is reduced marginal productivity (profitability).

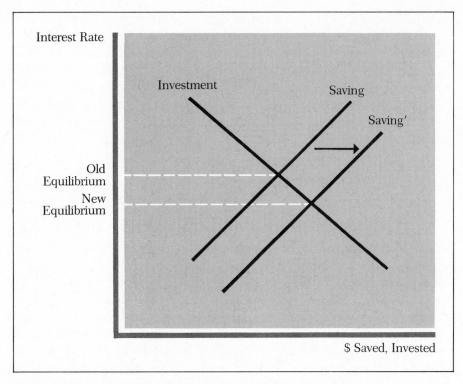

Figure 2 / Increased Saving Calls Forth Increased Investment

But not really. The excess of saving over investment puts down-ward pressure on the rate of interest, as savers try to lend out their funds. Some people will give in to their baser instincts as the rate of interest declines and spend a greater part of their income (saving less and enjoying it more). At the same time, the decline in the rate of interest encourages businessmen to expand their investments. As Figure 2 shows, the rate of interest will settle at a lower equilibrium, at which point all that is saved out of current income is still invested by entrepreneurs.

But where in all this does money fit in? The interest rate is in-fluenced only by the saving of the public (determined by their habits of thriftiness) and by capital investment of entrepreneurs (deter-mined by the productivity of capital). Money plays no role in this area of the Classical system. It influences neither employment, the rate of interest, nor GNP. Real things are determined by real forces. Total goods and services produced and total employment are determined by the supply of capital, the labor force, and existing technology; the interest rate is determined by the thriftiness of the public and the productivity of capital. Money plays no role in the real sector of the economy. Instead it is treated separately—via the second pillar of the classical edifice, the Quantity Theory—where it determines the price level.

The Quantity Theory of Money

Money, according to the Classicists, is a veil to be pierced by the analytical mind of the economist examining the determinants of real economic activity. Money affects the price level, but nothing else. An increase in the supply of money leads to an increase in the prices of all goods and services, but everything else—most notably the level of real economic activity, the rate of interest, and people's real income—remains unchanged. This conclusion expresses the quantity theory of money. It implies that money is neutral with respect to the real sector of the economy. The logic behind this is as follows.

We start with the *equation of exchange,* which is not the quantity theory but simply an *identity,* a truism:

$$(1) \qquad\qquad MV = Py$$

where M is the supply of money, V is velocity or its rate of turnover, P is the price level, and y is the level of *real* income.

The physical output of goods and services is represented by (lower-case) $y;$ that is what is produced by labor and capital given the technology currently available. Putting that in value terms (in dollars) requires that it be multiplied by an average level of prices for these goods and services—an index of prices—represented by $P.$ In other words, P times y is the total *value* of goods and services produced in the economy, namely GNP[3]—it is usually represented by

---

[3]Throughout this book when we use the term GNP we mean the dollar value of goods and services produced. The phrase *real* GNP or *full employment* GNP is used to

upper-case *Y*. On the left-hand side, the stock of money (in dollars) is represented by *M*. When multiplied by its velocity, the number of times such dollars are used in the purchase of goods and services, the product *MV* also equals total spending, or GNP. That is the equation of exchange. It says that total spending *(MV)* equals the value of what is bought *(Py)*.[4]

The equation of exchange was originally put forth in a slightly different form. The level of real income on the right-hand side was replaced by *T,* the total level of transactions. The total level of transactions exceeds the level of GNP because there are many transactions that are excluded from GNP. Purchases and sales of *financial* assets and of *existing* assets—such as stocks and bonds, old homes, and works by the Great Masters (the 1952 Marilyn Monroe calendar) —are not part of current production and hence are not included in GNP.[5] When the equation of exchange is written as:

$$(2) \qquad\qquad MV = PT$$

the velocity figure on the left-hand side is called transactions velocity.

Equation (1) is the most frequently used version of the equation of exchange. It is really the most meaningful approach, since our main concern is with GNP and not with total transactions. Thus all our subsequent discussion will be in terms of equation (1) and the "income" velocity of money. Irving Fisher, the brilliant Yale economist who is unfortunately known for his advice to buy just before the stock market crashed in 1929, was the most eloquent expositor of the equation of exchange as we have just presented it.[6]

---

distinguish real output from the nominal value. As long as prices remain unchanged, movements in the dollar value of GNP (also called nominal GNP) and real output are one and the same. For a discussion of how price indices are constructed, see any basic text on economics, such as William J. Baumol and Alan S. Blinder. *Economics* (New York: Harcourt Brace Jovanovich, 1979) pp. 107–110.

[4]As we saw in Chapter 1, velocity is *defined* as GNP ÷ *M*, or, in these terms, *Py* ÷ *M*. Substituting *Py* ÷ *M* for *V* on the left-hand side of (1) yields *Py* = *Py*, which is accepted as a truism even by those from Missouri.

[5]See Baumol and Blinder, *Economics,* Chapter 17, for a summary of GNP accounting.

[6]See Irving Fisher, *The Purchasing Power of Money* (New York: Macmillan, 1911).

"Now for those lessons I promised you. . . .
When savings exceeds investment. . . ."

There is still another version of the equation of exchange, how-ever, associated with economists at Cambridge University, in En-gland. So before discussing how we progress from the simple iden-tity expressed by equation (1) or (2) to the quantity theory as used by Fisher and other Classical economists, let us give equal time to our friends across the Atlantic.

The Cambridge economists viewed the equation of exchange in a slightly different light. Instead of concentrating on the rate of turn-over of a given stock of money during the year (its velocity), they concentrated on the fraction of GNP that people hold in the form of money. Simple algebraic manipulation of equation (1) produces the Cambridge "cash-balance approach" to the equation of exchange:

(3) $$M = kPy$$

where k is the fraction of GNP that people have command over in the form of money balances. Obviously $k = 1/V$, so equations (1) and (3) are equivalent from an algebraic standpoint (for some unknown reason, when the Cambridge economists divided both sides of equation (1) by V they changed $1/V$ to the letter k). And (3), like its predecessors, is still a truism—an identity that must be true by definition.

This latest version does represent a different orientation, however. In fact, equation (3) readily lends itself to interpretation as a *demand for money equation,* where people *want* to hold cash balances in a certain ratio to the value of GNP (say, one-third or one-fourth of GNP), to use in carrying out the anticipated level of transactions associated with that level of GNP.

But we are running a bit ahead of ourselves. It is time to convert the equation of exchange, whatever its form, from an algebraic identity—which it has been so far—into an analytical tool. Let's move, in other words, from the *equation of exchange* (an identity) to the *quantity theory of money* (a cause-and-effect hypothesis).

We started this section by saying that the quantity theory implied that increases in the supply of money cause increases in the price level. We can now be even more precise: According to the quantity theory of money, a change in the money supply produces a *proportionate* change in the price level—for example, if the money supply doubles, so does the price level. This cause-and-effect conclusion follows from two basic propositions (a nice word for assumptions) of the Classical school. First, on the right-hand side of equation (1), $MV = Py,$ y is assumed fixed at full employment (now you know why we started out with Jean Baptiste Say). Second, velocity is assumed to be fixed by the payment habits of the community, or, in the Cambridge cash-balances version, k is fixed because of the stable proportion of GNP that people want to hold in the form of money balances. If $MV = Py$ and V and y are assumed to be fixed, then if M doubles it follows that P *must* double. For example, if V and y are fixed at 4 and 100 respectively, then a supply of money equal to 25 is consistent with a *P* equal to 1. If *M* doubles to 50, *P* must double to 2.

To understand the process involved, we need only recall the discussion in Chapter 1 of how people react to changes in the money supply brought about by central bank operations. Start out in equilibrium, with everyone satisfied with the liquidity of his portfolio. Assume the Federal Reserve doubles the money supply. Liquidity rises. If people were formerly satisfied with their liquidity position, now they will try to get rid of their excess money balances by spending more. This increase in the demand for goods and services drives up prices, because total real output cannot expand—it is fixed at the full employment level by virtue of Say's law. If people were in equilibrium before a doubling of *M,* they will stop trying to spend the increased money balances only after their total expenditures have also doubled. Since real output is fixed, a doubling of total spending must cause prices to double. End result: Money stock held by the public has doubled, *money* GNP has doubled, the price level has doubled, *V* is the same as before, and so is *real* GNP.

Note carefully that Classical economists (as well as their Monetarist descendants) insist on clearly distinguishing the real versus nominal consequences of anything in general, and money in particular. A change in the money supply leaves the real amount of goods and services produced (real GNP) unchanged, but increases the dollar value of GNP (nominal GNP). As we will see in the next chapter, Keynesians are much less concerned with the real versus nominal distinction.

Money Demand and the Quantity Theory

The two versions of the quantity theory, *MV = Py* and *M = kPy,* are algebraically equivalent and also produce the same cause-and-effect implications for the relationship between money and prices. For explaining the transmission mechanism as we just have, and for what is to come later, the cash-balance version (*M = kPy*) is superior (in keeping with the best British tradition). The cash-balance equation can be interpreted as a demand for money function, as we mentioned above. Assume that *k* = ¼. Then if *Py* or GNP equals $400, this means that people want to hold one fourth of GNP, or $100, in cash balances; if GNP climbs to $600, the amount of money demanded rises to $150; and if GNP doubles to $800, money demand doubles to $200.

The fraction of GNP that people want to hold in the form of money, *k,* is determined by many forces. It is essentially a *transactions demand* for money. Thus, since money is used as a medium of exchange, the value of *k* is influenced by the frequency of receipts and expenditures; if you are paid weekly, you can manage with a smaller daily average cash balance than if you are paid monthly. Second, the ease with which you can buy on credit (the use of credit cards) also influences *k* by permitting people to reduce the average balance in their checking accounts. Money is also used as a temporary abode of purchasing power—waiting in the wings until you summon it and exercise control over real goods and services. Thus an individual may hold more or less, depending upon whether he or she expects to be out of a job for four months or two months of the year. For the community as a whole, so the argument goes, all these factors average out and are fairly stable, hence the public winds up wanting to hold a stable and/or predictable level of money balances relative to GNP.

Looking at the cash-balance version of the quantity theory ($M = kPy$) as a demand for money equation, it is easy to see that the doubling of prices (and hence money GNP) produced by a doubling of the money supply follows directly from the equilibrium condition that the amount of money demanded must equal the supply. When M doubles, people have twice as much money as they want to hold (money supply exceeds the amount demanded), given that nothing else has changed. So they start to spend it. They stop spending when they want to hold the increased money supply (when the amount of money demanded grows into equality with the supply). That occurs when money GNP has doubled.

It is also possible to look at this new equilibrium position in a slightly different way. Namely, the *real* amount of money that people hold is the same in both the initial and final positions. The real amount of money is given by the nominal money supply deflated by the price level, or *M/P,* where that tells you the amount of real goods and services that is "controlled" by the cash balances people hold. For example, if you hold a $1,000 checking account and the price index is unity, you control $1,000 worth of goods and services; if you have a $2,000 checking account but the price level has doubled, you still control the same real volume of goods and services.

The cash-balance version of the quantity theory, in fact, emphasizes that people try to fix their *real* money balances, not the dollar value of their cash holdings. Thus when the supply of money doubles, the public has twice as many *real* balances as it wants, given the old price level and real GNP. People try to get rid of those excess real balances by spending. But since the output of goods and services is fixed at full employment, only prices respond to the increased demand for goods. Prices will continue to rise until people stop trying to spend those extra real balances. And that happens when they have none left, that is, after prices have doubled so that real balances are back to their original level ($M/P = 2M/2P$ is a famous theorem in Boolean algebra).

Aggregate Demand and Supply: A Summary

In keeping with the best tradition of Classical economics, it is useful to summarize the discussion thus far within a supply/demand framework. This will serve us well later in bridging the Classical and Keynesian outlooks and will also form the foundation for analyzing inflation.

Figure 3 may not look exactly like the supply/demand graph you learned to love in basic economics, but it really is. Price is measured on the vertical axis and quantity is on the horizontal axis. In the macroeconomic framework, price refers to the price level of all goods, P, and quantity refers to the aggregate real output of all goods and services, y.

The supply schedule in Figure 3 is a vertical line to represent the classical assumption that the volume of goods and services that can be produced is fixed at full employment (y_{FE}). In particular, changes in the price level do not influence the supply of goods and services. (We encounter similar vertical supply schedules at the microeconomic level for many commodities in the very short run as well as for things like land in the long run.)

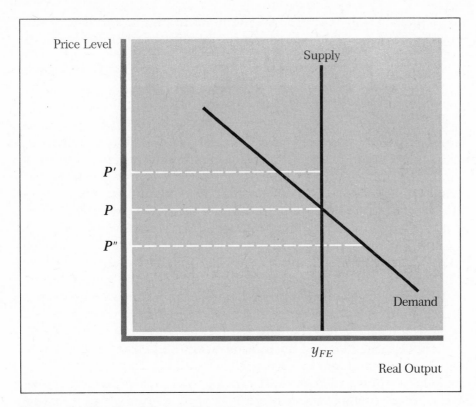

Figure 3 / The Equilibrium Price Level

The demand schedule in Figure 3 is negatively sloped. While this is the normal shape, the reason is somewhat different in the macro-economic context. The aggregate demand schedule is drawn for a given level of the money supply *(M)*. And as we have just seen, a given stock of money buys more goods and services with a lower price level. Hence a lower price level means that the amount of goods and services demanded is greater.[7]

[7]Note that the normal microeconomic reasons for demand rising when prices fall are not relevant in the macroeconomic context. First, lower prices usually generate a larger amount demanded because a particular commodity is cheaper and consumers substitute it for other goods. But in the macro framework we are dealing with all goods together, and all prices are falling, hence the "substitution effect" is not relevant. Second, lower prices usually increase the amount demanded because people's incomes can now buy more. But in the macro framework all prices, including the

The intersection of supply and demand in Figure 3 indicates the equilibrium price level. Since the supply of goods is fixed by Say's law, the demand schedule tells us only what price level will clear the market. If the price level were higher than P (as at P' in Figure 3), the aggregate demand for goods and services would be too low and businessmen would have to lower prices to sell all of their output. If the price level were lower than P (as at P''), the aggregate demand for goods and services would exceed what is available and businessmen would raise prices to ration the existing supply (and to make a handsome profit). Thus P is the equilibrium price level.

Note that this discussion shows that price flexibility is the key to the Classical school's argument that the level of real output would be at full employment. If the price level in Figure 3 were for some reason stuck at P', then aggregate demand for real goods would be below full-employment output (y_{FE}). That's why we said earlier, in our discussion of Say's law, that flexible wages and prices would insure that all goods would be sold and all labor employed. Now we see clearly that if this weren't the case, aggregate demand for real goods would be too low. Downward rigidity in prices is one of the elements Keynes focused on in analyzing the behavior of GNP at less than full employment, as we'll see in the next chapter.

Figure 4 allows us to identify the demand schedule more precisely. In particular, when there is a shift in the entire demand curve we see that the price level rises from P to P'. Our discussion in the previous sections showed that increases in the money supply raise the price level. From Figure 4 we see that this occurs because higher levels of M increase the aggregate demand for goods and services. In particular, in Figure 4 at the old price level, P, the public had just the right amount of real cash balances (given the old money supply). When the supply of money is increased, the demand for goods and services at every price level goes up, because real cash balances are higher. This is represented in the figure by a rightward shift of the demand curve. The net result of this increased demand,

(continued)
price of labor (wages), are falling. Thus the "income effect" of price decreases is irrelevant. That's why we appealed to our real money supply discussion. In particular, even though prices are falling, the stock of money is fixed by the central bank. Thus, as the value of real balances increases, because prices are falling, the amount demanded for all goods taken together rises.

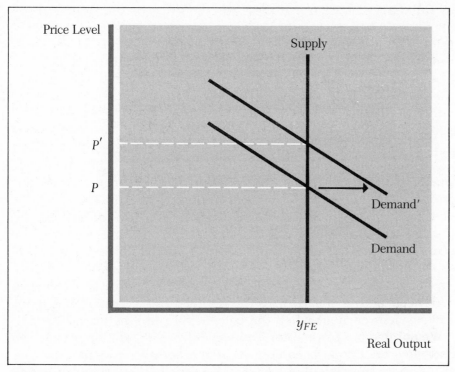

Figure 4 / An Increase in Aggregate Demand Raises Prices

however, is simply to raise the price level to P' because the aggregate supply of goods and services is fixed at full employment.

Our algebraic discussion in the previous sections was more specific than the graphics because we could show that changes in the money supply lead to proportional changes in prices under the quantity theory. But the pictures emphasize an important dimension as well: the quantity theory is really a specific statement of the aggregate demand for goods and services. In particular, this theory emphasizes that changes in the money supply raise prices by changing aggregate demand.

We have also just identified the source of the popular notion that inflation stems from "too much money chasing too few goods." In the context of Classical thinking, continued expansion in the money supply raises the aggregate demand for goods; with a fixed supply of goods, the result is rising prices, which is exactly what we mean by inflation. The Classical message, therefore, is that inflation is a monetary phenomenon: unless the money supply increases, the price level is stable. As we will see in Chapter 20, this is not the same conclusion reached by the Keynesian story on inflation.

Real Versus Nominal Rates of Interest

Once inflation enters the picture, we must return to amend our discussion of interest rate determination. Until now there was no need to consider the distinction between the real rate of interest and the nominal rate. The reason is that real and nominal yields are the same when the inflation rate is zero. Thus our discussion above, showing how saving and investment determined the rate of interest, was unambiguous: a given nominal rate of interest (in terms of dollars earned) is the same as the real yield (in terms of real goods and services earned) when the price level remains unchanged.

We pointed out in Chapter 5, however, that if inflation occurs, the real yield on a bond is calculated as the nominal rate less the rate of inflation. In particular, a $1,000 one-year bond that promises $50 in interest has a 5 percent nominal yield. But if the rate of increase in the price level is 2 percent, then it takes $1,020 next year just to buy what $1,000 would have purchased a year earlier. Thus only $30 of the $50 interest payment represents additional real goods and services that can be bought. In this case, therefore, the *real* yield is $30 per $1,000, or 3 percent. A convenient rule of thumb is as follows: the real yield is equal to the nominal rate minus the rate of inflation.

All of this is more arithmetic than economics. But Irving Fisher, of quantity theory fame, was the first to put the common-sense arithmetic together with some economic analysis. In particular, Fisher argued that if savers and investors expected inflation, they would force up the nominal rate of interest to include an inflation premium. The real rate would remain unchanged at the level determined by saving and investment, just as the nineteenth-century Classical economists said. But the nominal rate would increase by the expected rate of inflation.

The argument is as follows. Savers who were previously satisfied with, say, a 5 percent yield on bonds when inflation was zero, will save less and lend less when the expected rate of inflation jumps to two percent—after all, their savings will buy fewer real goods next year. Investors, meanwhile, will want to borrow even more funds when they expect 2 percent inflation—after all, they'll be investing in goods and services that can be sold at even higher prices next year. Thus at the old interest rate of 5 percent there is a greater demand for funds and a smaller supply. The level of interest rates is forced up to bring saving and investment back into equality. When the nominal yield rises to 7 percent, and the real rate of interest is back at 5 percent, lenders and borrowers will once again have consistent saving and investment plans.

More specifically, unless the nominal rate of interest rises by the expected rate of inflation, the real rate of interest (the nominal rate minus the expected rate of inflation) will be too low. As we saw in Figure 1, when the real rate is below equilibrium, desired investment exceeds saving and the real rate of interest is pushed up. So Fisher's addendum to the purely Classical interest theory was that, in equilibrium, the nominal rate of interest would increase by the expected rate of inflation and the real rate would remain unchanged (determined by saving and investment at full employment).

Modern Monetarist Modifications

While Monetarists adhere to virtually all the tenets of Classical economics, they have been known to use the quantity theory as a framework for describing the relationship between M and Py rather than just M and P. This approach recognizes the fact that real output may deviate temporarily from full employment, and represents an attempt at describing what influences GNP (which is Py) rather than just the price level. No doubt part of the Monetarist thrust in this direction stems from Keynesian preoccupation with GNP and the Monetarist desire to show that the quantity theory can do the job just as well.

A Monetarist reading of the quantity theory experiments discussed above would go something like this. Start with $MV=Py$ and assume that velocity is 4 and the money supply is $50. Thus the total value of GNP is $200. If the money supply increases to $100, the dollar value of GNP must rise to $400. If this increased money supply occurs during a period of unemployment, then real output (y) will increase. On the other hand, if the economy is already at full productive capacity, then prices alone will respond as in the Classical tradition.

It must be emphasized, however, that this broader view of the quantity theory can never wander very far from the first pillar of Classical economics: Say's law. Modern Monetarists still view the invisible hand as pushing the economy toward the full employment level of production (y_{FE}). Any increases or decreases in y stemming from expansions or contractions in M are viewed as temporary. As we will see in Chapter 20, much of this discussion hinges on a more precise specification of the aggregate supply and demand schedules that were just introduced.

A second modification of Classical thought occurred with Milton Friedman's revival of the quantity theory during the 1950s.[8] Friedman replaced the idea of the stability of velocity with the less militant notion that it is predictable. Or, looked at another way, money demand may not be a fixed fraction of GNP, but it is related to Py in a close and predictable way. Obviously this provides a looser linkage between changes in money and prices (or GNP), one that must be described in statistical terms rather than with a simple arithmetical example.[9] Nevertheless, if people respond in a predictable way to changes in the money supply, much of the Classical heritage is sustained.

Perhaps the most important Classical tradition that is upheld by modern Monetarists is the inherent stability of the economy at full employment. This explains the Monetarist rejection of governmental attempts to fine-tune economic activity. A higher level of economic activity requires more capital and labor or technological im-

[8]See Milton Friedman, "The Quantity Theory of Money—A Restatement" in his *Studies in the Quantity Theory of Money* (University of Chicago Press, 1956).
[9]The collection of essays cited in footnote 8 was Friedman's first attempt at statistical confirmation of the quantity theory. We will survey some of the more recent evidence in Chapter 22.

"Mr. Semple, who wants to stimulate the economy, help the cities, and clean up the environment, I'd like you to meet Mr. Hobart, who wants to let the economy, the cities, and the environment take care of themselves. I'm sure you two will have a lot to talk about."

Drawing by Stan Hunt; © *1976 by The New Yorker Magazine, Inc.*

provements; more money only leads to inflation. The answer to cyclical downturns is to wait for the natural upturn. Government intervention is unnecessary, and potentially damaging.

To some extent, these are the implications of Classical economics that sparked the Keynesian revolution. While modern Monetarists have popularized the notion of a self-correcting economy, enticing even some Keynesian disciples, there are still significant areas of disagreement between the two schools of macroeconomics. In the next chapter we outline the Keynesian viewpoint and then return to a Monetarist-Keynesian dialogue.

Summary

1. Modern Monetarism traces its roots to Classical economics. The two main concepts of Classical thinking on money and aggregate economic activity are Say's Law and the Quantity Theory.

2. Say's law emphasizes that the economy is inherently stable at full employment. Any deviations from that level of economic activity are only temporary. A key mechanism promoting stability is the flexibility of interest rates. Saving and investment are brought into equality through variations in the interest rate.

3. The quantity theory of money states that the impact of money in Classical economics is limited to the price level. Increases in the money supply raise prices, and decreases in money reduce the price level. Money is neutral with respect to the real sector of the economy. There is a clear distinction between real and nominal magnitudes.

4. At the heart of the quantity theory is a stable demand for money. More particularly, the demand for cash balances is a predictable fraction of GNP. This stability allows the quantity theory to predict that changes in money supply will be reflected in spending, and hence in prices.

5. The quantity theory can also be viewed as a statement about what determines the aggregate demand for goods and services. In particular, it says that increases in the money supply raise aggregate demand. With aggregate supply fixed at full employment, the impact of an increase in the money supply is to raise prices.

6. The real rate of interest is determined by saving and investment. When expectations of inflation emerge, the nominal rate of interest is forced up to include an inflation premium, while leaving the real rate unchanged.

7. Modern Monetarists treat the quantity theory more flexibly than their Classical ancestors. Money influences spending in a predictable way rather than in a rigid numerical fashion. Moreover, if the economy is at less than full employment, even real output might respond to changes in the money supply. But the natural tendency toward full employment eliminates any systematic impact on real output of changes in money supply.

Suggestions for Further Reading

Two books by Irving Fisher, *The Theory of Interest* (Macmillan, 1930) and *The Purchasing Power of Money* (Macmillan, 1911) are the most comprehensive treatments of Classical interest theory and the quantity theory, respectively. More recently, Milton Friedman has "modernized" the quantity theory; see "The Quantity Theory of Money—A Restatement" in his *Studies in the Quantity Theory of Money* (University of Chicago Press, 1956).

Appendix

GNP Definitions
and Relationships

This is a review of basic aggregate economic relationships that are relevant for both Monetarist and Keynesian analyses. We discuss the circular flow of income and output, the cleavage between saving and investment, and other paradigms of praxeology and catallactic concepts. Of course, if you have forgotten the meaning of some of the simple terms in the last sentence, you should read on to refresh your memory.

The Circular Flow of Spending, Income, and Output

Let's start by taking a simplified view of the economy, dividing its participants into two groups: business firms and households. Firms produce goods and services for sale; households buy these goods and services and consume them. Households are able to buy the goods and services produced by firms because they also supply firms with all the land, labor, capital and entrepreneurship required for production; hence they receive as income the total proceeds of production. The total value of the goods and services produced is called gross national product (GNP), or more simply national income (Y), and it can be measured by either the total output sold by firms *or* the

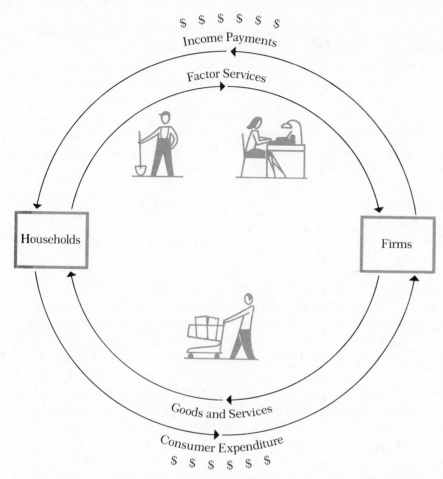

Figure 1 / The Circular Flow of Spending, Income, and Output

total income received by households (in the form of wages, rent, interest, and profits).

These relationships are summarized in Figure 1, the inner circle recording flows of *real* things (factors of production to firms and goods and services to households), the outer circle recording the associated *money* flows (income payments to households and money expenditures to firms). The money flow relationship can be written symbolically as $C = Y$, where C stands for household spending on consumer goods and Y stands for national income or GNP.

As long as firms sell all their output, they will continue to produce at that level. As long as we assume that all the income received by households is spent on the goods and services produced, production equals sales, output equals demand, and we are in equilibrium (no tendency for anything to change). But if we keep this up much longer, you will have fallen asleep in the very position you are now in, maybe still holding this book (also equilibrium). So we modify things a bit to make our hypothetical economy more like the real one.

Saving and Investment

Households don't spend all their income; they usually save some fraction. Saving represents a leakage in the circular flow. Total income of households (which is equal to the total value of goods and services produced by firms) does not all return to firms in the form of consumption expenditures. Saving (S) is defined simply as total income (Y) minus consumption spending (C)—i.e., $S = Y - C$. It may not have anything to do with putting the money in a bank, under the mattress, or in the stock market. Households may do any of these things with their savings—that is, with the excess of their income over their spending on consumer goods. For now we are not concerned with their financial transactions, just with the fact that failure to spend all income implies that total expenditure is less than total income (and total production). If things remained that way, output would exceed sales and firms would want to cut back production.

But all is not lost. Consumer goods are not the only thing that firms produce. Firms themselves add to their stock of production facilities or to inventories—they buy goods and services for their own use, which we call investment spending (I). If firms *want to invest (I)* exactly what households *want to save (S),* then all that is produced will once again be sold, but this time to both households (for consumption) and business firms (for investment). And, of course, the level of output will be one of equilibrium (hooray). This happy state of affairs is summarized in Figure 2 and can be represented as $C + I = Y$. Note that we can also describe the situation as one in which

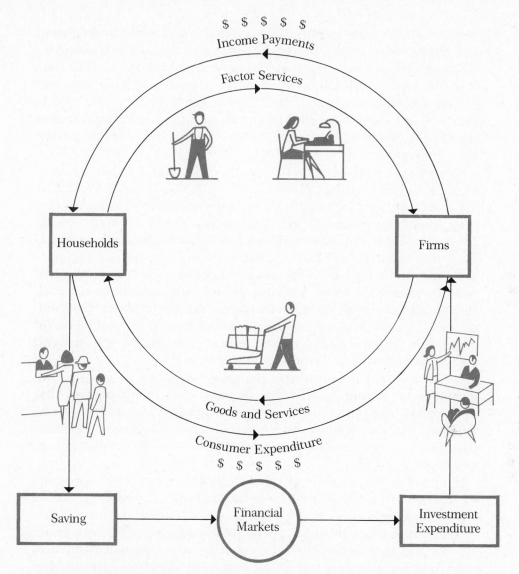

Figure 2 / The Circular Flow Including Saving and Investment

the leakage from the household spending stream (saving) is equal to business spending on investment, or, in symbols, $S = I$.

In Figure 2 we have labeled the connecting link between saving and investment the financial markets. Decisions to save are often made by people very different from those who invest—saving is done by all the little guys in the economy who scrimp to hold their spending down in order to prepare for a rainy day, while investment is done by corporate executives sitting around a huge oval desk with thirteen phones and four secretaries. These seemingly diverse groups are brought together by financial markets, with the savings of ordinary people borrowed by the corporate executives and then spent on investment goods, so that both groups may continue along their merry way.

The word "investment" is frequently confusing because it is used to mean different things. Here it means the purchase of "real" productive facilities, like factories and machine tools, whereas in common usage "investment" often refers to purely financial transactions, like buying stocks and bonds. Buying stocks and bonds can have implications for "real" investment (the purchase of factories and machine tools), but they are clearly different things. We will usually reserve the term "investment" for buying productive facilities, as we are using it here. In later chapters, however, we will occasionally fall into common parlance and use it for buying financial assets, like stocks and bonds; in that case, the purely financial meaning will be clear from the context.

It is important to emphasize that our discussion of equilibrium output as occurring when saving equals investment requires that households *want to save* the same amount as business firms *want to invest*. As we noted earlier in this chapter, Classical economics assumed that the interest rate would bring desired saving and investment together.

We have to distinguish this condition (where desired S = desired I) from one in which S and I are equal simply by definition. That is, saving is defined as $Y - C$. But $C + I = Y$, so that I also equals $Y - C$. Thus, by definition, S must always equal I, since both equal $Y - C$. But *this* equality is an ex post accounting identity, always true by definition. It is not an ex ante behavioral equality arising from what people *want* to do. Only when people *want* to save what firms *want* to invest will income be in equilibrium (remain unchanged). A concrete example is given in the next chapter.

So far we have ignored the government (wishful thinking?). It too introduces a leakage between income payments and household consumption expenditures—namely, taxes *(T)*. When the government collects taxes, households have less to spend on consumer goods (and less to save). If some other form of spending does not increase when taxes are levied, production once again would exceed the sum of all types of expenditures, and economic activity would decline. But the government could lend these funds to business firms so they can increase investment spending, or the government itself can buy goods and services from business firms.

If *desired* spending in the form of consumption *(C)*, investment *(I)*, and government *(G)* expenditure equals total output, or $C + I + G = Y$, then that level of production will be maintained. Note that we can also describe the situation as one in which total leakages from the spending stream, saving plus taxes, equals total spending injections in the form of investment and government expenditure, or $S + T = I + G$. For simplicity, we may sometimes refer to the left-hand side as total saving and the right-hand side as total investment.

Although we have now relaxed many of the hypothetical assumptions that populated our simple economy, we have still not introduced foreigners—exports and imports. Such a radical step is usually reserved for an entirely separate section in most textbooks. Ours is no exception. We believe (firmly) that the American Way of Life is best preserved when the outsiders are sealed off from the normal folks.[1]

Another Catallactic Concept[2]

We can look at the same subject, total spending in the economy, from a slightly different angle. So far we have viewed total spending as consisting of three categories, $C + I + G$. This breakdown is in terms of who does the spending—consumers, business firms, or government. But total spending could also be viewed as consisting of the quantity of money in existence *(M)* multiplied by the average number of times each dollar is spent on goods and services during a given period of time, which, as we noted in this chapter, is called velocity *(V)* or the rate of turnover of money.

---

[1] Ancient tablets unearthed by archaeologist Mel Brooks reveal that the first national anthem in the history of the world was *"Let Them All Go To Hell Except Cave 76."*

[2] Literally: exchange concept. Paradigm of praxeology = model of human action.

This way of looking at total spending ($M \times V$) is in terms of *what* is spent rather than *who* does the spending. An analogy: If two people are alternating driving a car, and one drives 50 miles and the other 30 miles, the total number of miles driven equals 80. A different way of finding the total miles driven is to calculate how many hours were spent driving and the average speed per hour—say, two hours at an average speed of 40 miles per hour. Total: 80 miles. This second way makes who is doing the driving irrelevant, just as with $M \times V$ it is irrelevant who is doing the spending. Since $M \times V$ just as $C + I + G$ equals total spending, we can also equate $M \times V$ with Y (as can be seen in Table 1 below). At times one way of looking at the process ($C + I + G = Y$) may be more fruitful, and at times the other ($M \times V = Y$) may be more illuminating.

We have seen in this chapter that Classical economists and their Monetarist descendants prefer the money-velocity link with GNP. We will see in the next chapter that Keynesian economists prefer to emphasize the impact on GNP of consumption, investment, and government spending. We have just shown that neither approach is superior from a purely formal standpoint. We will have to judge their relative merits on the basis of how well they explain the behavior of the economy.

Table 1 Components of Spending = Income, 1960–1980 ($ in billions)

Year	C	$+$	I	$+$	G	$=$	GNP	$=$	M	$\times$	V
1960	$325		$82		$100		$507		$142		3.57
1970	622		151		220		993		217		4.58
1980	1673		418		535		2626		416		6.31

Source: *Annual Reports,* Council of Economic Advisors.

18

The Keynesian
Framework: I

JOHN MAYNARD KEYNES, first baron of Tilton (1883–1946), did many things differently. We are not concerned here with his ability to make a fortune speculating in the market while simultaneously teaching at King's College, Cambridge; nor with his infatuation with the finer things in life—ballet, drama—and his editorial supervision for many years of the technical *Economic Journal;* nor with his unique abilities in the fields of mathematics, philosophy, and literature. Rather, we are concerned with his contribution to economics in his book, *The General Theory of Employment, Interest and Money,* published in 1936; how it revolutionized the thinking of all economists since, how it replaced Classical economics as the conventional wisdom, and how it led to a different outlook on employment, interest, and money.

Before going into the details of Keynes's contributions to macroeconomics and monetary theory and the refinement of his ideas at the hands of other economists (collectively labeled Keynesians), it will be helpful to set the stage by noting an essential difference in Keynes's outlook compared with that of his Classical teachers. Keynes was concerned with the short run, while Classical economists were preoccupied with the long run. Keynes's attitude toward the concern of his Classical mentors is best illustrated by his now-famous dictum: "In the long run, we are all dead."

Classical economics explained why fluctuating prices and interest rates would continuously push economic activity toward full employment. But Keynes argued that these free market forces could take considerable time to work themselves out. And in the short run there could be lengthy periods of underemployment. While it is difficult to delineate the borderline between the short run and long run, the six years of worldwide depression preceding the publication of Keynes's magnum opus seemed too long to wait for Classical market forces to restore full employment.

Keynes was preoccupied with what determined the level of economic activity during those lengthy recession or depression intervals between the full employment points of the Classical school. Real output could increase without any increase in the price level if we started out in a sufficiently depressed state. Thus, in terms of the aggregate supply and demand framework of Figure 3 in Chapter 17, Keynes was concerned with what determined actual output when the aggregate supply function was horizontal—that is, when real output could increase without raising prices. All of Keynes's basic analysis assumes that the price level is fixed. Therefore, throughout this chapter, all changes in GNP represent both nominal *and* real changes.

Keynes obviously had to focus on the aggregate demand for goods and services, since full employment supply was irrelevant for his particular problem. Theoretically, he could have chosen the quantity theory to describe aggregate demand, just as he had done in his Classical life before 1936. But in his new incarnation he had other plans for money, quite different from the quantity theory. Moreover, he believed he had to introduce a new set of analytical tools to deal with unemployment, since Classical economics had almost nothing to say about such matters. Keynes wanted to design a model of GNP determination that would explain how economic activity could be in equilibrium at *less* than full employment. Who or what was to blame for a depressed level of economic activity? To what extent is money the culprit?

A model is like a map. It does not include every detail of the actual terrain, but incorporates only those characteristics that are essential in explaining how to go from one point to another. Don't be turned off, therefore, if Keynes's model appears to be highly aggregative, ignoring many specifics and making many heroic assumptions. That is precisely what models are supposed to do: strip away the superfluous detail and get down to basics. The ultimate test, of course, is whether that simplified view of the world cuts through to explain actual behavior.

When Saving Doesn't Equal Investment

The Appendix to the previous chapter showed that for GNP to be at an equilibrium level—that is, no tendency for change—all that is produced must be sold to consumers or willingly added to the capital stock as investment by business firms. We also said that this equilibrium condition could be stated in a different way: Total saving *desired* by households must equal total investment *desired* by firms. In that way the leakage out of the spending stream in the form of saving would be made up by desired investment spending by firms, and everyone could continue along his merry way.

We also mentioned in the Appendix that ex post (after all is said and done) saving is always equal to investment. Only in the ex ante (desired) sense is equality of saving and investment an equilibrium condition. Let's take a very specific example of these relationships to set the stage for our discussion in the rest of the chapter.

Assume entrepreneurs produce $1,000 billion of output (Y) at full employment and expect to sell $800 billion to consumers (C) and want to use the remaining $200 billion for investment (including inventory accumulation). They will continue producing at that rate only if their sales are realized. If consumers plan to buy $800 billion in consumer goods and services and therefore *desire* to save $200 billion, all is well. But what if consumers decide they want to spend only $700 billion on consumer goods, which means they want to save $300 billion? What will give?

Assuming that consumers succeed in implementing their spending plans, entrepreneurs will wind up selling only $700 billion, although they have produced $800 billion in consumer goods and services. Clearly their selling plans have been disappointed, and they wind up with an *extra* $100 billion in (unwanted) inventories. In fact, they *wind up* investing $300 billion (the same as saving): their planned capital accumulation of $200 billion plus $100 billion of *unintended* inventory accumulation. Saving (S) equals investment (I) ex post, but *desired* savings exceeds *desired* investment by $100 billion.

The key Classical-Keynesian confrontation involves precisely such circumstances: What happens when *desired* saving exceeds desired investment? The Classics had a series of simple answers based on a single principle—*prices adjust* when there is an excess supply of or demand for any good (or all goods together). Therefore, when there is an excess supply that isn't being sold, entrepreneurs reduce their prices to get rid of unsold inventories, workers lower their wage demands to stave off unemployment, and the rate of interest (the *price* of borrowing) decreases when saving exceeds investment. The fall in the interest rate lowers desired saving (increasing desired consumer spending directly) and raises desired investment, until desired saving and investment are again equal and entrepreneurs are content with their previous (full employment equilibrium) level of production. All of this was stated more formally in the preceding chapter.

But Keynes was not sympathetic. Prices are sticky and probably wouldn't decline as inventories piled up. Wages are notoriously resistant to decreases and, even more important, fluctuations in the rate of interest do not equilibrate desired saving and desired investment. The rate of interest is determined in the money market; it equilibrates the supply and demand for money, not saving and investment. (And that is why Keynes dropped the quantity theory, as we will see in greater detail below.)

Assuming that the rate of interest doesn't bring saving into equality with investment, what happens as a result of the undesired inventory accumulation? Keynes thought that the level of real output, rather than prices, would respond most quickly. Entrepreneurs with unwanted accumulating inventories would probably cut back production. Output would fall as long as desired saving exceeded desired investment. Since the price level was unchanged, both real output and the associated level of nominal GNP would decline. How far? Until desired S equaled desired I, when a new equilibrium income, lower than before, would be reached. To help us see how far GNP would fall when desired saving exceeds desired investment,

Keynes invented the consumption function (or, looked at another way, the saving function).

Consumption and Simple GNP Determination

Let's start out with an equilibrium level of GNP so that we can see how discrepancies between desired saving and investment force changes in that level. Figure 1 is the familiar Keynesian cross diagram. (There was exactly one diagram in all of Keynes's *General Theory,* and it was a description of Classical interest theory! The figure shown here was made popular by Paul Samuelson.) The level of GNP (in dollars) is labeled Y and is measured on the horizontal axis, and expenditures (in dollars) are measured on the vertical axis.[1] The line drawn from the origin at an angle of 45° marks off equal magnitudes on each axis (remember isosceles triangles from basic geometry?); hence it traces the equilibrium condition $E = Y,$ or expenditure equals income (which also equals production).

Expenditure takes two forms: consumption and investment (we'll ignore the government for a while). Keynes argued that consumption spending (C) depends mainly on the level of income (Y)—more income, more consumption. In Figure 1, therefore, desired consumption is a simple linear function of Y:

$$C = a + bY$$

The letter b is the slope of the line, or $\Delta C/\Delta Y$, the change in consumption per unit change in income (see point X in Figure 1). It is called the marginal propensity to consume and is assumed to be less than 1. For example, if b is .8, that means an increase in Y of $100 raises C by $80. (It also means that saving goes up by $20.)

The a in the consumption function is the constant term. It records the level of C if Y were zero (presumably people eat even if they

[1]Throughout this chapter the level of GNP in dollar terms (Y) used in the figures corresponds to real GNP as well. This stems from the Keynesian assumption of fixed prices. When the analysis introduces variable prices, the real versus nominal distinction will be emphasized.

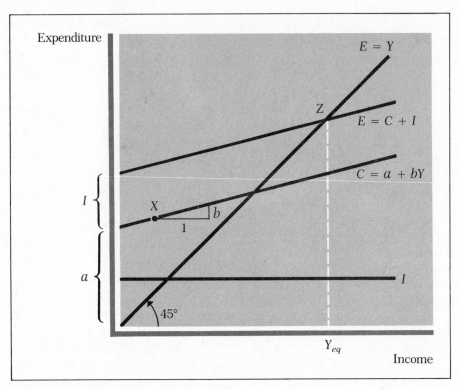

Figure 1 / Spending Determines Income

have no income—many of us have relatives like that), and it also sums up all other influences on consumption besides income. For example, if you had owned Xerox when it was Haloid (only as far back as 1958), you would now be consuming a lot more than if you owned Franklin National when it was Solvent (1973). Thus the consumption function might shift up or down, recorded by larger or smaller values for *a*, if people are wealthier or poorer, although our equation still says they would consume $8 out of every $10 *increment* in earned income.

As far as investment (*I*) is concerned, Keynes agreed with the Classics that it is a function of the rate of interest on bonds. Entrepreneurs compare the expected rate of return on a prospective investment with the rate of interest.[2] They invest as long as the rate of return exceeds the rate of interest and continue up to the point at which the expected return on the last investment just equals the rate of interest. If the rate of interest declines then investment projects with lower expected returns become profitable, hence investment will increase. For now we take the rate of interest as given. We also take expectations as given, which is an even more questionable proposition. Under such conditions, assume that investment is some constant amount (say $200 billion), as indicated by the horizontal line labeled I in Figure 1.

Equilibrium output is represented by the line $E = Y$, where total desired expenditure (E) equals total production Y. Total desired expenditure is the sum of desired C and desired I, or, in Figure 1,

---

[2]Note that since prices are fixed and inflationary expectations are zero, all nominal rates are the same as real rates.

The rate of return on an investment is determined by the expected future dollar revenues on the project and the current cost of the investment. In particular, if an investment is expected to generate $105 next year and requires a cash outlay of $100, we can calculate the rate of return quite simply. It is that rate of discount which equates the expected future revenues with the current cost, or $100 = \dfrac{105}{1 + q}$, where q is the rate of discount or, in our terminology, the rate of return. In our case it is clearly equal to .05, or 5 percent. We call q the rate of discount because it reduces (discounts) the $105 that is due next year to its current value (time is money). See Chapter 5 for a similar discussion.

Looked at another way, $100 put out at 5 percent for 1 year (100×1.05) produces $105 one year hence. This perspective also gives a clue as to how one ought to treat revenues two years hence. Namely, $100 left at 5 percent for two years produces 100×1.05 after one year, or $105, which is then reinvested and generates $110.25 after the next year ($105 \times 1.05 = \$110.25$). In general, therefore, if R_2 is the expected revenue two years from now, it must be discounted twice or

$$C = \frac{R_2}{(1 + q)(1 + q)} = \frac{R_2}{(1 + q)^2}$$

The general formula for the rate of return is as follows. If revenues of $R_1 \, R_2 \ldots R_n$ are expected over the next n years, then the rate of discount q which equates C, the current cost, to the expected stream of revenues, as in

$$C = \frac{R_1}{(1 + q)} + \frac{R_2}{(1 + q)^2} + \ldots + \frac{R_n}{(1 + q)^n}$$

is called the rate of return on the investment project. Relax—you have at least 13 seconds to perform the necessary computations.

line $E = C + I$, which is the vertical addition of C (= $a + bY$) and I. The point at which the total desired expenditure line ($E = C + I$) crosses the expenditure-equals-production line ($E = Y$) is equilibrium income (Y_{eq}). Point Z in Figure 1 is an example. At the level of production Y_{eq}, desired expenditure equals production.

It is also true that *desired* saving equals desired investment at that same income level. Desired saving is given by the difference between income and desired consumption (i.e., $S = Y - C$). It can be measured by the vertical difference between the 45° line and the consumption function. In Figure 1 the only point at which saving (the vertical difference between the 45° line and the consumption function) equals investment (the difference between the $E = C + I$ line and the consumption function) is at income Y_{eq}.

In Figure 2 we have plotted the saving function explicitly, where Y is measured along the horizontal axis and dollars saved or invested are on the vertical axis. Saving is defined as $Y - C$, so that

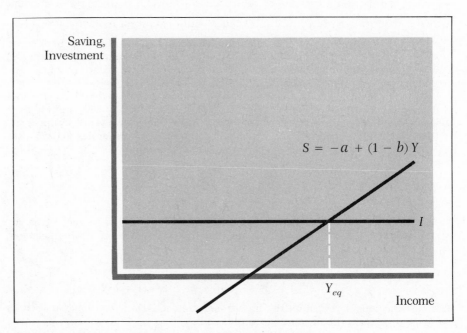

Figure 2 / Saving and Investment Determine Income

desired saving, S, equals $Y - (a + bY)$. Rearranging terms (and factoring the Y term) gives:

$$S = -a + (1 - b)Y$$

which is called the saving function. The marginal propensity to save equals 1 minus the marginal propensity to consume (out of each dollar increment in Y, a person spends b cents and saves $1 - b$ cents). From Figure 2 it is also clear that only at income Y_{eq} is desired saving equal to investment. At higher levels of income, desired saving exceeds desired investment; at lower levels of income, desired saving is less than desired investment.

Changes in GNP

Will production and income stay at level Y_{eq} in Figure 1 forever? It will if the consumption function (and hence the saving function) remains where it is, and if desired investment is also unchanged. Is that good? Yes, *if* Y_{eq} is the full employment level of economic activity. But Keynes not only wouldn't guarantee that it would be full employment, he was convinced that it would be only a fortuitous accident if it were. He reasoned that the level of economic activity is subject to wide swings because the level of investment is highly unstable. The consumption function was quite stable—you could always count on dumb households to consume a predictable percentage of income. But if entrepreneurs became uncertain about future sales prospects—especially about what other businessmen were planning to do—then desired investment spending would decline and GNP would fall.

There are two ways to see *how far* GNP declines when desired investment spending falls. Let us first look at what happens in terms of total spending (investment and consumption) when desired investment falls—the wide angle approach of Figure 1. We can then look at it from the standpoint of the investment-saving relationship —the isolated-camera on S and I of Figure 2.

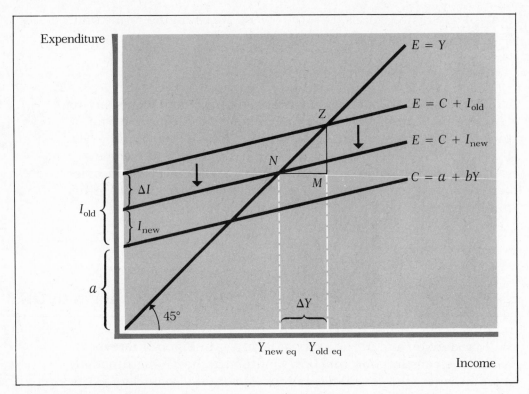

Figure 3 / A Decline in Investment Spending Reduces Y by a Multiple of the Change in Investment

In Figure 3 we have replotted Figure 1's equilibrium point Z and the equilibrium income associated with the old total spending function $E = C + I_{old}$. If desired investment now falls to I_{new}, then the total desired spending function declines to $E = C + I_{new}$, the new equilibrium point is at N, and income declines to $Y_{new\ eq}$. The decline in income is written as ΔY (the change in Y), and is measured by the change in income along the horizontal axis or by the distance MN (constructed parallel to the horizontal axis). As can be seen in Figure 3, the decline in income *exceeds* the decline in investment: the decline in income is ZM, which is equal to MN by construction, while the drop in investment is only part of ZM.

Why does income change by some *multiple* of the change in investment spending? Quite simply, because when investment changes and income begins to decrease (or increase), there is a further *induced* change in consumer spending. Consumption is a function of income, and whenever there is a change in Y, consumption spending is affected by the amount $b\Delta\dot{Y}$, where b is the marginal propensity to consume.

How large is the ΔY associated with a particular ΔI? GNP will change by the sum of the changes in both components of expenditure, namely $\Delta I + \Delta C$. Algebraically:

$$\Delta Y = \Delta I + \Delta C$$

But we know that, after all is said and done, $\Delta C = b\Delta Y$ (from our consumption function). Substituting $b\Delta Y$ for ΔC we have:

$$\Delta Y = \Delta I + b\Delta Y$$

We can now solve for the unknown value of ΔY by isolating the ΔY terms on the left side. We do this by subtracting $b\Delta Y$ from each side, which yields:

$$\Delta Y - b\Delta Y = \Delta I$$

Factoring the ΔY terms on the left side gives us:

$$\Delta Y(1 - b) = \Delta I$$

Dividing both sides by $(1 - b)$ produces:

$$\Delta Y = \Delta I \frac{1}{1 - b}$$

where $1/(1 - b)$ is known as the *multiplier*. If b, the marginal propensity to consume, equals .8, then the change in income will be 5 times the initial change in investment. If $b = .5$, the change in income will be 2 times the initial ΔI. [3]

The second way of looking at this process is to impose our desired S equals desired I condition for equilibrium. In Figure 4 we see that at income $Y_{\text{old eq}}$ investment I_{old} equals desired saving. When investment falls to I_{new} and income is still at $Y_{\text{old eq}}$, desired saving

[3]The multiplier is sometimes derived by more explicit use of the successive rounds of consumption flowing from the initial ΔI. This is called period analysis, and it goes something like this. Initially ΔI produces a direct change in income, ΔY, equal to the

exceeds desired investment and income must fall. Income falls enough to reduce desired saving until it is equal to investment. But we know from our saving function (see point R in Figure 4) exactly how much saving changes per unit ΔY:

$$\Delta S = (1 - b)\Delta Y$$

Since desired ΔS must equal desired ΔI in equilibrium, we can impose the following condition:

$$\Delta I = \Delta S$$

and then directly relate ΔI to ΔY by substituting $(1 - b)\Delta Y$ for ΔS. Hence:

$$\Delta I = (1 - b)\Delta Y$$

Dividing both sides by $(1 - b)$ produces:

$$\Delta Y = \Delta I \frac{1}{1 - b}$$

(*continued*)

ΔI. But then consumption changes by $b\Delta Y$ (which is equal to $b\Delta I$). This leads to a further change in consumption, $b(b\Delta I)$. This goes on, with the successive additions to GNP getting smaller and smaller because b is less than unity, hence b^2 is smaller than b, b^3 is smaller than b^2, and so on. The total ΔY is equal to the initial change in investment plus all of the subsequent changes in consumption (which stem from the initial $\Delta I = \Delta Y$). Or $\Delta Y = \Delta I + b\Delta I + b^2\Delta I + b^3\Delta I + \ldots + b^n\Delta I$. The right-hand side is a geometric progression whose sum is given by

$$\Delta I \times \frac{(1 - b^n)}{(1 - b)}$$

Since b is less than unity, b^n approaches zero as n gets large, hence we have

$$\Delta Y = \Delta I \times \frac{1}{(1 - b)}$$

which (surprisingly enough) is the same expression we derived in the text! These successive rounds of consumption were lumped together in the text into one $b\Delta Y$, by saying "after all is said and done," while here we build it up from each round of ΔY.

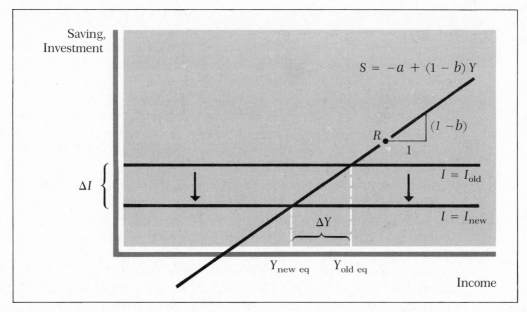

$$S = -a + (1 - b)\,Y$$

Figure 4 / A Decline in Investment Spending Reduces Y by a Multiple of the Change in Investment

which, to our great chagrin, is the same multiplier formula as before.

Autonomous Versus Induced Changes in GNP

Figures 3 and 4 suggest that anything that shifts the *position* of the total desired spending function will alter GNP. Such shifts in the position of the spending function are produced by *autonomous* spending changes (autonomous = independent; in our case, independent of GNP). The larger the size of the autonomous change in spending, the greater will be the change in economic activity.

But the multiplier story was based on the fact that autonomous spending changes also *induce* further changes in spending—in our case, via the consumption function. The larger the propensity to spend out of increments in income, or the larger the *slope* of the spending function (the larger b is), the greater will be the induced change in spending, and thus the greater will be ΔY.

Now you can see why Keynes divided spending into the two categories of consumption and investment. What he was really interested in was induced versus autonomous spending decisions. He argued that consumption spending is largely induced, while investment spending is largely autonomous (independent of income, but a function of the expected rate of return on capital and the rate of interest). Of course, investment prospects might be influenced by sales (current and future), which are certainly related to GNP. Similarly, desired consumption may change independently of current income—the constant term in the consumption function, a, shifts when Xerox goes from $1 per share to $100 per share. Nevertheless, Keynes still felt consumer spending was largely induced (by Y), while investment spending was largely independent (of Y).

It is worth noting that the multiplier expression derived above can be modified quite simply to take account of other sources of ΔY. In particular, ΔY is related to *any* autonomous change in spending (ΔA) by the same $1/(1 - b)$ factor. Or:

$$\Delta Y = \Delta A \frac{1}{1 - b}$$

For example, if the consumption function shifts upward, then A equals the difference between the old and new levels of autonomous consumption spending. Just like ΔI, this produces a direct change in Y which then causes further changes in Y via the conventional reaction of consumption of income.

The great problem of macroeconomics, according to Keynes, was that changes in autonomous spending would spark fluctuations in economic activity—rather wide fluctuations, via the multiplier, if the induced component of expenditure were large. These wide fluctuations in GNP would be associated with unemployment when GNP fell below its full employment level as a result of a decline in autonomous spending. What to do? The Classical response to such a situation was to do nothing—laissez faire. Keep hands off and let the long run work things out. But that was not the Keynesian response.

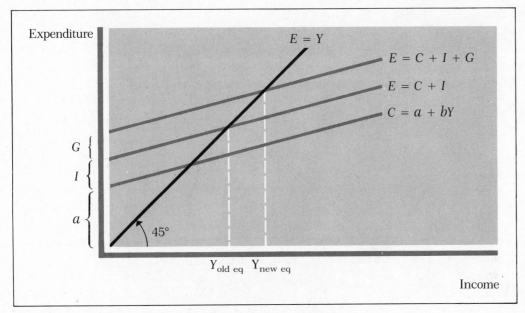

Figure 5 / Adding Government Spending Raises Income

Government to the Rescue

Keynes was the original Big Spender. If the private sector doesn't spend enough to keep everyone employed, let George do it (King George, of course). Government spending and taxation could be manipulated to offset the autonomous forces buffeting GNP and thereby restore full employment.

It is not very difficult to add government expenditure and taxes to our simple model. GNP is equal to the total of all expenditures in the economy—consumption, investment, and government:

$$C + I + G = Y$$

Assuming that government spending is some fixed level, G, we can simply add another line to Figure 1 for autonomous government spending. This is done in Figure 5, where $Y_{new\ eq}$ is the new equilibrium level of income when government spending is added.

"There are plenty of jobs around. People just don't want to work."

Drawing by Drucker; © 1972 The New Yorker Magazine, Inc.

The government usually finances its expenditures by taxation. Taxes do not lower spending directly, in the same sense that government expenditure directly changes spending. Rather, taxes reduce the amount of income that households have available for consumption expenditure. Consumption is not so much a function of GNP but of *disposable* income, where that is defined as equal to income minus taxes $(Y - T)$. We therefore have a new consumption function, written as:

$$C = a + b(Y - T)$$

Or, after carrying out the multiplication we can write the consumption function as:

$$C = a + bY - bT$$

It is easy to see from either way of writing the consumption function that when taxes go up by $10, consumption declines by b times that amount (or if $b = .8$, by $8). The reason is quite simple: People treat a dollar of income taken away by the government the same way they treat any other decline of a dollar's worth of income—they reduce consumption expenditure by the marginal propensity to consume times the change.

Taxes, in fact, introduce the same type of leakage between income and spending that saving does. From the standpoint of our model it makes no difference whether people reduce their consumption because they just happen to feel like it or because the government says it would be nice if they did (curiously, if you don't feel like it in the second case, you wind up getting a striped uniform and free room and board for between one and five years). In either case, the consumption function shifts downward. Figure 6 shows the equilibrium levels of GNP with and without taxes. Figures 5 and 6 also suggest that changes in both government spending and taxes produce multiplier effects on GNP. In this respect they are just like any other kind of autonomous expenditure. But there is one big differ-

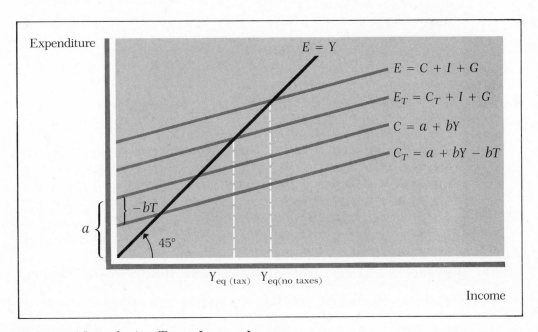

Figure 6 / Introducing Taxes Lowers Income

ence: Both taxes and government spending can be changed by government policy.[4]

The moral of the model of GNP including government expenditure and taxation is that the economy need not be buffeted about by autonomous changes in investment spending. Entrepreneurs may cut their desired investment spending if they get nervous, but nothing need happen to GNP as long as the government keeps its collective head and either increases *its* spending or lowers taxes so that consumers can increase theirs. In either case, the autonomous decline in investment spending could be offset by government *fiscal policy* (fiscal means pertaining to the public treasury or revenue, from the Latin *fiscus*). Whether or not the timing and magnitude of changes in G and T would be appropriate, given the institutional setup, is another matter (and will be discussed in later chapters). But the possibility of improving on the workings of the free market is certainly evident.

This returns us to an issue mentioned earlier: Is fiscal policy even necessary? Why doesn't income remain at full employment, with desired saving and investment brought into equality via fluctuations in the rate of interest, as the Classical economists said would happen? Why did Keynes, a truly Classical economist before he became a Keynesian, reject the Classical theory of interest rate determination? And what did he put in its place?

Money and the Rate of Interest

Our exposition of the Keynesian model so far is very much like its Classical counterpart in at least one respect—money doesn't matter. While the Classics said economic activity was set at the full employment level, and Keynes said it would settle at the point where total desired expenditure equaled production—which might be less than full employment—up to this point *neither* model has the money supply affecting real economic activity. The Classics, as we saw in the previous chapter, deflected its impact to the price level. Keynes,

---

[4]We will ignore the fact that taxes vary with the level of income. It does change the nature of the model slightly, but for our purposes we are better off without that complication.

the financial wizard of Cambridge, took a bolder position: The rate of interest is a monetary phenomenon. It is not determined by saving and investment, the way the Classics said, but by the supply of and demand for money.[5] Keynes also said that money might affect the level of economic activity, but only to the extent that it first influenced the rate of interest. Changes in the rate of interest would then alter desired investment spending, and thereby change the level of GNP.

The first order of business in investigating the rate of interest is to establish the framework by noting how Keynes divided the decision-making in his model of macroeconomic activity. So far, the analysis of income and expenditure revolves around two decisions: (1) household choice between spending income and saving it, with the latter defined simply as nonconsumption; (2) business firm decisions regarding the level of investment spending. These parts of the Keynesian system deal only with *flows:* consumption, saving, investment, and income over a given time period. It is, in the accountant's terminology, the "income statement" of the economy, with an implicit time dimension. We have also noted that none of these decisions involve any financial transactions; they deal only in *real* goods and services.

Money introduces an entirely new dimension to the macro model. Money is a *financial asset,* which is held in an individual's portfolio just as one holds a savings account at a bank, a corporate equity, or a Treasury bond. In other words, money is part of an individual's wealth—part of a person's balance sheet, in accountant's terms. The interest rate is determined by the third decision in the Keynesian scheme of things: (3) decisions of the public regarding the composition of its financial asset holdings.

Let's divide the public's portfolio into two types of assets: money and everything else. As we've seen before, money can be defined in many specific ways. For our purposes, the main distinction is that money has a fixed rate of interest, without any risk. Sometimes the rate is fixed at zero, as with currency; but that's not necessarily so, as with some checking accounts. The key is no capital losses or gains are incurred on the asset called money. Money is also used as the

---

[5]Obviously, since prices are fixed and inflation is not part of the picture, Keynes is referring to the real rate of interest when claiming it is a monetary phenomenon. The Classical picture of the real rate is Figure 1 of the last chapter, which shows saving and investment as determining the real rate of interest.

medium of exchange (to finalize transactions). Thus money is the most liquid of all assets, where liquidity is defined as the ability to turn an asset into the medium of exchange quickly with little or no loss in value. For lack of a better name, we'll call all other assets "bonds." The price of a bond can vary in terms of the medium of exchange, so the owner can suffer capital losses or reap capital gains. The realized rate of interest on a bond can be above or below what was expected at the time it was purchased, as we saw back in Chapter 5.

Money is a riskless asset, and bonds are risky assets. If people are risk averters—that is, if they dislike risk—then they will demand a higher expected return (interest rate) on risky assets compared with riskless assets. Thus a choice is necessary: How much of one's port-folio should go into money and how much into bonds?

It is important to note that the more bonds and less money held in a portfolio, the greater the uncertainty over total portfolio yield. For example, if I have $100, all in cash, my return is certain. If I put it all into bonds yielding 10 percent, I expect my return to be just that: 10 percent. But if interest rates rise substantially after my purchase, my $100 bond might be worth (could be sold for) only $75. In this case my expected 10 percent yield turns out to be minus 15 percent: the $10 in interest minus the capital loss of $25. If I had held $50 in cash and invested only $50 in bonds, I would have lost only half as much. More bonds in a portfolio mean more risk.

Our composite bond in this analysis includes all risky assets—equities, corporate bonds, municipals, even long-term government bonds. We'll assume that an efficient combination of risky assets has been derived. In Chapter 26 we'll return to the structure of yields on risky securities. For now we are concerned only with the choice between money and the composite bond of Keynes. It is this decision that determines the overall expected return, the "average" interest rate, on bonds.

The demand for money, called *liquidity preference* by Keynes, is a function of the rate of interest. In Figure 7 the horizontal axis measures the quantity of money, while the rate of interest is on the vertical axis.[6] The demand-for-money function is negatively sloped

---

[6]Since the rate of inflation is zero, the distinction between the real and the nominal rate of interest made in the last chapter doesn't exist. Thus the rate of interest on the vertical axis is the real rate, which is also equal to the nominal rate.

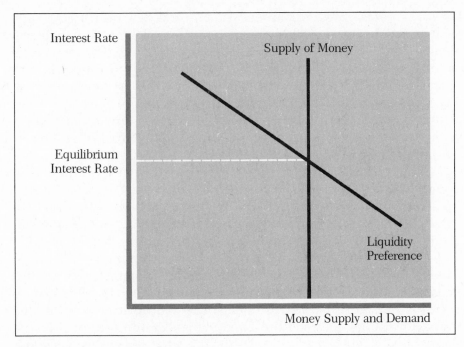

Interest Rate

Supply of Money

Equilibrium
Interest Rate

Liquidity
Preference

Money Supply and Demand

Figure 7 / Keynesian Interest Theory

—the lower the rate of interest, the larger the amount of money demanded.

There are a number of reasons for this negative relationship between quantity of money demanded and rate of interest. Keynes argued that people had an idea of some "normal" rate of interest, as though the rate of interest were attached to its "normal" level by a rubber band. When the rate of interest *declines,* more and more people become convinced that it will snap back to its "normal" level, i.e. that interest rates *will rise in the future.* If they hold bonds when rates are rising, they will suffer capital losses. In other words, the public, trying to avoid capital losses, would want to hold fewer bonds (but more money) as interest rates decline. This relationship has been called the speculative demand for liquidity because people are speculating on future bond prices.

A less restrictive approach to the negative relationship between demand for speculative money balances and the interest rate stresses interest rates as compensation for risk bearing.[7] A high rate of interest means that the cost of being liquid and safe (holding money) is great, in terms of the interest forgone. A high interest rate is an inducement to hold a large portion of one's assets in bonds (bond demand is high) and only a little in cash. At lower interest rates, the opportunity cost of (what one gives up by) holding money is much less. Since it feels good to be liquid, the amount of money demanded is greater at lower rates of interest. In more formal terms, people are risk averse—they don't like risk. There must be an inducement to hold a riskier portfolio, one with a larger amount of bonds. The inducement is a higher rate of interest.

Either approach to the demand for money explains its negative relationship to interest rates (as interest rates fall the amount of money demanded rises). Coupled with a fixed supply of money, determined by the central bank (a rather bold assumption), the rate of interest is in equilibrium when the amount of money demanded equals the supply. We know that the interest rate is in equilibrium then (as in Figure 7), because below the equilibrium rate the demand for money exceeds the fixed supply. If the rate of interest momentarily fell *below* the equilibrium rate, people would want more money than they have and would try to sell bonds to get it. The attempt to sell bonds drives down bond prices and interest rates up, until—at the equilibrium rate—people are satisfied with their portfolios of money and bonds.

At a rate of interest *above* the equilibrium rate, people would have more money than they want. They would try to get rid of their excess money balances by purchasing bonds. Bond prices would be driven up and interest rates down, until people were again happy with their holdings of money and bonds. This is at the equilibrium interest rate, of course.[8]

[7]This approach was first formally presented in James Tobin's article, "Liquidity Preference as a Behaviour Toward Risk," *Review of Economic Studies* (1958). It is less restrictive than Keynes's original discussion, because it does not require people to expect a "normal" level of interest rates. It also puts the money versus bonds decision within a general model of portfolio choice (see Chapter 23).

[8]It should not be too difficult to see why Keynesian analysis can look at the supply of and demand for money, rather than looking at the bond market directly, and say that the rate of interest is determined by equilibrium in the money market. As long as the total size of the public's portfolio, its wealth, is fixed—and in the short run this is a reasonable assumption—then a change in the demand for money relative to supply would be reflected in a one-to-one relationship by an opposite change in the demand

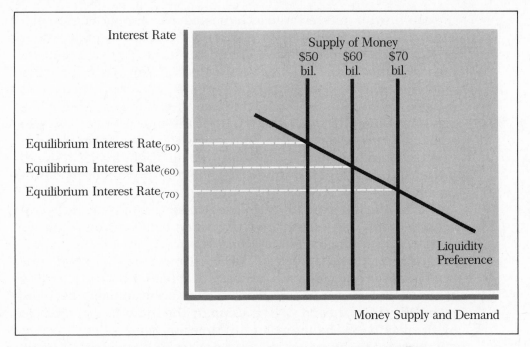

Figure 8 / Effect of Changing the Money Supply on the Interest Rate

Monetary Policy

What causes the rate of interest to change? Clearly, if either the demand for money or the supply of money shifts position, the equilibrium interest rate would change. For now, assume that the money demand function is given, and let us examine the impact of changes in the money supply on interest rates and economic activity.

In Figure 8, let's start out with the money supply at $60 billion and

---

for bonds relative to supply. In other words, if the demand for money goes up, it necessarily implies that people want to hold fewer bonds, and vice versa. Looking only at the supply and demand for money does not cost us any information in this scheme of things. A change in one market is automatically reflected in the other.

A more sensitive assumption embedded in this analysis is that money and bonds are substitutes only for each other: An excess demand for one means there is an excess supply of the other. Neither is considered a direct substitute for real goods and services. This turns out to be a distinction between modern Monetarists and Keynesians, as we shall see in Chapter 20.

the equilibrium interest rate as indicated. Assume the central bank increases the money supply (the magic word, as Captain Marvel said, is Shazam) from $60 to $70 billion. At the old rate of interest, the amount of money that people are now holding is greater than what they want. People try to dispose of their excess money balances (reduce their liquidity) by buying bonds, driving up the price of bonds and the interest rate down until the interest rate has fallen sufficiently to make people content to hold the new level of cash (and stop trying to buy bonds). This happy state of affairs occurs at the lower equilibrium interest rate$_{(70)}$, when the amount of money demanded now equals the new supply.[9]

The implications of the increased money supply for economic activity are clear—a lower interest rate on bonds means higher investment spending, *ceteris paribus* (a key phrase meaning everything else held constant, often used by economists to produce unexpected results and confound ordinary people in the street). In terms of our GNP-determining diagrams earlier in the chapter, the investment line shifts up and GNP goes up by the increase in I (induced by the decline in the interest rate) times the multiplier.

A decrease in the money supply produces just the opposite results. We start once again with a money supply of $60 billion in Figure 8, and this time let the central bank *decrease* the money supply to $50 billion (the magic word is obviously Mazahs). At the old equilibrium rate of interest, the amount of money that people are now holding is less than the amount they want to hold. People try to sell bonds to get more cash, bond prices decline, and interest rates rise until people are satisfied with their new money balances. They stop try-

[9]Since some forms of money balances pay interest—such as some checking accounts—it is at least conceivable that the larger supply of money could be absorbed by a higher interest payment on money balances rather than a lower interest rate on bonds. The excess supply of money requires only a decrease in the differential between the rate on bonds and the rate on money (so that people are induced to hold relatively more of the latter). One reason all bond rates fall, rather than the rate on money rising, has to do with the zero interest rate on currency and the fact that currency and demand deposits exchange on a one-to-one basis. Thus the rate of interest paid by banks on demand deposit balances cannot wander very far from the zero rate paid on currency. As a result, the major burden of adjustment to changes in the supply of money falls on all other rates of interest, rather than the own-rate on money. For a similar discussion, see James Tobin "A General Equilibrium Approach to Monetary Theory," *Journal of Money Credit and Banking* (February 1969).

ing to sell bonds when a new equilibrium is established at the higher interest rate $_{(50)}$.[10]

The implications for aggregate economic activity are the reverse of the case in which the money supply was increased. This time we have a higher interest rate on bonds and investment will decline; GNP goes down by the drop in I (induced by the rise in the interest rate) times the conventional multiplier.

The negative relationship between the demand for money and the rate of interest is an important component of the Keynesian model of GNP determination. It provides a link between changes in the supply of money and the level of economic activity.

But what Keynes giveth, Keynes can take away. If an increath in the money supply does *not* lower the interest rate, investment spending will not be affected. Keynes proceeded to question the efficacy of monetary policy under certain conditions. He argued, for example, that at very low interest rates the money demand function becomes completely flat. In Figure 9 it is easy to see that a very flat demand for money function means that increases in the money supply could no longer reduce the rate of interest. In particular, an increase in the money supply from $50 billion to $60 billion lowers the interest rate, but a further increase to $70 billion fails to produce any additional decline.

What causes the money demand function to enjoy the horizontal position? Keynes argued that at very low interest rates everyone would expect interest rates to rise to more "normal" levels in the future. In other words, everyone would expect bond prices to fall,

[10]An interesting sidelight: When the interest rate is above the equilibrium level, the public has more money than it wants and it tries to get rid of its excess cash (by buying bonds). When the interest rate is below the equilibrium level, the public wants more money than it has and it tries to get its hands on more cash (by selling bonds). *But it never succeeds, because the supply of money*—which is the amount the public has—*is determined not by the public but by the Federal Reserve.* When people buy or sell bonds to one another, all they do is shuffle the money supply around among themselves, moving it from one pocket to another. What the public *does* succeed in doing is changing the price of bonds—or the interest rate—until it reaches the (equilibrium) level where people are *content* to hold the same amount of money they held all along.

It is also interesting to note that when the money supply changes, the Keynesian result is that the interest rate adjusts to induce people to hold the new level of cash balances. In the classical world, when the money supply changes, the prices of all goods and services adjusts until people restore their *real* cash balances to their original level.

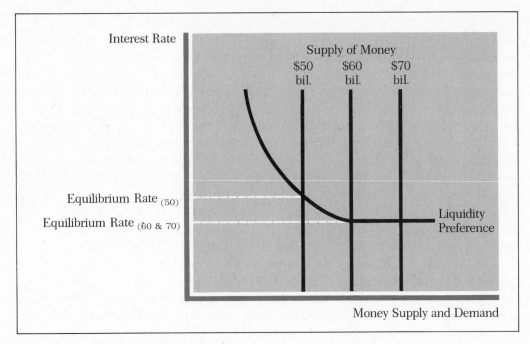

Figure 9 / Keynesian Liquidity Trap

therefore no one would want to hold bonds and the demand for liquidity (money) would be infinite. Any increase in money supply would simply be held by the public (hoarded), and none of the increased liquidity would spill over to the bond market. No one, in fact, would willingly hold bonds. In this "liquidity trap," as Keynes called the flat portion of the money demand function, monetary policy does not alter interest rates and therefore is completely ineffective. More generally, the flatter the liquidity preference function, the less effective monetary policy is in changing interest rates, hence in influencing GNP.

It should be obvious that monetary policy will also be less effective in changing GNP if investment spending is not very responsive to changes in the rate of interest. An interest insensitive investment function means that even a large change in the rate of interest will not alter investment spending very much. Thus a given change in the money supply will raise GNP by less if investment spending does not respond to interest rates.

Modern Keynesians have pointed out, however, that investment spending is not the only linkage between money supply and GNP. Consumers may also change their spending in response to variations in the interest rate. In particular, we noted above that consumer wealth—the value of stocks and bonds—influences consumption expenditure. A lower rate of interest means that the prices of bonds rise. Thus consumers will spend more when interest rates fall because they feel wealthier. In terms of our earlier diagrams, this wealth effect of a decrease in the interest rate causes the consumption function to shift upward.

We can conclude by noting that a change in the money supply will have a larger impact on GNP when the interest rate changes by a lot and when investment and consumption expenditures are sensitive to interest rates. The interest rate influences expenditure through changes in the cost of borrowed funds as well as via a somewhat more modern wealth effect.

Transactions Demand and Monetary Policy

The concept of a speculative demand for money, related to the rate of interest, was a Keynesian innovation. Before Keynes came along Classical economists had emphasized that the only reason people would want to hold money was for transactions purposes—to buy goods and services—as we saw in the previous chapter. An increase in GNP leads to an increase in the amount of money demanded (at every rate of interest), because people need more cash to carry out the higher level of transactions. Keynes also acknowledged this transactions demand, although he did not himself appear to realize all of its implications.[11]

Figure 10 shows how a change in the demand for money (at every rate of interest) affects the interest rate. We start out with a given

[11]Keynes also discussed a precautionary demand for money: People hold cash to provide for unforeseen contingencies. This demand was considered constant or was lumped together with transactions balances. In the next chapter we expand on the implications of transactions demand. In particular, since changes in income alter transactions demand and interest rates, we determine the level of income and interest rates simultaneously.

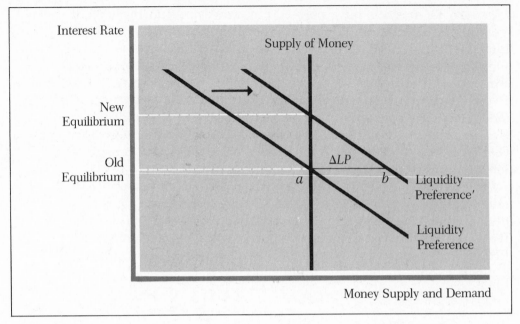

Figure 10 / A Shift in the Demand for Money Changes the Interest Rate

money supply and a given money demand (liquidity preference) function. Together they determine the equilibrium interest rate. Now suppose that people become more nervous than normal, perhaps because they expect a decrease in money supply. They seek ultimate relief by building up the proportion of cash in their portfolios. In other words, at every rate of interest people want more money (and fewer bonds) than before. Say the demand for money increases (ΔLP) by the amount *ab*. This happens at each rate of interest, so that we now have a new money demand function to the right of the old. At the old equilibrium rate of interest, there is now a larger amount of money demanded than the fixed supply. To get more cash, people try to sell bonds, driving bond prices lower and interest rates higher until a higher equilibrium interest rate is established. The case of a decrease in the demand for money can be treated symmetrically. The money demand function shifts to the left and the interest rate declines.

Something similar happens when the level of income changes. Say income rises. People now demand more money balances at every rate of interest to carry out the higher level of transactions, the demand for money function shifts to the right, and the rate of interest rises. In an economy that is growing, perhaps because investment spending is rising, the rate of interest would rise because of the increase in transactions demand for money. Unless, of course, the central bank expands the supply of money to provide for those transactions balances.

Now you know why we said back in Chapter 1 that "easy" or "tight" money is not really a matter of increases or decreases in the money supply in an absolute sense, but rather increases or decreases relative to demand. In a growing economy, the money supply must increase because the demand for money will rise along with the growth in GNP. Unless the central bank increases the money supply, interest rates will rise.

The transactions demand for money is probably affected by the interest rate as well as by income. It is very likely that higher interest rates reduce the demand for transactions balances. For example, assume you are paid $2,000 monthly (probably dropped out of school and became an apprentice plumber). You deposit the entire amount in the bank, spend it evenly over the month, and wind up at zero. Your *average* daily cash balance is $1,000. This is your transactions demand. But if interest rates on bonds were sufficiently high, you'd be willing to go to the cost and trouble to take half your salary at the beginning of the month ($1,000) and buy a bond, put the other $1,000 in your bank to be spent during the first fifteen days, and then when that runs out sell the bond and spend the second $1,000 over the last half of the month. What this means is that your average daily cash balance is only $500 (you go from $1,000 to zero evenly over fifteen days). What you gain from this is the higher interest on the funds invested in the bond market. And as long as the gain exceeds the costs, it's worth doing.

Your initial reaction might be: It would take an awfully high rate of interest to make me go through such shenanigans. That could be —but if you were a large corporation with a few million dollars in idle cash, the investment of that money could be very profitable. Most economists agree that the transactions demand for money, like

How Rockwell Makes Killing On High Rates

By Thomas Petzinger Jr.

Staff Reporter of THE WALL STREET JOURNAL

PITTSBURGH — While record interest rates are burdening and even bankrupting some businesses, others are making a killing in the short-term money markets.

With a lot of cash, it's easy. Rockwell International Corp., the diversified manufacturer, is a prime example. The short-term cash held by Rockwell earned $78.8 million in the fiscal year ended Sept. 30, compared with $507.5 million of pretax income from Rockwell's automotive, electronics, aerospace and general manufacturing operations. "The way things are going, we should run well over $100 million in interest income this year," says Robert A. DePalma, Rockwell's chief financial officer.

Rockwell has about 18 domestic cash investments totaling $570 million, mainly in bank certificates of deposit and time deposits held abroad, earning interest at rates as high as 20.375% a year. Even counting another $200 million in cash invested by Rockwell operations in Canada and Europe, that's "really a small part of the corporation's total assets" of $4.43 billion, says William L. Neely, treasurer. But he says it's "a hell of a big number in terms of the total earnings of the company."

Prime Rate "Madness"

For manufacturers, high interest rates raise the cost of financing their own operations and make it harder for their customers to buy. Bank lending rates, ranging from 20% to 21½% on short-term credit to the biggest and most creditworthy companies, are driving some manufacturers into court and are delaying others' expansion plans. Rockwell itself is encountering a downturn in its automotive business, which supplies parts for the depressed automobile and truck industry. "This 20% prime is madness, absolute madness," Mr. DePalma says.

Although its windfall interest income is helping Rockwell through hard times, some analysts worry over the temptation to sacrifice long-term investment for short-term gain. At Rockwell, managers "are all well aware of the fact that we're making 20%"— on cash—"and they're maybe going to make 10%" on other assets, Mr. Neely says. "When they see their margins shrinking, they reduce their operating assets, mainly inventories and receivables, in order to maintain their overall return, and they turn the cash over to me." Nonetheless, he insists that Rockwell will continue to plough money into expansion and improvement. "You can't stop the lifeblood of the company, which is capital," he says. "The liquidation of this company isn't in the cards."

At most large companies, cash management has grown sophisticated ever since the cost of money began climbing in the mid-1960s, from a long-term rate of less than 5%. Now most big companies collect and disburse cash through computers linked with their banks. Credits and debits get posted electronically, permitting companies to earn interest almost instantaneously

Getting the Last Buck

The companies release the cash at the last possible minute. Like others, Rockwell doesn't stick cash in its checking account before writing a check, but waits until the check will be presented for payment. Meanwhile the float, the cash that will go to settle the check, earns interest. "We've always been intense about wringing the last buck out of excess cash," Mr. Neely says.

At rates above 20%, the intensity turns to obsession. When Rockwell collects cash at a remote office outside its computer network, for example, "We're sure as hell going to double our effort to pick it up and get it deposited on Friday instead of Monday, even if it means flying there to get it," says L. Richard Cribbs, Rockwell's cash management director. On Friday, Dec. 5, Rockwell collected $15 million from a customer and, although no airplane heroics were needed, got it deposited in a time account that day at a New York bank at an annual rate of 20%. By Monday, the deposit had earned about $25,000 in interest.

Rockwell International Corp.'s Cash Moves This Month

Date	Amount Invested In Eurodollars	Maturity	Rate
12/2	$20 million	2 days	17⅛%
12/5	$15 million	3 days	20
12/8	$25 million	30 days	20⅛
	$35 million	30 days	20⅜
12/16	$35 million	182 days	19⅛
12/17	$15 million	overnight	20⅜
12/22	$35 million	28 days	20¾

News Item/ High Interest Rates Reduce Demand for Transactions Balances

the speculative demand, is a function of the rate of interest.[12] For some purposes it can be ignored or played down—but not if you are a corporate treasurer.

An interesting sidelight on the transactions demand discussion is the role played by credit cards. The easiest way to look at this is that credit cards permit a transaction to take place without a cash balance. In other words, people could theoretically invest all their cash at the beginning of the month in bonds, pay for everything via those little plastic cards, and then at the end of the month sell the bonds, put the proceeds into the bank, and write one check to the credit card company (which could be the bank itself). Although this is an extreme example, it indicates how credit cards get into the model and how their growth affects the economy. Greater use of credit cards reduces the demand for money (at every interest rate), thereby lowering interest rates, permitting investment and GNP to increase.

Expectations and Monetary Policy

Most simple economic models assume that expectations are exogenous, that is, they are determined outside the system.[13] This one is no exception. An important implicit assumption is that changes in the money supply are imposed by our central bank, the Federal Reserve, and that such policy changes are unanticipated. Under such circumstances, monetary policy alters the interest rate by more or less, depending upon the conditions described above.

[12]The interest sensitivity of transactions demand was first pointed out by William J. Baumol, "The Transactions Demand for Cash: An Inventory Theoretic Approach," *Quarterly Journal of Economics* (November 1952). For an application of modern cash management techniques stemming from Baumol, see Rita M. Maldonado and Lawrence S. Ritter, "Optimal Municipal Cash Management," *Review of Economics and Statistics* (November 1971). A somewhat more general treatment of household behavior is Robert J. Barro and Anthony M. Santomero, "Household Money Holdings and the Demand Deposit Rate," *Journal of Money, Credit, and Banking* (May 1972).

[13]More sophisticated economic models require that expectations for variables in the model (such as interest rates) conform with the predictions of the model. This is called "rational expectations" and will be discussed in Chapter 20.

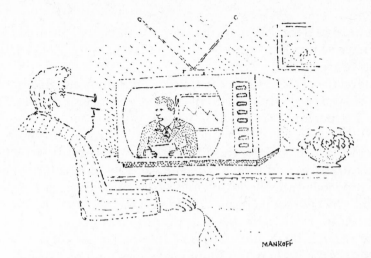

"On Wall Street today, news of lower interest rates sent the stock market up, but then the expectation that these rates would be inflationary sent the market down, until the realization that lower rates might stimulate the sluggish economy pushed the market up, before it ultimately went down on fears that an overheated economy would lead to a reimposition of higher interest rates."

Drawing by Mankoff; © 1981 by the New Yorker Magazine Inc.

But whether an increase or decrease in the stock of money causes a *simultaneous* movement in interest rates in the predicted direction depends crucially on whether or not the change in policy was anticipated. In particular, if everyone expects the Federal Reserve to cut back on the money supply next week or next month, a change in interest rates is likely to occur beforehand, with little or no effect at the time the money supply is actually altered. The reasoning is simple: If everyone expects the Fed to reduce the money supply in the future—and therefore expects interest rates to rise—then profit-maximizing bondholders will try to sell bonds *now* to avoid expected capital losses. Bond sales will drive down bond prices, driving up interest rates until they just about equal the expected rate next period. Thus when the money supply is, in fact, cut back next week or next month, rates don't move at all.

Incorporating expectations about policy movements into our model is possible but cumbersome. It is simulated by a shift in the demand for money function at every interest rate. In our particular example, when saying that bondholders want to sell to avoid capital losses, we are saying, in effect, that the demand for bonds decreases —or, in terms of our picture, that the demand for money increases at every rate of interest. That means the money demand function shifts to the right, as in Figure 10, increasing the rate of interest with the same supply of money.[14]

Thus an anticipated monetary policy will change interest rates before it is implemented. This is not especially surprising once it is put into the framework of our model, but it can be troublesome for policy-makers when portfolio managers get into the habit of forecasting stabilization behavior.

Aggregate Demand and Supply

So far we have described all the factors that can influence the aggregate demand for goods and services according to Keynes. As we mentioned at the very beginning of this chapter, since Keynesian analysis assumes prices are fixed because of a depressed state of the economy, all the impacts on aggregate demand discussed up to now correspond to changes in real output as well. It will be useful, nevertheless, to put the Keynesian model into a formal supply/demand framework, just as we did for Classical economics in Chapter 17. This will highlight the similarities and differences between Keynes and the Classics, it will permit a brief insight into Keynesian causes of inflation, and it will also let us see what is meant by supply-side economics.

In Figure 11 we put the price level on the vertical axis and the quantity of real output on the horizontal axis. Recall that nominal GNP, what we have labeled capital Y, is really Py, or the price level

[14]In the example of the previous paragraph, when the *anticipated* decrease in the money supply actually takes place, there is no increase in the level of rates precisely because the demand for money simultaneously decreases by the same amount at that time. The reason is people no longer expect the Fed to reduce the money supply. Thus, the demand for money returns to its original position.

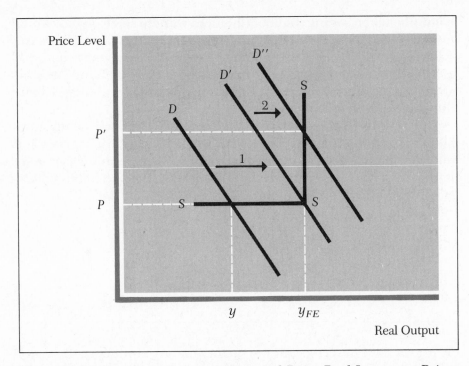

Figure 11 / Increases in Aggregate Demand Raise Real Income or Prices Depending upon the Shape of Aggregate Supply

times real output. Thus Figure 11 can be viewed as decomposing Y into its price and output components.[15]

The aggregate supply schedule in Figure 11 is in two parts: a horizontal segment, which reflects the fact that prices do not increase at less than full employment; and a vertical part, which is the Classical school's supply schedule showing that only prices increase (not real output) after full employment (assumed equal to output y_{FE}) is reached.

The aggregate demand schedule (D) is negatively sloped for the same reason as in the Classical world: a lower price level raises the real supply of money balances and this increases the aggregate

[15]Don't get nervous simply because until now aggregate demand ($C + I + G$) has been plotted in the figures against income (Y). We did not permit the price level to vary under that analysis. Now we are interested in how aggregate demand for real output varies when the price level changes, so Figure 11 plots demand as a function of price. They are simply different pictures tailored to answer different questions.

demand for goods and services. But in the Keynesian world, this rise in the real supply of money has a very specific channel of influence on real output. It occurs through the impact of rising real balances on the interest rate (as in Figure 8 above) and the impact of a lower interest rate on investment spending and hence GNP. Note that the increase in money supply in Figure 8 can occur either because the central bank raises cash balances or because a given supply of cash balances is worth more in real terms because the price level has fallen.

Equilibrium real output is given by the intersection of aggregate demand and supply in Figure 11. If we start with D, the level of real output is y and the price level is P. This combination of P and y would correspond with the equilibrium level of aggregate demand $(Py = Y)$ from, say, Figure 5 above. Thus far, Figure 11 adds nothing to our analysis since we had assumed all along that prices were fixed. The only plus is we now know that prices are fixed at some level, P (big deal).

If aggregate demand increases from D to D' in Figure 11, when aggregate supply is horizontal, the level of real output rises from y to y_{FE} and the price level remains at P. The rightward shift in the aggregate demand schedule can result from an increase in any of the autonomous expenditure categories discussed above. Thus D could shift to D' because of an increase in investment (I) or government expenditure (G), or because of a decrease in taxes which increases consumer spending (C). Note also that an increase in the money supply (M) will also shift D to D'.[16] What Figure 11 emphasizes for us is that the multiplier effects of autonomous expenditures on nominal income (ΔY) correspond to increases in real income (from y to y_{FE}).

But if aggregate demand increases further, from D' to D'', after aggregate supply has become vertical, then shifts in aggregate demand will result in price increases (from P to P') rather than increased real output. While the Keynesian analysis would still show a ΔY due to changes in autonomous spending, Figure 11 tells us that the increased nominal GNP is the result of higher prices ($P'y_{FE}$ minus Py_{FE}) rather than higher real output (as would be the case with Py_{FE} minus Py).

---

[16]An increase in M shifts D because at *every* price level there are more cash balances, which lowers interest rates and raises investment spending.

Thus when the economy is at or near full employment, Keynesian aggregate demand analysis can be used together with the aggregate supply curve to explain upward pressure on prices, or inflation. Anything that shifts the aggregate demand schedule to the right—whether it is increased government spending, increased consumer spending, or increased money supply that increases investment spending—will force up the price level. Notice that this explanation of what influences the price level is somewhat different from that of Classical economics. In Chapter 17 we showed that, according to Classical thinking, shifts in the aggregate demand schedule reflect changes in the money supply; in fact, the aggregate demand schedule embodies the quantity theory. This is a fundamental distinction between the Classical/Monetarist view of inflation and the Keynesian theory, and will be discussed again in Chapter 20.

At this point it is appropriate to explain the role of so-called supply-side policies in macroeconomics. Keynes himself had little reason to focus on aggregate supply, since in the depressed economy of the simple Keynesian model there are more than enough goods and services to go around. But in a full employment setting, the only way to increase real output is to expand productive capacity. That would be represented in Figure 11 by a rightward shift in the vertical segment of aggregate supply (y_{FE} would shift to the right). Supply-side economics focuses primarily on the impact of government policies on the aggregate supply schedule. Although this is very different from the Keynesian focus, the two are by no means contradictory.[17]

As we mentioned early in Chapter 17, the productive capacity of the economy is determined by the supply of labor, capital, and available technology. Policies that increase any of these production factors will increase potential real output. The government does not directly control any of these, but its tax policies influence the willingness of households and business firms to supply labor and invest in capital. In particular, higher tax rates may very well discourage work and investment, because labor and entrepreneurs are denied some fraction of the income they earn.

[17]Note that the quantity theory is in the same boat as Keynesian analysis because it focuses almost exclusively on aggregate demand.

According to supply-siders, the main consequence of reducing tax rates is increased production incentives. This contrasts with the Keynesian emphasis that a reduction in taxes raises aggregate demand. Up to now we have considered the effect of a tax reduction only on the aggregate demand schedule in Figure 11; supply-siders contend that the tax impact on the aggregate supply schedule can be even more important. Thus they *could* argue that if taxes were reduced when the economy was at full employment this need not cause prices to rise. In particular, if the vertical portion of the aggregate supply schedule shifted to the right by more than the movement in aggregate demand, prices could even fall. Whether this is in fact the case depends upon empirical evidence.

The role of Keynesian, Monetarist, and supply-side mechanisms in the inflationary process will be discussed in greater detail in Chapter 20. Meanwhile, in the next chapter we treat you to the pleasure of a more complicated Keynesian aggregate demand model.

Summary

1. Keynesian analysis maintains that the level of production is determined by the aggregate demand for goods and services. This differs from Classical economics, which argued that production occurs at full employment. The main difference between Keynes and the Classics is that Keynes did not think that fluctuating prices and interest rates would push the level of economic activity toward full employment, especially in the short run.

2. The Keynesian model focuses on the determinants of aggregate demand in order to pinpoint the level of production. Demand is divided into consumption, investment, and government expenditure. To Keynesians the consumption function is a key behavioral relationship because it allows them to explain how consumer spending varies with income. Thus when there is a change in exogenous spending (such as an increase in investment), income changes by some multiple (because of induced consumption spending).

3. Government expenditure and taxation play an important role in influencing the level of aggregate demand. Changes in taxes and government expenditures have multiplier effects on income and can be used to offset the effects on GNP of autonomous changes in investment.

4. According to Keynesians, the demand for and supply of money determine the level of interest rates. This differs from the Classical quantity theory, in which the supply of and demand for money determine the price level. The Keynesian result stems from the behavioral assumption that the demand for money is interest sensitive (plus the fact that the price level does not vary).

5. Changes in the money supply alter the level of interest rates in the Keynesian world. The impact on economic activity is then determined by the response of investment spending and the subsequent multiplier effects on GNP. The greater the impact of money supply changes on interest rates, and the larger the sensitivity of spending to interest rate changes, the more effect monetary policy will have on GNP.

6. All of Keynesian analysis focuses on the aggregate demand for goods and services. It assumes that aggregate supply is sufficient to accommodate increased demand without raising prices. Any increases in aggregate demand at full employment will raise prices and cause inflation, according to Keynesians. Supply-side policies emphasize the need to generate increased real output at or near full employment.

Suggestions for Further Reading

Keynesian ideas all stem, of course, from John Maynard Keynes, *The General Theory of Employment, Interest and Money* (New York: Harcourt, Brace, 1936). Having become a true classic (defined as a book that is no longer read, just referenced), it has been interpreted on many levels. One of the best interpretations is Alvin Hansen, *A Guide to Keynes* (New York: McGraw-Hill, 1953). A more advanced treatise is Axel Leijonhufvud (pronounced Leijonhufvud), *On Keynesian Economics and the Economics of Keynes* (Oxford University Press, 1968).

19

The Keynesian Framework: II

WHY CONFUSE THINGS with a more complicated model of GNP determination? Is it worth the effort? Haven't we said that a good model is like a good map—it tells you how to get from one place to another without detailing every curve in the road, every bump in the terrain? True enough. But sometimes a few complications make life more interesting. Versatility is the password. Being adaptable to more than one use is a desirable characteristic for a model.

The more complex model of GNP determination is known as *IS-LM* analysis. Among its many attractions, it shows how monetary and fiscal policy interact with each other; it shows what determines the relative multiplier effects of each; it provides a partial integration of the Classical and Keynesian systems into one conceptual framework; and it demonstrates some of the fundamental features distinguishing the Classical and Keynesian outlooks. As in the previous chapter, most of the analysis assumes a fixed price level, so that real and nominal magnitudes are still the same. In the next to last section we will analyze the implications of flexible wages and prices and at the end we will show how the *IS-LM* model collapses into an aggregate demand schedule.

337

Money, Interest, and Income

In Chapter 17 we noted that the Classical economists stressed the transactions demand for money. Keynes, as we saw in Chapter 18, also discussed this transactions demand, although he did not himself seem to perceive all its ramifications. In particular, because transactions demand increases with income, the rate of interest rises as income rises. Thus not only does the interest rate help determine income; in addition, income helps determine the interest rate.[1] Causation runs both ways—from the interest rate to income and from income to the interest rate. Fortunately, this is not an insurmountable problem. The economy winds up with a determinate level of each, but our model must be reformulated to take this into account.

We begin, in Figure 1, with three alternative money demand functions, each associated with a different level of economic activity.[2] The liquidity preference function associated with Y_1 is for a level of GNP which is less than Y_2, which in turn is less than Y_3. Each level of GNP has its own liquidity preference function, because at higher income levels more money is demanded for transactions purposes (at every rate of interest). The horizontal distance between any two demand-for-money functions is equal to the difference in the demand for money at the two levels of GNP. If we use the Classical formulation coming out of Cambridge (as discussed in Chapter 17), we can write:

$$\text{demand for money} = kY$$

or

$$\Delta \text{ demand for money} = k\Delta Y$$

The latter implies that the demand for money will change by k times the change in the level of GNP (where k equals, for example,

---

[1]The one exception is the liquidity trap, introduced in the last chapter, where the rate of interest is given and is independent of everything except public psychology.

[2]The discussion in the remainder of the chapter will be based on geometric analysis. For those who prefer algebra, the Appendix to the chapter presents the entire model, and its implications, in equation form.

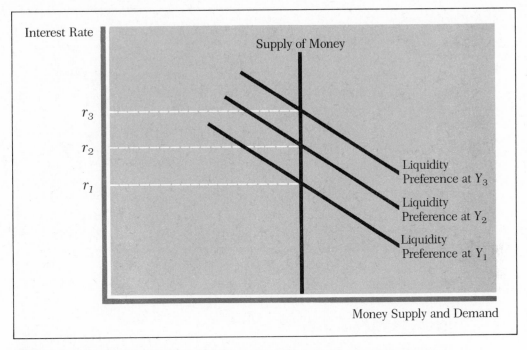

Figure 1 / How to Derive the *LM* Curve: at Higher Levels of Income, the Demand for Money Rises and so do Interest Rates

.25). In terms of Figure 1, this means that the horizontal distance between any two liquidity preference curves equals $k\Delta Y$.

The demand for money is really a function of two variables—income and the interest rate. The equilibrium condition (amount of money demanded = money supply) no longer provides an interest rate; rather, it provides combinations of income (Y) and the interest rate (r) which satisfy the condition that money demand equals money supply *when the money supply is fixed.* In fact, according to Figure 1, a positive relationship between Y and r is needed to keep the amount of money demanded equal to the fixed money supply. A higher level of GNP (compare Y_2 with Y_1) is associated with a higher interest rate (r_2 versus r_1). This relationship between Y and r that satisfies the equilibrium condition in the money market is plotted in Figure 2, where the interest rate is still on the vertical axis but now we have *income* on the horizontal axis. The line is labeled *LM* because it is the locus of combinations of Y and r that satisfy the

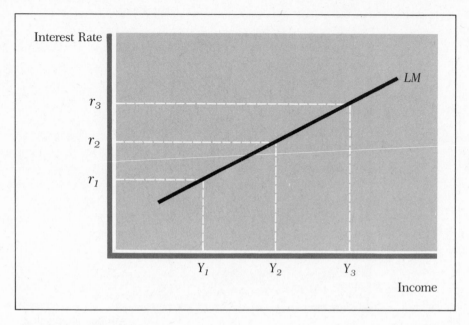

Figure 2 / The *LM* Curve

*l*iquidity-preference-equals-*m*oney-supply equilibrium condition.

How should you "read" the *LM* curve? In either of two ways. For a series of alternative interest rates, it tells you what the resulting income would have to be to make the demand for money equal to the (fixed) supply of money. *At higher interest rates,* there is less money demanded, *so income must be higher* to increase the demand for transactions balances if the total demand for money is to remain equal to the (fixed) supply. *Or,* for a series of alternative income levels, Figure 2 tells you what the resulting interest rate would have to be to make the demand for money equal to the fixed supply. *At higher income levels,* more transactions money is desired, *so the interest rate must be higher* to shrink the demand for money balances if the total demand is to remain equal to the fixed supply.

Before you write to the folks back home and tell them that the wise men from Wall Street said that an increase in the interest rate raises GNP, or that an increase in GNP raises the interest rate, rest assured that nothing of the sort has been said—so far. In fact, we can't even determine Y and r as yet, much less say anything about how each of these variables changes. All we have is one relationship (equation or equilibrium condition) and two variables, Y and r, and you remember enough high school algebra to know that you need at least two equations to determine the equilibrium values of two variables.

We *will* produce another relationship between Y and r—based on the equilibrium condition in the market for goods and services (the $C + I + G = Y$ or the $I = S$ equilibrium condition). This great unification and solution, which will knock your socks off, is scheduled to take place in about ten pages. But before that cataclysmic experience, it will be helpful for subsequent policy discussions to elaborate on the factors determining the slope of the LM curve and shifts in its position. Both of these help determine the relative size of monetary and fiscal policy multipliers.

All About *LM*

The determinants of the slope of the LM curve are best illustrated by going over the reasons for its positive slope. Take point A in Figure 3. Assume that the amount of money demanded equals the fixed money supply at that point, hence combination Y_1 and r_1 lies on the LM curve. To see whether a second (Y, r) combination that also satisfies the equilibrium condition (money demand = money supply) lies above and to the right of A (like point B), or below and to the right (like point D), let us first pick a point C which differs from A only in the level of income.

At point C, the rate of interest is still r_1 but income is Y_2 (above Y_1). Since income is higher at point C than at point A, the transactions demand for money is greater at C. Since nothing else is changed, point C must have a larger demand for money than the (fixed) supply. To set matters right, the interest rate must *rise* to reduce the demand for money and thereby restore the equality between demand and supply.

The slope of line AB (the LM curve) in Figure 3 is determined by two factors. *The first is the size of the gap between money demand and supply at point C.* If the increment in the amount of money demanded per unit ΔY is large, then the amount demanded will be a lot higher at C than at A, and the increase in r needed to restore

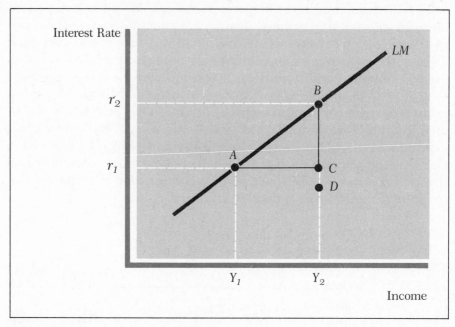

Interest Rate

r_2

r_1

A

B

C

D

LM

Y_1

Y_2

Income

Figure 3 / The Slope of the *LM* Curve

equilibrium (to lower the amount demanded) will be large. In other words, if transactions demand is great, then the level of r needed to maintain demand-supply equality at Y_2 will be great, point B will be higher than otherwise, and the slope of the *LM* curve will be steeper.

The second factor influencing the slope of the LM curve is the interest-sensitivity of money demand. For a given excess of money demand over supply at point C in Figure 3, the greater the interest-sensitivity of liquidity preference, the *smaller* the necessary increase in the rate of interest to restore equilibrium. This is so because when liquidity preference is highly interest-sensitive, then even a small increase in r reduces the amount of money demanded by a lot. In other words, at Y_2 the rise in r needed to insure demand-supply equality will be smaller the greater is the sensitivity of demand to r; point B will be lower than otherwise, and the slope of the *LM* curve will be flatter.

To summarize: The slope of the *LM* curve will be steeper the greater is the income sensitivity of the demand for money, and the less is the interest sensitivity of demand for money; the *LM* curve will be flatter the less is the income sensitivity of the demand for money, and the greater is the interest sensitivity.

Monetary Policy and the *LM* Curve

What causes the *LM* curve to shift *position* (in contrast to a change in its slope)? It does get boring in the same position, so the monetary authorities rush to the rescue. An increase in the supply of money moves the *LM* curve to the right, and a decrease in the money supply moves the *LM* curve to the left. By shifting the position of the *LM* curve, the Federal Reserve can increase or decrease the potential equilibrium level of GNP associated with a given interest rate. Let's see why a change in the money supply shifts the *LM* curve.

In Figure 4 we start with the *LM* curve associated with money supply M_1. All points on that curve satisfy the condition that the amount of money demanded $= M_1$. Take point *a,* with interest rate r_1 and income Y_1. Now increase the money supply to M_2. At point *a* the new larger money supply now exceeds the demand for money. What can restore equilibrium between the demand for money and money supply? Clearly, if *income* rises, the transactions demand for money will go up, hence some point to the right of *a,* say point *b,* will now represent equilibrium between demand and supply. Therefore, the new *LM* curve, $LM(M_2)$, the one with combinations of Y and r that satisfy demand equal to the new larger money supply, must be to the right of the old *LM* curve. (A similar argument shows that the *LM* curve must shift to the left if there is a decline in money supply.)

We can say exactly how far to the right (or to the left) the new *LM* curve must be. If the supply of money increases by $\Delta M,$ the amount of money demanded must change by the same amount in order to restore equilibrium. But we know that the transactions demand for money changes by k times the change in income ($k\Delta Y$). So income must change until $k\Delta Y$ equals ΔM (assuming nothing else changes, which is what we are doing by looking at the horizontal differences

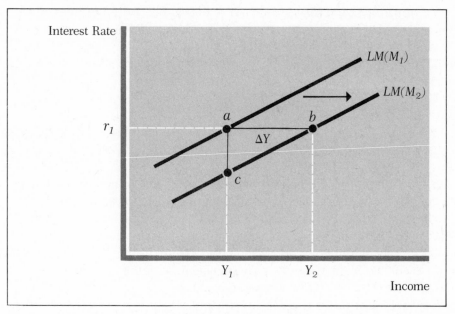

Figure 4 / An Increase in the Money Supply Shifts the *LM* Curve to the Right

between two *LM* curves—namely, the interest rate is being held constant). The demand for money will increase to match the enlarged supply when $k \Delta Y = \Delta M$, or when $\Delta Y = \Delta M/k$, which we can also write as $\Delta Y = 1/k \times \Delta M$. In other words, the horizontal distance between two *LM* curves is equal to $1/k \times \Delta M$ (or the difference in Figure 4 between Y_1 and Y_2 is $1/k \times \Delta M$).[3]

But a change in income is not the only way for a change in the money supply to be absorbed into the economy. The interest rate can fall, and this would also raise the amount of money demanded. This is represented in Figure 4 by point *c,* which lies directly below point *a*—i.e., we are still at income Y_1, *but this time it is the interest rate that has fallen* to restore equilibrium between the amount of money demanded and the new (larger) supply of money.

[3]Recall from Chapter 17 that when there is no interest sensitivity of the demand for money, then $1/k$ equals velocity. Under those conditions, the horizontal distance (which holds the rate of interest constant) between the two *LM* curves equals ΔM times velocity. This will be important in Chapter 21.

Unfortunately, we cannot as yet say exactly where the new increased money supply leads us. *Will it all be absorbed by increases in GNP, or will it all be absorbed by declines in the interest rate?* That question is a biggie! Our introductory discussion of Chapter 1 suggested that expansion in M will lead to *both* a higher GNP and a lower interest rate. Hence, if we start out at point a in Figure 4, the new equilibrium of the economy lies somewhere *between* points b and c. The Classical economists, however, said an increase in M will all be absorbed by transactions demand. In our case, GNP would increase and the economy will go to point b. We cannot yet answer the question because we don't really know where we started from. In order to find out where the devil we are, we must introduce the goods sector of the economy—saving and investment.

The Goods Market

Economic activity and interest rates are affected by behavior in the market for goods and services as well as in the money market. The counterpart to the money-demand-equals-money-supply equilibrium condition is the equilibrium between desired saving and investment (or total desired expenditure equals production). The equilibrium levels of GNP and interest rate must satisfy two equilibrium conditions: the condition that $I = S$ as well as money demand = money supply; which is a good thing, because with two variables, Y and r, we need two equations if both variables are to be determined (simultaneously).

To describe the combinations of Y and r needed for equilibrium in the goods market we must recall the investment function from Chapters 17 and 18. Desired investment spending is negatively related to the rate of interest; a fall in the rate of interest raises the level of investment spending. A higher level of investment spending, in turn, implies a higher level of GNP. These relationships are best depicted graphically. We will then discuss them in more general terms.

In Figure 5(a) the saving function is drawn together with three alternative levels of investment, each one associated with a different rate of interest. "Investment (r_1)" assumes rate of interest r_1, "investment (r_2)" assumes rate of interest r_2 (a higher rate than

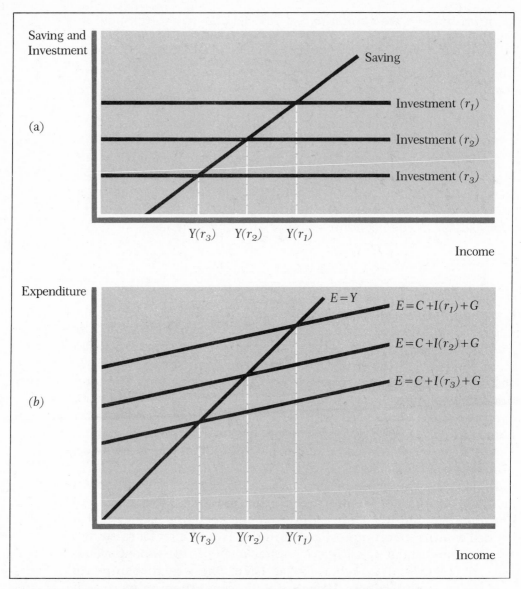

Figure 5 / How to Derive the *IS* Curve: at Lower Rates of Interest the Level of Investment is Higher, and so is the Level of Income

r_1), and so on. Figure 5(b) depicts the same situation, but from the total expenditure point of view. The three total expenditure lines are associated with the three different levels of investment.

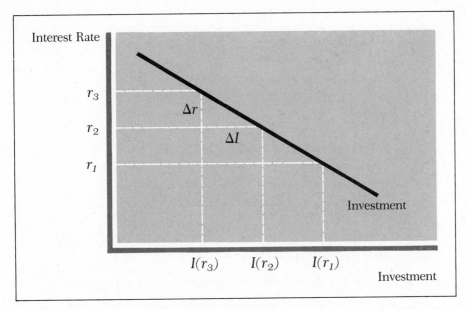

Figure 6 / The Investment Demand Function

The alternative levels of investment are derived from the investment function in Figure 6, where the rate of interest is measured on the vertical axis and the level of investment is on the horizontal axis. Interest rate r_3 is the highest rate and is associated with the lowest level of investment $I(r_3)$; interest rate r_1 is the lowest rate and is associated with the highest level of investment $I(r_1)$. The change in the amount of investment per unit change in the rate of interest ($\Delta I / \Delta r$) measures the sensitivity of investment spending to changes in the rate of interest.

It should be obvious from Figures 5(a) and 5(b) that there is a negative relationship between Y and r as far as the product market is concerned. Lower interest rates are associated with higher income levels as long as the equilibrium condition—saving equals investment—is satisfied. This relationship between Y and r is summarized in Figure 7, with r measured on the vertical axis and Y on the horizontal axis. (At this point, *we* are having difficulty distinguishing the horizontal from the vertical and who's on what—so keep your eyes open.) The locus of points satisfying the investment-equals-saving equilibrium condition is called the *IS* curve.

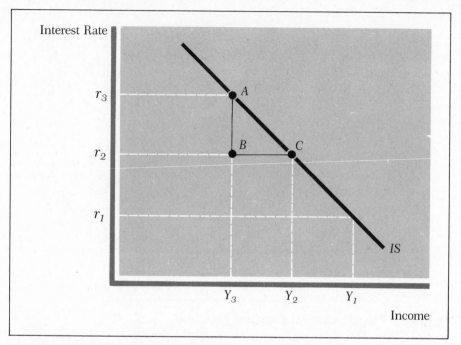

Figure 7 / The *IS* Curve and Its Slope

How should you "read" the *IS* curve? As with the *LM* curve, in either of two ways. For a series of alternative interest rates, it tells you what income must be to make saving equal to investment. *At higher interest rates,* there is less investment, *so income must be lower* to shrink saving (which is a function of income) to the point where it equals the smaller volume of investment. *Or,* for a series of alternative income levels, it tells you what the interest rate must be to make saving equal to investment. *At higher income levels,* saving is larger, *so the interest rate must be lower* to expand investment to the point where it equals the larger volume of saving.

Perhaps now you can appreciate our advice earlier in the chapter, with respect to the *LM* curve, suggesting that you not pass on that particular information about the relationship between *Y* and *r*. Now there are two relationships between *Y* and *r*. While more of a good thing is usually better, it can lead to embarrassing situations. In our case, however, it will rescue our model from indeterminacy.

But before presenting the Missouri Compromise (named after those who refused to believe it was possible), let's take a quick look at the factors that determine the slope and position of the *IS* curve; these are the things, along with the factors that determine the slope and position of the *LM* curve, that influence the relative magnitudes of the monetary and fiscal policy multipliers on GNP.

All About *IS*

To see why the *IS* curve looks the way it does, what makes it flatter or steeper, what moves it to the right or to the left, let us examine its negative slope in greater detail. Take point *A* in Figure 7 and assume that combination (r_3, Y_3) satisfies the condition saving equals investment: hence *A* lies on the *IS* curve. Now let us move to point *B*, which differs from *A* only in having a lower interest rate (r_2 compared with r_3). But a lower rate of interest implies a higher level of investment. Hence, if $I = S$ at point *A*, then *I* must *exceed* *S* at point *B*. In order to restore equilibrium, saving must be brought up to equality with investment. There's no better way to do it (in fact, no other way at all in our model) than for income to rise, say to Y_2, which raises saving (by the marginal propensity to save times ΔY). At point *C* saving is once again equal to investment, and it too is admitted to that select group of points on the *IS* curve.

The slope of the *IS* curve is determined by the size of the discrepancy between *I* and *S* at point *B*—that is, by the sensitivity of investment to a unit change in the interest rate—and by the responsiveness of saving to increases in income (the marginal propensity to save). For example, if investment is very sensitive to changes in *r* (in Figure 6, if the investment function were flatter, so that ΔI per unit Δr were larger), then investment would exceed saving by a lot at point *B* in Figure 7. In order to increase saving by a lot, income would have to rise a lot; point *C* would be further to the right than it is, and the *IS* curve would be flatter. If the marginal propensity to save were very large, however, the increase in *Y* need not be very large to restore equilibrium, point *C* would be more to the left, and the *IS* curve would be steeper.

All of this could be said in somewhat less formal terms. The fall in the rate of interest at point B compared with point A raises investment spending. This ΔI, in turn, raises the level of GNP by ΔI times the "simple" multiplier, $1/(1 - b)$, of the previous chapter. This increase in GNP is measured from point B to point C. (Note that this assumes quite explicitly that the rate of interest remains the same both before and after the increase in Y; and that is accomplished by drawing a *horizontal* line from B to C.) Hence the slope of the IS curve is flatter the more sensitive is investment spending to changes in the rate of interest, and the larger is the multiplier effect. This is perfectly consistent with the story just told in terms of the marginal propensity to save, because the larger the marginal propensity to save $(= 1 - b)$, the smaller the multiplier of the simple Keynesian model.

To summarize: A *highly* interest sensitive investment function and a *low* marginal propensity to save imply a flat IS curve; a low interest-sensitivity of investment and a high marginal propensity to save imply a steep IS curve.

The *position* of the IS curve (in contrast to its slope) is altered by any change in autonomous spending, e.g., government spending, private investment that is independent of the rate of interest, or private consumption spending that is independent of income (or, looked at from another standpoint, private saving that is independent of income, such as changes induced by government taxation). Such shifts in autonomous spending disturb the $I = S$ (or $E = Y$) equilibrium condition. The equilibrium combinations of Y and r will, therefore, be altered. This can be seen by looking either at saving equals investment equilibrium or output equals expenditure equilibrium. We will spare you the agony of doing it both ways (just this once), and concentrate on the expenditure equals output approach.

In Figure 8 let's start out with IS curve $IS(G_1)$. At every point, saving equals investment and desired total expenditure equals income. Now assume government spending goes up, from G_1 to G_2. From Figure 5(b) it is clear that under such conditions each of the total expenditure functions would shift upward, producing a higher level of Y for each interest rate. In Figure 8, therefore, an increase in G implies a shift to the right of the IS curve,

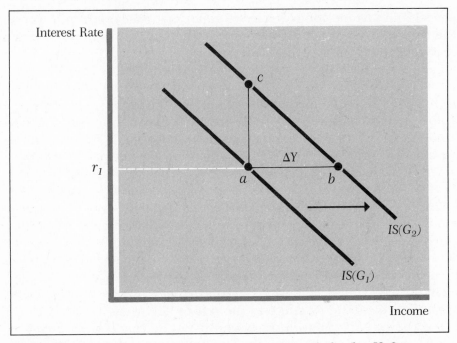

Figure 8 / An Increase in Government Spending Shifts the *IS* Curve to the Right

say to $IS(G_2)$—that is, a higher level of *Y* for each rate of interest.[4]

Similar shifts in the *IS* curve would be brought on by increases or decreases in investment spending that are independent of the rate of interest. How does something like that come about? If entrepreneurs suddenly expect higher future dollar returns on investment projects, the rate of return discussed in Chapter 18 will increase and some investment spending will be undertaken that otherwise would not have been. Keynes thought such shifts would, in fact, occur quite often and in substantial magnitude. Entrepreneurs are a fickle group, very sensitive to anything (war and

---

[4]An increase in taxes, on the other hand, implies a lower level of consumption in Figure 5(b), hence each of the total expenditure lines is lower than before and the level of *Y* associated with each rate of interest is less. Result: The *IS* curve shifts to the left.

peace) and anyone (presidents and reporters) that might influence the future profitability of their investments. Their actions tend to shift the investment demand function (Figure 6) to the right or left, thereby shifting the *IS* curve to the right or left as well.

We can also say exactly how much the *IS* curve shifts to the right or left due to a change in autonomous spending. A change in autonomous spending, ΔA, produces a change in GNP by the amount ΔA times the Chapter 18 multiplier, $1/(1 - b)$, assuming no changes in other categories of spending (besides consumption via the change in income). In Figure 8, the horizontal distance between two *IS* curves—e.g., point *a* to point *b*—measures the difference between two levels of income, assuming some type of autonomous spending has increased but the rate of interest remains constant. That would equal ΔA times our old multiplier friend $1/(1 - b)$. Therefore, an increase in autonomous spending—such as a change in government spending—shifts the *IS* curve to the right by ΔA times $1/(1 - b)$, while a decrease in autonomous spending shifts the *IS* curve to the left by ΔA times $1/(1 - b)$.

But there really is *another* possibility. The increase in autonomous spending need not raise GNP if some other category of spending simultaneously contracts. If, at the same time that government spending goes up, private investment spending is discouraged (because the rate of interest rises), it is conceivable that GNP could remain unchanged. This possibility is recognized explicitly in Figure 8 by point *c*, which is directly above *a*, implying no change at all in GNP. Instead, the rate of interest has risen sufficiently so that total spending remains the same: Income equals desired expenditure at point *c* as well as point *b*, saving equals investment at both points, and so both are on the new *IS* curve.

Keynesians seem to agree that a change in government spending will raise GNP a lot, hence we will wind up near point *b* when *G* goes up. The Classical economists, on the other hand, felt that the level of output would be unaffected by changes in any particular category of expenditure. An increase in *G* would be accompanied by a decrease in some other kind of spending, leaving income unchanged (we would move to point *c*). We can't really tell what will happen until we bring the *IS* curve together with the *LM* curve, derive equilibrium *Y* and *r* simultaneously, and then examine the way these variables respond to monetary and fiscal policy within that *general* equilibrium framework.

The Simultaneous Determination of Income and Interest: *IS* and *LM* Together

The equilibrium levels of GNP and the interest rate must satisfy equilibrium in the money market (money demand = money supply or $LP = M$), *and* in the product market ($I = S$). In Figure 9 we have drawn an *LM* curve for a given money supply, and an *IS* curve for a given level of government expenditure and taxation and a given investment function (relating I to r). The equilibrium Y and r must be at the intersection point of the *IS* and *LM* curves, point E, since only at that point does saving equal investment *and* liquidity preference (LP) equal the money supply. At any other point, one or both of these equilibrium conditions are violated, and dynamic forces will move income and the interest rate toward point E.

Let's see what happens if the economy is not at point E in Figure 9. Take point A on the *IS* curve. Saving equals investment, but money demand is less than money supply. (The latter is so because point A is directly above point B, which is on the *LM* curve. At point B we know $LP = M$. Since point A has a higher rate of interest, the amount of money demanded is less, and with a given money supply we have LP less than M.) People want to hold less money than they have at point A. To get rid of the money they start to buy bonds, driving bond prices higher and the interest rate lower. As the interest rate falls, investment rises and so does income—and, believe it or not, we are sliding down the *IS* curve toward E.

At point B, money supply equals money demand because we are on the *LM* curve, but investment exceeds saving (point B is directly below A; at A we know $S = I$; at B the interest rate is lower, hence I exceeds S). The excess of I over S leads to an increase in production as entrepreneurs try to replenish falling inventories. As income rises, the rate of interest is driven up because the money supply is fixed and people start to sell bonds in order to get additional transactions balances. We are now climbing up the *LM* curve toward E.

At points to the right of E, dynamic forces would lead to a fall in the level of income. At C we have $LP = M$, but desired investment is less than desired saving (see if you know why—hint: compare with D). Entrepreneurs cut back their production in order to reduce inventory accumulation. As GNP falls there is a reduction in the need for transactions balances, people start buying bonds with the

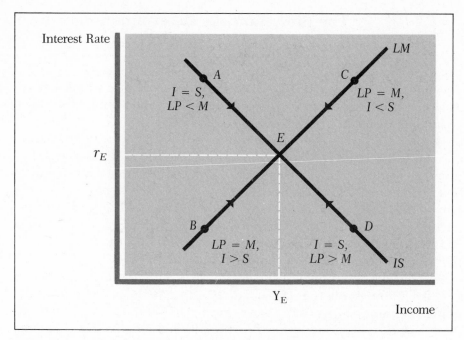

Figure 9 / The Simultaneous Determination of Income and Interest (Fantastic!)

extra cash, bond prices rise, and interest rates decline—we return to E by sliding down the LM curve. Finally, at point D investment equals saving, but LP exceeds M. People try to sell bonds to get more cash, bond prices fall, interest rates rise; investment spending starts to fall and income falls along with it—we climb the IS curve until we get to E.

Equilibrium point E has the nice property that if the economy is not there, dynamic forces will restore that particular combination of Y and r. It is a *stable* equilibrium. As long as the IS and LM curves remain in the same position, any deviation of income from Y_E will set forces in motion to restore that level of output; the same is true of interest rate r_E.

But there is nothing sacred about income Y_E. It may or may not be a full employment level of output. We have noted no tendency for the economy to insure that Y_E is full employment, although we will suggest a few things later on. If Y_E happens to be full employment,

"Look, the point is that where the LM *and* IS *curves intersect you get equilibrium in both the money market and the product market."*

all is well. But if it isn't, and the army of unemployed becomes restless, the government may step in to produce full employment. As we noted in the previous chapter, it could use monetary policy or fiscal policy. We have all the tools to do a complete analysis of the impact of such policies on GNP.

Monetary and Fiscal Policy

Monetary Policy: We have now reached the point where we can put all of our slopes and shifts to good use. Figures 10, 11, and 12 summarize the way monetary policy influences economic activity, and the factors affecting the size of the multiplier effects on GNP within the *IS–LM* framework.

In Figure 10, if we start with *LM* and *IS,* the equilibrium level of income is *Y* and the interest rate is *r.* An increase in the money

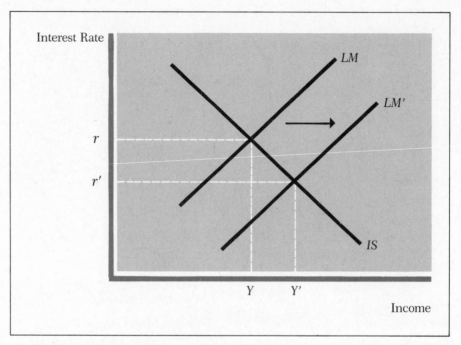

Figure 10 / An Expansionary Monetary Policy

supply, for example, shifts the *LM* function to *LM',* reducing the interest rate to *r'* and increasing GNP to *Y'.*[5]

Figure 11 shows that an increase in money supply (*LM* shifts to *LM'*) raises GNP by more, the *flatter is the IS curve.* With the relatively steep *IS* curve, the increase in income is only to Y_s, while with the flatter *IS* curve the increase is to Y_f. The flatter *IS* curve can be due to a highly interest-sensitive investment function.[6]

---

[5]All the examples are in terms of increases in the money supply. A decrease would simply shift the *LM* curve to the left and all of the changes would be just the reverse. Note again that since the price level is fixed, all the changes in dollar income correspond to changes in real income as well.

[6]The wealth effect of interest rates on consumption also makes the *IS* curve flatter, thereby increasing the impact of a change in the money supply on GNP. The reasoning is as follows: A decline in the rate of interest not only increases investment spending directly but also increases wealth (by raising bond prices) and thereby induces consumers to spend more. For a given decline in the rate of interest, therefore, both investment and consumption go up, which causes income to rise by a larger amount.

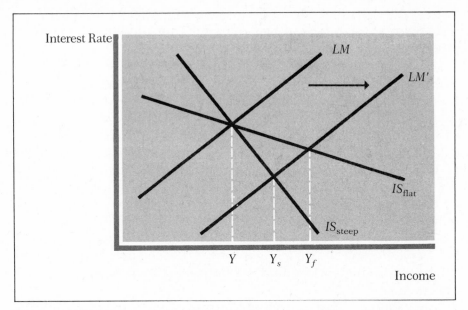

Figure 11 / Monetary Policy is More Effective the Flatter the *IS* Curve

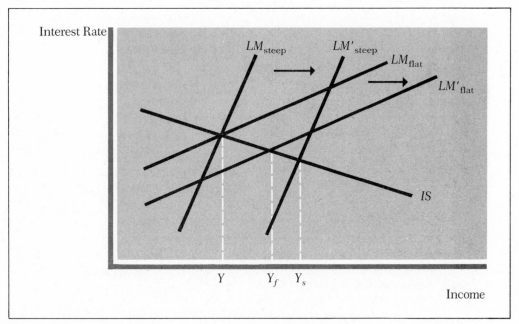

Figure 12 / Monetary Policy is More Effective the Steeper the *LM* Curve

Hence, the fall in r due to an increase in M raises the level of investment by a lot. The impact of monetary policy on GNP is more powerful under such conditions.

Figure 12 is somewhat more complicated. It illustrates that an increase in the money supply is more powerful *the less the sensitivity of money demand* to changes in the interest rate. If the demand for money is rather insensitive to changes in the rate of interest, the *LM* curve is steeper. An increase in money supply would shift LM_{steep} to LM'_{steep} or LM_{flat} to LM'_{flat}.[7] The former implies an increase in GNP from Y to Y_s, while the latter implies a shift from Y to Y_f. The explanation is as follows: The *less* the interest sensitivity of the demand for money, the *larger* the decline in the rate of interest when money supply is increased (because the amount of money demanded increases only slightly when there is only a small fall in r); therefore, with a big drop in r (needed to increase money demand), the induced increases in investment spending and GNP are large.

Fiscal Policy: The nature of the impact of fiscal policy on GNP is summarized in Figures 13, 14, and 15. An increase in government spending (or a decrease in taxes) shifts the *IS* curve to the right.[8] In Figure 13 there is a shift from *IS* to *IS'*. Equilibrium GNP goes from Y to Y' at the same time that the interest rate is driven *up* from r to r'. The interest rate goes up because there is increased transactions demand for money associated with the rise in GNP and, with a fixed money supply, r must rise to keep $LP = M$.

Up to now this interest rate effect has been suppressed in evaluating the impact of ΔG (or any change in autonomous spending) on economic activity. It has significant consequences, however. It *reduces* the size of the autonomous expenditure multiplier, hence the power of fiscal policy, because the increase in the interest rate reduces investment spending at the same time that government expenditure is going up. If the rate of interest had remained un-

---

[7]Notice that the *horizontal* distances between the two sets of curves are identical because the income sensitivity of the demand for money is the same in both cases; hence the *potential* increase in GNP due to the increased money supply is the same (at the old equilibrium interest rate).

[8]A decrease in government spending or an increase in taxes shifts the *IS* curve to the left, and all of the impacts are the reverse of those in the text.

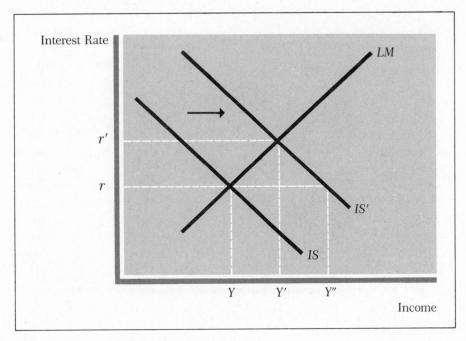

Figure 13 / An Expansionary Fiscal Policy

changed, the increase in GNP would have been to Y''. The size of the horizontal shift in the IS curve is equal to ΔG times $1/(1 - b)$, and the increase from Y to Y'' is equal to that. But the actual increase in GNP is less (only to Y'), because the interest rate goes up and investment spending is reduced somewhat (now you know why we called $1/(1 - b)$ the "simple" multiplier). In fact, this decrease in investment when government spending rises has come to be known as the "crowding out" effect.

The size of the government expenditure multiplier (and thus the effectiveness of fiscal policy) is greater, the smaller is the offsetting effect of rising interest rates on investment spending. In Figure 14 the rightward shift in the IS curve has a smaller impact on GNP with the steeper LM curve compared with the flatter LM curve. When a steep LM curve is due to small interest sensitivity of liquidity preference, for example, the increased transactions demand for money as GNP rises requires a large increase in the rate of interest

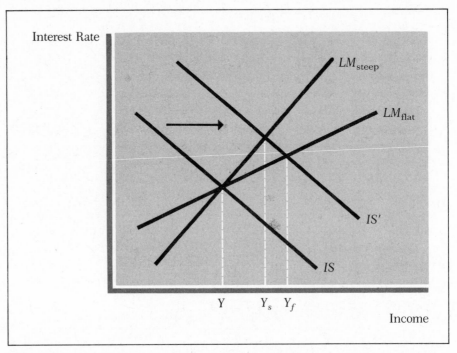

Interest Rate

LM_{steep}

LM_{flat}

IS'

IS

Y Y_s Y_f

Income

Figure 14 / Fiscal Policy is More Effective the Flatter the *LM* Curve

to bring total money demand back into equality with money supply. The large rise in the rate of interest cuts off a large amount of private investment—there is a large "crowding out" effect—hence the net impact on GNP is relatively small.[9]

Figure 15 is another rather complicated diagram. It indicates that the less the interest sensitivity of investment, the larger is the government expenditure multiplier, and thus the more effective is fiscal policy. If investment spending is insensitive to changes in the rate of interest, the *IS* curve is steeper. An increase in government spending either shifts IS_{steep} to IS'_{steep}, raising GNP to Y_s, or shifts IS_{flat} to IS'_{flat}, raising GNP to Y_f. The increase in the rate of interest

[9]The steep *LM* curve can also be due to a large transactions demand for money. In this case, the increase in Y produces a large rise in the demand for money, forcing the rate of interest to rise by a lot in order to bring money demand back into equality with the fixed money supply.

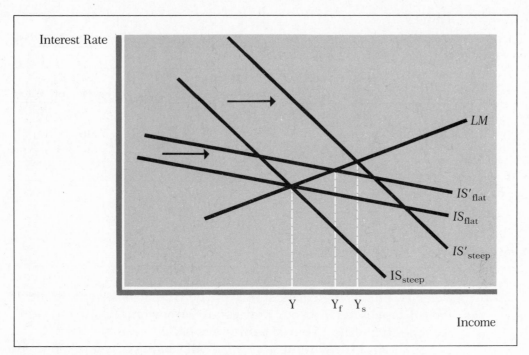

Figure 15 / Fiscal Policy is More Effective the Steeper the *IS* Curve

cuts off more investment the greater the sensitivity of investment to the rate of interest; hence the rise in income is smaller under such circumstances.[10]

As a reward for reading this far and still remaining conscious (check your pulse), Table 1 summarizes the factors influencing the relative effectiveness of monetary policy and fiscal policy. Start at the top of columns (1) and (2), with the statement, for example, "If *LP* is very sensitive to *r*" and then proceed to the extreme left-hand column for *"Then* (A), (B), (C) and (D)." The implications of each statement for *IS–LM* analysis and monetary and fiscal policy are recorded in the table.

[10]Notice that the horizontal distances between the two sets of *IS* curves are identical. This is so because, holding the rate of interest constant, the *potential* increase in GNP due to an increase in government spending is the same (because the marginal propensity to consume is assumed to be the same).

Table 1

	(1)	(2)
Then	If *LP* is very sensitive to r	If *I* is very sensitive to r
(A) The *LM* curve is	flatter	—
(B) The *IS* curve is	—	flatter
(C) Monetary policy is	less effective	more effective
(D) Fiscal policy is	more effective	less effective

Keynes and the Classics

Velocity, one of the cornerstones of the Classical system, seems to have disappeared from our Keynesian framework. Where has velocity gone? It has disappeared behind the *LM* curve. Since a particular *LM* function is drawn for a *given* money supply, as one moves up along an *LM* function, the income velocity of money is necessarily going up. Income is rising but the money supply is constant, so Y/M $(= V)$ has to rise. In Figure 16, three different *IS* curves produce three different levels of GNP, as well as three different levels of velocity: V_1 (equal to Y_1/M) at *a*; V_2 $(= Y_2/M)$ at *b*; and V_3 $(= Y_3/M)$ at *C*. V_3 is greater than V_2, which is greater than V_1.

The rightward shifts in the *IS* curve in Figure 16, associated with (for example) increased levels of government spending, succeed in raising GNP by raising velocity. In fact, velocity goes up because the demand for money is sensitive to the rate of interest. The rise in the rate of interest induces the public to hold less speculative balances (or, more generally, make more economical use of all money balances), permitting more cash to be used for carrying out transactions.

If the demand for money were totally *insensitive* to the interest rate, then velocity would be constant and GNP would not be affected by shifts in autonomous spending. An interest insensitive demand for money means that money demand depends *only* on income. For a given supply of money, there is only one level of income at which

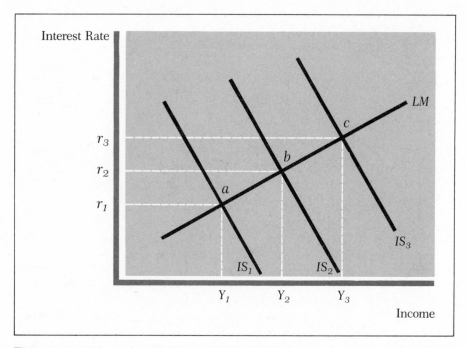

Figure 16 / When the *IS* Curve Shifts, both Income and Velocity Rise

the equilibrium condition, *LP = M,* is satisfied. The *LM* curve is vertical at that level of GNP, as shown in Figure 17—implying that no matter how high government spending rises, the level of GNP cannot go up because then *LP* would exceed *M.*

It is the fixed money supply that prevents GNP from rising under such circumstances. If autonomous spending goes up, illustrated by the rightward shifts in the *IS* curve in Figure 17, the result is an increase in the rate of interest, cutting off investment spending. The rate of interest rises until the fall in interest-sensitive investment spending is equal to the autonomous increase in spending, resulting in no increase in GNP. The "crowding out" effect is complete. (We will return to the implications of a vertical *LM* curve in Chapter 21.)

Another feature of *IS–LM* analysis is that it integrates the Classical and Keynesian theories of interest rate determination. In Chapter 18 the simplified Keynesian view was that the interest rate was a purely monetary phenomenon, determined by the supply and de-

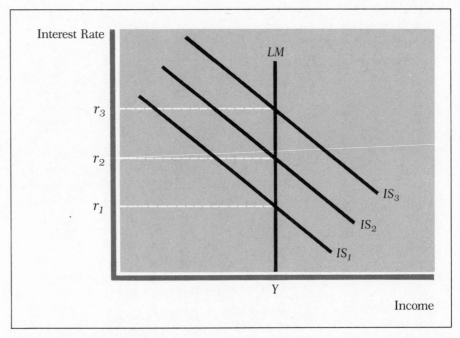

Figure 17 / When the *LM* Curve is Vertical, Shifts in the *IS* Curve Raise Neither Income nor Velocity

mand for money. The Classical school, on the other hand, argued that the interest rate was a "real" phenomenon, determined exclusively by saving and investment.[11] In our current treatment both monetary factors, embodied in the *LM* curve, and real factors, embodied in the *IS* curve, affect the interest rate. An increase in the money supply, by shifting the *LM* curve to the right, lowers the rate of interest, as Keynes suggested. An increase in autonomous investment, by shifting the *IS* curve to the right, raises the rate of interest, as the Classics suggested.

This partial rehabilitation of Classical interest rate theory forces us back to the question we raised earlier: Why don't variations in the rate of interest automatically bring about full employment in the

[11]Recall once again that this controversy refers to the real rate of interest. As long as inflationary expectations are zero, real rates equal nominal rates. Moreover, as long as inflationary expectations are unchanged, changes in nominal interest rates correspond to changes in real rates.

Keynesian system, as the Classical economists argued would happen? Having resurrected this much of Classical theory, can we bring Say's law back to life as well?

When Will Full Employment Prevail?

The Classical argument that the level of economic activity would tend toward full employment can be put into the Keynesian *IS–LM* framework quite simply. Figure 18 shows an equilibrium level of income Y and interest rate r associated with *IS* and *LM*. Let's assume that the level of GNP that would generate full employment is Y_{FE}.[12] Quite clearly, economic activity at Y is too low to justify employing all those who want to work at the going wage rate. Unemployment is the result.

The Keynesian apparatus makes it perfectly clear that the only way employment will increase is for aggregate economic activity to increase; only if desired spending increases will GNP increase beyond Y toward Y_{FE}. So far we have no reason to suspect that either the *IS* curve or the *LM* curve will shift to the right, hence no reason to suspect that output Y will not remain at that level unless there are increases in government spending or the money supply.

But the Classical economists said we needn't wait for government intervention. With less than full employment, workers would lower their wage demands and prices would be lowered as entrepreneurs tried to sell the output they produced with the increased labor that they hired (more workers would presumably be hired at lower wage rates). However, if both prices *and wages* are falling, there is no reason to expect consumers to spend more—goods cost less but individuals receive less money for their work, so their *real* income hasn't increased. Investment spending is also not likely to be affected directly. Entrepreneurs pay less for their inputs because of

[12]Since the price level is flexible under the current analysis, the horizontal axes in Figures 18 through 20 must be identified with real income (since nominal and real are no longer identical). The level of full employment income Y_{FE} corresponds to the full employment level of real output in Figure 11 of the last chapter. Since inflationary expectations are still not part of the picture, the vertical axis still represents both nominal and real rates of interest (they are still the same).

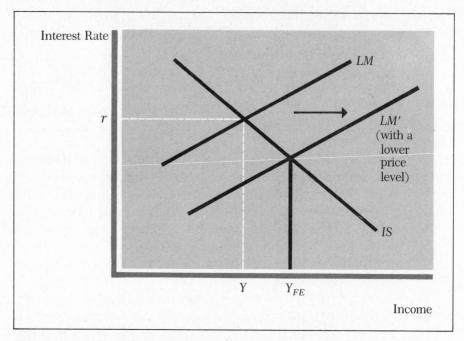

Figure 18 / The Classical Position: Lower Prices Shift the *LM* Curve to the Right and Automatically Produce Full Employment

the decline in prices, but they must also expect to receive a smaller dollar return on outputs; the two are likely to cancel each other and expected profitability should be more or less unchanged. Indeed, all our behavioral relationships are in *real* terms; people see through falling prices accompanied by falling incomes, so consumption, investment, and money-holding decisions are unaffected by equal movements in dollar incomes and prices. If no one is induced to increase spending, aggregate demand will remain at its old level, workers just hired will be fired, and the level of employment will be back where it started.

Nevertheless, the Classical economists had an ace in the hole: One thing clearly affected by a fall in the price level is the real value of the supply of money. As we saw in previous chapters, if the money supply is fixed at $1,000 and the price level is one, its real value (in purchasing power) is the same as if the money supply were $2,000 and the price level were doubled. But if we start out with a $2,000 money supply and the price level is cut in half—presto, the real money supply doubles (e.g., from $2,000/2 to $2,000/1)! This increase in the real value of the money supply due to falling prices is the mechanism through which the economy would move itself from a position of less than full employment to full employment. Here's how.

In terms of Figure 18, falling prices shift the *LM* curve to the right for the same reason that an increase in money supply does—falling prices increase the real value of the money supply and thereby create an excess of (real) money supply over the demand for money. Falling prices continue as long as people are unemployed, so that the increased real value of the money supply continues to shift the *LM* curve to the right, lowering the interest rate and increasing desired investment. This process would continue until the *LM* curve in Figure 18 is shifted from *LM* to *LM'* (the latter associated with a lower price level than at the original position), at which point economic activity is at full employment.

The Keynesian attack on this Classical mechanism was not confined to the argument that prices and wages are sticky and inflexible and not likely to fall very promptly. The Classical school, in fact, stressed that unemployment was the result of such downward inflexibility in wages and prices. Keynes said, however, that there were at least two other circumstances that would stall the move toward full employment. First, at the end of the last chapter we noted that in the case of a *liquidity trap* an increase in the money supply would not lower the interest rate. As long as the liquidity preference function is perfectly horizontal, an increase in the money supply, real or nominal, is associated with the same rate of interest. The *LM* curve is flat under such conditions,[13] and no matter how far the price level declines, the interest rate won't fall, investment spending will remain unaltered, and so will aggregate output and employment. This situation is depicted in Figure 19.

The second case in which falling prices fail to work is when investment is highly *insensitive* to the rate of interest. The *IS* curve is very steep. Under such conditions, declining prices and the in-

[13]Recall that the *LM* curve is flatter the greater the interest sensitivity of money demand. In the liquidity trap, money demand is infinitely interest-elastic, hence the *LM* curve becomes totally flat.

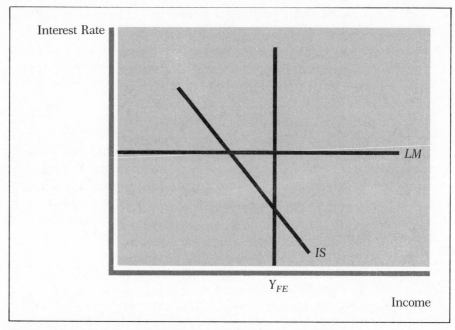

Figure 19 / An Extreme Keynesian Position: A Liquidity Trap

duced reduction in the rate of interest will be unable to raise invest-ment to a sufficiently high level to generate full employment spend-ing, as in Figure 20.

But Classical economics wasn't built on such a fragile link be-tween the monetary sector and spending on goods and services. The Classical argument that we have just presented based the automatic tendency toward full employment on the rightward shift *in the* LM *curve,* due to increases in the real value of the money supply. This is a thoroughly "Keynesian" mechanism, in the sense that money affects the economy only through the interest rate. But falling prices not only lower the interest rate—they also make people's real money balances worth more and this might have a more direct impact on economic activity. People would be wealthier in addition to being more liquid. And if more liquidity wouldn't help (because of, say, the liquidity trap), more wealth (in the form of real balances) certainly would. A cash balance of $10 may not mean you're very rich if the price level is unity. But if the price level fell to 1/10 of what it was,

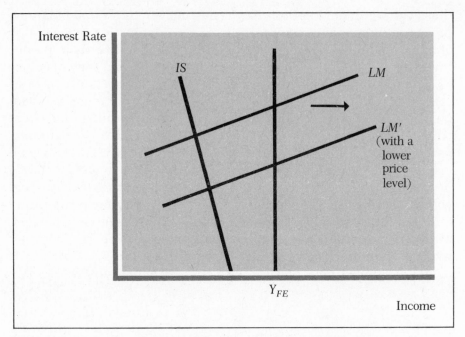

Figure 20 / Another Extreme Keynesian Position: Investment Unresponsive to the Interest Rate

you'd have $100 in purchasing power; a drop to 1/100 would make your $10 bill worth $1,000 (in purchasing power); and a decline in the price level to 1/100,000 of what it was would make you a millionaire!

As we noted in our discussion of the consumption function in Chapter 18, an increase in wealth raises desired consumption at every level of income.[14] In terms of Figures 19 and 20, *the IS curve* would now shift to the right until it intersects the *LM* curve at the full employment level of GNP. Prices then stop falling, and all those who want jobs are employed (with so many millionaires, perhaps the unemployment problem would be eliminated by the army of the wealthy pulling out of the labor force). In other words, the complete

[14]The wealth effect just discussed is called the real balance effect to distinguish it from the influence of interest rates on wealth. As we mentioned in footnote 6, the interest-rate-induced wealth effect merely changes the slope of the *IS* curve (it depends on the interest rate and the interest rate is on the vertical axis). The real balance effect *shifts* the *IS* curve because it alters spending at every rate of interest.

Classical argument has *both* Keynesian curves, the *IS* and *LM,* moving to the right as a result of falling prices. Changes in the real value of money balances affect the rate of interest and indirectly influence investment spending (the rightward shift in *LM*), but they may also affect consumption spending directly (the rightward shift in *IS*).

Keynes would say all this is fine, but by the time it comes about all those who wanted jobs will have passed through the Great Unemployment Window in the Sky. The Classical "do it yourself" path to full employment is lengthy and arduous. Unemployment can last a very long time if the economy is left to its own devices, with no help from its friends. So the Keynesian prescription is fiscal policy. Monetarists reflect their Classical ancestry by maintaining that flexible wages and prices will do the job. In the next chapter we use aggregate supply and demand analysis to describe these alternative viewpoints. It will be useful therefore to see how the *IS-LM* model developed here meshes with that broader framework.

IS-LM and Aggregate Demand

Recall from the end of Chapter 17 that the aggregate demand curve relates the price level to the demand for real output. The *IS-LM* model pictures the relationship between the interest rate and GNP. The connecting linkages between these models are twofold. First, as we mentioned above, once the price level is variable, it is necessary to distinguish carefully between real and nominal magnitudes. In particular, we must emphasize that the *IS-LM* model really describes the relationship between interest rates and the aggregate *demand* for real output; it tells us only that the demand for real output is increased when the interest rate falls; whether real output actually goes up depends upon whether the price level is forced up or whether real production can increase. Until now we have assumed that prices are fixed, hence changes in demand correspond to changes in real output. But in general, the division between price and real output movements depends on the shape of the aggregate supply curve, as we saw in Chapter 18.

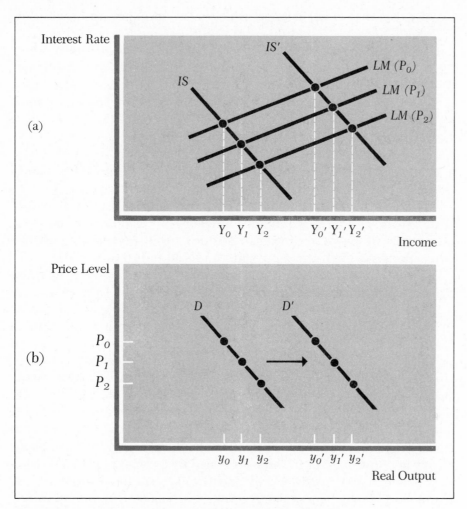

Figure 21 / Deriving Aggregate Demand from *IS-LM*

The second link between the models is the effect of changes in the price level on real money balances, and hence on the interest rate. In particular, in the previous section we showed that a lower price level shifts the *LM* curve to the right, lowers the interest rate and raises real GNP. Now we realize that it is more accurate to say that the *demand* for real output increases when the price level falls.

With this overview, it is relatively easy to generate a complete aggregate demand schedule from the *IS-LM* model. Different price levels are associated with a family of *LM* curves, as in Figure 21(a). Given the curve *IS* in Figure 21(a), we have a number of equilibrium real income or output levels (y_0, y_1 and y_2) associated with price levels P_0, P_1 and P_2. Figure 21(b) plots the demand for real output as an explicit function of those prices. The result is *D*, which is exactly what we call the aggregate demand curve.

It is also fairly easy to see the underlying factors causing the aggregate demand schedule to change position. Figure 21(a) shows that a rightward shift in the *IS* curve to *IS'* generates higher levels of GNP for any given price level. Thus the aggregate demand curve shifts from *D* to *D'* when any category of exogenous spending pushes the *IS* curve to the right. It follows that decreases in exogenous spending push the aggregate demand curve to the left.

Less obvious but also true, an increase in the stock of money shifts aggregate demand to the right. The reasoning is as follows: An exogenous increase in the money supply causes *each* of the *LM* curves in Figure 21(a) to shift rightward (use your imagination); thus, a higher level of demand for real GNP is associated with any given price level, and that's represented by a demand schedule like *D'* compared with *D* in Figure 21(b). Similarly, decreases in the money supply will cause the aggregate demand curve to shift to the left.

It is possible to describe in greater detail how the *IS* and *LM* curves combine to determine the slope and the size of the shifts in the aggregate demand schedule. For our purposes, you are no doubt happy to know, it is more important simply to recognize the connection between the *IS-LM* world and the aggregate demand/supply framework. We will explore the implications in the next chapter.

Summary

1. The main advantage of *IS-LM* analysis is that it shows the behavior of the money market and the product market in a single diagram. Keynes's earlier treatment ignored some crucial interactions. An important mechanism is that the interest

rate both influences GNP (through investment) and is affected by it (through the demand for money).

2. The simple Keynesian fiscal policy multiplier ignores the fact that an expansion in aggregate demand raises interest rates. Thus in the *IS-LM* model the impact of fiscal policy on GNP is tempered by rising interest rates that crowd out private investment.

3. Monetary policy raises GNP by lowering the interest rate and encouraging investment. The impact on GNP will be reduced, therefore, when either the interest rate can't be lowered much (because money demand is very interest sensitive) or when investment spending is relatively insensitive to the interest rate.

4. Velocity, the cornerstone of Classical economics, is hidden behind the *LM* curve of the Keynesian model. Fiscal policy raises GNP by increasing the velocity of the existing money supply.

5. Flexible wages and prices will push aggregate demand toward full employment equilibrium even in the Keynesian world. That process is tempered by a very interest sensitive money demand and by very interest insensitive investment. Nevertheless, given enough time, wage-price flexibility will generate full employment even according to *IS-LM* analysis.

Suggestions for Further Reading

The original presentation of the *IS-LM* model was in John R. Hicks, "Mr. Keynes and the 'Classics': A Suggested Interpretation," *Econometrica* (April 1937). An advanced treatment of Classical versus Keynesian macroeconomics is Don Patinkin, *Money, Interest, and Prices* (New York: Harper & Row, 1965), especially Chapters 9–14. A good advanced historical survey of topics in monetary theory is Harry G. Johnson, "Monetary Theory and Policy," *American Economic Review* (June 1962). An updating of Johnson's survey is Stanley Fischer, "Recent Developments in Monetary Theory," *American Economic Review* (May 1975).

Appendix

The Simple Algebra of Income Determination

For the algebraically inclined, much of the discussion in Chapters 18 and 19 can be summarized succinctly in equation form. The economy is divided into two sectors: the goods or product market, comprising the demand for goods and services; and the monetary sector, comprising the demand for and supply of money.

The Model

The product market can be described by four functional relationships (behavior equations) and one equilibrium condition (an identity). All the functional relationships are assumed to be linear, an assumption that simplifies exposition without doing excessive damage to real world applications. The functional relationships:

(1) $C = a + b\,(Y - T)$ Consumption (C) function
(2) $I = d - n(\mathrm{R})$ Investment (I) function
(3) $T = e + t(Y)$ Tax (T) function
(4) $G = \overline{G}$ Government spending (G)

and the equilibrium condition:

(5) $C + I + G = Y$ or $S + T = I + G$

where Y stands for GNP (income) and R for the interest rate. In each equation, the first lower-case letter represents the constant term of the function, and the second lower-case letter the coefficient of the independent variable (or the slope of the function); i.e., b is the marginal propensity to consume ($\Delta C / \Delta(Y - T)$), and n is the interest sensitivity of the investment function ($\Delta I / \Delta R$). Government spending is indicated by $\overline{G}$, and is exogenously fixed (imposed on the system from outside).

The *monetary sector* of the economy consists of two functional relationships and one equilibrium condition:

(6) $L = f - h(R) + k(Y)$ Liquidity preference (L) or demand-for-money function

(7) $M = \overline{M}$ Money supply (M)

(8) $L = M$ Equilibrium condition

The *IS* and *LM* Functions

By solving equations (1) through (5), we find the *IS* function:

(9) $Y = \dfrac{a - be + \overline{G} + d}{1 - b + bt} - \dfrac{n}{1 - b + bt} R$

By solving equations (6) through (8), we find the *LM* function:

(10) $Y = \dfrac{\overline{M} - f}{k} + \dfrac{h}{k}R$ or $R = \dfrac{kY + f - \overline{M}}{h}$

Equilibrium Income and Interest

By solving (9) and (10) simultaneously, we obtain equilibrium income (Y) and interest rate (R):

(11) $Y = \dfrac{1}{1 - b + bt + \dfrac{nk}{h}} \left(a - be + d + \overline{G} - \dfrac{nf}{h} + \dfrac{n\overline{M}}{h} \right)$

$$(12)\ R = \frac{1}{h(1 - b + bt) + nk}[ka - kbe + kd + k\overline{G}$$
$$+ f(1 - b + bt) - \overline{M}(1 - b + bt)]$$

Multiplier Effects: On Income

From (11) one can derive the multiplier effects on income, and from (12) one can derive the multiplier effects on the interest rate, that follow from a change in government spending (ΔG), an autonomous shift in the consumption or investment function (Δa or Δd), a shift in the tax function (Δe), a change in the money supply (ΔM), or an autonomous shift in the demand for money (Δf).

The multiplier effects on income, from (11), are:

$$(13) \qquad \frac{\Delta Y}{\Delta G\ \text{or}\ \Delta a\ \text{or}\ \Delta d} = \frac{1}{1 - b + bt + \dfrac{nk}{h}}$$

$$(14) \qquad \frac{\Delta Y}{\Delta e} = -\frac{b}{1 - b + bt + \dfrac{nk}{h}}$$

$$(15) \qquad \frac{\Delta Y}{\Delta M\ (\text{or}\ -\Delta f)} = \frac{n}{h(1 - b + bt) + nk}$$

Multiplier Effects: On the Interest Rate

The multiplier effects on the interest rate, from (12), are:

$$(16) \qquad \frac{\Delta R}{\Delta G\ \text{or}\ \Delta a\ \text{or}\ \Delta d} = \frac{k}{h(1 - b + bt) + nk}$$

$$(17) \qquad \frac{\Delta R}{\Delta e} = -\frac{kb}{h(1 - b + bt) + nk}$$

(18)
$$\frac{\Delta R}{\Delta M \ (\text{or} \ - \ \Delta f)} = - \ \frac{(1 - b + bt)}{h(1 - b + bt) + nk}$$

Policy Implications

A number of policy implications are contained in the above multiplier formulas. Among the more important are the following:

1. As (13) indicates, in the complete Keynesian system the multiplier effect on income of a change in government spending is *smaller* than the simple $\dfrac{1}{1 - b}$ that is typically taught in beginning economics courses. It is smaller by the addition of $bt + \dfrac{nk}{h}$ to the denominator. Here's what it means: t represents tax rates (they cut back consumer spending); k is the transactions demand for money (as income rises, the amount of transactions money desired increases, raising interest rates); n is the interest-sensitivity of investment spending (as interest rates rise, they cut back investment spending); modified by h, the interest-sensitivity of the demand for money (if liquidity preference is very responsive to interest rates, it will take only a small rise in rates to induce people to reduce their cash holdings enough to provide the additional money needed for transactions purposes).

2. Compare (13) and (14): as long as b is less than unity, an increase in government spending will increase income by more than an equal increase in taxes will lower income. The multiplier for a change in government spending is larger than the multiplier for a tax change.

2a. It follows from the above that a simultaneous and equal increase in both government spending and taxes—that is, a balanced budget change in government spending (financed entirely by higher taxes)—will not leave income unchanged, but will increase it. Balanced budgets are not neutral with respect to income.

3. Equation (15) indicates that monetary policy will be *less* powerful in affecting income the larger is h (the responsiveness of liquidity preference to interest rates) and the smaller is n (the responsiveness of investment spending to interest rates).[1]

3a. As a special case of the above, if h is *infinite* (Keynesian liquidity trap) or n is *zero* (investment completely insensitive to interest rates), then the multiplier for $\Delta M = 0$ and monetary policy is useless.

3b. Under such circumstances ($h = \infty$ or $n = 0$), it follows that fiscal policy is the only alternative.

4. Conversely, (15) also indicates that monetary policy will be *more* powerful in affecting income the smaller is h and the larger is n.

4a. As a special case of the above, if h is *zero* (liquidity preference completely insensitive to interest rates), then—from (13)—the multiplier for $\Delta G = 0$ and fiscal policy is useless.

4b. On the other hand, under such circumstances ($h = 0$) monetary policy is both necessary *and sufficient* to control income. If $h = 0$, equation (15) indicates that the multiplier for $\Delta M = \frac{1}{k}$; so long as k is constant in the liquidity preference function, a change in the money supply will always change income by the constant $\frac{1}{k}$. That is, $\Delta M \times \frac{1}{k} = \Delta Y$, which is—surprise!—the same as the quantity theory of money ($M \times$ velocity $= Y$, with velocity constant and equal to $\frac{1}{k}$).

---

[1]The effect of changes in h, n, or any of the other coefficients on the size of the multipliers can be verified by numerical examples (putting in actual numbers for each coefficient, calculating the multiplier, and then changing one of the coefficients and recalculating the multiplier), or by using calculus (take the derivative, for example, of $\Delta Y/\Delta M$ with respect to n, h, or k). Note also that the points made under 3a, 3b, 4a, and 4b are not discussed in this chapter. They correspond to points that will be made in the next two chapters.

20

A Monetarist-Keynesian Dialogue

AT AN ECONOMICS CONFERENCE in the late 1960s, Robert Solow, a prominent Keynesian from MIT, commented on a paper presented by Milton Friedman: "Another difference between Milton and myself is that everything reminds Milton of the money supply; well, everything reminds me of sex, but I try to keep it out of my papers."

Monetarists do, in fact, make so much of the money supply that they are rather easy to caricature. It appears frequently in their professional papers circulated among economists; it figures prominently in their policy recommendations to the government; and some have even shown how it can make money in the stock market. But so far, at least, no evidence has been presented on its qualifications as an aphrodisiac. Don't, however, rule out the possibility.

The President of the United States will use very different approaches in economic policy-making depending on whether his orientation is Keynesian or Monetarist. As a Keynesian, he would spend considerable time pressing Congress for countercyclical tax and expenditure legislation. If he were a Monetarist, he would spend more effort trying to convince everyone that things will get better by themselves; but to provide a proper noninflationary environment he would ask the Federal Reserve to keep money supply growth under control.

The basic Monetarist and Keynesian viewpoints were described in detail in Chapters 17 and 18. It is now time to distill their collective wisdom to see how and why their policy recommendations differ. We begin with the question of whether the private sector, if left alone, will generate a stable level of output that is close to full employment. The monetary and fiscal policy alternatives are then described. Next, we turn to inflation, with special attention to its consequences for interest rates. We conclude with an evaluation of the Monetarist prescription for long-run economic stability.

As it turns out, much of the Monetarist-Keynesian dialogue can be conveniently carried on within the aggregate supply and demand framework used toward the end of Chapters 17 and 18. Thus, we put the details of the Monetarist and Keynesian macro models on the back burner and consider the price and real output effects through the somewhat more general supply/demand analysis.

Is the Private Sector Inherently Stable?

Monetarists tend to believe that aggregate demand will be relatively unaffected by autonomous shifts in investment spending. Keynesians argue that unless there is an active attempt at stabilization, the level of economic activity and unemployment will fluctuate considerably when buffeted by entrepreneurial animal spirits.

Monetarists, reflecting their Classical ancestry, argue that any exogenous decrease in investment spending would be countered automatically by either increased consumption or interest sensitive investment spending. The mechanism could be attributed, somewhat mysteriously, to the fixed money stock, hence a relatively fixed level of aggregate demand based on the quantity theory; or, in keeping with Classical interest theory, to a reduction in interest rates that would follow a downward shift in the investment function. The drop in interest rates would, in turn, stimulate investment spending, reduce saving (thereby increasing consumption), and make up for the initial drop in investment.

Keynesians are less impressed with the automatic offsets to gyrations in investment spending. First, the mysterious quantity theory linkage between money and aggregate demand is simply not part of the picture. Moreover, the interest rate does not necessarily respond to a drop in investment. And even if the interest rate did decline, there's no guarantee that it would induce very much additional spending.

Fluctuations in the price level are another source of stability, according to Monetarists. If, for example, consumption and investment didn't rise fast enough to offset the initial decline in investment spending, the resulting unemployment would drive down prices. A fixed money stock with lower prices means a larger real supply of money. This could stimulate spending directly via the quantity theory. Alternatively, the larger real supply of money would lower interest rates—in good Keynesian fashion—and investment spending would increase still further. The Keynesian response to such expected price effects is twofold: First, prices rarely decline; and second, the spending effects are too slow to rely on to restore full employment.

These arguments can be put somewhat more elegantly in terms of aggregate demand and supply. Recall from Chapters 17 and 18 that the aggregate demand schedule shows how the quantity of real output demanded varies with changes in the price level. In particular, decreases in prices increase the amount of goods and services demanded because real money balances increase when the price level falls.[1]

The quantity theory approach of Monetarists assumes a direct and powerful impact of increased real money balances on the demand for output. When people have more real cash balances, they want to spend more—period. Monetarists don't even need falling interest rates to stimulate spending; with more money balances people simply go out and spend more on real goods and services. For Keynesians, on the other hand, there are many things that can intervene between real money balances and demand. In particular, interest rates may not fall very much when money balances increase because people may simply hold the additional cash balances. In addi-

---

[1]Recall that a decrease in the price level does not increase people's real income directly, because a falling price level means both goods prices and factor prices (wages) are falling. Thus falling prices do not directly expand aggregate demand via a simple Keynesian consumption function argument.

tion, desired spending may not be very responsive to decreases in interest rates. The transmission mechanism of money to aggregate demand is less reliable and less powerful, according to Keynesians, because there is no direct link between money and real spending decisions except through the interest rate.

All of this implies that the slope of the aggregate demand schedule, measuring how much of an increase in amount demanded occurs when prices fall, is flatter (and more stable) for Monetarists than for Keynesians. This slope is an important indication of how much of an offsetting (automatic) increase in aggregate demand occurs when unemployment and excess capacity cause prices to decline.

Of equal if not greater importance is the stability (or predictability) of the entire aggregate demand schedule—whether it stays put or jumps around a lot. According to Monetarists, the major factor determining aggregate demand is the stock of money. Once that is fixed, the amount of real output demanded depends upon the price level—lower prices mean more goods and services demanded. That's the message of the quantity theory: People spend real cash balances if they have more than they need for transaction purposes. Thus Monetarists argue that, once the stock of money is fixed, there will be relatively little impact on aggregate demand because of exogenous shifts in spending. For example, if investment spending falls, Monetarists expect interest rates to decline, which reduces saving and increases consumption. Thus the aggregate demand curve doesn't shift much with exogenous changes in investment. For Keynesians, however, changes in investment do not necessarily generate offsetting movements in consumption expenditures. Thus the aggregate demand schedule will be pushed to the left if exogenous investment falls, because at every price level fewer goods are demanded.

Now let's tell the story in terms of Figures 1 and 2, where the former has the Monetarist vertical aggregate supply curve and the latter has the simple Keynesian horizontal supply curve (S) as well as a somewhat more realistic upward sloping supply curve (S'). Start with aggregate demand curve D in each figure, so that real output is at the full employment level. Now ask what happens if businessmen suddenly decide to invest less than they have been. From the Monetarist view of Figure 1, the demand schedule, D, may

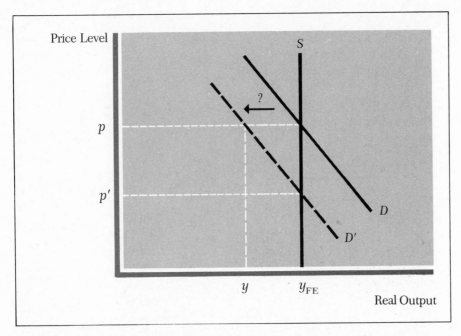

Figure 1 / Monetarist Response to Declines in Exogenous Investment: Real Output Remains at the Full Employment Level

simply stay put, in which case aggregate economic activity remains at y_{FE}. Some other form of spending will increase to take the place of the drop in investment. But if the aggregate demand curve shifts to D' in Figure 1, and the level of aggregate demand falls to y at the old price level P, the resulting unemployed labor and unused capacity cause wages and prices to fall toward P'. As prices fall, the real quantity of money expands and aggregate demand increases along the new demand curve D'. Prices fall until demand is brought back into equality with aggregate supply at y_{FE}.

In the Keynesian presentation of Figure 2, the leftward shift from D to D' most certainly takes place as a result of the fall in exogenous investment. If that happens, the story can end right there, when it has hardly begun. If prices are rigid even in the face of unemployment and excess capacity, the supply curve is S and aggregate demand and real output remain at the depressed level y. The Monetarist incentive to increase spending—falling prices—never appears.

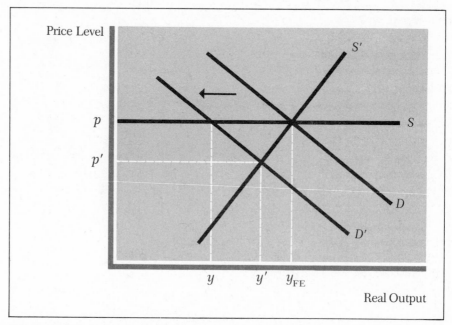

Price Level

S′

p ───────────────────── S

p′

D

D′

y   y′ y_{FE}

Real Output

Figure 2 / Keynesian Response to Declines in Exogenous Investment: Real Output Falls Below the Full Employment Level

The more realistic Keynesian case occurs when prices fall some-what when production is below full capacity, and wages also decline *but at a slower pace.* This produces an aggregate supply curve that looks like S′ in Figure 2. With supply curve S′, aggregate real output is above y (where it would be if prices didn't fall) but is still below full employment output y_{FE}.[2] The problem is that wages and prices

[2]Here's another way of looking at it. The vertical supply curve in Figure 1 occurs as follows. With a decline in goods prices, businessmen will hire the same number of workers and produce the same level of output (y_{FE}) only if their wage expenses fall in the same proportion. Under those circumstances, their profit margins remain the same, so their incentive to produce y_{FE} is sustained. Another way of putting it is that when wages (W) and prices (P) fall at the same rate, businessmen's *real* wage expense (W/P) remains unchanged and they will hire the same number of workers as before. On the other hand, if wages fall less than prices, then businessmen will fire some workers and cut back their output of goods and services. That is represented in Figure 2 by the positive slope in supply curve S′: When prices fall, the supply of real output declines below the level that would fully employ all labor (and capital).

do not fall far enough to stimulate sufficient new aggregate demand along D' to offset the decrease in exogenous investment.

Note that in both of the figures, if the demand curve were flatter, the fall in prices would not have to be that large to encourage more aggregate demand along the new demand curve D'. This would also reflect the Monetarist point of view: Falling prices with a fixed stock of money will generate full employment because aggregate demand is very sensitive to increases in real money balances.

An important point to remember is that the upward sloping Keynesian aggregate supply curve S' is only a short-run relationship. Even Keynesians recognize that with production below full employment there will be continued downward pressure on wages. As wages fall more, there will be an incentive for producers to move back to full employment production. Eventually, therefore, the vertical aggregate supply curve comes into the picture, even for Keynesians. But the essential message is that the entire process can take considerable time. Thus, Keynesians argue, we should try to push up aggregate demand by monetary and fiscal policies.

To summarize: Monetarists tend to think that the aggregate demand curve is stable, given a particular money supply, and that the aggregate supply schedule is vertical. These conditions imply that exogenous shifts in investment leave real output unchanged. Keynesians argue that the aggregate demand curve is quite sensitive to exogenous changes in investment and that the aggregate supply schedule is not vertical. These circumstances imply that entrepreneurial animal spirits buffet the level of real output.

Monetary and Fiscal Stimulus

Suppose the Keynesians have a point, and aggregate demand shifts to D' when businessmen are discouraged and cut back on their investment expenditures. Let's also put the economy into Figure 2 with the upward sloping supply schedule S'. Thus the reduction in aggregate demand reduces real output to y'. If we don't want to wait for further price adjustments to set matters right, then something must be done to push up aggregate demand. Monetary and fiscal policies are the two discretionary tools available to government poli-cy-makers for precisely such circumstances.

According to the Monetarists, if the central bank increases the money supply, the aggregate demand schedule shifts to the right, reflecting increased demand for goods and services.[3] The transmis-sion mechanism of an increase in money to spending is direct and certain. Extra cash balances do not first go into the bond market (as with Keynesians), where prices are forced up and interest rates pushed down. Rather, there is direct substitution between money and real goods.

For Keynesians, on the other hand, an increase in the money sup-ply may very well shift the aggregate demand schedule rightward, but the impact is less certain than for Monetarists. The problem is that the transmission mechanism between money and spending is not quite so direct. Extra money balances are first spent in financial markets; and the additional demand for bonds drives up bond prices and drives down interest rates. But how much of an increase in aggregate demand occurs depends upon the size of the drop in inter-est rates (which may not be that large if people simply hold some of the extra cash balances) and on the sensitivity of spending to a fall in rates.

According to Keynesians, falling interest rates can generate in-creased spending in a number of ways. The so-called cost of capital effect is the traditional impact of lower borrowing costs on the de-mand for investment goods. The wealth effect focuses on the impact of interest rates on securities prices—lower interest rates mean higher bond prices and people respond to such capital gains by consuming more. Finally, the credit availability effect (to be dis-cussed in Chapter 22) asserts that lenders may simply increase the amount of funds offered to borrowers, thereby permitting them to expand their spending plans. When all these channels of money to spending are operative, then the impact of expanding the money supply on aggregate demand is quite potent. But in this very specific outlook, there's many a possible slip 'twixt the cup and the lip.

---

[3]Do not be confused on this point. Increases in real balances caused by falling prices are reflected in the *slope* of the aggregate demand curve because prices are on the vertical axis; increases in real balances caused by an increase in the stock of money *shift* the aggregate demand curve because at each price level (on the vertical axis), more goods and services will be demanded (measured on the horizontal axis).

How to Score (Old-Timers' Day)

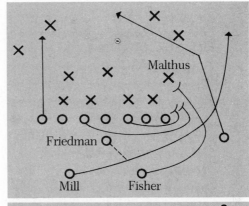

Monetarist Power Sweep

Milty Friedman hands off to J. S. Mill—who streaks down the right sideline behind a big block (actually a clip) by Swifty Irving Fisher that completely upends Big Tommy Malthus.

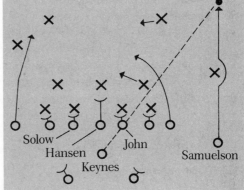

Keynesian Long Bomb

J. M. Keynes hits Poor Paul Samuelson with a TD pass—fantastic blocking by the unsung heroes of the front line, led by Bob Solow, Alvin Hansen, and Elton John (betcha didn't know he was a closet Keynesian).

The Keynesian analysis is a *credit,* as opposed to a strictly *monetary,* chain of causation. In a sense, money per se is seen as not too important until it finds its way into the hands of a potential spender. To a Monetarist, anyone holding money is a likely spender. But to a Keynesian, a loan transaction may be necessary to move money from its current owner, who may be holding it idle, to a borrower who wants to spend it. Thus the Keynesians take a credit view, concerned with financial assets, credit availability, the direction of interest rates, the reaction of lenders and borrowers to rate changes, and the role of financial markets as conduits for funds.

To a Monetarist, all this is excess baggage, more harmful than helpful (Monetarists love that phrase; it seems to fit just about anything Keynesians do). It is money per se that counts, and its effects on GNP are not roundabout but direct. To look at anything else is only a distraction.

The Keynesian answer to the somewhat less certain effects of monetary policy is to focus on fiscal policy to stimulate aggregate demand. We started out with a reduction in autonomous investment expenditure that pushed the aggregate demand curve to the left. A simple solution is to offset that decrease by exogenously increasing government spending or raising consumer expenditure by a discretionary reduction in tax rates.

A Monetarist questions whether *any* exogenous shifts in expenditure, whether generated by businessmen or the government, influences aggregate demand. We saw above that, according to Monetarists, interest rates would fall to counteract the effects of decreased investment on aggregate demand. A symmetrical argument maintains that interest rates will rise when government spending goes up. Thus the government spends more but others, businessmen and consumers, are induced to spend less because interest rates rise.

This process has often been called by a special name: crowding out. Because it has received considerable attention as a central issue dividing Monetarists and Keynesians, it is worth some further elaboration.

We begin by noting that, initially, an increase in government spending raises aggregate demand directly, before anything else has happened. But the public's need for day-to-day transactions money is likely to rise along with aggregate demand. If the supply of money does not increase simultaneously, the public will find itself short of cash, will presumably sell off some financial assets to try to get additional money, and will thereby drive up interest rates. This "crowding out" effect may inhibit private investment spending, at least partly offsetting the expansionary impact of the government's spending. In brief, both the execution and the net impact of fiscal policy appear to be inextricably bound up with monetary implications. Moreover, it is especially important to consider how the government finances the increased expenditure (or the reduction in taxes).

The Keynesian position on these matters is that any fiscal action, no matter how it is financed, will have a significant effect on aggregate demand. Keynesians do not deny that interest rates are likely to rise unless new money is forthcoming to meet cash needs for day-to-day transactions. Thus they admit that a government deficit financed by money creation is more expansionary than one financed by bond sales to the public, and that both are more expansionary than increased government spending financed by taxation. However, Keynesians do not believe that the decrease in private investment spending caused by higher interest rates will be great enough to offset fully the government's fiscal actions. They think that the net effect will be significant, and in the right direction, regardless of what financing methods are used.

One reason for this conclusion is that higher interest rates have dual effects. They may reduce private investment spending, but they may also lead people to economize on their cash balances, thereby supplying part of the need for new transactions money from formerly idle cash holdings. Put somewhat differently, even if an expansion in government spending is not financed by new money, the velocity of existing money will accelerate (in response to higher interest rates), so that the old money supply combined with the new velocity will be able to support a higher level of spending and GNP.

The Monetarist view is that unless an increase in government spending is financed by new money creation, it will not alter aggregate demand. Since velocity is seen as more or less stable, a direct link exists between the money supply and aggregate demand.

If an increase in government spending is financed by printing money, it will indeed increase spending. But according to the Monetarists, it is not the deficit that is responsible—it is the additional money. Furthermore, a deficit is a very clumsy way to go about increasing the money supply. Why not simply have the Federal Reserve engage in open market operations? That would accomplish the same purpose, a change in the money supply, without getting involved in budget deficits or surpluses.

As the Monetarists see it, a fiscal deficit financed in any other way —as by selling bonds to the public—will not affect aggregate demand. True, the government will be spending more. But others will wind up spending less. Net result: No change in total spending. The rise in government spending will *initially* increase aggregate demand. However, this will increase the demand for cash for transactions purposes and drive up interest rates, and bond sales to finance the government's expenditures will drive up rates still further. The public will be buying government bonds and financing the government, instead of buying corporate bonds and financing business firms. Business firms will be "crowded out" of financial markets by the government. The rise in interest rates will reduce private investment spending by as much as government spending is increased, and that will be the end of the story. Government fiscal policy, unaccompanied by changes in the supply of money, merely changes the proportion of government spending relative to private spending.

Another way to express Monetarist objections to the Keynesian emphasis on fiscal policy is to put them in terms of the long run versus the short run. As Monetarists see it, Keynesians concentrate too much on first-round (or short-run) effects, and tend to ignore subsequent long-run financial implications. The magnitude of the long-run financial aspects of a fiscal deficit or surplus is, in fact, much greater than the direct spending impact.

For instance, assume a budget deficit is produced by an increase in government spending financed by money creation. The increase in government spending is a once-and-for-all expansion. But the deficit must be financed continuously. After a year, if the deficit is financed by creating money, the change in the money supply will equal the increase in government spending. But if the deficit persists through the next year (because the level of government spending *remains* at the higher level), the money supply will again rise by the same amount. The same will hold true in the next year and the next. In other words, as the Monetarists view it, deficit spending may work eventually not because of its direct spending effects, but rather because of the long-run monetary effects that deficits produce.

Inflation

As long as we are on the subject of deficits and money creation, we can turn to a somewhat related area of dispute between Monetarists and Keynesians: inflation. In Chapter 2 we discussed the historical evidence on money and inflation. We can now look more carefully at what underlies the Monetarist contention that inflation is largely a monetary phenomenon.

Once again the debate turns on what influences the aggregate demand schedule. This is evident in Figure 3, which shows that if we start at full employment (where we always tend to be), with aggregate demand D and price level P, anything pushing demand to D' and D'' raises prices to P' and P''. The dynamics of P rising to P' and then P'' is precisely what we mean by inflation: rising prices. Thus Monetarists contend that since the aggregate demand schedule is likely to be stable at D unless the money supply changes, the main culprit behind shifts to D' and D'' is the Federal Reserve.

Keynesians, on the other hand, are not so quick to blame the Fed when inflation gets out of control. Any group of suddenly overexuberant spenders—government, business or consumers—can push up aggregate demand and generate increases in prices. Obviously, the Keynesian position permits the blame for inflation to be attributed to expanding government deficits when the economy is at full em-

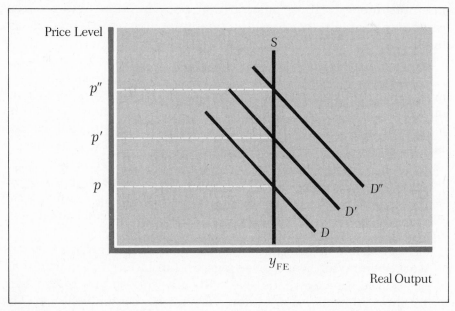

Figure 3 / Anything Shifting Aggregate Demand to the Right Causes Inflation

ployment. Monetarists, on the other hand, cannot rail against deficits per se as causing inflation. Only if the deficit induces the Federal Reserve to expand the money supply (see Chapter 16) will inflation follow.

Shifts in the aggregate supply schedule can also be charged with generating inflation. In fact, the cost-push variety of inflation mentioned in Chapter 2 forces up prices precisely because it shifts the supply schedule in Figure 3 to the left. Higher costs (such as occurred with energy during the 1970s) restricts production and this produces a period of rising prices. But Monetarists stress that such a once-and-for-all "supply shock" cannot account for persistent inflation; it is more of a one-shot deal. Except, of course, if those shocks keep coming, then we have a multiple-shock deal.

A second issue dividing Monetarists and Keynesians on inflation concerns the Phillips Curve. As described in Chapter 2, the Phillips Curve for the 1960s showed a predictable trade-off between inflation and unemployment. In particular, it indicated that lower rates of unemployment could be obtained only if we were willing to tolerate a faster rate of increase in prices. Monetarists, led by Milton Friedman, deny that there is a permanent trade-off between inflation and unemployment, arguing instead that once inflation was incorporated into people's decisions, the unemployment rate would return to its original level. And the data for the 1970s in Charts 1 and 2 of Chapter 2 can be interpreted as supporting that contention.

Once again we can explain the underlying conflict in terms of our aggregate supply/demand framework, but this time the issue turns on the shape of supply function. Figure 3 is the Monetarist picture: a vertical supply curve showing no change in real output (or employment) when inflation takes place. Figure 4 is the Keynesian picture: a positively sloped supply curve showing that as prices rise because of shifts in aggregate demand, real output expands *beyond* y_{FE}. This higher level of real output is produced by reducing the unemployment rate below what is normally considered full employment.

This situation, unfortunately, requires some explaining in terms of worker behavior, wage-price lags, and inflationary expectations. Rest assured, however, that we will only expose you to the bare minimum (we really don't know very much more ourselves). The explanation for the positively sloped supply curve was hidden in footnote 2 earlier in this chapter. The key to variations in the supply

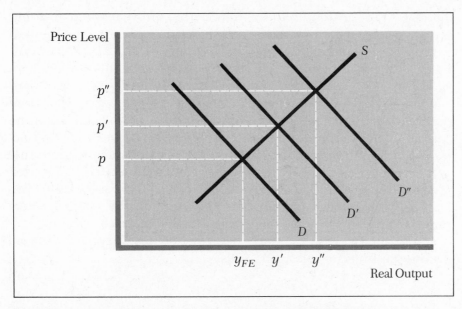

Figure 4 / Inflation Causes Higher Real Output (and Lower Unemployment) with a Positively Sloped Supply Curve

of real output is that wages change more slowly than prices when the overall price level changes. This means that when the price level falls, declining wages lag behind falling goods prices, and the real value of labor's compensation increases. That's why fewer workers are employed and less is produced when the price level declines. The other side of the coin is that when the price level rises, wages increase more slowly than prices, labor's real compensation falls, and more workers are hired. And that's the end of the story when it is told by unreformed Keynesians.

But economists of all persuasions now recognize that a lower real wage cannot permanently induce workers to spend less time playing tennis and more time at the factory or behind the desk. Thus, after a while, labor will demand that wages be adjusted upward, especially if people are working harder than before. Some workers may feel reluctant to do so right away because of a long-run relationship with their employer, one that transcends what could be only a temporary erosion in the value of their paychecks. But as the inflation reality sinks in and workers come to expect a permanently higher rate of inflation, their wage demands become more vociferous. Wages will be pushed up by competitive pressure among employers.

But once wages catch up to the higher rate of price increase, there is little incentive for businessmen to produce more than they started with. Thus, production eventually returns to y_{FE} and unemployment goes back to what is normally considered a full employment rate.

What we have just described is a slow but steady transition from the upward-sloping supply curve in Figure 4 to the vertical aggregate supply curve in Figure 3. Thus, after everything has adjusted, including inflationary expectations and labor-business contractual agreements, the aggregate supply curve must be vertical. Of course, the never-ending question is: How long can a "temporary" situation last? As we pointed out in Chapter 2, the greater the prominence of inflationary expectations, the less time it will take for workers to try to adjust their wages. And that's why the Phillips Curve disappeared during the inflation-plagued 1970s.

Inflation and Interest Rates

The role of inflationary expectations finds its way into still another area of the Monetarist-Keynesian discussion: How do interest rates respond to changes in the money supply? In this area, however, we cannot appeal to the aggregate supply/demand framework for expositional help. English will have to suffice (sorry; we don't like it any more than you do).

Milton Friedman has argued that an *expansionary* monetary policy *raises* interest rates and a *contractionary* monetary policy *lowers* interest rates; just the reverse of standard Keynesian analysis. How does Milton do it? Here's the point: An increase in the money supply *may initially* lower interest rates, if the increased liquidity is spent on financial assets. But that is only the beginning. Once aggregate demand responds to the increased money supply (as it must in the Monetarist world), the transactions demand for money will increase, thereby driving interest rates upward. But this is hardly new. Mainstream Keynesians certainly wouldn't disagree. The Monetarists argue, however, that the "income effect" of the increased money supply will overwhelm the initial "liquidity effect" so that the interest rate snaps back past its original level.

If pressed on this last point, Keynesians might even acquiesce again. After a while interest rates *could* pass the original equilibrium; but it all depends on the speed and strength of the response in GNP to monetary expansion. Keynesians would focus their attention on the interim period—before GNP expands. And this interim period is sufficiently long to justify the following statement: Expansionary monetary policy *means* lower interest rates, and contractionary policy *means* higher rates.

But there's more. Inflationary expectations play a key role in the response of interest rates to monetary policy. In particular, if expectations of inflation are generated by an expansionary monetary policy, then this will cause a *further* increase in the level of *nominal* interest rates. The reason is as follows: Suppose that when the expected rate of inflation is zero, the equilibrium interest rate is 5 percent. As we said in Chapter 17, if lenders expect prices to rise by 2 percent during the next 12 months and want to receive 5 percent in real terms, they will demand 7 percent from borrowers. As long as borrowers expect the same rate of inflation, they will go along with the higher nominal rate of interest. After all, if they were ready to pay 5 percent with no inflation, they should be equally eager to borrow money at 7 percent with 2 percent inflation—they will be paying off the loan in "cheaper" dollars.[4]

What might lead *both* borrowers and lenders to expect inflation and then arrive at a higher nominal rate of interest? You guessed it —an expansionary monetary policy. When such inflationary expectations are tacked on to the income effect, Monetarists contend that it is virtually certain that these two will dominate the initial liquidity impact and expansionary monetary policy will lead to higher nominal interest rates. An analogous argument can be made for contractionary monetary policy lowering interest rates.

Notice, by the way, that the Classical distinction between real and nominal rates is crucial in these arguments. Increases in money lead to inflation via the quantity theory. The interest rate (the *real* interest rate—the Classicists never spoke about fake rates) is deter-

---

[4]Borrowers would like to pay only 5 percent. But as we saw in Chapter 17, competition for funds forces them to pay what lenders demand, unless they are willing to pass up some investment projects. But inflation will increase the expected *dollar* returns on investments so that if a project was worth undertaking before it would be just as worthwhile with inflation and the higher nominal interest rate.

mined by savers and investors. They "pierce the veil" of money and refuse to let inflation interfere with their agreed-upon *real* rate of interest. Thus the "inflation premium" described by Irving Fisher is added to the real rate and increases in money supply raise the nominal rate of interest.

The story just told of nominal interest rates rising due to the inflationary expectations generated by expansionary monetary policy has taken on an added dimension called rational expectations. In particular, inflationary expectations that incorporate the predictions of economic models, such as the quantity theory of money, as well as the predictable behavior of policy-makers, are called rational expectations. They are rational in the sense that all potentially relevant information is brought to bear on the formulation of expectations. Nothing is left out, especially the predictions of economic models.

The consequences of such apparently innocuous logic are simply amazing. In particular, if policy-makers are expected to increase the money supply in an effort to lower interest rates, there will, in fact, not even be any temporary liquidity effect on real interest rates, since such anticipated money stock movements will have already been incorporated in portfolio decisions. For example, the liquidity effect of the anticipated increase in money stock will have already raised bond demand to take advantage of anticipated capital gains; thus no further bond price increases occur when the money stock actually increases. All that's left is the quantity theory effect which says that increases in money stock raise prices. Thus the anticipated rate of inflation generated by expansionary monetary policy pushes up nominal interest rates. There simply aren't any intermediate steps. Rational expectations provide a closer link between money and prices and between money growth and inflation and sever the usual Keynesian connection between money and interest rates.[5]

Lest this be dismissed as idle theorizing, the *New York Times* article reprinted here lends credibility to the entire mechanism. Of course, journalists are at least as gullible as the rest of us—their discussions carry no more weight than pedantic academic analyses.

Nevertheless, the rational expectations story sounds convincing. Remember, however, the simple quantity theory operates only at or

[5]For an exposition, see Frederic Mishkin, "Efficient Markets Theory: Implications for Monetary Policy," *Brookings Papers on Economic Activity* (1978:3).

WALL STREET FEARS OVER MONEY SUPPLY ARE SAID TO WORSEN

SHARP RISE COULD LIFT RATES

'Considerable Alarm' Is Expected if Bulge Develops at It Did in '77 —Inflationary Effect Seen

By JOHN H. ALLAN

Many of Wall Street's money market economists are beginning to worry that the nation's money supply is about to mushroom, touching off a sharp rise in interest rates this spring.

A year ago, when the basic money supply expanded $5.4 billion in early April, short-term interest rates were quick to respond. The rate on three-month Treasury bills jumped a half-point to 5 percent by mid-May.

Overly rapid growth in the money supply is regarded as one of the chief ingredients of an inflationary economy, and the behavior of money is watched closely for clues to the future behavior of business activity and prices. Over the past several years, the Federal Reserve has frequently responded to faster money supply growth by encouraging short-term interest rates to rise.

Indicators Due Out

Jeffrey A. Nichols, chief economist at Argus Research Corporation, warned that when the monetary indicators come out this Thursday, they could show "substantial" rise. The money supply has increased sharply during the first week of each of the past four quarters, he noted, adding that he "would not be at all surprised" if it happened again this week.

Seasonal distortions continued "to plague the reported data" even after the Federal Reserve's recently announced revisions in the statistics, Mr. Nichols observed. The revisions were made to take into account money deposit at banks that do not belong to the Federal Reserve System, as well as seasonal shifts.

According to Allen Sinai of Data Resources, a Lexington, Mass., investment advisory concern, growth in the money supply has already begun a series of increases that will raise it toward the upper limits of the Federal Reserve's short-run targets.

'Considerable Alarm' Seen

"Within a couple of weeks, there will be considerable alarm over the monetary growth rates," Mr. Sinai predicted.

Last Thursday afternoon, the Federal Reserve reported that the basic money supply, which is known as M-1 and which consists of money on deposit in checking accounts at commercial banks plus currency in circulation, rose $600 million to average. That took it to an estimated seasnally adjusted $341.3 billion in the week ended March 29. (The figures are reported after a one-week lag.)

With this $600 million increase, M-1 showed a two-month growth rate of 1.2 percent, well within the Federal Reserve's targeted range of 1 percent to 6 percent. For the latest 52 weeks, however, M-1 has shown a 6.9 percent growth rate, compared with the 6.5 percent maximum that the Federal Reserve would like to promote for the year from the fourth quarter of 1977 to the final three months of 1978.

The concern among some money market economists is that M-1 will soon begin to expand more rapidly, pushing the growth rate above the Fed's short-run target and further above the long-term maximum as well.

"The financial markets are ticking away like a time bomb," Mr. Sinai declared, asserting that the pressure of a rebounding economy, diminished liquidity and tighter money would push interest rates "significantly higher" over the next few weeks.

Some Express Optimism

This pessimistic outlook is not universal, of course.

The money-supply figures for this week "should not be as excessive as at the beginning of (recent) quarters," William E. Gibson, money market economist at Smith Barney, Harris Upham & Company said.

Higher interest rates in response to "surging monetary growth" can be expected late in April or early in May, not sooner, he indicated.

The Federal Reserve early last week "made every effort to convince the markets that short-term rate policy had not been changed," Mr. Gibson noted.

According to Alan C. Lerner, vice president at Bankers Trust Company, confidence in the Carter Administration's anti-inflation strategy "has all but evaporated" as the Federal budget deficit has continued so large so late in the current business expansion.

With G. William Miller, the Federal Reserve chairman, forecasting higher inflation and with the President not expected to offer a strong anti-inflation program when he speaks tomorrow, the stage may be set for a move toward tighter monetary policy, Mr. Lerner reasoned.

Aubrey G. Lanston & Company said in its highly regarded weekly letter this week, "the Administration can't be expected to urge greater monetary restrain." "It would be nice, however," the firm concluded, "if the Administration should indicate that it no longer will stand in opposition to such action."

News Item / Money Supply and Expectations Confounding the Conventional Wisdom

New York Times, April 10, 1978

near full employment. At lower levels of economic activity, there is considerable slippage between money and prices. Even near what we designate as full employment there are wage and price rigidities because of contractual arrangements that interfere with any proportional relationship between money and prices.

Most observers recognize, therefore, that it takes time for the inflation premium to be fully reflected in nominal interest rates. In the short run, lenders may have to settle for lower real interest rates. Instead of the nominal rate rising by 2 percent in our example above, it may rise by less, and therefore the real rate would fall somewhat when expected inflation jumped by 2 percent. Eventually, as lenders adjust their cash balances and borrowers alter their investment plans, the real rate returns to its long-run equilibrium level and the nominal rate rises above the real rate by the full expected rate of inflation.

How long is the long run? Ah, if we only knew the answer to that question, how simple life would be. We get closer to Irving Fisher's result even in the short run—say within six months—as the delay in borrower and lender reactions gets shorter. Furthermore, when expectations of inflation respond quickly to economic forces, the Fisher result is likely to occur still more quickly. On the other hand, when delays are long and expectations of inflation respond slowly, then it takes longer for nominal rates to rise by the full amount of the expected inflation. As a general rule, it is a good bet that an increase in nominal rates of interest will closely follow a jump in inflationary expectations, but nominal interest rates are unlikely to respond immediately by the full amount Fisher suggested.

Can we really be this far into a book on money and not be sure which way interest rates respond to monetary ease or stringency? Yes and no—unequivocally.

We can summarize the discussion as follows. An increase in the money supply will immediately reduce both the nominal rate and the real rate of interest because of a liquidity effect. As inflationary expectations respond to the monetary expansion, nominal rates are driven up but by less than the inflationary surge. Thus the nominal rate could very well be above the original level of nominal (and real) rates while the real rate can be below it. After borrowers and lenders have completed all their adjustments, the real rate of interest will be back where we started and the nominal rate will have increased by the expected rate of inflation.[6] So now you can answer just about anything you want to the question of what happens to interest rates when the money supply expands, as long as you keep the real and nominal straightened out (don't worry, not many people can do that). To really confuse matters you might try to explain how decreases in the money supply produce an opposite set of results.

Should a Robot Replace the Federal Reserve?

We started this chapter with a discussion of whether the private sector is inherently stable. If the self-correcting mechanisms described above operate properly, there is little need for active monetary and fiscal policies to prevent economic fluctuations. In fact, these stabilizing mechanisms form the Monetarist argument against government attempts at "fine-tuning" the economy. It's simply not needed.

Keynesians claim that since the strength of these self-correcting forces is uncertain, we should use countercyclical monetary and fiscal policies to help insure full employment production. They implicitly assume that attempts at leaning against the economic trends —expansionary policy in recessions and contractionary policy during inflations—can only help. The problem is that attempts at countercyclical policy can actually wind up causing greater instability than would have otherwise been the case.

Milton Friedman was the first to point out the potentially destabilizing impacts of government countercyclical policy. To explain the argument we must recognize that the effects of changes in monetary policy or fiscal policy take time to work themselves out. In particular, there are lags in the impacts of monetary and fiscal policy on GNP. The empirical evidence on lags is presented later, in Chapter 22. For now it is sufficient to recognize that it takes time for changes in interest rates to alter business spending decisions and it takes

---

[6]The fact that expansionary monetary policy cannot reduce interest rates permanently explains why it is impossible for the central bank to make congressmen happy by forcing down the cost of credit. It also explains why bondholders will not be forever wealthier because of increases in the money supply.

time even for households to adjust their consumer expenditures to increased disposable income. Putting this little addendum on lags with our aggregate demand story, we are able to show the potential damage of stabilization efforts. An alternative philosophy—rules rather than discretion—is proposed by Monetarists to mitigate the problem.

Assume that the Federal Reserve forecasts a recession six months from now. If the forecast is correct, and if a current expansion in the money supply would have an impact six months hence, well and good. But what if the Federal Reserve's crystal ball is not clear, and it is more than a year before the main impact of today's monetary policy is reflected in the economy? Then the effects of today's expansionary monetary policy are likely to be felt *after* the economy has passed the trough and is already on its way up.

As Figure 5 illustrates, the impact of today's easy money may exacerbate tomorrow's inflation. Tight money will have similarly delayed effects; it may be imposed with the best of intentions, to curtail a boom, but its real impact, being delayed, might accentuate

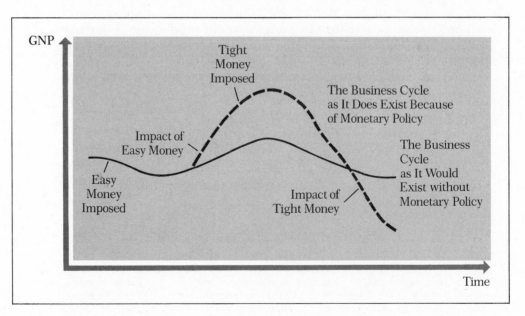

Figure 5 / Friedman's Alleged Perverse Effects of Countercyclical Monetary Policy

a recession. Monetary policy is a destabilizer rather than a stabilizer!

On these grounds—the precarious nature of economic forecasting and the alleged length, variability, and unpredictability of the time lags involved—Friedman and some other Monetarists have given up on orthodox monetary policy. Friedman argues that the economy has been and is now inherently stable and that it would automatically tend to stay on a fairly straight course, as Figure 5 indicates, if only it were not being almost continuously knocked off the track by erratic or unwise monetary policies. Conclusion: Quarantine the central bank. The best stabilization policy is no stabilization policy at all. Hasn't it all been said before:

> They also serve who only stand and waite.
> —John Milton

What Professor Friedman proposes instead is that the Federal Reserve be instructed by Congress to follow a fixed long-run rule: Increase the money supply at a steady and inflexible rate, month in and month out, year in and year out, regardless of current economic conditions. Set the money supply on automatic pilot and then leave it alone.

The specific growth rate—3, 4, or 6 percent—is less important than the principle. Once a figure is decided upon, no tinkering is permitted. But in point of fact, the actual money supply growth rate is intended to keep prices stable and employment high by allowing aggregate demand to grow at the same rate as the economy's real productive capacity. And this is illustrated in Figure 6 with our by now familiar aggregate supply and demand framework. But in this context, we allow the aggregate supply curve to shift rightward to reflect growth in capital and the labor force. Stable prices and full employment will be achieved when growth in the money supply pushes the aggregate demand schedule to the right along with aggregate supply (as in Figure 6).

The main advantage of a rule is that it would eliminate forecasting and lag problems and therefore remove what Friedman sees as the major cause of instability in the economy—the capricious and unpredictable impact of discretionary countercyclical monetary policy. As long as the money supply grows at a constant rate each year, be it 3, 4, or 6 percent, any decline into recession will be temporary. The liquidity provided by a constantly growing money supply

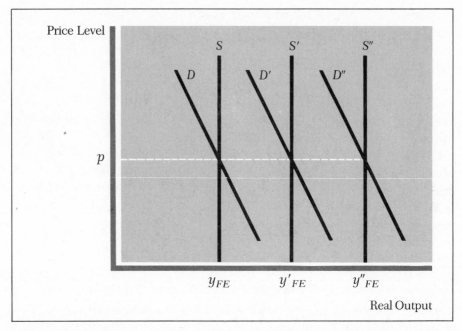

Figure 6 / Aggregate Demand and Supply Shifting Together over Time According to a Fixed Monetary Rule

will cause aggregate demand to expand. Similarly, if the supply of money does not rise at a more than average rate, any inflationary increase in spending will burn itself out for lack of fuel. Anyway, any discretionary deviations by the central bank would interfere with the natural course of the economy and only make matters worse.

The United States Congress has been impressed enough to come part of the way toward a Friedman-type rule, in preference to allowing the Federal Reserve to rely entirely on its own judgment and discretion. In March 1975 both the House of Representatives and the Senate passed House Congressional Resolution 133, which instructed the Federal Reserve to "maintain long-run growth of the monetary and credit aggregates commensurate with the economy's long-run potential to increase production." It also required that the Fed report quarterly to Congress on its target monetary and credit growth rates for the next twelve months. In November 1977 these provisions were incorporated into the Federal Reserve Act itself.

Whether one believes in a fixed rule or not, such reporting procedures can hardly be anything but beneficial. They force the Fed to continuously assess its policies in quantitative terms without shackling it with an inflexible formula. The result should be smoother monetary growth and the elimination of the extremely high (and extremely low) monetary growth rates that have often had harmful effects in the past.

Given the present state of knowledge, it is difficult to justify legislation at the present time that would circumscribe the Federal Reserve's actions more rigidly. Serious research on the subject is only in its early stages, and no consensus is apparent among economists who have worked in the area. It should be noted, however, that the variability of GNP before World War II (even excluding the Great Depression) was much larger than variability since World War II, and it is only in the latter period that stabilization policy has been active.[7]

Some proponents of activist stabilization policies argue that as long as there are some immediate impacts of policy on GNP, past errors of timing can be corrected. Thus expansionary monetary policy that acts too slowly to forestall a recession can be prevented from exacerbating the next round of inflation by a still more restrictive monetary policy. This possibility argues against a rule that would tie the hands of the stabilization authorities. Of course, the problem here is that ever larger doses of stimulus or restraint might be required to offset the detrimental lagged consequences of past policy. And that means that slight miscalculations might leave the system vulnerable to an explosion in either direction.

It is ironic—and perhaps instructive—that in the final analysis the extremists from both camps, Monetarist and Keynesian, have collectively ganged up on the Federal Reserve. The extreme Monetarists want to shackle it, because their concern with time lags leads them to believe it is both mischievous and harmful. The extreme Keynesians want to subordinate it to fiscal policy.

In the middle, squabbling but making more common cause than they had thought possible, are the moderates: moderate Monetarists,

---

[7]See Martin N. Baily, "Stabilization Policy and Private Economic Behavior," *Brookings Papers on Economic Activity* (1978:1).

"But didn't Milton say not to touch the steering wheel once we're moving?"

who believe that the forecasting-lag problem is not so great as to negate all the stabilizing effects of countercyclical monetary policy; and moderate Keynesians, who believe that monetary policy has a powerful impact on spending, and should be used along with fiscal policy with considerable caution.

It seems clear, after all is said and done, that central banking is still at least as much art as science. We simply do not know enough yet to legislate an eternal rule, or even a rule for the next six months, that the Federal Reserve must follow under any and all circumstances. Meanwhile, for better or worse, we appear to have no alternative but to rely on our best knowledge and judgment in the formulation of monetary policy. We can only try to make sure that the decision-makers are able and qualified men and women with open minds and the capacity to learn from experience.

Summary

1. The Monetarist argument that the private sector is inherently stable stems from the automatic tendency for falling interest rates and prices to raise aggregate demand whenever exogenous spending falls. Keynesians claim that in the short run wages are less flexible than prices and this will produce variations in real output when there are exogenous shifts in aggregate demand.

2. Monetarists claim that the transmission mechanism between money and spending is direct. Additional cash balances are spent directly on real goods and services. According to Keynesians, however, the linkage between money and spending occurs through the interest rate, and in this case there is room for considerable slippage.

3. If aggregate demand falls below full employment output and prices simply do not respond, the Monetarist outlook suggests that an expanded money supply would be the most reliable way to increase spending. Keynesians recommend active fiscal policy to set matters right. Monetarists claim that much of the expansionary impact of fiscal policy will disappear because rising interest rates crowd out private investment.

4. Inflation is basically a monetary phenomenon, according to Monetarists, because aggregate demand depends primarily on the money supply. Keynesians claim that fiscal policy or other exogenous spending can cause inflation as well. The existence of a Phillips Curve trade-off between inflation and unemployment depends upon the lags of wages and expectations behind changes in the price level. Even Keynesians would agree that in the long run there is no trade-off; but in the short run there is considerable disagreement.

5. Real interest rates initially fall after an increase in the money supply, but once inflationary expectations take hold, nominal rates rise. After a while the real rate will return to its original level, but as long as inflationary expectations remain, the nominal level of rates will be higher.

6. The Monetarist case for a fixed rule to circumscribe stabilization policy stems from the possibility that the lagged effects of

policy changes might cause greater instability in GNP. The key problem is accurately anticipating the timing of policy impacts on aggregate demand. Monetarists propose a fixed rule to prevent destabilizing effects. Keynesians believe the inflexibility imposed by a rule cannot be justified given the present state of knowledge about the impact of policy on demand.

7. Many of these Monetarist-Keynesian arguments can be traced to differing views of the aggregate supply and demand curves. Monetarists tend to believe aggregate demand is stable once money supply is fixed; Keynesians see no reason to assume such stability. Monetarists say the aggregate supply curve is usually vertical; Keynesians claim it is horizontal some of the time and upward sloping much of the time.

Suggestions for Further Reading

A good summary of both sides of the Monetarist-Keynesian dispute on several issues is in Yung Chul Park, "Some Current Issues in the Transmission Process of Monetary Policy," International Monetary Fund *Staff Papers* (March 1972). An excellent discussion of the points of disagreement between Monetarists and Keynesians is Leonall C. Andersen, Lawrence R. Klein, and Karl Brunner in the September 1973 issue of the Federal Reserve Bank of St. Louis *Review.* In an attempt to settle matters once and for all, a conference was held at Brown University in 1974. The proceedings are available in Jerome L. Stein, ed., *Monetarism* (New York: North-Holland, 1976). Finally, the *Journal of Political Economy* has sponsored an aptly titled volume: *Milton Friedman's Monetary Framework: A Debate with His Critics* (University of Chicago Press, 1974). They make it easy for you to order it by taking Mastercharge or Visa (why not American Express?).

An excellent modern treatment of inflation and interest rates is Thomas Sargent, "Rational Expectations, the Real Rate of Interest, and the Natural Rate of Unemployment," *Brookings Papers on Economic Activity* (No. 2, 1973). Another useful advanced paper is Robert J. Gordon, "Recent Developments in the Theory of Inflation and Unemployment," *Journal of Monetary Economics* (April 1976).

Professor Friedman's views on a rule for monetary policy are spelled out in his *A Program for Monetary Stability* (Bronx, N.Y.: Fordham University Press, 1959). The original statement on this subject was made by Henry Simons in "Rules Versus Authorities in Monetary Policy," *Journal of Politi-*

cal Economy (February 1936). A formal examination of Friedman's hypothesis using modern control techniques is Stanley Fischer and J. Phillip Cooper, "Stabilization Policy and Lags," *Journal of Political Economy* (July/August 1973).

For opposing positions, see John M. Culbertson, "Friedman on the Lag in Effect of Monetary Policy," *Journal of Political Economy* (December 1960), and R. S. Sayers, *Central Banking After Bagehot* (Clarendon Press, 1957). The views of Harry G. Johnson, Abba P. Lerner, Paul Samuelson, and others on rules versus authorities can be found in Volume 2 of the *Hearings* of the House Committee on Banking and Currency, *The Federal Reserve System After Fifty Years* (88th Congress, 1964).

Finally, for an eloquent defense of countercyclical policy together with a concise treatment of the Monetarist-Keynesian debate, see Franco Modigliani, "The Monetarist Controversy, or Should We Foresake Stabilization Policies?" *American Economic Review* (March 1977).

21

The Monetarists and the Keynesians (in Pictures)*

MODEST PETROVICH MOUSSORGSKY, the nineteenth-century Russian composer, published his popular *Pictures at an Exhibition* in 1874. Maurice Ravel later orchestrated these piano pieces and provided a royal introduction to *Pictures*—lots of horns (but no singing violins). Surely the Monetarist-Keynesian dispute deserves as much consideration. Unfortunately, when we suggested to Basic Books that they orchestrate a 45 rpm record with every copy of this book—perhaps the Beatles' *Taxman,* in honor of fiscal policy—they turned us down with icy stares. So we offer you the next best thing: the Monetarist-Keynesian dialogue in pictures!

In Chapter 20 we presented the Monetarist and Keynesian views on money and aggregate economic activity within an aggregate supply/demand framework, and showed that many of the policy issues dividing Monetarists and Keynesians focus on the impact of prices on both aggregate demand and supply. We also noted, however, that Monetarist and Keynesian views differ specifically on how aggregate demand is influenced by monetary and fiscal policy. In addition, they differ on interest rate–related impacts. The *IS-LM* model

*This chapter uses analytical techniques developed in Chapter 19. If you skipped Chapter 19, skip this one too.

developed in Chapter 19 can be used to highlight these aspects of the discussion. In fact, we showed toward the end of Chapter 19 that the *IS-LM* model captures with great precision the forces underlying the aggregate demand schedule. Thus it is perfectly consistent with the aggregate supply/demand framework, although it focuses attention on GNP and interest rates rather than the price level and real output.

Since the orientation of the *IS-LM* model is somewhat different from aggregate supply and demand, we begin the discussion in this chapter with the polar positions of Monetarists and Keynesians regarding the respective roles of monetary and fiscal policy on aggregate demand. We then turn to the stability of the private sector, the impact of money on interest rates, and finally inflation. Along the way we describe some distinctions between real and nominal impacts of monetary and fiscal policy. As we will see, there are omissions from the previous chapter's discussion where there is no *IS-LM* counterpart to the dialogue.

Monetary and Fiscal Policy

Over strenuous objections from Monetarists, and recognizing that such an approach can risk doing an injustice to their cause, we can represent an oversimplified Monetarist position within the *IS-LM* framework. In fact, near the end of Chapter 19 the Monetarist "special case" in the Keynesian model was set forth: a demand for money unresponsive to interest rates—depending on income only—producing a vertical *LM* function (see Figure 17 in Chapter 19 and the discussion related to it).

In that world, things are very simple. Velocity is constant. With a fixed money supply, GNP can't change and neither does velocity. The impact of a change in money supply on the level of income equals ΔM multiplied by velocity (V). This can be seen in Figure 1. Start with *LM* and *IS* and equilibrium income Y. An increase in the money supply shifts the *LM* curve to the right by $\Delta M \times V$ (see footnote 3 of Chapter 19). The new equilibrium level of income is Y' and it is obvious that the change in income from Y to Y' equals

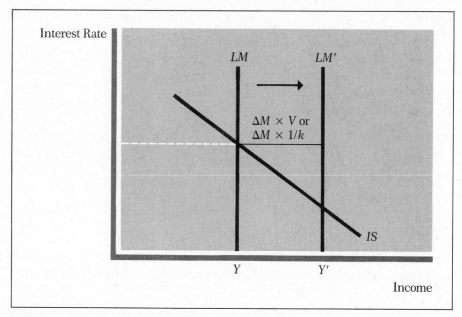

Figure 1 / When the *LM* Curve is Vertical, an Increase in the Money Supply Increases Income by Δ*M* Times Velocity

Δ*M* × *V in this case.* Income continues to rise until all of the increased money supply is absorbed into increased transactions demand.

On the other hand, as Figure 2 shows, when the *LM* curve is not vertical but is positively sloped (as is the case when the demand for money that underlies it is somewhat responsive to the rate of interest), then the increase in income due to a change in the money supply will be less than in Figure 1. In Figure 2 we have superimposed a set of positively sloped *LM* curves (*LM* and *LM'*) on the Monetarist case of Figure 1. While the horizontal distance between the two *LM* curves is the same as before, the increase in income is clearly less than before.[1] Why? Because the increase in the supply of money lowers the interest rate, and at lower interest rates people will hold some of the increased money supply in the form of "idle"

[1]The horizontal distance between the two *LM* curves is the same as before, but now it is simply called Δ*M* × 1/*k*, because 1/*k* = *V* only when the interest-sensitivity of liquidity preference equals zero.

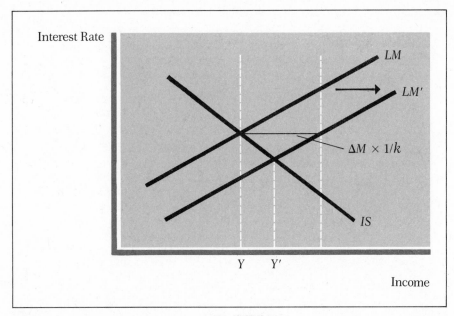

Figure 2 / When the *LM* Curve is not Vertical, an Increase in the Money Supply is Less Powerful in Increasing Income

balances rather than for transactions purposes. Thus the velocity or rate of turnover of the *total* money supply falls (some of it is now being held "idle"). But we are running a bit ahead of ourselves; let's wait until we come to the Keynesian analysis of money to complete this part of our story.

Let us reemphasize that the Monetarists are playing the game under protest—they don't like the rules of the Keynesian *IS-LM* apparatus. It forces them into a situation where the change in money supply first lowers the interest rate, which increases investment, and thereby GNP. Monetarists do not like to restrict the channels through which money influences spending to interest rates. Thus while the vertical *LM* curve does convey some of the Monetarist flavor—i.e., the stability of velocity—it still leaves a Keynesian taste. Moreover, as we stressed in Chapter 17, the assumption of stability in velocity is replaced by predictability in modern versions of Monetarism.

The Keynesian reservations about the potency of monetary policy can be summarized in a number of "special cases" in the *IS-LM*

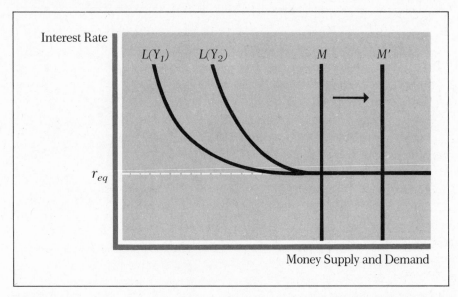

Figure 3 / With a Liquidity Trap, an Increase in the Money Supply from *M to M′* does not Shift the *LM* Curve (see Figure 4)

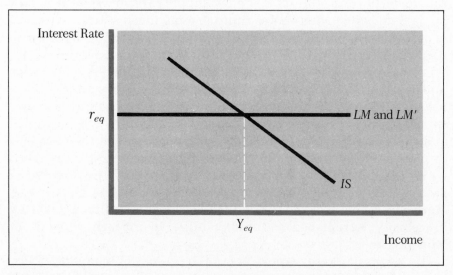

Figure 4 / With a Liquidity Trap, an Increase in the Money Supply, Since it does not Shift the *LM* Curve, does not Change Income

model. First, an increase in money supply would not affect anything if the *LM* curve were horizontal at the relevant level of GNP, i.e., if the liquidity trap were a reality.

Figure 3's supply and demand for money functions form the basis for constructing Figure 4's *LM* functions. If we increase the money supply from M to M' in Figure 3's liquidity trap, then we get no shift in the *LM* function in Figure 4. The *LM* curve with M (namely, *LM*) is the same as with M' (namely, *LM'*). As can be seen in Figure 4, when the *IS* curve intersects *LM* (or *LM'*), producing equilibrium income Y_{eq}, an increase in the money supply from M to M' does not lower the interest rate. All of the increased money supply is held as idle balances. Equilibrium income is unchanged. More money and the same level of GNP implies a decrease in velocity—the hallmark of the Keynesian critique of monetary policy.

A second category of pitfalls for monetary policy concerns the *IS* curve. Even if the liquidity preference function is well-behaved, so that an increase in the money supply succeeds in lowering the rate of interest, there may still be no impact on GNP if investment is completely unresponsive to the rate of interest. From Chapter 19 we know that the *IS* curve is very steep if investment has little interest sensitivity; with zero interest sensitivity, the *IS* curve is vertical. Under such conditions, changes in the money supply do not affect income even though they may change the rate of interest. Figure 5 illustrates that situation. Start with *IS* and *LM* and equilibrium income *Y*. Then, an increase in the money supply causes a rightward shift in the *LM* curve to *LM'*, which merely lowers the interest rate with no impact on GNP. Once again, the money supply has gone up but GNP hasn't, with velocity falling as a result.

To summarize: Monetary policy works in the Keynesian world when both the *IS* curve and the *LM* curve are "normal." Pathological cases of horizontal *LM*s and vertical *IS*s require fiscal medicine rather than monetary prescriptions to alter GNP. More generally, even when we are untroubled by horizontal *LM* curves and vertical *IS* curves, the impact of money on GNP is not the simple ΔM times a fixed velocity. For example, an increase in M may very well produce falling interest rates, more investment, and higher GNP. But GNP is not likely to rise in direct proportion to the change in M because interest rates decline, increasing the speculative demand for idle money along with the transactions demand. In other words, velocity is likely to decline.

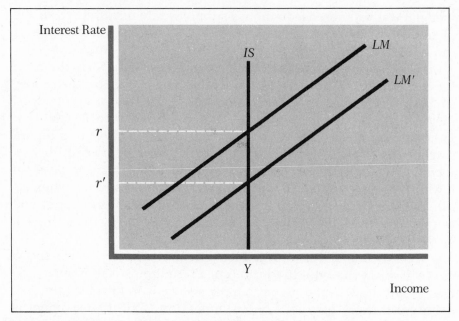

Figure 5 / When the *IS* Curve is Vertical, Monetary Policy is Ineffective

The Monetarist and Keynesian polar cases in *IS-LM* analysis produce symmetrical results for fiscal policy. In particular, fiscal policy has a zero impact with a vertical *LM* curve, while it is completely effective (with no offsetting crowding out due to interest rate effects on private investment) with a horizontal *LM* curve.

Figure 6 illustrates these points. Let's start at point *a* with income *Y* and interest rate *r*. An increase in government spending (or a reduction in taxes) shifts the *IS* curve from *IS* to *IS'*. If the *LM* curve were *LM,* the new equilibrium would be at *b,* and the entire impact is absorbed by a higher interest rate with no increase at all in GNP. In this case there is complete crowding out. But if the *LM* curve were *LM',* the new equilibrium would be at *c* and the impact is entirely on GNP, with no rise at all in the interest rate; in fact, since the rightward shift in the *IS* curve equals ∆G times 1/(1 − *b*), which also equals the change in GNP, the simple multiplier of Chapter 18 has returned in full bloom.

The general case of the positively sloped *LM* curve produces results that lie between the extremes, as we saw in Chapter 19. An

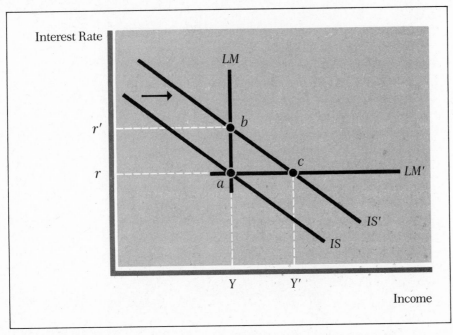

Figure 6 / When the *LM* Curve is Vertical, Fiscal Policy is Completely Ineffective; When it is Horizontal, it is Totally Effective

increase in government expenditure raises GNP, but by less than the "full multiplier" of the simple Keynesian system. This is because the interest rate goes up, cutting off some private investment (there is partial but not total crowding out). The rise in the rate of interest does not lower investment by as much as government spending increases because the higher rate of interest also reduces the demand for money, permitting once idle speculative balances to be used for carrying out the increased transactions associated with higher levels of GNP. It would seem, therefore, that unless the economy is characterized by the extreme case of zero interest sensitivity of the demand for money (producing a vertical *LM* curve), even Monetarists would agree that fiscal policy could have some impact on GNP.

Not so fast, says Professor Friedman. The shape of the *LM* curve is only part of the story. Perhaps more important, the financing

"In theory, yes, Mrs. Wilkins. But also in theory, no."

Drawing by Stan Hunt; © 1976 by The New Yorker Magazine, Inc.

aspects of fiscal policy—especially in the long run—tend to dominate the direct impacts of a change in government spending or taxation. The *IS-LM* model is not readily adapted to illustrate such effects, despite some attempts.[2]

Is the Private Sector Inherently Stable?

The vertical and horizontal *LM* curves depict extreme Monetarist and Keynesian positions, respectively. Moderate wings in both camps assert only that the *LM* curve is "quite vertical" on the one

[2]For example, William L. Silber, "Fiscal Policy in *IS-LM* Analysis: A Correction," *Journal of Money Credit and Banking* (November 1970), and Alan S. Blinder and Robert M. Solow, "Analytical Foundations of Fiscal Policy," in *The Economics of Public Finance* (Washington, D.C.: Brookings Institution, 1974), pp. 52–53.

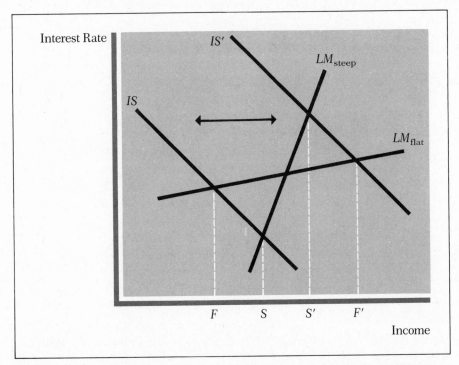

Figure 7 / A Flatter *LM* Curve Means Wider Fluctuations in GNP Due to Exogenous Shifts in Investment

hand or "somewhat flat" on the other. Such tendencies are sufficient to demonstrate the stability or instability of economic activity in the face of exogenous shifts in private investment.

Figure 7 shows two alternative *LM* curves: LM_{steep} and LM_{flat}. There are two *IS* curves representing shifts in autonomous investment. As can be seen in the picture, with LM_{steep} the induced fluctuation in GNP due to the shifting *IS* curve is *S* to *S'*. When the *LM* curve is LM_{flat}, however, the fluctuation in GNP is much wider, between *F* and *F'*. The key to the smaller fluctuation in GNP with LM_{steep} is that the level of interest rates fluctuates more than with LM_{flat}. Thus, when the *IS* curve shifts from *IS'* to *IS*, the interest rate falls a lot, inducing a large amount of endogenous investment to offset a large part of the decline in autonomous investment. With a flatter *LM* curve, the fall in the rate of interest is smaller and in-

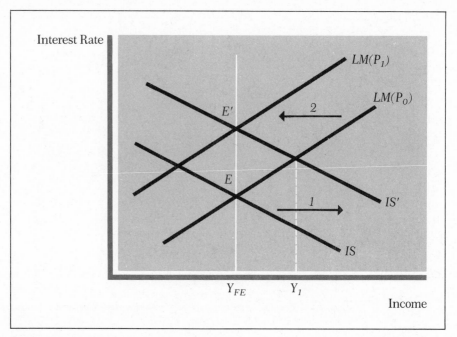

Figure 8 / At Full Employment Fluctuations in the Price Level Help Stabilize Economic Activity

duced investment is less. Thus a steeper *LM* curve stabilizes the level of economic activity associated with a particular stock of money because the interest rate fluctuates more. That's not quite how Monetarists would necessarily tell the story, but it's close enough.

When the economy operates near its full employment capacity, fluctuations in the price level help to stabilize the economy. Figure 8 shows the intersection of *IS* and $LM(P_0)$ at Y_{FE}. We introduced Y_{FE} at the end of Chapter 19 to represent the dollar value of full employment GNP. The *LM* curve is labeled with a particular price index, P_0, since changes in the price level will affect the position of *LM*. Moreover, at full employment, we assume that prices rise in response to increases in aggregate demand. A shift in autonomous spending pushes *IS* to *IS'* and raises demand to Y_1.[3] As a result prices

[3]Once the price level is variable, we must identify the horizontal axis with real income rather than nominal income. This was also done in Figures 18 through 20 of Chapter 19. We're just reminding you of the switch.

rise. With a fixed stock of money, this reduces the *real* supply of money and the *LM* curve is pushed back toward the full employment line. This process stops once aggregate demand is back at full employment—in our picture this occurs at the intersection between *IS'* and *LM*(P_1).

At the new equilibrium E' we have both a higher price level and a higher rate of interest.[4] The higher price level (caused by an exogenous increase in spending) reduced the real supply of money, raised interest rates, and pushed back aggregate demand to the full employment level. Thus, the fixed supply of money together with flexible prices and interest rates insulates full employment economic activity from exogenous changes in investment. The process would be reversed (lower prices and lower interest rates) if there were a decrease in exogenous investment (shifting *IS* to the left). Notice that Figure 8 has the elements of an inflation story, as we will see shortly.

The Interest Rate: Where Does It Go and Why?

Some of the disagreement discussed in Chapter 20 about how the rate of interest responds to changes in the money supply can be illustrated within the *IS-LM* framework.[5] In Figure 9, let's start out with *IS* and *LM;* equilibrium is at *E* with income *Y* and interest rate *r*. An increase in the money supply shifts the *LM* curve to *LM'* and the new equilibrium is *E'*, with interest rate *r'* and income *Y'*.

[4]The interest rate on the vertical axis is, as usual, the real rate of interest.
[5]The distinction between nominal and real interest rates produced by inflationary expectations is not made in the simple *IS-LM* world. Hence, that aspect of the argument discussed in Chapter 20 will not be reproduced here. As long as price expectations don't interfere, the two rates are equal. The Keynesian apparatus is not really geared to the real versus nominal rate distinction, although there have been some attempts. See William Gibson, "Interest Rates and Monetary Policy," *Journal of Political Economy* (May/June 1970); and Thomas Sargent, "Anticipated Inflation and Nominal Interest," *Quarterly Journal of Economics* (May 1972), and by the same author, "Rational Expectations, the Real Interest Rate, and the Natural Rate of Unemployment," *Brookings Papers on Economic Activity* (No. 2, 1973). See also Stephen F. LeRoy, "Interest Rates and the Inflation Premium," Federal Reserve Bank of Kansas City *Monthly Review* (May 1973).

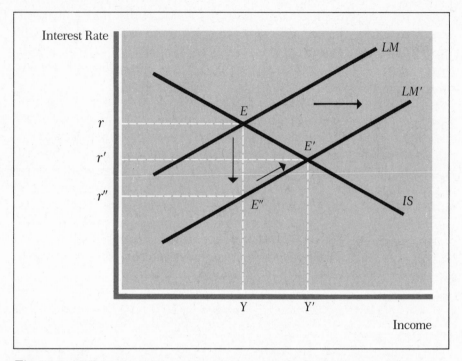

Figure 9 / When the Money Supply Goes Up, Can the Interest Rate be Far Behind?

How does the economy move from E to E'? Technically, this is a question in economic dynamics: the path of movement between one equilibrium and another. And while geometry is all right for comparing two equilibrium points (called comparative static analysis), as we have been doing, it has serious drawbacks in dynamics. Ever mindful of student desires, we decided to spare you the differential equations (if you promise to pay attention).

We start by assuming that immediately after the increase in money supply the level of income will remain unchanged, and the entire adjustment to the increased money supply will come in the form of a reduction in the rate of interest. This means the economy moves from E to E'' in Figure 9, and that the interest rate must initially fall to r'' to keep the amount of money demanded equal to the new supply at the same level of GNP. But E'' is not equilibrium because, although it is on the *LM* curve where money demand equals money supply, it is not on the *IS* curve, hence investment is not equal to saving. The fall in the interest rate means desired investment has gone up but so far saving hasn't. As a result—with investment greater than saving—production, income, and hence GNP begin to rise. The economy, therefore, moves up along the new *LM* curve toward *E′*.

This dynamic story suggests that even according to Keynesians the initial decline in the rate of interest (to r'') will be sharper than the ultimate response (the new equilibrium rate is at r'). Initially, the increased liquidity drives the interest rate way down. As income begins to rise, the interest rate is driven up. The liquidity effect of the increased money supply is partly offset by the income effect. Nevertheless, the negative slope of the *IS* curve does suggest that, in the traditional Keynesian model, the *equilibrium* interest rate after an increase in the money supply must be below the old rate. The income effect on interest rates does not swamp the liquidity effect.

There are other possibilities (even without introducing price expectations) that generate a *higher* equilibrium interest rate after an increase in money supply without departing from the Keynesian spirit. One obvious possibility is a modestly upward sloping *IS* curve. Don't panic—we don't intend to go into this case; it introduces too many complications. We mention it just so that you are aware of it. And you can see (use your imagination) that if the *IS* curve is positively sloped, the new equilibrium interest rate will lie above the old.[6]

The Role of Flexible Prices

When we discussed the stability of the private sector a few pages back, we showed that permitting price flexibility in the *IS-LM* model added considerably to the self-correcting mechanisms of the system. Price flexibility has even more startling effects on the real impacts of monetary and fiscal policy.

[6]A positively sloped *IS* curve occurs under conditions that are described in William L. Silber, "Monetary Policy Effectiveness: The Case of a Positively-Sloped *IS* Curve," *Journal of Finance* (December 1971).

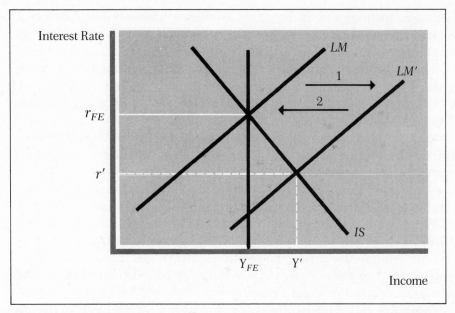

Figure 10 / An Increase in Money Supply at Full Employment Doesn't Lower the Interest Rate

In the first instance, when the economy is operating at or near full employment, the Keynesian interest rate mechanism gives way completely to Classical/Monetarist arguments. In particular, at full employment the rate of interest is independent of movements in the money stock. This can be seen in Figure 10, starting with IS and LM intersecting at Y_{FE} and r_{FE}. The latter is the real rate of interest since, as usual, we are assuming the absence of any inflationary expectations. As always, an increase in money supply shifts LM to LM', apparently pushing down the interest rate from r_{FE} to r_1 and raising aggregate demand to Y_1. But the excess of aggregate demand over Y_{FE} causes prices to rise. This reduces the real supply of money, pushing LM' back toward LM. After all is said and done, prices have risen until the LM curve is back where it started, since otherwise prices would keep on rising. And when LM' is back at LM, the real rate of interest is restored to its original level. Thus, at full employment, increases in money supply cannot reduce the interest rate below r_{FE}. Similar reasoning shows that *decreases* in the money stock will not raise interest rates above r_{FE} if prices fall when aggregate demand is below full employment.[7]

The interest rate r_{FE} has a special name. It's called the natural rate of interest and is defined as that rate which equates saving and investment at full employment. It is determined by the intersection point between the *IS* curve and the Y_{FE}–line. Shifts in the money stock can't change r_{FE}. Only shifts in the *IS* curve can, as we saw earlier in Figure 8. Thus at full employment only saving and investment (including government spending) determine the interest rate; money has nothing to do with it. At full employment, classical interest theory pops out of the Keynesian picture!

The implications for the effect of expansionary monetary policy on interest rates at full employment are twofold: (1) The real rate of interest is unchanged by increases in money supply. (2) Nominal rates (not shown in the figures) will rise if inflationary expectations are generated by the increased money stock. The latter is quite likely, especially in the long run. Borrowers and lenders recognize that excessive expansion in money stock means rising prices. This will no doubt lead them to agree upon an inflation premium attached to the real rate of interest. With the real rate fixed at r_{FE}, the net result is an increase in nominal rates by the expected rate of inflation.

The analysis of fiscal policy under flexible prices adds another dimension to the crowding out mechanism. In particular, we see that at full employment an increase in government expenditure is crowded out in real terms, even if the *LM* curve has a positive slope. Return to Figure 8 above, which shows a rightward shift in the *IS* curve at Y_{FE}. We can now use that same picture to represent an increase in government spending at full employment. Initially there is an increase in aggregate demand to Y_1, with investment demand declining (along the *IS* curve) to offset only part of the increase in government expenditure. A positively sloped *LM* curve permits such an expansion in aggregate demand. But that's not the end of the story. With aggregate demand, Y_1, exceeding full employment production, Y_{FE}, prices rise (from P_0 to P_1), pushing LM (P_0) back

---

[7]This type of price flexibility is also what underlies the monetarist vertical aggregate supply curve of Chapter 20.

toward $LM(P_1)$ and raising the interest rate still further. That process will continue until the new equilibrium, E', is reached. At that point the real interest rate has increased by enough to cut off an amount of investment spending equal to the initial increase in government expenditure. How do we know? Simple. If that weren't the case, aggregate demand would still be above Y_{FE}, prices would still be rising, and so would the interest rate. (The logic is simply nauseating.)

Two points are worth noting in this example: First, the interest rate at full employment is obviously affected by shifts in the real sector of the economy, represented by the *IS* curve (even though it is unaffected by shifts in the monetary sector). Second, notice that nominal GNP is higher at E' compared with E. How do we know? Because real GNP is still at Y_{FE}, but prices are higher (P_1 versus P_0). Thus, while there is real crowding out at full employment even with a positively sloped *LM* curve, there isn't nominal crowding out as with the vertical *LM* curve.

The story at full employment is decidedly Monetarist-Classical, even when cloaked in a Keynesian framework. But that's not really as devastating to Keynesian protagonists as it initially seems. After all, at full employment Keynes was as Classical an economist as Milton Friedman and John Stuart Mill put together.

Inflation

The *IS-LM* model with price flexibility at full employment can tell either a Monetarist or a Keynesian story about demand-pull inflation. In particular, we can identify when inflation is purely a monetary phenomenon and when it isn't. It should be recognized, however, that we implicitly assume a vertical aggregate supply schedule when describing variable prices, hence we cannot discuss the Phillips Curve controversy of Chapter 2.

We begin by noting again that aggregate demand is given by the intersection of the *IS* and *LM* curves. Start, in Figure 11, with *IS* and *LM* intersecting at the full employment income (Y_{FE}), so that the equilibrium income and the full employment income are one and

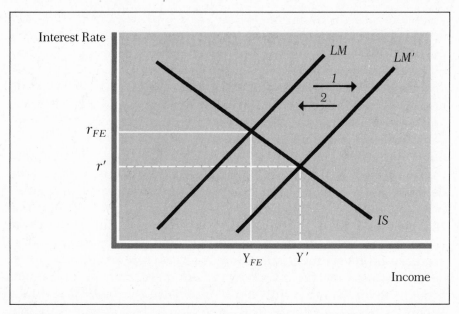

Figure 11 / At Full Employment, an Increase in the Money Supply Shifts the *LM* Curve to the Right and Produces Inflation

the same. Now if *either* curve shifts to the right, aggregate demand for goods and services will exceed the economy's capacity to produce such output at the current price level; upward pressure on prices results. The process of rising prices is exactly what we mean by inflation.

For example, in Figure 11 assume the money supply is increased: the *LM* curve shifts to *LM'* and aggregate demand rises to *Y'*. Aggregate demand exceeds full employment output and prices are bid up, illustrating a classic case of demand-pull inflation. The increased price level then reduces the *real* supply of money, and the *LM* curve begins to shift back toward its original position. The interest rate is pushed up and investment spending is reduced. Rising prices stop when aggregate demand is back at its old level—when the *LM* curve is back where it started. Note that in this case both the money supply and the price level are higher than before, but the *real* money supply and *real* output are unchanged.

An increase in the money supply raises prices, but the inflation provides its own cure—prices stop rising once the *real* supply of money falls back to its original level. Indeed, unless the nominal money supply is increased again (producing another rightward shift in *LM*), inflation has stopped. Continuous injections of money, of course, will cause continuous rightward shifts in the *LM* curve, and continuous inflation. Large and continued injections of money cause continuously large rightward shifts in the *LM* curve, and produce hyperinflation.

As long as the *LM* curve is positively sloped—that is, as long as the demand for money is sensitive to changes in the interest rate—inflation can occur even if the money supply is constant. In Figure 12, again start with *IS* and *LM* intersecting at the full employment income. This time the *IS* curve shifts to *IS'*—perhaps because of an increase in government spending. Aggregate demand, now *Y'*, exceeds Y_{FE} and prices start rising. But here too the inflation is brought to an eventual halt *if the money supply is held constant.* Rising prices—say from *P* to *P'*—reduce the real supply of money; because of that the *LM* curve shifts to the left (to *LM'* in Figure 12), and once again aggregate demand is at Y_{FE}, at which point the inflationary pressure ends.

In this case it is not increased money that causes inflation; the money supply, as we stressed, is held constant. Rather, it is the increased government (or consumer or investment) spending that raises aggregate demand above the full employment level. But the higher level of transactions associated with the increased price level (at the same level of *real* income, Y_{FE}) must be financed in some way. Total transactions have risen from $P \times Y_{FE}$ to $P' \times Y_{FE}$. This increased level of nominal income can be financed with the existing money supply because velocity has gone up ($P' \times Y_{FE}/M$ is greater than $P \times Y_{FE}/M$). Velocity increases because the demand for money is sensitive to the interest rate. As the interest rate rises, the amount of desired speculative money balances contracts, releasing funds for transactions purposes. (In Figure 12, velocity at point *b* is higher than at point *a*.)

While holding the money supply constant assures that the inflationary pressure of a once-and-for-all increase in the *IS* function will disappear, *continuous* rightward shifts in the *IS* curve—pro-

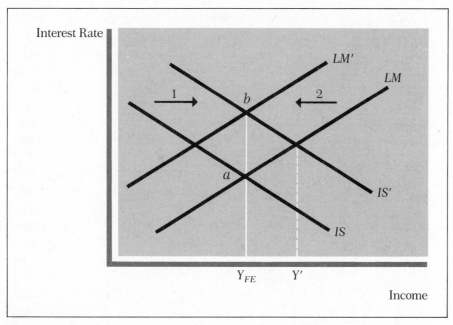

Figure 12 / At Full Employment, a Shift in the *IS* Curve to the Right Produces Inflation even Without an Increase in the Money Supply

duced, let us say, by ever increasing government expenditures—could *apparently* cause continuous inflation. But appearances are deceiving; inflation could not continue indefinitely, regardless of a rightward-shifting *IS* curve, if the money supply is really held constant. Here's why:

We just noted that rightward shifts in the *IS* curve can create inflation only when money demand is at least somewhat sensitive to interest rates; when the interest rate goes up, desired holdings of speculative money balances go down, permitting such funds to be used to carry out transactions. But it is generally agreed that speculative balances will eventually become depleted. In other words, the interest sensitivity of money demand decreases with higher and higher interest rates, until it becomes zero when there are no more speculative balances left. At that point, the entire money supply is being used for transactions balances, and money GNP can rise no

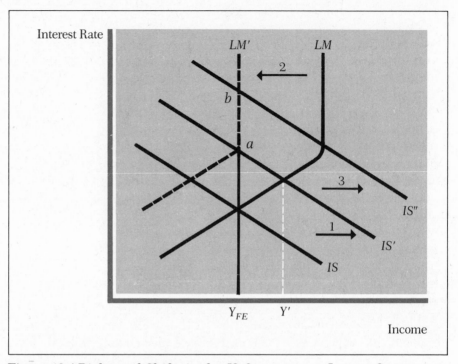

Figure 13 / Rightward Shifts in the *IS* Curve can no Longer Cause Inflation when the *LM* Curve Becomes Vertical

further.[8] Put somewhat differently, the velocity of money has reached its upper limit and can rise no further.

When this great moment arrives, the *LM* curve becomes vertical (zero interest-sensitivity), and further rightward shifts in the *IS* curve have no impact on aggregate demand. The only result is a higher interest rate. Here's the picture. Start out with *IS* and *LM* in Figure 13, intersecting again at the full employment income; shifting the *IS* curve to *IS'* produces aggregate demand *Y'*. Prices rise (say from *P* to *P'*), shifting *LM* to *LM'* and the new equilibrium to point *a*. The *LM* curve is now vertical, however, at level of real income Y_{FE}

[8]In Chapter 18 we suggested that even the transactions demand for money is sensitive to the interest rate, because at higher interest rates it pays to economize on transactions balances. While this may very well be true, it is usually assumed that the transactions demand for money is less interest elastic than speculative demand. Or, put somewhat differently, given the technology of the payments system at any specific time, there is a maximum rate of turnover—velocity—of a particular stock of money; therefore, the *LM* curve becomes vertical at high interest rates.

with the new price level (or at nominal income $P' \times Y_{FE}$).

Any further rightward shift in the *IS* curve, say to *IS"*, cannot raise aggregate demand because the existing money supply—remember, the money supply is being held constant—cannot support any higher level of transactions. Instead, the increased (say) government spending of so many billion dollars is fully offset by the rate of interest rising high enough to *reduce* private investment by the same amount; total spending remains the same, with the increase in government spending "crowding out" an equal amount of private investment spending. The economy moves from point *a* directly to point *b* without suffering any inflation, just a higher rate of interest.

Our story is almost complete. The *IS-LM* analysis has demonstrated the seemingly pretentious contentions of Monetarists that inflation can occur only for a short while in the absence of increases in the money supply. Sooner or later a constant money supply keeps inflation in check. But we also know that Monetarists recommend that long-run price stability requires a moderate but continuous constant rate of growth in the money supply. Thus we should show that increases in money supply do not always produce inflation. And that, too, can be illustrated in the *IS-LM* world.

Increases in the money supply will not necessarily be inflationary if we recognize that full employment GNP grows over time—as the labor force and the stock of capital grow, and as technological progress increases productivity, enabling the economy to produce more real goods and services. In terms of our picture, the Y_{FE} line shifts to the right as the productive capacity of the economy increases. Aggregate demand *must* increase if we are merely to stay in the same place as far as the unemployment picture is concerned.

In Figure 14, if we start out with *IS* and *LM*, all is well when full employment GNP is represented by Y_{FE}. But by next year full employment output becomes Y'_{FE}, and unless aggregate demand increases via rightward shifts in the *LM* and/or *IS* curves, the current level of demand will be too small to generate full employment. In a growing economy, therefore, increases in the money supply (producing rightward shifts in the *LM* curve—say to *LM'*) are needed simply to maintain full employment.[9] Only if the rightward shift in

[9]It is also usually recommended that as output grows, not only should the money supply increase, shifting *LM* to the right, but taxes should be reduced (or government spending increased) in order to shift the *IS* curve to the right as well. Which curve does most of the shifting to accommodate growth will affect the rate of interest and therefore the *composition* of aggregate demand, in terms of the proportion of consumption relative to investment spending.

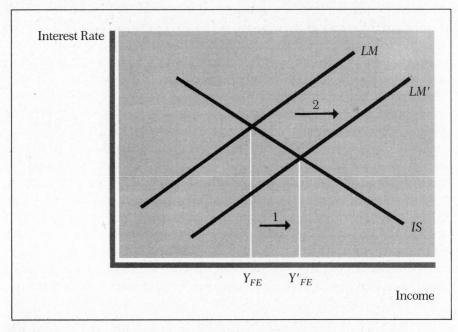

Figure 14 / Over Time, the Full Employment Level of Income Moves to the Right, so that More Money Finances Real Growth Rather than Inflation

the *LM* curve intersects the *IS* curve *beyond* Y'_{FE} will the increased money supply be inflationary. In other words, only if increases in the money supply exceed the transactions needs of a growing economy will inflationary pressures be generated.

Finally, a reminder. The *IS-LM* framework of analysis is fully appropriate only when inflation is of the demand-pull variety. Remember that at the very start of this section we assumed that no Phillips Curve problem exists. When inflation is due mainly to supply or cost-push factors—like aggressive union wage demands or the dramatic 400 percent increase in international oil prices that was imposed in 1973–1974—then it is difficult to handle the analysis within the constraints of the *IS-LM* framework. Only the aggregate supply/demand model can be used in that context.

Summary

1. The *IS-LM* version of the Monetarist-Keynesian dialogue focuses attention on GNP and interest rates. In addition, we supplement the discussion by introducing flexible wages and prices at full employment. Nevertheless, the *IS-LM* model captures only part of the debate. It cannot easily articulate the real versus nominal interest rate analysis nor can it depict in a simple way the financing side of fiscal policy.

2. The "special" (or extreme) Monetarist and Keynesian slopes of the *IS-LM* diagram help to highlight the polar positions on monetary and fiscal policy. In particular, a vertical *IS* curve and a horizontal *LM* make monetary policy impotent and fiscal policy supreme. A vertical *LM* curve, on the other hand, causes fiscal policy to lose its potency (complete crowding out) and raises monetary policy to its ultimate power (fixed velocity).

3. The demonstration that a steep *LM* curve insulates GNP from exogenous investment shocks highlights the stabilizing role of fluctuating interest rates on economic activity. Flexible prices add to that stabilizing mechanism.

4. The interest rate initially overadjusts to a change in the money supply, since the level of income responds only with a delay. Thus an expansionary monetary policy will usually lower interest rates by more in the short run than in the long run.

5. Price flexibility at full employment restores the results of Classical interest rate theory: the level of the real rate of interest is determined only by saving and investment. A change in the money supply cannot alter the real rate; it can only influence nominal rates by changing inflationary expectations. Price flexibility at full employment also causes fiscal policy's impact on real GNP to be completely crowded out even with a positively sloped *LM* curve.

6. Demand inflation can result from either increases in money supply or autonomous increases in spending as long as the *LM* curve is not vertical. At some point inflation becomes a purely monetary phenomenon because the interest sensitivity of money demand disappears (and *LM* becomes vertical).

Suggestions for Further Reading

Two advanced articles on the complete Monetarist position, both by Milton Friedman, are: "A Theoretical Framework for Monetary Analysis," *Journal of Political Economy* (March/April 1970), and "A Monetary Theory of Nominal Income," *Journal of Political Economy* (March/April 1971). Another formal exposition is by Karl Brunner and Allan H. Meltzer, "Mr. Hicks and the Monetarists," *Economica* (February 1973). For an interesting discussion by leading Monetarists and Keynesians over the nature of the issues, see the comments by Karl Brunner, Allan Meltzer, James Tobin, Paul Davidson, Don Patinkin, and Milton Friedman in "A Symposium on Friedman's Theoretical Framework," *Journal of Political Economy* (September/October 1972). For a more complex treatment of inflation, see Rudiger Dornbusch and Stanley Fischer, *Macroeconomics* (New York: McGraw-Hill, 1981).

Appendix

Interest Rates Versus the Money Supply Under Uncertainty

IN CHAPTER 15 we discussed the advantages and disadvantages of using the money supply versus the interest rate as a target of monetary policy. Monetarists generally prefer a money supply target while Keynesians prefer an interest rate objective. At this point we can formalize the underlying analysis to demonstrate the pluses and minuses of each.[1]

The simplest point to demonstrate is that hitting a particular target in terms of the interest rate implies loss of control over the money supply, while hitting a money supply target implies loss of control over the interest rate. We don't even need IS and LM curves for that, just money demand and money supply curves. In Figure 1 let's assume that r^* is the target interest rate, and we start out with the original money supply and liquidity preference curves M and LP. If the demand for money shifts to LP' then the Fed must accommodate the demand by shifting the supply curve to M' if the rate of

[1]The bulk of this discussion is based on an article by William Poole, "Rules of Thumb for Guiding Monetary Policy," in *Open Market Policies and Operating Procedures— Staff Studies* (Board of Governors of the Federal Reserve System, 1971). Poole also offers a simple demonstration within the *IS-LM* framework that monetary policy with an interest rate target minimizes *variability* in GNP when there are random fluctuations in the demand for money (and thus in the *LM* curve), while monetary policy with a money supply target minimizes *variability* in GNP when there are random fluctuations in the *IS* curve. This will be shown below as well.

433

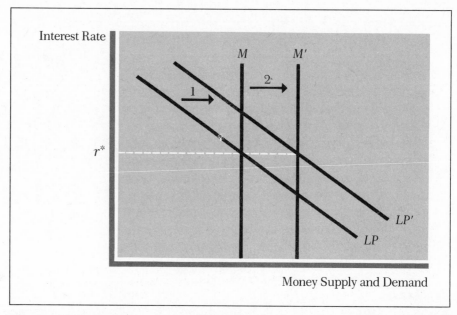

Figure 1 / If the Federal Reserve Wants to Peg the Interest Rate, It Has to Abandon Control Over the Money Supply

interest is to remain at r^*. Therefore, to peg the interest rate the Federal Reserve must be willing to relinquish control over the money supply. Figure 2 shows why keeping control over the money supply implies greater fluctuations in the rate of interest: with money supply fixed, shifts in the demand for money produce interest rates between r' and r''.

Is it always better for the Fed to specify a target for the money supply rather than the interest rate, or vice versa? The answer is— it depends. Consider the situation where the major source of instability in GNP comes from unanticipated movements in the *IS* curve. In Figure 3 we have the *IS* curve shifting back and forth between *IS* and *IS'*. With a money supply target set by the Fed and a stable demand function for money, we have the upward sloping money market equilibrium curve pictured in Figure 3. The level of GNP varies between *A* and *B*.

Compare this variability in GNP with what occurs when the Fed sets the interest rate as its policy target. Under such conditions we

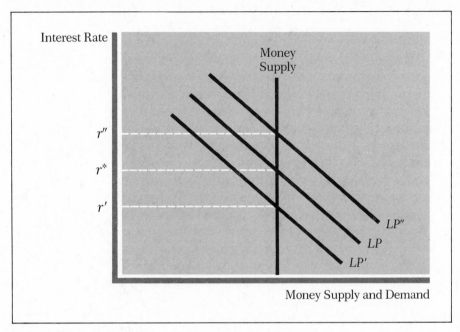

Figure 2 / If the Federal Reserve Wants to Peg the Money Supply, It Has to Abandon Control Over the Interest Rate

have the horizontal money market equilibrium curve in Figure 3.[2] GNP varies between X and Z. Clearly the money supply target is superior—it insures a smaller variability in GNP when the major source of instability is in the *IS* curve. A victory for the Monetarists.

When the game is played in the Keynesian ballpark, things turn out just the reverse. Here the demand for money is highly unstable. If the money supply is fixed by the Fed, and the demand for money

[2]The *LM* curve is flat under such circumstances because the Fed accompanies any increased demand for money with an increased supply, as we saw in Figure 1. Hence higher levels of Y (which increase the demand for money) are associated with the same level of interest, r^*. Notice that the definition of the *LM* curve is slightly different: it is the combination of Y and r with a *given* Federal Reserve policy and not a *given* money supply. That's why we've called the *LM* curve by its formal name: the money market equilibrium curve.

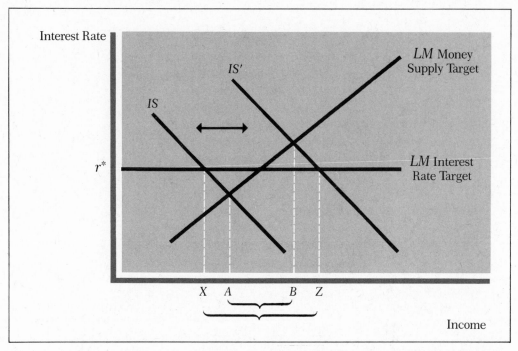

Interest Rate

IS'

IS

LM Money
Supply Target

r^*

LM Interest
Rate Target

X A   B Z

Income

Figure 3 / With an Interest Rate Target, an Unstable *IS* Curve Leads to Wider Variation in GNP than if the Fed had a Money Supply Target

shifts, then the *LM* curve moves between *LM* and *LM'* in Figure 4. With a fixed *IS* curve, GNP varies between *A* and *B*. But if the Fed uses an interest rate target, the relevant "*LM* curve" is again horizontal and there is no instability in GNP whatsoever. It stays put at *X*.

Monetarists insist that the most stable relationship in the economy (if not the world) is the demand for money. The Keynesian consumption function is much less stable. The *IS* curve is therefore the major source of GNP instability. Figure 3 tells the truth—a money supply target is best. Keynesians argue that if anything is unstable it is Monetarists themselves. Not being psychiatrists, they'll settle for an unstable demand function for money. The *LM*

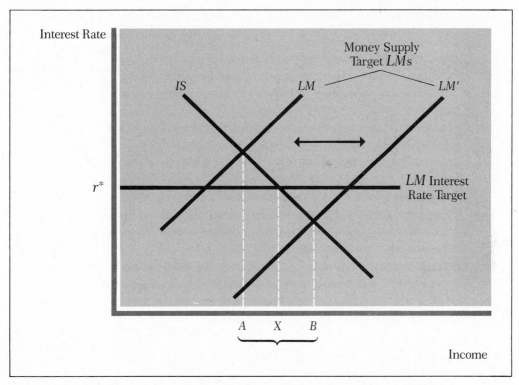

Figure 4 / With a Money Supply Target, an Unstable *LM* Curve Leads to
Wider Variation in GNP than if the Fed had an Interest Rate Target

curve is therefore the major source of GNP variability. Figure 4 tells
the truth—an interest rate target is best.

As in most Monetarist-Keynesian disputes, the ultimate resolution
lies in empirical evidence. No one believes that either the *IS* curve
or the *LM* curve is perfectly stable. Unfortunately, there has been
virtually no formal analysis of the *relative* stability of the underlying behavior in the real sector (*IS*) versus the monetary sector
(*LM*). At least one observation does seem possible, however. Keynesians are the first to admit that investment is unstable. Hence, in
order to assume a fixed or relatively stable *IS* curve, an accurately

offsetting fiscal policy (such as G increasing whenever autonomous investment decreases) must be assumed. This makes the Keynesian case somewhat weaker than the Monetarist argument.[3] What this probably proves, in a somewhat broader context, is that if you want to win a debate you should never—but never—admit anything.

[3]Actually, the Monetarist case for a money supply target gets support from some Keynesians as well. The money supply acts as a built-in stabilizer, with interest rates fluctuating up and down to keep investment from rising too steeply or falling too far. There is an even more advanced argument in favor of the money supply target, based on rational expectations. See (at your own risk) Thomas Sargent and Neil Wallace, "Rational Expectations, the Optimal Monetary Instrument, and the Optimal Money Supply Rule," *Journal of Political Economy* (April 1975).

22

Empirical Evidence on the Effectiveness of Monetary Policy

THEORY, LIKE PUNISHMENT, is said to be good for the soul. But even the most philosophical among us realize that humans—and yes, even students—also require rewards that are somewhat more concrete. Having poked into every nook and cranny of the Monetarist-Keynesian dialogue over the effectiveness of monetary and fiscal policy, the time has come to reveal the Truth (with a capital T). Since many people believe that numbers are Truth, here they are aplenty.

What are the facts about the behavior of velocity? How powerful is the impact of monetary policy on economic activity? How are interest rates affected? What particular categories of spending are most influenced by money? After all, if monetary policy is to alter GNP, it cannot do it by mystic incantations; it has to do it by changing the consumer spending of households, the investment spending of business firms, or the expenditures of governments—federal, state, or local. In contrast to the theoretical discussion of previous chapters, we now turn to the *empirical* evidence.

Living with Velocity

We have seen that part of the Monetarist-Keynesian debate hinges on the behavior of velocity—Monetarists contending that it is relatively stable and that any changes are highly predictable, while

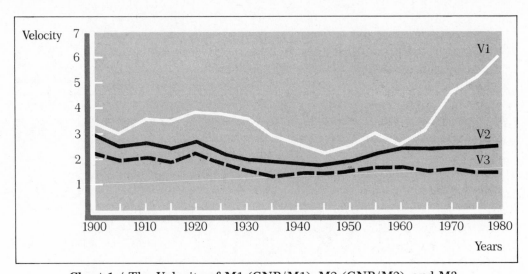

Chart 1 / The Velocity of M1 (GNP/M1), M2 (GNP/M2), and M3 (GNP/M3) Between 1900 and 1980
SOURCES: *Historical Statistics of The United States,* Department of Commerce, and *Federal Reserve Bulletin*

Keynesians argue that either contention is an exaggeration. The facts are that velocity is neither perfectly stable nor fully predictable. Unfortunately for the Federal Reserve, it does not operate in a world designed for its own convenience. With a money supply of $400 billion, a miscalculation of only 0.1 in velocity means a $40 billion swing in GNP. And with a money supply of $800 billion, the GNP jump is twice as large. But all is not necessarily lost. While velocity is not fixed, neither do its movements appear to be random or perverse. If the Federal Reserve could discover the underlying determinants of fluctuations in velocity, it might still be able to coexist with such a moving target.

With that in mind, examining the past may provide a clue to developments in the future. Chart 1 plots the historical course of three measures of velocity, each one associated with a different money supply concept. The velocity figures for V1 are based on M1, V2 on M2, and V3 on M3. Two broad generalizations emerge from the picture. First, while none of the velocity measures has been completely stable during the twentieth century, the meanderings of V2 and V3 have been quite tame. Of course, we just pointed out that even small miscalculations in velocity mean wide swings in GNP, especially for the more inclusive definitions of money. Nevertheless, the rather narrow range of movement in V2 and V3 is impressive. The second glaring message of Chart 1 is that V1 looks like it's on a space-flight trajectory. Those who prefer the narrow definition of money have some explaining to do.

First the facts. Velocity of M1 reached a peak of about 4 with the onset of the 1920s. It fell almost continuously during the Great Depression and World War II to an all-time low of about 2 in 1946. Since then, however, V1 has skyrocketed. It rose to 2.5 in 1950 and to 3.5 in 1960, passed its previous peak of 4 in 1965, pushed past 5 in 1975, and now stands well over 6. Why has the velocity of M1 gone on its own trip, apparently giving Monetarism a bad name and making life difficult for the Federal Reserve? If we have a reasonable explanation, we may be able to claim that V1's behavior is predictable, and that's enough for most reasonable people.

The main reason for the post–World War II rise in velocity of M1 lies in the relatively narrow historical definition of M1, demand deposits plus currency, and the increasing attractiveness of other categories of financial assets—bonds as well as stocks, savings and loan shares as well as savings accounts in commercial banks—as prudent and desirable outlets in which to invest excess cash. These assets are highly liquid, almost as liquid as money, and yet they offer much higher interest rates compared with demand deposits. Attractive yields on financial assets other than money have led more and more people to wonder why they should ever hold any idle cash aside from what they need for day-to-day transactions purposes. Traditional concepts about how much cash on hand is really necessary for doing business have also come under reexamination. If money for day-to-day transactions purposes can be pared down, then some of it can be lent to earn higher interest. The money then moves to borrowers who can use it for current purchases. As a result, a larger volume of current spending flows from the same stock of money.

Corporate treasurers, in particular, have found that it pays dividends to scrutinize their cash holdings intensively. Could they manage to get along with somewhat less in the till than they had previously thought of as "normal," and invest a portion in high-yielding time deposits at commercial banks or in U.S. Treasury bills? Increasingly the answer has been "yes," and imaginative new techniques of cash management have been developed to facilitate the process (as well as some not so imaginative old techniques, such as becoming "slow payers" when bills come due).

This trend has not escaped the attention of consumers. They have learned to economize on money by substituting lines of credit at retail stores and financial institutions in place of cash reserves; in addition, the growing use of credit cards has drastically reduced household needs for day-to-day transactions money. What was formerly held in the form of demand deposits or currency, for emergency use or for current payments, now shifts to interest-bearing savings deposits or higher yielding money market mutual funds.

In summary, it is clear that velocity has not been completely stable, nor has it fluctuated randomly or perversely.[1] There is a discernible pattern in the movements of M1 velocity during the postwar period—a persistent long-run rise (with minor short-run dips during recessions). Even though we may not be able to pinpoint all the specific determinants, we can still see broad cause-and-effect relationships.

Higher interest rates lead to an increase in velocity by inducing business firms and households to economize on money. They hold less, lend out the excess, and others (the borrowers) can then spend it. Once learned, techniques of cash management are not easily forgotten, so that even in recessions, when interest rates fall, velocity does not drop back very far.

Furthermore, the long-run upward trend in M1 velocity over the past quarter-century suggests that fundamental structural relationships between the money supply and the spending habits of the community are apparently in the process of transition. New payment methods have been introduced (credit cards and automated funds transfers are prime examples), as financial innovation occurs side by side with technological innovation in industry. Such financial innovation, however, rarely takes root overnight. Established payment habits change only gradually.

Thus, although velocity is not fixed, neither is it likely to change drastically in the short run. And this is especially true for V2 and V3.

---

[1]An early attempt at demonstrating the predictability of velocity is Karl Brunner and Allan H. Meltzer, "Predicting Velocity: Implications for Theory and Policy," *Journal of Finance* (May 1963).

The Federal Reserve may be able to live with such moving targets. By gaining further insight into what makes velocity move, the central bank might be able to establish a range of probabilities as to where velocity is likely to be tomorrow and the day after, and act on that basis. In other words, a morning line on velocity (not unlike the one your local bookie puts out on the races at Hialeah)—provided the odds were unemotionally calculated and continuously reassessed in the light of emerging evidence—might still enable the Federal Reserve to come out a winner.

The Demand for Money

We have just suggested that the historical movement in the velocity of M1 stems from many factors, including movements in interest rates, technology, and innovations in financial markets. To focus more precisely on the relative importance of each of these requires that we disentangle their separate influences. Only a formal application of statistical techniques to historical data on the money stock, interest rates, income, and other variables will permit us to identify the individual relationships. Indeed, economists have spent considerable effort estimating statistical counterparts to the money demand equations discussed in earlier chapters.[2] And the reasons for the effort are not difficult to understand—after all, the Monetarist and Keynesian heritages have a large stake in the outcome of such studies.

Just about every statistical study has shown that both the interest rate and the level of GNP influence money demand. In particular, higher interest rates significantly reduce the demand for cash balances. This result, by itself, contradicts extreme forms of Monetarism which assume zero interest sensitivity of money demand. On the other hand, none of the empirical investigations has ever isolated the Keynesian liquidity trap. More important, the estimated

[2]See David Laidler, *The Demand for Money: Theories and Evidence* (New York: Dun-Donnelley Corp., 1977) for a review of the empirical evidence on money demand.

interest elasticity of money demand has generally been quite low.[3] Thus the Monetarist outlook gains considerable support after all.

The question of the interest sensitivity of money demand has historically been an important issue dividing Monetarists and Keynesians. But once the extreme positions—zero and infinite interest elasticity—have been ruled out, the more sophisticated problem focuses on the *stability* of the money demand equation. After all, given the statistical results, the specific numbers are less important than how reliable they are in forecasting future money demand. As long as the historical estimates are reliable predictors of money demand, then the Federal Reserve can gauge the proper amount of money to add to or subtract from the economy in order to hit a particular target of economic activity. On the other hand, if the particular estimates change a lot, or if the demand for money jumps around for no apparent reason, then changes in the money supply will be useless predictors of economic activity. Monetarists would obviously be unhappy at such results, and so would ecumenical Keynesians who view both monetary and fiscal policies as potentially important stabilization weapons.

Most of the evidence suggests that the demand for money was quite stable until the mid-1970s; the predictive power of statistical money demand equations was quite good. Then, about the middle of 1974, the estimated demand equations for money went adrift. People were holding smaller money balances than the historical relationships suggested. This led to the celebrated mystery story—the case of the missing money.[4]

Mysteries are fun to read, but they pose problems for the authorities unless they can be solved. Explanations for the surprising shortfall in money holdings have ranged from technological developments, such as automated transfers of funds, to financial innovations, such as the use of money market mutual funds as substitutes for ordinary checking accounts. If the answer were primarily technological, then the shift in money demand in the mid-1970s

[3]In terms of the microeconomic division between elastic (greater than one) and inelastic (less than one) demand curves, the interest sensitivity of money demand has been estimated as low as 0.15 and as high as 0.7 (see the Laidler book cited in footnote 2, especially pp. 122–130).
[4]See Stephen M. Goldfeld, "The Case of the Missing Money," *Brookings Papers on Economic Activity* (1976, No. 3).

would be a less troublesome once-and-for-all event. But a significant source of the shortfall in money demand since 1974 stems from financial innovation.[5] And many of these developments have been stimulated by rising interest rates (see Chapter 6).

Fortunately, it is somewhat premature to indict money demand as a hopeless case of manic-depression. First, the stability until the mid-1970s was quite impressive. Second, there was a confluence of forces during the 1970s, including bursts of inflation and unprecedented volatility in interest rates, that combined to generate unique pressures for change. Finally, and closely related to the last point, the regulatory environment was too antiquated to accommodate a smooth transition within established historical relationships. For example, much of the innovative response to rising interest rates stemmed from the regulatory prohibitions against paying interest on demand deposits. Now that this restraint has loosened somewhat (again, see Chapter 6), there will be less incentive to circumvent regulations and destroy historical relationships in the process.

Time Lags in Monetary Policy

The empirical evidence just presented on velocity and money demand provides some comfort to those promoting the relationship between money and economic activity. But the simple velocity and money demand approaches, even with carefully calculated probabilities, leave much to be desired as a guideline for Federal Reserve policy-making. In particular, they ignore time lags between changes in monetary policy and the impact on economic activity. They also ignore the more sophisticated statistical methodology used to construct entire models of the economy so that the impact of monetary policy can be simulated more elaborately. Both lags and econometric models add flesh to the skeleton of our theoretical models. First we look at lags and then we introduce the power of econometric modeling.

[5] See Gillian Garcia and Simon Pak, "Some Clues in the Case of the Missing Money," *American Economic Review* (May 1979).

The FDIC's Chief Bank Examiner on the trail of the missing money.

By their own admission, Federal Reserve officials are not omniscient. If the economy starts to slip into a recession, it takes time before the experts realize what is happening so they can take steps to correct it. Similarly, if inflation begins to accelerate, it takes a while before the evidence verifies the fact.

Prompt recognition of what the economy is doing is not as easy as it sounds. For one thing, the available data are often inadequate and frequently mixed: New car orders will rise while retail department store sales are falling; farm prices may be dropping while employment in urban areas is rising. Furthermore, the economy rarely proceeds on a perfectly smooth course, either up or down. Every upsweep is interrupted from time to time by erratic dips; every decline into recession is punctuated irregularly by false signs of progress, which then evaporate. Is a change only a brief and temporary interruption of an already existing trend, or is it the start of a new trend in the opposite direction? No one is ever perfectly sure.

This problem of getting an accurate "fix" on what is happening in the economy, or what is likely to happen in the near future, is called the *recognition lag* in monetary policy. In 1975, for example, preoccupation with massive inflation continued even as the economy slipped into the worst recession since the 1930s.

As soon as the recognition lag ends, the *impact lag* begins, spanning the time from when the central bank starts using one of its tools, such as open market operations, until an effect is evident on the ultimate objective—aggregate spending in the economy. It may take weeks before interest rates change significantly after a monetary action has begun. Changes in credit availability and money supply also take time. And a further delay is probable before actual spending decisions are affected. Once monetary policy does start to influence spending, however, it will most likely continue to have an impact on GNP for quite a while. All of this was swept under the rug in the theoretical models discussed in earlier chapters. But now it's time to add some flesh to that bare-bones description of the real world.

Regarding the *recognition* lag, rough evidence suggests that the Federal Reserve generally starts to ease about half a year or more after a boom has already run its course, whereas it starts to tighten only about three months after a business cycle has reached its trough. This evidence is less than definitive, and it is likely that under some circumstances the monetary authorities will sense what is going on and take action more promptly than under other circumstances. Nevertheless, the inference that the central bank is typically more concerned with preventing inflation than with avoiding recession probably contains a grain of truth.

The *impact* lag is most conveniently discussed, along with the strength of monetary policy, in terms of the results that formal econometric models of the economy have produced. An econometric model is a mathematical-statistical representation that describes how the economy behaves. Such a model gives empirical content to theoretical propositions about how individuals and business firms, lenders and borrowers, savers and spenders react to economic stimuli. After such relationships are formalized in mathematical expressions, data on past experience in the real world are used to estimate the precise behavioral patterns of each sector. A model, therefore, is based on real-world observations jelled into a formal pattern by the grace of statistical techniques. Thrown into a computer, the model simulates the economy in action and grinds out predictions based on the formal interactions the model embodies.

Our knowledge of how best to construct such a model is far from complete. The same data can produce different results depending on the theoretical propositions used to construct the model. As one cynic put it, "If one tortures the data long enough, it will confess."

A Keynesian model, for instance, would incorporate behavioral assumptions different from those of a Monetarist model, and hence grind out an alternative set of predictions. A Monetarist model might relate total GNP to money supply directly, on the basis of a predictable velocity assumption. A Keynesian model, on the other hand, would spend considerable time trying to explain the determinants of consumption spending, investment spending, and liquidity preference. With regard to monetary policy in particular, the Keynesians' model would try to articulate explicitly the linkages between money supply, interest rates, and real spending decisions. And if something is left out, they have only themselves to blame.

Since both Monetarists and Keynesians are presumably interested in the truth, it is reasonable to assume that their models have been specified with that objective in mind. Let's review the evidence to see if some consensus emerges.

The Impact of Monetary Policy on GNP

The Federal Reserve Board, working with economists at the Massachusetts Institute of Technology and the University of Pennsylvania, has developed an econometric model of the behavior of economic aggregates in the United States. Many other economists have done similar work at other universities and financial institutions. But our discussion will be based primarily on the Federal Reserve–MIT–Penn model, called the Federal Reserve model for short, which was prepared specifically to evaluate the impact of stabilization policies on economic activity. The results of Monetarist models, such as the one constructed at the Federal Reserve Bank of St. Louis, will be contrasted with the Fed model.

It is important at the outset to emphasize that these econometric models are evolutionary phenomena, constantly revised and altered to reflect new and different perspectives about economic reality. Moreover, the numerical estimates of how the economy responds to a change in monetary policy (and fiscal policy as well) vary with the specific conditions of economic activity. Thus the numbers reported below provide a general flavor of how the models simulate economic and financial responses to policy, but they should be viewed as impressionistic. In fact, we must append the Surgeon General's warning: These numbers are dangerous to your health. They cannot be distributed without prescription. Minors will not be admitted, even with parental guidance.

The Federal Reserve's model articulates rather carefully the impact of monetary policy on various categories of spending. Indeed, the channels of transmission are clearly set out in mathematical splendor. We will give some of the details below, but at this point it is best to concentrate on an overview of the model's findings for monetary policy.

As a first approximation to measuring the impact of monetary policy, let us look at what the Federal Reserve's model says about the effect of changes in the money supply on (nominal) GNP. An increase in the money supply of $1 billion produces an increase of about $3 billion in GNP after one year, and at the end of two years GNP is nearly $6 billion above its initial level. After three years, economic activity is still rising, producing an increase of more than $10 billion in GNP above its original level.

The main implication of these results is that there is a rather long lag before the full effects of an increase in the money supply are felt on spending. If the Federal Reserve undertakes an expansionary monetary policy now, it will have to contend with the effects of such policies well into the future. This can create serious problems for monetary policy, as we saw in Chapter 20.

Monetarists, especially those of the St. Louis variety, are unhappy with the Fed model. They don't like the detailed description of the transmission mechanism between money and economic activity, suspecting that the architects of the model may have unwittingly left out some of the *direct* links between money and spending. Exactly what these links are is not for us to know—but money works in mysterious ways, so we must have faith. The Federal Reserve

Bank of St. Louis pits the midwestern virtue of simplicity against the sophisticated system produced by the Boston-Philadelphia-Washington Establishment.

The simple St. Louis model relating GNP directly to money produces a much faster and initially larger impact of money on economic activity. According to the St. Louis model, an increase of $1 billion in the money supply raises GNP by over $5 billion after one year, roughly double the impact derived from the Federal Reserve model over the same time interval. After one year, however, the St. Louis model finds no additional impact of money on GNP.

The Fed economists counter that the little black box connecting money and GNP in the St. Louis model does not lend itself to scientific evaluation. It is impossible to tell how much of the change in GNP is really due to changes in money supply and how much is due to other things that are changing at the same time. In short, the St. Louis model is too simple to be trusted by Easterners.

Some economists have argued that the effectiveness of monetary policy is asymmetrical—monetary policy is more effective in stopping inflation than in getting us out of recession. They reason that the high interest rates and curtailed availability of credit that characterize tight money cannot help but force restrictions on spending, while the low interest rates and ample credit availability that are typical of easy money will not necessarily induce people to borrow and spend.

The Federal Reserve model provides some support for an asymmetrical response to tight versus easy money. In particular, a *decrease* of $1 billion in the money supply lowers GNP by $4 billion after one year and by $8 billion after two years. Thus the impact of tight money is more than one-third larger than the impact of easy money. The St. Louis model, however, makes no distinction between periods of easy and tight money. According to the Monetarists, money is money and if you want it and don't have it, it is just as disturbing as when you have it and don't want it. (Yes, the sentence is written correctly; we checked it three times, and so did the proofreaders.)

Returning to the question of time lags, it should be noted that it takes time for an open market operation by the Federal Reserve to have an impact on the money supply. Reserves provided through open market purchases, for example, must work their way through the banking system as banks make loans and buy securities. If we measure the lag in monetary policy from the time when the Federal Reserve injects reserves through open market operations, then we must add on a few months to the delayed response in GNP to monetary policy.

Fiscal Policy and Crowding Out

The theoretical discussions in earlier chapters indicated a clear distinction between Monetarist and Keynesian views on the effectiveness of fiscal policy. Monetarists contend that tax and expenditure policies merely displace private spending, leaving little net impact of fiscal policy on GNP. Keynesians, on the other hand, argue that the "crowding out" effects of government policies are incomplete, implying that fiscal policy generates much of the traditional multiplier effect on GNP. It should be clear by now that this dispute can be resolved only by resort to empirical evidence.

Let us first see how the Federal Reserve's model treats the crowding out issue. Figure 1 shows the simulated response in nominal GNP (left side) and real GNP (right side) to a $10 billion expansion in government expenditure. In each of the pictures there are three lines, each representing alternative monetary policies accompanying the expansionary fiscal policy. The solid line shows the effect with a monetary policy that keeps the three-month Treasury bill rate unchanged. That assumption implies an expansion in the money stock to accommodate rising demand as GNP goes up. The dotted line assumes a monetary policy that keeps bank reserves (but not necessarily the money supply) unchanged. The dot-dash line simulates the results with a constant money stock.

It is evident from the pictures that this last monetary policy causes a substantial amount of crowding out, as we would expect. The fixed money stock policy forces rates of interest to rise as GNP increases; this cuts off certain categories of investment spending, as we will see in greater detail below. Note, however, that there isn't complete crowding out of nominal GNP, although in the right-hand picture there is crowding out of real GNP after about two years.

The multiplier effects of government spending are much more expansionary with more accommodating monetary policies. Thus the Fed model confirms the crucial role of money for the size of the fiscal policy multipliers. But the Fed model maintains that complete crowding out does not take place even with a fixed money stock assumption.

The original version of the Monetarist model developed at the Federal Reserve Bank of St. Louis reported complete crowding out of fiscal effects within the first year after government spending was increased. One of the problems with this revolutionary result was that the St. Louis model was silent on the specific categories of private spending that were crowded out by the government's expenditure. This agnosticism of the St. Louis model made its results highly suspect, according to most Keynesians. In point of fact, more recent estimates of the Monetarist model are less adamant on the absence of any fiscal effects on GNP.[6]

It seems that the empirical evidence on fiscal policy confirms significant crowding out, but only if the contractionary effects on private spending are given time to work themselves out. This brings us to the question of the role of interest rates within the framework of our models. First let's look at how changes in money supply influence the level of rates, and then we can turn to the specific categories of spending that are most sensitive to interest rates movements.

The Impact of Money on Interest Rates

According to both Monetarists and Keynesians, the initial liquidity impact of an expansionary monetary policy reduces the level of interest rates. Similarly, both Monetarists and Keynesians recognize that inflationary expectations generated by excessively expansionary monetary policy will raise interest rates. The key difference of opinion, as we explained back in Chapter 20, focuses on how long it takes for inflationary expectations to counteract the initial liquidity effects.

[6]See, for example, Benjamin M. Friedman, "Even the St. Louis Model Now Believes in Fiscal Policy," *Journal of Money, Credit and Banking* (May 1977).

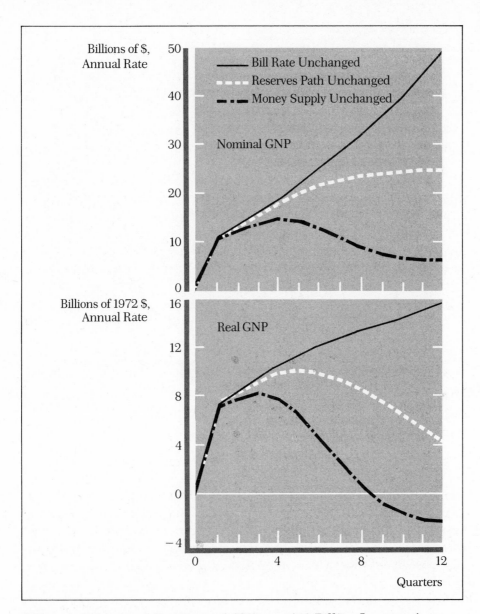

Figure 1 / Simulated Response of GNP to a $10 Billion Increase in Government Spending
SOURCE: Congressional Budget Office

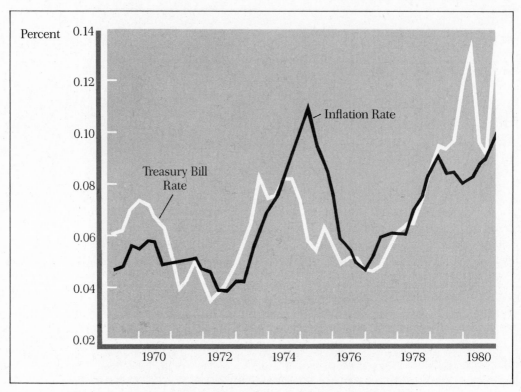

Chart 2 / Interest Rates Move With the Rate of Inflation

Chart 2 illustrates that the levels of short-term interest rates during the 1970s are rather closely related to actual movements in the rate of inflation. Thus a broad sweep of the data clearly shows the impact of inflation on the rate of interest. But the chart also shows substantial intervals of independent movements in the level of interest rates. And to identify the separate role of monetary policy in this area, it is once again necessary to consult the statistical evidence.

Most econometric models report that interest rates decline and remain below their original levels for six months to a year after an expansionary monetary policy, and that they are above their original levels for a similar period after a contractionary monetary policy. The Fed model, for example, shows that a $1 billion increase in reserves via open market purchases by the Federal Reserve lowers the corporate bond rate by one-fourth of 1 percentage point initially; after some slight readjustment upward during the next twelve months, it levels off and remains below its original level for a considerable length of time.

The more sensitive three-month Treasury bill rate reacts with greater gyrations to an open market purchase. Immediately following a $1 billion purchase of government securities by the Federal Reserve, the bill rate declines by more than 1 percentage point. But after a year the bill rate is only one-half of 1 percentage point below its original level, and it eventually comes to rest about one-third of 1 percentage point below its starting point.

Under certain conditions, the Federal Reserve model does suggest that interest rates could rise above their original levels in response to an expansionary monetary policy: namely, when inflationary price expectations are especially strong. Even here, however, the decline in rates lasts through at least a year of expansion. In contrast, there are some Monetarist models that show the Treasury bill rate snapping back to its original level and going above it within six months after an expansionary monetary policy.[7]

It should be emphasized that the response of inflationary expectations depends crucially on the initial state of the economy. At levels of economic activity that are very close to full employment, or when saver and investor concerns about inflation are especially strong, an upward jump in inflationary expectations due to expansionary monetary policy can be even quicker than we just indicated. Thus while the formal models show a relatively slow adjustment, their predictions are based on the average historical experience. Any particular historical event can show more sensitivity than the average if the specific conditions are ripe.

At this point it seems useful to go one step further in examining the behavior of interest rates. Rising rates should cut off some spending and falling rates should be stimulative. Let us see which categories of spending are most sensitive to movements in interest rates. In this way we can isolate the channels through which mone-

---

[7]One example is William E. Gibson, "Interest Rates and Monetary Policy," *Journal of Political Economy* (May/June 1970). For a recent result showing virtually no reduction in long-term interest rates due to expansionary monetary policy see Fredrick Mishkin, "Monetary Policy and Long-Term Interest Rates," *Journal of Monetary Economics* (January 1981).

tary policy operates as well as identifying the categories of private spending that are likely to be crowded out by fiscal actions.

Business Investment

One would expect interest rates and all types of investment spending to move in opposite directions: An increase in interest rates, for example, should lower business spending on plant and equipment. If the cost of borrowing rises, so our theory said, business firms should presumably be less willing to incur new debt to build new factories or buy new machines. The simple historical record shows, however, that interest rates and business investment almost always move in the *same* direction. As in most cases where fact contradicts economic theory, one of them must give ground—and it is usually fact.

In the historical record, many things are happening simultaneously, so separate strands of cause and effect are not sorted out. Investment spending on plant and equipment is influenced by a number of factors besides interest rates—sales expectations, changes in anticipated profitability, pressures from competitors, the degree of capacity currently being utilized, and expectations regarding inflation, to name only some. An increase in interest rates may inhibit investment, and yet investment may, in fact, rise if a number of these other elements shift sufficiently to offset its effect.[8]

Econometric methods, such as those used in constructing the Federal Reserve model, permit us to sort out the effects of individual variables. For our particular concern, we can examine the impact of interest rates on investment, holding all other influences constant. The Fed model shows, for example, that an increase of 1 percentage point (say from 10 to 11 percent) in the corporate bond rate lowers business spending on new plant and equipment by about

---

[8]Recall our theoretical discussion of the investment function in Chapter 18. The negative relationship between interest rates and investment was drawn with the explicit assumption that all other factors remained constant (*ceteris paribus* to the rescue once again!).

half a billion dollars after one year, by about $2.5 billion after two years, and by $4 billion after three years.

In this instance, the time delay of interest rate effects is clearly quite substantial. Most investment decisions are not made today and executed tomorrow. Decisions regarding installation of new machinery and construction of new plants are usually made far in advance. Thus an increase in interest rates does not promptly affect investment in plant and equipment. What it does affect is current decisions that will be implemented months or years in the future.

Residential Construction

The impact of monetary policy is felt more promptly and more powerfully on residential construction expenditures. In particular, an increase of 1 percentage point in the interest rate lowers spending on housing by $3 billion within a year. In addition to this interest rate effect, residential construction is also affected by monetary policy through credit rationing activities by financial institutions engaged in mortgage lending. In fact, credit availability is often emphasized by modern Keynesians as a significant channel through which monetary policy influences spending.

In the case of residential construction and mortgage lending, the use of credit rationing by lenders has been especially prevalent because of regulatory interference with the flows of funds into the mortgage lending institutions. Recall from Chapters 6 and 7 that ceilings on deposit rates that savings and loan associations, for example, could pay on passbook savings accounts meant that when other interest rates rose, deposit interest rates could not remain competitive. This forced mortgage lenders to reduce the amount of funds offered to potential homebuilders. Note that such credit rationing activities mean that tight monetary policies curtail spending even without raising the explicit cost of borrowing.

The Federal Reserve's model builds credit rationing into the transmission mechanism of money to spending. But this specific case of mortgage credit rationing is likely to become less important in the future as financial regulations are relaxed and as institutions

Consumer Lending Dries Up

Interest Rate Run-Up Brings Bank Cutbacks

By STEVE LOHR

In response to the recent surge in interest rates, banks and other lenders are cutting back on loans to individuals and making funds for consumer borrowing increasingly scarce.

For their part, consumers seem to be retrenching again as well. The most recent measures of auto, housing and retail sales have all shown declines, following brief periods of earlier strength. And economists warn that without a pickup in consumer spending and loan activity the economic recovery could be arrested, or, at a minimum, flattened and stretched out much longer than previous such recovery periods.

"All this talk we had been hearing recently about a consumer comeback is mostly just that—talk," observed Richard D. Perry, vice president of consumer loan services for the Bank of America, the San Francisco-based bank that is the nation's largest. "The consumer is quite apprehensive about taking on new debt."

Simply put, high interest rates mean two things: that inflation is a problem and that the Federal Reserve Board, through credit-tightening moves, is trying to combat that inflation by making borrowed funds more expensive.

By Nature Self-Limiting

High interest rates are by nature self-limiting. As individuals and institutions decide the cost of money is more than they can afford, economic activity slows, bringing down inflation and interest rates as well.

The economy currently appears to be at the point at which high interest rates should begin to slow it. The prime rate has advanced precipitously from 10¾ percent in early August to 15½ percent —moving up last week by a full point, an uncommonly large increment. Economists predict that rates will probably

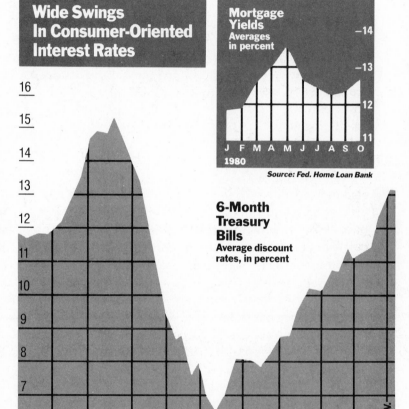

Wide Swings In Consumer-Oriented Interest Rates

16
15
14
13
12
11
10
9
8
7

JAN. | FEB. | MARCH | APRIL | MAY | JUNE | JULY | AUG. | SEPT. | OCT. | NOV.

1980

Mortgage Yields Averages in percent

−14
−13
−12
−11

J F M A M J J A S O
1980

Source: Fed. Home Loan Bank

6-Month Treasury Bills Average discount rates, in percent

peak soon, with the prime around 17 percent, and then retreat in the next month or two. In fact yesterday the stock market soared on the apparently growing belief that the peak was approaching.

But for the moment, in states such as New York—where usury laws place ceilings on interest charges to consumers—bankers say they will be increasingly tight-fisted with funds. Otherwise, they argue, they would be lending to consumers at rates below what the banks themselves must now pay for funds in the money markets.

"We're not making personal loans," Richard M. Kovacevich, senior vice president of Citibank, said in an interview. "We can't afford to make them at these rates."

At some banks still making personal loans, potential borrowers must be present or past customers; they must have had previous savings and checking accounts, as well as loans with that institution, to be eligible for new loans. At others, credit lines to customers have been cut back.

News Item / The Impact of Monetary Policy

New York Times, November 13, 1980

become less specialized. Thus the Federal Reserve's estimates may have to be revised further as the financial environment evolves in new directions.

Construction expenditures by state and local governments also appear sensitive to the actions of the monetary authorities. Municipal bond flotations are often reduced, postponed, or canceled during periods of high and rising interest rates. Many municipal governments have self-imposed interest rate ceilings that eliminate them from the market when rates go up. In other instances, when interest costs become too large, local voters are reluctant to approve bond issues for school construction and other projects, since the higher interest burden implies the immediate or eventual imposition of higher property or sales taxes.

The Federal Reserve model indicates that a 1 percentage point rise in the interest rate cuts state and local government spending by almost $2 billion after six months. Subsequently, however, the impact declines as the municipalities rethink their problems and, typically, proceed sooner or later with much of their planned expenditures.

Consumer Spending

The last major item on the monetary policy hit list is consumer spending. In this case the Federal Reserve model includes the wealth effect of modern Keynesians to channel the impact of interest rates to spending. In particular, a lower interest rate raises the value of stocks and bonds according to the model and this increases the level of consumer spending.

The importance of the wealth effect in the overall impact of monetary policy is quite substantial, according to the Federal Reserve's formulation. About one third of the impact of monetary policy on GNP after one year stems from the effects of changes in wealth on consumer spending. This is more than four times the response in plant and equipment expenditure and just about equal to the powerful effect of monetary policy on residential construction.

Perhaps the most important message of the entire set of empirical results is that there are significant long-run impacts of monetary policy on spending. While at first glance this seems to bolster the role of the Federal Reserve in the countercyclical efforts of the government, the potentially destabilizing impacts discussed in Chapter 20 become even more threatening. The Federal Reserve model suggests that monetary policy is a force to be reckoned with but is almost too powerful to harness for delicate fine-tuning of economic activity.

Summary

1. The historical behavior of GNP relative to M1 rules out the simple notion that velocity is fixed and unchanging. Although M2 velocity and M3 velocity are somewhat more stable historically, it is more important to concentrate on the predictability of velocity, rather than its stability.

2. Most statistical investigations of money demand lend credibility to the position that the demand for money, hence the behavior of velocity, is predictably related to economic activity and interest rates. Although innovations in technology and financial practices have confounded some of the historical regularities, there is reason to believe that a less cumbersome set of government regulations will mitigate the problem.

3. The impact of monetary policy on economic activity, as well as the associated time delays, are best illustrated by the results of econometric models. The main implication of the Federal Reserve's model is a rather substantial impact of money on GNP, but with a long lag before the full effects are completed. Monetarist models also show a sizable impact for monetary policy, but without substantial delayed effects beyond a year.

4. Fiscal policy has an impact on GNP, according to the models, but there is also evidence of significant crowding out. In particular, if government spending increases when the money supply is held constant, the rising rates of interest will cut off substantial amounts of private spending.

5. Interest rates increase and decrease with the rate of inflation. The relationship is not close enough, however, to negate the fact that increased money supply growth will lower short-term interest rates for a while (perhaps six months) before inflationary expectations take over.

6. Tight monetary policy and rising rates of interest have the most significant contractionary effects on residential construction. Consumer spending is also discouraged through a wealth effect of higher interest rates on stock and bond values. Business plant and equipment spending responds to higher interest rates with a significant delay (more than a year).

Suggestions for Further Reading

A comprehensive empirical test of the alternative specifications of money demand is found in Stephen M. Goldfeld, "The Demand for Money Revisited," in *Brookings Papers on Economic Activity* (No. 3, 1973). For an overview of the consequences of financial and technological innovations for velocity and money demand, see Thomas D. Simpson and Richard D. Porter, "Some Issues Involving the Definition and Interpretation of Monetary Aggregates," in *Controlling Monetary Aggregates III,* Federal Reserve Bank of Boston (October 1980).

To see how they broke from the starting gate in the Monetarist-Keynesian Correlation Derby, first read Milton Friedman and David Meiselman, "The Relative Stability of Monetary Velocity and the Investment Multiplier in the United States, 1897–1958," in *Stabilization Policies,* by the Commission on Money and Credit (Englewood Cliffs, N.J.: Prentice-Hall, 1963). Then read Michael E. DePrano and Thomas Mayer, "Tests of the Relative Importance of Autonomous Expenditures and Money," *American Economic Review* (September 1965), and also Donald D. Hester, "Keynes and the Quantity Theory," *Review of Economics and Statistics* (November 1964).

There are four excellent references on the Federal Reserve model: Frank de Leeuw and Edward M. Gramlich, "The Federal Reserve–MIT Econometric Model," in the *Federal Reserve Bulletin* (January 1968); Robert H. Rasche and Harold T. Shapiro, "The FRB-MIT Econometric Model: Its Special Features," *American Economic Review* (May 1968); Frank de Leeuw and Edward M. Gramlich, "The Channels of Monetary Policy: A Further Report on the Federal Reserve–MIT Model," *Journal of Finance* (May 1969); and Franco Modigliani, "Monetary Policy and Consumption," in *Consumer*

Spending and Monetary Policy (Federal Reserve Bank of Boston, 1971). A detailed evaluation of fiscal policy multipliers is found in the background paper of the Congressional Budget Office, *Understanding Fiscal Policy* (Government Printing Office, April 1978).

The two best expositions of the St. Louis model are Leonall C. Andersen and Jerry Jordan, "Monetary and Fiscal Policy: A Test of Their Relative Importance in Economic Stabilization," Federal Reserve Bank of St. Louis *Review* (November 1968), and Leonall C. Andersen and Keith Carlson, "A Monetarist Model for Economic Stabilization," Federal Reserve Bank of St. Louis *Review* (April 1970). For a discussion of the pros and cons of the St. Louis Monetarist approach, once again see Alan Blinder and Robert Solow in *The Economics of Public Finance,* especially pp. 63–78. For some political economy on this, see William L. Silber, "The St. Louis Equation: Democratic and Republican Versions and Other Experiments," *Review of Economics and Statistics* (November 1971).

A formal investigation of how interest rates reflect inflation is found in Eugene Fama, "Short Term Interest Rates as Predictors of Inflation," *American Economic Review* (June 1975). For a critique of that study, see John A. Carlson's "Comment," in the *American Economic Review* (June 1977). Finally, for a surprising result on monetary policy and interest rates, see Frederick Mishkin, "Monetary Policy and Long-Term Interest Rates," *Journal of Monetary Economics* (January 1981).

Part V
Financial Markets and Interest Rates

23

Risk and
Portfolio Choice

RISK IS a double-edged sword: it complicates decision-making but makes things interesting. That is true of life in general and monetary-financial economics in particular. At this point we'll stick to the economic perspective, although the end of our chapter will hint at issues with broader appeal.

Our main concern is setting the framework for decisions regarding the allocation of wealth among alternative assets. This is what is meant by portfolio selection. In accountants' terminology, we will examine the balance sheet decisions of the individual. The most interesting elements concern how to choose among assets with varying degrees of risk. This will set the stage for the discussions in the next few chapters on the structure of credit flows and interest rates on various assets.

Before our foray into risky decision-making, however, it is useful to describe the financial sector without risk. It's certainly not the world as we know it, but it is a good point of departure.

A World of Certainty

Without risk there are no disappointments. All plans proceed as conceived; all expectations are fulfilled; no promises are broken. Life is perfectly predictable, and so is the financial sector.

One person's promise to repay a loan is as good as anyone else's. No one is a welcher—not even your brother-in-law. Under such ideal conditions the same interest rate is applicable to each and every loan. Anyone trying to charge more will not succeed in making a loan; anyone charging less will be deluged with requests for funds. All promissory notes are perfect substitutes for each other; hence they must sell for the same price, which means they offer the same yield. Thus the interest rate is the same for all—it is the yield earned by lenders on a riskless loan, one that will be repaid in full by all borrowers, without a shadow of a doubt, at a designated time in the future.

Since this is a rather peculiar world, to say the least, it's worth asking whether there will be any borrowing or lending at all under such mythical conditions? The answer is yes, as long as individuals differ regarding the desired time patterns of their consumption. Those preferring instant gratification (IG) may want to consume more today than their current income, while prudent providers (PP) may want to consume less than their current income. The PPs lend to the IGs at the unique rate of interest. That rate is determined, in fact, by the balancing of the total demand for funds by the IGs with the total supply of funds from the PPs.

The rate of interest doesn't have anything to do with risk since there isn't any. Rather, the interest rate influences people's consumption and investment decisions. If more people want to borrow —either to buy a new hat (consumption) or to build a new factory (real investment)—than want to lend, the rate of interest will be pushed up by the unsatisfied (and still-eager) borrowers. The rise in the rate of interest causes some to rethink their borrowing and spending plans, while others may decide to save and lend more— with a higher interest rate it pays to be a prudent provider. Thus the key decisions influenced by the rate of interest are consumption, saving, and investment.[1] There are no portfolio problems because every financial asset is the same.

[1]This discussion underlies the classical school's interest rate theory described in Chapter 17.

Sources of Uncertainty

At the very least, the world as we know it is rife with unanticipated disappointment. Borrowers, however well intentioned, may be simply unable to fulfill their promises to repay borrowed funds. Factories built to produce polyester fabrics may become obsolete because of renewed enchantment with natural fibers. The manufacturer who borrowed funds with every intention of repaying out of expected polyester sales cannot pay the promised interest and/or principal on his loan. Either event is called a default, and the lenders' expected return is either reduced or wiped out.

Default risk is associated with all promissory notes of individuals and private corporations. The obligations of the federal government, on the other hand, are not so flawed. Federal taxing power, together with the authority to coin money, means that payment of interest and principal on federal obligations is never in doubt. There is, however, still another source of uncertainty affecting even the yields of default-free government securities: the risk of fluctuations in the level of the interest rate—sometimes called market risk or capital uncertainty.

A two-year government bond selling for its $1,000 face value and bearing an interest coupon of $60, payable at the end of each year, has an expected yield of 6 percent. There is no question that this bond will yield 6 percent if held to maturity. If you buy it you'll receive $60 per annum plus $1,000 at maturity. That's 6 percent, given the initial $1,000 outlay. But in our world of uncertainty, it's just possible that you will have to sell unexpectedly before maturity —say, at the end of one year. To whom do you sell? To someone else, to someone who wants to lend funds for one year (the original two-year bond now has one year to maturity). At what price? Aha! That's the big question. Can you get $1,000 for the bond, thereby realizing 6 percent, as expected? Not necessarily. It depends on the yield on newly issued one-year government securities. If the going rate of interest on one-year securities is 6 percent, the old bond sells for $1,000 and the yield is as expected. But if, for some reason, yields have risen to 7 percent, so that new bonds bear a coupon of $70 per $1,000, then you'll be offered less. In fact, you'll be offered about

$990, or just enough to make the $60 coupon yield 7 percent to the new holder; that, after all, is the going rate of interest.

What has happened to the two-year government bond sold after one year? Instead of yielding 6 percent, the expected yield to maturity, its actual yield turns out to be only 5 percent—the $60 coupon *minus* a capital loss of $10. The *holding-period* yield can be less than the original expected yield to maturity if the level of interest rates rises. Thus bonds that are sold before maturity have uncertain yields even if all coupon payments are made on time and even if the face value is paid at maturity. And, in our uncertain world, it's not unlikely for bondholders to need funds before their investments mature.

Still more uncertainty would be evident if we considered real interest rates rather than nominal yields. Government bonds do not promise payments in real goods and services—just nominal payments—a certain number of dollars. But we have already sufficiently complicated our simple world to examine the principles of portfolio choice under uncertainty.

Obviously there are many rates of interest on securities that differ with respect to maturity and issuer. Or, more generally, securities have different expected yields and varying degrees of risk. How can or should these securities be combined under rational decision-making? We have already mentioned the principle of diversification in connection with financial intermediaries in Chapter 6. We are also familiar with its usage in everyday discussion. As we will see below, portfolio diversification is desirable under certain circumstances and can be optimally designed given specific interrelationships between securities.

Risk Aversion and Portfolio Analysis

One of the most important *assumptions* of modern portfolio analysis is risk aversion. People are assumed to dislike risk. That doesn't mean they'll never indulge—they will if the price is right. And in the context of securities in a portfolio, the right price translates into a sufficiently high expected yield.

The simplest example illustrating risk aversion is the preference for a security which is certain to pay 5 percent compared with one having an equal chance of paying either 8 percent or 2 percent. The second security has an average return of 5 percent: about half the time its yield is 8 percent, and about half the time its yield is 2 percent. Its *expected* yield is 5 percent, where the formal definition of expectation is the sum of the possible outcomes multiplied by their respective probabilities: $8\% \times \frac{1}{2}$ plus $2\% \times \frac{1}{2} = 5\%$. Note that the *expected* yield is nothing more than the average yield.

Why does a risk averter prefer the certain return of 5 percent to an equal chance of 8 percent or 2 percent, even though the expected values of the two securities are identical? Simply put, the extra pleasure when the return is 8 percent is less than the additional pain when the return is 2 percent. Sound familiar? It should, because it's nothing more than diminishing marginal utility of money: each additional dollar is worth less (although you always want more!).

Would the risk averter ever be indifferent between a security paying a fixed yield with certainty, such as a 5 percent savings deposit in a commercial bank, and a bond whose return is uncertain? Yes, but only if the bond had a higher expected return to compensate for the undesirable uncertainty. For example, if the bond's equally probable outcome was either 10 percent or 2 percent, so that the expected return would be 6 percent (10 percent $\times \frac{1}{2}$ plus 2 percent $\times \frac{1}{2} = 6$ percent), then our risk-averting portfolio manager might be indifferent. If the possible outcomes are 12 percent and 2 percent, so that the expected return is 7 percent, then he might even prefer the risky venture—since the compensation in terms of higher expected yield might be enough to induce risk-taking. The required trade-off of higher return per unit of risk—the degree of risk aversion—is a subjective measure, quite different for every individual.

Does all this mean that someone who is not a risk averter must have deep-seated emotional problems? Not at all—he or she is simply a risk lover (also known as a compulsive-degenerate gambler). We observe that most people in the real world are risk averters. Not because they tell us so in any direct way, but because most people hold diversified portfolios—many different securities rather than just one with the highest possible return. Diversification is the salvation of the risk averter, but mere child's play to the risk lover.

Before proceeding to the principles of diversification and portfolio selection, it is useful to note that we have used what is formally called a probability distribution to represent the outcomes of our financial investment. Each of the possible "events" (8 percent and 2 percent) has a probability of occurring (½ in our case) and the sum of the probabilities is unity (at least one of the possible outcomes must occur). Moreover, we have used a statistic called the arithmetic mean (the common average) to summarize the most likely outcome—the expected value. In this vein, we can try to specify more carefully the meaning of risk.

Uncertain outcomes make for risky investments. While the expected value of our equally probable 8 percent and 2 percent investment is 5 percent, sometimes the return will be 3 percent more than the mean (8 minus 5 is 3) and sometimes the return will be 3 percent less (2 minus 5 is -3). The deviation of actual returns from expected returns is a useful measure of risk. Formal statistical techniques suggest a slightly more complicated approach—just to terrorize the uninitiated. Deviations of actual outcomes from the mean can be either positive or negative. In fact, if one were to add them up, the pluses and minuses would cancel! We could apply either of two arithmetic operations to avoid the canceling problem: (1) take absolute values; (2) square the deviations (recalling that a negative number squared is a positive number). The second is used in calculating what is called the standard deviation, which we now describe in somewhat greater detail.

In addition to the magnitude of the deviation around the expected value, risk should also be related to the probability of such events actually occurring. Thus if the 2 percent outcome has only a 1 in 10 chance of actually occurring, this represents less of a risk than if it has a probability of ½. In calculating the standard deviation, the squared deviations around the mean are "weighted" by their probabilities of occurring; that is, they are multiplied by their respective probabilities. This makes the standard deviation a still more intuitive measure of risk. The final step in the calculation is to restore the numbers to their original scale by taking the square root of the entire mess. In our example, we have the following: $(8 - 5)^2 \times ½ + (2 - 5)^2 \times ½ = 9 \times ½ + 9 \times ½ = 9$, the square-root of which is 3. In particular, for this investment the standard deviation of the probability distribution of returns is 3 percent. With a more complicated probability distribution, the numerical results are not quite so simple.

A potential drawback of the standard deviation is the use of both positive and negative deviations around the expected value. Shouldn't risk measure only the disappointments—that is, when actual outcomes are below expectations? That's a reasonable suggestion. But when the probability distribution is symmetrical above and below the mean, it makes no difference (below the mean is just half the total). Since there is evidence suggesting that security returns have this symmetry (they are normally distributed), and since the standard deviation has nice statistical properties (whatever that means), much of portfolio analysis uses the standard deviation to measure risk.

We are now prepared for one of the most fundamental propositions of modern portfolio theory:[2] An asset may seem very risky when viewed in isolation, but when combined with other assets, the risk of the portfolio may be substantially less—even zero! To illustrate this we also consider the central problem of portfolio analysis: how to choose an efficient portfolio.

Portfolio Selection

Take two assets (please). The first we'll call asset A for Adventure Inc. We're not quite sure what business they're in, but it's a good one. In good times it pays 16 percent and in bad times it pays 2 percent —clearly a cyclical industry. An expected return of 9 percent—but with fairly large uncertainty over the actual outcome—varying directly with the pulse of economic activity. Now consider asset B for Barbiturates Inc. We know pretty much what they do. In good times they lose money, producing a return of minus 2 percent. But in bad times they rake it in, earning 12 percent for the misanthropic investors. The expected return is 5 percent, with substantial variance in

[2]The original work on modern portfolio theory is Harry Markowitz, *Portfolio Selection* (New York: Wiley, 1959). Major extensions are summarized in William F. Sharpe, *Portfolio Theory and Capital Markets* (New York: McGraw-Hill, 1970).

the actual results. Note, however, that asset B's outcomes are coun-tercyclical—they are better when the economy is worse.

Could it make sense to buy both of these highly risky investments —apparently exposing oneself to all sorts of disappointment? The answer is definitely yes. In fact, dividing your funds equally between assets A and B yields a return of 7 percent, in both good times and bad—there is no uncertainty at all.[3]

Does that mean I would definitely prefer the half-and-half combi-nation to either A or B by itself? Well, I know I prefer it to B because B's expected return is only 5 percent and it is uncertain at that, while the half-and-half portfolio gives me 7 percent and no risk. In this case, the risk averter clearly chooses the combination portfolio. Less clear is whether he chooses the fifty-fifty strategy or puts all his money in A. While A has uncertainty, it also has a higher expected return (9 percent versus 7 percent). The choice of A versus the com-bination depends upon the precise nature of the risk averter's pref-erences—whether the extra 2 percent expected return compensates for the increase in risk.

The principal lesson derived from the example is twofold. First, the uncertainty of return of an individual asset is *not* by itself a measure of its riskiness. Rather it is the contribution of the asset's uncertain return to total portfolio risk that matters. Second, a key determinant of the latter is the interrelationship between the varia-bility of the assets' returns. This is so important it has a name of its own—covariance.[4]

[3]Here's the arithmetic: Start with $200. Put $100 in A and $100 in B. In "good times" A pays $16 (= 16 percent of $100) and B loses $2. The investor earns $14 ($16 minus $2) on $200 invested, or 7 percent (14/200). In "bad times" the $100 in A earns $2 while the $100 in B earns $12, for a total of $14, which is once again 7 percent. Note: The standard deviation of the returns on the half-and-half portfolio is zero even though each security's return had a positive standard deviation.
[4]Covariance has a simple intuitive definition: comovement. It also has a precise mathematical measurement. In our case, the deviation of each security's return from its mean is derived; the product of the paired observations is then weighted (as in the standard deviation) by the probability of each of the paired observations actually occurring. Positive covariance indicates that when one security's return is above its mean, so is the other. Negative covariance indicates when one security's return is above its mean, the other is below.

The term "correlation" used in the following sentence of the text also has specific mathematical connotation. It is the covariance divided by the product of the standard deviations. It rescales covariance so that *perfect* comovement is +1.0 and perfectly

In the example just given, assets A and B are perfectly negatively correlated: when asset A's realized yield is low, that of B is high, and vice versa; and the magnitudes are such that there is perfect offset. That's why combining the two reduces risk (in this case to zero). Indeed, this *is* the principal of portfolio diversification: Hold a number of assets (rather than one) so that the exposure to risk is reduced. An asset such as B, whose returns are countercyclical (high when everything else is low), is an ideal addition to a risk averter's portfolio.

But assets such as B are relatively hard to come by. If portfolio diversification to reduce risk depended on finding assets with "negative covariance of returns," we'd be in for tough times (and lots of risk). But the magic of portfolio diversification extends to other cases as well. In particular, as long as assets do not have *precisely* the same *pattern* of returns, then holding a group of assets reduces risk.[5]

Take the case where each asset yields either 6 percent or 2 percent, but the outcomes are independent of good times or bad times, *and of each other,* like the flip of a coin. Does dividing the portfolio between two such assets, X and Y, reduce risk? Well, if I hold both X and Y and *both* happen to yield 6 percent or both happen to yield 2 percent, I'm in the same situation as with holding just one. But it's also possible, in fact *just* as possible, that when X is yielding 6 percent, Y yields 2 percent, or when X yields 2 percent, Y yields 6 percent. In these cases, uncertainty is zero and the return is the average—4 percent. In fact, if I held many, many such assets, all with an equal chance of 6 percent or 2 percent, and the outcome of each one were *independent* of every other asset, then I'd be virtually certain of always earning 4 percent. About half of the outcomes would be 6 percent and half would be 2 percent.

You should recognize that the key condition in this last example is the word "independent." When asset returns are relatively inde-

---

(*continued*)

offsetting movement is -1.0, with intermediate relationships between these two extremes. A zero correlation means that the returns of the two securities are independent.

[5]The same pattern of returns translates into a correlation coefficient of $+1.0$ (the returns on all assets are above or below their respective means at the same time and are proportional to their standard deviations).

pendent (zero covariance), putting many together tends to produce the average return just about all of the time. Risk is thereby reduced to zero. Does that mean that most people who hold diversified portfolios have zero risk? No, it doesn't, because most assets are affected in a systematic way by economic conditions—hence most asset returns are not completely independent of each other.

Some Implications

The examples of portfolio diversification just given permit some refinement in the first principles discussed earlier. The standard deviation of returns is a good measure of risk when analyzing a security by itself. It is also a good measure of risk for an entire portfolio. But it is a relatively poor measure of the risk contribution of a single security to an entire portfolio. That depends much more on the covariance of returns with other securities; more precisely, the *average covariance* of a security's returns with all others. The reason lies in the magic of diversification: the risk contribution to a portfolio of a security's returns that are substantially independent of all other returns is nearly zero. This *nonsystematic* risk is diversified away as the number of securities held increases (as in our coin flipping example). Only the *systematic* movement of the return on a security with all others adds to portfolio risk.

If most asset holders are risk averse, then it also follows that they will demand extra compensation—higher expected returns—in proportion to the systematic risk of a security. Thus investors will pay attention to a risky security only if it also promises to pay a higher expected yield.

This information is just about all that is necessary for the first step in portfolio decision-making: separate *efficient* from *inefficient* *portfolios.* In fact, in our earlier example, asset B was ruled out because it had the same risk as the half-and-half portfolio (zero) but yielded less (5 percent versus 7 percent). A portfolio consisting only of asset B is inefficient. More generally, efficient portfolios have the following characteristics: greatest possible return for a given risk; lowest risk for a given return.

After calculating the various combinations of assets that produce efficient portfolios, investors choose that portfolio which matches their risk-return preferences. In our earlier example, we could not say whether asset A (yielding 9 percent with risk) dominated the half-and-half combination (yielding 7 percent and no risk). Both of these are efficient portfolios. Which is preferred depends upon the subjective trade-off between risk and return demanded by an individual.

Actually, the final choice of portfolio composition can be separated into two distinct decisions: first, derive the efficient combination of risky securities, and second, determine how much cash to hold versus the risky assets. We have already discussed the second issue in Chapter 18 under the demand for money. In Chapter 26 we discuss the choice among risky assets within the context of the structure of interest rates.

At this point, however, we can already anticipate a fundamental fact of life in financial markets. Securities with greater risk must offer investors higher expected yields. Or, looked at somewhat less charitably: If you want to earn a higher expected yield, you will have to accept greater risk. This result stems directly from risk-averse behavior by individual investors and their search among efficient portfolios for what suits them best. If a security that is more risky does not offer the opportunity to earn a higher expected yield, then investors will simply ignore it in constructing their preferred portfolio. The only way issuers of such securities can entice potential investors is to offer higher yields to compensate for the extra risk.

It's worth emphasizing that all of our analysis holds only for risk averters. For risk lovers this has been a classroom exercise, useful primarily in preparation for the final exam. How many of you are really risk lovers? Although it sounds like an enjoyable avocation, fewer people than you think actually meet the standard.

The fact that most people hold many financial assets supports the assumption of risk aversion. A risk lover would not find it sensible to hold a diversified portfolio. He or she chooses to invest in an asset with large possible capital gains (and losses, although he usually puts the latter in parentheses). That doesn't necessarily mean that people won't gamble occasionally—putting down a dollar in a lottery for a one-in-two-million chance of winning a million dollars has some psychic appeal (the mere thought of winning is enough to make you buy two tickets). An occasional trip to Las Vegas—while not an appropriate risk-averter activity—has its other compensations. But when it comes to putting *all* your assets to work—would you take a fifty-fifty chance of doubling your money or losing it all? If your answer is no, you're a risk averter; if the answer is yes, you're a risk lover. If you are the former, then some of the principles of diversification suggested here can help in deciding on the assets you should place in your portfolio. If you are the latter—see you on the next junket to Vegas (bring all of your money and jewelry and clothes and whatever else you can muster up and join the ASCPA—Anonymous Spurners of Conventional Portfolio Analysis).

Summary

1. In a world without risk there is no problem of portfolio choice; one asset is as good as any other. In fact, each and every asset offers the same yield.

2. Risk stems from uncertainty over the payments that will actually be received from investing in an asset. There are two sources of risk: (1) if the debtor defaults on principal or interest, actual payments will be less than promised; and (2) if an asset is sold before maturity, the price received may be less than expected. Both circumstances cause the actual yield on an asset to differ from what was expected.

3. Investors must, in general, be compensated for bearing risk. An investor will prefer an asset that always yields 5 percent to one that yields 5 percent *on average* but at any particular time may yield less or more. This preference is called risk aversion.

4. Risk-averse investors will try to combine securities in a portfolio in order to reduce risk. Such risk reduction through portfolio diversification occurs because the uncertain outcomes on each security can offset each other somewhat.

5. Do not judge the riskiness of a security by its own variability of possible outcomes. More important to a risk averter is whether the security's uncertain outcomes offset some of the risks on other securities in the portfolio.

6. Decisions about how to combine risky assets influence the structure of yields on securities. In particular, investors who want to earn higher yields on average will have to invest in more risky securities.

Suggestions for Further Reading

The seminal book by Harry Markowitz, *Portfolio Selection* (New York: Wiley, 1959), is still the best place to start. For a masterful introduction see William J. Baumol, *Portfolio Theory: The Selection of Asset Combinations* (New York: General Learning Corp., 1970). A leading text on investments is Edwin J. Elton and Martin J. Gruber, *Modern Portfolio Theory and Investment Analysis* (New York: J. Wiley and Sons, 1981).

24

Flow of Funds Accounting: A Framework for Financial Analysis

ACCOUNTING gives off bad vibes. It is widely believed to be the world's dullest profession. Kids grow up wanting to be movie stars or athletes but never accountants. This is unfortunate, because it is easier to be an accountant than a Faye Dunaway or a Reggie Jackson. Those jobs are already taken. It is also unfortunate because accounting is often more exciting than it looks.

Flow of funds accounting, for example, was first discovered by a Swedish fashion model named Inga, who stumbled upon it while taking skiing lessons in the Himalayas. She broke her tibia trying to make a hairpin turn and invented flow of funds while recuperating.

Flow of funds accounting, for those who have not read Inga's autobiography *(Everything You Always Wanted to Know About Flow of Funds But Were Afraid to Ask),* is used to analyze borrowing and lending in financial markets. It traces financial transactions by recording the payments each sector makes to other sectors and the receipts it receives from them—just as a family might keep track of its money by recording all its payments and receipts.

Flow of funds accounting is useful in many ways. As we shall see, it provides a useful framework for analyzing what happens in various financial markets (Chapter 25). It can also be thought of as tracing the financial flows that interact with and influence the "real" saving-investment process we discussed in Part IV. It records the maze of financial transactions underlying real saving and investment.

To appreciate all these implications, however, we will first have to learn what flow of funds accounting is all about. Specifically, it is a record of payments between and among various sectors. This is done via sector "sources and uses of funds" statements, which is what most of this chapter is devoted to explaining. You need not commit all the accounting details to memory; it will be sufficient to understand the main concepts that emerge. Let us begin by seeing how a typical sector "sources and uses" statement is constructed.

A Generalized Sector Income Statement

A sector "sources and uses of funds" statement is nothing more than the integration of its income statement with its balance sheet. Taking first things first, a simplified income statement, general enough to apply to any sector, would look something like the following:

(1) A Generalized Income Statement for a Single Sector:

Uses of Funds (on Current Account)	Sources of Funds (on Current Account)
Current expenditures	Current Receipts
Saving (Addition to Net Worth)	

$$\Sigma = \Sigma$$

An income statement like the above merely lists a sector's current receipts during a period of time as a source (inflow) of funds, and its current expenditures as a use (outflow) of funds. Current receipts differ depending on which sector is involved; they consist mainly of wages and salaries for the household sector, sales receipts for the business sector, and tax revenues for the government. Similarly, the composition of current expenditures also differs, depending on which sector we are looking at.

In all cases, however, one sector's payments become another sector's receipts: as tax payments, a major *use* of funds for households and business firms, become tax receipts, a major *source* of funds for the government. As we shall see, it is this mutual interaction that gives the eventual flow of funds matrix its interlocking nature.

Saving, on the left-hand side, is defined as any excess of current receipts for a sector over and above its current spending. It is the same as our old definition of saving from Chapter 17: saving equals income minus consumer spending. When it involves the government sector it is usually called a budget surplus, and when applied to the business sector it is frequently labeled either retained earnings or addition to net worth. In any case, since it is defined as the difference between current receipts and current expenditures, it is the balancing entry on an income statement. Thus summation equality signs are at the bottom of income statement (1).

A Generalized Sector Balance Sheet

Let us leave income statements for a moment and move over to balance sheets. Income statements show current receipts and expenditures over a *period* of time (say during the year 1984), whereas a balance sheet shows not receipts and expenditures but assets and liabilities, and not over a period of time but at an *instant* in time (say on December 31, 1984). A simplified balance sheet, general enough to apply to any sector, would look something like the following:

(2) *A Generalized Balance Sheet for a Single Sector:*

Assets	Liabilities and Net Worth
Financial Assets a. Money b. Other Real Assets	Liabilities Net Worth

$$\Sigma = \Sigma$$

As with income statements, the principal difference between the balance sheets of different sectors is in the characteristic items that appear under each heading—consumer durable goods such as furniture and automobiles are typical real assets for consumers, inventories and capital equipment are typical real assets for business firms, and so on. Also like income statements, balance sheets must balance, in this case because the net worth entry is defined as the difference between total assets and total liabilities. Thus our simplified balance sheet also contains summation equality signs.

On the balance sheet above, assets are divided into two broad categories, real and financial. A *real* asset, like a car or a calculator, appears on only one balance sheet, that of its owner. A *financial* asset, however, like money or bonds, always appears on two balance sheets: that of whoever owns it (as an asset), and that of whoever owes it (as a liability). This is because every financial asset is a *claim* by someone against someone else—an IOU of some sort—like a government bond (an asset to whoever owns it, a liability of the government) or a bank deposit (again an asset to the owner, a liability of the bank).[1]

While only *financial* assets appear on two different balance sheets, *all* liabilities do, because all liabilities—by definition—represent debts owed to others. Thus any time a liability is listed on anyone's balance sheet, a corresponding financial asset must be rung up on some other balance sheet.

Converting Balance Sheet Stocks to Flows: Saving and Investment

To analyze financial trends during a year we need data on flows over a period of time, not stocks on a balance sheet at an instant in time. But all is not lost. We can convert balance sheet stocks (of goods or

[1] A complication arises in this connection with respect to corporate equities (corporate stocks), because they are financial assets to whoever holds them but are not, legally, liabilities of the issuing corporation. For most purposes, the simplest way to handle this is to assume that corporate stocks and bonds are roughly the same thing, despite their legal differences, and treat them both as liabilities of the corporation. (In other words, we ignore the problem.)

of money) into flows by comparing two balance sheets for the same sector, two balance sheets "snapped" at different times. For example, we can take the balance sheet of a household on December 31, 1984, and then again on December 31, 1985. By comparing them, and seeing what *changes* have taken place in each entry, we can translate stocks into flows: we can tell how much furniture was purchased or how much cash was accumulated *during the year* 1985.

Going back to our simplified balance sheet (2), let's take the bottom pair of entries, real assets and net worth—ignoring financial assets and liabilities for the time being—and see how we can convert those stock figures, snapped at a moment in time, into flows covering a period of time. The change (Δ) between two dates could be displayed like this:

(3) *A Partial Sector Sources and Uses of Funds Statement, on Capital Account*:

Uses of Funds (on Capital Account)	Sources of Funds (On Capital Account)
Δ Real Assets (Investment)	Δ Net Worth (Saving)

Since (3) is derived from only part of the balance sheet, it need not balance, so there are no summation equality signs at the bottom. Notice also that the column headings are different from (2): "Assets" and "Liabilities and Net Worth" have been replaced by "Uses of Funds" and "Sources of Funds," the same as in income statement (1). Now, however, they refer to uses and sources of funds on *capital* rather than current account—that is, to long-term uses and sources instead of short-term ones.

On the uses side, the change in real assets refers to capital expenditures, as contrasted with an income statement's current expenditures. Capital expenditures involve the purchase of *real* assets with an expected useful life of a year or more; the term is synonymous

---

(*continued*)

A related problem, which also remains unresolved, is that both bonds and stocks are traded on organized markets and change in price, so they may be valued differently by the holder and the issuing corporation. For example, a $100 bond issued by a corporation may rise in price to $120; to the holder it is now a $120 financial asset, but to the corporation it is still a $100 liability. The difference is capital gains to the bondholder, although the bondholder receives no funds inflow unless the bond is sold.

with real investment spending (or simply *investment* spending), as we have been using that term throughout this book.[2] Such capital expenditures are not included in an income statement; in accordance with conventional accounting practice, income statements are confined to current expenditures—the purchase of assets with an expected useful life of less than a year.

A distinction has to be made between "investment" spending as economists use the word (it always refers to the purchase of *real* assets with a useful life of a year or more, like houses or machine tools), and the use of the word in general conversation, where it often refers to the purchase of *financial* assets, like stocks or bonds. When we say simply investment, we always have reference to buying real assets; if we want to refer to the purchase of financial assets, we will always say, explicitly, financial investment.

On the sources side, the change in a sector's net worth during the period is exactly the same thing as "saving" on its income statement covering that time interval. This deserves a word of explanation, since it is not immediately obvious (even though the fact that "saving" is frequently labeled "addition to net worth" should provide a clue that they are one and the same). On a balance sheet, net worth is defined as equal to a sector's total assets minus its total liabilities. A change in net worth must therefore equal any change in total assets less any change in total liabilities. On an income statement, in contrast, saving refers to an excess of current receipts over current expenditures. But any excess of current receipts over current expenditures (flows) must imply a resulting buildup of total assets or a reduction of liabilities, or some combination of the two. Conclusion: Saving on a sector's income statement must become an equivalent change in net worth on its balance sheet.

Put somewhat differently, as a "use" of funds on current account (on the income statement), saving means *not* spending. It means retention or accumulation. As such, it represents an addition to one's wealth or net worth and becomes available as a "source" of funds for capital account.[3]

---

[2]Real investment can be recorded on either a net or gross basis, depending on whether or not depreciation is deducted from original value.

[3]As with investment, saving can be measured on a net or a gross basis, depending on whether or not depreciation is deducted. It should be noted that even if depreciation is deducted, so that saving is measured on a net basis, depreciation will still be a

Since statement (3) is derived from only part of the balance sheet, and thus does not have to balance, it follows that an individual unit or sector may or may not invest (that is, buy capital goods) just equal to its current saving. It may save more than it invests, or invest more than it saves. If a unit or sector invests an amount equal to its current saving it is called a balanced budget sector. If it saves more than it invests it is called a surplus sector, and if it invests more than it saves it is called a deficit sector.[4] (Read this paragraph again—these will be useful concepts later on.)

How could a sector invest more than it saves? One way is simply to borrow enough to finance its deficit, which brings us to the other pair of balance sheet entries—liabilities and financial assets.

Converting Balance Sheet Stocks to Flows: Borrowing, Lending, and Hoarding

So far we have ignored the possibility of changes in liabilities and financial assets, the remaining entries on (2), our generalized sector balance sheet. Such changes between two balance sheet dates would look like this:

(4) A Partial Sector Sources and Uses of Funds Statement, on Capital Account:

Uses of Funds (Financial, on Capital Account)	Sources of Funds (Financial, on Capital Account)
Δ Financial Assets Other than Money (Lending)	Δ Liabilities (Borrowing)
Δ Money (Hoarding)	

---

source of funds for capital account, since it represents a noncash "expense" rather than an actual current outlay of funds.

[4]Alternatively, a surplus unit is one that spends (on consumption plus real investment) *less* than its current income, and a deficit unit is one that spends *more* than its current income.

"Hold it, gentlemen, hold it! I had it the wrong way around. It isn't assets that are in excess of ninety-seven million. It's liabilities!"

Drawing by Chon Day; © 1969 The New Yorker Magazine, Inc.

Since (4), like (3), is derived from only partial balance sheets, it need not balance and thus contains no summation equality signs. But whereas (3) dealt with nonfinancial or "real" sources and uses of funds, (4) is concerned with *financial* transactions—with *borrowing* (an increase in outstanding liabilities) as a source of funds, and with *lending* (an increase in holdings of financial assets other than money) and *hoarding* (increased money holdings) as uses of funds.

Strictly speaking, we should separate short-term financial transactions from long-term, comparable to our distinction between short- and long-term spending on real assets. However, in flow of funds accounting such distinctions are rarely made with respect to financial transactions, and all borrowing and lending, regardless of duration, are typically considered as on capital account.

The three possibilities in (4)—borrowing, lending, and hoarding—do not exhaust all the potential financial sources or uses of funds open to a sector. For instance, another possible financial *source* of funds, in addition to borrowing, is selling some holdings of financial assets. Still another source of funds is *dis*hoarding. And an additional possible *use* of funds would be to repay one's debts. These alternatives do not appear on (4) because only *net* changes are considered there, and it is implicitly assumed that they are all positive. Potential negative changes would add the three just mentioned.

By convention, if the net change in any entry turns out to be negative over a period, it is kept on the side where it presently appears in (4) but preceded by a minus sign. If the net change in financial assets for a sector turns out to be minus, for example, as when a person liquidates some of his government bonds, it would be recorded on the uses side but preceded by a minus sign and referred to as a negative use of funds. But a negative use is actually a source of funds—aha! Another useful concept.

A Complete Sector Sources and Uses of Funds Statement

Believe it or not, if we string together everything we've done so far we will have before us, in all its pristine glory, Inga's remarkable discovery—a complete sector sources and uses of funds statement. Lo and behold:

(5) = (1) + (3) + (4) *A Complete Sector Sources and Uses of Funds Statement:*

Uses of Funds		Sources of Funds
Current Expenditures		Current Receipts
Saving (addition to *NW*)	$\Sigma = \Sigma$	
Δ *RA* (Investment)		Δ *NW* (Saving)
Δ *FA* (Lending)		Δ *L* (Borrowing)
Δ *M* (Hoarding)		
	$\Sigma = \Sigma$	
	$\Sigma = \Sigma$	

Above the dashed line is the income statement, below the dashed line the changes in the balance sheet. Since the income statement must balance, as must the aggregate changes in the balance sheet, the summation of all the sources must equal the summation of all the uses of funds, and therefore we have summation equality signs all over the place.

We are now able to define more precisely what we mean by a sector's sources and uses of funds:

Sources of funds consist of (a) *current receipts;* (b) any *increase in a liability* item (borrowing); or (c) any *decrease in an asset* item (selling off assets, dishoarding).

Uses of funds consist of (a) *current expenditures;* (b) *any increase in an asset* item—increased holdings of real assets (investment), of financial assets (lending), or of money (hoarding); or (c) any *decrease in a liability* item (debt repayment).

We could simplify (5) by eliminating current receipts from sources and current expenditures from uses, taking only the difference between them—saving—as a source of funds (if positive, or as a use if negative). That is what we have, in effect, if we look only below the dashed line (which is the way the flow of funds accounts are published by the Federal Reserve).

"I called in you people from Accounting because I wanted to ask you if you're having fun."

Drawing by Weber; © 1978 by The New Yorker Magazine, Inc.

The requirement that everything below the dashed line must balance means that each sector's investing + lending + hoarding must equal its saving + borrowing. As we know, however, a sector might save more than it invests (a surplus sector), or invest more than it saves (a deficit sector). If it does have a discrepancy between its saving and its investing, this necessarily implies a corresponding differential between its *financial* sources and uses of funds. To be more specific: A surplus sector, with saving greater than investment, *must* dispose of its surplus by lending, repaying debts, or hoarding (building up its cash holdings) in an amount equal to its surplus. And a deficit sector, with investment in excess of its saving, *has to* finance its deficit by borrowing, selling off financial assets, or dishoarding (running down its cash holdings) in an amount equal to its deficit.[5]

These conclusions flow from the fact that below the dashed line, as well as above it, the sum of all a sector's uses of funds must equal the sum of all its sources. Putting the same thing rather formally:

For any one sector:

investment + lending + hoarding = saving + borrowing

So if:

saving > investment, then lending + hoarding > borrowing

And if:

investment > saving, then borrowing > lending + hoarding

The Flow of Funds Matrix for the Whole Economy

Early in this chapter we said that flow of funds accounting records payments between and among sectors via sector sources and uses of funds statements. Since one sector's payments become another sector's receipts, when we put all these individual sector statements

---

[5]A deficit sector might also finance its deficit by issuing new money. However, only two sectors are legally able to exercise that unique option—banks (by creating demand deposits) and the government (by creating dollar bills). If they did so, it would be entered on their statement (5) as an increase in their liabilities (borrowing), because while money is an asset to whoever owns it, it is a liability of whoever issues it.

together we get a flow of funds *matrix* for the economy as a whole, an interlocking grid that reveals financial relationships among all the sectors. When the flow of funds matrix was first published by the Federal Reserve in 1955, it contained the complete statements for each sector in the form of statement (5) above. Since 1959, however, it has consisted of only partial sector sources and uses statements, namely that part of (5) below the dashed line. Current receipts and current expenditures are not shown explicitly, but they are implicitly included in that the difference between them—saving (or dissaving)—is there.

Assuming a total of three sectors and omitting some detail, the flow of funds matrix appears essentially as follows:

(6) *Flow of Funds Matrix for the Whole Economy:*

	Sector A		Sector B		Sector C		All Sectors	
	U	S	U	S	U	S	U	S
Saving ($\triangle NW$)		s		s		s		S
Investment ($\triangle RA$)	i		i		i		I	
Borrowing ($\triangle L$)		b		b		b		B
Lending ($\triangle FA$)	l		l		l		L + H	
Hoarding ($\triangle M$)	h		h		h			
	$\Sigma = \Sigma$		$\Sigma = \Sigma$		$\Sigma = \Sigma$		$\Sigma = \Sigma$	

NOTE: The small letters within the matrix represent the data for sector saving (s), investment (i), borrowing (b), lending (l), and hoarding (h), and are placed in the appropriate space where such data would be entered. The capital letters similarly represent the aggregate sum totals for the whole economy. Thus $s + s + s = S$, $i + i + i = I$, etc. (Roman "U" and "S" represent uses and sources of funds.)

This matrix is nothing more than the placing of the sector sources and uses statements side by side, each in the form of that part of (5) below the dashed line. The resulting matrix forms an interlocking self-contained system, showing the balanced sources and uses of funds for each sector, interrelations among the sectors, and the aggregate totals of saving, investment, borrowing, lending, and hoarding for the economy as a whole.

For each individual sector, as we know, its investment + lending + hoarding must equal its saving + borrowing. Since that is true for each individual sector, it is also true in summation for all the sectors taken together, i.e., for the economy as a whole.

In addition, something else is true for the economy as a whole which need not be true for any one sector taken by itself: Saving must equal investment. (Haven't we met that one somewhere before?) We developed that relationship in "real" terms in Chapters 17 and 18, and now here it is again, emerging this time from the financial side:

For the whole economy:

investment + lending + hoarding = saving + borrowing

But since one sector's financial asset is another sector's liability:

lending + hoarding = borrowing

Therefore:

investment = saving

The conclusion that saving must equal investment applies only to the entire economy taken in the aggregate, but not to any single sector taken by itself. As we have seen, any single sector may save more than it invests, or invest more than it saves. But since saving must equal investment for the economy as a whole, it follows that for each sector that saves more than it invests there must, somewhere, be other sectors that invest correspondingly more than they save.[6]

In coming chapters we shall have frequent occasion to use this framework in analyzing financial institutions and markets, and the interdependencies among them. The economic function of financial markets, after all, is to provide channels through which the excess funds of surplus units (whose saving exceeds their investment) can be transferred to potential deficit units (who want to invest more

---

[6]This is true not only because the economy-wide total of saving must equal investment, but also because a surplus sector must dispose of its surplus, as we have seen, by lending, repaying debts, or hoarding an amount equal to its surplus. This in turn implies the existence of deficit sectors to borrow, reduce their financial assets, or dishoard.

Similarly, deficit sectors, which invest more than they save, necessarily imply the existence of surplus sectors. A deficit sector must finance its deficit by borrowing, selling off financial assets, or dishoarding. This in turn implies the presence of surplus sectors to do the lending, buying of the securities, or hoarding.

than they are saving). The flow of funds matrix enables us to trace these transactions and see how various spending flows are financed.

Summary

1. Flow of funds accounting combines sector income statements and balance sheets to construct sector sources and uses of funds statements.
2. Any one sector can save more or less than it invests, and lend more or less than it borrows. One that saves more than it invests is called a surplus sector: it is likely to be a net lender. One that invests more than it saves is called a deficit sector: it is likely to be a net borrower.
3. For the whole economy, however, saving must equal investment and lending plus hoarding must equal borrowing.
4. The flow of funds matrix for the whole economy is an interlocking grid of sector sources and uses statements. It shows borrowing and lending relationships between and among all the sectors. By examining it we can analyze who lent to whom and who borrowed from whom.

Suggestions for Further Reading

The best source of information on the actual construction of the accounts is *Introduction to Flow of Funds* (Board of Governors of the Federal Reserve System, June 1980). Also see A. D. Bain, "Flow of Funds Analysis," *Economic Journal* (December 1973). The usefulness of the flow of funds is exemplified by James S. Earley, Robert J. Parsons, and Fred A. Thompson, *Money, Credit, and Expenditure: A Sources and Uses of Funds Approach* (New York University, Center for the Study of Financial Institutions *Bulletin,* No. 3, 1976).

25

Forecasting Interest Rates

FORECASTING—whether of ball games, prize fights, or interest rates—is a hazardous profession. The accuracy of predictions may have progressed some since crystal balls gave way to mathematical models and computer technology, but not as much as you might think. This perhaps explains why a lot of people are back to fiddling with tea leaves, ouija boards, and tarot cards. Be forewarned, however: No matter how you go about predicting the future, the odds are against you.

People forecast interest rates because the stakes are high, just as they try to forecast stock prices for the same reason. If stock prices are going to rise, you'll gain by buying now rather than later. If they are going to fall, you're better off selling rather than buying. The same with bonds, or with any marketable asset for that matter, so that the temptation to forecast is almost irresistible. A financial institution can't make sensible portfolio decisions without some estimate, explicit or implicit, of future trends in financial asset prices —which means, in light of the inverse relationship between asset prices and interest rates, some estimate of future trends in interest rates.

This is particularly true with respect to long-term bonds, as contrasted with short-term money market instruments, since even a small change in long-term interest rates involves a substantial change (in the opposite direction) in long-term bond prices. A bank buying $100,000 of long-term government bonds at a 10 percent interest rate would suffer losses of $16,500 (on paper, anyway) when yields rose to 12 percent. If the bank could *anticipate* such a change in long-term interest rates, it could temporarily invest the $100,000 in short-term Treasury bills, wait until long rates have risen, and *then* switch the funds from bills to bonds.

To put it briefly, economic forecasting is important because rational decision-making is impossible without some conception of the shape of things to come. Decisions about whether to spend or not to spend, whether to borrow (or lend) now or to postpone borrowing (or lending) for six or nine months, whether to buy securities today or to hold cash for the present, whether borrowing or lending should be short- or long-term—all these and many others hinge on what the future is expected to bring. So economic forecasting, although it is still more art than science, is inescapable.

Forecasting Techniques

We are already familiar with one method of forecasting interest rates—with an econometric model of the economy, such as the Federal Reserve model discussed in Chapter 22. Based on empirically estimated consumption and investment functions, expectations regarding fiscal and monetary policies, and interrelations among these and other factors, such models have primarily been used for GNP forecasts. In the process of grinding out their GNP numbers, however, they simultaneously predict related variables, such as unemployment, price inflation—and interest rates.

But interest rate forecasts made via large-scale econometric models have been less than fully satisfactory. The theory behind them appears sound enough: Theoretical models[1] typically explain how both GNP and the interest rate are *jointly* determined by the same factors—consumer spending, investment spending, inflation, government spending, the supply of and demand for money, and so on.

[1]See the discussion of interest rates in Chapter 20.

So, in principle, a good GNP forecast should simultaneously produce a good interest rate forecast. But knowing and doing are different things, and in practice interest rate forecasts are generally much farther from the mark than GNP forecasts. Indeed, a portfolio manager who made his decisions primarily on the basis of interest rate forecasts generated by econometric models would probably be out of a job long before he finished reading all his computer printouts.

There are several reasons for the failure of econometric models in this respect. First, most such models still emphasize the goods and services sector of the economy rather than the financial sector, since their main purpose has traditionally been (and still is) projecting GNP and its components rather than interest rates. The underlying financial relationships are not nearly as fully refined in such models as the relationships regarding real spending decisions (the Federal Reserve model does, however, have a rather well-developed financial sector).

"And so, extrapolating from the best figures available, we see that current trends, unless dramatically reversed, will inevitably lead to a situation in which the sky will fall."

Drawn by Lorenz; © 1972 The New Yorker Magazine, Inc.

Second, even in the underlying theoretical models, which also evolved with GNP more than interest rates in mind, the *immediate* determinants of interest rates are not *explicitly* taken into account. Every participant in financial markets knows that interest rates—the price of credit—respond directly to lending and borrowing pressures, or more generally to the supply of credit and the demand for credit, as any price is determined by supply and demand. None of the standard theoretical models, however, be they Classical or Keynesian, incorporate the supply and demand for credit *explicitly* into their framework.

In Classical theory, for example, the interest rate is determined by saving and investment, as we saw in Chapter 17. Classical economists were not fools; they were well aware that lending and borrowing determine interest rates. But by focusing attention on saving and investment, they thought they were getting *behind* the superficial determinants to the basic underlying forces that explain the reasons for lending and borrowing. Lending was assumed to be directly related to saving, and borrowing to investment. That might be useful for long-run analysis, but it is not very helpful when it comes to forecasting interest rates over the next six to twelve months. You can save without lending (if you hold the money), and there can be lending without saving (banks do it all the time by creating money when they lend). Similarly, you can invest without borrowing (by using current income, or retained earnings), and you can borrow without investing (as when people borrow to speculate in the stock market). So Classical theory's determinants of interest rates—saving and investment—are far removed from the immediate determinants in the market place—lending and borrowing.

Nor does Keynesian theory do much better. In basic Keynesian analysis, as we saw in Chapter 18, interest rates are viewed as determined by the supply of money and the demand for money (liquidity preference). The supply of money, however, is a far cry from lending or the supply of credit. And the demand for money is not the same thing as borrowing or the demand for credit.

In other words, credit and money supply are different things. Credit is a flow concept, involving an amount over a period of time, while money is a stock, at a moment in time. In addition, they simply refer to different economic variables: If you lend a friend $10, the supply of credit is expanded, but the money supply is unaffected.

In the more complex Keynesian analysis, as in Chapter 19, saving and investment also become important in interest rate determination, and this is a step in the right direction. But lending and borrowing still remain hidden somewhere behind the scenes; our job in this chapter is to flush them out. Indeed, most practicing financial analysts approach interest rate forecasting directly via the supply of and demand for credit (or loanable funds). They also add an inflation premium to their predictions. Let's take a closer look at how they do it. We'll then draw some comparisons with our theoretical models.

The Supply and Demand for Loanable Funds: The Level of Interest Rates

The supply and demand for credit—or loanable funds—approach to interest rate determination amounts to a straightforward application of supply and demand analysis. In any competitive market, whether for wheat, hula hoops, or tickets to rock concerts, interaction between supply and demand determines price and quantity

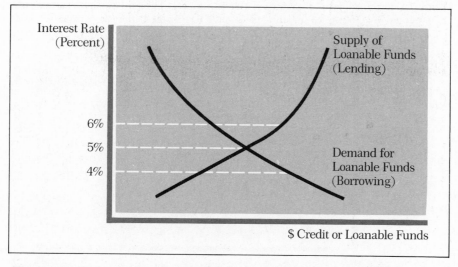

Figure 1 / Borrowing and Lending Determine the Interest Rate

exchanged. Financial markets are no different. The rate of interest is the price of credit or loanable funds, and whether it falls or rises depends on the relative eagerness of suppliers and demanders of loanable funds.

Take the standard supply-demand diagram (shown in Figure 1) illustrating price determination with supply and demand schedules. If, at a particular rate of interest (say 6 percent), lenders—the suppliers of loanable funds—are particularly anxious to lend, and borrowers rather reluctant to borrow, then the rate of interest will fall. On the other hand, if the rate of interest were only 4 percent, where borrowers—the demanders of credit—are more eager to borrow than lenders are to lend, the rate of interest is likely to rise.[2]

Forecasting interest rates by estimating the planned (or ex ante) demand for and supply of credit thus amounts, in principle, to: (1) projecting, at existing interest rates, the likely demand for credit (borrowing) during the coming year; (2) independently projecting, at existing interest rates, the likely supply of credit (lending); and then, (3) assessing the change in interest rates that will take

[2]Instead of talking about the supply of and demand for credit or loanable funds determining the rate of interest, we could talk about the same thing in terms of the demand for securities and the supply of securities determining the price of securities (see the diagram below). To supply credit (lend) is equivalent to *demanding* financial assets (securities)—financial institutions lend, for example, by purchasing financial assets. To demand credit (borrow) is the same as *supplying* securities—business firms borrow by selling their bonds or other IOUs. Look at the diagram below and

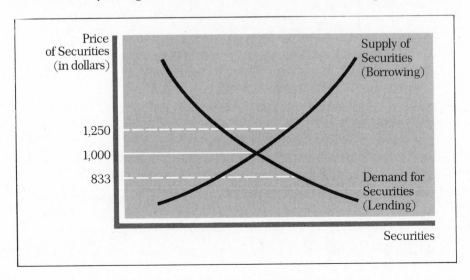

place in the market to bring the two into equality (since, ex post, the actual amount of borrowing will have to equal the actual amount of lending—you can't borrow unless someone else lends).

Most forecasters use a standard format for their trial-and-error worksheets. First they list, at existing interest rates, all the likely *demands* for credit—in terms of the dollar volume of various financial *instruments* that will be offered in the market as potential borrowers seek funds (such as corporate bonds, mortgages, government bonds). Second, they independently list, at existing interest rates, all the probable *supplies* of credit in terms of *who* will be wanting to lend how much. The third step is to hold your breath and compare the totals: If demand (borrowing) equals supply (lending), interest rates are likely to stay where they are and a vacation is in order; if demand exceeds supply, interest rates are likely to rise; and if supply exceeds demand, interest rates are likely to fall—and in the last two cases the Caribbean cruise must be postponed, since there's more work to be done.[3]

---

compare it with Figure 1 in the text. At a price of $833 (which corresponds, let us say, to the 6 percent *yield* in Figure 1, assuming a 5 percent *coupon* on a $1,000 bond), relative eagerness to buy securities—or lend—would drive up the price of securities, just as Figure 1 shows that it would drive *down* the rate of interest. And at a price of $1,250, corresponding to a 4 percent yield, relative eagerness to sell securities—to borrow—would drive down the price of securities, just as Figure 1 shows that such circumstances would drive *up* the rate of interest.

[3]This forecasting procedure implicitly assumes that financial markets are competitive, so that supply and demand pressures will be reflected in price (interest rate) changes. It rules out, therefore, the popular conspiracy theory of interest rate determination—the view that interest rates are rigged by a few insiders with substantial market power.

It is extremely doubtful that any one person, institution, or group of institutions has anywhere near enough power to rig interest rates in this country. There are too many lenders engaged in the business of lending, and therefore too many alternatives open to most would-be borrowers, to permit any tightly knit clique of lenders (or borrowers, for that matter) to control the price of credit. Lenders charging more than prevailing rates will price themselves out of the market and lose business to their competitors. Borrowers trying to borrow at cheaper rates will find themselves outbid for funds by others who are willing to pay the market price. Even the Federal Reserve does not have enough power to set interest rates at whatever level it pleases, whenever it wishes. The central bank may control the supply of credit, but it does not control the demand, and both are involved in the determination of its price. (Actually, the central bank does not even control the supply of credit; what it controls, and only imperfectly, is the supply of bank reserves.)

Table 1 Credit Projections for the Year 198?
(In billions of dollars)

	Approximation		
	1	2	3
*Demand for credit**			
in the form of:			
Mortgages	50	—	—
Corporate bonds	20	—	—
Government securities	15	—	—
State and local bonds	10	—	—
Business loans	35	—	—
Consumer loans	25	—	—
All other	5		
Total demand	160		
*Supply of credit**			
from:			
Commercial banks	55	—	—
Savings and loan associations	30	—	—
Mutual savings banks	10	—	—
Insurance companies	15	—	—
Pension funds	13	—	—
Finance companies	9	—	—
Credit unions	2	—	—
Nonfinancial business firms	6	—	—
Individuals and others	5		
Total supply	145		

*Since financial institutions are *intermediaries* in credit markets, their borrowing of funds from households and others (in the form of deposits, etc.) is not included in the final demand for credit; correspondingly, the supply (lending) of funds by households and others to financial institutions is not included in the final supply of credit.

The next step—there usually is one and it may be repeated several times—consists of making a stab at the extent of the rate changes, and then, given the new rates, at adjusting credit demands and supplies. Higher rates imply smaller amounts of credit demanded, larger amounts supplied. Lower rates are likely to involve larger amounts demanded, smaller amounts supplied. The process is continued with successive iterations until supply and demand equalize, since after all is said and done every successful borrower implies a lender, and vice versa.

The format of Table 1 illustrates the procedure. The first two steps, shown in column 1 of the table, involve the projection of likely demands for and supplies of funds at current interest rates. Demand and supply should be projected independently, of course, without reference to one when doing the other. Here the total demand for funds adds up to $160 billion, total supply only $145 billion. Conclusion: Interest rates are likely to rise.

But by how much? All we really have so far is two *points,* at existing interest rates, on a demand and supply diagram as in Figure 2(A). The extent of the rate increase depends on the interest sensitivity of demand and supply. If they both react significantly to a small change in rates (i.e., if they are both interest-elastic), a *small* rise in rates will be enough to reduce the amount demanded and increase the amount supplied so that they become equal, as in Figure 2(B). But if they both respond sluggishly or imperceptibly to higher interest rates—that is, if they are interest-inelastic, as in 2(C), then it will take a *considerable* rise in rates before demand and supply coincide.

Columns 2 and 3 in Table 1 are for successive approximations in demand and supply as the totals are adjusted toward equality. In the end, the forecast for the year ahead has to have total demand and total supply equal, since that is the way they must turn out ex post. A favorite candidate for *residual* adjustment to equate supply to demand is the lender category "individuals and others," which historically—especially in recent years—has been exceedingly volatile in response to changes in interest rates. As we saw in Chapter 6, this has been largely in reaction to Regulation Q rate ceilings, with households shifting to direct purchases of securities when market interest rates rise above Q ceilings, and then putting their funds back in financial intermediaries when market rates return to more normal levels. (As the footnote to Table 1 indicates, in order to avoid counting the same thing twice, only the *direct* purchase of securities by households is included in the supply of credit from "individuals and others"; funds channeled by individuals and others through financial intermediaries are considered as supplied to the market by the financial institutions.)

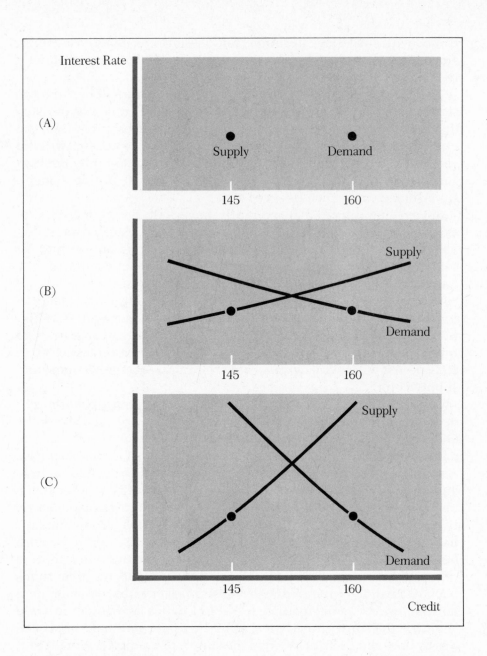

Figure 2 / The Same Initial Excess of Demand Over Supply May Raise Interest Rates a Little (B) or a Lot (C)

So far we have confined ourselves to overall pressures on interest rates. But of course there are many interest rates. In recognition of that, and to assist in thinking through the adjustment process, a matrix worksheet along the lines of Table 2 is frequently utilized. It allocates specific kinds of securities (demands for credit) among all potential purchasers (suppliers of credit). Filling it in shows how particular sectors of the financial market, and particular interest rates, are likely to be affected by supply and demand forces during the coming year.

For example, if the demand for credit by state and local governments (the supply of municipal bonds) is expected to be $10 billion during the year (from Table 1), but on the first round the matrix shows that the only likely buyers of such securities are commercial banks ($3 billion) and individuals ($2 billion), then the municipal bond area will be a prime candidate for higher yields. Other sectors may have less pressure, or even more. In this way forecasts can be made for a variety of interest rates. Of course, the matrix will have to be changed in second- and third-round iterations—with our state and local example, either the realized demand for funds will have to be reduced and/or the supply increased, until they are equal. At the end, the demand has to add up to the supply for each kind of security and also in the aggregate, in the lower right-hand corner of the matrix.[4]

In recent years one of the most important influences on interest rate forecasts has been the expected rate of inflation. Back in Chapter 20 we saw that higher rates of inflation cause lenders to demand higher nominal rates of interest as compensation for the erosion in their purchasing power. Borrowers are forced to pay higher rates if they want the funds. Most forecasters tack on an inflation premium to the interest rate forecast arrived at in the supply-demand exercise just described.

---

[4]We have simplified both tables for illustrative purposes. Most important, we have not taken the maturity of the securities into account. If relative pressures on short-term rates versus long-term rates are of concern, then a separation should be made along such lines. That is, the demand for credit should divide government securities, for example, into short-term and long-term governments, and supply should similarly be segmented. More on the structure of interest rates in the next chapter.

Table 2 Matrix Worksheet for Specific Types of Credit

Supply of Credit From	Demand for Credit in Form of								Total Supply↓
	Mort- gages	Corpo- rate bonds	Govt. bonds	Munic- ipal bonds	Busi- ness loans	Cons. loans	All other		
Commercial banks	—	—	—	3	—	—	—	=	55
Savings & loans	—	—	—	—	—	—	—	=	30
Mutual savings banks	—	—	—	—	—	—	—	=	10
Insurance companies	—	—	—	—	—	—	—	=	15
Pension funds	—	—	—	—	—	—	—	=	13
Finance companies	—	—	—	—	—	—	—	=	9
Credit unions	—	—	—	—	—	—	—	=	2
Nonfinancial business	—	—	—	—	—	—	—	=	6
Individual and others	≡	≡	≡	2 ≡	≡	≡	≡	=	5
Total Demand→	50	20	15	10	35	25	5	=	160/145

This simple inflation-adjustment procedure is based on the following implicit analysis. If inflation is expected to be two percentage points higher, say 9 percent rather than 7 percent, then at the old nominal interest rate borrowers will want more funds and lenders will offer fewer funds. This excess demand for funds puts upward pressure on nominal yields. The nominal rate of interest rises until it equates the supply of and demand for funds.[5]

Do forecasters increase their nominal rate forecasts one-to-one with a jump in inflationary expectations? Sometimes. Irving Fisher's dictum that nominal rates rise by the expected rate of inflation is valid only in a world without taxes or risk. It hardly needs emphasizing that life is complicated by both. Taxes, in particular,

[5]See Benjamin M. Friedman, "Who Puts the Inflation Premium into Nominal Interest Rates?" *Journal of Finance* (June 1978).

suggest that nominal rates will go up by more than inflation to maintain aftertax yields. On the other hand, allowing for an adjustment period suggests that nominal rates go up by less than expected inflation. Thus forecasters often take the route of least resistance—the "more thans" offset the "less thans" and the usual outcome is in the middle, a one-to-one jump.

Care must be taken, however, to match the period over which inflation is expected to accelerate with the maturity of the bond yield that is forecast. If inflation is expected to increase from 7 to 9 percent for one year and then drop back to its previous level, then only yields on one-year bonds should jump by two percentage points. Longer term maturities would reflect only one year of higher expected inflation. Thus, the near-term inflation outlook affects short-term yields while the long-run inflation outlook affects long-term yields. And that's one of the factors determining the maturity structure of interest rates, as we'll see in the next chapter.

In a similar vein, forecasters would reduce their interest rate forecast if the expected rate of inflation were to decrease. Thus if inflationary expectations have been running at 10 percent per annum, and the nominal rate of interest is, say, 14 percent, a decrease of inflationary expectations to 8 percent would mean a forecast reduction in interest rates to 12 percent if nothing else changed.

Behind Supply and Demand

Although the supply and demand for loanable funds approach to interest rate forecasting may at first glance appear far removed from the econometric model of the economy method discussed earlier in this chapter, down deep they are based on identical factors. To fill in all the blanks in the two tables above, one has to bring to bear just about everything that is included more formally in a typical large-scale econometric model of the whole economy. Indeed, just about every subject we have discussed in this entire book becomes relevant at some point in filling in the blanks to make a loanable funds interest rate forecast.

To take the first step in the entire process—*that is, to project likely demands for credit during the coming year*—one must first forecast sector spending decisions. To estimate how much people will want to *borrow,* we first have to get an accurate idea of how much they will want to *spend* (consume and invest). To forecast spending decisions, however, means we are in effect forecasting GNP.

More than that, we also have to forecast sector sources and uses of funds statements, to discover the extent to which various kinds of spending will have to be financed by borrowing compared with other forms of financing, such as retained earnings and/or dishoarding. Some spending may also be financed by the sale of financial assets, and this should be *added* to the demand for funds (supply of securities) in financial markets. It doesn't matter, so far as interest rates are concerned, whether the government floats a new issue of Treasury bills or business firms sell some "old" Treasury bills out of their portfolios to finance their inventory spending. The sale of one's own liabilities (borrowing) or of someone else's liabilities (selling off financial assets) both draw funds out of financial markets; any act of borrowing *or* sale of securities adds to the demand for loanable funds and contributes to upward pressure on interest rates.

Indeed, it is this very possibility—the sale of "old" securities by their owners—that makes the prediction of interest rates so hazardous. We seem to be able to forecast real output and employment much better than we can predict interest rates. In large part this is due to the very nature of financial markets as contrasted with markets for real goods and services. There is a large supply of *existing* securities—securities that have been issued in the past—always overhanging financial markets, and decisions with respect to holding or dumping these can be made on short notice and executed rapidly. Only a small fraction of the transactions in most financial markets consist of current lending and borrowing exchanges; most transactions involve the trading of already existing securities. In addition, although financial markets are no more susceptible to waves of optimism or pessimism than other markets, in financial markets such shifts in sentiment can more easily be translated into immediate buy or sell orders. Thus decisions with respect to buying or selling "old" securities can swamp the influence of current lending and borrowing, with consequent unforeseen effects on market interest rates. To put it briefly, forecasting interest rates is—for similar reasons—no different from predicting what is going to happen in the stock market, and even the weather man often does better than *that.*

Turning to the supply of loanable funds, we again have to use a GNP forecast, this time as a basis for estimating the flow of savings into financial institutions, which will be a significant determinant of their ability to supply credit to ultimate borrowers. Another determinant of the ability of financial institutions—especially commercial banks—to make loans and buy securities will, of course, be Federal Reserve policies. Easy money policies that expand bank reserves and the money supply will correspondingly augment the supply of loanable funds, in contrast to tight money policies that keep a lid on monetary growth. Thus money supply and money demand enter the picture.[6]

Finally, in assessing the changes in interest rates that are likely to take place due to discrepancies between ex ante demand and supply, the interest-elasticities of each kind of credit demand and supply become crucial, as noted earlier with reference to Figure 2. So also do the interest-elasticities of various kinds of spending: higher interest rates may discourage some spending from proceeding as originally planned, and lower interest rates may stimulate additional spending. These feedbacks from interest rates to spending and thereby to GNP thus require a revised GNP forecast—which means starting our method of successive approximations over again from the very beginning. So we have, in effect, come full circle. All the forces in our theoretical model—saving, investment, money supply, money demand—are embedded somewhere in the loanable funds framework, although not always right on the surface.

It should be pointed out that similar feedback effects take place between and among various interest rates, since financial instruments are substitutes for one another both in lender portfolios and in the options open to borrowers. If corporate bond yields rise, for example, some lenders will make marginal shifts out of government securities and into the now relatively more attractive corporates,

[6]Debt repayment should also be added to the supply of loanable funds, just as liquidation of financial assets should be added to the demand. Debt repayment involves the purchase of one's own liabilities, compared with lending, which is the purchase of someone else's liabilities. But any purchase of securities injects funds into financial markets, regardless of whose liability the securities might represent.

thereby slowing the rise in corporate yields but starting an upswing in government yields. At the same time, corporations, faced with higher bond interest rates, may decide to float fewer bonds and take out more bank loans instead—which will also slow the rise in corporate bond yields but put upward pressure on bank lending rates. Thus, because of *substitutability* on the part of both lenders and borrowers, all interest rates tend to move up and down more or less together, although the differentials among them may widen or narrow, as we will see in the next chapter.

Summary

1. Practical forecasting of the level of interest rates focuses on the supply of and demand for credit, or, looked at another way, on the supply of and demand for securities. This is also called the loanable funds approach to interest rate determination. It is most closely related to Classical economics, which viewed saving and investment as the forces underlying the supply of and demand for funds.

2. Financial market practitioners try to forecast the supplies of and demands for credit by various sectors of the economy on the basis of projected incomes and planned spending decisions. An excess of supply over demand leads to a lower interest rate forecast, and an excess of demand over supply leads to a higher one.

3. Changes in inflationary expectations are usually added to or subtracted from the interest rate that would bring supply and demand into balance.

4. The forces underlying the supply and demand projections include the level of GNP, saving, investment, government spending, money supply, and just about everything else we have said would influence the level of interest rates. Thus, while the loanable funds approach may look a little different from either the Classical or Keynesian formulations, everything is still in place, just as you'd expect from a good practitioner.

Suggestions for Further Reading

Annual supply and demand for credit projections are published each year
—usually in late January or early February—by Salomon Brothers *(The
Supply and Demand for Credit)* and by Bankers Trust Company *(Credit
and Capital Markets)*. The address of the former is 1 New York Plaza, New
York, New York, 10004, and the latter is Post Office Box 318, Church Street
Station, New York, New York, 10015. See also William C. Freund and Edward D. Zinbarg, "Application of Flow of Funds to Interest-Rate Forecasting," *Journal of Finance* (May 1963). Also Michael J. Prell, "How Well Do
the Experts Forecast Interest Rates?" in the Federal Reserve Bank of Kansas City *Monthly Review* (September-October 1973).

If you want to learn more about loanable funds interest theory and liquidity preference interest theory, a good place to start is Joseph W. Conard, *An
Introduction to the Theory of Interest* (Berkeley: University of California
Press, 1959). Also see Friedrich A. Lutz, *The Theory of Interest,* 2d ed.
(Chicago: Aldine, 1968).

26

The Structure
of Interest Rates

BURT REYNOLDS is not easily ruffled. He is hardly ever caught off guard. But once, while he was at one of those swinging dinner parties in Washington (actors campaigning for politicians), he met his one-time economics instructor, Dr. Mark Etz. Reynolds was standing in the corner, surveying the scene, when Etz walked up to him, puffing on his ever present pipe, and said: "Young man, I've just realized something. There are more interest rates out there than hair on your chest." Reynolds was dumfounded. He could hardly believe his ears. He was caught with his pants down, as it were. He had always thought there was only one—*the* interest rate that Etz had talked about all term long.

To make sure you won't be caught in equally embarrassing circumstances, we now take note of the many different interest rates on various types of financial instruments. The structure of yields on different maturities of the *same* class of securities is explored first. We then turn to the relationship between yields on different categories of securities (such as government bonds versus corporate bonds).

508

The Term Structure of Rates and the Yield Curve

The relationship between yields on different maturities of the same type of security is called the *term structure* of interest rates (from "term to maturity"). For government bonds we might compare the yields on three-month Treasury bills, one-year notes, and ten-year bonds.

The relationship between yield and maturity is sometimes depicted graphically by a *yield curve,* as in Figure 1, where yield is measured on the vertical axis and term to maturity is on the horizontal axis. Often the yield curve is upward sloping—that is, short-term securities yield less than long-term securities (curve *A*). Sometimes it is rather flat—short-term yields equal long-term yields (curve *B*). And sometimes the yield curve is even downward sloping —short-term interest rates are *above* long-term rates (curve *C*).

What determines the shape of the yield curve? A straightforward

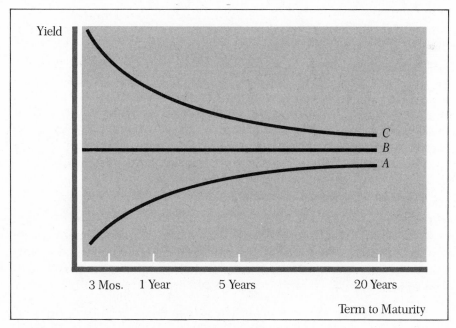

Figure 1 / Three Alternative Yield Curves

case can be made for a basic supply-demand approach. For example, when the supply of short-term securities rises, the short-term interest rate is pushed up to induce investors to buy the added supply. Similarly, when the supply of long-term securities rises, the long-term rate is forced up. But a simple supply-demand approach is vulnerable because it may ignore important relationships between the markets for short-term and long-term securities. The unadulterated supply-demand model is a "segmented markets" theory of the term structure.[1]

There are many—and here financial analysts and economists often find much common ground—who argue that short-term securities and long-term securities are very good substitutes for each other in investor portfolios—not for every investor but for enough so that their decisions *collectively* make a significant impact on the market. For such investors the important feature of the security they buy is what it yields over the period for which they want to invest (also called the "holding period" yield). This implies that long-term rates are related in a very special way to short-term rates. Let's illustrate that with a particular example.

Say you are the portfolio manager of a bank and you want to invest funds for two years. Suppose you could buy a one-year Treasury security today yielding 5 percent, and you expect that next year the rate on one-year securities will be 7 percent. If you buy the one-year security today and reinvest in a one-year security next year, you expect an average return over the two years of about 6 percent. If you had the option of buying a *two-year* Treasury security today that yielded 6½ percent, you'd jump at it (so would everyone else). On the other hand, if two-year Treasury securities were yielding only 5½ percent, you wouldn't touch them (neither would anyone). This means that unless the two-year security yields exactly 6 percent (the average of the current and expected short term rates), portfolio managers would try to buy it (if it yielded more) or sell it (if it yielded less). Thus buying and selling pressure by portfolio managers will maintain the long-term rate as an average of the current short-term rate and the expected future short-term rate.[2]

[1] The clearest exposition of this theory is John M. Culbertson, "The Term Structure of Interest Rates," *Quarterly Journal of Economics* (November 1957).
[2] In Chapter 28 we discuss futures markets for Treasury securities. These institutions provide additional investment opportunities for portfolio managers. It turns out that prices in the futures market mirror the implicit interest rates discussed here.

A somewhat more general statement is as follows: The relationship between the yield on a two-year (long-term) security and a one-year (short-term) security depends on the expected future short-term rate. If next year's *expected* short-term rate is above the current short-term rate, then the current long-term rate will be above the current short-term rate and the yield curve will be upward sloping. On the other hand, if next year's expected short-term rate is below the current short term rate, the yield curve will be downward sloping.[3]

The key to this "expectations" theory of the term structure is that short-term securities and long-term securities are very good substitutes for each other in investor portfolios. In fact, they're perfect substitutes: If expected "holding period" yields are the same, the portfolio manager is indifferent between "shorts" and "longs." Instead of a segmented market, there is a single market. Note in this case that if the supply of longs goes up and the supply of shorts goes down, it makes absolutely no difference as far as yields are concerned. Investors will happily exchange long-term securities for short-term securities, with no change in yields, as long as expected future short-term rates are unchanged.

There are few who argue that all investors are unconcerned about differences between short-term securities and long-term securities. It is simply a fact of life—embedded in the mathematics of bond prices—that the *prices* of short-term securities are less volatile than those of long-term securities. If you have to sell a security before it reaches maturity and interest rates have increased, a short-term security will have fallen in price much less than a long-term one. If you might have to sell to raise cash, you'll prefer short-term securities. Commercial banks, for example, prefer short-term securities precisely because their needs for cash are often unpredictable.

---

[3]The story of the downward sloping yield curve is as follows. If the current one-year rate is 5 percent and investors expect next year's one-year rate to be 3 percent, portfolio managers could earn an average return of 4 percent by investing in two successive one-year securities. If the current rate on a two-year security were above 4 percent all investors would buy it, forcing up the price and reducing the yield. If the current two-year rate were below 4 percent, no one would buy it, forcing down the price and raising the yield. Thus the two-year security must yield 4 percent when the current one-year security yields 5 percent and the expected one-year rate is 3 percent. Since the short-term (one-year) rate is 5 percent and the long-term (two-year) rate is 4 percent, we have exactly what we call a downward sloping yield curve.

Recognition of the greater capital uncertainty of long-term securities leads to the "liquidity premium" modification in the expectations theory of the term structure. If most investors are like commercial banks and prefer the capital certainty of short-term securities, while most bond issuers prefer to issue long-term securities, then investors on balance will demand a premium for holding longs. This is often called a liquidity premium, but it is really a risk premium —a reward for exposure to the capital uncertainty of long-term securities. Thus in our previous numerical example a two-year security would have to yield more than the average of the current one-year rate and next year's expected one-year rate. Otherwise investors wouldn't want to hold the riskier two-year security.

There is some evidence suggesting that there are liquidity premiums embedded in long-term interest rates. But to leave it at that would be misleading, because some investors actually have a *preference* for long-term securities. Life insurance companies and pension funds, for example, don't worry that much about surprising needs for cash. Their liabilities are actuarially predictable. In fact, they want to make sure they earn at least 8 (or 10 or 12) percent on their assets over the next ten (or twenty or thirty) years. That way they're sure of a profit—because they promise to pay pension holders something less than that. These institutions therefore prefer long-term securities.

Since some institutions prefer long-term securities while others prefer short-term issues, it would seem that the supply-demand approach to explaining the term structure could make a healthy comeback. For example, when the supply of five-year securities increases relative to other maturities, the yield on such issues will have to increase above the "expectations theory average" in order to induce investors to leave their preferred maturity ranges and to invest in the unfamiliar "five-year" territory. The same would be true for any increased supply of a particular maturity category. Thus the yields on various maturities would seem to have relatively little to do with expectations.

Not so fast, say the proponents of the expectations theory. While many institutions have preferred maturity ranges for their investments, they can also be induced rather easily to switch between shorts and longs when yields get out of line with expectations. Commercial banks, for example, require only a "liquidity premium" to invest in longer-term securities. A large increase in the supply of five-year bonds may therefore initially push up the yield to a higher level than is warranted by the expectations theory alone. But commercial banks will then be lured away from their one-year notes by the increased yields on five-year bonds. And pension funds will be enticed as well. Both these actions mitigate the upward pressure on five-year bond yields caused by the increased supply of securities in that maturity category. In the process, the role of expectations is restored.

These modifications in the expectations theory of the term structure of interest rates make the theory conform more closely to reality. A further step is to recognize that investors do not usually have precise numerical predictions of short-term rates for next year or the year after. More likely, investors form expectations of when the "level" of rates is relatively high and when the "level" of rates is relatively low. While this sounds fairly innocuous, it provides a powerful explanation of when the yield curve is likely to be upward sloping (curve *A* in Figure 1) or downward sloping (curve *B*).

When interest rates are high relative to what they have been, investors generally expect them to decline in the future. Falling interest rates mean rising bond prices, and those investors who are holding long-term bonds in their portfolio will reap their just reward—big capital gains. Therefore, when all rates are relatively high, investors will prefer to hold long-term securities rather than short-term securities (because the potential capital gains on shorts are relatively low). This additional demand for long-term securities drives their prices up and their yields down—relative to short-term securities. Thus long-term yields are below short-term yields when the overall level of rates is high (the yield curve is downward sloping).

Similarly, when the general level of rates is low and yields are expected to rise in the future, investors prefer not to hold long-term securities because they are likely to incur large capital losses. This drives the price of long-term securities down (and the yield up) thereby producing long-term rates above short-term rates (an upward sloping yield curve).

Chart 1 illustrates the accuracy of these conjectures with yield curves during the mid-1970s. The actual yield curve on August 30, 1974, was downward sloping, and that's when the overall "level" of rates was quite high by the then current historical standards. On the other hand, the most sharply upward sloping curve is for January

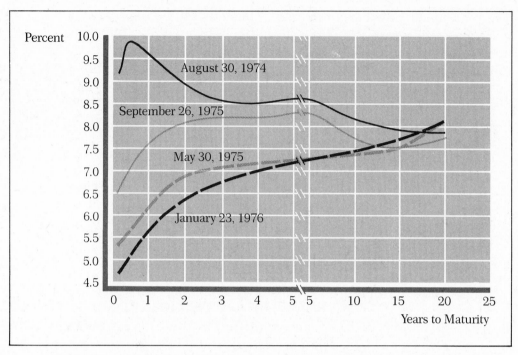

Chart 1 / Yields on U.S. Government Securities. When the "Level" of Rates is High, the Yield Curve is Likely to be Downward Sloping

23, 1976, when the "level" of rates was relatively low.

We could continue with more details on the term structure relationship. But we've gone about as far as we should without recognizing that nicely shaped curves such as those drawn in Figure 1 and Chart 1 hardly ever occur in nature. Not that the yield curve for any of the dates listed in Chart 1 is wrong. It's just that the yield curve depicts the relationship between yield and maturity, and there are other factors which influence yields—even on a relatively homogeneous group of securities such as government bonds.

There are many different issues of government bonds and each one differs in some respect (besides maturity) from the others. Some have coupons of 3 percent, others of 8 percent. Some are accepted at par (face value) in payment of estate taxes, even though they are selling well below par. These features affect the relative yields on

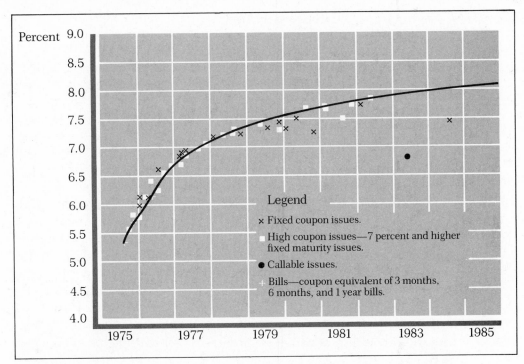

Chart 2 / Yields of Treasury Securities, May 30, 1975 (Based on Closing Bid Quotations)

bonds of identical maturity.[4] Chart 2 shows Chart 1's May 30, 1975, yield curve under a microscope. As you can see, there are little dots of different shapes around various portions of the yield curve; they represent the *precise* yields of *specific* issues. The yield curve is drawn freehand to approximate the yield-maturity relationship. In the next section the specific features of different bonds are examined to help explain yield differentials among bonds of identical maturity.

[4]Take the following example. In 1958 the government issued a bond due in 1990 with a 3½ percent coupon. The bond was sold at par or face value ($1,000) and yielded 3½ percent—the going rate at that time for long-term governments. In early 1975 the government issued another bond due in 1990, this time with a coupon of 8¼ percent. The yield of 8¼ percent was the going rate for long-term governments in the beginning of 1975. In May 1975 both the 3½ percent coupon and the 8¼ percent coupon had the same number of years to maturity—fifteen. They should have both yielded

The Risk Structure of Interest Rates

We've just seen that government securities of the *same* maturity can have different yields. Once we step away from the safety of governments, the riskiness, marketability, and tax aspects of bonds play the dominant role in explaining yield relationships. Indeed, for lack of a better name, this is often called the risk structure of interest rates, even though other factors besides the relative risk of default come into play. We'll take a look at the relationship between yields on governments, corporates, municipals, and mortgages, staying away from term structure influences by looking at long-term bonds only. By long-term we mean bonds with twenty years to maturity.[5]

As with term structure theory, a straightforward supply-demand analysis can be tried in explaining yield relationships. For example, as the supply of corporate bonds rises relative to, say, governments, the yield on corporates should increase. But as with the term structure, a simplistic supply-demand approach ignores important relationships between these markets which dominate the yield structure. In particular, because all bonds are substitutes for each other

---

(*continued*)

exactly the same thing—8¼ percent. In particular, the price of the 3½ percent coupon bond should have fallen until the bond yielded exactly what other available government bonds of the same maturity yielded. If not, why would anyone gave held the 3½s rather than the 8¼s? In point of fact, the price of the 3½s fell quite a bit—you could buy $1,000 worth for only $781. But at that price, the yield was about 5.7 percent, quite a bit less than the 8¼ percent. The main reason for this is that the 3½s are acceptable at par ($1,000) in the payment of estate taxes. Such "flower bonds," as they are irreverently called, are in great demand among wealthy elderly persons. Thus the yield is well below other government bonds of identical maturity.

It should also be noted that the 3½s would yield less than the 8¼s even without the estate tax feature. The coupon interest on a bond is taxed at regular income tax rates. Any appreciation in the price of a bond is treated as capital gains—which, let us assume, is taxed at half the normal rate. If I held the 8¼s to maturity I'd have to pay income tax on the entire $82.50 (per $1,000 bond) each year. If I held the 3½s to maturity, I'd have to pay regular income tax on the $35 (per bond) each year. I'd have a capital gain of $219.00 ($1,000 paid at maturity minus the cost of $781.00) which is taxed half as much as regular income. Thus investors prefer the 3½s to the 8¼s; hence they would yield less even without being "flower bonds."

[5]In the good old days (1900), long-term really meant long-term—bonds of forty years maturity were common. See Benjamin Klein, "The Impact of Inflation on the Term Structure of Corporate Financial Instruments," in W. Siber, ed., *Financial Innovation* (Lexington, Mass.: Heath, 1975).

in investor portfolios, as soon as one yield begins to rise relative to others, investors switch into that security. This substitution process holds down the widening yield differentials among securities.

In fact, when you think about it, every security entitles the holder to receive exactly the same thing—a stream of dollar payments in the future. One reason investors pay a different price for each of these contracts is that sometimes people break their promises. They don't wind up doing what they said they'd do. In religion you do penance for such transgressions, in the financial world you go bankrupt. So, bonds are risky—they may not pay either the interest or the principal. Since the federal government has substantial taxing power and since it can always print money to pay off its bonds, there is no risk of default on government securities.[6] But for corporations, individuals, and even (especially?) municipal governments, the risk of default is prominent. Since people usually have to be paid to bear more risk, yields on corporate bonds exceed those on governments, as is evident in Chart 3. For the same reason, yields on lower quality corporate bonds exceed the yields on the issues of higher quality corporations. In fact, bond rating services such as Moody's and Standard and Poor's classify both corporate and municipal bonds into different risk classes—from AAA (the best and the brightest) to BBB (fair but fragile) to DDD (dead in default). The yields on higher rated bonds are lower than those on lower rated bonds.

Municipal bonds—the debt issued by state and local governments —have a number of interesting features. The default risk of such bonds used to be considered quite low, with the only significant bankruptcies occurring during the Great Depression. The taxing power of state and local governments is the ultimate backing for municipal bonds. But the taxing power of states and cities is limited by people's willingness to stay put and subject themselves to the burden of ever increasing local taxes. Americans just don't sit still for very long, especially when hit by the tax prod. As a result of this and the *de facto* defaults of New York City in 1975 and Cleveland in 1978, default risk considerations exert considerable influence on the yield relationships between municipals and other bonds.

---

[6]But there is a risk of inflation if the government prints money to pay off its debt. And if the public thinks this is a real possibility, *nominal* yields will be very high even on "risk-free" governments.

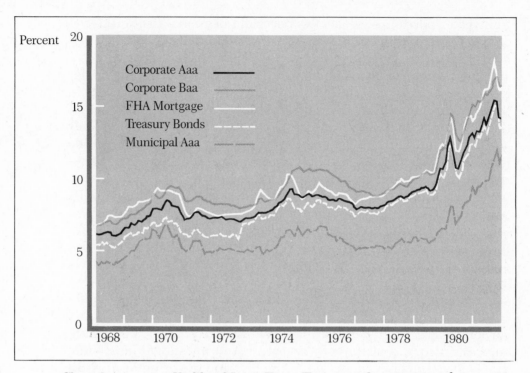

Chart 3 / Average Yields of Long-Term Treasury, Corporate, and Municipal Bonds and Mortgages

The tax-exempt status of interest payments on municipal bonds is, however, the most important influence on municipal yields versus governments and corporates. Say you pay 50 percent of your income in taxes. If the yield on a government bond is 8 percent, you'll get $80 per $1,000 invested, but after the tax man cometh you'll wind up with only $40—or an after-tax yield of 4 percent. But if you own a municipal bond which pays $80 per $1,000 invested, you keep it all because the interest on the municipal bond is immune from the Internal Revenue Service. If the municipal bond had no chance of default and if everyone were in the 50 percent bracket, then investors would refuse to buy government bonds and would buy all the municipals they could lay their hands on if both yielded 8 percent before taxes. This would drive down the price of governments and push up the price of municipals. When would investors be indifferent between the two? Clearly, if the municipal bond yielded 4 percent and the government bond yielded 8 percent, they would both pay their owners $40 *after* taxes and the market would be in equilibrium.

Of course, not everyone is in the 50 percent tax bracket—that's reserved for rock stars and brain surgeons. At a lower income tax rate, the yield on municipals will have to be higher—say 5 percent versus 8 percent on governments.[7] Furthermore, municipal bonds ain't what they used to be in terms of their default-free reputation. This tends to push such rates even closer to the yield on fully taxable U.S. government bonds. As can be seen in Chart 3, the yields on municipal bonds have usually stayed well below comparable maturity governments, as dictated by tax considerations. But in 1970, in response to default jitters brought on by the Penn Central bankruptcy, the yields on municipal bonds were forced toward yields on fully taxable governments. This is a truly classic example of the response of interest rates to risk exposure.

Let us now turn to the yields on mortgages versus the rest. Compared with corporate bonds, mortgages are probably somewhat more risky because they are liabilities of individuals with unfamiliar credit ratings. But this cannot explain the pattern traced in Chart 3, because the mortgage rate recorded is for mortgages that are insured or guaranteed by government agencies: either the Federal Housing Administration (FHA) or the Veterans Administration (VA). And yet the yields on such mortgages exceeded the yields on governments throughout the period. Something must be lurking in the background. And although mortgages have a number of "special features," the one which is most important from our standpoint is called marketability.

Securities that are traded in organized markets such as the stock exchanges can be readily sold to someone else if the investor has to raise cash. The ready marketability of an asset is a desirable characteristic from an investor's standpoint. An individual can sell the asset on short notice without a large drop in price. Bonds with good marketability will therefore yield less than those without this

---

[7]If your tax rate is t, the yield on governments is G, and the yield on municipals is M, then after-tax yields are equal when $G(1 - t) = M$. Hence, the ratio of M to G equals $(1 - t)$. With a tax rate of 37.5 percent, the equilibrium yield on governments would be 8 percent compared with 5 percent on municipals.

characteristic. An excellent market exists for trading government bonds. It is not located in any particular building. Rather, banks and government securities dealers stand ready to buy and sell government bonds at quoted prices. A similar but somewhat less organized network exists for corporate and municipal bonds. Within each of these groups—governments, corporates, and municipals—some issues are more marketable than others, and yields on the less marketable securities have to be higher to make them attractive to potential purchasers. All of this will be discussed further in Chapter 28.

For understanding the trends in yield differentials, we must focus on the fact that mortgages have never had any secondary market to speak of. That helps explain why FHA mortgage yields were above even the yields on corporate bonds until 1967 (not shown in Chart 3), and have been intertwined with such rates since, despite the fact that FHA mortgages are free of credit risk. The marketability issue certainly helps explain why yields on government-insured mortgages exceed the yields on regular government obligations, although insurance fees and certain administrative headaches play a well-earned role. In recent years, most notably since 1970, government-related agencies such as the Government National Mortgage Association and the Federal Home Loan Mortgage Corporation (see Chapters 7 and 28) have fostered a secondary market in mortgages. The fact that the FHA mortgage rate recently stayed below corporate rates has been attributed by some to the development of a secondary market.

Our discussion of yield differentials has touched upon many specific features of bonds. So many, in fact, that it's hard to see how anyone can ignore them. How did we talk about interest rates for twenty-five chapters without mentioning each and every one? How could our analysis of movements in the *level* of interest rates have been accurate when the level is made up of so many very different parts? A quick glance at Chart 3 indicates that while rate differentials can and do change, all rates still move more or less together. Much of the *overall* movement is determined by monetary policy, inflation, and the course of economic activity, as we stressed in the previous chapter. Our focus in this chapter has put those overall movements under a microscope, producing a different perspective. Sometimes one approach is preferable and sometimes the other. It depends on what you're looking for.

Summary

1. The relationship between yields on short-term and long-term securities is frequently illustrated graphically by a yield curve. The yield curve can be upward sloping (short-term rates are below long-term rates), downward sloping (short-term rates are above long-term rates), or flat (the yields on shorts and longs are the same).

2. The basic expectations theory maintains that the shape of the yield curve is determined by investors' expectations of future short-term interest rates. In particular, if short-term rates are expected to rise the yield curve will be upward sloping, while if short-term rates are expected to fall the yield curve will be downward sloping. A specific result is that long-term rates are averages of current and expected future short-term rates.

3. There are a number of modifications to the pure expectations theory that allow other influences on rate structure besides expectations. For example, since investors are usually considered risk averse, and since long-term securities have greater capital uncertainty than short-term securities, a liquidity premium is likely to be attached to long-term yields. In addition, some investors, such as life insurance companies, prefer long-term securities because they can "lock in" a guaranteed return on the funds. This suggests that there are preferred maturity ranges for investors and changes in supplies of securities will alter yields on different maturities.

4. The fundamental role of expectations in shaping the yield curve is emphasized by the following empirical regularity: When the overall level of rates is high compared with that of the recent past, the yield curve slopes downward; when the level of rates is low compared with recent experience, the yield curve slopes upward.

5. Default risk helps to explain the excess of corporate bond yields over comparable maturity government bonds. The probability of default also influences the structure of yields within the corporate bond market.

6. Municipal bonds yield less than government bonds because the interest payments on municipals are exempt from income

taxes. Nevertheless, when default probabilities on municipal debt increase, their tax-free yields can approach taxable yields on governments.

7. The ready marketability of a bond reduces the yield necessary to pay investors. Governments are the most marketable bonds while individual mortgages are the least.

Suggestions for Further Reading

There are many excellent studies of the term structure of interest rates. A good survey as well as advanced material is found in Burton Malkiel's *The Term Structure of Interest Rates* (Princeton, N.J.: Princeton University Press, 1966). A somewhat more difficult study is by Richard Roll, *The Behavior of Interest Rates* (New York: Basic Books, 1970). There have been numerous specific analyses as well, such as J. Huston McCulloch, "An Estimate of the Liquidity Premium," *Journal of Political Economy* (February 1975); and Edward J. Kane, "The Term Structure of Interest Rates: An Attempt to Reconcile Teaching With Practice," *Journal of Finance* (May 1970).

The risk structure of interest rates has a less organized career. An early article on the subject is Lawrence Fisher, "Determinants of Risk Premiums on Corporate Bonds," *Journal of Political Economy* (June 1959). A somewhat more general analysis is Dwight M. Jaffee, "Cyclical Variations in the Risk Structure of Interest Rates," *Journal of Money, Credit, and Banking* (July 1975). An interesting analysis of risk and term structure together is in Philip Cagan's "A Study of Liquidity Premiums on Federal and Municipal Securities," in *Essays on Interest Rates,* ed. Jack Guttentag and Phillip Cagan (New York: National Bureau of Economic Research, 1969). For an analysis of the impact of marketability on mortgage yields, see Deborah G. Black, Kenneth D. Garbade, and William L. Silber, "The Impact of the GNMA Pass-Through Program on FHA Mortgage Costs," *Journal of Finance* (May 1981).

A survey of rate structure issues is found in James C. Van Horne's excellent paperback *Financial Market Rates and Flows* (Englewood Cliffs, N.J.: Prentice-Hall, 1978). Finally, for the nitty-gritty on specific features of bonds such as call provisions, intermarket spreads and swap opportunities, loss recovery periods, cushion bonds, perpetuities, and the magic of compounding, see Sidney Homer and Martin Liebowitz, *Inside the Yield Book* (Englewood Cliffs, N.J.: Prentice-Hall, 1970). Don't miss the discussion on page 101 on the yield pickup swap and the net gains to the swapper.

Appendix

The Nuts and Bolts of Debt Management

The first section of this chapter discussed the relationship between short- and long-term yields on government securities. We also touched on the question of whether changes in relative supplies of government debt affect the structure of rates. We now turn to a more prosaic matter: How does the U.S. Treasury "manage" the government's obligations?

We now have a national debt—federal government securities outstanding—totaling more than $1 trillion. The national debt is essentially the result of past and present fiscal policy, mostly past. It is the sum of all past deficits, less surpluses, in the federal budget. Given a national debt of $1 trillion, its day-to-day management has implications for the functioning of financial markets, monetary policy, and economic stability. How can the debt be refinanced most smoothly when portions of it come due? How much of the debt should be in the form of short-term Treasury bills, how much in the form of long-term Treasury bonds? First we'll discuss the statistics, then the techniques, and finally the objectives of debt management.

Of the $1 trillion in government debt outstanding, only about $700 billion is in marketable form; that is, only $700 billion can be bought or sold in the open market by investors. The remaining $300 billion is divided up as follows: about $200 billion in various government trust accounts (such as social security), $65 billion in familiar U.S. savings bonds, about $15 billion in special foreign issues, and $20 billion in special state and local government series. These non-marketable issues are largely outside normal Treasury debt management considerations. This is best illustrated by savings bonds. Individuals buy and redeem them at will—with the Treasury passively accommodating the public's preferences.

Of the $700 billion in marketable government debt outstanding, about $125 billion is held by the Federal Reserve as a result of current and past open market purchases. That leaves about $575 billion of marketable government debt held by the private sector of the economy—banks, insurance companies, nonfinancial corporations, and individuals.

The magnitude of the debt management problem is best appreciated by noting that more than $300 billion in government debt obligations come due each year and must be paid off. How? By refinancing it, of course—that is, by reborrowing the $300 billion once again, either from the same investors who choose to replace maturing issues or from others who want to get in on the act. The Treasury can replace maturing issues with short-term Treasury bills (up to one year to maturity), intermediate-term Treasury notes (one to ten years maturity), or long-term bonds (usually above ten years to maturity, sometimes twenty or thirty). And that's what debt management policy is all about: choosing the maturities to issue when replacing debt obligations.

Given the magnitude of the housekeeping details, the Treasury follows a number of well-established practices. The routine permits the financial markets to prepare properly for Treasury operations. Treasury bills are conventionally issued with original maturities of 91 days (three-month bills), 182 days (six-month bills) and 364 days (fifty-two-week bills). New supplies of 91- and 182-day bills are auctioned weekly (on Monday), while the fifty-two-week bills are auctioned monthly.

As described in more detail in the Appendix to Chapter 5, the Federal Reserve Banks conduct these bill auctions as fiscal agents for the Treasury. Investors submit their bids to a regional Federal Reserve Bank by submitting either a competitive or a noncompetitive tender. Large investors (above $500,000) must submit competitive tenders: that is, they must state a bid price for a specific amount of bills. The Treasury either accepts or rejects these bids on a price priority basis. Smaller investors can submit noncompetitive tenders: that is, they state an amount they wish to buy; and they receive that quantity at the average price of the auction. Large banks and other government securities dealers are especially cautious in these auctions, calculating their bid prices with great care and waiting until the very last minute before submitting their orders. Small price differences can mean quite a lot when buying $100 million bills.

One popular category of bills that appears on an irregular basis is the tax anticipation bill. These bills are issued to bridge the Treasury's temporary cash flow problems. Corporations find them especially attractive because they can be used at par to pay corporate profits taxes even though their scheduled maturities are usually one week after tax payments are due. Because of this special demand by corporations, these tax anticipation bills yield somewhat less than comparable maturity bills.

Treasury notes and bonds differ from bills both because of their longer maturities and because they carry semiannual coupon payments. Bills are sold at a price discount, reflecting the interest yield, while notes and bonds are usually sold at par. The only difference between a note and a bond is that the former cannot be issued with an original maturity above ten years. These coupon issues also follow a scheduled auction pattern. Two-year notes are issued about a week before the end of every month, four-year notes are issued during the second month of every quarter, with seven- and ten-year notes sometimes included in the package; bonds of fifteen- and twenty-five-year maturities are also offered during these quarterly "refunding" operations. These notes and bonds are usually issued via auctions similar to those for Treasury bills.

With this vast array of instruments and techniques at the Treasury's disposal, plus the network of securities dealers that make a secondary market in government obligations (to be discussed in Chapter 28), it would seem relatively easy to manage even the rather large public debt currently outstanding. And in some sense it is quite easy, because Treasury obligations always get sold, and with few hangups. But while the mechanics are quite straightforward, the role and objectives of debt management are sometimes unclear.

What are the objectives of day-to-day debt management? One goal is to minimize the interest cost of the debt to the taxpayers. But this can hardly be the only objective. If it were, the Treasury could minimize the interest cost—indeed, reduce it to zero—by simply printing money and buying back all the outstanding securities. It could thus replace its interest-bearing debt (bills and bonds) with its non-interest-bearing debt (money). Obviously, the Treasury does not "monetize the debt," because to do so would probably result in massive inflation, and the Treasury also has the objective of managing the debt to promote economic stability.

These two objectives—minimizing interest cost and economic stabilization—often dictate opposite policy actions. Minimizing the interest cost suggests that when we are in a recession, and interest rates are low across the board, the Treasury should refund its maturing issues with new long-term bonds, thus insuring low interest payments for itself well into the future. During boom periods, when interest rates are typically high, the Treasury should refinance by selling short-term issues, Treasury bills, so the government does not have to continue paying high rates after yields have fallen to more normal levels.

Stabilization objectives call for just the opposite policies. When we are in a recession, the last thing we want to do is raise long-term interest rates, which is precisely what pushing long-term securities onto the market is likely to accomplish. Boom periods, when we *do* want to raise long rates (to reduce investment spending), are when we should sell long-term bonds.

Thus the objective of minimizing interest costs dictates lengthening the maturity structure of the debt (more long-term bonds relative to short-term bills) during recession periods, and shortening the maturity structure during boom periods. For purposes of economic stabilization we should do the opposite—try to shorten the maturity structure during recessions and lengthen it during prosperity.

A complication that makes it difficult to lengthen the maturity structure of the federal debt is the archaic 4¼ percent legal ceiling on government bond interest rates. By virtue of a law passed in 1917, the Treasury is not allowed to pay more than a 4¼ percent interest rate on bonds with ten or more years to maturity. Since long-term market interest rates have generally been well above 4¼ percent in recent years, the Treasury has been unable to offer competitive yields on long-term securities and thus has had no choice but to borrow via shorter-maturity issues. (In a daring break with tradition, Congress grabbed the bull by the tail and faced the situation squarely; it has modified the law and permitted the Treasury to issue a limited amount of bonds at rates above 4¼ percent.)

Debt management policy must be administered in coordination with monetary and fiscal policy. If minimizing the interest cost is the primary goal of Treasury debt management, then monetary and fiscal policy will have to take appropriate action to offset this counterstabilization debt policy. If economic stabilization is the primary objective of debt management, the monetary and fiscal authorities can take this into account and reduce the forcefulness of their own actions.

Coordination between the monetary and debt management authorities is also essential on a continuing basis because of the vast magnitude of the Treasury's frequent refunding operations. When the Treasury refinances a large volume of maturing issues and issues longer-term obligations, it often needs central bank help. If the Federal Reserve is pursuing a tight money policy, for example, it may become somewhat less aggressive and resort to a policy of keeping an "even keel" in the bond markets as the date of a refinancing approaches. In effect, the central bank could mark time while the Treasury went through the mechanics of the refunding operation. It is difficult enough for the Treasury to roll over so much debt without being forced to cope with additional complications resulting from aggressive actions of the monetary authorities.

Monetary policy, fiscal policy, and debt management are often considered the three main tools of stabilization policy. In fact, however, debt management has typically been the runt of the litter. Perhaps that is just as well. Given the power of monetary and fiscal policy to implement national economic goals, perhaps debt management can make its most significant contribution by successfully accomplishing the more limited but not unimportant task of continuously refinancing a very large volume of government securities without unduly disturbing the nation's financial markets.

27

The Stock Market and Interest Rates

WHY DO STOCK PRICES go up and down? Not so much particular stocks, like IBM or Xerox, but why does the entire stock market soar or shudder, with all stocks more or less rising or falling together? How important are changes in interest rates in driving stock prices up or down?

It is a fact of life that the total supply of stocks in existence is more or less fixed. What changes is not so much the number of shares lying around—in vaults, under mattresses, and concealed between the pages of the family Bible—but the price of each.

For example, at the end of 1980 the market value of all the publicly held shares of stock in existence amounted to something like $1,600 billion. In the early 1960s it was about $500 billion, and in the early 1950s less than $200 billion. And yet in the past thirty years corporations have raised relatively little money by issuing new equity—perhaps $150 billion or so. This means that almost all of that $1,600 billion represents price appreciation of existing shares.

The fact that the total supply outstanding is relatively fixed does not, of course, imply that the amount offered on the market need be fixed. People who have bought, and even some who haven't, can always sell. Thus in recent years stocks have been drifting out of the hands of individual investors, who on balance have been selling, into the plush suites of institutional investors, who have been buy-ing. In 1960 pension funds, mutual funds, insurance companies, and other institutional investors held about 15 percent of the market value of outstanding shares; now they hold about 30 percent. But 70 percent, or over $1,100 billion, is still held by individuals, about 25 million of them, and each and every one is out to make a killing.

Strangely enough, given the widespread interest in the stock mar-ket, economists have generally had very little to say about it. The most popular postwar college textbook, Paul Samuelson's *Econom-ics,* is estimated to have sold over three million copies since it first appeared in 1948. Considering the royalties accruing to so popular an author, and a leading economist in the bargain, one would think he might have both the wherewithal and the training to discover the secret of what makes the market tick. But if Paul has found out, he isn't telling! The latest edition of *Economics* contains only nine pages on the stock market (out of 861).

Some economists are less reticent than Professor Samuelson about letting us in on why stock prices fluctuate. Their explanations have ranged from the influence of sunspots on men's emotional behavior to the conspiratorial machinations of shadowy figures in high places. However, the explanations that are of most interest to us here deal with money and interest rates.

A Money Supply View of Stock Prices

The belief that fluctuations in the money supply provide the key to movements in stock prices is based on a series of cause-and-effect hypotheses that contain elements of both Monetarist and Keynesian thinking. In its simplest form, the reasoning is as follows: When the Federal Reserve increases the money supply at a faster than normal rate, the public, finding itself with more cash than it needs for cur-rent transactions, spends some of its excess money buying financial assets, including stocks. Since the supply of equities is more or less fixed, especially in the short run, this incremental demand raises their price. Some stocks will go up more than others and some may go down, depending on the prospects for particular companies, but overall the *average* of stock prices will rise.

Or the transmission process might be somewhat more complex, but with similar results. The increase in the money supply may first lead the public to step up its *bond* purchases, thereby raising bond prices. Higher bond prices mean lower interest rates. With bonds yielding less, some potential bond purchasers are likely to switch over to the now relatively more attractive stock market. The demand for stocks expands because their substitute, bonds, has become more expensive—just as the demand for Yamahas will expand when their alternative, Hondas, become more expensive (not to mention the Suzuki).

Or it could be an even more roundabout process. The larger money supply leads to lower interest rates, more investment spending—creating more household income and thereby more consumer spending (through the multiplier)—a higher GNP, and along with it larger corporate profits. Enlarged corporate profits spur stock purchases and higher stock prices.

In any case, the result is the same. Whether the chain of causation is direct, from the money supply to stock prices, or indirect, through the bond market and interest rates, or through GNP, an increase in the money supply at a faster than normal pace is seen as accelerating the demand for stocks, leading to higher stock prices.

Conversely, decreases in the money supply—or increases at a slower rate than necessary to provide for the transactions needs of a growing economy—leave the public with shortages of funds. Result: among other things, a cutback in stock purchases—again, either directly or because, with higher interest rates, bonds become more attractive buys, or because corporate profits decline as GNP falls. This reduced demand for stocks lowers their prices.

Conclusion: A rapidly expanding money supply leads to higher stock values; inadequate monetary growth leads to a falling market.

Persuasive as the underlying reasoning seems, all too often the facts simply do not bear it out. Evidently too many other cross-currents simultaneously impinge on the stock market, such as business expectations and political developments. Like so many other single-cause explanations in economics, this simplified view of stock price determination contains too much truth to ignore but not enough to make it very reliable in the clutch.

Consider 1929, and the couple of years before and after. From mid-1927 to mid-1928, the money supply increased by 1.6 percent;

from mid-1928 to mid-1929, it increased by 1.2 percent. The stock market, meanwhile, going its merry way, *doubled.*

In the next two years, from mid-1929 to mid-1931, the money supply contracted by about 5 percent each year. If the stock market was merely reacting to changes in the money supply, it was by all odds the biggest overreaction in history, because the proverbial bottom dropped out and the market promptly lost all the gains it had made in the previous two years and then some.

Furthermore, it is not at all clear precisely what is cause and what is effect. Did the market crash because the money supply contracted? Or did the money supply contract because the market crashed (as banks called speculative margin loans and demand deposits were wiped off the books)? The latter explanation is as logical as the former.

The 1929 market collapse, as many see it, was due to a number of interrelated factors: an unwarranted mood of euphoric optimism prior to the crash, excessive speculative activity, fundamental weakness in underlying business conditions, and so on. The money supply, if it influenced the breakdown at all, did so only as one among many causes.

None of which is meant to imply that the money supply was or is unimportant. If it had been rapidly and forcefully restored to its 1929 level by 1930, or even 1931, the depression initiated by the stock market collapse would probably not have been either as severe or as long as it turned out to be. That the Federal Reserve stood by, wringing its hands, while the money supply declined by 30 percent from 1929 to 1933 undoubtedly intensified and prolonged what we now call the Great Depression. But that is a very different thing from saying that movements in the money supply caused or could have given one even a vague idea of the heights or the depths to which stock prices went from 1927 to 1931. As a matter of fact, most of the drop in the money supply occurred *after* 1931; by that time, however, the market was too weary to do much reacting, either over or under.

To come closer to the present, in 1940 the stock market fell 15 percent even though the money supply was then rising 15 percent (on top of a similar rise the year before). In 1962, again, the market tumbled despite an increasing money supply. And in 1973–1974 the stock market fell by more than 40 percent, even though the money supply increased by 11 percent over that two-year period.

On other not infrequent occasions, however, it is true that declines in stock prices *were* preceded or accompanied by declines in the rate of growth of the money supply, as in 1957, 1960, 1969, and 1981. And often increases in stock prices were indeed associated with increases in the growth of the money supply, as in 1967, 1968, and 1975.

In at least some of these instances, however, both stock prices and the money supply might conceivably have been reacting to a third causal force, perhaps an upturn in business conditions stimulated by the outbreak of war ( ) peace ( )—check one—a spurt in consumer spending, or something else. An improvement in business conditions, regardless of cause, typically leads to an expansion in bank business loans, a larger money supply, brighter profit prospects, and thereby higher stock prices. As the history of business cycles indicates, such upswings (or downturns) are capable of generating a cumulative push that can work up considerable momentum, carrying *both* the money supply and stock prices along with it.

Chart 1 provides some idea of the pitfalls involved in reading a cause-and-effect relationship into two sets of statistics simply because they move together. The unbroken line indicates the movement of stock prices, annually, from the end of 1960 through the end of 1966, using stock prices at the end of 1960 as the base (= 100).

The thin dashed line, on a similar index basis, is the movement of the money supply annually, also from the end of 1960 through the end of 1966. Over this particular six-year period, changes in the money supply clearly bore little relationship to turning points in stock prices.

Finally, the chart includes a third line (*W*). Its movements are obviously closely related to changes in stock prices. Almost without exception, the line labeled *W* and the line tracing stock prices move up and down together.

Cause and effect? The line labeled *W,* make of it what you will, is an annual index (1960 = 100) of the number of times members of the old Washington Senators baseball team struck out each year, over the period 1960 through 1966. (Source: *The Sporting News's Official Baseball Guide and Record Book,* Annual, 1960–1966.) For at least those years, evidently, an investor trying to forecast turning points in the stock market would have been better off spending time reading the box scores than checking money supply figures.

Monetary Policy and Wall Street

Once we expand our horizon to encompass more than the money supply alone, however, there is widespread agreement that monetary policy, *in general,* frequently does have a considerable influence on the stock market. It is by no means the only influence, and is often overshadowed by other forces and events, but nevertheless it is widely believed that on balance monetary policy has had a substantial effect on stock prices at times in the past, especially since the mid-1960s, and is likely to continue to do so in the foreseeable future.

This is quite aside from the power of the Federal Reserve to set margin requirements on stock purchases. In an attempt to prevent

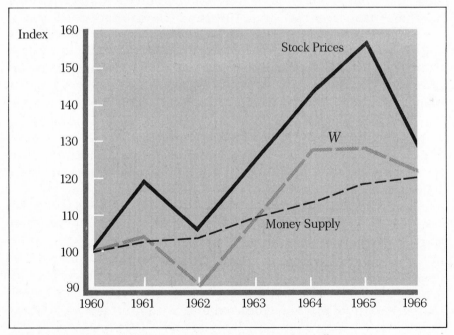

Chart 1 / Stock Prices and Other Variables, 1960–1966
SOURCE: For Stock Prices: Dow-Jones Industrials, monthly closing averages for December of each year (December 1960 = 100). For Money Supply: Demand deposits plus currency, monthly averages for December of each year (December 1960 = 100)

a repetition of the speculative wave, financed heavily with borrowed funds, that carried the market to dizzy heights until the fall of 1929, Congress in the 1930s authorized the Federal Reserve to impose margin (or minimum down payment) requirements on the purchase of stocks. If the margin requirement is 100 percent, then 100 percent cash must be put up and no borrowing at all is permitted. If the margin requirement is 80 percent, that much of one's own cash must be put up when buying a security and only the remaining 20 percent can be financed by borrowing from a bank or a broker. Of course, you could always finance the entire amount by borrowing from your brother-in-law and no one would be the wiser (except perhaps, in the long run, your brother-in-law).

High margin requirements have probably helped restrain speculation in stocks, especially by those who could least afford it. Nevertheless, if the Federal Reserve had only this device to influence the market, it would be relying on a weak reed indeed. Margin requirements are 100 percent at Santa Anita and Hialeah racetracks, but at last report speculative activity by those who could not afford it as well as by those who could appeared unimpaired.

The impact of overall monetary policy on stock prices stems not so much from the Federal Reserve's power to set margin requirements as from its influence over the money supply, the entire spectrum of interest rates and financial markets, current and expected business conditions, and—last but far from least—the expected rate of inflation. It is in the recent past, rather than twenty or thirty years ago, that the effects of monetary policy on stock prices are most clearly visible. The credit squeezes of 1966, 1969, 1974, and 1981 are prime examples—stock prices tumbled in each of those episodes.

Indeed, these events appear to have impressed so many in recent years that expectations about the immediate future course of monetary policy have now become one of the main topics of conversation among stock market analysts. Every week stock market participants eagerly await the release of the Federal Reserve's money supply figures, fearful of making commitments without this knowledge in hand.

If the figures show that the money supply is growing *faster* than the Fed's announced guidelines—say the Fed is aiming to increase the money supply by 4 to 6 percent annually, but the weekly figures reveal that in fact it has been increasing by 9 percent—then Wall

Street concludes that the Fed will *soon be tightening* to get the money supply back on track.

Alternatively, if the figures show that the money supply is growing *more slowly* than the Fed's announced guidelines—again, say the Fed is aiming to increase the money supply by 4 to 6 percent, but this time the weekly figures reveal that in fact it has been increasing by only 1 percent—then Wall Street concludes that the Fed will *soon be easing* to get the money supply back on the track.

Views on Wall Street are mixed as to precisely what such figures imply for stock prices. If the money supply has been growing faster than the Fed's target, so that *tightening* is in order, then some see this as heralding a fall in stock prices, but others view it as signaling an upturn. Those who see tighter money as precipitating a fall in the stock market reason that tighter money means higher interest rates (lower bond prices); this will make bonds relatively more attractive than stocks, resulting in lower stock prices as well. On the other hand, others see tighter money as signaling an *upturn* in stock prices on the logic that inflation has been bad for stock prices; tighter money will stop inflation, which in turn will eventually bring interest rates down and thereby stimulate higher stock prices.

The same divergence of views exists for the implications of easier money. If the money supply has been growing more slowly than the Fed's target, so that *easing* is in order, some see this as likely to produce higher stock prices. They reason that easier money means lower interest rates (higher bond prices); this will make stocks relatively more attractive than bonds, resulting in higher stock prices. Others, however, come to the opposite conclusion. They see easier money as fueling inflation, which in turn will eventually bring higher interest rates and thereby depress stock prices.

By and large, the first group (tighter money will depress stock prices, easier money stimulate them) seemed to hold the predominant opinion in the early seventies. But as inflation accelerated during the decade, the second group gained adherents (tighter money will stimulate stock prices, easier money depress them).

Both groups, however, had their problems (and so have we). One problem is difficulty in interpreting the weekly Federal Reserve statistics, which are often ambiguous. One money supply measure may overshoot the target at the same time as another money supply measure undershoots it. Which measure should be used? Or the

Prime Surges to 20%; Dow Tumbles 17.83

Bond Prices Continue to Fall Sharply

By VARTANIG G. VARTAN

A record-tying prime rate — and fears of further interest rate increases — sent stock prices tumbling yesterday. The Dow Jones industrial average plunged 17.83 points, to 916.21.

Bond prices continued to fall sharply, creating record yields in many fixed-income securities.

Major banks raised their basic lending charge for blue-ribbon clients by a full percentage point, to 20 percent. This marked the seventh increase since the beginning of November, when the prime stood at 14½ percent. It was 20 percent in April.

David Jones, a money market economist for Aubrey G. Lanston & Company, dealers in Government securities, said he expected the prime rate to reach 22 percent within the next several weeks.

"That could be the peak," Mr. Jones said. "But, over the near term, there is significant upward momentum in rates reflecting the pressure applied by the Federal Reserve."

Gathering storm clouds for the stock market also included trepidation that rising rates could restrain economic growth in 1981 and posssibly lead to a renewal of last spring's recession.

The Dow industrials, along with other popular market indicators, have been battered steadily in recent sessions. On Monday, the Dow dropped 22½ points in response to rising interest rates and mounting investor fears of a possible Soviet invasion of Poland.

Just three weeks ago, on Nov. 20, the Dow finished above the 1,000 mark for the first time in almost four years. Analysts attributed that performance to hopes that President-elect Ronald Reagan would take forceful steps to restrain inflation and revive the economy.

April's Peak Is Equaled, Chase Leading Way

By ROBERT A. BENNETT

In an ominous sign for the economy, the prime lending rate rose a full percentage point yesterday, to 20 percent, reaching the record set last April shortly after President Carter declared a national emergency to deal with inflation.

Bankers predicted that, if the Federal Reserve System continued to pursue its restrictive monetary policies, the prime would climb even further.

"If rates stay at this level for any sustained period, it would have a dire impact on the economy," said Alfred Brittain 3d, chairman of the Bankers Trust Company.

Small Concerns Vulnerable

Economists say that small and medium-sized companies are especially vulnerable to the high interest rates. "These rates are putting us out of business," said Russell M. Rockwell, owner of the Rockwell Equipment Company in Hamilton, Ohio, in a telephone interview yesterday. The company, which has sales of about $1 million a year, is a distributor of agricultural and industrial equipment.

"I don't think the Federal Reserve knows what it's doing," Mr. Rockwell said. "It's like a 2-year-old kid squeezing the kitten to death, and he doesn't realize he's doing it."

One farm-equipment producer has 12 dealers in the Ohio-Kentucky region in the process of liquidation, Mr. Rockwell reported. His own company is now paying 20¼ percent for its money, and "I expect that to go up," Mr. Rockwell said.

Companies that deal in high-priced goods and operate on small profit margins are particularly affected by high interest rates, economists say. If sales slump, as they have, the dealers must borrow to finance their inventories. The higher the rate of interest, the more expensive these costs become.

News Item / Interest Rates and Stock Prices   *New York Times, December 11, 1980*

money supply may overshoot the target on the basis of the past week's or month's data but undershoot it on the basis of the past two or three months' data. Which time span should be used?

Not to mention the potentially biggest problem of all: The Federal Reserve may have changed its money supply target. There is a one-month lag between meetings of the Federal Reserve's Open Market Committee and release to the public of what transpired. If the Fed changed its target from a 4–6 percent annual growth rate to 1–3 percent, then 1 percent is right on target and does not imply future easing. Someone who acts as though it does imply future easing could be making a serious mistake.

But then whoever said making money in the stock market is easy! The lesson, once again, is that Fed watching is helpful in anticipating stock market trends, but it is no short cut to getting rich because too many other things are simultaneously affecting stock prices.

Summary

1. Changes in the money supply alone have been an unreliable guide to predicting fluctuations in the stock market.

2. Monetary policy in general, however, has been more dependable. Monetary policy affects interest rates and expectations about future interest rates affect stock prices.

3. When interest rates fall (bond prices rise), bonds become less attractive relative to stocks, funds shift out of bonds and into stocks, and stock prices are likely to rise.

4. On the other hand, when interest rates rise (bond prices fall), stocks become less attractive relative to bonds, funds shift out of stocks and into bonds, and stock prices are likely to fall.

5. Wall Street now spends a lot of time analyzing monetary policy, hoping for clues to what is going to happen to stock prices. Such analysis has been helpful but so far it has offered no easy road to riches.

Suggestions for Further Reading

For attempts to quantify the relationship between the money supply and stock prices, see Michael W. Keran, "Expectations, Money, and the Stock Market," Federal Reserve Bank of St. Louis *Review* (January 1971); K. E. Homa and Dwight M. Jaffee, "The Supply of Money and Common Stock Prices," *Journal of Finance* (December 1971); and Michael J. Hamburger and Levis A. Kochin, "Money and Stock Prices: The Channels of Influence," *Journal of Finance* (May 1972). For a critical analysis of these efforts, see the discussion by Merton H. Miller in the same May 1972 issue of the *Journal of Finance*. Also see James E. Pesando, "The Supply of Money and Common Stock Prices," *Journal of Finance* (June 1974); and Robert D. Auerbach, "Money and Stock Prices," Federal Reserve Bank of Kansas City *Monthly Review* (September–October 1976).

One of the early attempts to examine the relationship between money and stock prices was Beryl W. Sprinkel, *Money and Stock Prices* (Homewood, Ill.: Irwin, 1964); this has since been revised and retitled *Money and Markets: A Monetarist View* (Irwin, 1971). An interesting study of the relationship between stock prices and economic activity is Barry Bosworth, "The Stock Market and the Economy," *Brookings Papers on Economic Activity* (No. 2, 1975).

If this chapter has tempted you to think you can beat the market, before you try to do so read Burton Malkiel's paperback *A Random Walk Down Wall Street* (New York: Norton, 1974). Or if you have the notion that other games of chance are more in your line, at least know what the odds are against you. You'll find them all in Edwin Silberstang's *The Winner's Guide to Casino Gambling* (New York: Holt, Rinehart, and Winston, 1980).

28

The Structure and Performance of Securities Markets

KATHARINE HEPBURN needs a script, Jackson Browne a guitar, Richard Avedon a camera, and Chris Evert a tennis racket. Each performer uses the props appropriate for the medium in question. Performances can be stimulating, comical, pleasurable, disappointing. That's how it is in the world of entertainment.

Well, it's not so different in financial markets. Brokers, dealers, specialists, and traders are the actors. Telephones, ticker tapes, and computer terminals are the props. Stocks, bonds, bills, and mortgages are the media. Performances are described as resilient, deep, broad, thin, liquid. Our task is to describe who goes with what and why. You can then decide whether to applaud or hiss after your next financial transaction.

Nature and Function of Securities Markets

In Chapters 25 and 26 we examined the forces that influence the equilibrium prices of different types of securities. For the most part we ignored the structure of these markets, taking it for granted that somehow the interested buyers and sellers of the securities would find their way to the marketplace. And that is precisely the main

539

assumption underlying the equilibrium price that emerges from the intersection of supply and demand curves: The price balances the supplies of and demands for the security by *all* potential market participants.

In practice, bringing all buyers and sellers together is not quite so simple. Trading interests are not costlessly uncovered, because buyers and sellers may be in different locations and therefore not aware of each other. Similarly, time may elapse between a buyer's arrival at the marketplace and the appearance of a compatible seller. Such geographical and temporal fragmentation make the prices at which transactions actually take place differ from the equilibrium price emerging from a theoretical Walrasian auction.[1] Real world trading at prices that straddle the true equilibrium is the best we can hope for. In fact, we might think of the ideal situation as actual transactions prices doing a little dance around the theoretical equilibrium price.

Securities markets are organized to help bring buyers and sellers together, so that both parties to the transaction will be satisfied that a fair and representative trading price has been arranged. There are three main types of market organization that facilitate the actual purchase and sale of securities: an auction market, a brokered market, and a dealer market. In each case, the aim is to match up buyers and sellers.

An auction market provides a forum where buyers and sellers can confront each other directly to bargain over price. By publicizing the auction, the marketplace hopes to attract many buyers and sellers, thereby increasing the likelihood that all will discover mutually agreeable trading interests. When there is a scarcity of ready buyers or sellers, it is possible to try a little harder to uncover potential traders. In particular, a person can pay a broker to search for the

---

[1]Leon Walras, a late-nineteenth-century French economist concerned with general equilibrium systems, conceptualized the equilibrium price as the outcome of the following type of auction. Buyers and sellers submit the quantities they want to buy and sell at a particular price to the auctioneer. If the quantity supplied exceeds what is demanded, the auctioneer asks for new orders at a lower price. If the lower price generates more buyers than sellers, the auctioneer raises the price and asks for still a new set of orders. Such recontracting takes place until a price emerges at which buying and selling interests are equal. And that is precisely the equilibrium price of the familiar supply demand diagram (see Figure 1 in Chapter 25). The only real world marketplace that operates this way is in London, where the price of gold is "fixed" twice a day.

other side of the transaction. In still other cases, a dealer emerges who stands ready to buy at his bid price from all sellers and sell at his offer (or asked) price to all buyers. In this type of market the dealer bridges the gaps between buyers and sellers by holding securities in his own inventory. He is compensated by the difference between his bid (buying) and asked (selling) prices.

The organizational structure of a market—the existence of brokers, dealers, exchanges—as well as the technological paraphernalia—such as ticker tapes, TV quotation screens, and telegraphic communications—are all mobilized to keep transaction prices as close to true (but unknown) equilibrium prices as is economically feasible. Easy access to a trading forum, with many potential buyers and sellers, means that a security can be bought or sold quickly with little discount from its equilibrium value. That is what is meant by marketability—a catch-all phrase indicating small deviations of actual transaction prices about the true equilibrium.

Good marketability implies that a security can be sold, liquidated, turned into cash, very quickly without triggering a collapse in price. A highly marketable security is more desirable to investors, so its equilibrium price will be higher, and its yield lower, relative to less marketable securities. The rest of our discussion is devoted to evaluating the marketability of various securities and to describing the market structures that characterize trading.

Primary Versus Secondary Markets

Before detailing the nature of trading in securities markets, it is important to carefully distinguish primary markets from secondary markets. Most of the popular markets, such as the New York Stock Exchange, are secondary markets, where existing securities are exchanged between individuals and institutions. The primary markets—markets for newly issued securities—are much less well-known.

New issues of stock or bonds to raise funds for General Motors, General Electric, or Colonel Sanders are not sold to saver-lenders on the floor of the New York Stock Exchange, the American Stock Exchange, or even the Midwest Stock Exchange in Chicago. Rather, the matchmaking takes place behind closed doors, aided by Wall

Street's investment bankers. The names Morgan Stanley, Goldman Sachs, Salomon Brothers, Lazard Frères, and Merrill Lynch dominate the list. They often act as brokers and dealers in secondary markets as well. But in their role as investment bankers they help

Newspaper Advertisement / An Underwriting Syndicate Floats a New Issue

distribute newly issued stocks and bonds to ultimate investors—insurance companies, pension funds, and individuals throughout the country.

These distributions are called underwritings: the investment banker guarantees an issuer of bonds a price (and implicitly a yield) on the new issue. Often a number of investment bankers band together in a syndicate to market a new issue; by sticking together they share the risk of adverse movements in interest rates between the time an issue is bought from the corporation and the time it goes out of the investment bankers' inventory—safely tucked away in some pension fund's portfolio for many years to come. The idea is to get rid of the issue as quickly as possible—within a day or two. That minimizes the risk exposure of the investment banking firm's capital. Announcements of successful underwritings, such as the one reproduced here, appear frequently in the financial press.

A number of features of this new-issue market are noteworthy. First, as with many—or most—markets, it is not located in any particular spot. Underwritings of new issues do not take place on the floor of an organized exchange. Rather, the marketplace is the conference rooms of investment banking firms, linked by telephone with each other, with corporations, and with ultimate investors. Second, the most important commodity sold by these market-makers is information, information about the yield required to sell an issue and who are the likely buyers. That's one of the most important functions of markets—dissemination of price and trading information. To market the new issue, investment bankers also sell the services of their capital—buying the issue outright from the corporation, thereby insuring that the firm pays only the agreed-upon yield. Subsequent adverse or favorable yield movements do not affect the issuing firm, just the vacation prospects of the investment bankers.

The near-invisibility of primary markets, compared with the immense popular recognition of secondary markets for equities, does not change the fact that both serve essential functions. Moreover, there is a close interrelationship between yields on securities in secondary markets and primary markets. One important clue to the required new-issue yield on a corporation's bonds, for example, is the recent yield on the firm's obligations in the secondary market. How useful these yields are depends, in part, upon the "quality" of secondary market yields. Are they close to equilibrium prices or do they reflect one or two transactions that might not be representative? Only by recognizing the nature of the secondary market can the yields recorded there be evaluated. Let's start by describing some alternative types of market structure.

Equity Trading: Auctions and Dealers

The New York Stock Exchange is the most visible secondary market, in part because equities of the largest corporations are traded there. But high visibility comes also from the fact that you can actually see the marketplace. Trading takes place on the floor of the exchange, at 11 Wall Street. Business is conducted by members of the exchange—those who own proverbial seats (at one time there were actual seats, but these have long since gone the way of the Model T). Transactions are recorded on the ticker tape, flashed on the floor itself as well as in brokerage offices throughout the country. This is a real marketplace, the same as the county fair, except it's a lot noisier. Nothing is left to the imagination, as is necessary in telephone markets.

Individual stocks are traded at particular locations, called posts, on the football-field floor. Traders receiving orders via telephone from brokerage offices throughout the country scurry about placing orders with particular specialists. It is the job of the specialist to maintain orderly trading for the securities he or she is in charge of. Specialists may simply match publicly tendered buy and sell orders submitted at the same price. Floor traders stand at the post and bid for orders that are not matched in the specialist's "order book." When none of these occur, specialists step in and buy for their own account (at the bid price) or sell from inventory (at the asked price) to prevent excessive gyrations in transactions prices and, it is hoped, to make a handsome profit. Thus trading through specialists on the floor of the exchange is a hybrid of an open auction and dealer trading: the specialist acts as both auctioneer and dealer.

Stock exchanges in the United States are all modeled along these lines. In addition to the NYSE there is the American Stock Exchange (Amex), the Midwest Stock Exchange, and so on, as indicated in Table 1. As shown in the table, each exchange has its own listings —securities which are traded primarily on it. Smaller companies are generally listed on the Amex and the regionals. Shares of large

Table 1 Number of Securities Listed on Exchanges (December 31, 1980)

	Equities	Bonds
American	925	232
Boston	47	1
Cincinnati	5	5
Midwest	15	0
New York	1,540	3,057
Pacific	51	33
Philadelphia (PBW)	17	22
Intermountain	35	0
Spokane	26	0

SOURCE: Securities and Exchange Commission, *Statistical Bulletin.*

NYSE-listed companies are also frequently traded on regional exchanges.

The markets are knitted together by electronic communications. Intermarket trading has reached a stage that effectively integrates these geographically separate market centers. Price discrepancies between General Motors quoted on the NYSE and on the Midwest Exchange are arbitraged away within seconds. That means if the price of General Motors is $50 on the NYSE but is quoted at $51 on the Midwest, an immediately profitable and riskless transaction (arbitrage) can be executed: buy at $50 in New York and sell at $51 in Chicago. The buying on the NYSE forces up the price, the selling on the Midwest forces down the price—with the process ending only when the prices are equalized.

Such price discrepancies rarely emerge nowadays. The regionals and the New York exchange are closely integrated. We have moved toward a national market system as mandated by congressional legislation in 1975, although there are some further steps that might be taken.[2]

[2]Movement toward a centralized market started back in 1975, when the consolidated ticker tape began reporting trades of NYSE-listed securities no matter where they were executed. Among the steps that remain to be taken: automated execution of trades based on most favorable price quotations.

While exchanges nominally conduct auctions, we've just seen that specialists sometimes act as dealers—buying and selling for their own account. The vast majority of common stocks do, in fact, trade in dealer markets. In fact, the dealers are the Merrill Lynches and E.F. Huttons that also act as investment bankers and operate nationwide brokerage offices. To be sure, the over-the-counter (OTC) securities are usually smaller than exchange-listed stocks, with less trading interest. But currently there are about 2,500 stocks traded under the Automated Quotation System of the National Association of Securities Dealers, called NASDAQ. And this might be very much closer to the future of securities markets than exchange-based trading.

Trading in OTC securities used to be a relatively haphazard operation, especially when compared with organized exchanges. Individual broker/dealer firms bought and sold OTC securities for their own account—they acted as dealers. For some OTC stocks, like Tampax, more than a dozen firms made a market—that is, they quoted bid and asked prices that account executives at brokerage firms could rely upon when selling or buying for their customers. For smaller OTC securities, perhaps only one or two firms will make a market. If you placed an order with your fortune-telling stockbroker to buy Fly-by-Night Air, Inc., he would call one or two dealers, get the lowest offer, and execute the trade. But you and he could never be sure that it was the best offer—and only you would really care. Moreover, the only record of market making would appear in the daily pink sheets, which record (on pink paper) bids and offers (not trades) toward the end of the day.

Dealers still quote bids and offers on OTC securities, but just about everything else changed for the larger OTC securities when NASDAQ was introduced in 1971. TV screens replaced telephones as the communications mechanism. Market makers now enter bids and offers via a terminal linked to the NASDAQ computer, and these quotes are flashed to subscribing brokerage offices throughout the country. The hunt-and-peck method of uncovering the best bids and offers has given way to computer search—a far more efficient technique. There were measurable improvements in the performance of OTC stock trading, as we'll see below.

A word about stockbrokers is in order. They are formally called account executives at a brokerage firm, and they are usually the closest contact an individual has with the stock market. Yet, in the purest sense of the word, they act only as agents, as your agent in executing your orders to buy and sell securities. They are not auctioneers, nor are they dealers in most securities. They charge a commission for filling your order at the best price. They have a fiduciary responsibility to get you the best deal. There are therefore potential conflicts of interest if your stockbroker's firm is also a dealer in an OTC security you want to sell (or buy). Legally and morally, he shouldn't sell to his firm unless it is the best bidder. But it is often difficult to monitor such responsibilities.

Bond Trading: Dealers and Brokers

The existence of New York Stock Exchange bond trading is one of the better-kept secrets on Wall Street. Compared with the immense visibility of stock transactions, bond trading is virtually invisible— even though NYSE bond transactions are recorded in the financial press alongside the stock tables. The low profile of bond transactions is caused by two factors: (1) the overwhelming proportion of bond trading takes place over-the-counter, through market-making dealers; (2) bonds are held primarily by institutional investors, rather than individuals. Both of these obscure bond trading from public view.

While the bonds of some large corporations are listed on the NYSE, most corporate issues and virtually all U.S. Government, federal agency, and municipal bonds are traded over-the-counter. As shown in Table 2, the volume of OTC trading in Treasuries and agencies simply dwarfs bond trading on the NYSE.

The telephone is still the dominant mechanism for uncovering the best bids and offers of the numerous bond-dealing firms. On the other hand, most dealers maintain extensive computer-based information systems to record the holdings of bonds by ultimate investors (insurance companies, pension funds, and other institutions). This helps the dealer unearth buyers and sellers when needed.

There are so many individual corporate debt issues that trades in a particular bond are sometimes days or weeks apart. It does not really pay to invest in highly automated trading facilities when the volume of transactions does not warrant the huge outlay.

The exception is the government bond market. Here the volume of trading is so large (see Table 2) that computer-based trading and sophisticated communications technology now dominate the marketplace. Each of the forty or so dealers supplement their telephone surveillance of other dealers with electronic monitoring of quotations in the brokers' market. Dealer quotes are closely intertwined by the relatively easy search process.

Unlike dealers, brokers act purely as middlemen—never buying or selling for their own account, merely matching buy and sell orders. The broker actively searches for compatible trading partners, rather than passively accepting (as would a pure auctioneer) only tendered bids and offers. On the other hand, brokerage is less risky than dealing because there is no inventory of securities to worry about. Thus the rewards to brokerage are commensurately less. Brokers earn a living by the sweat of their brow; dealer earnings must also cover the cost of ulcers.

Electronic linkage in the government securities market is provided by the brokerage firm of Garvin Guy Butler, through a subsidiary known as Garban. Bids and offers are flashed on computer screens to the more than forty dealers in governments. The bids can

Table 2 Comparative Stock and Bond Volume for 1980

Security	Volume
Treasuries (OTC)	Average Daily Volume of 18.3 billion; Approximate Annual Volume (assuming 250 trading days per year) = $4.6 trillion
Agencies (OTC)	Average Daily Volume of $3.3 billion; Approximate Annual Volume (assuming 250 trading days per year) = $825 billion
Bonds—NYSE	Approximate Annual Volume of $5.0 billion
Equities—NYSE	12.3 billion shares traded for the year; Annual Volume of $398 billion
Equities—OTC (NASDAQ)	6.4 billion shares for the year

SOURCES: *Federal Reserve Bulletin; Wall Street Journal.*

be "hit" and the offers "taken" by telephoning the office of Garban. Thus, while technology permits instantaneous search of the market, it does not, as yet, permit electronic trading.

Most other trading in the OTC bond market is still done via telephone search among various dealer firms. An investor can search by himself—such as a life insurance company portfolio manager telephoning a number of bond dealers to locate the best bid for a corporate bond the company has decided to sell. Alternatively, a property and casualty insurance company might turn to a broker in the municipal bond market to search for the most favorable price on a particular purchase or sale. Brokers in the municipal bond market typically accumulate these purchase and sale interests early during a trading day, disseminate them via teletype to their customers, and then hope for a matching set of interests. For some investors, it pays to be patient and to wait until the end of the day before deciding where to buy or sell.

Money Market Trading

Short-term debt instruments, such as Treasury bills and municipals under one year to maturity, trade in the OTC market just like their longer-term relatives. So do negotiable bank certificates of deposit (CDs) and bankers acceptances. These are very active markets, with numerous dealers quoting bids and offers. In fact, in the government bond market, the investment banker dealers are supplemented by commercial bank dealers, such as Citibank, Chase, and Bankers Trust. It pays a trader to shop around to get the best deal—not so much because of the wide discrepancies in market quotes but because the huge dollar amounts make even small price differentials worth the extra time and effort.

Commercial paper, the short-term debt of prime-rated corporations, does not trade in a secondary market. Rather, if an investor would like to sell his paper before it comes due, he turns to the issuer, who stands ready (usually) to redeem before maturity. Companies that employ dealers to sell their commercial paper are absolved of this nuisance; the dealer usually makes a limited secondary market—agreeing to buy back paper from its customers only.

The most unique form of trading structure is in the shortest of all money market instruments—federal funds. These are unsecured one-day obligations of a commercial bank. The borrowing bank buys federal funds and the lending bank sells federal funds, with the transfer occurring immediately (same-day funds). There is, in essence, only a primary market. Banks deal directly with each other in buying and selling, with large money-market banks doing most of the buying. There are two major federal funds brokers: Garvin Guy Butler and Mabon Nugent. They match purchase and sale orders communicated to them via telephone.

The unique aspect of the operation is that a seller (lender) of federal funds must approve of the buyer (borrower) because the latter has an unsecured obligation to repay the funds on the following day.[3] That's why federal funds can't be resold—they are not negotiable. We might not mind if Citibank owed us money but would not have relished the thought of their transferring that obligation to Franklin National Bank on the eve of that bank's demise. That's why, even if the price is right, federal funds brokers must check with the parties involved before completing a transaction, and the brokers have to try harder for some banks than for others.

Mortgage Trading: A New Industry

The secondary market for mortgages would be virtually nonexistent if it weren't for government intervention. As mentioned in Chapter 26, the Federal National Mortgage Association and the Federal Home Loan Mortgage Corporation buy mortgages from savings and loan associations, savings banks, and mortgage bankers. But there's virtually no trading in individual mortgages. There just aren't any buyers.

[3]Overnight repurchase agreements with government bonds accomplish the same transfer of funds but with the bonds serving as security. The federal funds market and the RP market are alternative sources of overnight funds for banks (see Chapter 8). The yields on these two sources move quite closely together. If they didn't, banks would arbitrage between the two markets, bringing their yields together—much as the prices of GM in New York and Chicago are held together.

Latest Financial Technology

The main difficulty with mortgages is the diversity of individual characteristics and the relatively small size of each issue. These preclude active market-making. A dealer would be inundated with unwanted detail if he bought and sold individual mortgage loans.

The secondary market in mortgages changed for good back in 1970, when the Department of HUD's Government National Mortgage Association announced that it would insure the timely payment of interest and principal on bundles of FHA-VA insured mortgages. These had to be at least $1 million lots of standardized individual mortgages—government insured, identical coupon, with a servicing fee paid to the originator of the mortgage to collect and "pass through" the interest and principal to the ultimate investor. Dealers viewed these "GNMA pass-through" instruments as quite similar to bonds and began to quote bids and offers on them. The volume outstanding of these neatly wrapped mortgages grew to more than $100 billion by 1981. Trading became extremely active.

The underlying mortgages thus gained marketability by disappearing into a package.

Conventional mortgages have recently joined their FHA-VA cousins in the pass-through parade. The Federal Home Loan Mortgage Corporation issues participation certificates in conventionals and a number of private firms, led by the Bank of America, have issued pass-throughs backed by conventional mortgages. The once nonexistent secondary market for mortgages now flourishes under the multicolored packaging of pass-throughs and participation certificates.

Financial Futures

The popular visibility of the markets for GNMAs, Treasury bills, and Treasury bonds was altered dramatically during the mid-1970s with the advent of futures markets on these securities. Unlike relatively invisible over-the-counter trading, futures markets are tangible operations. From the visitors' gallery, the Chicago Board of Trade (CBT), which sponsors futures trading in Treasury bonds and GNMAs, and the Chicago Mercantile Exchange (CME), which conducts Treasury bill futures trading, both look very much like the New York Stock Exchange. People scurry about placing orders at different points on the floor. These specific locations are called pits on the futures exchanges rather than posts as on the stock exchange, but that's a difference of form, not substance. As with the stock exchanges, the futures markets conduct trading through an open auction.[4] In particular, direct confrontation between buyer and seller is most prominent. Individuals on the floors of the exchanges bid and offer futures contracts on behalf of customers throughout the country.

Futures contracts on Treasury bonds, GNMAs, and Treasury bills trade alongside the more traditional contracts on agricultural commodities such as soybeans, corn, cattle, and pork bellies. And in a

---

[4]Unlike the stock exchanges, however, there is no specialist in futures market trading.

sense they are quite similar to the older futures contracts. The main characteristic of a futures contract is that it deals in rights and obligations regarding a specific standardized commodity, rather than the actual commodity itself. For example, in January 1983 a person could buy a Treasury bill contract that confers the right and obligation to receive $1,000,000 of 90-day Treasury bills at a specific date in the future, say March 1984. The seller of such a contract has the right and obligation to deliver those Treasury bills on the specified date. The key point for negotiation is the price at which the contractual obligations are set. And that's what gets determined by the often frenetic bidding and offering on the floor of a futures exchange.

Recall from our discussions in Chapters 25 and 26 that once the price of a particular security is fixed, the yield is simultaneously determined. Thus when trading in Treasury bill futures fixes the price of a three-month Treasury bill that must be delivered at some future date, it is simultaneously fixing the yield on such bills. If a portfolio manager wanted to make certain that he could buy Treasury bills (or Treasury bonds or GNMA securities) at a fixed yield at some date in the future, he could buy a futures contract obligating the seller to deliver the securities at that time. Why would someone take on such a risky obligation? Obviously, if a person were a speculator and thought that actual yields would be even higher later (so that securities prices would be lower), he could make a profit by contracting to deliver securities at what turns out to be a high price. In particular, on the delivery date of the futures contract he could buy the securities at a low price and deliver them at the contractually fixed higher price.

In point of fact, prices of futures contracts are determined by the interplay of speculators, who buy or sell with the hope of guessing correctly about actual prices that will prevail in the future, and hedgers, who buy or sell because they want to fix the price today of a transaction they will have to make in the future.[5] In the process, the risks of future price fluctuations of the underlying asset are transferred from hedgers to speculators. And this is one of the main contributions of futures markets to economic welfare.

[5]For example, a mortgage banker who is originating mortgage loans that will be ready for packaging and sale in three months can eliminate the risk of price changes by selling a GNMA futures contract today at a fixed price.

It is important to recognize that prices in the futures markets in these securities are closely related to prices determined in the so-called spot or cash markets, where the actual securities are traded. For example, suppose that the price for Treasury bonds to be delivered in one month on the Chicago Board of Trade was $73 per $100 face value. If at the same time a bond were offered at a price of $70 by one of the government securities dealers discussed above, it might very well pay someone (anyone) to buy from the dealer at $70, sell a futures contract at $73, hold the securities for a month, and deliver the bonds on the futures contract. In fact, such buying by arbitrageurs in the spot market and their selling in the futures market would force the prices in the two markets into alignment.[6]

The main advantages of futures markets over the spot market for the underlying commodity are as follows. First, by trading in rights and obligations of a specific standardized commodity, such as an 8 percent coupon, twenty-year Treasury bond, the futures market cuts through the often bewildering detail of the cash markets. Instead of an array of prices on many different categories of Treasury bonds, a single price emerges for a standardized instrument. This consolidation facilitates the price discovery and price dissemination function of markets. Second, and closely related to the first point, the large volume of trading in the standardized commodity makes it cheaper and easier for most people to transact in futures contracts.

If someone wanted to profit because he expected interest rates to fall in the future, he could go to a dealer and buy a Treasury bond; if rates actually fell, he would reap capital gains because the price of his bonds would rise. But it is usually much easier to buy a futures contract for delivery of Treasury bonds either three or six or nine months in the future. And if actual bond prices rise, so will the prices on the futures contracts (the arbitrageurs will see to that). Moreover, it isn't even necessary to take delivery of the bonds in order to reap the profit. The futures contract can simply be sold at the higher price. In fact, most futures contracts are concluded by an offsetting sale rather than physically delivering the product. Thus futures contracts provide a convenient forum for investors in the Treasury securities markets.

---

[6]The prices would not be identical because the purchase in the cash market must be financed at some interest rate. Thus, futures prices will usually be above spot market prices by the amount of the financing charge (the one month interest rate).

Efficiency of Secondary Market Trading

Now that the major forms of market organization have been described, we can ask the big question: Do they measure up? How well do the various securities markets match buyers and sellers? The general criterion for performance was described earlier in the chapter: transaction prices should hover about the true equilibrium price. Since we never observe the latter, a number of proxy performance measures are used—the most popular of which is the bid-asked spread. But as we'll see, there's much more to a good performance than narrow bid-asked spreads.

Figure 1 illustrates the relationship between the bid-asked spread and the theoretical equilibrium. Sellers on the supply curve and buyers on the demand curve could transact at the equilibrium price if they waited for each other. Impatient sellers are confronted by the bid price by a dealer who hopes to turn around and sell at the asked

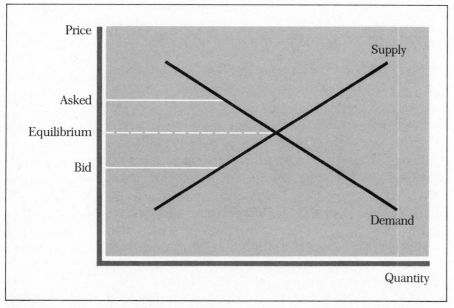

Figure 1 / Bid-asked Spreads Cause Actual Transactions Prices to Hover About the True Equilibrium Price

price to eager buyers. The spread is the dealer's reward for holding what he's bought even though he doesn't want it. As is obvious from the figure, a smaller spread means that transactions prices will be closer to the equilibrium price.

The dealer will quote a narrow bid-asked spread if: (1) the expected volume of transactions is large; and (2) the anticipated risk of large price changes is low. Large volume means it's easy to turn over inventory since there are frequent orders to buy and sell. Low volatility of price changes means that the risk exposure of the dealer's inventory is small. Both mean the dealer can be forced to quote narrow bid-asked spreads and still stay in business—committing his capital and skill to market-making. Since dealers are no more benevolent than the rest of us, the element forcing dealers to quote narrow spreads is competitive pressure.

Table 3 shows a number of sample bid-asked quotations from the *Wall Street Journal.* First some basic explanations of the numbers. All bonds are quoted as a percent of par. Thus, on February 2, 1982, the Treasury 14 percent coupon notes due in June 1985 could be sold at 98 8/32 (the bid price) per $100 face value and could be bought at 98 12/32 (the asked price) per $100 face value. Since minimum denominations of most notes and bonds are $1,000, that means it costs $983.75 to buy while I get $982.50 if I sell a $1,000 Treasury note. The spread (asked minus bid) recorded in the last column is ⅛ or 12.5 cents per $100, or $1.25 per $1,000 transaction. In other words, if I bought a $1,000 Treasury note and decided to sell immediately because I just got a hot stock tip, my schizophrenia would cost me $1.25. A $2,000 round trip, as they call it, costs $2.50, a $3,000 trade, $3.75 and so on. This is a measure of the liquidity costs of the security: the transactions costs of buying and selling.

As can be seen in the first few lines of the table, government notes, bonds and GNMAs have very small bid-asked spreads. The short-term Treasury note has the narrowest spread—suggesting correctly that short-term money market instruments have the most liquid market.

The bond of the Federal Home Loan Bank Board has a ½ point spread—or $5 per $1,000, compared with the ¼ point or $2.50 per $1,000 round-trip transaction in the Treasury bond. This suggests that federal agency securities have less liquidity than Treasury obligations, which is true.

Table 3 Bid and Asked Quotations on Securities

Name of Market	Particular Issue		Bid	Ask	Spread
	Coupon	Maturity			
1. *Governments and Agencies*					
Treasury Note	14	June 1985	$98\frac{8}{32}$	$98\frac{12}{32}$	$\frac{1}{8}$
Treasury Bond	$14\frac{1}{4}$	Feb 2002	$98\frac{6}{32}$	$98\frac{14}{32}$	$\frac{1}{4}$
GNMA	14	—	$89\frac{8}{32}$	$89\frac{16}{32}$	$\frac{1}{4}$
Federal Home Loan Bond	14	June 1984	$98\frac{8}{32}$	$98\frac{24}{32}$	$\frac{1}{2}$
2. *Tax Exempts*					
Kansas Turnpike	$3\frac{3}{8}$	1994	83	86	3
Massachusetts	$6\frac{1}{2}$	2000	$53\frac{1}{2}$	$56\frac{1}{2}$	3
Municipal Assistance Corporation of New York	$10\frac{1}{4}$	1993	85	89	4
3. *OTC Stocks*					
Tampax		—	$31\frac{5}{8}$	$31\frac{7}{8}$	$\frac{1}{4}$
Banc One		—	$38\frac{3}{4}$	$39\frac{1}{4}$	$\frac{1}{2}$

SOURCE: *Wall Street Journal*, February 2, 1982.

The tax-exempt market in the second section of the table indicates $30 and $40 round-trip costs for long-term municipals. The liquidity is much less than in either the Treasury market or the agency market.

The explanation for the variation in the spreads lies primarily in the volume of trading in the particular issues. Short-term Treasury bills and notes are more actively traded than Treasury bonds. GNMA volume is greater than agency trading, while the individual municipal issues trade most infrequently.

The last section of Table 3 records the bids and offers for two OTC securities. Tampax trades on a ¼-point spread and Banc One Corporation on a ½-point spread. Like point spreads in football, these quotations must be scrutinized before jumping to costly conclusions. It would seem, for example, that both securities have smaller liquidity cost than the Federal Home Loan Bond. In fact, the reverse is the case. Quotations in the equity market are *per share.* Thus, to buy 100 shares of Tampax costs $3187.50 (31⅞ times 100), with an immediate sale netting $3162.50. Thus the cost is $25.00 for a $3000.00 transaction. A $3,000 round trip in the agency market costs only $15. The lesson is clear: Bid-asked spreads must be related to the price of the security and the implied cost of trading or liquidating a fixed dollar amount. In general, higher transaction costs on equities versus bonds reflect the greater risk of price fluctuation a dealer is exposed to.

But there's more to the story than bid-asked spreads.[7] For one thing, we haven't mentioned bid-asked spreads on the organized exchanges. The reason is that they aren't published in the newspapers even though a specialist will quote a spread at his post. IBM, a very active NYSE security, was selling at $63 on February 2, 1982 and was quoted on a spread of no more than ⅛. That's $12.50 per $6,000 round trip—not much more than it would cost to trade $6,000 in Treasury notes, and considerably less than the liquidity cost in the agency market. For trades of that size, equities are just about as liquid as Treasury or agency securities, if not more so.

The real difference between liquidity in Treasuries or agencies and liquidity in *any* equity lies in the size of transaction that can be handled without causing either a widening of the bid-asked spread or a shift up (in the case of a buy) or down (for a sale) in the implicit equilibrium price. Quotes in equities must be good for at least a round lot—100 shares. Quotes in the Treasury market must also be good for a round lot—either $1 million or $500,000 in face value. A $5 or $10 million order in Treasuries can also be filled without much trouble. But for equities, there's simply no way to liquidate a $5 million block of stock—or even a $1 million position—without causing the specialist to back away after the purchase of 100 or 200 shares. Thus the bid-asked spread measures the liquidity cost of normal-sized transactions, and what's normal in the Treasury and agency markets would be abnormal in any common stock. In fact,

[7]Even the bid-asked spread itself is not as unambiguous as it seems. In competitive dealer markets, bids and offers are quoted by each market-maker. The quotations in Table 3 are averages. Unless all quotes are identical, a potential trader is confronted with price dispersion. It pays to search among dealers for the most favorable quote, but this search adds to the cost of executing a trade. See Kenneth D. Garbade and William L. Silber, "Price Dispersion in the Government Securities Market" *Journal of Political Economy* (August 1976).

blocks of stock are not brought to the auction market on the exchange floor unless a trade has been arranged beforehand by dealers. While the public auction of organized exchanges looks good and has distinct advantages, it simply cannot handle the large trades of institutional investors.[8]

This discussion suggests a somewhat more sophisticated measure of market performance, one that focuses on the ability of a market to absorb large trading volume without causing wild gyrations in transactions prices. The qualitative description of such markets is relatively easy: they have breadth, depth, and resiliency. A market is deep if it is easy to uncover buy and sell orders above and below current transactions prices; if these orders exist in large volume, then the market has breadth; if new orders quickly pour in when prices move up or down, the market is called resilient.

All these characteristics imply low transactions price volatility. For example, even if a dealer's bid and asked quotes are good for 100 shares only, if a larger purchase order produces sales from the crowd surrounding an exchange trading post or causes institutions that continuously monitor dealer quotes to call in sell orders, then prices won't gyrate much. Markets which are *not* broad, deep, and resilient are called thin markets; only a small volume of trading can be absorbed without producing wide price swings.

Having said all that, there's not much else to do. There just aren't any good measures of this aspect of liquidity. Simply looking at price volatility is not enough—part of everyday price movements are equilibrium price changes and do not reflect poorly on a market's liquidity.

One important observation can be made, however, concerning the impact of communications technology on the ability of any market to absorb large orders without becoming "disorderly." Traders who can continuously monitor quotations on TV screens like NASDAQ can participate more quickly in buying and selling if prices deviate from their view of equilibrium. When prices fall, they buy; when prices rise, they sell. This very process contributes to price stability and liquidity. Moreover, once in place, the reduction in price

[8]Institutional investors can trade among themselves through a computerized brokerage service called Instinet. Trading interests are recorded via computer terminal and then transmitted to other subscribing institutions. When there is a match, the trade is recorded and executed.

volatility also leads to narrower bid-asked spreads, since dealer inventories are subject to less risk.[9]

We have extended our discussion of secondary market trading efficiency, marketability, and liquidity to the point of no return. Price changes should be small when trading is motivated by liquidity needs; that's the characteristic of highly marketable securities. But new information affecting the underlying value of the security should be reflected quickly in equilibrium price changes. Indeed, if prices of financial assets did not reflect news about bankruptcies, earnings trends, lawsuits, and whatever else affects the payments promised by the issuer of the financial instrument, then the market would be inefficient. Some call this aspect of a market allocational efficiency. Up to now we have analyzed the operational efficiency of financial markets. Actually, the popular discussion of "efficient capital markets" focuses on allocational efficiency, without calling it by that name. We discussed some aspects of efficient capital markets in Chapter 23 in the context of portfolio theory. We'll add a few thoughts on the subject in the next section, within the framework of regulation of securities markets.

Efficient Capital Markets and Regulation

A vast literature has developed during the past fifteen years based on a relatively straightforward proposition: The current price (hence, expected yield) of a security fully reflects all publicly available information. Put somewhat differently: There is no unexploited, publicly available, information that would lead to superior investment performance. If securities prices fully reflect all available information, the capital market is called efficient.

It's hard to argue with the statement that markets will be efficient. If securities prices didn't reflect all publicly available information, market pressures would quickly force them to do so. Suppose a news flash that an OTC-traded company had discovered how to make oil

[9]See Anthony Santomero, "The Economic Effects of NASDAQ: Some Preliminary Results," *Journal of Financial and Quantitative Analyses* (January 1974), for evidence that NASDAQ significantly reduced bid-asked spreads on OTC securities.

out of used textbooks were ignored by dealers. Everyone else would find the price of the security relatively cheap in view of the fantastic profits the company will reap. Buy orders pour into brokerage offices and sell orders disappear. Dealers will meet their commitment to sell 100 shares at the old price and then will more than double the quoted asking price to avoid selling what they don't have at ridiculously low prices. As soon as the dealer quotes a price sufficiently high to reflect the rosy profit outlook, buy orders drop to normal (the security is no longer such a bargain), sell orders reappear (let's take some profits), and the new equilibrium price fully reflects all publicly available information.

There's nothing wrong with that story. It happens all the time. The problem arises in the implications for buying and then selling securities. The implication is quite simple: Don't trade. If prices quickly incorpoate all information affecting the fortunes of a company, then you can't earn above-average returns by selling so-called overvalued securities or buying undervalued ones. There aren't any bargains. Moreover, the fancy charts sold by investment advisers, suggesting that you buy when the price of a stock rises by 5 or 10 percent, aren't worth the paper they are printed on.

Needless to say, securities analysts have little use for such academic ranting and raving. How quickly do you think markets absorb new information? Within a day or two is the best estimate of academic researchers.[10] If that's the case, there is little to gain from buying or selling after reading the investment bulletins of your favorite brokerage house. By the time you've finished, there's nothing to do but watch which way the price of your security went.

Allegations that manipulation, deception, and misinformation helped turn the 1929 stock market collapse into a national disaster led Congress to enact the Securities and Exchange Act of 1934. The Act provided for the establishment of the Securities and Exchange Commission to prevent fraud and promote equitable and fair opera-

---

[10]One of the first articles testing market efficiency is Eugene Fama, Lawrence Fisher, Michael Jensen, and Richard Roll, "The Adjustment of Stock Prices to New Information" *International Economic Review* (February 1969). For a general review see Eugene Fama, "Efficient Capital Markets," *Journal of Finance* (May 1970). A specific example appears in Kenneth Garbade, William Silber, and Lawrence White, "Market Reaction to the Filing of Antitrust Suits," *Review of Economics and Statistics* (November 1982).

tions in securities markets. The focal point of SEC regulations is the disclosure of information that might be relevant for the pricing of securities. There are two major aspects of disclosure requirements: (1) In the primary markets, corporations issuing new securities must file a registration statement with the SEC, disclosing all information that might be pertinent to investors; (2) in secondary markets, no person, especially corporate insiders, may trade on nonpublic information.

Our discussion of market efficiency made specific reference to publicly available information. It's quite possible—indeed, quite probable—that nonpublicly available information can be used to make extra profits or avoid undesirable losses. The SEC insists that no investor should be at a disadvantage when purchasing or selling securities. Not only must there be full disclosure of all pertinent information, but misinformation and dissemination of false or misleading reports are specifically prohibited.

The SEC's job is not an easy one. It has enlisted the aid of the various organized exchanges and the National Association of Securities Dealers in supervising brokers, dealers, and transactions in secondary markets. The exchanges and the NASD take these disciplinary and supervising responsibilities seriously. And with good reason. The specter of more detailed SEC involvement in day-to-day operations is more than enough to encourage vigorous self-regulation.

It would be a mistake, however, to assume that manipulation, fraud, misinformation, and deception have disappeared from financial transactions simply because the SEC plays watchdog. Markets are efficient because investors and traders scrutinize and search and screen all information for themselves. *Caveat emptor et venditor* are still the watchwords that insure market efficiency.

Regulatory Challenges: Options and Futures

Regulatory supervision of the stock and bond markets is undergoing severe testing because of the proliferation of trading in put and call options, as well as the successful innovation of futures contracts for financial assets. Neither options nor futures are new inventions. Puts and calls have traded in OTC markets since the nineteenth century, and organized commodities exchanges have traded agricultural futures for at least as long. But in the mid-1970s put and call options were standardized and trading was inaugurated on the Chicago Board Options Exchange (CBOE) and then on the American Stock Exchange. Futures in financial instruments, as we saw above, were innovated by the Chicago Board of Trade and the Chicago Mercantile Exchange.

Trading activity in options and financial futures has skyrocketed in recent years, causing the SEC, the Federal Reserve, and the U.S. Treasury to worry about the implications of options on stocks and futures on bonds for the underlying markets. First let's briefly describe options; then we'll discuss the legitimacy of government concern.

An option contract confers the right to buy or sell a particular stock at a specified price (the exercise or striking price) within a certain time interval. A call option gives the right to buy (call the stock) and a put option the right to sell (put the stock). Examples are: a call option to buy 100 shares of Eastman Kodak at a price of $70 per share (the exercise price) expiring six months from now, or a put option to sell 100 shares of Kodak at a price of $70 expiring six months from now.

How much, if anything, are such options worth? Well, if Kodak's stock price increases to $80, the call option is worth at least $10—because I can take it to the writer (seller) of the option and demand the stock for $70—which I could then immediately sell on the New York Stock Exchange for $80. The call option confers at least $10 in capital gains. The put option won't be worth very much since Kodak stock sells for $80, hence a contract conferring the right to sell the stock at $70 has little value. But if Kodak's price had dropped to $50, then the put option at $70 would be worth quite a bit—at least $20. The reason is: I can buy the stock at $50 on the New York Stock Exchange and take it to the writer (seller) of the put option, who must buy the stock at $70—the put entitles me to a capital gain of $20 if I choose to exercise (execute) the contract. The possibility of stock prices fluctuating, plus the right to exercise the contract, gives value to put and call options.

As we saw above, a futures contract is a firm agreement to deliver, at some future date, a standardized product; there are no options in this case.[11] The price at which delivery is to be made is agreed upon now. The buyer of the futures contract must receive the product and the seller is bound to deliver it. In financial futures, the product to be delivered is securities: $1 million in U.S. Treasury bills, $100,000 in GNMAs, and so on. The precise maturity of the bills and the coupon of the GNMAs are specified beforehand.

Despite clear differences in the contractual agreements, options and futures do share common features. Both are useful for speculation because they are highly leveraged instruments—that is, the amount of money that must be put up (to insure that buyers and sellers honor their contracts) is small relative to the price swings that are experienced. Both are traded through clearing corporations which intervene between buyers and sellers—permitting each to concentrate on expected price movements and not on the reliability of the other party to fulfill the contractual obligation. Both options and futures fulfill legitimate economic functions—providing portfolio managers with additional opportunities for risk reduction.

But one of the most important characteristics shared by options and futures is that each is suspected of potentially disrupting or destroying the spot markets for the commodities—in our case, the underlying stocks and bonds. Trading in stock options on the Chicago Board Options Exchange now surpasses trading in some underlying stocks on the NYSE. What will happen to the liquidity of stock trading? Will the options market dominate the stock market, like the proverbial tail wagging the dog? Do the futures markets in Treasury bills and GNMAs create greater instability in spot prices?

The Federal Reserve, the Treasury, and the SEC share a substantial concern about these issues. They have a common interest in the viability of liquid and efficient secondary markets. But so far there is no empirical evidence demonstrating that options and futures are detrimental to the underlying financial markets. That doesn't, of course, mean these issues shouldn't be investigated most carefully. But it does mean that the regulators' reflex of curbing financial

---

[11]The key difference between an option and a future is that the buyer of the future has both the right *and* the obligation to receive the product, while the buyer of the option has acquired only the right to receive the product. For example, when prices fall the owner of the option can simply walk away from his contract while the owner of the futures contract must accept delivery at the lower price.

innovations simply because they are new must be restrained. Until detrimental evidence is uncovered, it is best to follow the precept: Let a hundred flowers bloom. Although it wasn't first enunciated to support innovative financial practices, it is a most appropriate maxim.

Summary

1. The equilibrium price that emerges from the familiar supply-demand picture assumes that all buyers and sellers have been brought together in the marketplace. Actual transactions prices in real world markets may differ from the theoretical equilibrium price because it is costly to bring together all potential traders.

2. Markets that trade existing securities are organized as either auction, broker, or dealer markets. In all cases, resources are devoted to uncovering compatible trading interests. The New York Stock Exchange is the best example of an auction market, while government and corporate bonds are traded primarily in dealer markets. Brokers are frequently used in the municipal bond market and also in trading government bonds and federal funds.

3. It is important to distinguish these secondary markets for securities from the primary market where newly issued securities are initially placed with investors. Virtually all corporations use investment bankers to help market new issues of stock and bonds.

4. Futures markets in Treasury securities and GNMA pass-throughs supplement the cash (or spot) markets in these securities. The standardized futures contract consolidates price and trading information that appears more diffusely in the markets for the underlying securities. Futures markets provide a vehicle for hedgers to transfer risk exposure to speculators.

5. The operating efficiency of secondary markets is measured by how close actual transactions prices conform to theoretical

equilibrium prices. A narrow bid-asked spread in a dealer market produces transactions prices that are close to the true equilibrium price. Other dimensions to operating efficiency include the size of order that can be accommodated at a given quotation. The market for Treasury securities is the most efficient secondary market.

6. Securities markets are highly efficient processors of new information. Most evidence suggests that current prices fully reflect all publicly available information. Regulatory supervision by the Securities and Exchange Commission is aimed at preventing fraud and promoting fair and equitable trading.

Suggestions for Further Reading

The classic article on the interrelationship between information and markets is George J. Stigler, "The Economics of Information," *Journal of Political Economy* (June 1961). Bid-asked spreads were brought into the picture by Harold Demsetz, in "The Cost of Transacting," *Quarterly Journal of Economics* (February 1968). A broad historical perspective on the impact of technology in financial markets is found in Kenneth D. Garbade and William L. Silber, "Technology, Communication, and Performance of Financial Markets: 1840–1975," *Journal of Finance* (June 1978). An excellent description of the structure of broker, dealer, and auction markets, as well as an analysis of futures contracts, appears in Kenneth D. Garbade, *Securities Markets* (New York: McGraw-Hill, 1982). Finally, a fascinating glimpse of the underwriting process in action can be found in Ernest Bloch, "Pricing a Corporate Bond Issue: A Look Behind the Scenes," *Monthly Review* of the Federal Reserve Bank of New York (October 1961).

Part VI
International Finance

29

Foreign Exchange Rates

SINCE the end of World War II, the rapid growth of multinational corporations, the expansion in world trade, and the explosion of tourism have highlighted the importance of international payments. Big banks and corporations used to do only a small part of their business overseas, but now most of them have branches worldwide. Foreign cars were a novelty in America thirty years ago, but now they are giving American automobile manufacturers nightmares. Only the wealthy could afford to vacation in Europe before World War II, but now tens of thousands of college students fly across the Atlantic every summer.

Any time a transaction takes place between the residents of two different countries, one kind of money has to be exchanged for another. What determines whether we will have to pay a little or a lot for a French franc or a German mark? Or, looking at the same thing from the other side of the fence, what determines whether the French or Germans will have to pay a lot or a little for an American dollar?

Exchanges of one kind of money for another are made on the foreign exchange market, which is worldwide. Many banks throughout the world buy and sell foreign monies, in the form of foreign currencies and deposits in foreign banks. So do foreign exchange dealers, for whom this sort of thing is the main business.

More familiar to most people are the currency exchanges, which do most of their transactions with tourists; they are found downtown, at airports, and at railroad stations in all the major tourist centers.

The foreign exchange rate is quoted in either of two ways: the price of 1 French franc, for example, is 25 American cents; or 1 American dollar costs 4 French francs. These are obviously equivalent statements.

The price of foreign money, the foreign exchange rate, like the price of anything that is bought and sold, is determined by demand and supply. The only problem is to identify the underlying determinants of the demand for and the supply of foreign money—usually called foreign exchange.

The Effect of the Balance of Payments on Exchange Rates

With respect to demand, whenever we import foreign goods, buy foreign stocks or bonds, or travel abroad, *we have to make payments to others.* Naturally enough, they want to get paid in their own money. So we have to get hold of foreign exchange, which we can do by going to a bank or currency exchange and buying some. Imports thus give rise to a *demand for foreign exchange.* (Notice that when we buy foreign money we do so by offering dollars; a demand for foreign money can also be thought of as a supply of dollars on foreign exchange markets.)

On the other hand, whenever we export our goods, sell our securities to others, or are host to foreigners traveling here, *payments have to be made to us.* Naturally, we also want to get paid in our own money. So foreigners have to buy American dollars, which they can do by going to a bank or currency exchange and offering their own money to get some dollars. Exports thus give rise to a *supply of foreign exchange.* (Notice that when they offer or supply foreign money they are trying to buy dollars; the supply of foreign exchange can also be viewed as a demand for dollars on foreign exchange markets.)

These underlying determinants of the demand for and supply of foreign exchange are conveniently summarized in a national *balance of payments,* which is an accounting record of all payments made across national borders. We will examine the balance of payments in more detail in the next chapter, but for the moment it is enough to say that for each country it shows the payments made to foreigners and the receipt of funds from them, in the same way that a family might keep a record of all its expenditures and receipts.

A deficit in the balance of payments is no different from a deficit in a household's budget. It means that collectively we are paying out more money abroad than we are taking in, possibly because we are importing more products than we are exporting. A surplus in the balance of payments is just the opposite. It means we are taking in more money from abroad than we are paying out. Balance of payments deficits and surpluses have an important influence on movements in exchange rates:

1.   A *deficit* in our balance of payments means that we are importing more than we are exporting, so that we are paying out more money abroad than we are taking in. This translates into a demand for foreign exchange greater than the supply. As a result, the price of foreign money will rise—foreign exchange will *ap*preciate in value relative to the dollar. The reason is that a deficit in our balance of payments means we are trying to buy more foreign money than foreigners want to sell to us—because they don't need as much of our money as we need of theirs. We can also think of this as a supply of dollars greater than the demand for them on the foreign exchange market, so the dollar will *de*preciate in value relative to other kinds of money.

2.   On the other hand, a *surplus* in our balance of payments means we are exporting more than we are importing, so that we are taking in more from abroad than we are paying out. This translates into a supply of foreign money (trying to buy dollars) that is greater than the demand, so the price of foreign money will fall—foreign exchange will depreciate (and the dollar will appreciate).

The Effect of Exchange Rates on the Balance of Payments

When exchange rates are free to respond to market forces of demand and supply, as just described, they generate self-correcting changes in imports and exports, and in other types of international transactions, which eliminate balance of payments deficits and surpluses. To see how this works, assume we are running a payments deficit. The price of foreign exchange will rise because our demand for foreign exchange exceeds supply. As a result, foreign goods and services will become more expensive for us, so we are likely to import less. At the same time, we will probably export more because foreigners will find our products less expensive (they can now get more dollars for the same amount of their money).

Less imports and more exports: our balance of payments deficit should decline.[1]

The same reasoning applies if we have a payments surplus. The price of foreign money will fall—increasing our imports (because foreign goods are now cheaper for us to buy) and decreasing our exports (our products are now more expensive for foreigners), thereby reducing our surplus.

Figure 1 illustrates these principles in the case of French francs. The dollar price for one franc is on the vertical axis (for example, 25 cents for one franc), and the number of francs is on the horizontal axis. The demand and supply curves for francs have the conventional shapes: the amount of francs demanded increases as their dollar price falls, since when francs become less expensive, French products become cheaper for us, we import more from France, hence we demand more francs. The amount of francs supplied decreases as their dollar price falls, since when francs become cheaper our goods become more expensive for the French, so we export less to them, hence they supply fewer francs on the foreign exchange market.

As drawn, the demand and supply curves for francs imply an equilibrium price of 25 cents for one franc. At that exchange rate, the demand for francs equals supply and our balance of payments shows neither a deficit nor a surplus (at least with respect to France).

What would happen if the exchange rate for some reason happened to be at only 20 cents? As Figure 1 shows, with the franc that cheap our imports would grow, increasing our demand for francs,

[1]Actually, the price elasticities of our exports and imports are important here, but we will ignore this complication. If you want to dig further into such details, see the discussion of the Marshall-Lerner condition in any textbook on international economics. For an advanced treatment see Rudiger Dornbusch. "Currency Depreciation, Hoarding, and Relative Prices," *Journal of Political Economy* (July/August 1973).

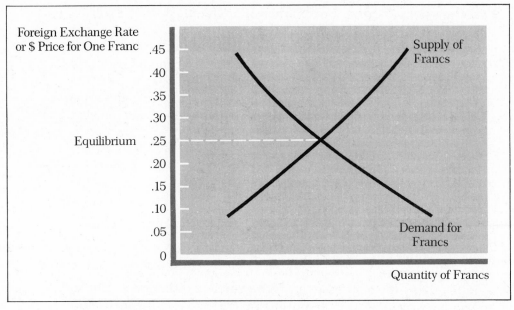

Figure 1 / Supply of and Demand for Foreign Exchange and Foreign Exchange Rates

and our exports would shrink, decreasing the supply of francs. But in a free market, such conditions could not last. The excess of demand over supply would push the exchange rate back up to 25 cents once again. At that price the exchange rate would be in equilibrium, and so would our balance of payments. Thus a freely fluctuating exchange rate keeps both supply and demand for foreign money in equilibrium and also balances the record of international payments.

As a final reminder, don't forget that in international transactions of one kind of money for another there is always a reciprocal exchange involved. The demand for foreign money implies a supply of dollars, and the supply of foreign money implies a demand for dollars. We have said that a deficit in our balance of payments means that the demand for foreign money exceeds the supply, so the dollar price of foreign money will *appreciate*. We could just as well say that a deficit in our balance of payments means that the supply of dollars on foreign exchange markets exceeds the demand for them, so the dollar will *depreciate*.

It all follows from the fact that when we have a payments deficit we are paying out more money abroad than we are taking in. American importers are paying out more dollars than foreigners need in order to buy our exports. This produces an excess supply of dollars in world financial markets and depresses the value of the dollar (which is the same thing as saying that it will depreciate).

Still to Come

Actually, foreign exchange rates that float freely in response to market forces of demand and supply are fairly new in international finance. From the end of World War II until the early 1970s, exchange rates were fixed by international agreement and were not allowed to react to pressures of the marketplace. The agreed-upon fixed exchange rates were supervised by the International Monetary Fund, an institution established at a monetary conference held in Bretton Woods, New Hampshire, in 1944. This fixed-rate system encountered periodic difficulties, however, and finally fell apart in 1973. In Chapter 31 we will see how fixed exchange rates worked and why they failed.

During the late nineteenth century and the first three decades of the twentieth, the international financial system operated under the gold standard, in which rates of exchange were also fixed. Nowadays a lot of people seem to be interested in returning to the gold standard, so we will examine it in Chapter 32.

First, however, as a special treat for all you accounting buffs, let's explore the balance of payments in greater detail. If accounting isn't your thing, feel free to pay a 50-peso fine and go directly to Chapter 31.

Summary

1. Our payments abroad create a demand for foreign exchange (which can also be viewed as a supply of dollars). Payments from foreigners to us create a supply of foreign exchange (or a demand for dollars).

2. An international balance of payments is an accounting record of all payments made across national borders. A deficit in our balance of payments means that collectively we are paying out more money abroad than we are taking in. A surplus means we are taking in more than we are paying out.

3. A deficit in our balance of payments translates into a demand for foreign exchange greater than the supply, leading to appreciation in the value of foreign exchange relative to the dollar. Alternatively, we could say that a deficit translates into a supply of dollars on world financial markets greater than the demand for them, leading to depreciation of the dollar relative to foreign monies.

4. If foreign exchange rates are left free to respond to market forces of demand and supply, movements in exchange rates will eliminate both deficits and surpluses. At the equilibrium exchange rate, the demand for and supply of foreign exchange (or the supply of and demand for dollars) are equal, and the balance of payments is in neither deficit nor surplus.

Suggestions for Further Reading

An informative booklet that fleshes out much of the material in this chapter is Roger M. Kubarych's *Foreign Exchange Markets in the United States* (Federal Reserve Bank of New York, 1978). The New York Fed will send you a copy free if you ask for one; write to the Public Information Department, 33 Liberty Street, New York, N.Y., 10045.

30

Balance of Payments Accounting

QUESTIONS ABOUT the balance of payments are asked so frequently that we feel it would be a service to mankind to correct at least a few of the major misconceptions that abound. For example, the question that arises most often is: What color is the balance of payments? Many people think it is purple, but that is wrong. It is generally wrong, anyway, because the balance of payments is purple only when the consumption function is lavender, and, as you recall, that is a special case. In fact, the balance of payments is usually a deep green, except when it has been left out in the rain too long.

The second most frequently asked question is that hardy perennial: How fat is the balance of payments? It is often said that economists don't know much, and even if they do, who cares? But here is a perfect example to the contrary. Econometric studies show very clearly that the balance of payments is usually too thin for its own good, especially in the Western Hemisphere. It certainly could use more vitamins and wheat germ.

And finally: Does the balance of payments really balance? The answer to that is definitely yes, unless it is shoved. But since most people seem to remain unconvinced, a further word of explanation is necessary.

Sources and Uses Once Again

Actually, a country's balance of payments is nothing more than a sector sources and uses of funds statement in disguise. Just as a sources and uses statement (Chapter 24) records a sector's receipts from and payments to other sectors, so a country's balance of international payments shows the country's receipts from and payments to other countries. The main difference is that in flow of funds accounting the sectors are subdivisions within a country (the household sector, the business sector, and so on), while in balance of payments accounting the sectors are divided into "our country" and "the rest of the world."

In principle we could construct a model balance of payments for a country, from the ground up, in exactly the same way we constructed our model sources and uses statement in 24. All you have to do is think about the United States as a sector, versus the rest of the world, and everything else follows just about the same way. In practice, however, things are a bit more complex, mainly because the entries in our balance of payments—as it is presented by the Department of Commerce—are artfully arranged so as to camouflage the fact that it is really nothing more than a simple sources and uses of funds statement. But lest you be too hard on the economists at the Department of Commerce for making life complicated, don't forget the ancient Buddhist adage: Simplicity is the enemy of Romance.

Without tearing aside the veil of mystery completely, let's return briefly to what we meant by sources and uses of funds when we were doodling with sector sources and uses statements back in Chapter 24.

1. *Sources* of funds consist of (a) *current receipts;* (b) any *increase in a liability* item (borrowing); or (c) any *decrease in an asset* item (selling off assets, dishoarding).

2. *Uses* of funds consist of (a) *current expenditures;* (b) any *decrease in a liability* item (debt repayment); or (c) any *increase in an asset* item—increased holdings of real assets (investment), financial assets (lending), or money (hoarding).

3. We concluded that *the sum of a sector's sources of funds must equal the sum of its uses of funds.* If a sector spends on current and capital goods more than its current receipts (deficit sector), it has to finance its deficit by borrowing, selling off assets, or dishoarding; if its consumption plus investment spending is less than its current income (surplus sector), it has no choice but to repay debts, lend, or hoard an amount equal to its surplus.

Sources and uses of funds have similar meanings and implications in a country's balance of international payments, except that now we have to adapt to the fact that in international transactions we are dealing with *another* country's money. A source or receipt of funds for us as a nation means we get an inflow of foreign money; a use or expenditure of funds for us as a nation means we part with foreign money, an outflow, as we spend abroad. So in international balance of payments accounting, sources and uses of funds become sources and uses of *foreign* monies.

What are some of our main *sources* of foreign money (or foreign exchange, as it is usually called)? Clearly, merchandise exports yield us foreign exchange. When your average Peruvian housewife subscribes to *Vogue,* she mails in some Peruvian money which can be taken to our local bank and changed into dollars. But the Peruvian money does not disappear; the U.S. bank now owns it. From the point of view of the United States, as a nation, we have acquired foreign exchange. (A unit of Peruvian money is called a sol. Remember that. It will probably be on the final.)

The same thing applies if foreign tourists travel across the highways and byways of America in search of Paradise (Montana) or Hell (Michigan). They need American money if they are to get a Big Mac at McDonald's, and to get dollars they have to go to a bank and hand over some sucres, bahts, kyats, or leva—the monies of Ecuador, Thailand, Burma, and Bulgaria respectively.

We similarly receive an inflow of foreign exchange when we export stocks or bonds (borrow from abroad), just as when we export goods—as when an oil sheik in Kuwait buys some U.S. Treasury bills or IBM stock (foreigners traditionally account for a little under 10 percent of the transactions on the New York Stock Exchange). In all these instances foreigners need to buy dollars, and in the process we as a nation acquire ownership of some of their kind of money.

Uses of funds on our balance of international payments come about when it is Americans who do the spending: when we import voodoo dolls from Haiti or love potions from Xanadu; when American tourists in blue jeans and headbands check in at the Sahara Hilton; and when Americans import stocks or bonds (lend to foreigners), as when we buy some United Kingdom Treasury bills in London. In all these instances we have to pay with foreign money, so we go to a bank or currency exchange and buy pounds or francs or what have you (or else use up some of the foreign exchange we had previously acquired). In the process, of course, foreigners acquire ownership of some of our kind of money.

In other words, the sources and uses of foreign exchange for the United States—our balance of international payments—correspond to the standard sources and uses of funds for a sector in domestic trade. Table 1 offers a somewhat formal presentation.

Does It Really Balance?

Does the balance of payments really balance? Of course it does. Just as on a sector sources and uses statement the sum of all a sector's sources of funds must equal the sum of all its uses, so on a nation's balance of international payments all the sources have to equal all the uses. The same logic applies to both.

Like a household, a country cannot incur a deficit by spending on current and capital goods more than its current receipts unless it finances that deficit by borrowing, selling off some assets, or drawing down its cash reserves.[1] It cannot incur a surplus by total spend-

[1]A complication arises in this connection with respect to certain kinds of direct foreign equity investment, similar to the complication regarding corporate equities and bonds mentioned in footnote 1 of Chapter 24. We resolved that problem by assuming that corporate stocks and bonds are roughly the same thing, and we will resolve this difficulty the same way.

Say that Volkswagen ships an entire automobile manufacturing plant, piece by piece, to Ohio. Our imports would rise, but we would *not* be financing this current deficit by borrowing, selling off assets, or dishoarding, since these imports are still owned by Germany. It is handled in the balance of payments accounts as a direct investment by foreigners in the United States (ownership interest). The simplest way
(*continued on page 580*)

Table 1 A Generalized Sources and Uses of Funds Approach to the Balance of Payments for the United States*

Uses of Foreign Exchange	Sources of Foreign Exchange
Current expenditures—as for:	*Current receipts*—as for:
Our merchandise imports	Our merchandise exports
U.S. tourist spending abroad	Foreign tourist spending here
Interest and dividends paid to people abroad	Interest and dividends received from abroad
Services rendered by foreign ships, airlines, etc.	Services rendered by U.S. ships, airlines, etc.
U.S. military spending abroad	Foreign military spending here
Unilateral transfers (gifts, remittances, etc) from U.S.	Unilateral transfers (gifts, remittances, etc.) to U.S.
Decreases in liabilities (debt repayment)—such as:	*Increases in liabilities* (borrowing)—such as:
Reductions in foreign holdings of U.S. securities	Purchases by foreigners of U.S. securities
Reductions in foreign bank loans to U.S. companies	Increases in foreign bank loans to U.S. companies
Reductions in foreign holdings of U.S. money, in the form of either U.S. currency or demand deposits in U.S. banks	Increases in foreign holdings of U.S. money, in the form of either U.S. currency or demand deposits in U.S. banks
Increases in assets—such as:	*Decreases in assets*—such as:
Direct investment by American firms abroad (ownership interest)	Direct investment by foreign firms in the U.S. (ownership interest)
Our purchases of foreign securities (lending)	Reductions in our holdings of foreign securities
Increases in U.S. bank loans to foreign companies (lending)	Reductions in U.S. bank loans to foreign companies
Increases in our holdings of foreign money, in the form of either foreign currency or demand deposits in foreign banks (hoarding)	Reductions in our holdings of foreign money, in the form of either foreign currency or demand deposits in foreign banks (dishoarding)
And our purchases of gold	And our sales of gold

*In the more traditional presentations of the balance of payments, sources of foreign exchange are usually called credits (or plus items), and uses are called debits (or minus items).

ing less than current receipts without disposing of that surplus via debt repayment, lending, or building up its cash reserves (hoarding). In brief, if a country's uses are greater than its sources in some categories, then its sources must be correspondingly greater than its uses on the remainder of the statement.

If all this is so—if the balance of payments always balances—then why all the fuss? How can people keep talking about a deficit in our balance of payments, which implies an inequality, when such an inequality appears to be an impossibility?

Again, as with sector statements, it all depends on precisely what you are measuring. A sector's *total* sources must equal its *total* uses, but within the totals particular pairs may not match up at all: a sector's current expenditures can exceed its current receipts, or vice versa; its saving may exceed its investment, or vice versa; its borrowing may exceed its lending, or vice versa. If you measure the grand totals, they are equal. But if you look behind them, you will find that those grand totals are usually made up of many (eventually offsetting) inequalities.

The typical items that adjust to make our balance of payments "balance" are increases or decreases in foreign holdings of U.S. dollars or short-term securities. For example, say we import more than we export: We have to pay for the difference, which we could do by giving a check to the foreign seller. He deposits the check in his bank to get francs or pesos, so his bank now has the check, which means that a foreign bank now owns demand deposits in an American bank. Our balance of payments would show more imports than exports, but this would be balanced by an increase in foreign holdings of a U.S. liability (demand deposits are a liability of the U.S. bank). In effect, we have financed our imports by borrowing from abroad—the lender is the foreign bank that now owns a demand deposit in a U.S. bank.

The foreign bank might decide to exchange that demand deposit for U.S. Treasury bills, to earn some interest. But that wouldn't change anything; from the point of view of the balance of payments,

(*continued from page 578*)
to think of this, consistent with footnote 1 in Chapter 24, is to assume that Germany's equity ownership of assets in the United States is roughly the same as if Germany acquired debt claims on this country (our borrowing). In other words, once again stocks and bonds are considered roughly the same thing.

that just substitutes one kind of U.S. liability for another. Or prior to August 1971 the foreign bank might, through its government, have used the demand deposit to buy some of our gold: in that case a U.S. gold sale (a source) would balance our imports (a use). No matter how you figure it, in the aggregate sources are always equal to uses.

So what does a balance of payments deficit (or surplus) mean?

Measure for Measure (or As You Like It)

Economists often talk about the *trade* deficit (or surplus), or the deficit *on current account.* Indeed, reference is frequently made to no less than *six* different balance of payments deficits—or surpluses —each of which results from selecting different categories in the payments accounts. Table 2 illustrates each of the six and their relationships to each other. Although at first glance Table 2 looks rather different from Table 1, way down deep it is the same thing.

Using Table 2 to illustrate the calculations, here are the particulars of each balancing act:

1.   The *trade balance* is the most old-fashioned of all, measuring only merchandise exports relative to imports. In Table 2 the merchandise trade balance has a $1 billion surplus, with exports $1 billion greater than imports. In Mercantilist days, in the 1600s and 1700s, this was the exclusive measure. A country with excessive imports would have to settle up by selling off some of its gold, clearly a Bad Thing. Adam Smith worked hard in his study in Kirkcaldy, Scotland, for many years and finally emerged with a big book attacking this narrow view of international finance, thereby becoming Famous. He pointed out that it was better to consume more goods than to hoard more gold, but many people are still not convinced to this very day.

2.   The *goods and services balance* adds services, including such transactions as military expenditures, tourist spending, and interest and/or dividends paid or received for past investments. In Table 2 services transactions alone show a surplus of $5 billion, so that the surplus of goods and services, which is a cumulative balance, is $6 billion.

Table 2 Illustrative U.S. Balance of Payments*
(In billions of dollars)

	Net Balance	Cumulative Net Balance
A. Merchandise Trade:		
1. Exports	+ 70	
2. Imports	− 69	
Merchandise Trade Balance	+ 1	+ 1
B. Services:		
1. Military Receipts	+ 2	
2. Military Payments	− 5	
3. Income on U.S. Investments Abroad	+ 18	
4. Payments for Foreign Investments in U.S.	− 9	
5. Receipts from Travel and Transportation	+ 9	
6. Payments for Travel and Transportation	− 11	
7. Other Services (net)	+ 1	
Balance on Services	+ 5	
Goods and Services Balance		+ 6
C. Transfer Payments:		
1. Private	− 1	
2. Government	− 3	
Balance on Transfer Payments	− 4	
Current Account Balance		+ 2
D. Long-term Capital:		
1. Direct Investment Receipts	+ 3	
2. Direct Investment Payments	− 5	
3. Portfolio Investment Receipts	− 4	
4. Portfolio Investment Payments	− 1	
5. Government Loans (net)	− 2	
6. Other Long-term (net)	− 2	
Balance on Long-term Capital	− 3	
Basic Balance		− 1
E. Short-term Private Capital:		
1. Nonliquid Liabilities	+ 1	
2. Nonliquid Claims	− 5	
Balance on Short-term Private Capital	− 4	

Table 2 Illustrative U.S. Balance of Payments*
(In billions of dollars)

	Net Balance	Cumulative Net Balance
F. Miscellaneous:		
1. Allocation of Special Drawing Rights (SDR)	0	
2. Errors and Omissions	2	
Balance on Miscellaneous Items	− 2	
Net Liquidity Balance		− 7
G. Liquid Private Capital:		
1. Liabilities to Foreigners	+ 4	
2. Claims on Foreigners	− 2	
Balance on Liquid Private Capital	+ 2	
Official Settlements Balance		− 5
The Official Settlements Balance is Financed by Changes in		
U.S. Liabilities to Foreign Official Holders:		
1. Liquid Liabilities	+ 5	
2. Readily Marketable Liabilities	+ 1	
3. Special Liabilities	− 2	
Balance on Liabilities to Foreign Official Holders		+ 4
U.S. Reserve Assets:		
1. Gold	0	
2. Special Drawing Rights	0	
3. Convertible Currencies	+ 1	
4. IMF Gold Tranche	0	
Balance on Reserve Assets	+ 1	
Total Financing of Official Settlements Balance		+ 5

*Pluses are sources of foreign exchange (or credits), and minuses are uses of foreign exchange (or debts). Official data are published monthly in the *Survey of Current Business* (U.S. Department of Commerce).

3.   The *current account balance* adds transfer payments, both private and governmental. Transfer payments are gifts flowing from one country to another. In Table 2 the current account balance has a $2 billion surplus, because the United States made $4 billion more transfer payments to the rest of the world than it received from the rest of the world, thereby shrinking the $6 billion goods and services surplus to only $2 billion on current account.

4.   The *basic balance* adds long-term securities transactions to the current account figures.[2] We have a *basic* deficit in our balance of payments when the sum of our current expenditures plus our net purchases of long-term foreign securities exceeds the sum of our current receipts plus foreign net purchases of long-term U.S. securities. In Table 2, for example, our basic deficit is $1 billion.

5.   The *net liquidity balance* also incorporates nonliquid short-term private capital movements, allocations of SDRs (see footnote 2 in Chapter 32), and errors and omissions (because many international transactions go unrecorded). Adding these elements brings the net liquidity deficit to $7 billion, as Table 2 shows.

6.   Finally, the *official settlements balance* brings in liquid short-term private capital movements. Table 2 indicates that foreigners bought $4 billion of short-term U.S. securities, while we bought $2 billion of theirs, yielding a $2 billion surplus in the liquid private capital accounts. Adding this to the net liquidity balance yields an official settlements deficit of $5 billion.

Why so many different measures of what constitutes a balance of payments deficit (or surplus)? Primarily to confuse the general public, one might surmise. The government can always publicize the measure that currently looks best—the one that shows the smallest

---

[2]Securities and bank lending transactions, by the way, whether short- or long-term, are generally called capital movements. Our purchases of foreign securities are a capital outflow from the U.S., while foreign purchases of our securities are a capital inflow. Imports of foreign securities, like imports of foreign goods, are a use of foreign exchange for us; exports of our securities, like exports of our goods, provide us with foreign exchange.

Note that section D of Table 2 includes three kinds of long-term securities transactions: direct investments, portfolio investments, and long-term loans. These distinctions are rather arbitrary. Foreign purchases of U.S. stocks, for instance, are classified as direct investments only if the foreigner acquires 25 percent or more of the enterprise. Otherwise it is considered a portfolio investment. All purchases of U.S. bonds by foreigners are considered portfolio investments.

deficit. In addition, however, each measure focuses on something a little different from the others.

Today, discussion centers mainly on the relative merits of the basic balance compared with the net liquidity balance and the official settlements balance. The details of these controversies are beyond the scope of this book, and if you are bewildered don't feel you're the only one. In 1976 the Department of Commerce threw up its hands and announced that it would no longer publish figures on any of these three balances. Now it just publishes the numbers on all the transactions and lets people themselves compute whichever balance makes them happiest.

Summary

1. A country's balance of international payments shows its receipts from and payments to other countries.

2. In the aggregate, the balance of payments always balances, because *total* receipts of foreign exchange have to equal *total* payments plus hoarding of foreign exchange.

3. However, subsections of the balance of payments need not balance. For example, merchandise exports can exceed or fall short of merchandise imports. There are six different measures of balance of payments deficits (or surpluses), each of which results from selecting different categories within the total.

Suggestions for Further Reading

One of the most useful articles on balance of payments accounting is Rita M. Maldonado, "Recording and Classifying Transactions in the Balance of Payments," in the *International Journal of Accounting* (Fall 1979). Also very helpful is Norman S. Fieleke, "Accounting for the Balance of Payments," in the Federal Reserve Bank of Boston's *New England Economic Review* (May/June 1971). An updated version has been published by the

Boston Fed titled "What is the Balance of Payments?" Write to the Federal Reserve Bank of Boston, zip code 02106, for a copy. (Remember to say please.)

Also useful is the analysis of alternative balance of payments measures in the 1970 and 1971 *Economic Report of the President.* If you really want to get down to the nitty-gritty, see the Bernstein Report, more formally titled *The Balance of Payments Statistics of the United States: Review and Appraisal,* Report of the Review Committee for Balance of Payments Statistics to the Bureau of the Budget (U.S. Government Printing Office, 1965).

Another committee has also examined the balance of payments format, and as a result extensive changes have been made in the way the figures are presented. See *Report of the Advisory Committee on the Presentation of Balance of Payments Statistics* in the June 1976 issue of the *Survey of Current Business,* published by the U.S. Department of Commerce.

31

Fixed Versus Floating Exchange Rates

FROM THE END of World War II until 1973, the world's international financial system was based on *fixed* exchange rates. When you spent a weekend in Amsterdam or a spring vacation in Rio, you knew before you started what the price of foreign money would be. Nowadays exchange rates *float,* and you're never sure how much it will cost to buy the money you'll need when you get there.

Fixed exchange rates have undeniable benefits. Within the United States, for example, a dollar costs a dollar no matter what state you're in. A common currency within a country is a domestic fixed exchange rate system and it has obvious advantages. It would be a mess if we had domestic floating rates—if dollars were stamped with each state's name on the top and had to be exchanged for a differently stamped dollar, at unpredictable cost, every time you went from one part of the country to another.

Since fixed exchange rates are good at home, why not internationally? On the basis of such thinking, the major countries agreed in 1944 to establish the International Monetary Fund to supervise fixed exchange rates. The fixed exchange rate system worked tolerably well for two decades, but intermittently produced international financial crises that eventually brought the whole system tumbling down.

How Fixed Rates Were Maintained

Remember how *floating* exchange rates work? When a country runs a balance of payments deficit, the supply of its money offered on world financial markets exceeds the demand, so that its money depreciates in value relative to other monies. But with *fixed* exchange rates, as they existed from the end of World War II until 1973, fluctuations in exchange rates were stopped before they could get started. By international agreement, under the International Monetary Fund, a deficit country that saw its money start to depreciate had to step in promptly and prevent the decline. How? By buying up its own money in order to absorb the excess of supply over demand at the pegged exchange rate.

As an illustration, say France is initially in a situation where the supply of and demand for francs is equal, so that the foreign exchange rate is in equilibrium. Suddenly the French people decide they no longer like French wine and pastry but prefer American soda pop and Twinkies, which they begin to import in huge quantities.

As Figure 1(a) shows, this change in tastes would shift the entire supply curve of francs to the right, as the French offer more francs (at every exchange rate) to buy the increased number of dollars they need to pay American soda pop and Twinkies exporters. At the old equilibrium exchange rate, France now has a deficit in its balance of payments, which translates into a supply of francs greater than the demand. With exchange rates free to fluctuate, the franc will depreciate and move down toward a new lower equilibrium level.

In Figure 1(b), however, the rate is fixed, or pegged, at an agreed-upon level, called par. Again the shift in the supply curve results in a supply of francs greater than the demand at the old equilibrium exchange rate. This excess of supply over demand is indicated in Figure 1(b) by the cross-hatched line (xxxxxxx). The French central

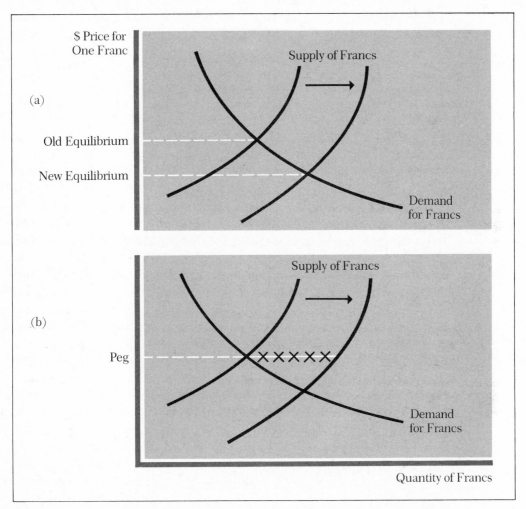

Figure 1 / In (a), with floating rates, the franc depreciates; in (b), with pegged rates, the French central bank prevents the decline by buying up francs (= ~~xxxxxxx~~).

bank steps in *and buys up this excess,* thereby preventing the franc from depreciating.

Of course, the French central bank can't buy up its own money by offering more of the same in exchange—which it could simply print —because that's what people are *selling,* not buying. It has to use *other* money to buy up its own, and this other money is called international reserves.

Traditionally, international reserves have been held in the form of gold, because of its general acceptability. Since the end of World War II, however, most foreign countries have held a substantial portion of their reserves in the form of U.S. dollars, which generally have been just about as acceptable as gold in making international payments. They also hold other kinds of "foreign exchange" among their reserves—pounds, marks, and so on—but mostly they hold U.S. dollars. Other nations acquire dollars when we run our deficits and then hold them as their reserves.

In general, countries use their reserves in the same way individuals and business use their cash balances—to bridge temporary gaps between the receipt and expenditure of funds, to tide them over periods when inflows of funds are slack, and to meet unexpected or emergency needs. *In particular,* with a system of fixed exchange rates, countries also used reserves to intervene in foreign exchange markets whenever the value of their money threatened to slide away from par (its agreed-upon fixed value). A foreign country generally used U.S. dollars for this purpose, paying out dollars to buy up any excess supply of its own money, thereby preventing its own money from depreciating relative to other monies. Or, if it was a surplus rather than a deficit country, selling its own money to keep it from *ap*preciating relative to others.[1]

International Financial Crises

A major difficulty with the fixed-rate system was that it contained no self-correcting pressures to help eliminate a country's balance of payments deficit and bring about an equilibrium in its exchange rate. With floating rates, as we saw in Chapter 29, the franc's depreciation would reduce the supply of francs offered on foreign ex-

---

[1]This means, by the way, that since dollars were the reserves of foreign countries, the United States was in the unique position of not having to intervene itself to keep *its* money from changing in value relative to other monies; since all the other countries were intervening to keep their monies from changing in value relative to the dollar, the dollar was automatically prevented from changing relative to them.

change markets, increase the demand for them, and eventually end downward pressure on the franc.

But if no depreciation is allowed, what is there to stop France from running balance of payments deficits forever? If it does so, then it must continue to pay out its reserves to buy up excess francs, and that's the catch. For France's foreign exchange reserves are not infinite. Sooner or later, when it starts to run out of reserves, it will have to stop "defending the franc." In international financial terminology, France will have to *devalue* the franc, lower its agreed-upon par value. At the new par value, the deficit will disappear, or so it is hoped. If not, France may have to devalue again.

The seeds of the old-fashioned international financial crises that used to erupt periodically when the world was on fixed exchange rates sprang from the ever present threat of devaluation by one country or another.

Once the international financial community senses that devaluation is a possibility, no matter how remote, it is likely to take actions that increase the probability of its occurrence. Anyone who owns francs, or liquid assets payable in francs, and suspects that the franc may be devalued, would be inclined to get out of francs and into some other kind of money—say West German marks—until the devaluation had been completed. Then, with the same marks, they could buy back more francs than they originally had. Such "speculative" sales of francs by private holders must of course be purchased by the French monetary authorities, as they try to prevent the franc from depreciating below par. This puts an added strain on their reserves, thereby increasing the likelihood of devaluation—which in turn stimulates renewed "speculative" activity.

International transfers of short-term funds stemming from fears of devaluation can feed on themselves in this fashion and rapidly build up to the point where they generate massive reserve drains. Such short-term flows of funds include the purchase of Treasury securities as well as shifts of time and demand deposits. Since devaluations are an ever present fact of life under a fixed exchange rate system, countries with balance of payments deficits have traditionally been viewed with some suspicion by those who manage large polls of mobile funds—treasurers of multinational corporations, bankers, oil sheiks, financial consultants to private investors, and others with similar responsibilities. Indeed, fund managers

STEVENSON

"O.K. The forward rate for marks rose in March and April, combined with a sharp increase in German reserves and heavy borrowing in the Eurodollar market, while United States liquid reserves had dropped to fourteen billion dollars, causing speculation that the mark might rise and encouraging conversion on a large scale. Now do you understand?"

Drawing by Stevenson; © 1971 The New Yorker Magazine, Inc.

often got nervous about holding a country's money as soon as that country's rate of inflation exceeded that of other countries, since this was taken as an early warning signal of future devaluation (a rise in prices that is more rapid than elsewhere hurts exports, encourages imports, and thereby invites balance of payments deficits).

Domestic Stabilization Policies under Fixed and Floating Exchange Rates

To what extent are domestic monetary and fiscal policies influenced or limited by the kind of exchange rate system that is in effect?

With fixed exchange rates, a country's domestic stabilization policies may be severely constrained by the requirement that it maintain exchange rate stability. With floating rates, on the other hand, it appears—on the surface, at least—that a country can do just about whatever it wants to domestically, because fluctuations in the exchange rate will automatically take care of such external factors as exports and imports.

Let's look at fixed rates first. Under fixed exchange rates, a country running a balance of payments deficit must use its international reserves to buy up its own money to prevent it from depreciating on the foreign exchange market. A country cannot run a payments deficit forever, because sooner or later it will run out of international reserves. Therefore it has to be concerned about the effects of its domestic policies on its imports and exports, including financial flows that respond to intercountry interest rate differentials.

Under a fixed-rate system, how much freedom do individual nations have to pursue their own independent domestic policies? Not too much, once you think about it. If Great Britain is running a payments deficit, for example, it can hardly ignore that fact and try to live the good life regardless. If it did, its rising prices and higher incomes relative to other countries would stimulate its imports and hamper its exports. Great Britain's balance of payments deficit would worsen and it would wind up desperately buying pounds to stop the pound from depreciating, in the process using up its scarce international reserves.

Under fixed exchange rate arrangements, with no automatic external mechanism to take care of payments imbalances, nations have to take deliberate *internal* measures to do the job. Which means that a chronic-deficit nation sooner or later has no choice but to use monetary and fiscal policies to contract imports, expand exports, and attract financial investments from abroad. Contracting imports and expanding exports requires holding down wages and prices at home, or at least holding the rate of inflation below that of other countries (so domestic products become relatively less expensive), and quite possibly inducing at least a mild recession. To attract financial flows from abroad requires tight money and higher interest rates at home. If a chronic-deficit nation decides it would rather not take such measures, it will run out of reserves as it tries to prevent its money from depreciating on international financial markets. So under fixed exchange rates, freedom of individual domestic action is severely limited by balance of payments considerations.

There is one exception to this principle, at least for a while: namely, a nation that is in the uniquely fortunate position of having *its* money used as reserves by the rest of the world. Say the United States runs continuous balance of payments deficits. What in any other case would soon be viewed as an excess supply of that country's money on world financial markets is not so promptly thought of as excess in the case of the dollar—since other countries want dollars to hold as part of their reserves. Until other countries start to feel that enough is enough, a reserve money country, such as the United States, can run balance of payments deficits with virtual impunity. In effect, since dollars represent a U.S. liability, everyone else is happily (?) lending to the United States. But eventually this tolerance comes to an end, and when that happens the dollar also starts to depreciate and then the United States is in the same boat as everyone else. Then our freedom to pursue strictly domestic objectives is also constrained, and "the discipline imposed by the balance of payments" becomes universal.

One illustration of this is the dilemma that intercountry interest rate differentials have posed for the Federal Reserve during recessions since the early 1960s. In a recession, should the Fed attempt to *lower* interest rates at home to stimulate domestic spending—and then see the balance of payments worsen as short-term funds move abroad in search of higher yields? Or should the Fed attempt to *raise* interest rates at home to attract funds from abroad, or at least deter funds from leaving, thereby bolstering the balance of payments— but then see the recession worsen as domestic spending is curtailed by high interest rates? At times the Federal Reserve's response to this problem has been to try to *twist* the structure of interest rates here at home, lowering long-term rates to encourage domestic business expansion while simultaneously keeping up short-term rates to prevent an outflow of funds abroad. However, as the Fed has discovered, it can twist the interest rate structure only so far. Under most circumstances it simply is not possible to lower long-term interest rates beyond a certain point without dragging short-term rates down with them.[2]

---

[2]For a possible explanation, see our discussion of the term structure of interest rates in Chapter 26.

The lesson to be learned from all of this is that no central bank can conduct an independent, wholly domestically oriented monetary policy within the framework of fixed exchange rates.

Floating rates are another story. Flexible foreign exchange rates are generally hailed as the one system that permits a country to pursue domestic policies unhampered by external balance of payments considerations. When a country runs a payments deficit its money depreciates, which reduces imports, stimulates exports, and automatically corrects the deficit.

Under this system, nations have much more freedom to pursue their own independent domestic stabilization policies. A deficit country can continue to use monetary and fiscal policies to maintain a prosperous economy. It does not have to induce a recession at home in order to make its exports more attractive and cut back on its imports; depreciation of its money on world financial markets will automatically take care of that.

All of which sounds too easy. There must be a catch. And sure enough, there is. It is true that deficits (and surpluses) will eventually be taken care of by exchange rate movements. But do *not* leap from that to the further conclusion that the adjustment process will be painless. Because it might be very painful indeed!

Think for a moment of what that adjustment process involves for a deficit country (say Great Britain): it means, for one thing, that its imports will cost more, because the United Kingdom, with its money depreciating, will have to pay more to acquire the marks and francs it needs for imports. If these imports are "essential"—like food for Great Britain or oil for the United States—the cost of living will rise and living standards will fall in the deficit country. This is inflation. If you have to pay a lot more for food, or for gasoline, you will have a lot less left over for other things. In addition, there will be less "other things" available, because England's exports are likely to expand. Since other countries can obtain pounds cheaply, foreigners will take a larger fraction of Great Britain's output—leaving less for the home folks. On both grounds—more expensive imports and more exports—life will become less comfortable in Great Britain. The U.K. will get rid of its payments deficit, but will find its standard of living declining in the process.

Unwilling to face this reality, many deficit countries try to pursue domestic policies that forestall such painful adjustments. A typical scenario goes somewhat as follows. As the cost of living rises in Great Britain, because of more costly essential imports, unions insist on correspondingly larger wage increases in an effort to maintain real wages. This drives up business costs, which are already higher because imported raw materials cost more. Result: a higher wage-price level. The central bank now expands the money supply by enough to support these higher wages and prices, and thereby nullifies the effects of the pound's depreciation.

On the export side, the higher British prices wipe out the export advantages of the depreciated pound: if the pound has depreciated by 10 percent but British price tags rise by 10 percent, foreigners find British goods no cheaper than before. And on the import side, if the pound depreciates by 10 percent, then home goods look more attractive to British residents than the now more expensive foreign products, but if British price tags rise by 10 percent, then foreign goods are no more expensive (relative to British goods) than before. Inflation in Great Britain—because of a refusal to lower living standards —has offset the balance of payments corrective effects of the pound's depreciation. The result: continued deficits and further depreciation of the pound, until sooner or later measures are taken that effectively cut back imports and stimulate exports—or, in other words, that reduce Britain's standard of living.[3]

Thus, while nations have considerably more freedom to pursue their own independent domestic stabilization policies with a system of floating exchange rates than they have with a system of pegged rates, this freedom is far from unlimited. If a country wants to import from abroad, it ultimately has no choice but to maintain a price level at which its products are competitive in export markets. Otherwise it cannot get the foreign exchange it needs to pay for its imports. This implies that a deficit nation cannot long permit inflation to continue at home at a faster rate than is taking place in the

---

[3]Britons *have* to lower their standard of living in the sense that they must consume less, produce less capital goods for home use, or accept fewer government services. $GNP = C + I + G +$ exports $-$ imports. Assume that $C + I + G = 110$ and exports $= 10$ and imports $= 20$. Thus $GNP = 100$. Keeping GNP at 100 but forcing exports to equal imports, say at 15 each, requires that $C + I + G$ equal no more than 100, as compared with 110 before. This assumes, however, that the British balance of payments deficit is due to an excess of merchandise imports; if it is due to excessive lending abroad (importing foreign securities), then the British can balance their books by lending less abroad.

countries with which it trades. This necessity cannot be ignored in deciding upon domestic monetary and fiscal policies, regardless of what kind of international monetary system may be in effect. Evidently the "discipline of the balance of payments" is unavoidable, whether we like it or not.

Floating Rates: Success or Failure?

Have floating exchange rates been a success? In some respects they undoubtedly have been an improvement over fixed rates. Had fixed rates still been in existence late in 1973, for example, it is not hard to imagine the financial crises of vast proportions that would have exploded when the Organization of Petroleum Exporting Countries (OPEC) announced a fourfold increase in oil prices. Floating rates have absorbed the shocks of that and similar episodes remarkably well.

But floating rates have nevertheless fallen far short of expectations. For one thing, they have not wiped out our chronic balance of payments deficit. If there was anything floating rates were expected to do, it was to rectify that situation by making our imports more expensive and our exports more competitive. But in fact our payments deficit has not really responded.

There are several explanations, none of them entirely satisfactory. One is that the balance of payments corrective process takes time—that although the payments deficit may get worse for a while in response to depreciation, eventually it will get better. Economists often refer to this as a J-curve phenomenon: At first things deteriorate, but at some point they turn around and improve dramatically. Things get worse initially because imports are resistant to the price increases caused by the depreciation of the dollar, implying that imports actually rise in dollar volume in the short run; similarly, it takes time before exports are stimulated. In the short run, therefore, the depreciation of the dollar is likely to enlarge the balance of payments deficit rather than contract it. *Eventually,* however, there will be a meaningful turnaround.[4]

[4]See Rudiger Dornbusch and Paul Krugman, "Flexible Exchange Rates in the Short Run," *Brookings Papers on Economic Activity* (No. 3, 1976).

Fed Sold Marks To Help Dollar

By MARIO A. MILLETTI

The Federal Reserve Bank of New York, attempting to support a skidding dollar, intervened heavily in the foreign-exchange markets from August to October by selling the equivalent of $236.8 million in West German marks, Fed officials said yesterday.

The officials, in their regular quarterly report, stressed that the intervention was not directed at maintaining a specific level for the dollar but was aimed instead at quelling disorderly or unsettled market conditions.

The Fed's operations, which amounted to a total of around $400 million, involved mainly buying and selling marks. "We haven't intervened in yen," said Scott E. Pardee, a vice president at the New York Fed. The mark and the Japanese yen recently have been the strongest currencies against the dollar.

Particularly Unsettled in October

The Fed's intervention occurred at about the same time that Treasury Secretary W. Michael Blumenthal made statements suggesting that the Government's policy was not to prop up the dollar, although he said that a strong and stable dollar was a necessity.

The currency markets were particularly unsettled in October, when most of the Fed's intervention took place, said Mr. Pardee and Alan R. Holmes, executive vice president in charge of the New York Fed's foreign desk.

Mr. Pardee attributed much of the market conditions to "more of a gambling atmosphere than we've had in really more than a year or so." Foreign-exchange dealers, he said, were ignoring favorable economic forces in the United States. He added that market actions often were determined by rumors—such as the one that Arthur F. Burns, chairman of the Federal Reserve Board, had resigned—and by unfavorable news stories.

"I thought the Government securities market was subject to rumor-mongering, but I must say the exchange market goes them one better because it is more international in scope," commented Mr. Holmes.

The Fed's October actions, which amounted to the equivalent of around $200 million, were one of its two or three largest monthly interventions, Mr. Pardee said. "We've had to operate more forcefully than we have had to since early 1975," he added.

The Fed's total market dealings from August to October were submerged in the record $30 billion of gross market interventions by all major central banks throughout the world, the Fed's report showed. The overall figure reflects, among other things, an unsuccessful major attempt by the Bank of England to limit a rise in the pound.

In the prior May through July period, Fed intervention amounted to the equivalent of $300 million compared with total major central bank interventions of $22 billion, a spokesman said.

News Item / Dirty Float

New York Times, December 1, 1977

An alternative explanation is that we have never really given floating rates a sufficient chance to float freely, so they could produce their results. Instead, nations have continuously intervened in foreign exchange markets, nudging exchange rates higher or lower, refusing to let the free market operate. Instead of "clean" floats, we have had managed or "dirty" floats.

So far, then, the verdict is mixed. Floating foreign exchange rates are neither a clear success nor an unmitigated disaster. Everything considered, they have probably been an improvement over fixed rates since they came into being in 1973. Many bankers and business executives would still prefer to return to fixed rates,[5] but the likelihood appears slim that it will happen in the near future.

Summary

1. With fixed exchange rates, a deficit country must intervene and buy up its own money to prevent its depreciation on the foreign exchange market. It uses its international reserves for this purpose, but this process ends when a country runs out of reserves.

2. International financial crises tend to develop under fixed rates when fears of devaluation lead to wholesale dumping of a country's money.

3. The United States was (and still is) more insulated than other countries with respect to payments deficits and the depreciation of its money, because the dollar is used as their international reserve by many other countries.

4. Nations have more freedom and flexibility in the exercise of independent domestic policies under floating rates than they do under fixed rates, but the "discipline of the balance of payments" exists under floating rates too.

5. Floating rates have not been a complete success since they were instituted in 1973, but they have probably been an improvement over fixed rates.

[5]For an expression of views along these lines, see "The Drift Back to Fixed Exchange Rates: Floating Rates Are Being Viewed Worldwide as a Costly, Failed Experiment," *Business Week* (June 2, 1975), pp. 60–63.

Suggestions for Further Reading

For two excellent insiders' views of the events discussed in this chapter, see Charles A. Coombs, *The Arena of International Finance* (New York: John Wiley & Sons, 1976); and Robert Solomon, *The International Monetary System, 1945–1976* (New York: Harper and Row, 1977).

On speculative flows of funds and international financial crises, see Donald L. Kohn, "Capital Flows in a Foreign Exchange Crisis," *Monthly Review* of the Federal Reserve Bank of Kansas City (February 1973); and Philip Rushing, "Reciprocal Currency Arrangements," *New England Economic Review* of the Federal Reserve Bank of Boston (November/December 1972).

In more general terms, see Abba P. Lerner, "What Would We Do Without the Speculator?" in his *Everybody's Business* (East Lansing: Michigan State University Press, 1961); and Milton Friedman, "In Defense of Destabilizing Speculation," in his *The Optimum Quantity of Money and Other Essays* (Chicago: Aldine, 1969). Also see the article by Friedman, "The Case for Flexible Exchange Rates," in his *Essays in Positive Economics* (University of Chicago Press, 1953).

For more advanced discussions of speculation, see William J. Baumol, "Speculation, Profitability, and Stability," *Review of Economics and Statistics* (August 1957), and Lester G. Telser, "A Theory of Speculation Relating Profitability to Stability," *Review of Economics and Statistics* (August 1959).

A lucid analysis of some of the issues discussed in this chapter is presented by Janice M. Westerfield in "Would Fixed Exchange Rates Control Inflation?" in the Federal Reserve Bank of Philadelphia *Business Review* (July/August, 1976). Also see Marina Whitman, "Global Monetarism and the Monetary Approach to the Balance of Payments," *Brookings Papers on Economic Activity* (No. 3, 1975); and Paul A. Volcker, "The Political Economy of the Dollar," Federal Reserve Bank of New York *Quarterly Review* (Winter 1978–79). Also valuable are Thomas M. Humphrey's articles on the international aspects of inflation in his *Essays on Inflation* (Federal Reserve Bank of Richmond, 1979).

32

The Gold Standard

DURING 1981 and 1982 an official blue-ribbon U.S. Gold Commission deliberated long and hard before deciding against a return to the gold standard. The United States was officially on a full-fledged gold standard from 1900 to 1933, and a lot of people would like to return to those good old days before double-bubble gum and the *Dukes of Hazzard.*

What is the gold standard and how is it supposed to work? Well, it's storytelling time.

An Island Paradise

Long ago and far away, the natives of a small island in a remote part of the world had a monetary system of which they were extremely proud. Although they lacked commercial banks and had no Federal Reserve, they had something many people consider much more important—a monetary standard. It was not a gold standard, but it was somewhat similar. It was a rock standard. Near the southeastern edge of the island, on a high cliff, sat a handsome and enormous rock, awesome to behold and thrilling to touch, and it was this that they decided should serve as "backing" for their money.

601

Naturally, the rock was too heavy, and indeed too valuable, to use as an actual means of payment. Instead, for circulating media itself, corresponding to our coins and dollar bills, they used special clamshells. People had confidence in these because boldly inscribed on them were the words:

Will Pay to the Bearer on Demand One Dollar in Rock

The very fact that this statement was made meant that no one ever demanded any rock. The assurance that it was there was sufficient.

For many years all went well. The economy was simple but prosperous, and those from the Great Civilizations across the sea who occasionally visited the island marveled at its stability and its thriving commerce. The natives were not reluctant to explain the reasons for their prosperity: hard work, thrift, clean living, and, above all, sound money. Sound as a rock.

Unfortunately, one night a severe storm struck the island. The inhabitants awoke the next morning to find the rock gone, evidently hurled into the sea by the furies of nature. Consternation! Panic! Luckily, however, they were saved from the potential consequences —worthless money and economic collapse—by an accident of fate that took place within the week. One of the younger natives, a child of no more than eight, perched on the very cliff where the rock had once been, was looking at a rainbow arching far out over the horizon. Following it down, he suddenly saw—or thought he saw—the rock, fathoms deep, under the water.

After much excitement, it was finally ascertained that on very clear days, when the sea was calm and the sun at a certain angle, some who had especially strong eyes could see it. Those who could not, which included almost everyone, were assured by those who could that the outlines of the boulder were indeed discernible. And so, the backing still there, confidence in the money was restored, and in a short while the island became more prosperous than ever.

Of course, all the outstanding clamshells had to be called in, so that the elders of the community could strike out the words:

Will Pay to the Bearer on Demand One Dollar in Rock

In their place was painstakingly inscribed:

Will Pay to the Bearer on Demand One Dollar
in Lawful Money

Now if anyone brought in a clamshell to be redeemed, it would simply be exchanged for another clamshell. As it turned out, however, no one bothered. After all, with the backing assuredly there, the money obviously was as good as rock.

End of story.

Our own monetary system, of course, has always been much more rational. Until 1933 all our money was redeemable in gold at the United States Treasury. Every dollar bill bore the following inscription:

The United States of America
Will Pay to the Bearer on Demand One Dollar in Gold

Then, overnight, it was declared illegal for anyone in this country to have gold in his possession, except for industrial or numismatic purposes. Gold ownership by Americans was made illegal by an Executive Order issued by President Franklin D. Roosevelt on April 5, 1933. The prohibition was formalized by the Gold Reserve Act of 1934. Accordingly, the inscription on the currency was solemnly, officially, and duly altered to:

The United States of America
Will Pay to the Bearer on Demand One Dollar
in Lawful Money

In 1947 a literal-minded citizen of Cleveland, A. F. Davis, sent the Treasury a $10 bill and respectfully requested, in exchange, the promised $10 in "lawful money." He received back, by return mail, two $5 bills.

Seventeen years later, in 1964, the venerable inscription was finally removed from our currency. All that remains is an unpretentious observation: "This note is legal tender for all debts, public and private." Also (in considerably larger print): "In God We Trust."

The Gold Standard Domestically

The main reason for the recent appeal of the gold standard is that it contains built-in automatic safeguards against inflation. It does this by linking the money supply to gold, making it virtually impos-

"Then it's agreed. Until the dollar firms up, we let the clamshell float."

Drawing by Ed Fisher; © 1971 The New Yorker Magazine, Inc.

sible to increase the money supply enough to support a sustained increase in the price level.

A return to the gold standard could be accomplished overnight by three simple acts:

1. *Impose a fixed ratio between gold held by the government and currency in circulation.* For every $1 of gold, for example, $4 of currency. The ratio need not be 100 percent; a less restrictive ratio, like 25 percent, would serve just as well, for the same reason that banks are not required to hold 100 percent reserves behind their demand deposit liabilities. Fractional gold reserves are based on the same logic as fractional bank reserves: Everyone is unlikely to want to turn money into gold at one and the same time, just as everyone is unlikely to want to turn demand deposits into currency simultaneously.

2. *Permit unlimited convertibility between gold and currency.* Since bank deposits are interchangeable with currency, in effect deposits would also be freely convertible into gold.

3. *Set an official fixed price of gold for conversions between currency and gold.* Say $400 = 1 troy ounce of gold, as an example. Since this automatically means that $1 is worth 1/400th of an ounce of gold, it is often expressed by saying that a country thereby "defines" its monetary unit in terms of a specific physical amount of gold: the dollar is defined as equal to 1/400th of an ounce of gold. *Devaluation*—legally redefining the dollar to be worth *less* (say 1/500th of an ounce of gold)—is thus the same as raising the official price of gold (to $500 a troy ounce).[1]

Neglecting small handling charges, Americans would then be free to convert $400 into one ounce of gold at the Treasury whenever they wish, or to turn in one ounce of gold and get $400. Of course, the U.S. Treasury must convince people that it can maintain enough gold in its coffers to make good on its promise to pay out one ounce of gold to anyone bringing in 400 dollar bills.

This convertibility between currency and gold is the lever that controls the money supply, and through the money supply presumably the price level. This is because many people are convinced, on the basis of experience, that over the long run gold will retain its value better than paper money. Expectations that prices are apt to rise will lead many people to demand gold in exchange for currency —and, since bank deposits are freely convertible into currency, to also exchange deposits for currency and then for gold.

With less gold in its vaults, the government is forced to contract the amount of currency in circulation. And since banks hold currency as reserves, they will have to call in loans and merely extinguish demand deposits. Thus money supply falls when gold flows out of the Treasury. Inflationary expectations thereby generate their

[1]Gold's weight is always expressed in troy ounces. A troy ounce is heavier than the ounce most American's are used to (the avoirdupois ounce). Specifically, 1 troy ounce = 1.1 avoirdupois ounces. A metric ton contains 32,150 troy ounces, so at $400 an ounce a ton of gold (about 80 standard-size gold bars) is worth a cool $12,860,000.

While we're on the subject, we might as well mention that gold—chemical element 79—melts at 1063° centigrade, boils at 2600° centigrade, and has a specific gravity of 19.3.

own remedy. With a smaller money supply, inflation is aborted before it can really get underway.

Now for the bad news. The gold standard has built-in safeguards against inflation, but not necessarily against recession and unemployment. Under the gold standard, the money supply is determined by the public, not by the Federal Reserve. Gold hoarding by the public reduces the money supply and the central bank, if it abides by the rules, can't do anything about it. This may be effective in minimizing inflation, but it is likely to intensify a recession—especially if fears arise that the government might possibly devalue the dollar. Governments are often tempted to devalue during recessions, in order to increase employment by expanding exports. As we will see in the following section, devaluation depreciates the foreign exchange value of a country's money, thereby inhibiting its imports and stimulating its exports.

If the public starts to suspect that the government may soon devalue—that is, raise the official price of gold—it makes sense to buy as much gold as possible now, before the price rises, and then sell it back to the government after the price has gone up. This is precisely what led the United States to abandon the gold standard in 1933.

In brief, the gold standard provides a powerful barrier against inflation but is far less effective when it comes to recession. It could even turn a mild recession into a major depression.

The Gold Standard Internationally

Under the international gold standard, each nation similarly agrees to tie its money supply rigidly to its gold stock, decides upon an official fixed price for gold, and then stands ready to buy or sell unlimited quantities at that price.

This necessarily results in fixed rates of exchange between one nation's money and another's: If France establishes 800 francs an ounce as the price it will pay for gold, and the United States decides upon $400 an ounce, then the par rate of exchange will be $1 = 2 francs, since both $1 and 2 francs buy equal amounts of gold. (Were the U.S. to devalue the dollar and raise the price of gold to, say, $800 an ounce, then the dollar would depreciate to a new exchange rate

I was born in 1929, when gold was selling for $20.67 an ounce...I married in 1968, in an outwardly happy marriage. That was the year gold began to go up again...For the past few years my wife has been having an affair with another man...

...Six months ago she went off to live with him...If I had bought gold in 1929 I could sell it today at 9 times the price at $180 an ounce, up from $20.67 then...Last week she came back 'to give our marriage another chance,' she says...'To give our marriage another chance?' I tell her, 'Until next time you leave, you mean'...

Some say gold stocks yes, gold bars no. I say gold bars yes, gold stocks no...Yesterday she left 'forever'...This morning she's back again...'I want to say something,' she says...

Drawing by Lou Myers; © *1975 The New Yorker Magazine, Inc.*

of $1 = 1 franc. This should stimulate U.S. exports, as mentioned above, because the French can now buy as many dollars as before with only half as many francs.)

This fixed exchange rate of $1 = 2 francs would be quite stable, not varying below or above par by more than the relatively small cost of shipping gold from one country to another. For instance, assume that the United States has a deficit in its balance of payments while France has a surplus. The excess supply of dollars on the foreign exchange market should lead to depreciation of the dollar relative to the franc—the dollar will start to fall in value from $1 = 2 francs to $1 = 1.9 francs and so on.

But it can only depreciate by the cost of shipping gold, which is a fairly modest sum. If an American importer of 800 francs' worth of French perfume is told by his local banker that he'll have to pay much more than $400 to get the 800 francs he needs, the importer will simply turn around and buy $400 worth of gold (1 ounce) from the U.S. Treasury and ship it to France at his own expense, thereby discharging his obligation to his French supplier. Doing this will be cheaper than operating through the foreign exchange office of the local bank. Thus the dollar can depreciate only to a lower limit, called our gold export point, which is below par by the cost of shipping gold abroad from the U.S.

Or assume that the United States has a balance of payments surplus and France has a deficit. This should lead to appreciation of the dollar relative to the franc—the dollar will start to rise in value from $1 = 2 francs to $1 = 2.1 francs and so on. But the same limit exists at that end too. If a French importer of $400 worth of American cowboy boots finds that his local bank is charging him much more than 800 francs to get the $400 he needs, the importer can simply buy an ounce of gold at the French Treasury for 800 francs and ship it here at his own expense. Thus the dollar can appreciate only to an upper limit—called our gold import point—which is above par by the cost of shipping gold from abroad to the United States.

International gold flows thereby produce fairly stable exchange rates under the gold standard. Such gold movements also provide a built-in antidote against inflation, since each country's money supply is supposed to be rigidly tied to its gold stock. Worse inflation here than abroad leads to a U.S. balance of payments deficit, because our goods become more expensive. The result is depreciation of the dollar on foreign exchange markets, followed promptly by *gold out-flows* that (a) stop the depreciation of the dollar and (b) force a contraction in our money supply, thereby stifling inflation. As inflation is brought under control, our exports should expand and our imports contract, thus improving our balance of payments position so that the gold outflow gradually ceases. It is a self-correcting system.

If the gold standard functions so smoothly, and contains inflation so effectively, why was it abandoned by the leading industrial countries fifty years ago?

Great Britain, the linchpin of the international financial system in the late nineteenth century and the early decades of the twentieth, suspended convertibility of the pound into gold—and thereby went off the gold standard—in September of 1931. The United States followed suit in March of 1933. The reasons were the same in both cases: substantial gold drains out of the Treasury, due to unsettled economic conditions and persistent rumors of devaluation.

Under the gold standard, a country losing gold is supposed to contract its money supply and put deliberate downward pressure on its economy. In the early 1930s both Great Britain and the United States were indeed losing gold (because of fears of devaluation), but understandably neither wanted to impose the tight money called for by the gold standard's rules. Both were in the midst of major depressions that no one wanted to make worse by monetary tightness.

The United States resumed convertibility of the (devalued) dollar into gold in 1934, for foreign central banks and governments only, and fixed exchange rates were reinstituted after World War II. However, the system collapsed again, in the early 1970s, under the weight of persistent U.S. balance of payments deficits, unstable world financial conditions, and recurrent rumors that the United States was once again preparing to devalue the dollar. Since then, of course, foreign exchange rates have for the most part floated unattached to gold, fluctuating daily with the tides of supply and demand.[2]

---

[2]In 1970 a step toward a substitute for gold in international finance was hesitantly taken with the introduction into the world's monetary system of International Monetary Fund Special Drawing Rights (SDRs), more commonly known as "paper gold". SDRs are a form of international reserve asset, usable only by central banks and governments to settle international debts in much the same way as gold. But instead

Will the Gold Standard Make a Comeback?

What are the probabilities that we will bring back the gold standard in the foreseeable future? Extremely low, for a number of reasons:

1.   It is difficult today, perhaps impossible, to establish a fixed relationship between a nation's gold stock and its money supply. The gold standard was the construct of a simpler monetary era. Most of our money now consists of bank deposits, not currency, and there is even considerable controversy about which deposits to include. As a result, we have several different money supplies—M1, M2, M3, and so on—and it is hard to justify why one and not the other should be tied to gold.

2.   Just as difficult is the choice of an appropriate official price for gold, given the wide swings in its free market price—between $200 and $875 a troy ounce—in recent years. Too low an official price would encourage wholesale gold flows from government to private hoards, too high a price the reverse.

3.   The gold standard has built-in safeguards against inflation but not against recession and unemployment. No democratically elected government could deliberately provoke heavy unemployment, simply because of gold outflows, and expect to remain long in office. Indeed, even prior to the 1930s the United States "sterilized" the domestic monetary effects of international gold flows by offsetting central bank open market operations—a clear violation of the gold standard's rules—in order to pursue domestic stabilization objectives unhampered by gold constraints.

Fundamentally, the gold standard is based on an illusion: namely, that human judgment in economic life can be replaced by a built-in self-correcting thermostat, so that monetary and financial disturbances are automatically set right without intervention by politicians and central bankers. In fact, human judgment is still involved, even with the gold standard. It is involved in fixing the ratio between the gold stock and the money supply; in selecting the official price of gold; in deciding whether or not to devalue, when, and by how much;

(*continued*)
of having to be panned, dredged, or mined from the earth, they are created out of thin air—just like demand deposits—by an entry on the books of the International Monetary Fund.

and in establishing priorities with respect to national economic goals.

Like it or not, politicians and central bankers will not disappear. In a democracy, our only hope is to try to fill their positions with able and qualified men and women who will do their best to promote the public interest in a world where truth is elusive.

Summary

1. The gold standard involves setting an official price for gold and then permitting unlimited convertibility at that price. The money supply is tied to the stock of gold in the Treasury. As a result, it is the public—not the Federal Reserve—that ultimately determines the country's money supply.

2. The gold standard provides a powerful barrier against inflation, but is far less effective against recession and unemployment.

3. Internationally, the gold standard results in fixed exchange rates, because flows of gold between countries keep the exchange rate from fluctuating by more than the cost of shipping gold.

4. These same gold flows also provide an automatic self-equilibrating mechanism that controls inflation and corrects balance of payments deficits. A country experiencing more inflation than others will have a balance of payment deficit, as a result of which it will lose gold. This will force a contraction in its money supply. With a smaller money supply, inflation should abate and the country's balance of payments position improve.

5. The gold standard broke down because of fears of devaluation —which led to large gold drains—and the refusal of nations to follow the gold standard's rules—which required that with less gold they sharply contract their money supplies.

6. It is not likely that the gold standard will be reestablished in the foreseeable future.

Suggestions for Further Reading

The conclusions of the U.S. Gold Commission are contained in its two-volume *Report to the Congress of the Commission on the Role of Gold in The Domestic and International Monetary Systems* (U.S. Government Printing Office, March 1982). Also see Michael David Bordo, "The Classical Gold Standard: Some Lessons for Today," in the *Review* of the Federal Reserve Bank of St. Louis (May 1981).

More required reading: Milton Friedman, "Commodity-Reserve Currency," in *Essays in Positive Economics* (University of Chicago Press, 1953), not to mention John Maynard Keynes, *A Treatise on Money* (New York: Harcourt, Brace, 1930), vol. 2, pp. 289 ff. This time Friedman and Keynes are on the same side of the fence.

Actually, you'll probably get a better appreciation of the role of gold in human affairs if you go to the movies and see Alec Guinness in *The Lavender Hill Mob* or Humphrey Bogart in *Treasure of the Sierra Madre*. And don't miss W. C. Fields in the Klondike in *The Fatal Glass of Beer*.

Index

Accounting: balance of payments and, 575–578; categories in, 581–584; sources and uses of funds approach in, 576–578

Alhadeff, David, 120

Andersen, Leonall C., 406, 462

Anderson, Gerald H., 162

Angell, Norman, 20

Anthony, Susan B. : dollars, $8n$

Atkinson, Thomas, 171

Auerbach, Robert D., 538

Automated teller machines, 166

Axilrod, Stephen, 246

Bach, G. L., 35

Bagehot, Walter, $195n$, 206

Baily, Martin N., $403n$

Bain, A. D., 490

Balance of payments accounting, 575–586; goods and services balance, 581; liquidity, 584; sources and uses, 576–578; trade balance and, 581

Balance of payments deficits, 569, 570, 571, 609

Balbach, Anatol B., 162

Ball, R. J., 35

Bankers Trust Company, 507

Banking Act of 1933, 92, 106

Banks (commercial banks), 36–52; asset and liability management, 122–141; bank capital, 128; business processing in, 36–42; buying and selling (standing and sitting), 122; deposit expansion, 42–51; deposit insurance, 106–109; discretionary funds management, 135; equity capital of, 128; financing government spending, 260; funds of, sources of, 124; funds of, uses of, 123; idle excess reserves, 254; liability management, 131–134; liquidity, 129–131; money position, 138–141; money position management, 138–140; monopoly threat of, 112–115; movements in bank reserves, 207–227; profitability, 129–131; regulation and structure, 100–121; reserve equation, 219; size of, 109–112

Barro, Robert J., 329

Barter economy, 9–11

Baumol, William J., $277n$, 476, 600, $329n$

Benston, George J., 121

Bernstein Report, 586

Black, Deborah G., 522

Black, Robert P., 80, 99, 153

Blinder, Alan S., $277n$, $416n$, 462

Bloch, Ernest, 566

Bogart, Humphrey, 612

Bonds, 69; coupon rate of, 74; prices and yields, 74–78; trading in, 547–549; yield to maturity, 74

Boorman, John T., 255

Bordo, Michael David, 612

Bosworth, Barry, 538

Bowden, Elbert V., 121

Bretton Woods conference, 573

Brimmer, Andrew, $182n$

Brokers: securities, 147

Brooks, Mel, $297n$

Brundy, James, 171

Brunner, Karl, 240, 406, 432

Budgets: deficits and money supply, 256–267

Burns, Arthur F., 179

Cagan, Phillip, 255, 522

Capital market, 69–71

Carlson, John A., 462

Carlson, Keith, 462

Carson, Deane, 99, 206

Certificates of Deposit: bank failures